ANNUAL EDITIONS

American Government 12/13
Forty-Second Edition

EDITOR

Bruce Stinebrickner
DePauw University

Bruce Stinebrickner is the Leonard E. and Mary B. Howell Professor of Political Science at DePauw University in Greencastle, Indiana, and has taught American politics at DePauw since 1987. He has also taught at Lehman College of the City University of New York (1974–1976), at the University of Queensland in Brisbane, Australia (1976–1987), and in DePauw programs in Argentina (1990) and Germany (1993). He served fourteen years as chair of his department at DePauw after heading his department at the University of Queensland for two years. He earned his BA *magna cum laude* from Georgetown University in 1968, his MPhil from Yale University in 1972, and his PhD from Yale in 1974.

Professor Stinebrickner is the coauthor (with Robert A. Dahl) of *Modern Political Analysis,* sixth edition (Prentice Hall, 2003), and has published articles on the American presidential selection process, American local governments, the career patterns of Australian politicians, and freedom of the press. He has served as editor of thirty-four earlier editions of this book as well as fifteen editions of its *State and Local Government* counterpart in the McGraw-Hill Contemporary Learning Series. His current research interests focus on government policies involving children (e.g., schooling, child custody, adoption, and foster care).

Currently in his fourth year on the Greencastle, Indiana, school board, Professor Stinebrickner is serving his second year as board president. He is also a member of the Greencastle Redevelopment Commission. In both his teaching and his writing, Professor Stinebrickner applies insights on politics gained from living, teaching, and lecturing abroad as well as serving in local government.

McGraw Hill

Connect Learn Succeed™

ANNUAL EDITIONS: AMERICAN GOVERNMENT, FORTY-SECOND EDITION

Published by McGraw-Hill, a business unit of The McGraw-Hill Companies, Inc., 1221 Avenue of the Americas, New York, NY 10020. Copyright © 2013 by The McGraw-Hill Companies, Inc. All rights reserved. Printed in the United States of America. Previous editions © 2012, 2011, and 2010. No part of this publication may be reproduced or distributed in any form or by any means, or stored in a database or retrieval system, without the prior written consent of The McGraw-Hill Companies, Inc., including, but not limited to, in any network or other electronic storage or transmission, or broadcast for distance learning.

Some ancillaries, including electronic and print components, may not be available to customers outside the United States.

This book is printed on acid-free paper.

Annual Editions® is a registered trademark of The McGraw-Hill Companies, Inc.

Annual Editions is published by the **Contemporary Learning Series** group within the McGraw-Hill Higher Education division.

1 2 3 4 5 6 7 8 9 0 QDB/QDB 1 0 9 8 7 6 5 4 3 2

ISBN: 978–0–07–8051135
MHID: 0–07–8051134
ISSN: 0891-3390 (print)
ISSN: 2158-3218 (online)

Managing Editor: *Larry Loeppke*
Senior Developmental Editor: *Jill Meloy*
Permissions Coordinator: *DeAnna Dausener*
Marketing Specialist: *Alice Link*
Senior Project Manager: *Joyce Watters*
Design Coordinator: *Margarite Reynolds*
Cover Designer: *Studio Montage, St. Louis, Missouri*
Buyer: *Susan K. Culbertson*
Media Project Manager: *Sridevi Palani*

Compositor: Laserwords Private Limited
Cover Image Credits: Beathan/Corbis (inset); © Comstock/PunchStock (background)

Editors/Academic Advisory Board

Members of the Academic Advisory Board are instrumental in the final selection of articles for each edition of ANNUAL EDITIONS. Their review of articles for content, level, and appropriateness provides critical direction to the editors and staff. We think that you will find their careful consideration well reflected in this volume.

ANNUAL EDITIONS: American Government 12/13
42nd Edition

EDITOR

Bruce Stinebrickner
DePauw University

ACADEMIC ADVISORY BOARD MEMBERS

Preface

In publishing ANNUAL EDITIONS we recognize the enormous role played by the magazines, newspapers, and journals of the public press in providing current, first-rate educational information in a broad spectrum of interest areas. Many of these articles are appropriate for students, researchers, and professionals seeking accurate, current material to help bridge the gap between principles and theories and the real world. These articles, however, become more useful for study when those of lasting value are carefully collected, organized, indexed, and reproduced in a low-cost format, which provides easy and permanent access when the material is needed. That is the role played by ANNUAL EDITIONS.

American Government 12/13 is the forty-second edition in an *Annual Editions* series that has become a mainstay in many introductory courses on the American political system. The educational goal is to provide a readable collection of up-to-date articles that are informative, interesting, and stimulating to students beginning their study of the American political system.

Everyone reading this book no doubt knows that in January 2009 Democrat Barack Obama was sworn in as president of the United States. That same month the 111th Congress convened, with both houses having substantial Democratic majorities. The forty-fourth president of the United States entered the White House facing a daunting array of challenges. Succeeding Republican George W. Bush, Obama became president amidst a severe economic recession that many Americans feared would become a second Great Depression. U.S. military forces had been fighting in Iraq and Afghanistan for most of the decade, and many Americans thought it was time to reduce the two wars' toll on American lives and pocketbooks and try to restore the nation's tattered image in the world. President Obama and the country faced other major challenges. These included skyrocketing healthcare costs while millions of Americans were left without insurance and timely access to appropriate medical care, shortcomings in financial institutions and regulations that had led to the economic meltdown, the threat of climate change thought by many to imperil the entire human race, the long-simmering problem of millions of undocumented immigrants living in the United States, and large budget deficits leading to mounting national debt.

No one should be surprised that as I write this preface in September 2011—well into the third year of the Obama presidency—the problems and challenges noted in the preceding paragraph have not all been resolved. Some of them have been addressed (e.g., healthcare reform, financial regulatory reform, troop surge in Afghanistan), with the long-term consequences unknown and unknowable at this time; some have been explicitly put aside (e.g., immigration policy) for later consideration. Government taxing and spending; Medicare, Medicaid, and Social Security entitlement programs; economic recovery; and deficits and the national debt have loomed large during Obama's presidency and have taken center stage during the past twelve months or so. The interesting

and challenging years of the Obama presidency may, for better or worse, wind up being a turning point in American history.

By November 2010 President Obama's approval ratings had sharply declined, and voters inflicted heavy losses on the Democratic party in the mid-term congressional elections. Republicans regained control of the House of Representatives and, when the 112th Congress convened in January 2011, Republican John Boehner replaced Democrat Nancy Pelosi as Speaker of the House. In addition, Republicans gained six seats in the Senate, bringing the Republican minority to a total of 47 seats, a sufficient number under Senate filibuster rules to block Democrats' policy initiatives. The political system shifted from "unified government" (wherein one party controls the presidency and both houses of Congress) to "divided government" (in which neither party controls all three elected entities in the legislative and executive branches).

In the dying days of the 111th Congress in December 2010, Democrats and Republicans reached a deal to avoid a government shutdown just before a previously enacted spending measure was due to expire. That uneasy compromise extended Bush-era cuts for another two years and included other provisions that were barely palatable to one side or the other. The brinkmanship and political unease of December 2010 foreshadowed what was to come once Speaker John Boehner and his fellow Republicans assumed majority control of the House of Representatives in January 2011.

The growth in deficit spending during the Obama presidency necessitated more government borrowing and the corresponding need for Congress to raise the national government's debt ceiling. Adjusting the debt ceiling has been a frequent and typically routine occurrence for decades, but 2011 proved to be something other than a routine year. In June and July, Americans—and indeed the world—watched the spectacle of Washington policymakers trying to reach a deal to raise the debt ceiling and thereby avoid a default by the United States government, an almost unthinkable prospect that many observers believed would produce a catastrophic worldwide financial collapse. Brinksmanship reared its head, just as it had in government shutdown crisis in December 2010. A last-minute deal in early August averted default even though the fallout from the weeks-long crisis included stock market volatility, downgrading of the U.S. government's credit rating, and another blow to an already fragile economic recovery.

The debt ceiling deal reached by President Obama, Speaker Boehner, and the Senate leadership was complicated. One element was the formation of the Joint Select Committee on Deficit Reduction. Dubbed by some a "super-committee," this twelve-member bipartisan congressional committee was charged with producing a package of spending and/or revenue measures that would substantially reduce annual deficits and thus begin to stabilize the burgeoning national government debt. The super-committee was instructed to bring its recommendations back to Congress by November 23, 2011. Unless Congress approved the recommendations within a month, substantial across-the-board spending cuts, which many observers saw as draconian in areas such as national defense, would automatically occur.

By the time this book appears in print, the outcome of the super-committee process will be known. But as I write this preface in September 2011, it is impossible to predict what will happen. Indeed, in the past week or so, President Obama and others have urged the super-committee to recommend even larger reductions than those mandated in August. As I have already mentioned, the closely related issues of taxing, spending, deficits, national debt, entitlements, and so forth have clearly assumed center stage in the American political system and seem likely to remain there for the foreseeable future.

No account of politics and policymaking over the past twelve months would be complete without mention of the Tea Party movement and its influential role in the American political system over the past several years. This movement seemed to arise from growing consternation with national government deficits among a number of Americans and coalesced around the core belief that national government spending needed to be markedly reduced. Tea Party candidates beat a number of more moderate candidates in Republican primaries before the 2010 congressional elections, and a sizable number of Tea Party adherents became members of the 112th Congress. Their membership in the House Republican caucus substantially complicated Speaker John Boehner's task in his negotiations with President Obama about taxing, spending, the debt ceiling, and the like.

On the national security front, the past twelve months have brought continued outbursts of violence in Iraq as American troops have been withdrawn. Meanwhile, U.S. troops in Afghanistan have suffered a growing number of casualties as they have sought to inflict crippling blows on the Taliban before beginning a phased military withdrawal in 2012. As everyone reading this preface probably knows, U.S. Navy Seals killed Osama bin Laden in a surprise raid on his hideout in Pakistan in early May 2011. Last, but not least, a series of popular uprisings began in Tunisia, Egypt, Libya, Syria, and elsewhere in the Middle East during the spring of 2011. Authoritarian regimes in Tunisia and Egypt were overthrown surprisingly quickly, but it took months before Libyan strongman Muammar el-Qaddafi and his government were toppled from power. During what came to be known as "Arab Spring," the Obama administration became openly involved in the overthrow of Qaddafi and cautiously supported the Libyan rebels with noncombatant assistance while the British and French military provided more active combat support.

On the domestic political scene, the 2012 presidential election campaign is already very much under way. More than a half-dozen aspirants are campaigning for the Republican presidential nomination, with Texas governor Rick Perry and former Massachusetts governor Mitt Romney the apparent frontrunners. President Obama is also on the campaign trail, giving speeches and appearing at fundraisers that will no doubt net him millions of dollars in campaign funds. And Republicans and Democrats on Capitol Hill are keeping an eye on their electoral prospects in the 2012 congressional elections. Whether the Tea Party movement will play the same sort of pivotal role in the 2012 elections as it did in 2010 remains to be seen.

As I have written in prefaces to earlier editions of this book, "every time I work on the preface for a new edition of this book, I am led to write that the coming year will be another interesting one for students of American politics." The past year has certainly proved no exception to this general rule; nor do I expect the coming year to be different in this respect.

As I write this preface, the coming presidential and congressional elections to be held in November 2012, some fourteen months from now, have begun to cast their shadows over the American political system. Can Congress and the president govern in a constructive manner while elected officials of both parties are understandably tempted to position themselves for the coming election campaign? Will the tepid economic recovery and the 9 percent unemployment rate change appreciably in the coming twelve months? How successful will the super-committee process be in reducing annual deficits and, in turn, stabilizing the long-term U.S. debt? Will President Obama be a one-term president? Who will be his Republican opponent, and to what extent will Obama's re-election chances depend on the identity of his opponent?

The next twelve months will likely provide answers or partial answers to many of the questions just posed, as well as others like them. Careful observation of American politics as it unfolds on a day-to-day basis can teach us a great deal about regularities and unpredictable aspects of the American political system. The selections in this book should help readers comprehend and even anticipate what will happen in the year to come and, more importantly, enhance their understanding of the characteristic functioning of the contemporary American political system.

The systems approach provides a rough organizational framework for this book. The first unit focuses on ideological and constitutional underpinnings of American politics from both historical and contemporary perspectives. The second unit treats the major institutions of the national government. The third covers the "input" or "linkage" mechanisms of the system—political parties, elections, interest groups, and media. The fourth and concluding unit shifts the focus to policy choices that confront the government in Washington and resulting "outputs" of the political system.

Each year thousands of articles about American politics appear, and deciding which to reprint in a collection of readings such as this can be difficult. Articles are chosen with an eye toward providing viewpoints from left, right, and center. Almost half of the selections in this book are new to this year's edition, a reflection of continuing efforts to help keep those who read this book abreast of important contemporary developments in the American political system. Other parts of the book have also been revised, of course, and I want to thank Anthony Baratta, a recent

Political Science major at DePauw, for help in updating the Internet references. Two new features introduced a year ago to aid students' learning appear again in this edition. Located at the beginning of each unit, *Learning Outcomes* direct attention to ideas, concepts, and issues that selections in the unit address. *Critical Thinking* questions at the end of each article enable readers to test their understanding of the article's content.

Next year will bring another opportunity for change, and you, the reader, are invited to participate in the process.

Bruce Stinebrickner
Editor

The Annual Editions Series

VOLUMES AVAILABLE

Adolescent Psychology

Aging

American Foreign Policy

American Government

Anthropology

Archaeology

Assessment and Evaluation

Business Ethics

Child Growth and Development

Comparative Politics

Criminal Justice

Developing World

Drugs, Society, and Behavior

Dying, Death, and Bereavement

Early Childhood Education

Economics

Educating Children with Exceptionalities

Education

Educational Psychology

Entrepreneurship

Environment

The Family

Gender

Geography

Global Issues

Health

Homeland Security

Human Development

Human Resources

Human Sexualities

International Business

Management

Marketing

Mass Media

Microbiology

Multicultural Education

Nursing

Nutrition

Physical Anthropology

Psychology

Race and Ethnic Relations

Social Problems

Sociology

State and Local Government

Sustainability

Technologies, Social Media, and Society

United States History, Volume 1

United States History, Volume 2

Urban Society

Violence and Terrorism

Western Civilization, Volume 1

World History, Volume 1

World History, Volume 2

World Politics

Contents

UNIT 1
Foundations of American Politics

The concepts in bold italics are developed in the article. For further expansion, please refer to the Topic Guide.

UNIT 2
Structures of American Politics

The concepts in bold italics are developed in the article. For further expansion, please refer to the Topic Guide.

The concepts in bold italics are developed in the article. For further expansion, please refer to the Topic Guide.

UNIT 3
Process of American Politics

The concepts in bold italics are developed in the article. For further expansion, please refer to the Topic Guide.

The concepts in bold italics are developed in the article. For further expansion, please refer to the Topic Guide.

UNIT 4
Products of American Politics

The concepts in bold italics are developed in the article. For further expansion, please refer to the Topic Guide.

The concepts in bold italics are developed in the article. For further expansion, please refer to the Topic Guide.

Correlation Guide

The *Annual Editions* series provides students with convenient, inexpensive access to current, carefully selected articles from the public press. **Annual Editions: American Government 12/13** is an easy-to-use reader that presents articles on important topics in the study of American government. For more information on *Annual Editions* and other *McGraw-Hill Contemporary Learning Series* titles, visit www.mhhe.com/cls.

This convenient guide matches the units in **Annual Editions: American Government 12/13** with the corresponding chapters in three of our best-selling McGraw-Hill American government textbooks by Harrison/Harris, Losco/Baker, and Patterson.

Annual Editions: American Government 12/13	**American Democracy Now, 2/e by Harrison/Harris**	**AM GOV 2012 by Losco/Baker**	**The American Democracy, 10/e by Patterson**
Unit 1: Foundations of American Politics	**Chapter 1:** People, Politics, and Participation **Chapter 2:** The Constitution **Chapter 3:** Federalism **Chapter 4:** Civil Liberties **Chapter 5:** Civil Rights	**Chapter 1:** Citizenship in Our Changing Democracy **Chapter 2:** The Constitution: The Foundation of Citizens' Rights **Chapter 3:** Federalism: Citizenship and the Dispersal of Power **Chapter 4:** Civil Liberties: Expanding Citizens' Rights **Chapter 5:** Civil Rights: Toward a More Equal Citizenry	**Chapter 1:** Political Thinking **Chapter 2:** Constitutional Democracy: Promoting Liberty and Self-Government **Chapter 3:** Federalism: Forging a Nation **Chapter 4:** Civil Liberties: Protecting Individual Rights **Chapter 5:** Equal Rights: Struggling toward Fairness The Struggle for Equality
Unit 2: Structures of American Politics	**Chapter 11:** Congress **Chapter 12:** The Presidency **Chapter 13:** The Bureaucracy **Chapter 14:** The Judiciary	**Chapter 11:** Congress: Doing the People's Business **Chapter 12:** The Presidency: Power and Paradox **Chapter 13:** Bureaucracy: Citizens as Owners and Consumers **Chapter 14:** The Courts: Judicial Power in a Democratic Setting	**Chapter 11:** Congress: Balancing National Goals and Local Interests **Chapter 12:** The Presidency: Leading the Nation Foundations of the Modern Presidency **Chapter 13:** The Federal Bureaucracy: Administering the Government **Chapter 14:** The Federal Judicial System: Applying the Law
Unit 3: Process of American Politics	**Chapter 6:** Political Socialization and Public Opinion **Chapter 7:** Interest Groups **Chapter 8:** Political Parties **Chapter 9:** Elections, Campaigns, and Voting **Chapter 10:** The Media	**Chapter 6:** Public Opinion: Listening to Citizens **Chapter 7:** Political Participation: Equal Opportunities and Unequal Voices **Chapter 8:** Interest Groups in America **Chapter 9:** Parties and Political Campaigns: Citizens and the Electoral Process **Chapter 10:** Media: Tuning In or Tuning Out	**Chapter 6:** Public Opinion and Political Socialization: Shaping the People's Voice **Chapter 7:** Political Participation: Activating the Popular Will **Chapter 8:** Political Parties, Candidates, and Campaigns: Defining the Voter's Choice **Chapter 9:** Interest Groups: Organizing Influence **Chapter 10:** The News Media: Communicating Political Images
Unit 4: Products of American Politics	**Chapter 15:** Economic Policy **Chapter 16:** Domestic Policy **Chapter 17:** Foreign Policy and National Security **Chapter 18:** State and Local Government	**Chapter 15:** Public Policy: Responding to Citizens **Chapter 16:** Foreign and Defense Policy: Protecting American Interests in the World	**Chapter 15:** Economic and Environmental Policy: Contributing to Prosperity **Chapter 16:** Welfare and Education Policy: Providing for Personal Security and Need **Chapter 17:** Foreign and Defense Policy: Protecting the American Way **Chapter 18:** State and Local Politics: Maintaining Our Differences

Topic Guide

This topic guide suggests how the selections in this book relate to the subjects covered in your course. You may want to use the topics listed on these pages to search the Web more easily.

On the following pages a number of websites have been gathered specifically for this book. They are arranged to reflect the units of this Annual Editions reader. You can link to these sites by going to www.mhhe.com/cls.

All the articles that relate to each topic are listed below the bold-faced term.

Internet References

The following Internet sites have been selected to support the articles found in this reader. These sites were available at the time of publication. However, because websites often change their structure and content, the information listed may no longer be available. We invite you to visit www.mhhe.com/cls for easy access to these sites.

Annual Editions: American Government 12/13

General Sources

The Daily Beast: Andrew Sullivan
andrewsullivan.thedailybeast.com

Political and social commentary by award-winning editor, journalist, and author Andrew Sullivan, with links to other useful sources.

Fact-checking
www.factcheck.org

www.opensecrets.org

www.politifact.com

If you are not sure you believe what a politician, blogger, television commentator, or organization is saying, here are three sites dedicated to fact-checking political assertions.

The Monkey Cage
www.themonkeycage.org

"Democracy is the art of running the circus from the monkey cage." (H.L. Mencken) Despite its humorous name and epigram, this is a serious blog written by political scientists to relate political science research to current political happenings.

Plain Blog About Politics
plainblogaboutpolitics.blogspot.com

"I'm a political scientist blogging about American politics, especially the presidency, Congress, parties, and elections." So reads Jonathan Bernstein's description of his blog. Go see for yourself.

National Review: The Corner
www.nationalreview.com/corner

Part of National Review Online, this blog addresses a whole range of political issues in a timely fashion and from a conservative perspective.

Think Progress
www.thinkprogress.org

Part of the Center for American Progress, this blog addresses a whole range of political issues in a timely fashion and from a liberal perspective.

UNIT 1: Foundations of American Politics

The American Scene
www.theamericanscene.com

Open this site for access to political, cultural, and Web commentary on a number of issues from a conservative political viewpoint.

Library of Congress
www.loc.gov/rr/program/bib/ourdocs/NewNation.html

The Library of Congress holds many of the most important documents in United States history, especially those that relate to the founding of the nation. Here you will find not only the original documents, but also a wealth of supplemental material such as correspondence among the founders, copies of relevant proceedings, and events taking place on key dates in the adoption of those documents.

National Archives and Records Administration (NARA)
www.archives.gov

This official site of the NARA, which oversees the management of all records of the national government, offers easy access to background information for students interested in the policymaking process, including a search function for federal documents and speeches, and much more.

The Pew Center for the People and the Press
http://people-press.org

The Pew Center conducts research on attitudes toward politics, the press, and public policy issues. This site contains a wealth of interesting information on what people in the United States and other nations are thinking.

UNIT 2: Structures of American Politics

Department of State
www.state.gov

View this site for understanding of the workings of a major executive branch department. Links explain what the department does, what services it provides, and what it says about U.S. interests around the world. Generally similar information about other executive branch departments can be found at their official websites (e.g., www.usda.gov, www.energy.gov, and www.usdoj.gov).

Federal Reserve System
www.federalreserve.gov

Consult this site to learn the answers to FAQs about the structure of the Federal Reserve System, monetary policy, and more. It provides links to speeches and interviews as well as essays and articles presenting different views on the Fed.

United States House of Representatives
www.house.gov

The official website of the House of Representatives provides information about current and past House members and agendas, the legislative process, and more. You can learn about events on the House floor as they happen.

United States Senate
www.senate.gov

The Senate website provides information about current and past Senate members and agendas, legislative activities, and committees.

United States Supreme Court
www.supremecourt.gov

The official website of the Supreme Court contains recent opinions, biographies of the nine justices, and some background information on the Court.

White House
www.whitehouse.gov

The White House website contains presidential speeches, press briefings, and issue positions of the incumbent president.

Internet References

UNIT 3: Process of American Politics

FiveThirtyEight
http://fivethirtyeight.blogs.nytimes.com

More than a polling site with a liberal bent, FiveThirtyEight includes fascinating detail about the science and limitations of polling and critiques of data from other sites. It provided perhaps the most accurate predictions of state and national elections in 2008. FiveThirtyEight (which refers to the number of votes in the Electoral College) originally had its own site, but is now hosted by *The New York Times.*

The Gallup Organization
www.gallup.com

Open this Gallup Organization home page for links to an extensive archive of public opinion poll results and special reports on a variety of topics related to American society, politics, and government.

Poynter Online
www.poynter.org

This site of the Poynter Institute for Media Studies provides extensive links to information and resources about the media, including media ethics and reporting techniques. Many bibliographies and websites are included.

Real Clear Politics
www.realclearpolitics.com

This site presents, in a timely and easily accessible manner, the latest published poll results on a variety of political topics, including, of course, how candidates are faring during election campaigns. There are also commentaries from a range of sources about campaigns and American politics more generally. Like FiveThirtyEight.com, it is a popular and authoritative source for so-called political junkies.

Tech President
techpresident.com

This site began as a "cross-partisan group blog covering how the 2008 presidential candidates were using the web, and . . . how content generated by voters affected the campaign." It has now expanded to how candidates and government offices at all levels are using the web and how voters are responding.

UNIT 4: Products of American Politics

American Diplomacy
www.unc.edu/depts/diplomat

American Diplomacy is an online journal of commentary, analysis, and research on U.S. foreign policy and its results around the world.

Cato Institute
www.cato.org

Conservative commentary on American politics.

Ezra Klein
http://voices.washingtonpost.com/ezra-klein

Liberal commentary on American politics.

Foreign Affairs
www.foreignaffairs.org

This website of the well-respected foreign policy journal is a valuable research tool. It allows users to search the journal's archives and provides indexed access to the field's leading publications, documents, online resources, and more. Links to dozens of other related websites are available.

Paul Krugman
krugman.blogs.nytimes.com

A Nobel Prize winning economist, *New York Times* columnist, and a liberal, Paul Krugman discusses mostly economic issues.

Tax Foundation
www.taxfoundation.org

The Tax Foundation (or what some commentators call the "Anti- Tax" Foundation) provides critical analysis of your tax bill and taxes in general.

UNIT 1

Foundations of American Politics

Unit Selections

Learning Outcomes

After reading this Unit, you will be able to:

- Distinguish, and provide examples of *empirical* writings about politics, which focus on what is (or was), and *normative* writings about politics, which focus on what ought to be.

- Compare and contrast the relative persuasiveness of normative writings that address the same political topic (for example, the U. S. Supreme Court's *Citizens United v. F.E.C.* decision in 2010) from different perspectives. Of the two opposing perspectives on the *Citizens United* decision presented in selection 13, which do you find more persuasive and why?

- Compare and contrast the relevance and utility—for *you*—of historic writings from a century or more ago with the relevance and utility of contemporary writings about American politics.

- Analyze the importance of various constitutional and legal issues for the actual functioning of the contemporary American political system, and defend your conclusions.

- Appraise the extent to which various political writings, including historic documents like the Declaration of Independence and the U. S. Constitution, are conservative or liberal, as those words are used today in the American political system.

- Determine whether the Constitution of the United States is a positive force for democratic government (as *The Federalist Papers* argue) or contains many troublesome undemocratic elements (as "It Is Time to Repair the Constitution's Flaws" (11) contends), and explain why.

- Investigate whether fundamental ideas and ideals that appear in the Declaration of Independence, the *Preamble* to the Constitution, and *Federalist Papers 51* and *10* reappear in contemporary writings about American politics such "Can America Fail?" (5), "Pledging Allegiance to Peace" (10), and "Obama in Libya" (14).

Student Website
www.mhhe.com/cls

This unit treats some of the less concrete elements of the American political system—historic ideals, contemporary ideas and values, and constitutional and legal issues. These dimensions of the system are not immune to change. Instead, they interact with the wider political environment in which they exist and are modified accordingly. Usually this interaction is a gradual process, but sometimes events foster more rapid change.

Human beings can be distinguished from other species by their ability to think and reason at relatively high levels of abstraction. In turn, ideas, ideals, values, and principles can and do play important roles in politics. Most Americans value ideals such as democracy, freedom, equal opportunity, and justice. Yet, the precise meanings of these terms and the best ways of implementing them are the subject of much dispute in the political arena. Such ideas and ideals, as well as disputes about their "real" meanings, play important roles in the practice of American politics.

Although the selections in this unit span more than 200 years, they are related to one another. Understanding contemporary political viewpoints is easier if the ideals and principles of the past are also taken into account. In addition, we can appreciate the significance of historic documents such as the Declaration of Independence and the Constitution better if we are familiar with contemporary ideas and perspectives. The interaction of different ideas and values plays an important part in the continuing development of the foundations of the American political system.

The first section of this unit includes several historic documents from the eighteenth century. The first is the Declaration of Independence. Written in 1776, it proclaims the Founders' views of why independence from England was justified and, in doing so, identifies certain "unalienable" rights that "all men" are said to possess. The second document, the Constitution of 1787, remains in effect to this day. It provides an organizational blueprint for the structure of American national government, outlines the federal relationship between the national government and the states, and expresses limitations on what government can do. Twenty-seven amendments have been added to the original Constitution in two centuries. In addition to the Declaration of Independence and the Constitution, the first section includes two selections from *The Federalist Papers,* a series of newspaper articles written in support of the proposed new Constitution. Appearing in 1787 and 1788, *The Federalist Papers* addressed various provisions of the new Constitution and argued that putting the Constitution into effect would bring about good government.

The second section treats contemporary political ideas and viewpoints. As selections in this section illustrate, efforts to apply or act on political beliefs in the context of concrete circumstances often lead to interesting commentary and debate. "Liberal" and

© Library of Congress, Prints and Photographs Division

"conservative" are two labels often used in American political discussions, but political views and values have far more complexity than can be captured by these two terms. Selections in the third section show that constitutional and legal issues and interpretations are tied to historic principles as well as to contemporary ideas and values. It has been suggested that throughout American history almost every important political question has, at one time or another, appeared as a constitutional or legal issue.

The historic documents and the other selections in this unit might be more difficult to understand than the articles in other units. Some of them may have to be read and reread carefully to be fully appreciated. But to grapple with the important material treated here is to come to grips with a variety of conceptual foundations of the American political system. To ignore the theoretical issues raised would be to bypass an important element of American politics today.

Internet References

The American Scene
www.theamericanscene.com

Library of Congress
www.loc.gov/rr/program/bib/ourdocs/NewNation.html

National Archives and Records Administration (NARA)
www.archives.gov

The Pew Center for the People and the Press
http://people-press.org

The Declaration of Independence

Thomas Jefferson

When in the Course of human events, it becomes necessary for one people to dissolve the political bands which have connected them with another, and to assume among the powers of the earth, the separate and equal station to which the Laws of Nature and of Nature's God entitle them, a decent respect to the opinions of mankind requires that they should declare the causes which impel them to the separation.—We hold these truths to be self-evident, that all men are created equal, that they are endowed by their Creator with certain unalienable Rights, that among these are Life, Liberty and the pursuit of Happiness.—That to secure these rights, Governments are instituted among Men, deriving their just powers from the consent of the governed.—That whenever any Form of Government becomes destructive of these ends, it is the Right of the People to alter or to abolish it, and to institute new Government, laying its foundation on such principles and organizing its powers in such form, as to them shall seem most likely to effect their Safety and Happiness. Prudence, indeed, will dictate that Governments long established should not be changed for light and transient causes; and accordingly all experience hath shewn, that mankind are more disposed to suffer, while evils are sufferable, than to right themselves by abolishing the forms to which they are accustomed. But when a long train of abuses and usurpations, pursuing invariably the same Object evinces a design to reduce them under absolute Despotism, it is their right, it is their duty, to throw off such Government, and to provide new Guards for their future security.—Such has been the patient sufferance of these Colonies; and such is now the necessity which constrains them to alter their former Systems of Government. The history of the present King of Great Britain is a history of repeated injuries and usurpations, all having in direct object the establishment of an absolute Tyranny over these States. To prove this, let Facts be submitted to a candid world.—He has refused his Assent to Laws, the most wholesome and necessary for the public good.—He has forbidden his Governors to pass Laws of immediate and pressing importance, unless suspended in their operation till his Assent should be obtained; and when so suspended, he has utterly neglected to attend to them.—He has refused to pass other Laws for the accommodation of large districts of people, unless those people would relinquish the right of Representation in the Legislature, a right inestimable to them and formidable to tyrants only.—He has called together legislative bodies at places unusual, uncomfortable, and distant from the depository of their public Records, for the sole purpose of fatiguing them into compliance with his measures.—He has dissolved Representative Houses repeatedly, for opposing with manly firmness his invasions on the rights of the people.—He has refused for a long time, after such dissolutions, to cause others to be elected; whereby the Legislative powers, incapable of Annihilation, have returned to the People at large for their exercise; the State remaining in the meantime exposed to all the dangers of invasion from without, and convulsions within.—He has endeavoured to prevent the population of these States; for that purpose obstructing the Laws for Naturalization of Foreigners; refusing to pass others to encourage their migrations hither, and raising the conditions of new Appropriations of Lands.—He has obstructed the Administration of Justice, by refusing his Assent to Laws for establishing Judiciary powers.—He has made Judges dependent on his Will alone, for the tenure of their offices, and the amount and payment of their salaries.—He has erected a multitude of New Offices, and sent hither swarms of Officers to harass our people, and eat out their substance. He has kept among us, in times of peace, Standing Armies without the Consent of our legislatures.—He has affected to render the Military independent of and superior to the Civil power.—He has combined with others to subject us to a jurisdiction foreign to our constitution, and unacknowledged by our laws; giving his Assent to their Acts of pretended Legislation:—For quartering large bodies of armed troops among us:—For protecting them, by a mock Trial, from punishment for any Murders which they should commit on the Inhabitants of these States:—For cutting off our Trade with all parts of the world:—For imposing Taxes on us without our Consent:—For depriving us in many cases, of the benefits of Trial by Jury:—For transporting us beyond Seas to be tried for pretended offences:—For abolishing the free System of English Laws in a neighboring Province, establishing therein an Arbitrary government, and enlarging its Boundaries so as to render it at once an example and fit instrument for introducing the same absolute rule into these Colonies:—For taking away our Charters, abolishing our most valuable Laws and altering fundamentally the Forms of our Governments:—For suspending our own Legislatures, and declaring themselves invested with power to legislate for us in all cases whatsoever.—He has abdicated Government here, by declaring us out of his Protection and waging War against us.—He has plundered our seas, ravaged our Coasts, burnt our towns, and destroyed the lives of our people.—He is at this time transporting large Armies of foreign Mercenaries to compleat the works of death, desolation and tyranny, already begun with circumstances of Cruelty & perfidy scarcely paralled in the most barbarous ages, and totally unworthy the Head of a civilized nation.—He has constrained our fellow Citizens taken Captive on the high Seas to bear Arms against their Country, to become the executioners of their friends and Brethren, or to fall themselves by their Hands.—He has excited domestic insurrections amongst us, and has endeavoured to bring on the inhabitants of our frontiers, the merciless Indian Savages, whose known rule of warfare, is an undistinguished destruction of all ages, sexes and conditions. In every stage of these Oppressions We have Petitioned for Redress in the most humble terms: Our repeated Petitions have been answered only by repeated injury. A Prince, whose character is thus marked by every act which may define a Tyrant, is unfit to be the ruler of a free people. Nor have We been wanting in attentions to our British brethren. We have warned them from time to time of attempts by their legislature to extend an unwarrantable jurisdiction over us. We have reminded them of the circumstances of our emigration and settlement here. We have appealed to their native justice and magnanimity, and we have conjured them by the ties of our common kindred to disavow these usurpations, which would inevitably interrupt our connections and correspondence. They too have been deaf to the voice of justice and of consanguinity. We must, therefore, acquiesce in the necessity, which denounces our Separation, and hold them, as we hold the rest of mankind, Enemies in War, in Peace Friends.—

WE, THEREFORE, the Representatives of the UNITED STATES OF AMERICA, in General Congress, Assembled, appealing to the Supreme Judge of the world for the rectitude of our intentions, do, in the Name, and by Authority of the good People of these Colonies, solemnly publish and declare, That these United Colonies are, and of Right ought to be FREE AND INDEPENDENT STATES; that they are Absolved from all Allegiance to the British Crown, and that all political connection between them and the State of Great Britain, is and ought to be totally dissolved; and that as Free and Independent States, they have full Power to levy War, conclude Peace, contract Alliances, establish Commerce, and to do all other Acts and Things which Independent States may of right do.—And for the support of this Declaration, with a firm reliance on the protection of divine Providence, we mutually pledge to each other our Lives, our Fortunes and our sacred Honor.

Critical Thinking

1. What are the three inalienable rights outlined in the Declaration of Independence?
2. Break down the main arguments for independence as outlined in the document.
3. From where do governments draw their power, according to the Declaration of Independence?

The Declaration of Independence, 1776.

The History of the Constitution of the United States

Constitution of the United States. The Articles of Confederation did not provide the centralizing force necessary for unity among the new states and were soon found to be so fundamentally weak that a different political structure was vital. Conflicts about money and credit, trade, and suspicions about regional domination were among the concerns when Congress on February 21, 1787, authorized a Constitutional Convention to revise the Articles. The delegates were selected and assembled in Philadelphia about three months after the call. They concluded their work by September.

The delegates agreed and abided to secrecy. Years afterward James Madison supported the secrecy decision writing that "no man felt himself obliged to retain his opinions any longer than he was satisfied of their propriety and truth, and was open to the force of argument." Secrecy was not for all time. Madison, a delegate from Virginia, was a self-appointed but recognized recorder and took notes in the clear view of the members. Published long afterward, Madison's Journal gives a good record of the convention.

The delegates began to assemble on May 14, 1787, but a majority did not arrive until May 25. George Washington was elected President of the Convention without opposition. The lag of those few days gave some of the early arrivals, especially Madison, time to make preparations on substantive matters, and Gov. Edmund Jennings Randolph presented a plan early in the proceedings that formed the basis for much of the convention deliberations. The essentials were that there should be a government adequate to prevent foreign invasion, prevent dissension among the states, and provide for general national development, and give the national government power enough to make it superior in its realm. The decision was made not merely to revise the articles but to create a new government and a new constitution.

One of the most crucial decisions was the arrangement for representation, a compromise providing that one house would represent the states equally, the other house to be based on popular representation (with some modification due to the slavery question). This arrangement recognized political facts and concessions among men with both theoretical and practical political knowledge.

Basic Features. Oliver Wendell Holmes, Jr., once wrote that the provisions of the Constitution were not mathematical formulas, but "organic living institutions *[sic]* and its origins and

growth were vital to understanding it." The constitution's basic features provide for a supreme law—notwithstanding any other legal document or practice, the Constitution is supreme, as are the laws made in pursuance of it and treaties made under the authority of the United States.

The organizational plan for government is widely known. Foremost is the separation of powers. If the new government were to be limited in its powers, one way to keep it limited would have been executive, legislative, and judicial power [given] to three distinct and non-overlapping branches. A government could not actually function, however, if the separation meant the independence of one branch from the others. The answer was a design to insure cooperation and the sharing of some functions. Among these are the executive veto and the power of Congress to have its way if it musters a super-majority to override that veto. The direction of foreign affairs and the war power are both dispersed and shared. The appointing power is shared by the Senate and the president; impeaching of officers and financial controls are powers shared by the Senate and the House.

A second major contribution by the convention is the provision for the judiciary, which gave rise to the doctrine of judicial review. There is some doubt that the delegates comprehended this prospect but Alexander Hamilton considered it in *Federalist* No. 78: "The interpretation of the laws is a proper and peculiar province of the Courts. . . . Wherever a particular statute contravenes the Constitution, it will be the duty of the judicial tribunals to adhere to the latter and disregard the former."

Another contribution is the federal system, an evolution from colonial practice and the relations between the colonies and the mother country. This division of authority between the new national government and the states recognized the doctrine of delegated and reserved powers. Only certain authority was to go to the new government; the states were not to be done away with and much of the Constitution is devoted to insuring that they were to be maintained even with the stripping of some of their powers.

It is not surprising, therefore, that the convention has been called a great political reform caucus composed of both revolutionaries and men dedicated to democracy. By eighteenth-century standards the Constitution was a democratic document, but standards change and the Constitution has changed since its adoption.

Change and Adaptation. The authors of the Constitution knew that provision for change was essential and provided for it in Article V, insuring that a majority could amend, but being restrictive enough that changes were not likely for the "light and transient" causes Jefferson warned about in the Declaration of Independence.

During the period immediately following the presentation of the Constitution for ratification, requiring assent of nine states to be effective, some alarm was expressed that there was a major defect: there was no bill of rights. So, many leaders committed themselves to the presentation of constitutional amendments for the purpose. Hamilton argued that the absence of a bill of rights was not a defect; indeed, a bill was not necessary. "Why," he wrote, in the last of *The Federalist Papers,* "declare things that shall not be done which there is no power to do?" Nonetheless, the Bill of Rights was presented in the form of amendments and adopted by the states in 1791.

Since 1791 many proposals have been suggested to amend the Constitution. By 1972 sixteen additional amendments had been adopted. Only one, the Twenty-first, which repealed the Eighteenth, was ratified by state conventions. All the others were ratified by state legislatures.

Even a cursory reading of the later amendments shows they do not alter the fundamentals of limited government, the separation of powers, the federal system, or the political process set in motion originally. The Thirteenth, Fourteenth, Fifteenth, and Nineteenth amendments attempt to insure equality to all and are an extension of the Bill of Rights. The others reaffirm some

existing constitutional arrangements, alter some procedures, and at least one, the Sixteenth, states national policy.

Substantial change and adaptation of the Constitution beyond the formal amendments have come from national experience, growth, and development. It has been from the Supreme Court that much of the gradual significant shaping of the Constitution has been done.

Government has remained neither static nor tranquil. Some conflict prevails continually. It may be about the activities of some phase of government or the extent of operations, and whether the arrangement for government can be made responsive to current and prospective needs of society. Conflict is inevitable in a democratic society. Sometimes the conflict is spirited and rises to challenge the continuation of the system. Questions arise whether a fair trial may be possible here or there; legislators are alleged to be indifferent to human problems and pursue distorted public priorities. Presidents are charged with secret actions designed for self-aggrandizement or actions based on half-truths. Voices are heard urging revolution again as the only means of righting alleged wrongs.

The responses continue to demonstrate, however, that the constitutional arrangement for government, the allocation of powers, and the restraints on government all provide the needed flexibility. The Constitution endures.

Adam C. Breckenridge, University of Nebraska-Lincoln

The Constitution of the United States

We the People of the United States, in Order to form a more perfect Union, establish Justice, insure domestic Tranquility, provide for the common defence, promote the general Welfare, and secure the Blessings of Liberty to ourselves and our Posterity, do ordain and establish this Constitution for the United States of America.

Article. I.

SECTION. 1. All legislative Powers herein granted shall be vested in a Congress of the United States, which shall consist of a Senate and House of Representatives.

SECTION. 2. The House of Representatives shall be composed of Members chosen every second Year by the People of the several States, and the Electors in each State shall have the Qualifications requisite for Electors of the most numerous Branch of the State Legislature.

No Person shall be a Representative who shall not have attained to the age of twenty five Years, and been seven Years a Citizen of the United States, and who shall not, when elected, be an Inhabitant of that State in which he shall be chosen.

Representatives and direct Taxes shall be apportioned among the several States which may be included within this Union, according to their respective Numbers, which shall be determined by adding to the whole Number of free Persons, including those bound to Service for a Term of Years, and excluding Indians not taxed, three fifths of all other Persons. The actual Enumeration shall be made within three Years after the first Meeting of the Congress of the United States, and within every subsequent Term of ten Years, in such Manner as they shall by Law direct. The Number of Representatives shall not exceed one for every thirty Thousand, but each State shall have at Least one Representative; and until such enumeration shall be made, the State of New Hampshire shall be entitled to chuse three, Massachusetts eight, Rhode-Island and Providence Plantations one, Connecticut five, New York six, New Jersey four, Pennsylvania eight, Delaware one, Maryland six, Virginia ten, North Carolina five, South Carolina five, and Georgia three.

When vacancies happen in the Representation from any State, the Executive Authority thereof shall issue Writs of Election to fill such Vacancies.

The House of Representatives shall chuse their Speaker and other Officers; and shall have the sole Power of Impeachment.

SECTION. 3. The Senate of the United States shall be composed of two Senators from each State, chosen by the Legislature thereof, for six years; and each Senator shall have one Vote.

Immediately after they shall be assembled in Consequence of the first Election, they shall be divided as equally as may be into three Classes. The Seats of the Senators of the first Class shall be vacated at the Expiration of the second Year, of the second Class at the Expiration of the fourth Year, and of the third Class at the Expiration of the sixth Year, so that one third may be chosen every second year; and if Vacancies happen by Resignation, or otherwise, during the Recess of the Legislature of any State, the Executive thereof may make temporary Appointments until the next Meeting of the Legislature, which shall then fill such Vacancies.

No Person shall be a Senator who shall not have attained to the Age of thirty Years, and been nine Years a Citizen of the United States, and who shall not, when elected, be an Inhabitant of that State for which he shall be chosen.

The Vice President of the United States shall be President of the Senate, but shall have no Vote, unless they be equally divided.

The Senate shall chuse their other Officers, and also a President pro tempore, in the Absence of the Vice President, or when he shall exercise the Office of President of the United States.

The Senate shall have the sole Power to try all Impeachments. When sitting for that Purpose, they shall be on Oath or Affirmation. When the President of the United States is tried the Chief Justice shall preside: And no Person shall be convicted without the Concurrence of two thirds of the Members present.

Judgment in Cases of Impeachment shall not extend further than to removal from Office, and disqualification to hold and enjoy any Office of honor, Trust or Profit under the United States: but the Party convicted shall nevertheless be liable and subject to Indictment, Trial, Judgment and Punishment, according to Law.

SECTION. 4. The Times, Places and Manner of holding Elections for Senators and Representatives, shall be prescribed in each State by the Legislature thereof; but the Congress may at any time by Law make or alter such Regulations, except as to the Places of chusing Senators.

The Congress shall assemble at least once in every Year, and such Meeting shall be on the first Monday in December, unless they shall by Law appoint a different Day.

SECTION. 5. Each House shall be the Judge of the Elections, Returns and Qualifications of its own Members, and a Majority of each shall constitute a Quorum to do Business; but a smaller Number may adjourn from day to day, and may be authorized to compel the Attendance of absent Members, in such Manner, and under such Penalties as each House may provide.

Each House may determine the Rules of its Proceedings, punish its Members for disorderly Behaviour, and, with the Concurrence of two thirds, expel a Member.

Each House shall keep a Journal of its Proceedings, and from time to time publish the same, excepting such Parts as may in their Judgment require Secrecy; and the Yeas and Nays of the Members of either House on any question shall, at the Desire of one fifth of those Present, be entered on the Journal.

Neither House, during the Session of Congress, shall, without the Consent of the other, adjourn for more than three days, nor to any other Place than that in which the two Houses shall be sitting.

SECTION. 6. The Senators and Representatives shall receive a Compensation for their Services, to be ascertained by Law, and paid out of the Treasury of the United States. They shall in all Cases, except Treason, Felony and Breach of the Peace, be privileged from Arrest during their Attendance at the Session of their respective Houses, and in going to and returning from the same; and for any Speech or Debate in either House, they shall not be questioned in any other Place.

No Senator or Representative shall, during the Time for which he was elected, be appointed to any civil Office under the Authority of the United States, which shall have been created, or the Emoluments whereof shall have been encreased during such time; and no Person holding any Office under the United States, shall be a Member of either House during his Continuance in Office.

SECTION. 7. All Bills for raising Revenue shall originate in the House of Representatives; but the Senate may propose or concur with amendments as on other Bills.

Every Bill which shall have passed the House of Representatives and the Senate, shall, before it become a Law, be presented to the President of the United States; If he approve he shall sign it, but if not he shall return it, with his Objections to that House in which it shall have originated, who shall enter the Objections at large on their Journal, and proceed to reconsider it. If after such Reconsideration two thirds of that House shall agree to pass the Bill, it shall be sent, together with the Objections, to the other House, by which it shall likewise be reconsidered, and if approved by two thirds of that House, it shall become a Law. But in all such Cases the Votes of both Houses shall be determined by Yeas and Nays, and the Names of the Persons voting for and against the Bill shall be entered on the Journal of each House respectively. If any Bill shall not be returned by the President within ten Days (Sundays excepted) after it shall have been presented to him, the Same shall be a Law, in like Manner as if he had signed it, unless the Congress by their Adjournment prevent its Return, in which Case it shall not be a Law.

Every Order, Resolution, or Vote to which the Concurrence of the Senate and House of Representatives may be necessary (except on a question of Adjournment) shall be presented to the President of the United States; and before the Same shall take Effect, shall be approved by him, or being disapproved by him, shall be repassed by two thirds of the Senate and House of Representatives, according to the Rules and Limitations prescribed in the Case of a Bill.

SECTION. 8. The Congress shall have Power To lay and collect Taxes, Duties, Imposts and Excises, to pay the Debts and provide for the common Defence and general Welfare of the United States; but all Duties, Imposts and Excises shall be uniform throughout the United States;

To borrow Money on the credit of the United States;

To regulate Commerce with foreign Nations, and among the several States, and with the Indian Tribes;

To establish an uniform Rule of Naturalization, and uniform Laws on the subject of Bankruptcies throughout the United States;

To coin Money, regulate the Value thereof, and of foreign Coin, and fix the Standard of Weights and Measures;

To provide for the Punishment of counterfeiting the Securities and current Coin of the United States;

To establish Post Offices and post Roads;

To promote the Progress of Science and useful Arts, by securing for limited Times to Authors and Inventors the exclusive Right to their respective Writings and Discoveries;

To constitute Tribunals inferior to the supreme Court;

To define and punish Piracies and Felonies committed on the high Seas, and Offences against the Law of Nations;

To declare War, grant Letters of Marque and Reprisal, and make Rules concerning Captures on Land and Water;

To raise and support Armies, but no Appropriation of Money to that Use shall be for a longer Term than two Years;

To provide and maintain a Navy;

To make Rules for the Government and Regulation of the land and naval Forces;

To provide for calling forth the Militia to execute the Laws of the Union, suppress Insurrections and repel Invasions;

To provide for organizing, arming, and disciplining, the Militia, and for governing such Part of them as may be employed in the Service of the United States, reserving to the States respectively, the Appointment of the Officers, and the Authority of training the Militia according to the discipline prescribed by Congress;

To exercise exclusive Legislation in all Cases whatsoever, over such District (not exceeding ten Miles square) as may, by Cession of Particular States, and the Acceptance of Congress, become the Seat of the Government of the United States, and to exercise like Authority over all Places purchased by the Consent of the Legislature of the State in which the Same shall be, for the Erection of Forts, Magazines, Arsenals, dock-Yards, and other needful Buildings;—And

To make all Laws which shall be necessary and proper for carrying into Execution the foregoing Powers, and all other Powers vested by this Constitution in the Government of the United States, or in any Department or Officer thereof.

SECTION. 9. The Migration or Importation of such Persons as any of the States now existing shall think proper to admit, shall not be prohibited by the Congress prior to the Year one thousand eight hundred and eight, but a Tax or duty may be imposed on such Importation, not exceeding ten dollars for each Person.

The Privilege of the Writ of Habeas Corpus shall not be suspended, unless when in Cases of Rebellion or Invasion the public Safety may require it.

No Bill of Attainder or ex post facto Law shall be passed.

No Capitation, or other direct, Tax shall be laid, unless in Proportion to the Census or Enumeration herein before directed to be taken.

No Tax or Duty shall be laid on Articles exported from any State.

No Preference shall be given by any Regulation or Commerce or Revenue to the Ports of one State over those of another; nor shall Vessels bound to, or from, one State, be obliged to enter, clear or pay Duties in another.

No Money shall be drawn from the Treasury, but in Consequence of Appropriations made by Law; and a regular Statement and Account of the Receipts and Expenditures of all public Money shall be published from time to time.

No Title of Nobility shall be granted by the United States: And no Person holding any Office of Profit or Trust under them, shall, without the Consent of the Congress, accept of any present Emolument, Office, or Title, of any kind whatever, from any King, Prince, or foreign State.

SECTION. 10. No State shall enter into any Treaty, Alliance, or Confederation; grant Letters of Marque and Reprisal; coin Money; emit Bills of Credit; make any Thing but gold and silver Coin a Tender in Payment of Debts; pass any Bill of Attainder, ex post facto Law, or Law impairing the Obligation of Contracts, or grant any Title of Nobility.

No State shall, without the Consent of the Congress, lay any Imposts or Duties on Imports or Exports, except what may be absolutely necessary for executing its inspection Laws: and the net Produce of all Duties and Imposts, laid by any State on Imports or Exports, shall be for the Use of the Treasury of the United States; and all such Laws shall be subject to the Revision and Controul of the Congress.

No state shall, without the Consent of Congress, lay any Duty of Tonnage, keep Troops, or Ships of War in time of Peace, enter into any Agreement or Compact with another State, or with a foreign Power, or engage in War, unless actually invaded, or in such imminent Danger as will not admit of delay.

Article. II.

SECTION. 1. The executive Power shall be vested in a President of the United States of America. He shall hold his Office during the Term of four Years, and, together with the Vice President, chosen for the same Term, be elected as follows.

Each State shall appoint, in such Manner as the Legislature thereof may direct, a Number of Electors, equal to the whole Number of Senators and Representatives to which the State may be entitled in the Congress: but no Senator or Representative, or Person holding an Office of Trust or Profit under the United States, shall be appointed an Elector.

The Electors shall meet in their respective States, and vote by Ballot for two Persons, of whom one at least shall not be an Inhabitant of the same State with themselves. And they shall make a List of all the persons voted for, and of the Number of Votes for each; which List they shall sign and certify, and transmit sealed to the Seat of Government of the United States, directed to the President of the Senate. The President of the Senate shall, in the Presence of the Senate and House of Representatives, open all the Certificates, and the Votes shall then be counted. The Person having the greatest Number of Votes shall be the President, if such Number be a Majority of the whole Number of Electors appointed; and if there be more than one who have such Majority, and have an equal Number of Votes, then the House of Representatives shall immediately chuse by Ballot one of them for President; and if no Person have a Majority, then from the five highest on the List the said House shall in like Manner chuse the President. But in chusing the President,

the Votes shall be taken by States, the Representation from each State having one Vote; a quorum for this Purpose shall consist of a Member or Members from two thirds of the States, and a Majority of all the States shall be necessary to a Choice. In every Case, after the Choice of the President, the Person having the greatest Number of Votes of the Electors shall be the Vice President. But if there should remain two or more who have equal Votes, the Senate shall chuse from them by Ballot the Vice President.

The Congress may determine the Time of chusing the Electors, and the Day on which they shall give their Votes; which Day shall be the same throughout the United States.

No Person except a natural born Citizen, or a Citizen of the United States, at the time of the Adoption of this Constitution, shall be eligible to the Office of President; neither shall any person be eligible to that Office who shall not have attained to the Age of thirty five Years, and been fourteen Years a Resident within the United States.

In Case of the Removal of the President from Office, or of his Death, Resignation, or Inability to discharge the Powers and Duties of the said Office, the Same shall devolve on the Vice President, and the Congress may by Law provide for the Case of Removal, Death, Resignation or Inability, both of the President and Vice President, declaring what Officer shall then act as President, and such Officer shall act accordingly, until the Disability be removed, or a President shall be elected.

The President shall, at stated Times, receive for his Services, a Compensation, which shall neither be encreased nor diminished during the Period for which he shall have been elected, and he shall not receive within that period any other Emolument from the United States, or any of them.

Before he enter on the Execution of his Office, he shall take the following Oath or Affirmation:—"I do solemnly swear (or affirm) that I will faithfully execute the Office of President of the United States, and will to the best of my Ability, preserve, protect and defend the Constitution of the United States."

SECTION. 2. The President shall be Commander in Chief of the Army and Navy of the United States, and of the Militia of the several States, when called into the actual Service of the United States; he may require the Opinion, in writing, of the principal Officer in each of the executive Departments, upon any Subject relating to the Duties of their respective Offices, and he shall have Power to grant Reprieves and Pardons for Offences against the United States, except in Cases of Impeachment.

He shall have Power, by and with the Advice and Consent of the Senate, to make Treaties, provided two thirds of the Senators present concur; and he shall nominate, and by and with the Advice and Consent of the Senate, shall appoint Ambassadors, other public Ministers and Consuls, Judges of the supreme Court, and all other Officers of the United States, whose Appointments are not herein otherwise provided for, and which shall be established by Law: but the Congress may by Law vest the Appointment of such inferior Officers, as they think proper, in the President alone, in the Courts of Law, or in the Heads of Departments.

The President shall have Power to fill up all Vacancies that may happen during the Recess of the Senate, by granting

Commissions which shall expire at the End of their next Session.

SECTION. 3. He shall from time to time give to the Congress Information of the State of the Union, and recommend to their Consideration such Measures as he shall judge necessary and expedient; he may, on extraordinary Occasions, convene both Houses, or either of them, and in Case of Disagreement between them, with Respect to the Time of Adjournment, he may adjourn them to such Time as he shall think proper; he shall receive Ambassadors and other public Ministers; he shall take Care that the Laws be faithfully executed, and shall Commission all the Officers of the United States.

SECTION. 4. The President, Vice President and all civil Officers of the United States, shall be removed from Office on Impeachment for, and Conviction of, Treason, Bribery, or other high Crimes and Misdemeanors.

Article. III.

SECTION. 1. The judicial Power of the United States, shall be vested in one supreme Court, and in such inferior Courts as the Congress may from time to time ordain and establish. The Judges, both of the supreme and inferior Courts, shall hold their Offices during good Behaviour, and shall, at stated Times, receive for their Services, a Compensation, which shall not be diminished during their Continuance in Office.

SECTION. 2. The judicial Power shall extend to all Cases, in Law and Equity, arising under this Constitution, the Laws of the United States, and Treaties made, or which shall be made, under their Authority;—to all Cases affecting Ambassadors, other public Ministers and Consuls;—to all Cases of admiralty and maritime Jurisdiction;—to Controversies to which the United States shall be a Party;—to Controversies between two or more States;—between a State and Citizens of another State;—between Citizens of different States;—between Citizens of the same State claiming Lands under Grants of different States, and between a State, or the Citizens thereof, and foreign States, Citizens or Subjects.

In all Cases affecting Ambassadors, other public Ministers and Consuls, and those in which a State shall be Party, the supreme Court shall have original Jurisdiction. In all the other Cases before mentioned, the supreme Court shall have appellate Jurisdiction, both as to Law and Fact, with such Exceptions, and under such Regulations as the Congress shall make.

The Trial of all Crimes, except in Cases of Impeachment, shall be by Jury; and such Trial shall be held in the State where the said Crimes shall have been committed; but when not committed within any State, the Trial shall be at such Place or Places as the Congress may by Law have directed.

SECTION. 3. Treason against the United States, shall consist only in levying War against them, or in adhering to their Enemies, giving them Aid and Comfort. No Person shall be convicted of Treason unless on the Testimony of two Witnesses to the same overt Act, or on Confession in open Court.

The Congress shall have Power to declare the Punishment of Treason, but no Attainder of Treason shall work Corruption of Blood, or Forfeiture except during the Life of the Person attained.

Article. IV.

SECTION. 1. Full Faith and Credit shall be given in each State to the public Acts, Records, and judicial Proceedings of every other State. And the Congress may by general Laws prescribe the Manner in which such Acts, Record and Proceedings shall be proved, and the Effect thereof.

SECTION. 2. The Citizens of each State shall be entitled to all Privileges and Immunities of Citizens in the several States.

A Person charged in any State with Treason, Felony, or other Crime, who shall flee from Justice, and be found in another State, shall on Demand of the executive Authority of the State from which he fled, be delivered up, to be removed to the State having Jurisdiction of the Crime.

No Person held to Service or Labour in one State, under the Laws thereof, escaping into another, shall, in Consequence of any Law or Regulation therein, be discharged from such Service or Labour, but shall be delivered up on Claim of the Party to whom such Service or Labour may be due.

SECTION. 3. New States may be admitted by the Congress into this Union; but no new State shall be formed or erected within the Jurisdiction of any other State; nor any State be formed by the Junction of two or more States, or Parts of States, without the Consent of the Legislatures of the States concerned as well as of the Congress.

The Congress shall have Power to dispose of and make all needful Rules and Regulations respecting the Territory or other Property belonging to the United States; and nothing in this Constitution shall be so construed as to Prejudice any Claims of the United States, or of any particular State.

SECTION. 4. The United States shall guarantee to every State in this Union a Republican Form of Government, and shall protect each of them against Invasion; and on Application of the Legislature, or of the Executive (when the Legislature cannot be convened) against domestic Violence.

Article. V.

The Congress, whenever two thirds of both Houses shall deem it necessary, shall propose Amendments to this Constitution, or, on the Application of the Legislature of two thirds of the several States, shall call a Convention for proposing Amendments, which, in either Case, shall be valid to all Intents and Purposes, as Part of this Constitution, when ratified by the Legislatures of three fourths of the several States, or by Conventions in three fourths thereof, as the one or the other Mode of Ratification may be proposed by the Congress; Provided that no Amendment which may be made prior to the Year One thousand eight hundred and eight shall in any Manner affect the first and fourth Clauses in the Ninth Section of the first Article; and that no State, without its Consent, shall be deprived of its equal Suffrage in the Senate.

Article. VI.

All Debts contracted and Engagements entered into, before the Adoption of this Constitution, shall be as valid against the United States under this Constitution, as under the Confederation.

This Constitution, and the Laws of the United States which shall be made in Pursuance thereof; and all Treaties made, or which shall be made, under the Authority of the United States, shall be the supreme Law of the Land; and the Judges in every State shall be bound thereby, any Thing in the Constitution or Laws of any State to the Contrary notwithstanding.

The Senators and Representatives before mentioned, and the Members of the several State Legislatures, and all executive and judicial Officers, both of the United States and of the several States, shall be bound by Oath or Affirmation, to support this Constitution; but no religious Test shall ever be required as a Qualification to any Office or public Trust under the United States.

New Hampshire	JOHN LANGDON
	NICHOLAS GILMAN
Massachusetts	NATHANIEL GORHAM
	RUFUS KING
Connecticut	Wm. SAML JOHNSON
	ROGER SHERMAN
New York . . .	ALEXANDER HAMILTON
New Jersey	WIL: LIVINGSTON
	DAVID BREARLEY
	Wm. PATERSON
	JONA: DAYTON
Pennsylvania	B FRANKLIN
	THOMAS MIFFLIN
	ROBt MORRIS
	GEO. CLYMER
	THOs. FITZSIMONS
	JARED INGERSOLL
	JAMES WILSON
	GOUV MORRIS
Delaware	GEO: READ
	GUNNING BEDFORD jun
	JOHN DICKINSON
	RICHARD BASSETT
	JACO: BROOM
Maryland	JAMES McHENRY
	DAN OF St THOs. JENIFER
	DANL CARROLL
Virginia	JOHN BLAIR
	JAMES MADISON Jr.
North Carolina	Wm. BLOUNT
	RICHd. DOBBS SPAIGHT
	HU WILLIAMSON
South Carolina	J. RUTLEDGE
	CHARLES COTESWORTH PINCKNEY
	CHARLES PINCKNEY
	PIERCE BUTLER
Georgia	WILLIAM FEW
	ABR BALDWIN

Article. VII.

The Ratification of the Conventions of nine States, shall be sufficient for the Establishment of this Constitution between the States so ratifying the Same.

Done in Convention by the Unanimous Consent of the States present the Seventeenth Day of September in the Year of our Lord one thousand seven hundred and Eighty seven and of the Independence of the United States of America the Twelfth In witness whereof We have hereunto subscribed our Names,

Go. WASHINGTON—Presidt. and deputy from Virginia
In Convention Monday, September 17th 1787.

Present The States of

New Hampshire, Massachusetts, Connecticut, Mr. Hamilton from New York, New Jersey, Pennsylvania, Delaware, Maryland, Virginia, North Carolina and Georgia.

Resolved,

That the preceeding Constitution be laid before the United States in Congress assembled, and that it is the Opinion of this Convention, that it should afterwards be submitted to a Convention of Delegates, chosen in each State by the People thereof, under the Recommendation of its Legislature, for their Assent and Ratification; and that each Convention assenting to, and ratifying the Same, should give Notice thereof to the United States in Congress assembled. Resolved, That it is the Opinion of this Convention, that as soon as the Conventions of nine States shall have ratified this Constitution, the United States in Congress assembled should fix a Day on which Electors should be appointed by the States which shall have ratified the same, and a Day on which the Electors should assemble to vote for the President, and the Time and Place for commencing Proceedings under this Constitution. That after such Publication the Electors should be appointed, and the Senators and Representatives elected: That the Electors should meet on the Day fixed for the Election of the President, and should transmit their Votes certified, signed, sealed and directed, as the Constitution requires, to the Secretary of the United States in Congress assembled, that

Ratification of the Constitution

State	Date of Ratification
Delaware	Dec 7, 1787
Pennsylvania	Dec 12, 1787
New Jersey	Dec 19, 1787
Georgia	Jan 2, 1788
Connecticut	Jan 9, 1788
Massachusetts	Feb 6, 1788
Maryland	Apr 28, 1788
South Carolina	May 23, 1788
New Hampshire	June 21, 1788
Virginia	Jun 25, 1788
New York	Jun 26, 1788
Rhode Island	May 29, 1790
North Carolina	Nov 21, 1789

the Senators and Representatives should convene at the Time and Place assigned; that the Senators should appoint a President of the Senate, for the sole Purpose of receiving, opening and counting the Votes for President; and, that after he shall be chosen, the Congress, together with the President, should, without Delay, proceed to execute this Constitution.

By the Unanimous Order of the Convention

Go. WASHINGTON—Presidt.

W. JACKSON Secretary.

ARTICLES IN ADDITION TO, AND AMENDMENT OF, THE CONSTITUTION OF THE UNITED STATES OF AMERICA, PROPOSED BY CONGRESS, AND RATIFIED BY THE SEVERAL STATES, PURSUANT TO THE FIFTH ARTICLE OF THE ORIGINAL CONSTITUTION.

Amendment I.

Congress shall make no law respecting an establishment of religion, or prohibiting the free exercise thereof; or abridging the freedom of speech, or of the press; or the right of the people peaceably to assemble, and to petition the Government for a redress of grievances.

Amendment II.

A well regulated Militia, being necessary to the security of a free State, the right of the people to keep and bear Arms, shall not be infringed.

Amendment III.

No Soldier shall, in time of peace be quartered in any house, without the consent of the Owner, nor in time of war, but in a manner to be prescribed by law.

Amendment IV.

The right of the people to be secure in their persons, houses, papers, and effects, against unreasonable searches and seizures, shall not be violated, and no Warrants shall issue, but upon probable cause, supported by Oath or affirmation, and particularly describing the place to be searched, and the persons or things to be seized.

Amendment V.

No person shall be held to answer for a capital, or otherwise infamous crime, unless on a presentment or indictment of a Grand Jury, except in cases arising in the land or naval forces, or in the Militia, when in actual service in time of War or public danger; nor shall any person be subject for the same offence to be twice put in jeopardy of life or limb; nor shall be compelled in any criminal case to be a witness against himself, nor

be deprived of life, liberty, or property, without due process of law; nor shall private property be taken for public use, without just compensation.

Amendment VI.

In all criminal prosecutions, the accused shall enjoy the right to a speedy and public trial, by an impartial jury of the State and district wherein the crime shall have been committed, which district shall have been previously ascertained by law, and to be informed of the nature and cause of the accusation; to be confronted with the witnesses against him; to have compulsory process for obtaining witnesses in his favor, and to have the Assistance of Counsel for his defence.

Amendment VII.

In Suits at common law, where the value in controversy shall exceed twenty dollars, the right of trial by jury shall be preserved, and no fact tried by a jury, shall be otherwise re-examined in any Court of the United States, than according to the rules of the common law.

Amendment VIII.

Excessive bail shall not be required, nor excessive fines imposed, nor cruel and unusual punishments inflicted.

Amendment IX.

The enumeration in the Constitution, of certain rights, shall not be construed to deny or disparage others retained by the people.

Amendment X.

The powers not delegated to the United States by the Constitution, nor prohibited by it to the States, are reserved to the States respectively, or to the people.

Amendment XI.
(Adopted Jan. 8, 1798)

The Judicial power of the United States shall not be construed to extend to any suit in law or equity, commenced or prosecuted against one of the United States by Citizens of another State, or by Citizens or Subjects of any Foreign State.

Amendment XII.
(Adopted Sept. 25, 1804)

The Electors shall meet in their respective states and vote by ballot for President and Vice-President, one of whom, at least, shall not be an inhabitant of the same state with themselves; they shall name in their ballots the person voted for as President, and in distinct ballots the person voted for as Vice-President, and they shall make distinct lists of all persons voted for as President, and of all persons voted for as Vice-President, and of the number of votes for each, which lists they shall sign and certify, and transmit sealed to the seat of the government of the United States, directed to the President of the Senate;—The President of the Senate shall, in the presence of the Senate and House of Representatives, open all the certificates and the votes shall then be counted;—The person having the greatest number of votes for President, shall be the President, if such number be a majority of the whole number of Electors appointed; and if no person have such majority, then from the persons having the highest numbers not exceeding three on the list of those voted for as President, the House of Representatives shall choose immediately, by ballot, the President. But in choosing the President, the votes shall be taken by states, the representation from each state having one vote; a quorum for this purpose shall consist of a member or members from two-thirds of the states, and a majority of all the states shall be necessary to a choice. And if the House of Representatives shall not choose a President whenever the right of choice shall devolve upon them, before the fourth day of March next following, then the Vice-President shall act as President, as in the case of the death or other constitutional disability of the President.—The person having the greatest number of votes as Vice-President, shall be the Vice-President, if such number be a majority of the whole number of Electors appointed, and if no person have a majority, then from the two highest numbers on the list, the Senate shall choose the Vice-President; a quorum for the purpose shall consist of two-thirds of the whole number of Senators, and a majority of the whole number shall be necessary to a choice. But no person constitutionally ineligible to the office of President shall be eligible to that of Vice-President of the United States.

Amendment XIII.

(Adopted Dec. 18, 1865)

SECTION 1. Neither slavery nor involuntary servitude, except as a punishment for crime whereof the party shall have been duly convicted, shall exist within the United States, or any place subject to their jurisdiction.

SECTION 2. Congress shall have power to enforce this article by appropriate legislation.

Amendment XIV.

(Adopted July 28, 1868)

SECTION 1. All persons born or naturalized in the United States and subject to the jurisdiction thereof, are citizens of the United States and of the State wherein they reside. No State shall make or enforce any law which shall abridge the privileges or immunities of citizens of the United States; nor shall any State deprive any person of life, liberty, or property, without due process of law; nor deny to any person within its jurisdiction the equal protection of the laws.

SECTION 2. Representatives shall be apportioned among the several States according to their respective numbers, counting the whole number of persons in each State, excluding Indians not taxed. But when the right to vote at any election for the choice of electors for President and Vice President of the United States, Representatives in Congress, the Executive and Judicial officers of a State, or the members of the Legislature thereof, is denied to any of the male inhabitants of such State, being twenty-one years of age, and citizens of the United States, or in any way abridged, except for participation in rebellion, or other crime, the basis of representation therein shall be reduced in the proportion which the number of such male citizens shall bear to the whole number of male citizens twenty-one years of age in such State.

SECTION 3. No person shall be a Senator or Representative in Congress, or elector of President and Vice President, or hold any office, civil or military, under the United States, or under any State, who, having previously taken an oath, as a member of Congress, or as an officer of the United States, or as a member of any State legislature, or as an executive or judicial officer of any State, to support the Constitution of the United States, shall have engaged in insurrection or rebellion against the same, or given aid or comfort to the enemies thereof. But Congress may by a vote of two-thirds of each House, remove such disability.

SECTION 4. The validity of the public debt of the United States, authorized by law, including debts incurred for payment of pensions and bounties for services in suppressing insurrection or rebellion, shall not be questioned. But neither the United States nor any State shall assume or pay any debt or obligation incurred in aid of insurrection or rebellion against the United States, or any claim for the loss or emancipation of any slave; but all such debts, obligations and claims shall be held illegal and void.

SECTION 5. The Congress shall have power to enforce, by appropriate legislation, the provisions of this article.

Amendment XV.

(Adopted March 30, 1870)

SECTION 1. The right of citizens of the United States to vote shall not be denied or abridged by the United States or by any State on account of race, color, or previous condition of servitude.

SECTION 2. The Congress shall have power to enforce this article by appropriate legislation.

Amendment XVI.

(Adopted Feb. 25, 1913)

The Congress shall have power to lay and collect taxes on incomes, from whatever source derived, without apportionment among the several States, and without regard to any census or enumeration.

Amendment XVII.

(Adopted May 31, 1913)

The Senate of the United States shall be composed of two Senators from each State, elected by the people thereof, for six years; and each Senator shall have one vote. The electors in each State shall have the qualifications requisite for electors of the most numerous branch of the State legislatures.

When vacancies happen in the representation of any State in the Senate, the executive authority of such State shall issue writs of election to fill such vacancies: Provided, That the legislature of any State may empower the executive thereof to make temporary appointments until the people fill the vacancies by election as the legislature may direct.

This amendment shall not be so construed as to affect the election or term of any Senator chosen before it becomes valid as part of the Constitution.

Amendment XVIII.

(Adopted Jan. 29, 1919)

SECTION 1. After one year from the ratification of this article the manufacture, sale or transportation of intoxicating liquors within, the importation thereof into, or the exportation thereof from the United States and all territory subject to the jurisdiction thereof for beverage purposes is hereby prohibited.

SECTION 2. The Congress and the several States shall have concurrent power to enforce this article by appropriate legislation.

SECTION 3. This article shall be inoperative unless it shall have been ratified as an amendment to the Constitution by the legislatures of the several States, as provided in the Constitution, within seven years from the date of the submission hereof to the States by the Congress.

Amendment XIX.

(Adopted Aug. 26, 1920)

The right of citizens of the United States to vote shall not be denied or abridged by the United States or by any State on account of sex.

Congress shall have power to enforce this article by appropriate legislation.

Amendment XX.

(Adopted Feb. 6, 1933)

SECTION 1. The terms of the President and Vice President shall end at noon on the 20th day of January, and the terms of Senators and Representatives at noon on the 3d day of January, of the years in which such terms would have ended if this article had not been ratified; and the terms of their successors shall then begin.

SECTION 2. The Congress shall assemble at least once in every year, and such meeting shall begin at noon on the 3d day of January, unless they shall by law appoint a different day.

SECTION 3. If, at the time fixed for the beginning of the term of the President, the President elect shall have died, the Vice President elect shall become President. If a President shall not have been chosen before the time fixed for the beginning of his term, or if the President elect shall have failed to qualify, then the Vice President elect shall act as President until a President shall have qualified; and the Congress may by law provide for the case wherein neither a President elect nor a Vice President elect shall have qualified, declaring who shall then act as President, or the manner in which one who is to act shall be selected, and such person shall act accordingly until a President or Vice President shall have qualified.

SECTION 4. The Congress may by law provide for the case of the death of any of the persons from whom the House of Representatives may choose a President whenever the right of choice shall have devolved upon them, and for the case of the death of any of the persons from whom the Senate may choose a Vice President whenever the right of choice shall have devolved upon them.

SECTION 5. Sections 1 and 2 shall take effect on the 15th day of October following the ratification of this article.

SECTION 6. This article shall be inoperative unless it shall have been ratified as an amendment to the Constitution by the legislatures of three-fourths of the several States within seven years from the date of its submission.

Amendment XXI.

(Adopted Dec. 5, 1933)

SECTION 1. The eighteenth article of amendment to the Constitution of the United States is hereby repealed.

SECTION 2. The transportation or importation into any State, Territory, or possession of the United States for delivery or use therein of intoxicating liquors, in violation of the laws thereof, is hereby prohibited.

SECTION 3. This article shall be inoperative unless it shall have been ratified as an amendment to the Constitution by conventions in the several States, as provided in the Constitution, within seven years from the date of the submission hereof to the States by the Congress.

Amendment XXII.

(Adopted Feb. 27, 1951)

SECTION 1. No person shall be elected to the office of the President more than twice, and no person who has held the office of President, or acted as President, for more than two years of a term to which some other person was elected President shall be elected to the office of the President more than once. But this Article shall not apply to any person holding the office of President when this Article was proposed by the Congress, and shall not prevent any person who may be holding the office of President, or acting as President, during the term within which this Article becomes operative from holding the office of President or acting as President during the remainder of such term.

SECTION 2. This Article shall be inoperative unless it shall have been ratified as an amendment to the Constitution by the legislatures of three-fourths of the several States within seven years from the date of its submission to the States by the Congress.

Amendment XXIII.

(Adopted Mar. 29, 1961)

SECTION 1. The District constituting the seat of Government of the United States shall appoint in such manner as the Congress may direct:

A number of electors of President and Vice President equal to the whole number of Senators and Representatives in Congress to which the District would be entitled if it were a State, but in no event more than the least populous State; they shall be in addition to those appointed by the States, but they shall be considered, for the purposes of the election of President and Vice President, to be electors appointed by a State; and they shall meet in the District and perform such duties as provided by the twelfth article of amendment.

SECTION 2. The Congress shall have power to enforce this article by appropriate legislation.

Amendment XXIV.

(Adopted Jan. 23, 1964)

SECTION 1. The right of citizens of the United States to vote in any primary or other election for President or Vice President, for electors for President or Vice President, or for Senator or Representative in Congress, shall not be denied or abridged by the United States or any State by reason of failure to pay any poll tax or other tax.

SECTION 2. The Congress shall have the power to enforce this article by appropriate legislation.

Amendment XXV.

(Adopted Feb. 10, 1967)

SECTION 1. In case of the removal of the President from office or of his death or resignation, the Vice President shall become President.

SECTION 2. Whenever there is a vacancy in the office of the Vice President, the President shall nominate a Vice President who shall take the office upon confirmation by a majority vote of both houses of Congress.

SECTION 3. Whenever the President transmits to the President pro tempore of the Senate and the Speaker of the House of Representatives his written declaration that he is unable to discharge the powers and duties of his office, and until he transmits to them a written declaration to the contrary, such powers and duties shall be discharged by the Vice President as Acting President.

SECTION 4. Whenever the Vice President and a majority of either the principal officers of the executive departments or of such other body as Congress may by law provide, transmit to the President pro tempore of the Senate and the Speaker of the House of Representatives their written declaration that the President is unable to discharge the powers and duties of his office, the Vice President shall immediately assume the powers and duties of the office as Acting President.

Thereafter, when the President transmits to the President pro tempore of the Senate and the Speaker of the House of Representatives his written declaration that no inability exists, he shall resume the powers and duties of his office unless the Vice President and a majority of either the principal officers of the executive department or of such other body as Congress may by law provide, transmit within four days to the President pro tempore of the Senate and the Speaker of the House of Representatives their written declaration that the President is unable to discharge the powers and duties of his office. Thereupon Congress shall decide the issue, assembling within forty-eight hours for that purpose if not in session. If the Congress within twenty-one days after receipt of the latter written declaration, or, if Congress is not in session, within twenty-one days after Congress is required to assemble, determines by two-thirds vote of both Houses that the President is unable to discharge the powers and duties of his office, the Vice President shall continue to discharge the same as Acting President; otherwise, the President shall resume the powers and duties of his office.

Amendment XXVI.

(Adopted June 30, 1971)

SECTION 1. The right of citizens of the United States, who are 18 years of age or older, to vote shall not be denied or abridged by the United States or by any state on account of age.

SECTION 2. The Congress shall have the power to enforce this article by appropriate legislation.

Amendment XXVII.

(Adopted May 7, 1992)

No law, varying the compensation for the services of the Senators and Representatives, shall take effect, until an election of Representatives shall have intervened.

Critical Thinking

1. In light of the procedures for ratifying the Constitution that appear in Article VII, consider the Preamble and its claim that "We the People" did "ordain and establish" the Constitution.
2. Name the three main branches of government as outlined in the Constitution, and identify a half-dozen or so of the powers shared between two or more branches.
3. What is a federal system? What powers do individual states retain in the U.S. federal system? What powers does the national government have?
4. What is the Bill of Rights? What are some of the key protections it specifies?

The Constitution of the United States, 1787.

Federalist No. 10

JAMES MADISON

To the People of the State of New York

Among the numerous advantages promised by a well-constructed Union, none deserves to be more accurately developed than its tendency to break and control the violence of faction. The friend of popular governments never finds himself so much alarmed for their character and fate, as when he contemplates their propensity to this dangerous vice. He will not fail, therefore, to set a due value on any plan which, without violating the principles to which he is attached, provides a proper cure for it. The instability, injustice, and confusion introduced into the public councils, have, in truth, been the mortal diseases under which popular governments have everywhere perished; as they continue to be the favorite and fruitful topics from which the adversaries to liberty derive their most specious declamations. The valuable improvements made by the American constitutions on the popular models, both ancient and modern, cannot certainly be too much admired; but it would be an unwarrantable partiality, to contend that they have as effectually obviated the danger on this side, as was wished and expected. Complaints are everywhere heard from our most considerate and virtuous citizens, equally the friends of public and private faith, and of public and personal liberty, that our governments are too unstable, that the public good is disregarded in the conflicts of rival parties, and that measures are too often decided, not according to the rules of justice and the rights of the minor party, but by the superior force of an interested and overbearing majority. However anxiously we may wish that these complaints had no foundation, the evidence of known facts will not permit us to deny that they are in some degree true. It will be found, indeed, on a candid review of our situation, that some of the distresses under which we labor have been erroneously charged on the operation of our governments; but it will be found, at the same time, that other causes will not alone account for many of our heaviest misfortunes; and, particularly, for that prevailing and increasing distrust of public engagements, and alarm for private rights, which are echoed from one end of the continent to the other. These must be chiefly, if not wholly, effects of the unsteadiness and injustice with which a factious spirit has tainted our public administrations.

By a faction, I understand a number of citizens, whether amounting to a majority or minority of the whole, who are united and actuated by some common impulse of passion, or of interest, adverse to the rights of other citizens, or to the permanent and aggregate interests of the community.

There are two methods of curing the mischiefs of faction: the one, by removing its causes; the other, by controlling its effects.

There are again two methods of removing the causes of faction: the one, by destroying the liberty which is essential to its existence; the other, by giving to every citizen the same opinions, the same passions, and the same interests.

It could never be more truly said than of the first remedy, that it was worse than the disease. Liberty is to faction what air is to fire, an aliment without which it instantly expires. But it could not be less folly to abolish liberty, which is essential to political life, because it nourishes faction, than it would be to wish the annihilation of air, which is essential to animal life, because it imparts to fire its destructive agency.

The second expedient is as impracticable as the first would be unwise. As long as the reason of man continues fallible, and he is at liberty to exercise it, different opinions will be formed. As long as the connection subsists between his reason and his self-love, his opinions and his passions will have a reciprocal influence on each other; and the former will be objects to which the latter will attach themselves. The diversity in the faculties of men, from which the rights of property originate, is not less an insuperable obstacle to a uniformity of interests. The protection of these faculties is the first object of government. From the protection of different and unequal faculties of acquiring property, the possession of different degrees and kinds of property immediately results; and from the influence of these on the sentiments and views of the respective proprietors, ensues a division of the society into different interests and parties.

The latent causes of faction are thus sown in the nature of man; and we see them everywhere brought into different degrees of activity, according to the different circumstances of civil society. A zeal for different opinions concerning religion, concerning government, and many other points, as well of speculation as of practice; an attachment to different leaders ambitiously contending for pre-eminence and power; or to persons of other descriptions whose fortunes have been interesting to the human passions, have, in turn, divided mankind into parties, inflamed them with mutual animosity, and rendered them much more disposed to vex and oppress each other than to co-operate for their common good. So strong is this propensity of mankind to fall into mutual animosities, that where no substantial occasion presents itself, the most frivolous and fanciful distinctions have been sufficient to kindle their unfriendly passions and excite their most violent conflicts. But the most common and durable source of factions has been the various and unequal distribution of property. Those who hold and those who are without property have ever formed distinct interests in society.

Those who are creditors, and those who are debtors, fall under a like discrimination. A landed interest, a manufacturing interest, a mercantile interest, a moneyed interest, with many lesser interests, grow up of necessity in civilized nations, and divide them into different classes, actuated by different sentiments and views. The regulation of these various and interfering interests forms the principal task of modern legislation, and involves the spirit of party and faction in the necessary and ordinary operations of the government.

No man is allowed to be a judge in his own cause, because his interest would certainly bias his judgment, and, not improbably, corrupt his integrity. With equal, nay with greater reason, a body of men are unfit to be both judges and parties at the same time; yet what are many of the most important acts of legislation, but so many judicial determinations, not indeed concerning the rights of single persons, but concerning the rights of large bodies of citizens? And what are the different classes of legislators but advocates and parties to the causes which they determine? Is a law proposed concerning private debts? It is a question to which the creditors are parties on one side and the debtors on the other. Justice ought to hold the balance between them. Yet the parties are, and must be, themselves the judges; and the most numerous party, or, in other words, the most powerful faction must be expected to prevail. Shall domestic manufactures be encouraged, and in what degree, by restrictions on foreign manufactures? are questions which would be differently decided by the landed and the manufacturing classes, and probably by neither with a sole regard to justice and the public good. The apportionment of taxes on the various descriptions of property is an act which seems to require the most exact impartiality; yet there is, perhaps, no legislative act in which greater opportunity and temptation are given to a predominant party to trample on the rules of justice. Every shilling with which they overburden the inferior number, is a shilling saved to their own pockets.

It is in vain to say that enlightened statesmen will be able to adjust these clashing interests, and render them all subservient to the public good. Enlightened statesmen will not always be at the helm. Nor, in many cases, can such an adjustment be made at all without taking into view indirect and remote considerations, which will rarely prevail over the immediate interest which one party may find in disregarding the rights of another or the good of the whole.

The inference to which we are brought is, that the *causes* of faction cannot be removed, and that relief is only to be sought in the means of controlling its *effects*.

If a faction consists of less than a majority, relief is supplied by the republican principle, which enables the majority to defeat its sinister views by regular vote. It may clog the administration, it may convulse the society; but it will be unable to execute and mask its violence under the forms of the Constitution. When a majority is included in a faction, the form of popular government, on the other hand, enables it to sacrifice to its ruling passion or interest both the public good and the rights of other citizens. To secure the public good and private rights against the danger of such a faction, and at the same time to preserve the spirit and the form of popular government, is then the great object to which our inquiries are directed. Let me add that it is the great desideratum by which this form of government can be rescued from the opprobrium under which it has so long labored, and be recommended to the esteem and adoption of mankind.

By what means is this object attainable? Evidently by one of two only. Either the existence of the same passion or interest in a majority at the same time must be prevented, or the majority, having such coexistent passion or interest, must be rendered, by their number and local situation, unable to concert and carry into effect schemes of oppression. If the impulse and the opportunity be suffered to coincide, we well know that neither moral nor religious motives can be relied on as an adequate control. They are not found to be such on the injustice and violence of individuals, and lose their efficacy in proportion to the number combined together, that is, in proportion as their efficacy becomes needful.

From this view of the subject it may be concluded that a pure democracy, by which I mean a society consisting of a small number of citizens, who assemble and administer the government in person, can admit of no cure for the mischiefs of faction. A common passion or interest will, in almost every case, be felt by a majority of the whole; a communication and concert result from the form of government itself; and there is nothing to check the inducements to sacrifice the weaker party or an obnoxious individual. Hence it is that such democracies have ever been spectacles of turbulence and contention; have ever been found incompatible with personal security or the rights of property; and have in general been as short in their lives as they have been violent in their deaths. Theoretic politicians, who have patronized this species of government, have erroneously supposed that by reducing mankind to a perfect equality in their political rights, they would, at the same time, be perfectly equalized and assimilated in their possessions, their opinions, and their passions.

A republic, by which I mean a government in which the scheme of representation takes place, opens a different prospect, and promises the cure for which we are seeking. Let us examine the points in which it varies from pure democracy, and we shall comprehend both the nature of the cure and the efficacy which it must derive from the Union.

The two great points of difference between a democracy and a republic are: first, the delegation of the government, in the latter, to a small number of citizens elected by the rest; secondly, the greater number of citizens, and greater sphere of country, over which the latter may be extended.

The effect of the first difference is, on the one hand, to refine and enlarge the public views, by passing them through the medium of a chosen body of citizens, whose wisdom may best discern the true interest of their country, and whose patriotism and love of justice will be least likely to sacrifice it to temporary or partial considerations. Under such a regulation, it may well happen that the public voice, pronounced by the representatives of the people, will be more consonant to the public good than if pronounced by the people themselves, convened for the purpose. On the other hand, the effect may be inverted. Men of factious tempers, of local prejudices, or of sinister designs, may, by intrigue, by corruption, or by other means, first obtain the suffrages, and then betray the interests, of the people. The question resulting is, whether small or extensive republics are more favorable to the election of proper guardians of the public weal; and it is clearly decided in favor of the latter by two obvious considerations.

In the first place, it is to be remarked that, however small the republic may be, the representatives must be raised to a certain number, in order to guard against the cabals of a few; and that, however large it may be, they must be limited to a certain number, in order to guard against the confusion of a multitude. Hence, the number of representatives in the two cases not being in proportion to that of the two constituents, and being proportionally greater in the small republic, it follows that, if the proportion of fit characters be not less in the large than in the small republic, the former will present a greater option, and consequently a greater probability of a fit choice.

In the next place, as each representative will be chosen by a greater number of citizens in the large than in the small republic, it will be more difficult for unworthy candidates to practise with success the vicious arts by which elections are too often carried; and the suffrages of the people being more free, will be more likely to centre in men who possess the most attractive merit and the most diffusive and established characters.

It must be confessed that in this, as in most other cases, there is a mean, on both sides of which inconveniences will be found to lie. By enlarging too much the number of electors, you render the representative too little acquainted with all their local circumstances and lesser interests; as by reducing it too much, you render him unduly attached to these, and too little fit to comprehend and pursue great and national objects. The federal Constitution forms a happy combination in this respect; the great and aggregate interests being referred to the national, the local and particular to the State legislatures.

The other point of difference is, the greater number of citizens and extent of territory which may be brought within the compass of republican than of democratic government; and it is this circumstance principally which renders factious combinations less to be dreaded in the former than in the latter. The smaller the society, the fewer probably will be the distinct parties and interests composing it; the fewer the distinct parties and interests, the more frequently will a majority be found of the same party; and the smaller the number of individuals composing a majority, and the smaller the compass within which they are placed, the more easily will they concert and execute their plans of oppression. Extend the sphere and you take in a greater variety of parties and interests; you will make it less probable that a majority of the whole will have a common motive to invade the rights of other citizens; or if such a common motive exists, it will be more difficult for all who feel it to discover their own strength, and to act in unison with each other. Besides other impediments, it may be remarked that, where there is a consciousness of unjust or dishonorable purposes, communication is always checked by distrust in proportion to the number whose concurrence is necessary.

Hence, it clearly appears, that the same advantage which a republic has over a democracy, in controlling the effects of faction, is enjoyed by a large over a small republic,—is enjoyed by the Union over the States composing it. Does the advantage consist in the substitution of representatives whose enlightened views and virtuous sentiments render them superior to local prejudices and to schemes of injustice? It will not be denied that the representation of the Union will be most likely to possess these requisite endowments. Does it consist in the greater security afforded by a greater variety of parties, against the event of any one party being able to outnumber and oppress the rest? In an equal degree does the increased variety of parties comprised within the Union, increase this security. Does it, in fine, consist in the greater obstacles opposed to the concert and accomplishment of the secret wishes of an unjust and interested majority? Here, again, the extent of the Union gives it the most palpable advantage.

The influence of factious leaders may kindle a flame within their particular States, but will be unable to spread a general conflagration through the other States. A religious sect may degenerate into a political faction in a part of the Confederacy; but the variety of sects dispersed over the entire face of it must secure the national councils against any danger from that source. A rage for paper money, for an abolition of debts, for an equal division of property, or for any other improper or wicked project, will be less apt to pervade the whole body of the Union than a particular member of it; in the same proportion as such a malady is more likely to taint a particular county or district, than an entire State.

In the extent and proper structure of the Union, therefore, we behold a republican remedy for the diseases most incident to republican government. And according to the degree of pleasure and pride we feel in being republicans, ought to be our zeal in cherishing the spirit and supporting the character of Federalists.

PUBLIUS

Critical Thinking

1. According to Madison, can the causes of faction be eliminated? Can its effects be controlled?

2. What, according to Madison, are the two key differences between a democracy and a republic?

3. What are the advantages of a republican form of government? Does Madison advocate a democratic or a republican government? Why?

4. "Extend the sphere and you take in a greater variety of parties and interests." So begins several sentences that present one of the most central claims in *Federalist No. 10*. Do you find that claim persuasive?

From *The Federalist No. 10*, 1787.

Federalist No. 51

James Madison

To the People of the State of New York

To what expedient, then, shall we finally resort, for maintaining in practice the necessary partition of power among the several departments, as laid down in the Constitution? The only answer that can be given is, that as all these exterior provisions are found to be inadequate, the defect must be supplied, by so contriving the interior structure of the government as that its several constituent parts may, by their mutual relations, be the means of keeping each other in their proper places. Without presuming to undertake a full development of this important idea, I will hazard a few general observations, which may perhaps place it in a clearer light, and enable us to form a more correct judgment of the principles and structure of the government planned by the convention.

In order to lay a due foundation for that separate and distinct exercise of the different powers of government, which to a certain extent is admitted on all hands to be essential to the preservation of liberty, it is evident that each department should have a will of its own; and consequently should be so constituted that the members of each should have as little agency as possible in the appointment of the members of the others. Were this principle rigorously adhered to, it would require that all the appointments for the supreme executive, legislative, and judiciary magistracies should be drawn from the same fountain of authority, the people, through channels having no communication whatever with one another. Perhaps such a plan of constructing the several departments would be less difficult in practice than it may in contemplation appear. Some difficulties, however, and some additional expense would attend the execution of it. Some deviations, therefore, from the principle must be admitted. In the constitution of the judiciary department in particular, it might be inexpedient to insist rigorously on the principle: first, because peculiar qualifications being essential in the members, the primary consideration ought to be to select that mode of choice which best secures these qualifications; secondly, because the permanent tenure by which the appointments are held in that department, must soon destroy all sense of dependence on the authority conferring them.

It is equally evident, that the members of each department should be as little dependent as possible on those of the others, for the emoluments annexed to their offices. Were the executive magistrate, or the judges, not independent of the legislature

in this particular, their independence in every other would be merely nominal.

But the great security against a gradual concentration of the several powers in the same department, consists in giving to those who administer each department the necessary constitutional means and personal motives to resist encroachments of the others. The provision for defence must in this, as in all other cases, be made commensurate to the danger of attack. Ambition must be made to counteract ambition. The interest of the man must be connected with the constitutional rights of the place. It may be a reflection on human nature, that such devices should be necessary to control the abuses of government. But what is government itself, but the greatest of all reflections on human nature? If men were angels, no government would be necessary. If angels were to govern men, neither external nor internal controls on government would be necessary. In framing a government which is to be administered by men over men, the great difficulty lies in this: you must first enable the government to control the governed; and in the next place oblige it to control itself. A dependence on the people is, no doubt, the primary control on the government; but experience has taught mankind the necessity of auxiliary precautions.

This policy of supplying, by opposite and rival interests, the defect of better motives, might be traced through the whole system of human affairs, private as well as public. We see it particularly displayed in all the subordinate distributions of power, where the constant aim is to divide and arrange the several offices in such a manner as that each may be a check on the other—that the private interest of every individual may be a sentinel over the public rights. These inventions of prudence cannot be less requisite in the distribution of the supreme powers of the State.

But it is not possible to give to each department an equal power of self-defence. In republican government, the legislative authority necessarily predominates. The remedy for this inconveniency is to divide the legislature into different branches; and to render them, by different modes of election and different principles of action, as little connected with each other as the nature of their common functions and their common dependence on the society will admit. It may even be necessary to guard against dangerous encroachments by still further precautions. As the weight of the legislative authority requires that it should be thus divided, the weakness of the executive may require, on the other hand, that it should be fortified. An absolute negative on the legislature appears, at first view, to be the natural defence with which the executive magistrate should be armed. But perhaps it would be neither altogether safe nor alone sufficient. On ordinary occasions it might not be exerted with the requisite firmness, and on extraordinary occasions it might be perfidiously abused. May not this defect of an absolute negative be supplied by some qualified connection between this weaker department and the weaker branch of the stronger department, by which the latter may be led to support the constitutional rights of the former, without being too much detached from the rights of its own department?

If the principles on which these observations are founded be just, as I persuade myself they are, and they be applied as a criterion to the several State constitutions, and to the federal Constitution, it will be found that if the latter does not perfectly correspond with them, the former are infinitely less able to bear such a test.

There are, moreover, two considerations particularly applicable to the federal system of America, which place that system in a very interesting point of view.

First. In a single republic, all the power surrendered by the people is submitted to the administration of a single government; and the usurpations are guarded against by a division of the government into distinct and separate departments. In the compound republic of America, the power surrendered by the people is first divided between two distinct governments, and then the portion allotted to each subdivided among distinct and separate departments. Hence a double security arises to the rights of the people. The different governments will control each other, at the same time that each will be controlled by itself.

Second. It is of great importance in a republic not only to guard the society against the oppression of its rulers, but to guard one part of the society against the injustice of the other part. Different interests necessarily exist in different classes of citizens. If a majority be united by a common interest, the rights of the minority will be insecure. There are but two methods of providing against this evil: the one by creating a will in the community independent of the majority—that is, of the society itself; the other, by comprehending in the society so many separate descriptions of citizens as will render an unjust combination of a majority of the whole very improbable, if not impracticable. The first method prevails in all governments possessing an hereditary or self-appointed authority. This, at best, is but a precarious security; because a power independent of the society may as well espouse the unjust views of the major, as the rightful interests of the minor party, and may possibly be turned against both parties. The second method will be exemplified in the federal republic of the United States. Whilst all authority in it will be derived from and dependent on the society, the society itself will be broken into so many parts, interests and classes of citizens, that the rights of individuals, or of the minority, will be in little danger from interested combinations of the majority. In a free government the security for civil rights must be the same as that for religious rights. It consists in the one case in the multiplicity of interests, and in the other in the multiplicity of sects. The degree of security in both cases will depend on the number of interests

and sects; and this may be presumed to depend on the extent of country and number of people comprehended under the same government. This view of the subject must particularly recommend a proper federal system to all the sincere and considerate friends of republican government, since it shows that in exact proportion as the territory of the Union may be formed into more circumscribed Confederacies, or States, oppressive combinations of a majority will be facilitated; the best security, under the republican forms, for the rights of every class of citizens, will be diminished; and consequently the stability and independence of some member of the government, the only other security, must be proportionally increased. Justice is the end of government. It is the end of civil society. It ever has been and ever will be pursued until it be obtained, or until liberty be lost in the pursuit. In a society under the forms of which the stronger faction can readily unite and oppress the weaker, anarchy may as truly be said to reign as in a state of nature, where the weaker individual is not secured against the violence of the stronger; and as, in the latter state, even the stronger individuals are prompted, by the uncertainty of their condition, to submit to a government which may protect the weak as well as themselves; so, in the former state, will the more powerful factions or parties be gradually induced, by a like motive, to wish for a government which will protect all parties, the weaker as well as the more powerful. It can be little doubted that if the State of Rhode Island was separated from the Confederacy and left to itself, the insecurity of rights under the popular form of government within such narrow limits would be displayed by such reiterated oppressions of factious majorities that some power altogether independent of the people would soon be called for by the voice of the very factions whose misrule had proved the necessity of it. In the extended republic of the United States, and among the great variety of interests, parties, and sects which it embraces, a coalition of a majority of the whole society could seldom take place on any other principles than those of justice and the general good; whilst there being thus less danger to a minor from the will of a major party, there must be less pretext, also, to provide for the security of the former, by introducing into the government a will not dependent on the latter, or, in other words, a will independent of the society itself. It is no less certain than it is important, notwithstanding the contrary opinions which have been entertained, that the larger the society, provided it lie within a particular sphere, the more duly capable it will be of self-government. And happily for the *republican cause,* the practicable sphere may be carried to a very great extent, by a judicious modification and mixture of the *federal principle.*

PUBLIUS

Critical Thinking

1. Explain the rationale for what has come to be called the "separation of powers."

2. *Federalist No. 51* argues that members of one branch should not be involved in the selection of members of another branch. Why, according to *Federalist No. 51*, is a "deviation" from this principle warranted in the case of the judiciary?

3. According to Madison, why is a system of independent "departments" (that is, branches) of government with separate powers necessary?

4. Which branch does Madison believe will be predominant? How does the structure of government outlined in the proposed constitution minimize or remedy the problem of that one branch being too powerful?

5. Explain what is meant by calling the United States a "compound republic" and summarize the advantages of being a "compound republic."

From *The Federalist No. 51*, 1787.

Can America Fail?

A sympathetic critic issues a wake-up call for an America mired in groupthink and blind to its own shortcomings.

KISHORE MAHBUBANI

I n 1981, Singapore's long-ruling People's Action Party was shocked when it suffered its first defeat at the polls in many years, even though the contest was in a single constituency. I asked Dr. Goh Keng Swee, one of Singapore's three founding fathers and the architect of its economic miracle, why the PAP lost. He replied, "Kishore, we failed because we did not even conceive of the possibility of failure."

The simple thesis of this essay is that American society could also fail if it does not force itself to conceive of failure. The massive crises that American society is experiencing now are partly the product of just such a blindness to potential catastrophe. That is not a diagnosis I deliver with rancor. Nations, like individuals, languish when they only have uncritical lovers or unloving critics. I consider myself a loving critic of the United States, a critic who wants American society to succeed. America, I wrote in 2005 in *Beyond the Age of Innocence: Rebuilding Trust Between America and the World,* "has done more good for the rest of the world than any other society." If the United States fails, the world will suffer too.

The first systemic failure America has suffered is groupthink. Looking back at the origins of the current financial crisis, it is amazing that American society accepted the incredible assumptions of economic gurus such as Alan Greenspan and Robert Rubin that unregulated financial markets would naturally deliver economic growth and serve the public good. In 2003, Greenspan posed this question: "The vast increase in the size of the over-the-counter derivatives markets is the result of the market finding them a very useful vehicle. And the question is, should these be regulated?" His own answer was that the state should not go beyond regular banking regulation because "these derivative transactions are transactions among professionals." In short, the financial players would regulate themselves.

This is manifest nonsense. The goal of these financial professionals was always to enhance their personal wealth, not to serve the public interest. So why was Greenspan's nonsense accepted by American society? The simple and amazing answer is that most Americans assumed that their country has a rich and vibrant "marketplace of ideas" in which all ideas are challenged. Certainly, America has the finest media in the world. No

subject is taboo. No sacred cow is immune from criticism. But the paradox here is that the *belief* that American society allows every idea to be challenged has led Americans to assume that every idea *is* challenged. They have failed to notice when their minds have been enveloped in groupthink. Again, failure occurs when you do not conceive of failure.

The second systemic failure has been the erosion of the notion of individual responsibility. Here, too, an illusion is at work. Because they so firmly believe that their society rests on a culture of individual responsibility—rather than a culture of entitlement, like the social welfare states of Europe—Americans cannot see how their individual actions have undermined, rather than strengthened, their society. In their heart of hearts, many Americans believe that they are living up to the famous challenge of President John F. Kennedy, "Ask not what your country can do for you—ask what you can do for your country." They believe that they give more than they take back from their own society.

There is a simple empirical test to see whether this is true: Do Americans pay more in taxes to the government than they receive in government services? The answer is clear. Apart from a few years during the Clinton administration, the United States has had many more federal budget deficits than surpluses—and the ostensibly more fiscally responsible Republicans are even guiltier of deficit financing than the Democrats.

The recently departed Bush administration left America with a national debt of more than $10 trillion, compared with the $5.7 trillion left by the Clinton administration. Because of this large debt burden, President Barack Obama has fewer bullets to fire as he faces the biggest national economic crisis in almost a century. The American population has taken away the ammunition he could have used, and left its leaders to pray that China and Japan will continue to buy U.S. Treasury bonds.

H ow did this happen? Americans have justified the erosion of individual responsibility by demonizing taxes. Every candidate for political office in America runs against taxes. No American politician—including

Although individual responsibility is a cherished part of the national creed, Americans have long reaped more in services and benefits from government than they pay in taxes.

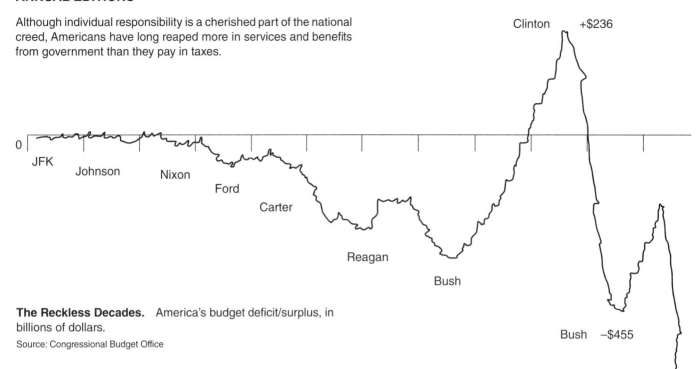

The Reckless Decades. America's budget deficit/surplus, in billions of dollars.

Source: Congressional Budget Office

President Obama—dares to tell the truth: that no modern society can function without significant taxes. In some cases, taxes do a lot of good. If Americans were to impose a $1 per gallon tax on gasoline (which they could easily afford), they would begin to solve many of their problems, reducing greenhouse-gas emissions, dependence on Middle East oil, and the production of fuel-inefficient cars and trucks.

The way Americans have dealt with the tax question shows that there is a sharp contradiction between their belief that their society rests on a culture of individual responsibility and the reality that it has been engulfed by a culture of individual irresponsibility. But beliefs are hard to change. Many American myths come from the Wild West era, when lone cowboys struggled and survived supposedly through individual ingenuity alone, without the help of the state. Americans continue to believe that they do not benefit from state support. The reality is that many do.

The third systemic failure of American society is its failure to see how the abuse of American power has created many of the problems the United States now confronts abroad. The best example is 9/11. Americans believe they were innocent victims of an evil attack by Osama bin Laden and Al Qaeda. And there can be no doubt that the victims of 9/11 were innocent. Yet Americans tend to forget the fact that Osama bin Laden and Al Qaeda were essentially created by U.S. policies. In short, a force launched by the United States came back to bite it.

During the Cold War, the United States was looking for a powerful weapon to destabilize the Soviet Union. It found it when it created a pan-Islamic force of mujahideen fighters, drawn from countries as diverse as Algeria and Indonesia, to roll back the Soviet invasion of Afghanistan after 1979. For a time, American interests and the interests of the Islamic world converged, and the fighters drove the Soviets out and contributed

to the collapse of the Soviet Union. At the same time, however, America also awakened the sleeping dragon of Islamic solidarity.

Yet when the Cold War ended, America thoughtlessly disengaged from Afghanistan and the powerful Islamic forces it had supported there. To make matters worse, it switched its Middle East policy from a relatively evenhanded one on the Israel-Palestine issue to one heavily weighted toward the Israelis. Aaron David Miller, a longtime U.S. Middle East negotiator who served under both the Clinton and George W. Bush administrations (and is now a public-policy scholar at the Woodrow Wilson Center), wrote recently that both administrations "scrupulously" road-tested every idea and proposal with Israel before bringing it to the Palestinians.

Americans seem only barely aware of the pain and suffering of the Palestinian people, and the sympathy their plight stirs in the world's 1.2 billion Muslims, who hold America responsible for the Palestinians' condition. And tragically, in the long run, a conflict between six million Israelis and 1.2 billion Muslims would bring grief to Israel. Hence, Americans should seriously review their Middle East policies.

The Middle East is only one of many areas in which American policies have harmed the world. From U.S. cotton subsidies, which have hurt poor African farmers, to the invasion of Iraq; from Washington's double standard on nuclear proliferation—calling on non-nuclear states to abide by the Nuclear Non-Proliferation Treaty while ignoring its own obligations—to its decision to walk away from the Kyoto Protocol without providing an alternate approach to global warming, many American policies have injured the 6.5 billion other people who inhabit the world.

Why aren't Americans aware of this? The reason is that virtually all analysis by American intellectuals rests on the assumption that *problems* come from outside America and America provides only *solutions*. Yet the rest of the world can see clearly that American power has created many of the world's major problems. American thinkers and policymakers cannot see this because they are engaged in an incestuous, self-referential, and self-congratulatory discourse. They have lost the ability to listen to other voices on the planet because they cannot conceive of the possibility that they are not already listening. But until they begin to open their ears, America's problems with the world will continue.

American thinkers and policy-makers have lost the ability to listen to other voices on the planet.

It will not be easy for America to change course, because many of its problems have deep structural causes. To an outsider, it is plain to see that structural failures have developed in America's governance, in its social contract, and in its response to globalization. Many Americans still cannot see this.

When Americans are asked to identify what makes them proudest of their society, they inevitably point to its democratic character. And there can be no doubt that America has the most successful democracy in the world. Yet it may also have some of the most corrupt governance in the world. The reason more Americans are not aware of this is that most of the corruption is legal.

In democracies, the role of government is to serve the public interest. Americans believe that they have a government "of the people, by the people, and for the people." The reality is more complex. It looks more like a government "of the people, by special-interest groups, and for special-interest groups." In the theory of democracy, corrupt and ineffective politicians are thrown out by elections. Yet the fact that more than 90 percent of incumbents who seek reelection to the U.S. House of Representatives are reelected provides a clear warning that all is not well. In *The Audacity of Hope* (2006), Barack Obama himself describes the corruption of the political system and the public's low regard for politicians. "All of which leads to the conclusion that if we want anything to change in Washington, we'll need to throw the rascals out. And yet year after year we keep the rascals right where they are, with the reelection rate for House members hovering at around 96 percent," Obama writes. Why? "These days, almost every congressional district is drawn by the ruling party with computer-driven precision to ensure that a clear majority of Democrats or Republicans reside within its borders. Indeed, it's not a stretch to say that most voters no longer choose their representatives; instead, representatives choose their voters."

The net effect of this corruption is that American governmental institutions and processes are now designed to protect special interests rather than public interests. As the financial crisis has revealed with startling clarity, regulatory agencies such as the Securities and Exchange Commission and the Commodity Futures Trading Commission have been captured by the industries they are supposed to regulate. And when Congress opens the government's purse, the benefits flow to special interests rather than the public interest. Few Americans are aware how severely special interests undermine their own national interests, both at home and abroad. The latest two world trade negotiating rounds (including the present Doha Round), for example, have been held hostage by the American agricultural lobbies. To protect 25,000 rich American cotton farmers, the United States has jeopardized the interests of the rest of the 6.8 billion people in the world.

When congress opens the government's purse, the benefits flow to special interests rather than the public interest.

Normally, a crisis provides a great opportunity to change course. Yet the current crisis has elicited tremendous delay, obfuscation, and pandering to special interests. From afar, America's myopia is astounding and incomprehensible. When the stimulus packages of the Chinese and U.S. governments emerged at about the same time, I scanned American publications in search of attempts to compare the two measures. I could not find any. This confirmed my suspicion that American intellectuals and policymakers could not even conceive of the possibility that the Chinese effort may be smarter or better designed than the American one.

An even bigger structural failure that American society may face is the collapse of its social contract. The general assumption in the United States is that American society remains strong and cohesive because every citizen has an equal chance to succeed. Because most Americans believe they have had the same opportunity, there is little resentment when a Bill Gates or a Sergey Brin amasses a great fortune.

This ideal of equal opportunity is a useful national myth. But when the gap between myth and reality becomes too wide, the myth cannot be sustained. Today, research shows that social mobility in the United States has declined significantly. In the 2008 report *The Measure of America,* a research group, the American Human Development Project, notes that "the average income of the top fifth of U.S. households in 2006 was almost 15 times that of those in the lowest fifth—or $168,170 versus $11,352." The researchers also observe that "social mobility is now less fluid in the United States than in other affluent nations. Indeed, a poor child born in Germany, France, Canada, or one of the Nordic countries has a better chance to join the middle class in adulthood than an American child born into similar circumstances."

Behind these statistics are some harsh realities. Nearly one in five American children lives in poverty, and more than one in 13 lives in extreme poverty. African-American babies are more than twice as likely as white or Latino babies to die before reaching their first birthday. People in more than half a million households experience hunger, data from the U.S. Department of Agriculture indicate. The education system is both inegalitarian and ineffective. In a recent international assessment of subject-matter literacy in 57 countries, America's 15-year-olds ranked 24th in mathematics and 17th in science. It should come as no surprise that though the United States ranks second among 177 countries in per capita income, it ranks only 12th in terms of human development.

More dangerously, many of those who have grown wealthy in the past few decades have added little of real economic value to society. Instead, they have created "financial weapons of mass destruction," and now they continue to expect rich bonuses even after they delivered staggering losses. Their behavior demonstrates a remarkable decline of American values and, more important, the deterioration of the implicit social contract between the wealthy and the rest of society. It would be fatal for America if the wealthy classes were to lose the trust and confidence of the broader American body politic. But many of America's wealthy cannot even conceive of this possibility. This explains why so few of the Richard Fulds and John Thains have apologized with any sincerity for the damage they have done.

America's latest responses to globalization also reveal symptoms of a structural failure. Hitherto, Americans have been champions of globalization because they have believed that their own economy, the most competitive in the world, would naturally triumph as countries lowered their trade and tariff barriers. This belief has been an important force driving the world trading system toward greater openness.

Today, in a sign of great danger for the United States and for the world, the American people are losing confidence in their ability to compete with Chinese and Indian workers. More and more American politicians are jumping on the protectionist bandwagon (although almost all of them dishonestly claim they are not protectionists). Even the American intelligentsia is retreating from its once stout defense of free trade. Paul Krugman of Princeton and The *New York Times,* who won the Nobel Prize for Economics in 2008, showed which way the wind was blowing when he wrote, "It's hard to avoid the conclusion that growing U.S. trade with Third World countries reduces the real wages of many and perhaps most workers in this country. And that reality makes the politics of trade very difficult."

At the moment of their country's greatest economic vulnerability in many decades, few Americans dare to speak the truth and say that the United States cannot retreat from globalization. Both the American people and the world would be worse off. However, as globalization and global capitalism create new forces of "creative destruction," America will have to restructure its economy and society in order to compete. It will need to confront its enormously wasteful and inefficient health care policies and the deteriorating standards of its public education system. It must finally confront its economic failures as well, and stop rewarding them. If General Motors, Chrysler, and Ford cannot compete, it will be futile to protect them. They, too, have failed because they could not conceive of failure.

Every problem has a solution. This has always been the optimistic American view. It is just as true in bad times as in good times. But painful problems do not often have painless solutions. This is equally true of the current economic crisis. To deal with it, American leaders must add an important word when they speak the truth to the American people. The word is *sacrifice.* There can be no solution to America's problems without sacrifice.

One paradox of the human condition is that the most logical point at which to undertake painful reform is in good times. The pain will be less then. But virtually no society, and especially no democratic society, can administer significant pain in good times. It takes a crisis to make change possible. Hence, there is a lot of wisdom in the principle, "never waste a crisis."

Let me suggest for purely illustrative purposes three painful reforms the United States should consider now. The goal of these suggestions is to trigger a serious discussion of reform in American discourse.

First, there is a silver bullet that can dispel some of the doom and gloom enveloping the world and admit a little hope. And hope is what we need to get the economic wheels turning in the right direction. As Amartya Sen, another Nobel laureate in economics, said recently, "Once an economy is in the grip of pessimism, you cannot change it just by changing the objective circumstance, because the lack of confidence in people makes the economy almost unrescuable. You have to address the confidence thing, and that requires a different type of agenda than we have." The completion of the Doha Round of world trade talks would go a long way toward restoring that confidence. The good news is that the deal is almost 95 percent cooked. But the last five percent is the most difficult.

One of the key obstacles to the completion of the Doha Round is the resistance of those 25,000 rich American cotton farmers. Millions of their poor West African counterparts will not accept a Doha Round agreement without a removal of the U.S. cotton subsidies that unfairly render their own crops uncompetitive. In both moral and rational terms, the decision should be obvious. The interests of the 6.8 billion people who will benefit from a successful Doha Round are more important than the interests of 25,000 American farmers. This handful of individuals should not be allowed to veto a global trade deal.

America's rich cotton farmers are also in the best position to make a sacrifice. Collectively, they have received more than $3 billion a year in subsidies over the last eight years, a total of about $1 million each. If they cannot make a sacrifice, who in America can? Where is the American politician with the courage to say this?

America has a second silver bullet it can use: a $1 per gallon tax on gasoline. To prevent the diversion of the resulting revenues into pork barrel projects, the money should be firewalled and used only to promote energy efficiency and address the challenge of climate change. Last year, the United States consumed more than 142 billion gallons of gas. Hence, even allowing for a change in consumption, a gas tax could easily raise more than $100 billion per year to address energy challenges.

This sounds like a painful sacrifice, one that America's leaders can hardly conceive of asking, yet it is surprising that Americans did not complain when they effectively paid a tax of well over $1 per gallon to Saudi Arabia and other oil producers when oil prices surged last year. Then, the price at the pump was more than $4 a gallon. Today, with world oil prices hovering around only $40 a barrel, the price per gallon is around half its peak price. A $1 tax would still leave gas relatively cheap.

This brings me to the third silver bullet: Every American politician should declare that the long-term interests of the country are more important than his or her personal political career. As leaders, they should be prepared to make the ultimate political sacrifice in order to speak the truth: The time has come for Americans to spend less and work harder. This would be an extraordinary commitment for politicians anywhere in the world, but it is precisely politics as usual that led the United States to today's debacle.

The latest budget presented to Congress by President Obama offers a great opportunity for change. Instead of tearing the budget apart in pursuit of narrow interests and larding it with provisions for special interests, Congress has the opportunity to help craft a rational plan to help people at the bottom, promote universal health care, and create incentives to enhance American competitiveness.

I know that such a rational budget is almost totally inconceivable to the American body politic. The American political system has become so badly clogged with special interests that it resembles a diseased heart. When an individual develops coronary blockages, he or she knows that the choices are massive surgery or a massive heart attack. The fact that the American body politic cannot conceive of the possibility that its clogged political arteries could lead to a catastrophic heart attack is an indication that American society cannot conceive of failure. And if you cannot conceive of failure, failure comes.

Critical Thinking

1. What does the author identify as the three systemic failures of American society?

2. How, according to the author, did groupthink contribute to the financial crisis of 2008–2009?

3. How does the author explain the 9/11 terrorist attacks in the context of American abuse of power?

4. What are some of the ways in which corruption is embedded in the American political system, according to the author?

5. What are the author's three "silver bullet" reforms that he suggests to stimulate discussion of reform in America?

KISHORE MAHBUBANI, dean of the Lee Kuan Yew School of Public Policy at the National University of Singapore, is the author most recently of *The New Asian Hemisphere: The Irresistible Shift of Global Power to the East* (2008).

What Makes a Country Great?

A new rating system compares more than gross domestic product, and it suggests that the U.S. lags many of its peers on health, education, and personal fulfillment.

BRUCE STOKES

Paris—The pursuit of happiness is one of America's promises to its citizens, enshrined in the Declaration of Independence. But today, Americans are a profoundly unhappy people. Their sour mood in the wake of the Great Recession reflects growing disillusionment with the exceptionalism of the American Dream and a widespread sense that the United States is in decline. The perceived fall from greatness, and who is to blame for it, are already shaping up as major themes for the 2012 campaign.

"Many in Washington—including the president—are really arguing over how best to manage the decline of our nation," Rep. Paul Ryan, R-Wis., the House Budget Committee chairman, charged in an early salvo last month.

But a very narrow set of objective economic indicators will fuel much of the debate over the United States' stature: annual growth of the gross domestic product, unemployment, and overall wealth. As it happens, the country's performance based on these metrics is remarkably good compared with other major industrial nations. Although the public gloom reflects doggedly high unemployment, it doesn't fully explain the broader sense of a national slide in stature. Looking at a wider array of measures about the quality of life may better explain that uneasiness.

One early version of such a tool now exists, just in time to help frame—and perhaps inform—the 2012 election debate about American exceptionalism.

In late May, the Organization for Economic Cooperation and Development, the Paris-based think tank supported by 34 industrialized nations, released its first-ever Your Better Life Index. The interactive database compares member countries along 11 separate lines, from indicators of wealth and income to measures of health, education, personal fulfillment, and leisure time. The goal, OECD officials say, is to help people identify their preferences and encourage public debates within countries about the broadest meaning of well-being.

"People around the world have wanted to go beyond GDP for some time," the organization's secretary-general, Angel Gurria, said. "This index is designed for them. It has extraordinary potential to help people help us deliver better policies for better lives."

America in Decline?

Republican presidential wannabes are already championing the exceptionalism of American life with a fervency that suggests they doth protest too much. Undeclared GOP presidential hopeful Mitt Romney has titled his new book, *No Apology: The Case for American Greatness.* Sarah Palin told an audience in Colorado last month that "America is not in decline. [There is] not a need for a fundamental transformation of America." There are many measures of success and decline, however. The U.S. economy is still the largest and wealthiest in the industrialized world. Relative to Europe and Japan, the United States is recovering quite well from the Great Recession. The International Monetary Fund expects America's economy to grow 2.8 percent this year, much better than the 1.8 percent expansion that the IMF forecasts for the European Union or the 1.4 percent it foresees in Japan. The U.S. is likely to outperform both of those economic rivals at least through 2016. Moreover, America ranks first in global competitiveness, up from third last year, in the International Institute for Management Development's annual ranking of nations' economic performance. That determination is based on an array of measures that include public finances, productivity, education, and basic infrastructure.

Nevertheless, China's economy is now expected to be larger than America's by 2016, thanks to years of stronger growth. The IMF foresees unemployment in the United States averaging 8.5 percent through 2011, about 2 points higher than joblessness in Germany and 4 points higher than in Japan. The U.S. government's deficit will remain close to 11 percent of the economy, higher than that of Japan and more than four times that of Germany. On its current trajectory, the federal debt will equal 90 percent or more of U.S. gross domestic policy by 2020, many analysts predict.

Given the trauma of the past several years, it's not a surprise that many Americans embrace a declinist worldview rather than an exceptionalist vision. In a November 2010 Allstate/*National Journal* Heartland Monitor poll, only 20 percent of Americans thought that the United States had the world's strongest economy. More than twice as many, 47 percent, picked China.

Asked which nation will have the best economy two decades from now, 37 percent chose China and 34 percent the United States. In the latest Heartland Monitor survey, taken last month, 58 percent of Americans thought that the country was on the wrong track.

In terms of its raw economic size and wealth, the United States is still No. 1. But America is doing poorly in managing its finances and creating jobs, a fact not lost on its citizens.

The Pursuit of Happiness

Money isn't everything, of course, and purely economic metrics are, at best, limited indicators of national well-being. Just ask any Washingtonian stuck on the Capital Beltway at rush hour. Traffic jams increase gasoline consumption, which shows up in economic data as a plus for the GDP, but they obviously don't improve the quality of life. Ill health can have the same effect, with increased spending and "production" of medical services reflected as a positive for the economy.

"The commonly accepted standard of social progress, GDP, is seriously deficient," said Richard Easterlin, an economics professor at the University of Southern California. "Instead of GDP, measures relating to the multiple dimensions of well-being, not just material gains, should be used in policy decisions and welfare evaluations."

To that end, in 2008, French President Nicolas Sarkozy asked three prominent economists—Joseph Stiglitz and Amartya Sen, both Nobel Prize winners, and Jean-Paul Fitoussi—to lead a commission to consider better measures of social progress. Their report called for a sea change in the way that economists and politicians think about the benefits of economic growth. They rejected the sole reliance on traditional economic measures and pushed for a broader array of quality-of-life indicators—people's health, education, and personal satisfaction, as well as a community's environmental quality. Widening the lens on life, they argued, would lead to better evaluations of public well-being and, perhaps, better policy decisions.

"What we measure affects what we do," the three economists concluded, "and if our measurements are flawed, decisions may be distorted."

The OECD's Your Better Life Index is an attempt to translate that vision into practice. The initiative includes objective quantitative indicators, such as life expectancy, unemployment, and household income, as well as subjective measures, such as peoples' perceptions of their own health, sense of community, and life satisfaction.

"We don't want to replace GDP," said Martine Durand, the OECD's chief statistician. "It's just that GDP doesn't capture all aspects of how people measure their lives."

The organization hopes that if citizens have a means of judging the broad success of their societies—from economic growth to work-life balance—they will hold their governments to a higher standard. "If you tell elected officials what is in the test, they will study for the test," one senior OECD official wryly observed.

The OECD began wrestling with these concepts seven years ago and recently decided to pull them all together, timed for release during the organization's 50th year and, serendipitously, during Sarkozy's year as leader of the G-20 group of the world's leading economies.

Aware of the political pitfalls inherent in crowning one country over the others as the best place to live, the OECD makes no attempt to come up with a single number encapsulating the "best" country in the world.

Instead, it ranks countries according to a slew of indicators that highlight particular values. Because different people have different priorities, the database allows them to assign their own weighting to those values and rank the countries accordingly.

If your only interest is earning money, for example, you might assign a maximum weighting of 5 to "income" and a zero to everything else. By that measure, the U.S. comes out solidly on top, after the city-state of Luxembourg. If your primary interest is joy of life, by contrast, you might place the greatest weight to surveys of "life satisfaction," "life-work balance," and perhaps "community." That would put Denmark at No. 1, followed closely by most other Western European countries, as well as Australia, Canada, and New Zealand. The United States ranks 17th. Put another way, America is a good place to make money, but it's not as much fun or as fulfilling to live there as in a lot of other countries.

The Better Life Index has clear shortcomings. It has no measure for inequality, despite a rising gap between the rich and the poor in the United States and in a number of other major economies. Human happiness is relative. It is not just a function of how people are doing, but how their lives stack up against those of their peers.

Moreover, the index has no indicator of environmental sustainability, such as carbon emissions or rates of natural-resource depletion that would link a nation's economic growth to the Earth's carrying capacity. Strong economic performance at the expense of future generations may create a better life for those living today, but be regretted by those alive tomorrow.

And the index itself is also built with limited statistical indicators. The environmental component is based solely on particular matter in the air of cities. The health component is based only on life expectancy and self-reported health.

Over time, the organization hopes to add other measures of well-being, such as inequality and sustainability. It also plans to include more countries in its comparisons, among them Brazil, China, India, Indonesia, Russia, and South Africa. Nevertheless, the index does point to real differences between what countries offer.

Income. As might be expected of the world's richest country, Americans enjoy the most disposable household income and have the greatest household financial wealth among the nations that make up the OECD index. Only the residents of tiny Luxembourg are better off, but that country has fewer people and a lower average household income than San Diego County.

Based on these economic metrics, Americans still top the list. At nearly $38,000 annually, after adjusting for purchasing power, Americans' after-tax income is two-thirds higher than the OECD average and outpaces the second-place Norwegians' income by more than $8,000 a year. Americans are also wealthier, on average, than their counterparts in every other OECD country. Adjusted for purchasing power, the average U.S. household has $98,000—about $5,000 more than the second-place Swiss.

Income and wealth indisputably help provide many Americans with a better life, giving them access to quality education, health care, and housing.

Jobs. For most people, the primary source of income is their job, which also affords them workplace friendships, a sense of self-esteem, and marketable skills. In 2010, 67 percent of Americans ages 15 to 64 had a paid job. Although this is roughly the OECD average, the employment rate in the United States has been falling, and America now trails 14 other advanced economies, led by Switzerland at 79 percent, in the proportion of its working-age population that holds a job.

Particularly troubling, the percentage of the U.S. labor force that has been unemployed for a year or longer was 2.85 percent in 2010, slightly higher than the OECD average, and that number is on the rise. The long-term unemployed tend to lose their job skills, making it even less likely that they will again find fulltime employment.

The United States' weak ranking on employment may be temporary. For years before the Great Recession, job creation was stronger here than in Western Europe and Japan. Given that U.S. aggregate economic growth is once again faster than that of Europe or Japan, the comparative job picture may improve as the recovery gains strength.

Work-life balance. Work and income enable Americans to afford both the necessities and the luxuries of life, but only if they have time to enjoy them. Americans work a lot of hours: 1,768 annually, or about a half-hour a week more than the average in other OECD countries. This nose-to-the-grindstone behavior outperforms even the Japanese and South Koreans, who have a reputation as hard workers. It also leaves Americans with less time for sleeping, eating, socializing, and sports and other recreational activities. In their attention to such personal care and leisure, Americans trail the laid-back Belgians, the siesta-seeking Spanish, and the industrious Germans.

Community. Americans' sense of exceptionalism has long been rooted in their strong communities, a phenomenon recognized by Alexis de Tocqueville in *Democracy in America* in the early 19th century. More recently, however, commentators such as Robert Putnam in *Bowling Alone: The Collapse and Revival of American Community* have lamented Americans' growing alienation. This theme has been picked up by politicians, who have called for policies that bolster families and communities. For their part, average Americans do not complain much about alienation. At the same time, there is nothing exceptional about Americans' sense of community.

As social creatures, people's well-being is framed by the frequency and quality of their personal relationships, which provide both emotional and practical support, such as job opportunities. Nine out of 10 Americans (92 percent) say they know someone they can rely on in a time of need, a percentage that is above the OECD average. Conversely, very few—only

3 percent—say they rarely spend time with family and friends, which is much better than average.

Nevertheless, if Tocqueville were writing about community today, he would find better evidence of exceptionalism in Australia, Canada, New Zealand, and Scandinavia, whose citizens are more likely than Americans to have tight bonds with family and friends.

Life satisfaction. Money can't buy you love, the Beatles advised us nearly a half-century ago. Now it is clear that it buys Americans only a modicum of satisfaction (hat-tip to the Rolling Stones). Given their wealth, Americans are happier than most people in other advanced societies, but they are not nearly as satisfied as Sarah Palin or Mitt Romney think they should be.

Human happiness is a subjective concept, the product of positive experiences and feelings that outweigh negative sentiments and add up to relative degrees of satisfaction with life. Economists have long disdained such ephemeral concepts, preferring more-quantifiable measures of fulfillment, such as income. But the profusion of public-opinion surveys makes it possible to map how people assess the quality of their lives.

Despite the recent recession, seven in 10 Americans are satisfied with their lives, and eight in 10 believe that their lives will be fulfilling five years from now. Three in four Americans (76 percent) report having more positive experiences, such as feelings of being rested or of pride in accomplishment, during an average day than they do negative ones, such as pain, worry, sadness, or boredom, according to Gallup surveys.

But Americans' self-assessment is only slightly above the OECD average, hardly a sign of exceptional happiness. Perhaps even more telling, the United States ranks nearly last among the relatively wealthy OECD countries—those whose citizens have average disposable household incomes above the organization's median of $22,000. The Nordics, Dutch, Canadians, Australians, Israelis, and even the recently financially troubled Irish and Spanish are all happier than Americans.

Economics of Happiness

The OECD's Your Better Life Index is the latest in a long series of efforts to grapple with what scholars call the economics-of-happiness debate.

This research is largely based on public-opinion data, drawing on the pioneering work done 50 years ago by Hadley Cantril, a social psychologist at Princeton University. Cantril showed people a 10-step ladder and asked them to place themselves on a step in response to various questions. Their answers were then correlated with their income, gender, age, and education. (There was one hitch: In some cultures, people had no idea what a ladder was.)

Cantril determined that the relationship between material well-being and happiness was tenuous at best, a finding that has been confirmed by more-rigorous and extensive surveys since then.

"Contrary to what economic theory assumes," the University of Southern California's Easterlin said, "more money does not make people happier. At a point in time, happiness varies directly with income. But over time, happiness does not increase when a country's income increases." This has come to be known as the Easterlin paradox.

Allen Parducci, another University of Southern California researcher, argues that the paradox can be explained by the fact that people's expectations ratchet up over time, in line with improvements in their income. A bigger paycheck ultimately leaves many people no happier.

This conclusion was borne out by the 2007 Pew Global Attitudes survey of public sentiment in 47 countries. An overwhelming majority of Americans (65 percent) were satisfied with their lives, but an even larger proportion of Mexicans (76 percent) said they were satisfied with theirs—even though the per capita income of Americans was four times higher. Clearly, satisfaction with life has to do with more than just money.

"Happiness research," said Carol Graham, a senior fellow at the Brookings Institution, "[has] allowed us to uncover significant amounts of public frustration among precisely those groups that should be satisfied or happy, according to our income-base measures."

What *does* make people happy? "A stable marriage, good health, and enough—but not too much—income are good for happiness," she said. "Unemployment, divorce, and economic instability are terrible for it."

The policy implications of the new happiness research are just beginning to become apparent. Not surprisingly, recent survey data show that happiness declined significantly among Americans in the wake of the 2008 financial crisis.

But after the Dow Jones industrial average stopped falling, individual happiness recovered much faster than Wall Street did. By June 2009, happiness exceeded precrisis levels, even though living standards remained depressed. "Once the uncertainty ended," said Graham, author of the forthcoming book *The Pursuit of Happiness,* "people seemed to be able to return to previous happiness levels, while making do with less income or wealth."

For a nation that faces years of austerity and for the politicians who must lead voters through these constrained times, these findings offer hope. People's expectations of life adjust to fit their new circumstances. A society and its politics can stabilize once economic turbulence subsides.

Don't expect much discussion in the upcoming election season about feeling better while having less. Candidates will cherry-pick their measures of America's decline or its relative success to fit their political narrative, and money and jobs are more tangible than such softer values as community ties and free time.

Still, the OECD index and the growing body of research into happiness could lead to a more nuanced debate.

The index suggests that the United States is neither as exceptional as some Americans would like to believe nor at the beginning of an epic decline. The U.S. is becoming a normal nation, one with great shortcomings but also much going for it. Most important, the index tells us nothing about the country's potential, which arguably remains limitless. That is the vision for politicians to paint, as long as they are clear and honest about America's starting point.

Critical Thinking

1. What is the Your Better Life Index, what organization developed and released it in 2011, and on what is the Index based?

2. On what sorts of statistical indicators have discussions of quality of life in different nations traditionally concentrated?

3. How does the U.S. compare with other OECD nations with respect to money and wealth, joys of life, and safety?

4. What light does the 2011 Better Life Index shed on the notion of American exceptionalism? On the notion of American decline?

The author is a senior fellow at the German Marshall Fund.

What They Don't Know

People are all fired up about the deficit, but their level of knowledge is way down when it comes to the causes.

Fred Barbash

With Washington tied in knots over the budget deficit, pollsters lately have been trying to get a sense of exactly where voters stand on the issue. What they're finding would not be terribly helpful to those trying to solve the problem.

That's because many Americans' perception of how federal spending is divvied up is just plain wrong. In fact, if their answers about the federal budget were even close to correct, slashing the deficit would be a breeze.

In a recent CNN-Opinion Research survey, 30 percent of the respondents guessed that a fifth or more of the budget goes for foreign humanitarian and development aid. The real figure is closer to six-tenths of 1 percent.

In a Bloomberg survey, 70 percent said cutting foreign aid would make a large dent in the deficit. Fewer than half said the same about cutting Medicare.

About 22 percent of the respondents, when surveyed, thought the Corporation for Public Broadcasting consumes more than a tenth of the budget. The reality is closer to a hundredth of a percent.

And about a quarter of those in the survey believed that more than 10 percent of taxpayer money pays for housing assistance for the poor. The real figure is about 1.2 percent.

At a time when the deficit is driving every debate in Washington, the fiscal intelligence of the citizenry is troubling but not surprising to experts on public opinion. Mostly, pollsters say, people are in a state of confusion on a broad variety of issues.

It isn't that they don't care. Between 80 percent and 90 percent of those responding in most surveys see the deficit as a "major problem." It's that they don't know. Not knowing in America is an old habit that should have faded over the years, given Americans' educational opportunities and access to information, but hasn't, according to those who study public opinion.

Failed quizzes about the budget only scratch the surface. Research demonstrates fundamental misunderstandings across the spectrum about government, about which level of government does what and which official is accountable for what. Presidents get blamed for local problems, mayors for national problems. Incumbent office holders can even get a boost on voting day if their local team wins a major championship just prior to an election.

This ignorance creates a vacuum that politicians and activists are all too happy to fill—with their own spin.

Multiple versions of reality or wishful thinking distort the debate, particularly on issues such as government spending. "It explains why people say, 'We don't like deficits,' and on the other hand say, 'Don't cut anything and don't raise taxes,'" said Bryan Caplan, a George Mason University scholar and author of an oft-cited book, "The Myth of the Rational Voter: Why Democracies Choose Bad Policies."

It explains why many think that "raising taxes on rich people will do it" on the deficit, says Andrew Kohut, president of the Pew Research Center. "Some knowledge about wealth might change that attitude."

The fact that there's so little understanding of the basic facts means there's little agreement on what is actually being debated, complicating matters further. "The lack of an agreed-upon playing field makes the deficit debate a disaster," says Brendan Nyhan, a political scientist at the University of Michigan who studies public opinion. "People are talking past each other."

Confusion is the norm for many Americans, and every month brings another illustration in the form of surveys showing just what Americans don't know. One of the most jaw-dropping recent results came from a Kaiser Family Foundation survey in which nearly half the respondents could not say whether the Obama administration's health care law was still law. A quarter thought it had been repealed. Another didn't know whether it existed or not.

A trove of data just before and after the 2010 midterm election showed serious misunderstandings among voters about virtually every issue they claimed to care about, from the economy to the wars in Afghanistan and Iraq to the economic stimulus bill and the 2008 financial industry bailout.

On the economy, almost two-thirds of voters surveyed in a Bloomberg poll believed incorrectly that the economy hadn't grown during 2010, when, in fact, it grew all that fiscal year.

In the immediate wake of the 2010 election, fewer than half of Americans, according to a Pew poll, didn't know exactly how it came out, whether Republicans had won the House, the House and the Senate, or neither.

The more systemic problem, and one that disturbs academics and others who study this phenomenon, is the gap demonstrated by a series of studies of what citizens need to know to hold officials accountable: What level of government is responsible for what; who has control over certain events, and who does not.

This vacuum in understanding, say public opinion experts, lets officials off the hook and also licenses their finger-pointing exercises as they try to shift responsibility elsewhere.

Overwhelmed with Information

It isn't news that the public is badly informed on public affairs. The dark arts practiced by political consultants are predicated on the idea that some proportion of voters will believe almost anything in part because their knowledge is limited. Thus the standard campaign ad can treat opinion as fact just as voters do in surveys: "Republicans voted to end Medicare" is one example; Democrats passing a "government takeover" of health care is another.

Nor is it a revelation that voters often choose "facts" to suit their opinions. The notion that public broadcasting eats up a sizable chunk of the budget gets life from Republican efforts to eliminate appropriations for National Public Radio. "Conservatives have heard a lot about this on Fox and so are very energized about this issue," says Kohut.

But civic-minded activists, indeed generations of civics teachers, used to hope that as people became better educated and as news became more accessible, America's political IQ would improve. That does not appear to have happened.

There's been no formal measure of public ignorance over time since the 1950s. But Kohut said he did a study in the 1990s showing that young people "knew less about what was going on in the world than they had in the '60s and '70s. Since then we've gone through a coaxial revolution and a digital revolution of news flows, and the levels of information are the same as they were in the early '90s."

Indeed, scholars and surveys suggest that the proliferation of new media outlets—cable television news, the Internet, Twitter and all the rest—have become part of the problem.

"The level of information saturation in the highly advanced economies is not all a good thing," said Clay Ramsay, research director for the Program for Public Consultation at the University of Maryland. "If you have so many choices" of information, "your sorting problem is increased to the point where you don't have time for it. You have your kids. You have your marriage. And you have your job. And then you have some time left over for the wider world. If you are constantly trying to thrash your way through extravagant competing claims because no one is helping you filter it out, your ability to see the world gets impaired."

"You have your marriage. And you have your job. And then you have some time left over for the wider world."

—Clay Ramsay, Program for Public Consultation

Studies by Pew and others have shown that people increasingly congregate primarily or exclusively at news sources they know will cater to their existing beliefs. Thus, they are less and less likely to hear information that conflicts with their point of view.

Research by Nyhan and others has confirmed empirically that the speed and ubiquity of new media sources, combined with mastery of the field by partisan activists, has brought the level of misinformation in America to new heights.

Nyhan studied the origin and spread of the claim that the Democratic health care bill included "death panels," which would determine who would get treated and who would not. In the study, titled "Why the 'Death Panel' Myth Wouldn't Die," he wrote that as politics has become more polarized, "legislators, pundits and interest groups have waged a vicious communications war against each other, making misleading claims about the other side and its policy agenda. These claims are then rapidly disseminated to the public via both the mainstream media, which often reports misleading rhetoric in a 'he said, she said' format, and the growing array of talk radio hosts, cable news shows and websites that cater to the demand for preference-consistent news and (mis)information."

People tend not to engage on issues, if they do at all, unless and until they feel they have a direct stake and a direct impact on the outcome. "To a certain degree, the public has the policy world and politics on a need-to-know basis," says Kohut. When people have a need to get interested, he says, they get informed.

Ilya Somin, a law professor at George Mason University who has researched voter ignorance extensively, says the voter who chooses not to know is behaving rationally. Individuals will do a lot of research in advance of decisions they really control, such as whether to buy a new car. But they have miniscule control over who gets elected to the presidency or to Congress, and thus choose not to spend a lot of time prepping in advance of election day. There's no incentive, Somin says, to become informed just to be a "better voter."

Congress itself hasn't done anything to improve voter understanding of the issues, particularly when it involves the complexities of the federal budget.

Political stalemate in Washington means that the annual appropriations process has broken down more often than not in the last decade. Lawmakers use continuing resolutions and omnibus spending bills rather than the more painstaking and deliberative process they designed for themselves to use.

So the civics class notion that the "president proposes and Congress disposes" in federal spending is very far from reality. It's hard enough for close observers of Congress to understand, much less people watching from afar.

Another distortion comes from the fact that much of the debate over the budget and spending happens around the edges. Two-thirds of all spending is mandatory—meaning interest payments on the debt and entitlement programs such as Medicare and Social Security—while only a third is spending that can be readily adjusted up or down on a yearly basis. Lawmakers are starting to talk about the need to get Medicare costs under control, but until now much of the noise in budget debates has been over a small slice of the pie. So that small slice takes on outsized importance in the minds of voters. Earmarks are a more minuscule sliver, and they have generated some of the loudest fights.

Another reason the voter may be confused is the sheer complexity of the issues at hand. If Congress decides not to raise the debt ceiling, the perception that the United States is in imminent danger of default might cause a spike in interest rates and do real harm to the economy. On the other hand, no one really knows what would happen, because the government has never before defaulted.

Studying the Ignorant Voter

The study of voter ignorance, which began in the 1940s, has become a modest industry in the academic world. Conservatives over the years associated the "ignorant voter" idea with supposedly elitist and paternalistic liberals. But libertarians such as Caplan and Somin have taken up the subject eagerly.

"Before you study public opinion, you ask why things aren't better," says Caplan. "After you study public opinion, you ask why things aren't worse."

Somin writes in the draft of his forthcoming book, "Democracy and Political Ignorance," that the "sheer depth of most individual voters' ignorance is shocking to many observers not familiar with the research." He sees public ignorance as "a type of pollution that infects the political system rather than our physical environment."

Much of the recent research by Somin, Caplan and others does indeed go to the heart of the political system, shedding light on why political professionals do what they do and why it so often works.

Nyhan and Jason Reifler of Georgia State University showed in an ambitious experiment how resistant voters can be to adjusting their version of reality even when presented with the corrective facts. Non-truth sticks, especially when it reinforces an existing bias.

That's why misleading ads, Nyhan said in an interview, are so popular with consultants—and even more so when such ads create a controversy, which serves to reinforce the falsehood. The consultants' position "may take a negative hit," he says, "but they know that once these things are out there, they're hard to walk back."

As proof, he says the "death panel" myth persists to this day.

How an Informed Public Would Do It

Ordinary opinion surveys give "the impression that, when it comes to the budget, the American public is simply a mass of incoherent and irrational feelings," according to a study by the Program for Public Consultation.

But the questions in such polls—about which programs should be cut, for example—are often asked in isolation from one another. As the study says: "It is as if we were to ask someone, 'Would you like to have some cake?' which would probably elicit a positive response. We could then ask, 'Would you like to eat some cake?' which would also probably elicit a positive response, and could lead us to say, 'So you want to have your cake and eat it, too?'"

What would happen, though, if people were given all the relevant information in an accurate form and asked to come up with a way to cut the cake?

Working with the president's fiscal commission late last year, the program, based at the University of Maryland, tried to find out. Researchers attempted to simulate the budget process by providing accurate data to 2,043 Americans and then conducting a detailed survey about what steps they would take to reduce the deficit for fiscal 2015.

On average, those surveyed found ways to reduce the projected deficit by $437 billion, about a third of which would come from discretionary spending cuts and two-thirds from increases in income and excise taxes.

The bulk of the proposed spending cuts were in the areas of defense and intelligence, subsidies for large farms and, to a lesser extent, reductions in veterans' benefits. In each case, they went well beyond anything proposed by the Obama administration or by congressional Republicans.

But those surveyed also favored some additional spending, including double the amount for energy conservation and renewable energy and a modest increase to the Environmental Protection Agency for pollution control.

About 75 percent of those in the survey agreed on an increase in income taxes on individuals, and a majority would concentrate that increase on people with incomes greater than $100,000 a year. About 65 percent agreed on an increase in the corporate tax.

Respondents weren't asked to address Medicare with precise numbers because of uncertainty about the impact of the health care overhaul law, but those surveyed were willing to take steps to keep the program solvent. The majority found it acceptable to raise the current 1.45 percent Medicare tax by 1 percentage point; increase Medicare physicians' premiums by 40 percent; and gradually raise the age of eligibility to 68, among other steps.

In a similar vein, the majority said it would raise the limit on wages subject to the Social Security payroll tax and increase the retirement age to at least 68.

The exercise avoided one big element in the entitlement debate, Medicaid, because of its complex mix of federal and state financing.

Those responding to the survey came with biases, and they showed. Even though they were given accurate numbers, many insisted that foreign aid was getting five times more money than it is. They "assumed there were substantial amounts of foreign aid hidden in some other areas of the budget," the report said.

"While there were variations by party identification in the results," the report said, "the degree of agreement is probably more noteworthy. Among a total of 31 areas, on average Republicans, Democrats and independents agreed on 22 areas—that is, all three groups agreed on whether to cut, increase or maintain funding."

Partisan and ideological disagreement centered on nine areas. Only Republicans wanted to cut mass transit, global health and money allocated to international organizations. Only Republicans would increase spending for homeland security.

Meanwhile, only Democrats would increase spending for housing programs, and only Democrats would cut nuclear weapons and money for law enforcement.

And only independents would increase spending for science, federal law enforcement and land management.

All things considered, "they were able on average to come up with extremely effective" solutions, said Clay Ramsay, research director of the program. This is "the public when presented with information and the ability to move it around," he says. In the real world, there's also "the public when it's not presented with any information" and "the public when it's been thoroughly agitated by serious money."

The difficulty with such an experiment, of course, is that those surveyed are free to be fearless. They don't have to get re-elected.

—Fred Barbash

While voter biases reinforce misinformation, voter ignorance is what licenses politicians and their operatives to dish it out. "People who are insiders understand what they can get away with," says Caplan.

The frailties of homo Americanus are on wider display than they have ever been, thanks to frequency and repetitiveness of polls in recent years. The Pew Research Center's regular surveys of political knowledge has become a standard index on the subject.

The last one, in March, showed that:

- 43 percent of the public didn't know the unemployment rate.
- 57 percent didn't know the name of the Speaker of the House.
- 60 percent didn't know that most U.S. electricity comes from coal.
- 62 percent didn't know that Republicans had a majority in the House.
- 71 percent didn't know that the single program on which the government spends the most money is Medicare.

WorldPublicOpinion.org, a project based at the University of Maryland, conducted a similar study in December 2010. It found "strong evidence that voters were substantially misinformed on many of the issues prominent in the election campaign," including the economic stimulus law, the health care overhaul, the state of the economy, climate change, campaign contributions and President Obama's birthplace.

Voters uniformly misattributed the origins of both the financial and auto bailouts, saying Obama started both, when in fact both began under President George W. Bush.

Only 10 percent of the voters knew that their taxes had gone down in recent years. About 38 percent of them believed they had gone up during Obama's presidency.

The Larger Problem

More revealing is the accountability gap that researchers documented most recently in an unpublished paper titled, "Systematically Biased Beliefs about Political Influence," by Caplan, Somin, Eric Cramton of the University of Canterbury and Wayne A. Grove of Lemoyne College in Syracuse.

"What we found," said Grove, an economist, "is that if you look item by item at the budget, the economy, and so on, you see that the public does not distinguish the role of Congress from the role of the president from the role of state and local officials." As a result, he said, "it's hard to hold politicians accountable," and the politicians know it, he added.

In addition to being wrong about who does what, voters tend to be wrong about the capacity of officials to influence events over which they have little or no control.

Politicians, political operatives, campaign advertising gurus and pollsters have operated for decades on this very assumption: that the electorate indiscriminately hands out blame and credit. Grove believes this phenomenon bears some responsibility for the deficit, for the intense focus now on spending and taxes, and for the deadlock as Republicans and the White House grapple with the debt ceiling.

Grove credits tea party activists with breaking the accountability code by focusing so much attention on the deficit, and by pointing directly at Congress, which is responsible for the red ink.

Grover Norquist, president of the anti-tax group Americans for Tax Reform, also illustrates how a single savvy activist, who understands government, can effectively use that knowledge to inform and mobilize voters who otherwise might stay on the sidelines.

Since Ronald Reagan was president, Norquist has made his organization a powerful force in Republican politics largely by eliciting from candidates signed pledges not to support any measure that looks like a tax increase, whatever it is called. Although the average American might not understand the intricacies of the tax code, they do understand a simple statement like that.

All but 14 sitting Republicans in the House and Senate have signed Norquist's pledge, and he has a proven track record of mobilizing voters against anyone who breaks it. Among those he is credited with helping to defeat was President George Bush in 1992, who famously broke his "read my lips" pledge against a tax increase.

In recent months, Norquist has figured prominently in the deficit debate, feuding with some GOP senators who think he's getting in the way of a possible compromise that would bring Republicans on board to raise the debt ceiling by Aug. 2 to avoid what Treasury Secretary Timothy F. Geithner says would be catastrophic consequences.

GOP leaders are demanding significant spending cuts as a condition of support for the debt limit increase, and most say they're unwilling to make revenue measures, or tax increases, part of the mix. Democrats say they'll talk about cuts if Republicans show more flexibility on revenue.

But when some Senate Republicans, including Oklahoma's Tom Coburn, signaled flexibility on taxes, saying they would consider eliminating some tax deductions and credits as a way to simplify the code and rid it of what they call unneeded "tax expenditures," Norquist said he would treat those as pledge violations. He certainly isn't the primary cause of the budget deadlock, but some argue that he contributes to it.

"Simplification of the tax code was something Republicans have talked about for a long time," says Maryland's Ramsay. "But Grover Norquist says 'no.' The question is why is that so potent. . . . Where does this depth of perception that he has this power come from? The biggest political decision was Grover Norquist sitting alone and deciding that reforming the tax code consisted of a tax increase. Had he decided the other way, the road might have been open" to agreement.

Norquist, in an interview, counters that he isn't standing in the way of a deal, only of a deal that includes tax increases. "There will be a deal," he said. "There just won't be tax increases." And he took issue with the suggestion that he personally is such a "potent" force. The power comes from the pledge, he says. "If I said tomorrow that we should raise taxes, it wouldn't matter" because the pledges would still be in effect.

What the pledge does, he says, is to save voters time and effort they would have to expend studying issues to determine what a candidate stands for. "The pledge reduces the cost of being an informed citizen," he says. Taxation "is an issue that tells you everything else you need to know about the person. If a candidate won't raise taxes, he won't be a spender either."

Activists such as Norquist may be simplifying things for voters. But some believe that the black-and-white inflexible distinctions they draw discourage political deal-making in Congress, Grove said. Meanwhile, citizens who might support compromise largely remain in the dark and on the sidelines. Recent polls do in fact show the public to be more receptive than Congress to a compromise of tax measures and spending cuts.

Kohut says, in his experience, voters ultimately catch up. But it can take time. He cites George W. Bush's proposal when he first ran for president to create personal accounts under Social Security. "When we started testing the idea of privatizing Social Security, the Bush initiative, we were getting 70 percent of the public saying they liked the idea. Once Bush wins and begins to talk about it, that 70 goes down to a 40. So you have to be very leery about asking questions about things people haven't thought about," Kohut says.

"Opinions do change when people get information," he says, "and they will get the information on things they've not thought about when they see an opportunity, or when they feel threatened."

For Further Reading

Debt talks, CQ Weekly, p. 1208; long cuts, p. 998; Norquist, p. 1132. For public budget see www.worldpublicopinion.org/pipa/pdf/mar05/FedBudget_Mar05_rpt.pdf.

Critical Thinking

1. How do the big majority of Americans view the national government's budget deficit?

2. How knowledgeable are Americans about the causes of the budget deficit and the proportion of national government spending allocated to different activities?

3. Identify several activities of the national government for which Americans significantly overestimate the amount of government spending.

4. Who is Grover Norquist and what has he done to mobilize voters who might otherwise be politically inactive?

From *CQ Weekly*, June 13, 2011, pp. 1260–1266. Copyright © 2011 by Congressional Quarterly, Inc. Reprinted by permission via Copyright Clearance Center.

Changing Faiths

PETER STEINFELS

American Grace is a scrupulously researched, extensively documented, and utterly clear book filled with findings that should rattle the assumptions of anyone, religious or secular, who cares about religion in American public life. Findings like these:

- "The evangelical boom that began in the 1970s was over by the early 1990s, nearly two decades ago. In twenty-first century America expansive evangelicalism is a feature of the past, not the present."

- "Cohorts of whom barely 5 percent say they have no religious affiliation are being replaced by cohorts of whom roughly 25 percent say they have no religion, massively increasing the nationwide incidence of nones."

- "The more often you say grace, the more likely you are to find a home in the Republican Party, and the less likely you are to identify with the Democrats."

- "Most Americans today are religious feminists."

- "There is little overt politicking over America's pulpits and, to the extent it happens, it is more common on the political left than the right."

- "Religious Americans are, in fact, more generous neighbors and more conscientious citizens than their secular counterparts. On the other hand, they are also less tolerant of dissent."

- "Regular churchgoers are more likely to give to secular causes than nonchurch-goers, and highly religious people give a larger fraction of their income to secular causes than do most secular people."

- "A whopping 89 percent of Americans believe that heaven is not reserved for those who share their religious faith. Americans are reluctant to claim that they have a monopoly on truth."

American Grace is not, however, a collection of believe-it-or-not findings about American religion. It tells a story and makes coherent arguments. The social science of many chapters takes on flesh and blood in congregational profiles that range from Episcopal churches in Massachusetts to a venerable African American church in Baltimore and booming "mega-churches" in Minnesota and California, from Chicago Catholic parishes turning Hispanic to a liberal suburban synagogue and a Utah Mormon ward incorporating an unusual number (for Mormons) of Democrats. And the book comes with more than a hundred striking graphs.

The book's story is one of a religious earthquake and two aftershocks. The earthquake was the disaffection from religion occurring in "the long Sixties." Church attendance plummeted. So did the percentage of Americans saying that religion was "very important" in their life. At every stage of their life, boomers would always lag behind their parents by 25 percent to 30 percent in regular churchgoing. The authors know well that these were the years of the civil-rights, anti-war, and women's liberation movements, of pot, acid, the pill, Roe v. Wade, and Watergate. But with a refreshing directness and only a bit of embarrassment, they emphasize sex. Between 1969 and 1973, the fraction of Americans stating that premarital sex was "only sometimes wrong" or "not wrong at all" doubled, from 24 percent to 47 percent, a startling change in four years—and then drifted up, never to decline. Attitudes toward premarital sex turn out to be one of the strongest predictors of a host of other political and religious changes, including that of the first great aftershock, the evangelical upsurge of the 1970s and 1980s.

That reaction to "the long Sixties" has been extensively analyzed. Less so the second great aftershock, the rise of the "nones" after 1990 when young people, in particular, began rejecting identification with any religion, though not necessarily with a variety of religious beliefs and practices. More and more young Americans, according to polls, came to view religion as "judgmental, homophobic, hypocritical, and too political," overly focused on rules rather than spirituality. "The Richter rating of this second aftershock is greater than that of the first aftershock and rivals that of the powerful original quake of the Sixties," Putnam and Campbell write.

The second aftershock, however, only exacerbated the so-called God gap. The slightly shrinking evangelical camp became all the more identified with Republican conservatism. The new nones, mostly of a liberal stamp to begin with, increased the identification of Democrats with secularism.

Not that the identification of religious groups with one party or another was new in American history. A century ago a Methodist (outside the South), whether churchgoing or not, was more than likely a Republican; a Catholic, whether churchgoing or not, was more than likely a Democrat. What is new is the identification of religiosity itself, regardless of faith, with political partisanship. Today a churchgoer, whether Methodist or Catholic, is more likely to be a Republican while their indifferent or lapsed counterparts are more likely to be Democrats.

What changed? Issues of family and personal, especially sexual, morality that were always religiously salient became politically salient, that is, posed sharp choices between the parties. This was particularly the case with abortion and same-sex marriage. Would recent history be different if the conflicts over abortion and same-sex relationships had been fought out as much within the parties as between them, as has often been the case with free trade, military spending, Middle East policy, aid to education, and a number of other issues? "When abortion was emerging as a major issue during the 1970s," Putnam and Campbell note, "Democrats were somewhat more likely to oppose abortion than Republicans because, in that period, Catholics were overwhelmingly Democratic and pro-life. It was not until the Democratic and Republican parties took distinctive stands on abortion in the 1980s that the issue became a predictor of party sympathies."

How does this new link between religiosity and political partisanship actually work on the ground? Knowing that "the image of the highly politicized church, especially among evangelicals, is entrenched in the folklore of contemporary politics," Putnam and Campbell go out of their way to test the data behind their conclusion that there is very little overt politicking in America's houses of worship, the major exceptions being Jewish and African American congregations.

They take similar care in concluding that religious Americans are more generous and active citizens than secular Americans, although George Washington and Alexis de Tocqueville might have predicted as much. Churchgoing Americans, it turns out, are twice as likely as their demographically matched secular neighbors to volunteer to help the needy and to be civically active. Not only do those in the most religious fifth of Americans give four times as high a proportion of their annual income to charity as those in the least religious fifth, but they give a higher proportion even to specifically secular causes. Neither this generosity nor this activism has to do with ideology. Cross-checking with other surveys, Putnam and Campbell conclude that on measures of generosity and civic engagement, religious liberals rank as high or higher than religious conservatives and higher than secular liberals.

But in examining the links between both religiosity and partisan politics and religiosity and civic contributions, Putnam and Campbell highlight something beyond simple religiosity, something featured in Putnam's best known book, Bowling Alone: The Collapse and Revival of American Community—the catalytic role of social networks. What translates traditional religious teaching into partisan politics is seldom overt politicking from the pulpit but rather the religious social networks—"echo chambers," the authors call them—of fellow congregants, who are increasingly like-minded about politics. What makes religious folks collect clothes for the poor, donate to the United Way, and attend town meetings is not just theology or exhortations by the clergy; it is involvement in the life of the congregation, having family and friends there, talking about religion with them, and participating in small groups. "Devout people who sit alone in the pews are not much more neighborly than people who don't go to church at all," they find. "Statistics suggest that even an atheist who happened to become involved in the social life of a congregation (perhaps a spouse) is much more likely to volunteer in a soup kitchen than the most fervent believer who prays alone." As their title suggests, Putnam and Campbell are relatively sanguine about America's religious future. Polarization and partisanship are not going away—evangelicals, for example, make up in zeal and high church attendance what they are losing in numbers—but they think partisanship will be muted for reasons having to do with "switching, matching, and mixing." American religion is a great churn. Putnam and Campbell estimate that "roughly 35-40 percent of all Americans and 40–45 percent of white Americans have switched at some point away from their parents' religion." People change their allegiances, intermarry, and have close friends and relatives of other faiths.

Putnam offers himself as exhibit A. He and his sister were raised as Methodists. At marriage, he converted to Judaism. His children were raised as Jews; one married a Catholic who is now secular, and the other's spouse was secular but converted to Judaism. Putnam's sister married a Catholic and converted to Catholicism. Her three children became evangelicals! No wonder that so many Americans refuse to believe, regardless of the tenets of their religion, that those of differing conviction are bereft either of spiritual truth or hope of salvation.

In fact, having family or friends of another religious tradition turns out to have a spillover effect, increasing acceptance of other traditions not represented in one's immediate circle. But it is not yet clear whether this acceptance extends to "foreign" faiths such as Islam. And in attending to overall patterns, Putnam and Campbell may be underestimating the potential impact of militant minorities. They report, for example, "During the 2000 presidential campaign, only 5 percent of churchgoers reported hearing their clergy endorse a candidate." Only? In an Ohio or Florida, that margin can determine who sends this nation into war or bankruptcy. And who can say that the two aftershocks of the last four decades won't be followed by another?

No doubt, other criticisms will be made of American Grace. Its statistical methodology will be poked and probed. Its theological descriptions will be found a bit rough and ready. Its historical framing could stretch across the Atlantic and back in time. No matter. This is an indispensable analysis of religious polarization, partisanship, and pluralism in American life.

Critical Thinking

1. What are the "earthquake" and the two "aftershocks" that have marked the last fifty years of Americans' religious beliefs?
2. While identification of religious groups with one party or another is not new in the U.S., what *is* new about the relationship between religion and political partisanship in the American political system?
3. How much overt politicking is there in houses of worship in the United States?
4. How do churchgoers compare with non-churchgoers in volunteering to help the needy and engaging in civic activities?
5. What is the role of social networks in explaining differences in political and civic behavior among churchgoers and secularists?

PETER STEINFELS is co-director of the Fordham University Center on Religion and Culture, a former religion correspondent and columnist for *The New York Times*, and the author of *A People Adrift: The Crisis of the Roman Catholic Church in America.*

Reprinted with permission from *The American Prospect,* by Peter Steinfels, November 2010, pp. 4 pages. www.prospect.org. *The American Prospect,* 1710 Rhode Island Avenue, NW, 12th Floor, Washington, DC 20036. All rights reserved.

Democratize the Grid

Jim Hightower

The Bible tells us that on the Sixth Day, God created man, allowing him to live in the lush garden and be steward of the whole Earth. But God's great mistake on that day was failing to demand a security deposit.

At last, though, humankind seems to grasp the fact that we're perilously close to environmental catastrophe, and governments around the world are beginning to respond. A green transformation is under way as growing majorities of people demand everything from strict regulation of climate-change pollutants to aggressive development of a new clean-energy economy.

In the past few years, freelance inventors, small companies, co-ops, professors, backyard mechanics, and a few mad scientists have made tremendous strides in the development of alternative fuel technologies. These technologies are already cheaper than fossil fuels when we factor in the tremendous savings they provide in the health and environmental costs we are now paying for oil and coal.

The fossil fuel lobbyists wail that renewables will hurt America's workers by eliminating jobs in oil refineries, strip mines, etc. "Save the workers," they cry! Such a show of compassion for labor might be heart warming if these same corporate interests had not spent the past couple of decades ruthlessly slashing hundreds of thousands of jobs, while relentlessly busting the wages, benefits, and unions of the declining workforce that remains.

Meanwhile, researchers at the Pew foundation found that clean energy jobs grew nearly two and a half times faster than those produced by all other sectors. Green energy is labor-intensive, employing not only engineers and scientists, but also huge numbers of skilled steelworkers, machinists, electricians, pipe fitters, operating engineers, sheetmetal workers, carpenters, and laborers.

This new energy can create a full-employment economy, including training and work programs for unemployed and low-income folks in our inner cities and rural areas.

To his credit, President Obama has boosted spending on alternatives. But the United States still invests less in renewables than most of the nations of Europe, including small ones like Denmark. And China already has higher fuel efficiency than we're supposed to have in a decade.

But chanting "USA! USA!" misses the point of green development. Its not that we have to beat China at a new Cold War game, as Thomas Friedman suggests in every other column of his in *The New York Times.* What if the USA does not become the "Number One, Gold Medal, Blue Ribbon, Worldwide Winner" in green technology sales? Does that make us a loser? No. And if we do become number one, does that make every other nation a loser? Of course not. The goal is a green Earth, which will make all of us winners.

We also need to get over the myth that bigger is better. Everyone from T. Boone Pickens to the communist leaders of China are viewing green energy in terms of the same old massive, centralized, corporatized structural model. But huge, centralized projects require equally huge corporations to run them.

For roughly the same price per kilowatt, renewable electricity can be produced by you with solar panels on your roof and wind generators in your community. Instead of building another centralized energy system that puts a handful of Exxons or Exelons in charge, the switch to green gives Americans a rare opportunity to restructure and democratize the energy economy so ownership is localized, financial benefits are broadly shared, and economic power is decentralized.

The Earth itself is telling us that there are very real physical limits to growth, that Earth's "carrying capacity" for human activity is fast being surpassed. We can no longer allow economists, corporate chieftains, politicians, the business media, and others to tell us that every increase in our country's Gross Domestic Product is happy news. We need to be sensible in our use of the Earth and restrained in our accumulation of things. Less really can be more.

Critical Thinking

1. According to Jim Hightower, how do alternative fuel technologies compare in cost with fossil fuels?
2. How has growth in clean energy jobs compared with growth of jobs in other sectors?
3. What effect, according to Jim Hightower, would growth in renewable energy sources such as solar power and wind turbines have on economic centralization?
4. What is Jim Hightower's reaction to the notion that increases in GDP are inevitably good news?

JIM HIGHTOWER produces The Hightower Lowdown newsletter and is the author, with Susan DeMarco, of "Swim Against the Current: Even a Dead Fish Can Go with the Flow."

Reprinted by permission from *The Progressive,* December 2010/January 2011, p. 76. Copyright © 2011 by The Progressive, 409 E Main St, Madison, WI 53703. www.progressive.org

Pledging Allegiance to Peace

Our country is the world, our countrymen are all mankind.

A Quaker argues that patriotism is deadly, no matter where or why it is practiced.

TONY WHITE

We love the land of our nativity only as we love all other lands. The interests, rights, liberties of American citizens are no more dear to us than are those of the whole human race. Hence, we can allow no appeal to patriotism, to revenge any national insult or injury.

—William Lloyd Garrison, abolitionist,
"Declaration of Sentiments Adopted
by the Peace Convention" (1838)

Most Americans take for granted that patriotism is a virtue. We are taught at home, in school, and by the media that love for and pride in our country rank among our highest moral duties. We are exhorted to patriotism daily by flags, songs, holidays, monuments, marches, speeches, images, and literature that extol the glory of our country. So deeply ingrained is our belief in the value of patriotism that even to question it is taboo. When someone criticizes our personal sense of patriotism—always a ready-made tactic for trashing peace activists—it stings, and makes us very defensive. We think they just don't understand what true patriotism is all about, and perhaps we are moved to buy a bumper sticker reading "Peace Is Patriotic."

But is patriotism peaceful? Based on my life experience, studies, intellect, and conscience, I am led undeniably to the conviction that patriotism is immoral: It is selfish and irrational, hinders our judgment, divides the world, contributes to militarization, causes war, and contradicts the teachings of Jesus.

Patriotism is selfish and irrational, hinders our judgment, divides the world, contributes to militarization, causes war, and contradicts the teachings of Jesus.

Patriotism is an attitude of favoritism toward "my country" and "my people." If egotism or pridefulness toward oneself is

a vice, then patriotism or pridefulness toward one's particular country is likewise deplorable.

Patriotism clouds our judgment; it hinders objectivity and detracts from our ability to assess political situations rationally. Patriotism biases us toward our country's perspective, encumbering our desire and ability to consider outside perspectives. Patriotism breeds conformity and closed-mindedness. Furthermore, it makes us overly trusting of those in power over us, and susceptible to abuses of that power.

This is evidenced by what happened after 9/11: Americans were swept up in a wave of feverish patriotism and fell in line with a corrupt agenda. As a prime example, take the USA Patriot Act—who would dare oppose such a noble-sounding ordinance? Never mind that it involves gratuitous violations of civil liberties; what freedom-loving U.S. citizen does not also love warrantless surveillance, wiretapping, search and seizure, as well as detention and no-fly lists? Clearly, the act was given that title because politicians know the efficacy of patriotism for manipulating public opinion.

That patriotic propaganda measures are increased during wartime should be reason enough to give us pause concerning patriotism. Notice also how many flags are displayed for U.S. holidays associated with war—Presidents Day (celebrating the birthdays of Washington and Lincoln, both notorious for leading war efforts), Memorial Day, Independence Day (celebrating the day war was declared by the colonists on Britain), and Veterans Day—and how few flags appear on other federal holidays: Martin Luther King Jr. Day (honoring a winner of the Nobel Peace Prize), Thanksgiving (purportedly celebrating gratitude and cooperation between European colonists and Native Americans), and Labor Day. The bond between patriotism and war is not even covert.

I personally experienced the intoxication of patriotism. Right after 9/11 (before I was a Quaker), I supported the Iraq war. I believed that the cause was just. Looking back, I realize that I was living in a fog, basing my opinions on fleeting, vague notions. Because I heard something about weapons of mass destruction (WMDs), I was able to watch "shock and awe" approvingly, naively envisioning the United States speedily wiping out terrorism by force across the world. I cringe when I recall arguing with someone publicly that the United States should ignore the United Nations' caution about entering Iraq.

When it became clear that Iraq had no WMDs or links to 9/11, and that the war was based on lies, I felt betrayed. I also felt guilty for my own poor judgment—how could I have been so gullible? Grappling with this, I eventually saw that I had fallen prey to the stupefying effects of patriotism.

In kindergarten, I learned a mysterious morning chanting ritual in which one robotically pledges one's life to a flag and to one nation under God, "invisible" (as my child's mind heard it) with liberty and justice for all. Now I understand what I was saying. And I understand that people, and certainly Christians, should not pledge at all, certainly not to a material object (an idol), certainly not to one particular nation among many, and certainly not to something under God. I also know now that no kingdom save an invisible one could truly have liberty and justice for all.

I remember getting emotional about the war song known as "The Star-Spangled Banner." In seventh grade, I even won third place in an essay contest on the topic "What does patriotism mean to me?" I virtually equated *America* with *freedom*—faulty reasoning on which the essay was based and for which I was rewarded.

Many of us are taught in school that "America is the greatest country in the world," while the darker aspects of our history are largely ignored or glossed over. So how could I not view the United States as innocent, and anyone who opposes it as unreasonable and even evil? How could I not assume that whatever the United States does is destined to work and that the president always speaks the truth?

Patriotism Divides the World

Anarchist Emma Goldman, in a 1908 speech on patriotism and militarization, said: "Patriotism assumes that our globe is divided into little spots, each one surrounded by an iron gate." Patriotism separates us from other little spots and builds pride in our us-ness, setting societies against each other under the pretext that to protect *us* we must be prepared to kill any of *them*. If all countries are encouraged to be prideful toward themselves, how can we be surprised when war occurs? Further, patriotism has a tendency to result in nativism, for example, in Nazi Germany and in discrimination against immigrants in the United States.

For patriotism to be a universal virtue would be illogical. If it were virtuous for every human being to be patriotic toward the same country, then this—while crude—would be self-consistent. But if it is right for the English to be patriotic toward England and the French toward France, then when England and France have a conflict of interest, morality will conflict with itself. Two leaders will disagree and both will be right, and two armies will clash and both will be doing the right thing.

Patriotism is a major factor contributing to militarism and war. It is the primary force that glorifies combat, and nothing contributes to the propagation of war more than military hero worship. As long as the view prevails that there is no more glorious, honorable, and heroic service than to train to become a killing machine, there will be war, as any leaders who fancy an attack will have legions of glory-seeking yes-men at their mercy. Military hero worship is what makes it possible for a decent person to murder on command in good conscience. Albert Einstein wrote in *The World as I See It* in 1931, "The greatest obstacle to international order is that monstrously exaggerated spirit of nationalism which also goes by the fair-sounding but misused name of patriotism."

Patriotism is contrary to the teachings of Christ. In the Sermon on the Mount, Jesus declared, "You have heard that it was said 'Love your neighbor and hate your enemy.' But I say to you, love your enemies."

In the context of Hebrew law, here referenced by Jesus, *neighbor* meant "fellow Israelite," that is, compatriot. Thus, *enemy,* used in contrast to this, would likely be understood to refer to a national enemy. Jesus was demanding that no distinction be made between countryman and foreigner.

In fact, allegiance to any current government is consent to violence. Governmental power is rooted in violence—in the military, as well as the armed police. No one sincerely committed to the principle of nonviolence can in good conscience give consent to an institution based on military force. We can contrive many rationalizations for the supposed necessity of government, but this contradiction cannot be denied. The United States Constitution, purporting to be the "supreme law of the land," grants the government the power to declare war.

We Christians are called to recognize a different law as supreme—since we cannot serve two masters, let us not be servants of men, but let our sole allegiance be to the Kingdom of God, a kingdom not of the worldly kind and so one that does not require its subjects to fight for it, for we have only one Master and are all brothers and sisters.

Leo Tolstoy, in his 1896 essay "Patriotism or Peace" (how's that for a bumper sticker slogan!), writes, "If Christianity really gives peace, and we really want peace, patriotism is a survival from barbarous times, which must not only not be evoked and educated, as we now do, but which must be eradicated by all means, by preaching, persuasion, contempt, and ridicule."

In "Patriotism and Government," published in 1900, Tolstoy writes: "It is immoral because, instead of recognizing himself as the son of God, as Christianity teaches us, or at least as a free man, who is guided by his reason, every man, under the influence of patriotism, recognizes himself as the son of his country and the slave of his government, and commits acts which are contrary to his reason and to his conscience."

The usual rebuttal to condemnation of patriotism is that some patriotism is bad, but not all; only excessive, imperialistic, blind, narrow-minded, exclusivist patriotism, go the many variations—but not our "healthy" patriotism.

Patriotism in its purest form—from which all others derive—is the desire for one's country to claim glory and power over all others due to its people's superiority. To say that excessive patriotism is bad, but that there is a "golden mean" of patriotism, is to say that excessively promoting violence is bad, but moderately promoting it is good. Non-imperialistic patriotism still implies acceptance of past imperialism. What country was not founded on or upheld by unjust conquest?

And yet we have no reservations in our allegiance. Patriotism itself blinds and narrows our minds; it is essentially a bias. This supposed "clear-sighted" patriotism doesn't exist, unless perhaps for self-interested manipulation of others, because to see patriotism clearly is to see its pernicious implications. If we remove all that is exclusivist about patriotism, nothing remains.

Most people will grant that my argument holds in the context of despotism. Some, however, may object that since our government is a democracy, the right to dissent is its distinctive mark and, in fact, what makes it worthy of patriotism in the first place. It follows that it is our patriotic duty to question authority, and that, as the late social historian Howard Zinn said, "Dissent is the highest form of patriotism."

Given the First Amendment, I can understand why someone might believe that dissent is patriotic, and I used to. But consider this statement by linguist and political activist Noam Chomsky: "The smart way to keep people passive and obedient is to strictly limit the spectrum of acceptable opinion, but allow very lively debate within that spectrum—even encourage the more critical and dissident views. That gives people the sense that there's free thinking going on, while all the time the presuppositions of the system are being reinforced by the limits put on the range of the debate."

In public discourse, there is a sense that we can disagree as we may, if only in the spirit of patriotism. Thus, it seems as though dissent needs patriotism to legitimize it. So while we may dissent on particular issues, a prerequisite is assent to the system as a whole—a system rooted in violence. Each time we patriotically dissent, we buy into this violent system all over again. Perhaps nothing reinforces the violent status quo more than patriotic dissent: It implies that whatever our disagreements, the one premise that even the most radical dissident dare not question is rule by violence.

To break from patriotism may seem shocking and painful. But I daresay that many people in the United States reading this do not really love the United States, though we think we do. What we really love is an idealized version of the United States. We love the values of equality and liberty in the Declaration of Independence. But these values did not originate in 1776; they existed long before, and will continue long after the United States is gone. And the actual United States has never really lived up to these ideals.

Inequality and lack of freedom were written into the U.S. Constitution with the institution of slavery, and have since continued through various forms of oppression. To this, we might retort that what we love is the tremendous courage and perseverance of the people of the United States in overcoming these injustices. But why give credit to the United States for what resides in the human heart? Have not people from all corners of the earth exhibited this same spirit? Most great reforms are initially opposed by governments, and thus much of the people's perseverance has actually been subject to persecution.

Some assert that patriotism keeps countries together. But why presuppose that this is good, that the status quo ought to be maintained? That this is even offered as a response reveals the depth of our indoctrination and directly reflects the view that the powerful have always endeavored to inculcate in the masses through patriotism—that whatever upholds the current establishment is good and necessary. If patriotism alone were keeping a country together, it would be an artificial basis propping up an outlived tradition. Political establishments should be maintained only as long as they are just and beneficial. A sound social organization should be able to self-persist organically, rendering patriotism superfluous at best.

If we want to achieve world peace and a form of society not based on violence, the time for change is now. But if we eradicate patriotism, what unifying principle can replace it? One answer is humanism. It unites not a particular group, but all people.

If we eradicate patriotism, what unifying principle can replace it? One answer is humanism.

If humanism proves too weak a sentiment, let us embrace universal love. This can happen when we realize our connection to others and the underlying unity of all things; when we experience the Divine inherent in ourselves and recognize this same divine essence in others; when, as Quaker founder George Fox wrote, we "walk cheerfully over the world, answering that of God in every one."

Critical Thinking

1. Why, according to Tony White, do most Americans take it for granted that patriotism is a virtue?

2. Why might patriotism be considered immoral?

3. In what way was the U.S. war against Iraq justified by falsehoods?

4. How does patriotism, in White's view, work to divide the world?

A Decent Proposal

In which I solve the G.O.P's gay-marriage problem.

BILL KELLER

Supporters of same-sex marriage say gay people are entitled to be fully equal citizens, including in their yearning to make families. Opponents say the state has no business bestowing the blessings of marriage on those who do not fit the traditional template.

What if you could satisfy both?

What if the state were empowered to grant civil unions, regardless of sexual orientation—in other words, to lay out all the rights and responsibilities of two adults who merge their lives, without recourse to the word "marriage"? The state can make you partners, but it can't make you husband and wife. The church—or synagogue or mosque or temple or ashram—has the authority to bless (or not) this contract as a marriage. Marriage, after all, is a sacrament. We don't expect the state to baptize or serve communion or absolve our sins.

Rest assured, the proposal is theoretical. In our real world, the concept of civil marriage is embedded in more than a thousand federal statutes. And as one advocate pointed out to me, many who aspire to equal marriage rights would see this as a cruel evasion, like closing public schools to avoid integration.

More to the point, advocates of same-sex marriage are winning without such a radical redefinition of terms.

Even before New York passed its law last week, the move toward legalization of same-sex marriage in America had become inexorable. It may feel excruciatingly slow for those who are waiting their turn, but it's just a matter of time until the country lives up to what it believes.

The latest Gallup poll shows that, for the first time, a majority of Americans favors marriage rights. And support will continue to surge thanks to demographics: among 18-to-34-year-olds, approval is now an overwhelming 70 percent. If Gallup polled high-school students, it would need a category called "Why are you even asking?"

The accumulation of state laws that extend marriage rights to gay couples is slow but steady. New York just doubled the percentage of Americans who live in states with more egalitarian marriage laws, to 11 percent; that percentage will double again if the California gay-marriage lawsuit prevails. Already, 41 percent of Americans live in states that afford some legal recognition for same-sex couples, even if that does not include the right to marry there.

Public opinion is moving because same-sex families are rapidly becoming mainstream. Two years ago, 581,300 same-sex couples told the Census they were living together. One in five of these couples is raising children. Their median household incomes are comfortably in the middle class—meaning that, unlike African-Americans in their fight for acceptance, gay people do not face a great gulf of class. (The statistics on gay couples come from Gary Gates, a demographer at U.C.L.A.)

If Larry Kramer's blistering play, "The Normal Heart," now confronting audiences on Broadway, represents the angry breakthrough politics of the early AIDS epidemic, the politics of gay marriage is couples living their lives as neighbors, parents, Little League coaches, colleagues, car-poolers. Marriage (unlike homosexuality) is a lifestyle choice, one that overrides a multitude of differences. It's a little harder to demonize people when their kids are having play dates with your kids.

President Obama, whose professed belief that marriage requires a man and a woman has always sounded more calculated than heartfelt, seems to have sensed that the climate is shifting enough for him to come out of his political closet. His views, as my colleague Sheryl Gay Stolberg reported, are "evolving."

The remaining bastions of resistance are evangelical Christians (including many black ministers), the Catholic Church and the Republican Party. But rank-and-file Catholics are actually far more supportive of same-sex marriage than other Christians—not to mention their own clerical hierarchy—and church leaders seem a little less eager than in the past to throw themselves on the barricades. As Michael Barbaro reported in The Times, Gov. Andrew Cuomo, a Catholic, persuaded the Archdiocese of New York to pull back its heavy artillery from the marriage debate.

The Republican electoral base remains unconvinced—only 28 percent of G.O.P. voters accept same-sex marriage, unchanged from a year ago—and so does most of the Republican presidential field. While no one expects the 2012 election to hinge on gay marriage, the issue may have weight, especially if one of the G.O.P.'s more vociferous social conservatives gets the nomination. Those views would be a potential liability in a general election where, according to Gallup, 59 percent of independent voters favor gay marriage.

The issue also creates a logical tangle for the Republican hopefuls. Their support for a constitutional amendment defining marriage as heterosexual collides with their outspoken respect for states' rights; and two states that embrace gay-marriage rights are those early political laboratories, Iowa and New Hampshire.

One of the most awkward contortions in the recent New Hampshire debate began when Michele Bachmann was asked whether, as president, she would try to repeal same-sex-marriage laws of individual states. "I'm running for the presidency of the United States," Bachmann declared. "And I don't see that it's the role of a president to go into states and interfere with their state laws."

The (presumably Republican) audience cheered. But minutes later, when the moderator polled the candidates on a constitutional amendment to lock in the more conventional definition of marriage, Bachmann backpedaled: "John, I do support a constitutional amendment on marriage between a man and a woman, but I would not be going into the states to overturn their state law."

My e-mails to the Bachmann camp asking how she would square that circle went unanswered.

A few lecterns down the stage from Bachmann, Representative Ron Paul, the feisty Texas libertarian, had an answer that caught my attention: "Get the government out of it."

"I don't think government should give us a license to get married," Paul said. "It should be in the church."

Paul, with his jihad against the Federal Reserve on the one hand and his support for legalizing heroin on the other, often seems to operate at an oblique angle to his party's mainstream. But I wonder if he might be on to something—an elegant way for Republicans to reconcile their less-is-better view of government with their fealty to the religious right.

Would Republican voters buy it? Maybe. Polls show that they are more amenable to civil unions than to anything called marriage. There's also something classically conservative about the idea. Theodore B. Olson, the former Bush solicitor general who is co-counsel on the California lawsuit for gay marriage, tells fellow Republicans that a good same-sex-marriage law embodies some of the party's most fundamental principles: freedom to live your life, stable families and (by not requiring churches to marry gay couples if that violates their beliefs) religious liberty. Paul's approach offers conservatives all of that plus a heaping helping of less-government-in-your-life.

And one other thing: a chance to avoid being on the wrong side of history.

Critical Thinking

1. What is the core of Keller's proposal specifying the proper role of governments with respect to marriage?

2. If Keller's proposal were implemented, would "marriage" no longer exist?

3. How have Americans' attitudes about same-sex marriage evolved?

4. Why does Keller suggest that the Republican party in particular would be well-served by his proposal?

BILL KELLER is executive editor of *The New York Times.*

It Is Time to Repair the Constitution's Flaws

SANFORD LEVINSON

In 1987 I went to a marvelous exhibit in Philadelphia commemorating the bicentennial of the drafting of the U.S. Constitution. The exhibit concluded with two scrolls, each with the same two questions: First, "Will You Sign This Constitution?" And then, "If you had been in Independence Hall on September 17, 1787, would you have endorsed the Constitution?" The second question emphasized that we were being asked to assess the 1787 Constitution. That was no small matter inasmuch as the document did not include *any* of the subsequent amendments, including the Bill of Rights. Moreover, the viewer had been made aware in the course of the exhibit that the Constitution included several terrible compromises with slavery.

Even in 1987, because of those compromises I tended to regard the original Constitution as what the antislavery crusader William Lloyd Garrison so memorably called "a covenant with death and an agreement with hell." So why did I choose to sign the scroll? I was impressed that Frederick Douglass, the great black abolitionist, after an initial flirtation with Garrison's rejectionism, endorsed even the antebellum Constitution. He argued that, correctly understood, it was deeply antislavery at its core.

The language of the Constitution—including, most importantly, its magnificent preamble—allows us to mount a critique of slavery, and much else, from within. The Constitution offers us a language by which we can protect those rights that we deem important. We need not reject the Constitution in order to carry on such a conversation. If the Constitution, at the present time, is viewed as insufficiently protective of such rights, that is because of the limited imagination of those interpreters with the most political power, including members of the Supreme Court. So I added my signature to the scroll endorsing the 1787 Constitution.

On July 3, 2003, I was back in Philadelphia to participate in the grand opening of the National Constitution Center. The exhibit culminated in Signers' Hall, which featured life-size (and lifelike) statues of each of the delegates to the constitutional convention. As one walked through the hall and brushed against James Madison, Alexander Hamilton, and other giants of our history, one could almost feel the remarkable energy that must have impressed itself on those actually in Independence Hall.

As was true in 1987, the visitor was invited to join the signers by adding his or her own signature to the Constitution. Indeed, the center organized a major project during September 2003 called "I Signed the Constitution." Sites in all 50 states were available for such a signing. Both the temporary 1987 exhibit and the permanent one that remains at the National Constitution Center leave little doubt about the proper stance that a citizen should take toward our founding document.

This time, however, I rejected the invitation to re-sign the Constitution. I had not changed my mind that in many ways it offers a rich, even inspiring, language to envision and defend a desirable political order. Nor did my decision necessarily mean that I would have preferred that the Constitution go down to defeat in the ratification votes of 1787–88. Rather, I treated the center as asking me about my level of support for the Constitution *today* and, just as important, whether I wished to encourage my fellow citizens to reaffirm it in a relatively thoughtless manner. As to the first, I realized that I had, between 1987 and 2003, become far more concerned about the inadequacies of the Constitution. As to the second, I had come to think that it is vitally important to engage in a national conversation about its adequacy rather than automatically to assume its fitness for our own times.

My concern is only minimally related to the formal rights protected by the Constitution. Even if, as a practical matter, the Supreme Court reads the Constitution less protectively with regard to certain rights than I do, the proper response is not to reject the Constitution but to work within it by trying to persuade fellow Americans to share our views of constitutional possibility and by supporting presidential candidates who will appoint (and get through the Senate) judges who will be more open to better interpretations. Given that much constitutional interpretation occurs outside the courts, one also wants public officials at all levels to share one's own visions of constitutional possibility—as well, of course, as of constitutional constraints. And that is true even for readers who disagree with me on what specific rights are most important.

So what accounts for my change of views since 1987? The brief answer is that I have become ever more despondent about many structural provisions of the Constitution that place almost insurmountable barriers in the way of any acceptable contemporary notion of democracy. I put it that way to acknowledge that "democracy" is most certainly what political theorists call an "essentially contested concept." It would be tendentious to claim that there is only one understanding—such as "numerical majorities always prevail"—that is consistent with "democracy." Liberal constitutionalists, for example, would correctly place certain constraints on what majorities can do to vulnerable minorities.

That being said, I believe that it is increasingly difficult to construct a theory of democratic constitutionalism, *applying our own 21st-century norms,* that vindicates the Constitution under which we are governed today. Our 18th-century ancestors had little trouble integrating slavery and the rank subordination of women into their conception of a "republican" political order. *That* vision of politics is blessedly long behind us, but the Constitution is not. It does not deserve rote support from Americans who properly believe that majority rule, even if tempered by the recognition of minority rights, is integral to "consent of the governed."

I invite you to ask the following questions:

1. Even if you support having a Senate in addition to a House of Representatives, do you support as well giving Wyoming the same number of votes as California, which has roughly 70 times the population? To the degree that Congress is in significant ways *unrepresentative,* we have less reason to respect it. It is not a cogent response, incidentally, to say that any such inequalities are vitiated by the fact that the House of Representatives is organized on the basis of population, putting to one side issues raised by partisan gerrymandering. The very nature of our particular version of bicameralism, after all, requires that both houses assent to any legislation. By definition, that means that the *Senate can exercise the equivalent of an absolute veto power* on majoritarian legislation passed by the House that is deemed too costly to the interests of the small states that are overrepresented in the Senate, especially those clustered together in the Rocky Mountain area and the upper Midwest.

2. Are you comfortable with an Electoral College that, among other things, has since World War II placed in the White House five candidates—Truman, Kennedy, Nixon (1968), Clinton (1992 and 1996), and Bush (2000)—who did not get a majority of the popular vote? In at least two of those elections—in 1960, for which evidence exists that Nixon would have won a recount, and in 2000—the winners did not even come in first in the popular vote. The fact is that presidential candidates and their campaign managers are not necessarily trying to win the popular vote, except as an afterthought. Instead they are dedicated to putting together a coalition of states that will provide a majority of the electoral votes.

3. Are you concerned that the president might have too much power, whether to spy on Americans without any Congressional or judicial authorization or to frustrate the will of a majority of both houses of Congress by vetoing legislation with which he disagrees on political, as distinguished from constitutional, grounds? At the very least, it should be clear from recent controversies that the present Constitution does not offer a clear understanding of the limits of presidential power, particularly during times of presidentially perceived emergencies.

4. Are you concerned about whether the country is well served by the extended hiatus between election day and the presidential inauguration some 10 weeks later, during which lame-duck presidents retain full legal authority to make often controversial decisions? Imagine if John Kerry had won the 2004 election, and President Bush had continued to make decisions about policy on Iraq, Iran, and North Korea that would have greatly affected his administration. Much of the hiatus is explicable only with regard to the need for the Electoral College to operate (which serves as an additional reason to eliminate that dysfunctional institution).

5. Are you satisfied with a Constitution that, in effect, maximizes the baleful consequences of certain kinds of terrorist attacks on the United States? If a successor to United Flight 93 were to succeed in a catastrophic attack on the House of Representatives and the Senate, we could find ourselves in a situation where neither institution could operate—because the Constitution makes it impossible to replace disabled (as distinguished from dead) senators or to fill House vacancies by any process other than an election. That would contribute to the overwhelming likelihood of a presidential dictatorship. The Constitution is written for what is termed "retail" vacancies, which occur only occasionally and are easily subject to being handled by the existing rules. Should "wholesale" vacancies occur, however, the present Constitution is nothing less than a ticking time bomb.

6. Do you really want justices on the Supreme Court to serve up to four decades and, among other things, to be able to time their resignations to mesh with their own political preferences as to their successors?

7. Finally, do you find it "democratic" that 13 legislative houses in as many states can block constitutional amendments desired by the overwhelming majority of Americans as well as, possibly, 86 out of the 99 legislative houses in the American states? No other country—nor, for that matter, any of the 50 American states—makes it so difficult to amend its constitution. Article V of our Constitution constitutes an iron cage with regard to changing some of the most important aspects of our political system. But almost as important is the way that it also constitutes an iron cage with regard to our imagination. Because it is so difficult to amend the Constitution—it seems almost utopian to suggest the possibility, with regard to anything that is truly important—citizens are encouraged to believe that change is almost never desirable, let alone necessary.

One might regard those questions as raising only theoretical, perhaps even "aesthetic," objections to our basic institutional structures *if* we feel truly satisfied by the outcomes generated by our national political institutions. But that is patently not the case. Consider the results when samples of Americans are asked whether they believe the country is headed in the right or the wrong direction. In April 2005, a full 62 percent of the respondents to a CBS poll indicated that they believed that the country was headed in "the wrong direction." A year later, a similar CBS poll found that 71 percent of the respondents said that the country was "on the wrong track," with unfavorable ratings for Congress and the president, and only a slim majority approving of the Supreme Court. Surely that comprehensive sense of dissatisfaction is related for most Americans to a belief that our political institutions are *not* adequately responding to the issues at hand. Serious liberals and conservatives increasingly share an attitude of profound disquiet about the capacity of our institutions to meet the problems confronting us as a society.

To be sure, most Americans still seem to approve of their particular members of Congress. The reason for such approval, alas, may be the representatives' success in bringing home federally financed pork, which scarcely relates to the great national and international issues that we might hope that Congress could confront effectively. In any event, we should resist the temptation simply to criticize specific inhabitants of national offices. An emphasis on the deficiencies of particular officeholders suggests that the cure for what ails us is simply to win some elections and replace those officeholders with presumptively more virtuous officials. But we are deluding ourselves if we believe that winning elections is enough to overcome the deficiencies of the American political system.

We must recognize that substantial responsibility for the defects of our polity lies in the Constitution itself. A number of wrong turns were taken at the time of the initial drafting of the Constitution, even if for the best of reasons given the political realities of 1787. Even the most skilled and admirable leaders may not be able to overcome the barriers to effective government constructed by the Constitution. In many ways, we are like the police officer in Edgar Allen Poe's classic *The Purloined Letter*, unable to comprehend the true importance of what is clearly in front of us.

If I am correct that the Constitution is both insufficiently democratic, in a country that professes to believe in democracy, and significantly dysfunctional, in terms of the quality of government that we receive, then it follows that we should no longer express our blind devotion to it. It is not, as Thomas Jefferson properly suggested, the equivalent of the Ark of the Covenant. It is a human creation open to criticism and even to rejection. You should join me in supporting the call for a new constitutional convention.

Critical Thinking

1. In what structural ways is the U.S. Congress unrepresentative of the population?

2. Why should the Electoral College be abolished, according to the author?

3. In what ways are the Constitution's current provisions for replacement of members of Congress a potential problem in the face of a catastrophic attack?

4. Why is Article V of the Constitution problematic?

5. What does the author suggest as a potential remedy to the important flaws in the Constitution?

SANFORD LEVINSON is a professor of law at the University of Texas Law School. This essay is adapted from *Our Undemocratic Constitution: Where the Constitution Goes Wrong (And How We the People Can Correct It)*, by Oxford University Press. Copyright © 2006 by Oxford University Press.

Debating *Citizens United*

One year ago a conservative majority of the Supreme Court opened the floodgates to unlimited independent election expenditures by corporations. This magazine decried the *Citizens United* ruling as a "dramatic assault on American democracy," and we called for the passage of a constitutional amendment stating that corporations don't have the same rights to political expression as individuals. We stand by that editorial. Tracking the role that corporate money plays in politics is an urgent priority for this magazine, as is championing electoral reform. But we're also committed to airing dissenting opinions. In this case, some First Amendment scholars and groups have supported the Court's decision as being consistent with free speech, and we've asked Floyd Abrams, a respected constitutional lawyer, to express those views. We've also invited another renowned advocate of civil liberties, Burt Neuborne, to reply. Their exchange follows.

—The Editors

FLOYD ABRAMS AND BURT NEUBORNE

Remember the First Amendment?

When the *Citizens United* decision was released, many commentators treated it as a desecration. People who would enthusiastically defend the free speech rights of Nazis, pornographers and distributors of videos of animals being tortured or killed were appalled that corporations and unions should be permitted to weigh in on who should be elected president.

That the opinion was based on the First Amendment seemed only to add to their sense of insult. Some dealt with that uncomfortable reality by simply ignoring what the opinion said. When President Obama denounced the opinion in his State of the Union address and elsewhere, he made no reference to the First Amendment. And this magazine chose to mention it only once in its four-page editorial in the February 15, 2010, issue ["Democracy Inc. [1]"] denouncing the ruling and urging the adoption of a constitutional amendment that would reverse it—an amendment that would, for the first time in American history, limit the scope of the First Amendment.

Now that almost a year has passed since the ruling, it is time to return to what the case actually does and does not say, to distinguish between myth and reality. A good deal of inaccurate press commentary, for example, has asserted that the Supreme Court in *Citizens United* declared unconstitutional requirements that contributors or other supporters of campaigns be identified, thus

leading to "secret" corporate contributions. Not a word of that is true. In fact, the Court said just the opposite, affirming by an 8-1 vote (with only Justice Clarence Thomas dissenting) the constitutionality of Congressionally imposed disclosure requirements because "prompt disclosure of expenditures can provide shareholders and citizens with the information needed to hold corporations and elected officials accountable."

Citizens United had no legal impact on the nondisclosure of the identity of contributors to certain not-for-profit groups organized under Section 501(c)(4) of the Internal Revenue Code, ranging from Moveon.org Civic Action to recent Karl Rove–created conservative entities like Crossroads GPS. That is because Congress has never required such disclosure. It could still do so, but if it doesn't, don't blame *Citizens United*.

Nor can *Citizens United* be held responsible for the results of the midterm election. As the *Washington Post* pointed out on November 3, in two-thirds of the Congressional races that flipped from Democratic to Republican, more money was spent by the losing Democrat. Viewing all sixty-three races, Democrats and their supporters spent $206.4 million while the generally victorious Republicans spent $171.7 million. So in the first post–*Citizens United* election, one thing is clear: the much predicted one-sided corporate takeover of the political system did not occur.

Citizens United concluded that the First Amendment bars Congress from criminalizing independent expenditures by corporations and unions supporting or condemning candidates for federal office. Concern about the constitutionality of such a law is not new. The Taft-Hartley Act, passed by an antiunion Republican Congress in 1947, was the first law barring unions and corporations from making independent expenditures in support of or opposition to federal candidates. That law was vetoed by the not-at-all conservative President Harry Truman on the ground that it was a "dangerous intrusion on free speech."

In fact, in those days it was not the conservative jurists on the Supreme Court but the liberal ones who were most concerned about the constitutionality of such legislation. In 1948, in a case commenced against the CIO, the four most liberal justices concluded that whatever "undue influence" was obtained by making large expenditures was outweighed by "the loss for democratic processes resulting from the restrictions upon free and full public discussion." Nine years later, in a case involving the United Auto Workers, a dissenting opinion of the three liberal giants, Justices William Douglas and Hugo Black and Chief Justice Earl Warren, rejected the notion that either a corporation or a union could be limited in its speech because it was "too powerful," since that was no "justification for withholding First Amendment rights from any group—labor or corporate."

The opinion of Justice Anthony Kennedy in *Citizens United* was written in that spirit. It was rooted in two well-established legal propositions. The first was that political speech, especially political speech about whom to vote for or against, is at the core of the First Amendment. There has never been doubt that generally, as Justice Kennedy put it, "political speech must prevail against laws that would suppress it, whether by design or inadvertence."

The second prong of Justice Kennedy's opinion addressed the issue (much discussed in this magazine and elsewhere) of whether the fact that Citizens United was a corporation could deprive it of the right that individuals have long held to support or oppose candidates by making independent expenditures. In concluding that the corporate status of an entity could not negate this right, Justice Kennedy cited twenty-five cases of the Court in which corporations had received full First Amendment protection. Many of them involved powerful newspapers owned by large corporations; others involved non-press entities such as a bank, a real estate company and a public utility company. Justice John Paul Stevens's dissenting opinion (unlike most of the published criticism of *Citizens United*) took little issue with this historical record, acknowledging, "We have long since held that corporations are covered by the First Amendment."

The dangers of any statute barring speech advocating the election or defeat of candidates for office were starkly illustrated through the justices' questioning of the lawyers representing the United States. There were two arguments. In the first, the assistant solicitor general defending the constitutionality of the statute was forced to concede that the same logic that the government used to defend the statute would, as well, permit the government to criminalize the publication of a book by a corporation urging people to vote for a candidate. In the second, then–Solicitor General Elena Kagan was required to acknowledge that the government's position would provide constitutional justification for applying Taft-Hartley to criminalize the publication of a political pamphlet. As these quite accurate responses indicated, the notion that no serious First Amendment challenge was raised in *Citizens United* is itself a myth.

Consider the group that commenced the case and the film it prepared. Citizens United is a conservative organization, partially funded by corporate grants. It prepared and sought to air on video-on-demand a documentary-style movie it had made castigating then–Senator Hillary Clinton when she was viewed as the leading Democratic presidential candidate in 2008. It was an opinionated, tendentious and utterly unfair political documentary—precisely what the First Amendment most obviously protects.

For me, that's the real issue here. Were the five jurists—yes, conservative jurists—right in concluding that this is the sort of speech that must be protected under the First Amendment? Or were the four dissenting jurists correct that the airing of that documentary could be treated as a crime? I know my answer to that question.

Corporations Aren't People

We don't know exactly where the corporate money came from in the midterm elections, or where it went. We know that more than $4 billion was spent by both sides, much of it on negative and misleading advertising. We also know that about $300 million, maybe much more, came from corporate treasuries. And we know that in fifty-three of seventy-two contested Congressional districts and at least three contested Senate races in which corporations heavily backed the Republican candidate over the Democrat, the Republican won. But we don't know how much corporations actually spent, or where, because the disclosure laws broke down and the Senate Republicans blocked every attempt to repair them. And we can only guess at the size of the massive tidal wave of secret corporate money ready to wash away the 2012 presidential election.

We do know this—thanks to the Supreme Court's 5-4 decision in *Citizens United* granting corporations a First Amendment right to spend unlimited sums to win an election, we are facing a second Gilded Age where American democracy is for sale to the highest corporate bidder. Justice Kennedy's opinion, touted by some as a great victory for free speech, begins with a glaring First Amendment mistake. Kennedy claims that the case is about the constitutionality of discriminating between two categories of First Amendment speakers—corporations and human beings. But that just begs the question. The real issue in *Citizens United* was whether corporations should be viewed as First Amendment speakers in the first place. The business corporation is an artificial state-created entity with unlimited life; highly favorable techniques for acquiring, accumulating and retaining vast wealth through economic transactions having nothing to do with politics; and only one purpose—making money. Human beings, on the other hand, die, do not enjoy economic advantages like limited liability and, most important, have a conscience that sometimes transcends crude economic self-interest. Those dramatic differences raise a threshold question, ignored by Justice Kennedy, about whether corporations are even in the First Amendment ballpark.

One hundred years ago, confronted by the same question, the Supreme Court ruled that corporations, as artificial entities, are not protected by the Fifth Amendment's privilege against self-incrimination. That's still the law. In 1988 Justice Kennedy wrote that huge corporations do not deserve the self-incrimination privilege because the privilege "is an explicit right of a natural person, protecting the realm of human thought and expression." Kennedy never explains in *Citizens United* why freedom of speech is not exclusively a "right of a natural person, protecting the realm of human thought and expression." The closest he comes is the argument that voters will somehow benefit from a massive, uncontrolled flow of corporate propaganda. But he never explains how a voter is helped by being subjected to an avalanche of one-sided speech just before an election from a corporation with an unlimited budget and an economic stake in the outcome, especially when the voter often doesn't even know the speech is coming from a corporation.

We invented the business corporation for one reason—its economic potential. It makes sense, therefore, to vest it with constitutional protection for its property. It is, however, a huge and unsupported jump to vest business corporations with noneconomic constitutional rights (like free speech and the privilege against self-incrimination) that flow from respect for human dignity. Robots have no souls. Neither do business corporations. Vesting either with free speech rights is legal fiction run amok.

Nor is it persuasive to argue that since newspaper corporations enjoy First Amendment protection, the electoral speech of oil companies and banks must be similarly protected. The short answer is that the First Amendment has a separate "press" clause that applies to newspapers but not to oil companies or banks. The fact that the First Amendment provides limited protection to commercial speech not only fails to support a general right of corporate free speech; it cuts strongly against it. Precisely because corporations lack human dignity, the Supreme Court has upheld bans on false, misleading and harmful advertising. A similar ban would wipe out most election ads by corporations.

Don't get me wrong. The government had no business trying to suppress the video from Citizens United, a ninety-minute right-wing hatchet job on Hillary Clinton. The video didn't fall under the campaign laws because it was necessary to take the affirmative step of downloading it, the equivalent of taking a book off a library shelf. The need for active collaboration by willing viewers should have ended the *Citizens United* case before it got started. In addition, the campaign statute applied only if 50,000 eligible voters were likely to view the video. How likely was it that 50,000 Democrats would have affirmatively downloaded a hatchet job on Hillary Clinton just before the primary? Moreover, lower court precedent had already recognized an exemption for electioneering communications with only tiny amounts of corporate funding, such as the less than 1 percent in *Citizens United*. Finally, the Supreme Court had already carved out a First Amendment safe harbor for nonprofit grassroots groups with *de minimis* corporate funding.

Justice Kennedy simply leapfrogged the numerous narrower grounds for a decision in order to overrule two precedents and grant as much power as possible to corporate America. Talk about "judicial activism." Given its inconsistent and gratuitous nature, *Citizens United* is good law only as long as five votes support it. The decision should not be treated as binding precedent once the Court's personnel change. In 2012, anyone?

In fairness, *Citizens United* only makes an already terrible system worse. Campaign finance law rests on four mistakes made by judges. Taken together they are a democratic disaster. First, the Supreme Court insists that unlimited spending during an election campaign is pure speech, not speech mixed with conduct. Second, the Court insists that avoiding huge concentrations of electoral power is not important enough to justify limits on massive campaign spending by the superrich. Third, the Court insists that while the spending of unlimited amounts of campaign money is virtually immune from government regulation, the contribution of money to a candidate may be restricted. Finally, the Court has ruled that while preventing corruption justifies regulating campaign contributions, it does not justify limiting independent expenditures. The Court simply ignores the sense of obligation—or fear—generated by huge independent political expenditures.

In the world the Supreme Court has built, the very rich enjoy massively disproportionate political power. What's worse, the exercise of that power can now take place in secret and can tap the almost unfathomable wealth available to our newly minted corporate co-citizens. Say "hello" to Citizen Exxon. Almost fifty years ago, Felix Frankfurter warned that we would rue the day we allowed judges to shape American democracy. Maybe he was right. The first decade of this century opened with the Supreme Court's coup in *Bush v. Gore,* and closed with a putsch granting First Amendment rights to huge corporations to spend as much as they want to buy an election. At the rate the Court is going, soon we will be able to be adopted by a corporation. Maybe even marry one. Until then, I'm afraid we'll just have to settle for being fucked by them.

Protecting Speech

What is it about the *Citizens United* case that seems to drive so many of its learned critics close to the edge? What is it that now drives my friend Burt Neuborne, a most sophisticated legal observer, to wind up sounding somewhat more like Lady Chatterley's gamekeeper than the esteemed scholar he is?

It certainly shouldn't be the impact of the ruling on the 2010 midterm elections. As the Campaign Finance Institute, a non-partisan research organization, concluded, "Party and non-party spending to help competitive Democrats and Republicans was about equal across the board. As a result, neither set of expenditures could be said to have tipped the electoral balance."

Nor should Burt be so agitated at the notion that for-profit corporations have First Amendment rights. That was not only well established in the law for many years before *Citizens United*—again, Justice Kennedy cited twenty-five prior cases in his opinion in which corporations had received full First Amendment rights—but has been essential to the protection of such rights for all.

Burt would limit such rights only to "press" entities. A free press is essential to a free society. But as Justice William Brennan, no slouch in defending First Amendment rights, repeated in an opinion he wrote twenty-five years ago, "The inherent worth of . . . speech in terms of its capacity for informing the public does not depend upon the identity of its source, whether corporation, association, union, or individual." Justice John Paul Stevens, the author years later of the dissent in *Citizens United,* joined that opinion, which also rejected out of hand the notion that "speakers other than the press deserve lesser First Amendment protection." Brennan and Stevens (then) were right; Burt isn't.

In the end, though, the issue isn't what speech Burt or I would allow. Or even what speech the Supreme Court should protect. It's what power Congress should have over speech. The McCain-Feingold law and other legislation held unconstitutional in *Citizens United* contained sweeping bans on speech. They made criminal, as Justice Kennedy pointed out, a Sierra Club ad within sixty days of an election condemning a member of Congress who favored logging in national parks. They barred unions from publishing pamphlets endorsing candidates for president. A ruling that protects such speech should be celebrated, not mocked.

The Censorship Canard

Not even Floyd Abrams, one of the best lawyers I know, can defend *Citizens United.* Floyd notes, correctly, that the case does not prevent Congress from requiring disclosure of corporate election expenditures. He fails to note, though, that Congress attempted to do just that but was blocked on a 59-39 Republican Senate filibuster vote. Thirty-nine senators representing a minority of the population are enough to prevent disclosure of corporate election spending. What are the odds that a wholly owned Congress dependent on massive corporate financial support will find sixty votes in the Senate for disclosure?

Floyd argues that First Amendment concern by liberals about corporate election speech isn't new. He cites Truman's veto of the Taft-Hartley Act and liberal justices' (unsuccessful) efforts to protect speech by the CIO and the UAW. He assumes that the First Amendment rights of unions and corporations are joined at the hip. But unions are free associations of individuals who join together to advance their economic and political interests. A union's money comes from its members' dues. If support for a union is required by law, a dissenter is entitled to a refund for any speech with which he or she disagrees. But corporations derive their funds from market transactions having nothing to do with politics. When you put gas in your car or buy a beer, do you think you are making a political contribution? If individuals associated with corporations want to form voluntary associations analogous to unions, that's fine—as long as they use their own money.

The twenty-five prior cases cited by Floyd allegedly recognizing corporate speech rights deal solely with commercial speech designed to flog a corporation's products or to the right of the press to carry on its constitutionally protected activities. Just because we let corporations sell soap and own newspapers doesn't mean we have to turn our democracy over to them.

Finally, Floyd plays the lawyer's trump—the ad horrendum argument—warning that corporate-financed books are next on the censorship radar. He ignores the First Amendment's press clause, which protects corporate publishers. More fundamental, though, he ignores the fact that a book needs a voluntary reader. The law struck down in *Citizens United* had nothing to do with books. It targeted only those forms of speech—TV and radio ads—that blast their way into your consciousness with no help from the hearer.

In the end, *Citizens United* licenses a small group of corporate managers to use a vast trove of other people's money to buy elections in secret, using forms of speech that cannot be easily avoided. Although 80 percent of Americans don't want to be bombarded with corporate electoral propaganda, *Citizens United* insists that unrestricted, massive corporate electioneering is really good for us. Even Floyd Abrams can't make that medicine go down.

Critical Thinking

1. How and why do Abrams and Neuborne differ on how corporations should be treated in the context of freedom of speech?

2. What are the key gaps between myth and reality in connection with the *Citizens United* decision, according to Floyd Abrams?

3. Does the *Citizens United* ruling prevent corporations' election spending from being disclosed? Why, according to Neuborne, is such disclosure not required and what are the consequences?

4. On what four mistakes made by judges, according to Neuborne, does current campaign finance law rest?

Floyd Abrams, a senior partner in the firm of Cahill Gordon and Reindel LLP, is the author of *Speaking Freely: Trials of the First Amendment* (2005). **Burt Neuborne**, the Inez Milholland Professor of Civil Liberties at New York University Law School, is the founding legal director of the Brennan Center for Justice at New York University. He served as national legal director of the ACLU during the Reagan administration, and has represented Senators John McCain and Russ Feingold in litigation over campaign finance reform.

Obama in Libya
A Clear and Arrogant Violation of Our Constitution

This is a condensed version of the speech Representative Kucinich gave on March 31 on the House floor.

DENNIS KUCINICH

MR. Speaker, the critical issue before this nation today is not Libyan democracy; it is American democracy. Our dear nation stands at a crossroads. The direction we take will determine not what kind of nation we are but what kind of nation we will become. Will we become a nation which plots in secret to wage war? Will we become a nation that observes our Constitution only in matters of convenience?

Will we become a nation which destroys the unity of the world community painstakingly pieced together from the ruins of World War II, a war which itself followed a war to end all wars?

Now, once again we stand poised at a precipice—forced to the edge by an Administration which has thrown caution to the winds and our Constitution to the ground.

It is abundantly clear from a careful reading of our Declaration of Independence that our nation was born from nothing less than the rebellion of the human spirit against the arrogance of power.

The power to declare war is firmly and explicitly vested in the Congress of the United States under Article I, Section 8 of the Constitution.

Let us make no mistake about it, dropping 2,000-pound bombs and unleashing the massive firepower of our Air Force on the capital of a sovereign state is in fact an act of war and no amount of legal acrobatics can make it otherwise.

It is that same arrogance of power which the former Senator from Arkansas, J. William Fulbright, saw shrouded in the deceit which carried us into the abyss of the war in Vietnam. We determined we would never again see another Vietnam. It was the awareness of the unchecked power and arrogance of the executive which led Congress to pass the War Powers Act.

The Congress through the War Powers Act provided the executive with an exception to unilaterally respond only when the nation was in actual or imminent danger: to "repel sudden attacks."

Today we are in a constitutional crisis because our chief executive has assumed for himself powers to wage war which are neither expressly defined nor implicit in the Constitution, nor permitted under the War Powers Act. This is a challenge not just to the Administration, but to Congress itself: The President has no right to wrest that fundamental power from Congress— and we have no right to cede it to him.

We, Members of Congress, can no more absolve our President of his responsibility to obey this profound constitutional mandate than we can absolve ourselves of our failure to rise to the instant challenge that is before us today.

We violate our sacred trust to the citizens of the United States and our oath to uphold the Constitution if we surrender this great responsibility and through our own inaction acquiesce in another terrible war.

We must courageously defend the oath that we took to defend the Constitution of the United States of America or we forfeit our right to participate in representative government.

How can we pretend to hold other sovereigns to fundamental legal principles through wars in foreign lands if we do not hold our own Presidents to fundamental legal principles at home?

We are staring into the maelstrom of war in Libya. And the code of behavior we are establishing today sets a precedent for the potential of evermore violent maelstroms ahead in Syria, Iran, and the horrifying chaos of generalized war throughout the Middle East. Our continued occupation of Iraq and Afghanistan makes us more vulnerable, not less vulnerable, to being engulfed in this generalized war.

In two years, we have moved from President Bush's doctrine of preventive war to President Obama's assertion of the right to go to war without even the pretext of a threat to our nation.

This Administration is now asserting the right to go to war because a nation may threaten force against those who have internally taken up arms against it. Our bombs began dropping even before the U.N.'s International Commission of Inquiry could verify allegations of murder of noncombatant civilians by the Qaddafi regime.

The Administration deliberately avoided coming to Congress and furthermore rejects the principle that Congress has any role in this matter. Yesterday we learned that the Administration would forge ahead with military action even if Congress passed a resolution constraining the mission. This is a clear and arrogant violation of our Constitution.

The Administration's new war doctrine will lead not to peace, but to more war.

The President cannot say that Libya is an imminent or actual threat. He cannot say that war against Libya is in our vital interest. He cannot say that Libya had the intention or capability of attacking the United States. He has not claimed Libya had weapons of mass destruction to be used against us.

Is this is truly a humanitarian intervention? What is humanitarian about providing to one side of a conflict the ability to wage war against the other side of a conflict, which will inevitably trigger a civil war turning Libya into a graveyard?

What are the fundamental principles at stake in America today?

First and foremost is our system of checks and balances built into the Constitution to ensure that important decisions of state are developed through mutual respect and shared responsibility in order to ensure that collective knowledge—indeed, the collective wisdom of the people—is brought to bear.

Our nation has an inherent right to defend itself and a solemn obligation to defend the Constitution. From the Gulf of Tonkin in Vietnam to the allegations of weapons of mass destruction in Iraq, we have learned from bitter experience that the determination to go to war must be based on verifiable facts carefully considered.

Finally, civilian deaths are always to be regretted. But, we must understand from our own Civil War 150 years ago that

nations must resolve their own conflicts and shape their own destiny internally. However horrible those internal conflicts may be, these local conflicts can become even more dreadful if armed intervention in a civil war results in the internationalization of that conflict.

The belief that war is inevitable makes of war a self-fulfilling prophecy.

The United States, in this new and complex world wracked with great movements of masses to transform their own governments, must itself be open to transformation, away from intervention, away from trying to determine the leadership of other nations, away from covert operations to try to manipulate events, and towards a rendezvous with those great principles of self-determination which gave us birth.

Critical Thinking

1. According to the U.S. Constitution in what institution is the power to declare war vested?

2. How do the provisions of the War Powers Act relate to the power to declare war?

3. To what extent did President Obama involve Congress before ordering U.S. military actions in connection with Libya?

4. To what does "arrogance of power" refer in the context of both the Vietnam War and U.S. military activities in connection with Libya?

DENNIS KUCINICH is now in his seventh term representing the Tenth District of Ohio in the U.S. House of Representatives.

Reprinted by permission from *The Progressive,* June 2011, pp. 26–27. Copyright © 2011 by The Progressive, 409 E Main St, Madison, WI 53703. www.progressive.org

UNIT 2

Structures of American Politics

Unit Selections

Learning Outcomes

After reading this Unit, you will be able to:

- Determine the extent to which "the Constitution provides only a bare skeleton" (to quote from the Unit 2 overview that appears below) of how the presidency, Congress, the Supreme Court, and the bureaucracy function today.

- Compare, contrast, and evaluate the performances of different presidents while in office.

- Compare and contrast the praise and criticisms of the U.S. Congress or its members in selections by Lee Hamilton, William G. Howell and Jon C. Pevehouse, Lawrence Lessig, and Eric Lipton. Then appraise the performance of the U.S. Congress and its members yourself.

- Compare and contrast the decisions of the Supreme Court under different chief justices.

- Describe and analyze the major roles that the bureaucracy plays in the operation of U.S. government.

- Describe, compare, and contrast shortcomings of (1) presidents, (2) Congress as a whole and individual members of Congress, (3) the Supreme Court as a whole and individual members of the Court, and (4) the bureaucracy as a whole and individual bureaucrats.

- Describe and evaluate congressional-presidential relations in the following two contexts: (1) foreign and military policymaking, and (2) the process of legislating, including vetoes by presidents and veto overrides by Congress.

- Compare and contrast congressional-presidential relations when operating under conditions of "unified" government and "divided" government.

- Identify the single most important point that Unit 2 selections make about each of the following institutions: the presidency, Congress, the Supreme Court, and the bureaucracy. Then explain why you think each of the four points you have identified is the most important point made about each of the institutions.

James Madison, one of the primary architects of the American system of government, observed that the three-branch structure of government created at the Constitutional Convention of 1787 pitted the ambitions of some individuals against the ambitions of others. Nearly two centuries later, political scientist Richard Neustadt wrote that the structure of American national government is one of "separated institutions sharing powers." These two eminent students of American politics suggest an important proposition: The very design of American national government contributes to the struggles that occur among government officials who have different institutional loyalties and potentially competing goals.

This unit is divided into four sections. The first three treat the three traditional branches of American government, and the last one treats the bureaucracy. One point to remember when studying these institutions is that the Constitution provides only a bare skeleton of the workings of the American political system. The flesh and blood of the presidency, Congress, judiciary, and bureaucracy are derived from decades of experience and the expectations and behavior of today's political actors.

A second and related point to note is that the way a particular institution functions is partly determined by the identities of those who occupy relevant offices. The presidency operates differently with Barack Obama in the White House than it did when George W. Bush was president. Similarly, Congress and the Supreme Court function differently according to who are serving as members and especially who hold leadership positions within the institutions. There were significant changes in the House of Representatives after Republican John Boehner succeeded Democrat Nancy Pelosi as Speaker in 2011 and, before that, when Pelosi took over from Dennis Hastert in 2007. In the Senate, within a two-year period beginning in January 2001, Republican majority leader Trent Lott was succeeded by Democrat Tom Daschle, who in turn was succeeded by Republican Bill Frist. These changes in Senate leadership brought obvious changes in the operation of the Senate. Changes were evident once again when Democrat Harry Reid succeeded Frist in 2007.

A third point about today's American political system is that in recent decades traditional branch vs. branch conflict has been accompanied and probably even overshadowed by increasing partisanship between the two major parties. In the first six years of George W. Bush's presidency, Republican members of Congress seemed to be substantially more influenced by the party affiliation that they shared with President Bush than the institutional loyalties that, in Madison's eyes, should and would pit Congress against the president. In turn, many observers think that during the first six years of this century, Congress did not satisfactorily perform its traditional function of "checking" and "balancing" the executive branch.

In the November 2006 elections Democrats regained majority control of both houses of Congress. For Democrats in the 110th Congress, party affiliation and a belief in institutional or branch prerogatives reinforced one another. Both their party differences with President Bush *and* the belief that Congress is and should be co-equal to the executive branch fueled opposition to the Iraq war and to other Bush actions. And President Bush no doubt had both party loyalties and executive branch prerogatives in mind as he contended with Democratic leaders and Democratic majorities in the 110th Congress. The 2008 elections brought Democratic control to all three elected institutions of the national government (Presidency, House of Representatives, and Senate), a situation that political scientists call "unified government." Thus, in January 2009, a new

© fStop/Getty Images

period of "unified government" (under Democratic control) began, but in January 2011 "divided government" returned after Republicans regained majority control of the House of Representatives in the November 2010 elections.

Some observers of the American political system, Woodrow Wilson among them, have argued that "unified government" is likely to be more effective and efficient than its counterpart, "divided government" (in which neither major party controls all three elective institutions). Others, most notably Professor David Mayhew of Yale University, arguably the most respected contemporary political scientist specializing in the study of American politics, have concluded that "unified governments" vary very little, if at all, from "divided governments" in what they accomplish. For nearly two-thirds of the time since World War II, Americans have lived under "divided government."

The first section of this unit contains articles on the contemporary presidency. They include both treatments of past presidents such as George W. Bush and Ronald Reagan and articles addressing the presidency of Barack Obama through the middle of his third year in office. Eight months after Bush became president in the aftermath of the controversial 2000 election, the 9/11 terrorist attacks on the World Trade Center and the Pentagon abruptly transformed his presidency. Americans of both parties rallied around President Bush in his efforts to respond decisively to the attacks, and Congress passed a resolution that authorized President Bush to invade Iraq. The resulting war in Iraq began in early 2003, and within a few weeks President Bush triumphantly declared the success of the invasion that had overthrown the regime of Iraqi president Saddam Hussein.

But the situation in Iraq grew worse instead of better in the next few years, and by the start of 2006, the majority of Americans opposed the Iraq war and disapproved of Bush's performance as president. The 2006 congressional elections gave voters the chance to express their views on the Bush administration and they did so forcefully, handing majority control of both houses of Congress to the Democrats. In November 2008, Democrat Barack Obama won the presidency over Republican John McCain, with widespread disapproval of Bush's performance as president being a key factor in that outcome. By the third year of Obama's presidency, polls showed substantial and growing disapproval of his overall performance as well as with many of his policy initiatives. It is in these contexts that articles in the first section of this unit assess the presidency of Barack Obama and some other recent presidencies.

The second section of this unit treats Congress, which has undergone noteworthy changes in the past four decades after more than a half-century of relative stability anchored by the extremely powerful seniority system instituted in the early twentieth century. In the 1970s, reforms in that seniority system worked to decentralize power on Capitol Hill. The unexpected Republican takeover of the House of Representatives as a result of the 1994 congressional elections brought even more changes. New Republican Speaker Newt Gingrich reduced the power of committees and the importance of the seniority system, imposed term limits on committee chairs, consolidated power in the Speaker's office, and became a prominent figure on the national scene. The 2006 congressional elections, as already noted, enabled Democrats to regain majority control of both houses. Representative Nancy Pelosi of California became the first woman Speaker of the House, and Republicans controlled neither house of Congress for the first time in a dozen years. Democrats increased their majorities in both houses of Congress in the 2008 elections, and, of course, a fellow Democrat, Barack Obama, won the White House. For the first year of the 111th Congress, Democrats (joined by two independents) controlled 60 seats in the Senate, making for what sometimes operated as a "filibuster-proof" majority. The 2010 elections returned majority control of the House of Representatives to Republicans and Republican John Boehner of Ohio succeeded Pelosi as Speaker in January 2011.

The Supreme Court sits at the top of the U.S. court system and is the focus of the third section in this unit. The Court is not merely a legal institution; it is a policymaker whose decisions can affect the lives of millions of citizens. The Court's decisive role in determining the outcome of the 2000 presidential election illustrated its powerful role in the American political system.

Membership of the nine-member Court—and, in turn, operation of the institution as a whole—was unusually stable between 1994 and 2005, one of the longest periods in American history during which no Supreme Court vacancies occurred. In July 2005, Associate Justice Sandra Day O'Connor announced her intention to resign and a few months later Chief Justice William Rehnquist died. President Bush's nominees to fill the two vacancies, John Roberts and Samuel Alito, became chief justice and associate justice, respectively. Less than four months into Barack Obama's presidency, Associate Justice David Souter announced his retirement. President Obama nominated Sonia Sontomayor to replace Souter, and she became the first Hispanic woman to sit on the Court. In 2010, President Obama nominated Elena Kagan to succeed retiring Associate Justice Stevens, and she became the fourth woman to serve on the Court and brought the number of women justices currently serving to three, an all-time high.

Like all people in high government offices, the chief justice and the associate justices have legal, policy, and political views of their own. Observers of the Court pay careful attention to the way the chief justice and the eight associate justices act on those views and interact with one another in shaping the decisions of the Court.

The bureaucracy of the national government, the subject of the fourth and last section in this unit, is responsible for carrying out policies determined by top-ranking officials. Yet the bureaucracy is not merely a neutral administrative instrument, and it is often criticized for waste and inefficiency. Even so, government bureaucracies must be given credit for many of the accomplishments of American government. Whether we like it or not, government bureaucracies wield great power in the conduct of American national government.

As a response to the September 11 terrorist attacks, Congress in 2002 passed a bill establishing the Department of Homeland Security, the biggest reorganization of the bureaucracy since the Department of Defense was founded in the aftermath of World War II. In the summer of 2004, the 9/11 Commission issued its report recommending the restructuring of the government's intelligence community. In response, Congress passed a bill later that year that established the position of Director of National Intelligence in an attempt to bring a clearer hierarchy and better communication to the government's intelligence establishment. More effective and efficient functioning of the bureaucracy has clearly become an important concern since the destruction of the World Trade Center, and efforts to improve government bureaucracy's performance in the areas of homeland security and intelligence gathering are continuing. On another front, in July 2010, Congress passed and the president signed the Dodd-Frank Wall Street Reform and Consumer Protection Act, which established a new government agency, the Bureau of Consumer Financial Protection. According to the U.S. Chamber of Commerce, the mammoth bill directs that bureaucrats formulate 350 rules, conduct 47 studies, and write 74 reports.

Student Website
www.mhhe.com/cls

Internet References

Department of State
www.state.gov

Federal Reserve System
www.federalreserve.gov

United States House of Representatives
www.house.gov

United States Senate
www.senate.gov

United States Supreme Court
www.supremecourt.gov

White House
www.whitehouse.gov

The Founders' Great Mistake

Who is responsible for the past eight years of dismal American governance? "George W. Bush" is a decent answer. But we should reserve some blame for the Founding Fathers, who created a presidential office that is ill-considered, vaguely defined, and ripe for abuse. Here's how to fix what the Founders got wrong—before the next G. W. Bush enters the Oval Office.

GARRETT EPPS

For the past eight years, George W. Bush has treated the White House much as Kenneth Grahame's Mr. Toad treated a new automobile—like a shiny toy to be wrecked by racing the motor, spinning smoke from the tires, and smashing through farmyards until the wheels come off. Bush got to the Oval Office despite having lost the popular vote, and he governed with a fine disdain for democratic and legal norms—stonewalling congressional oversight; detaining foreigners and U.S. citizens on his "inherent authority"; using the Justice Department as a political cudgel; ordering officials to ignore statutes and treaties that he found inconvenient; and persisting in actions, such as the Iraq War, that had come to be deeply unpopular in Congress and on Main Street.

Understandably, most Americans today are primarily concerned with whether Barack Obama can clean up Bush's mess. But as Bush leaves the White House, it's worth asking why he was able to behave so badly for so long without being stopped by the Constitution's famous "checks and balances." Some of the problems with the Bush administration, in fact, have their source not in Bush's leadership style but in the constitutional design of the presidency. Unless these problems are fixed, it will only be a matter of time before another hot-rodder gets hold of the keys and damages the country further.

The historian Jack N. Rakove has written, "The creation of the presidency was [the Framers'] most creative act." That may be true, but it wasn't their best work. The Framers were designing something the modern world had never seen—a republican chief executive who would owe his power to the people rather than to heredity or brute force. The wonder is not that they got so much wrong, but that they got anything right at all.

According to James Madison's *Notes of Debates in the Federal Convention of 1787,* the executive received surprisingly little attention at the Constitutional Convention in Philadelphia. Debate over the creation and workings of the new Congress was long and lively; the presidency, by contrast, was fashioned relatively quickly, after considerably less discussion. One important reason for the delegates' reticence was that George Washington, the most admired man in the world at that time, was the convention's president. Every delegate knew that Washington would, if he chose, be the first president of the new federal government—and that the new government itself would likely fail without Washington at the helm. To express too much fear of executive authority might have seemed disrespectful to the man for whom the office was being tailored.

Washington's force of personality terrified almost all of his contemporaries, and although he said little as presiding officer, he was not always quiet. Once, when an unknown delegate left a copy of some proposed provisions lying around, Washington scolded the delegates like a headmaster reproving careless prep-schoolers, and then left the document on a table, saying, "Let him who owns it take it." No one did.

Even when Washington remained silent, his presence shaped the debate. When, on June 1, James Wilson suggested that the executive power be lodged in a single person, no spoke up in response. The silence went on until Benjamin Franklin finally suggested a debate; the debate itself proceeded awkwardly for a little while, and was then put off for another day.

Many of the conversations about presidential authority were similarly awkward, and tended to be indirect. Later interpreters have found the original debates on the presidency, in the words of former Supreme Court Justice Robert H. Jackson, "almost as enigmatic as the dreams Joseph was called upon to interpret for Pharaoh."

In the end, the Framers were artfully vague about the extent and limits of the president's powers. Article I, Section 8 of the Constitution, which empowers Congress, runs 429 words; Article II, Section 2, the presidential equivalent, is about half as long. The powers assigned to the president alone are few: he can require Cabinet members to give him their opinions in writing; he can convene a special session of Congress "on extraordinary occasions," and may set a date for adjournment if the two houses cannot agree on one; he receives ambassadors and is commander in chief of the armed forces; he has a veto on legislation (which Congress can override); and he has the power to pardon.

The president also *shares* two powers with the Senate—to make treaties, and to appoint federal judges and other "officers of the United States," including Cabinet members. And, finally, the president has two specific *duties*—to give regular reports on the state of the union, and to "take care that the laws be faithfully executed."

All in all, the text of Article II, while somewhat ambiguous—a flaw that would be quickly exploited—provided little warning that the office of president would become uniquely powerful. Even at the convention, Madison mused that it "would rarely if ever happen that the executive constituted as ours is proposed to be would have firmness enough to resist the legislature." In fact, when citizens considered the draft Constitution during the ratification debates in 1787 and 1788, many of their concerns centered on the possibility that the Senate would make the president its cat's-paw. Few people foresaw the modern presidency, largely because the office as we know it today bears so little relation to that prescribed by the Constitution.

The modern presidency is primarily the intellectual handiwork not of "the Framers" but of one Framer—Alexander Hamilton. Hamilton's idea of the presidency can be found in a remarkable speech he gave to the convention, on June 18, 1787. In it, Hamilton argued that the president should serve for life, name Cabinet members without Senate approval, have an absolute veto on legislation, and have "the direction of war" once "authorized or begun." The president would be a monarch, Hamilton admitted, but an "elective monarch."

Hamilton's plan was so far from the mainstream of thought at the convention that none of its provisions was ever seriously discussed. Nonetheless, Hamilton was and remains the chief theorist of the presidency, first in writing his essays for *The Federalist* and then in serving as George Washington's secretary of the Treasury. In this latter role, acting as Washington's de facto prime minister, Hamilton took full advantage of the vagueness and brevity of Article II, laying the groundwork for an outsize presidency while the war-hero Washington was still in office.

In *The Federalist*, Hamilton had famously proclaimed that "energy in the executive is a leading character in the definition of good government." Just how much energy he favored became clear during America's first foreign crisis, the Neutrality Proclamation controversy of 1793. When Britain and France went to war, many Americans wanted to aid their Revolutionary ally. But Washington and the Federalists were rightly terrified of war with the powerful British Empire. Washington unilaterally proclaimed that the United States would be neutral.

France's American supporters, covertly aided by Thomas Jefferson, fiercely attacked Washington for exceeding his constitutional authority. The power to make treaties, they said, was jointly lodged in the president and the Senate; how could Washington unilaterally interpret or change the terms of the treaty of alliance with France?

Under the pen name "Pacificus," Hamilton wrote a defense of Washington's power to act without congressional sanction. The first Pacificus essay is the mother document of the "unitary executive" theory that Bush's apologists have pushed to its limits since 2001. Hamilton seized on the first words of Article II: "The executive power shall be vested in a President of the United States of America." He contrasted this wording with Article I, which governs Congress and which begins, "All legislative powers herein granted shall be vested in a Congress of the United States." What this meant, Hamilton argued, was that Article II was "a general grant of . . . power" to the president. Although Congress was limited to its enumerated powers, the executive could do literally anything that the Constitution did not expressly forbid. Hamilton's president existed, in effect, outside the Constitution.

That's the Bush conception, too. In 2005, John Yoo, the author of most of the administration's controversial "torture memos," drew on Hamilton's essay when he wrote, "The Constitution provides a general grant of executive power to the president." Since Article I vests in Congress "only those legislative powers 'herein granted'," Yoo argued, the more broadly stated Article II must grant the president "an unenumerated executive authority."

Hamilton's interpretation has proved durable even though there is little in the record of constitutional framing and ratification to suggest that anyone else shared his view. In times of crisis, power flows to the executive; too rarely does it flow back. And while Washington himself used his power wisely (Jeffersonians found out in 1812 that pulling the British lion's tail was poor policy), it was during his administration that the seeds of the "national-security state" were planted.

The system that the Framers developed for electing the president was, unfortunately, as flawed as their design of the office itself. When Madison opened discussion on presidential election in Philadelphia, he opined that "the people at large" were the "fittest" electorate. But he immediately conceded that popular election would hurt the South, which had many slaves and few voters relative to the North. To get around this "difficulty" he proposed using state electors. Electoral-vote strength was based on a state's total population, not on its number of voters—and the South received representation for three-fifths of its slaves both in the House of Representatives and in the Electoral College.

Scholars still debate whether the Framers foresaw the prospect of a contested presidential election, followed by a peaceful shift of power. (Remember that, as Shakespeare pointed out in *Richard II*, kings left office feet first.) Some members of the founding generation believed that a duly elected president would simply be reelected until his death, at which point the vice president would take his place, much like the Prince of Wales ascending to the throne.

Perhaps as a result, the mechanics of presidential election laid out in the Constitution quickly showed themselves to be utterly unworkable. The text of Article II contained no provision for a presidential ticket—with one candidate for president and one for vice president. Instead, each elector was supposed to vote for any two presidential candidates; the candidate who received the largest majority of votes would be president; the runner-up would be vice president. In 1800, this ungainly system nearly brought the country to civil war. Thomas Jefferson and Aaron Burr ran as a team; their electors were expected to vote for both of them. Jefferson assumed that one or two would drop Burr's name from the ballot. That would have given Jefferson the larger majority, with Burr winning the vice presidency. But due to a still-mysterious misunderstanding, all the electors voted for both candidates, producing a tie in the electoral vote and throwing the election to a House vote.

The ensuing drama lasted six days and 36 ballots before Hamilton threw Federalist support to Jefferson (as much as he despised Jefferson, he regarded Burr as "an embryo-Caesar"). This choice began the chain of events that led to Hamilton's death at Burr's hands three years later. More important, the imbroglio exposed the fragility of the election procedure.

In 1804, the Electoral College was "repaired" by the Twelfth Amendment; now the electors would vote for one candidate for president and another for vice president. This was the first patch on Article II, but far from the last—the procedures for presidential election and succession were changed by constitutional amendment in 1933, 1951, 1961, and 1967. None of this fine-tuning has been able to fix the system. In 1824, 1876, 1888, and 2000, the Electoral College produced winners who received fewer popular votes than the losers, and it came startlingly close to doing so again in 2004; in 1824, 1876, and 2000, it also produced prolonged uncertainty and the prospect of civil unrest—or the fact of it.

Even when the election system works passably, a president-elect must endure another indefensible feature of the succession process. In England, a new prime minister takes office the day after parliamentary elections; in France, a newly elected president is inaugurated within a week or two. But when Americans choose a new leader, the victor waits weeks—nearly a quarter-year—to assume office. The presidential interregnum is a recurrent period of danger.

Originally, a new president didn't take office until March 4. This long delay nearly destroyed the nation after the 1860 election. During the disastrous "secession winter," Abraham Lincoln waited in Illinois while his feckless predecessor, James Buchanan, permitted secessionists to seize federal arsenals and forts. By March 1861, when Lincoln took office, the Civil War was nearly lost, though officially it had not even begun.

In 1932, Franklin Roosevelt crushed the incumbent, Herbert Hoover, but had to wait four months to take office. During that period, Hoover attempted to force the president-elect to abandon his proposals for economic reform. Roosevelt refused to commit himself, but the resulting uncertainty led the financial system to the brink of collapse.

The Twentieth Amendment, ratified in 1933, cut the interregnum nearly in half, but 11 weeks is still too long. After his defeat in 1992, President George H. W. Bush committed U.S. troops to a military mission in Somalia. The mission turned toxic, and Bill Clinton withdrew the troops the following year. Clinton was criticized for his military leadership, perhaps rightly—but the Constitution should not have permitted a repudiated president to commit his successor to an international conflict that neither the new president nor Congress had approved.

As the elder Bush did, an interregnum president retains the power of life or death over the nation. As Clinton did, an interregnum president may issue controversial or corrupt pardons. In either case, the voters have no means of holding their leader accountable.

The most dangerous presidential malfunction might be called the "runaway presidency." The Framers were fearful of making the president too dependent on Congress; short of impeachment—the atomic bomb of domestic politics—there are no means by which a president can be reined in politically during his term. Taking advantage of this deficiency, runaway presidents have at times committed the country to courses of action that the voters never approved—or ones they even rejected.

John Tyler, who was never elected president, was the first runaway, in 1841. William Henry Harrison had served only a few weeks; after his death, the obscure Tyler governed in open defiance of the Whig Party that had put him on the ticket, pressing unpopular proslavery policies that helped set the stage for the Civil War.

Andrew Johnson was the next unelected runaway. Politically, he had been an afterthought. But after Lincoln's assassination, Johnson adopted a pro-Southern Reconstruction policy. He treated the party that had nominated him with such scorn that many contemporaries came to believe he was preparing to use the Army to break up Congress

by force. After Johnson rebuffed any attempt at compromise, the Republican House impeached him, but the Senate, by one vote, refused to remove him from office. His obduracy crippled Reconstruction; in fact, we still haven't fully recovered from that crisis.

American political commentators tend to think loosely about exertions of presidential authority. The paradigm cases are Lincoln rallying the nation after Fort Sumter, and Roosevelt, about a year before Pearl Harbor, using pure executive power to transfer American destroyers to embattled Britain in exchange for use of certain British bases. Because these great leaders used their authority broadly, the thinking goes, assertions of executive prerogative are valid and desirable.

Certainly there are times when presidential firmness is better than rapid changes in policy to suit public opinion. Executive theorists in the United States often pose the choice that way—steady, independent executive leadership or feckless, inconstant pursuit of what Hamilton called "the temporary delusion" of public opinion. But not all shifts in public opinion are delusive or temporary. An executive should have some independence, but a presidency that treats the people as irrelevant is not democratic. It is authoritarian.

Lincoln and Roosevelt asserted emergency powers while holding popular mandates. Lincoln had just won an election that also provided him with a handy majority in Congress; Roosevelt was enormously popular, and in 1940 his party outnumbered the opposition 3-to-1 in the Senate and by nearly 100 seats in the House.

But sometimes a president with little or no political mandate uses the office to further a surprising, obscure, or discredited political agenda. Under these circumstances, what poses as bold leadership is in fact usurpation. The most egregious case arises when a president's policy and leadership have been repudiated by the voters, either by a defeat for reelection or by a sweeping rejection of his congressional allies in a midterm election. When that happens, presidents too often do what George Bush did in 2006—simply persist in the conduct that has alienated the country. Intoxicated by the image of the hero-president, unencumbered by any direct political check, stubborn presidents in this situation have no incentive to change course.

When the voters turn sharply against a president mid-term, his leadership loses some or all of its legitimacy, and the result can be disastrous. Clinton was decisively repudiated in November 1994. After the election, the administration and the new Republican Congress remained so far apart on funding decisions that the government had to shut down for 26 days in 1995 and 1996. This episode is now remembered for Clinton's political mastery, but it was actually a dangerous structural failure. (Imagine that the al-Qaeda attacks of September 11, 2001, had happened instead on December 20, 1995, when the stalemate had forced the executive branch to send most of its "nonessential" employees home.)

To sum up, while George W. Bush may have been a particularly bad driver, the presidency itself is, and always has been, an unreliable vehicle—with a cranky starter, an engine too big for the chassis, erratic steering, and virtually no brakes. It needs an overhaul, a comprehensive redo of Article II.

Constitutional change is a daunting prospect. But consider how often we have already changed the presidency; it is the Constitution's most-amended feature. And this is the moment to think of reform—the public's attention is focused on the Bush disaster, and ordinary people might be willing to look at the flaws in the office that allowed Bush to do what he did.

So how should the presidency be changed?

First, voters should elect presidents directly. And once the vote is counted, the president-elect (and the new Congress) should take office within a week. Americans accustomed to the current system will object that this would not allow enough time to assemble a Cabinet—but in England and France, the new chief executive considers ministerial nominations before the election. A shorter interregnum would force the creation of something like the British shadow cabinet, in which a candidate makes public the names of his key advisers. That would give voters important information, and provide the president with a running start.

Next, Article II should include a specific and limited set of presidential powers. The "unitary executive" theorists should no longer be allowed to spin a quasi-dictatorship out of the bare phrase *executive power;* like the responsibilities of Congress, those of the president should be clearly enumerated.

It should be made clear, for example, that the president's powers as commander in chief do not crowd out the power of Congress to start—and stop—armed conflict. Likewise, the duty to "take care that the laws be faithfully executed" needs to be clarified: it is not the power to decide which laws the president wants to follow, or to rewrite new statutes in "signing statements" after Congress has passed them; it is a duty to uphold the Constitution, valid treaties, and congressional statutes (which together, according to the Constitution, form "the supreme law of the land").

After a transformative midterm election like that of 1994 or 2006, the nation should require a compromise between the rejected president and the new Congress. A president whose party has lost some minimum number of seats in Congress should be forced to form the equivalent of a national-unity government. This could be done by requiring the president to present a new Cabinet that includes members of both parties, which the new Congress would approve or disapprove as a whole—no drawn-out confirmation hearings on each nominee. If the president were unwilling to assemble such a government or unable to get congressional approval after, say, three tries, he would have to resign.

This would not give Congress control of the executive branch. A resigning president would be replaced by the vice president, who would not be subject to the new-Cabinet requirement. This new president might succeed politically where the previous one had failed (imagine Al Gore becoming president in 1995, and running in 1996—and perhaps in 2000—as an incumbent). And that possibility would discourage the new congressional majority from simply rejecting the compromise Cabinet. Resignation might be worse for them than approval.

As a final reform, we should reconsider the entire Hamiltonian concept of the "unitary executive." When George Washington became president, he left a large organization (the Mount Vernon plantation) to head a smaller one (the federal government). But today, the executive branch is a behemoth, with control over law enforcement, the military, economic policy, education, the environment, and most other aspects of national life. That behemoth is responsible to one person, and that one person, as we have seen, is only loosely accountable to the electorate.

In other areas, the Framers solved this problem neatly: they divided power in order to protect against its abuse. Congress was split into the House and the Senate to ensure that the legislative process would not be so efficient as to absorb powers properly belonging to the other branches. The problem now is not an overweening Congress but an aggrandized executive branch; still, the remedy is the same. We should divide the executive branch between two elected officials—a president, and an attorney general who would be voted in during midterm elections.

As we are learning from the ongoing scandal of the torture memos, one of the drawbacks of a single executive is that Justice Department lawyers may consider it their job to twist the law to suit the White House. But the president is not their client; the United States is. Justice Department lawyers appointed by an elected attorney general would have no motive to distort law and logic to empower the president, while the White House counsel's office, which does represent the president, would have every incentive to monitor the Justice Department to ensure that it did not tilt too strongly against the executive branch. The watchmen would watch each other.

This arrangement would hardly be unprecedented: most state governments elect an attorney general. The new Article II could make clear that the president has the responsibility for setting overall legal policy, just as governors do today.

None of these changes would erode the "separation of powers." That happens only when a change gives one branch's prerogatives to another branch. These changes refer in each instance back to the people, who are the proper source of all power. The changes would still leave plenty of room for "energy in the executive" but would afford far less opportunity for high-handedness, secrecy, and simple rigidity. They would allow presidential firmness, but not at the expense of democratic self-governance.

It's not surprising that the Framers did not understand the perils of the office they designed. They were working in the dark, and they got a lot of things right. But we should not let our admiration for the Framers deter us from fixing their mistakes.

Our government is badly out of balance. There is a difference between executive energy and autocratic license; between leadership and authoritarianism; between the democratic firmness of a Lincoln and the authoritarian rigidity of a Bush. The challenge we face today is to find some advantage in Bush's sorry legacy. Reform of the executive branch would be a good place to start.

Critical Thinking

1. What powers are assigned to the president acting alone? What powers are shared with the legislative branch? What two specific duties does the Constitution assign to the president?

2. How was the vice presidential selection process as originally outlined in the Constitution flawed? How have those challenges been addressed?

3. What are the problems associated with the relatively long time span between election results and inauguration day?

4. What four specific reforms to the presidency does the author propose? Do you favor them?

5. Do you agree that "our government is badly out of balance"? Why or why not?

Veto This!

When presidents veto a bill, they're exercising strength—or showing weakness. They usually win the override battles but sometimes lose the war for public approval.

CARL M. CANNON

The first presidential veto in American history was exercised, fittingly enough, by George Washington. He informed Congress in writing on April 5, 1792, that having "maturely considered the Act passed by the two Houses," he felt obligated to send it back on the grounds that it was unconstitutional. The legislation had to do with the number of citizens that each member of the House would represent. Having defeated the British on the field of battle—thereby giving the members of Congress their jobs to begin with—President Washington was accorded a high level of deference. No serious attempt to override the veto transpired, and Congress rewrote the measure to satisfy his objections.

Washington issued a single veto in his second term as well. This time, the dispute was on policy grounds, as the former general didn't cotton to the minutiae of a congressional plan for reorganizing the armed forces. He issued that veto on February 28, 1797; again, the veto stood. With these two actions, Washington initiated a tug-of-war between the executive and legislative branches of the federal government that persists to this day. The veto, a forgotten power during George W. Bush's first term, has now emerged as a prime battleground in the twilight months of his presidency.

"One thing that needs to be underscored is that because President Bush is a 'lame-duck' president, it doesn't mean that he is no longer powerful," said Chris Kelley, a political science professor at the University of Miami in Ohio. "The veto is a powerful weapon that the president simply must use from time to time."

Alexander Hamilton would have agreed. At the dawn of the Republic, Hamilton told his fellow Founders that the presidential veto (Latin for "I forbid") was "a qualified negative" that would serve as a brake on the passions of a popularly elected legislature. For five years, Bush did not avail himself of this authority, making him the only president except for John Quincy Adams to go an entire four-year term without vetoing anything that Congress sent him.

Was Bush practicing good government, or bad government? The answers to that question—and to the questions about Bush's newfound fondness for the veto—are partly political, partly theoretical. The political portion of the question is the voters' to answer. It will be addressed on the 2008 campaign trail, where presidential and congressional candidates from both parties are parsing Bush's recent vetoes to boost their candidacies. The theoretical component has even more movable parts and is the continuation of an argument more than 200 years old.

The first U.S. president to use the prerogative to veto *major* legislation solely over policy objections was Andrew Jackson. He was also the first to see the veto's potential as a political tool: In 1832, Jackson vetoed the enabling legislation to extend the charter of the villified Second Bank of the United States. Although his economic reasoning was specious, his political antenna was flawless, and the 1832 bank veto helped to assure Jackson's re-election.

For the better part of two centuries, political scientists and constitutional scholars have debated the propriety of Jackson's willingness to use the veto as a political tool, even while the principle became the standard for all subsequent presidents. Two rival theories of what constitutes a good-government use of the veto emerged.

The first, in the words of Stephen Skowronek, a political science professor at Yale University, is that the Jackson veto precedent "made a mockery of the premier operating principle" of Jeffersonian democracy, that is, deference to people's representatives in Congress. Jackson's veto was an artifice, these critics have said over the years, that short-circuited the separation of powers and contributed to the rise of the "imperial presidency" so disfavored by the Founders. In substituting the whims of one person for the will of the people, the veto also—and inevitably—soured relations between the branches of government.

"The veto tilts the balance of power in Washington too far toward the status quo."

—Sanford Levinson,
University of Texas professor

This was the precise complaint leveled against Bush last week when he vetoed a $35 billion, five-year expansion of the State Children's Health Insurance Program that passed both chambers of Congress with comfortable majorities and enjoyed bipartisan support.

"You [had] consensus across party and ideology, and a unity on the most important domestic issue, health care," Rep. Rahm Emanuel, D-Ill., said. "Except for one person."

But one person is all it takes—if that person is the president.

"I think that this is probably the most inexplicable veto in the history of the country," Sen. Edward Kennedy, D-Mass., declared on the Senate floor. "It is incomprehensible: It is intolerable. It's unacceptable."

But accept it Congress must—unless Democrats can muster a two-thirds vote in each chamber to override. And that's where critics of the veto say that the system goes off the rails. "Put simply, the veto tilts the balance of power in Washington too far toward the status quo," says Sanford Levinson, professor of law and government at the University of Texas (Austin).

Levinson, author of a recent book, *Our Undemocratic Constitution: Where the Constitution Goes Wrong (and How We the People Can Correct It)*, asserts that anyone who thinks that judicial review of legislation passed by majorities has an autocratic tinge to it ought to be more worried about the presidential veto. He says that the Supreme Court has invalidated some 165 laws throughout U.S. history, while presidents have vetoed about 2,550 bills—only 106 of which Congress has managed to override. "If judicial activism is anti-democratic," he wrote recently, "then the presidential veto is, well, *very* anti-democratic."

There is, however, a second school of thought, represented by such scholars as Ronald C. Moe and Louis Fisher, who wrote about separation-of-powers issues for the Congressional Research Service. In this view, the presidential veto has a positive impact on the political process. For starters, the threat of a veto gives Congress an incentive to draw legislation more carefully, encouraging compromise. The veto can serve, as Alexander Hamilton suggested it might, as an additional brake against "improper laws" passed in the heat of the moment. "It establishes a salutary check upon the legislative body, calculated to guard the community against the effects of faction, precipitancy, or of any impulse unfriendly to the public good, which may happen to influence a majority of that body," Hamilton wrote.

Implicit in this view of checks and balances is a sophisticated notion: namely, that bad ideas, once signed into law, are more difficult to repeal than they were to enact. A contemporary illustration of Hamilton's fear may be the innocent sounding "Anti-Drug Abuse Act." Congress passed it hurriedly in 1986 without hearings, partially as a response to the cocaine-induced death of University of Maryland basketball star Len Bias. Coming as cheap crack, cocaine was turning urban streets into shooting galleries, the law prescribed far harsher sentences for possessing or dealing crack than it did for having powder cocaine.

That provision has put tens of thousands of young African-Americans in federal prison for far longer terms than white drug abusers, who tend to traffic in powder cocaine. President Reagan signed the law a week before the 1986 election. Eric Sterling, then a Democratic House aide who helped to draft the

bill, wistfully recalls wishing that Reagan had vetoed it. Sterling, who now heads the Criminal Justice Policy Foundation, has been trying for the better part of two decades to persuade Congress to repeal the 1986 statute that mandates harsh terms for low-level cocaine dealers. "The Framers would have offered this law as a perfect example of the proper use of the presidential veto," Sterling said. "The problem is that by virtue of [these laws'] popularity, they are the hardest vetoes to cast."

Who's in Charge?

Mirroring the ongoing philosophical discussion about the proper role of presidential vetoes, another conversation is taking place on a more practical political level: Are vetoes a sign of strength or weakness in a chief executive? Does it help a president to issue vetoes, or hurt him and his party? These, as Bush and his suddenly fractious Republicans are discovering during the current term of Congress, are not academic questions. Once again, there are two sides to the equation; and once again, it is clear that the dispute won't be settled in Bush's presidency.

Let's call the first viewpoint the Rodney King school of thought. Why *can't* we all get along? This argument holds that presidential vetoes are, almost by definition, a sign that the chief executive lacks power, leadership ability, and a large enough following to shape events. In other words, a president who has to veto has failed to persuade, can't compromise, can't get the White House's own legislation through Congress, and is unable to take the issue over the heads of Congress to the people.

"A strong president needs fewer vetoes because he's able to exercise sufficient control over the congressional agenda, whether through decisive influence over legislative formulation or judicious use of veto threats that make it unlikely bills the president would oppose would land on his desk," says Robert Spitzer, professor of political science at the State University of New York (Cortland).

Framed this way, Capitol Hill has more say-so in setting the veto-agenda than is generally acknowledged these days in Washington. In an influential 1978 book on the politics of the veto, political scientists Thomas Romer and Howard Rosenthal explored this point. The authors outlined a "monopoly agenda control model" in which Congress, not the president, determines the fate of veto threats. In their theory, the agenda-setter is the pivotal legislator on any given issue, who presents the White House with take-it-or-leave-it proposals. Thus, the president is essentially in a reactive, and therefore, subordinate, position. This is something of a postmodern (or, at least, post–Franklin Roosevelt) view, and it probably is not a coincidence that Romer and Rosenthal were doing their research when Gerald Ford was president.

Ford was a creature of the House, but as president he was also a captive of the huge Democratic majorities he inherited as voters in 1974 reacted against the Republican Party of Richard Nixon, Spiro Agnew, and Watergate. Despite serving as president for barely half a term, Ford has the distinction of tying for second place on the all-time list of presidential vetoes that were overridden by Congress. Ford, overridden 12 times, shares that dubious silver medal with President Truman, who recorded the lowest Gallup Poll job-approval rating in history.

The record-holder is Andrew Johnson, overridden 15 times, who was impeached by the House and nearly convicted in the Senate. The precipitating act of impeachment was Johnson's veto of a bill he believed—correctly, the Supreme Court later ruled—was unconstitutional.

"Many conventional presidency scholars argue that the use of a veto indicates a weak president, since the power of the presidency resides in his ability to bargain and persuade the Congress to go along with his policies," Kelley said. "Thus if he uses a veto, it means that his credibility with the Congress is low. Those who point to Ford as a failed president often will examine both his vetoes and the overrides."

Nolan McCarty, acting dean of the Woodrow Wilson School of Public and International Affairs at Princeton University, has described two other models for vetoes. In one, the White House and Congress have incomplete information about exactly what will precipitate a veto. Bush, for example, threatened to veto an expansion of the student loan program, but then didn't, perhaps leading wishful Democrats to believe that he would feel pressured to sign the SCHIP bill. The absence of a dominant

Presidents Usually Win

Congress is rarely able to muster the two-thirds majority of votes in both chambers to override a presidential veto. This list, based on a compilation by the Congressional Research Service, does not include pocket vetoes after Congress adjourned.

President	Vetoes	Overrides	Vetos that Stuck	Major Overrides
TRUMAN	180	12	Natural-gas deregulation 1950 Coastal tidelands 1946, 1952	Taft-Hartley labor relations 1947 Income-tax cuts 1947, 1948 McCarran Internal Security 1950 McCarran-Walter immigration quotas 1952
EISENHOWER	73	2	Natural gas 1956 Farm spending 1956, 1958 Housing programs 1959 Pollution control 1960	TVA spending 1959 Federal pay 1960
KENNEDY	12	0	Federal pensions 1961	
JOHNSON	16	0	Cotton quotas 1968	
NIXON	26	7	Minimum-wage increase 1973	Water Pollution Control 1972 War Powers Act 1973
FORD	48	12	Oil price controls 1975	Freedom of Information Act 1974
CARTER	13	2	Nuclear reactor 1977	Oil import fee 1980
REAGAN	39	9	Textile quotas 1988	South Africa sanctions 1986 Water projects 1987 Highway funding 1987
G.H.W. BUSH	29	1	Minimum-wage increase 1989 Job discrimination 1990 China trade status 1992 Family-medical leave 1990, 1992 Taxes 1992 Stem-cell research 1992 Campaign finance 1992	Cable TV 1992
CLINTON	36	2	Spending reductions 1995 Appropriations 1995 Bosnia arms embargo 1995 "Partial-birth" abortion 1996, 1997 Product liability 1996 Tax cuts 1999 Estate-tax repeal 2000	Line-item vetoes 1998 Securities litigation 1995
G.W. BUSH	4	0	Stem-cell research 2006, 2007 Iraq war limits 2007	

legislative actor is what leads to the impasse. "When there is such uncertainty," McCarty wrote, "vetoes may occur because the Legislature overestimates its ability to extract concessions from the president."

In the wake of Bush's SCHIP veto, perhaps the nation's capital finds itself in that fluid state of affairs—meaning that, eventually, compromise legislation will emerge. The president has left the door open, and Congress is home to a handful of moderate Republicans who hope that Bush and the Democrats will walk through that door together. Of course, there is another, less pleasant, place to be. McCarty describes this model as "Blame-Game Vetoes."

When one party accuses the other of making "war on children," it is a safe bet that partisan advantage, not meaningful negotiation, is at the frontal cortex of the party's collective brain. Not that the Democrats tried to hide it. "We're not going to compromise," Senate Majority Leader Harry Reid said flatly after Bush's recent veto. House Speaker Nancy Pelosi vowed that Democrats would try to override and to make the issue "a hard vote for Republicans." New Jersey's Democratic governor, Jon Corzine, said, "I hope we override the veto before we start worrying about compromise."

To produce legislation, the process usually needs to work the other way around. But this is the blame game. SCHIP "has got to be up there with motherhood and apple pie," Rep. Jim Cooper, D-Tenn., told the *Los Angeles Times,* apparently with a straight face. "This is Tiny Tim. And who is against Tiny Tim? The only person in all of literature was Ebenezer Scrooge."

So who is winning the blame game? The early signs were a thumbs-down for George W. Scrooge and a thumbs-up for the Democrats. Public opinion polls showed that the voters, egged on by Democrats and media editorialists, thought that Bush's veto was wrongheaded, if not heartless. Eventually, White House aides and a few Republicans joined the fray, raising various arguments to support Bush's position: Some of the "children" covered under this bill would be nearly 25 years of age; the earning power of some eligible families tops $80,000 a year; some people opting into the program already have private health insurance; the Democrats' plan would be funded with a regressive $1-a-pack tax on cigarettes—that kind of thing. There was truth (or some truth, anyway) to all of these assertions, but Bush did not make them in the days leading up to the veto. Speaking to reporters at the White House, Bush simply said he had "philosophical" differences with the Democrats.

That was code, pure and simple, intended for the ears of fiscal conservatives, who have grown disenchanted with the GOP leader who has run up huge budget deficits in each year of his presidency. Translated, Bush's words meant: "OK, OK, I'll quit spending tax dollars like a drunken sailor."

In this new spirit, Bush has threatened to veto 10 of 11 pending appropriations bills. Until now, nobody knew for sure whether he was serious. In his first term, Bush vetoed nothing. In year five of his presidency, despite threatening 133 vetoes, Bush issued a single one, on embryonic-stem-cell research. This year, he vetoed a similar stem-cell bill, along with a spending measure aimed at curbing escalation of the Iraq war. Now Bush has issued his fourth veto. Has he found his groove? Perhaps. But some believe that he waited too long.

"It's an hour too late," says Frank Luntz, the Republican communications guru who helped fashion the 1994 Contract with America. "And a dollar too short."

Situational Ethics

Until Democrats reclaimed Congress in the 2006 elections, the premium in Bushworld was indeed on getting along. Rodney King would have approved. In the first term, Nicholas Calio, then-White House director of legislative affairs, told *National Journal* that the two top Republicans in the House, Speaker Dennis Hastert and Majority Leader Tom DeLay, made it a point of pride to send no bill to 1600 Pennsylvania Avenue that would be vetoed. "It's a real principle with the speaker and DeLay," Calio said. John Feehery, Hastert's spokesman at the time, went further, asserting that his boss believed that to invite a presidential veto signaled "a breakdown in the system."

"We don't want to make political points with this president," Feehery added, "because we agree with him on almost everything." Congressional Republicans challenged Bush's veto threats only once, in 2002, on a campaign finance overhaul. Bush didn't like the bill, but he put his signature on it anyway, the overt evidence of his displeasure was that he didn't invite one of its principal authors, Sen. John McCain, R-Ariz., to the signing ceremony.

Another reason that Bush hasn't relied on the veto is that he routinely uses "signing statements" to assert that he will implement new legislation in ways that conform with his thinking and that of White House lawyers and policy makers. On other occasions, particularly as regards national security, this president hasn't even given that much deference to congressional intent: If White House lawyers deem a law, such as the statutes regarding the wiretapping of suspected foreign terrorists, to be technologically out-of-date, well, this administration just writes its own hall pass.

Thus, Bush's first term featured an odd combination of co-operating closely with Capitol Hill Republicans on some occasions and simply ignoring Congress on others. Along the way, Team Bush overlooked historic examples showing that sometimes a veto—along with a healthy dose of chutzpah—is just what it takes to make a president look strong. Truman, in his first term, lamented during several crippling national strikes that he lacked the executive authority to force trade union leaders to the bargaining table. Congress gave Truman that power in the Taft-Hartley Act. He promptly vetoed it, putting himself at long last in organized labor's good graces. Congress overrode the president's veto, and Truman happily used the power vested in him some dozen times. Moreover, he turned around and won re-election in 1948, with, yes, the help of labor. For a president, this is as good as it gets—veto nirvana.

Republicans were in charge of both ends of Pennsylvania Avenue during most of the first six years of Bush's presidency, so the chances for such showdowns were small. But Democrats ran the show when Franklin Roosevelt was president—and he vetoed 635 of their bills. According to presidential scholar William Leuchtenburg, Roosevelt would instruct White House aides to look for legislation that he could veto, "in order to remind Congress that it was being watched."

Alan Greenspan, who is old enough to remember FDR, believes that Bush—and the country—would have been well served if this president had done the same. "My biggest frustration remained the president's unwillingness to wield his veto against out-of-control spending," Greenspan wrote in his new book, *The Age of Turbulence: Adventures in a New World*. "Not exercising the veto power became a hallmark of the Bush presidency. . . . To my mind, Bush's collaborate-don't-confront approach was a major mistake."

Many movement conservatives couldn't agree more. They think that Bush's belated embrace of the veto might save the GOP's soul and give the Republican base a principle to be excited about. "The GOP needs to regain its brand on spending," says Grover Norquist, president of Americans for Tax Reform. "The Democrats are acting now in 2007 and 2008 as they did in 1993 and 1994: taxing, spending. And here the GOP can highlight its differences with vetoes and veto-upholding. It is a truly selfless act by Bush as he isn't running, but the GOP House and Senate guys are, and they need their brand back. This autumn's fight, which I hope to be long and drawn out and repetitive, will do for the GOP what they should have been doing over the past six years."

Other Republicans, most notably moderates who face tough re-election fights next year, are unnerved by Bush's newfound fiscal conservatism, and especially by his willingness to veto a children's health bill to prove it. "I believe this is an irresponsible use of the veto pen," said Sen. Gordon Smith, an Oregon Republican who faces a spirited challenge in 2008. "It's the White House that needs to give," added another Senate GOP centrist, Susan Collins of Maine.

The noises emanating from the White House don't give these worried Republicans much reassurance. "Good policy is good politics," said White House spokesman Tony Fratto last week. "If members stand on principle, they'll be just fine."

Principles can be in the eye of the beholder, however, especially in Washington, where situational ethics are routinely on display. Dan Mitchell of the libertarian Cato Institute points out that the money at stake in the health care initiative is small compared with the excess spending that Bush accepted when Republicans controlled Congress. "There certainly does seem to be a legitimate argument that the president only objects to new spending when Democrats are doing it," Mitchell said.

Bush might have more moral sway had he, back in 2002, vetoed a bipartisan and pork-laden $190 billion farm bill. Half a century ago, Dwight Eisenhower did just that. The Democrats pounced, thinking they had Ike right where they wanted him. "The veto of the farm bill," then-Senate Majority Leader Lyndon Johnson said, "can be described only as a crushing blow to the hopes and the legitimate desires of American agriculture." That was one description. Another was "fiscal restraint," something that Eisenhower had managed to make sexy—with his veto pen.

By the end of the 1959 Christmas recess, an unnamed White House aide was telling *Time* magazine, "When those congressmen come back in January, they're going to be so anxious to find something to cut that they'll cut their own wrists if necessary." On his way out of office, with high approval ratings and a federal budget nearly in balance, Eisenhower was *Time's* "Man of the Year."

Similar battle lines are drawn for the upcoming year, during which Democrats will try to hold their congressional majorities and recapture the White House. Will they succeed? They will if Sen. Hillary Rodham Clinton has anything to say about it. "With the stroke of a pen, President Bush has robbed nearly 4 million uninsured children of the chance for a healthy start in life and the health coverage they need but can't afford," the New York Democrat and 2008 presidential front-runner said after Bush's veto.

"This is vetoing the will of the American people," Clinton added. "I was proud to help create the Children's Health Insurance Program during the Clinton administration, which today provides health insurance for 6 million children."

Hillary Clinton was right about her role in SCHIP. The part of the story that she may be forgetting, however, is that her husband got traction as president after the Republicans took over Congress and he began wielding his veto pen—36 times before leaving office.

"Clinton's skillful and aggressive use of the veto was a hallmark of his domestic presidency after the Republicans gained control of Congress in 1994," wrote Charles Cameron, a political science professor at Princeton and the author of *Veto Bargaining: Presidents and the Politics of Negative Power*. "In some respects, he was more successful opposing Congress than he had been leading it, when the Democrats controlled the institution."

Reagan faced a House controlled by the opposition party and he, too, issued a spate of vetoes, 78 (half of them pocket vetoes). Congress overrode nine—matching Roosevelt's tally. The overrides didn't hurt either man's legacy. At least one of the 2008 presidential candidates has apparently taken this lesson to heart. Republican Mitt Romney, who as Massachusetts governor faced an overwhelmingly Democratic Legislature for four years, boasts of vetoing hundreds of appropriations while serving in Boston—and says he'd happily do it all over again in Washington.

"If I'm elected president, I'm going to cap nondefense discretionary spending at inflation minus 1 percent," he said recently. "And if Congress sends me a budget that exceeds that cap, I will veto that budget. And I know how to veto. I like vetoes."

Critical Thinking

1. Summarize two rival theories of what constitutes a "good-government use of the veto" by a president.

2. Consider whether vetoes are a sign of strength or weakness in a president.

3. Why are presidential vetoes difficult to override?

4. How do "signing statements" lessen the inclination of a president to use his veto power?

5. Compare President George W. Bush's use of the veto in his first term versus his second term. Why did his approach change?

ccannon@nationaljournal.com.

What Happened to Obama's Passion?

Drew Westen

It was a blustery day in Washington on Jan. 20, 2009, as it often seems to be on the day of a presidential inauguration. As I stood with my 8-year-old daughter, watching the president deliver his inaugural address, I had a feeling of unease. It wasn't just that the man who could be so eloquent had seemingly chosen not to be on this auspicious occasion, although that turned out to be a troubling harbinger of things to come. It was that there was a story the American people were waiting to hear—and needed to hear—but he didn't tell it. And in the ensuing months he continued not to tell it, no matter how outrageous the slings and arrows his opponents threw at him.

The stories our leaders tell us matter, probably almost as much as the stories our parents tell us as children, because they orient us to what is, what could be, and what should be; to the worldviews they hold and to the values they hold sacred. Our brains evolved to "expect" stories with a particular structure, with protagonists and villains, a hill to be climbed or a battle to be fought. Our species existed for more than 100,000 years before the earliest signs of literacy, and another 5,000 years would pass before the majority of humans would know how to read and write.

Stories were the primary way our ancestors transmitted knowledge and values. Today we seek movies, novels and "news stories" that put the events of the day in a form that our brains evolved to find compelling and memorable. Children crave bedtime stories; the holy books of the three great monotheistic religions are written in parables; and as research in cognitive science has shown, lawyers whose closing arguments tell a story win jury trials against their legal adversaries who just lay out "the facts of the case."

When Barack Obama rose to the lectern on Inauguration Day, the nation was in tatters. Americans were scared and angry. The economy was spinning in reverse. Three-quarters of a million people lost their jobs that month. Many had lost their homes, and with them the only nest eggs they had. Even the usually impervious upper middle class had seen a decade of stagnant or declining investment, with the stock market dropping in value with no end in sight. Hope was as scarce as credit.

In that context, Americans needed their president to tell them a story that made sense of what they had just been through, what caused it, and how it was going to end. They needed to hear that he understood what they were feeling, that he would track down those responsible for their pain and suffering, and that he would restore order and safety. What they were waiting for, in broad strokes, was a story something like this:

"I know you're scared and angry. Many of you have lost your jobs, your homes, your hope. This was a disaster, but it was not a natural disaster. It was made by Wall Street gamblers who speculated with your lives and futures. It was made by conservative extremists who told us that if we just eliminated regulations and rewarded greed and recklessness, it would all work out. But it didn't work out. And it didn't work out 80 years ago, when the same people sold our grandparents the same bill of goods, with the same results. But we learned something from our grandparents about how to fix it, and we will draw on their wisdom. We will restore business confidence the old-fashioned way: by putting money back in the pockets of working Americans by putting them back to work, and by restoring integrity to our financial markets and demanding it of those who want to run them. I can't promise that we won't make mistakes along the way. But I can promise you that they will be honest mistakes, and that your government has your back again." A story isn't a policy. But that simple narrative—and the policies that would naturally have flowed from it—would have inoculated against much of what was to come in the intervening two and a half years of failed government, idled factories and idled hands. That story would have made clear that the president understood that the American people had given Democrats the presidency and majorities in both houses of Congress to fix the mess the Republicans and Wall Street had made of the country, and that this would not be a power-sharing arrangement. It would have made clear that the problem wasn't tax-and-spend liberalism or the deficit—a deficit that didn't exist until George W. Bush gave nearly $2 trillion in tax breaks largely to the wealthiest Americans and squandered $1 trillion in two wars.

And perhaps most important, it would have offered a clear, compelling alternative to the dominant narrative of the right, that our problem is not due to spending on things like the pensions of firefighters, but to the fact that those who can afford to buy influence are rewriting the rules so they can cut themselves progressively larger slices of the American pie while paying less of their fair share for it.

But there was no story—and there has been none since.

In similar circumstances, Franklin D. Roosevelt offered Americans a promise to use the power of his office to make their lives better and to keep trying until he got it right. Beginning in his first inaugural address, and in the fireside chats that followed, he explained how the crash had happened, and he minced no words about those who had caused it. He promised to do something no president had done before: to use the resources of the United States to put Americans directly to work, building the infrastructure we still rely on today. He swore to keep the people who had caused the crisis out of the halls of power, and he made good on that promise. In a 1936 speech at Madison Square Garden, he thundered, "Never before in all our history have these forces been so united against one candidate as they stand today. They are unanimous in their hate for me—and I welcome their hatred."

When Barack Obama stepped into the Oval Office, he stepped into a cycle of American history, best exemplified by F.D.R. and his distant cousin, Teddy. After a great technological revolution or a major economic transition, as when America changed from a nation of farmers to an urban industrial one, there is often a period of great concentration of wealth, and with it, a concentration of power in the wealthy. That's what we saw in 1928, and that's what we see today. At some point that power is exercised so injudiciously, and the lives of so many become so unbearable, that a period of reform ensues—and a charismatic reformer emerges to lead that renewal. In that sense, Teddy Roosevelt started the cycle of reform his cousin picked up 30 years later, as he began efforts to bust the trusts and regulate the railroads, exercise federal power over the banks and the nation's food supply, and protect America's land and wildlife, creating the modern environmental movement.

Those were the shoes—that was the historic role—that Americans elected Barack Obama to fill. The president is fond of referring to "the arc of history," paraphrasing the Rev. Dr. Martin Luther King Jr.'s famous statement that "the arc of the moral universe is long, but it bends toward justice." But with his deep-seated aversion to conflict and his profound failure to understand bully dynamics—in which conciliation is always the wrong course of action, because bullies perceive it as weakness and just punch harder the next time—he has broken that arc and has likely bent it backward for at least a generation.

When Dr. King spoke of the great arc bending toward justice, he did not mean that we should wait for it to bend. He exhorted others to put their full weight behind it, and he gave his life speaking with a voice that cut through the blistering force of water cannons and the gnashing teeth of police dogs. He preached the gospel of nonviolence, but he knew that whether a bully hid behind a club or a poll tax, the only effective response was to face the bully down, and to make the bully show his true and repugnant face in public.

In contrast, when faced with the greatest economic crisis, the greatest levels of economic inequality, and the greatest levels of corporate influence on politics since the Depression, Barack Obama stared into the eyes of history and chose to avert his gaze. Instead of indicting the people whose recklessness wrecked the economy, he put them in charge of it. He never

explained that decision to the public—a failure in storytelling as extraordinary as the failure in judgment behind it. Had the president chosen to bend the arc of history, he would have told the public the story of the destruction wrought by the dismantling of the New Deal regulations that had protected them for more than half a century. He would have offered them a counternarrative of how to fix the problem other than the politics of appeasement, one that emphasized creating economic demand and consumer confidence by putting consumers back to work. He would have had to stare down those who had wrecked the economy, and he would have had to tolerate their hatred if not welcome it. But the arc of his temperament just didn't bend that far.

The truly decisive move that broke the arc of history was his handling of the stimulus. The public was desperate for a leader who would speak with confidence, and they were ready to follow wherever the president led. Yet instead of indicting the economic policies and principles that had just eliminated eight million jobs, in the most damaging of the tic-like gestures of compromise that have become the hallmark of his presidency—and against the advice of multiple Nobel-Prize-winning economists—he backed away from his advisers who proposed a big stimulus, and then diluted it with tax cuts that had already been shown to be inert. The result, as predicted in advance, was a half-stimulus that half-stimulated the economy. That, in turn, led the White House to feel rightly unappreciated for having saved the country from another Great Depression but in the unenviable position of having to argue a counterfactual—that something terrible might have happened had it not half-acted.

To the average American, who was still staring into the abyss, the half-stimulus did nothing but prove that Ronald Reagan was right, that government is the problem. In fact, the average American had no idea what Democrats were trying to accomplish by deficit spending because no one bothered to explain it to them with the repetition and evocative imagery that our brains require to make an idea, particularly a paradoxical one, "stick." Nor did anyone explain what health care reform was supposed to accomplish (other than the unbelievable and even more uninspiring claim that it would "bend the cost curve"), or why "credit card reform" had led to an increase in the interest rates they were already struggling to pay. Nor did anyone explain why saving the banks was such a priority, when saving the homes the banks were foreclosing didn't seem to be. All Americans knew, and all they know today, is that they're still unemployed, they're still worried about how they're going to pay their bills at the end of the month and their kids still can't get a job. And now the Republicans are chipping away at unemployment insurance, and the president is making his usual impotent verbal exhortations after bargaining it away.

What makes the "deficit debate" we just experienced seem so surreal is how divorced the conversation in Washington has been from conversations around the kitchen table everywhere else in America. Although I am a scientist by training, over the last several years, as a messaging consultant to nonprofit groups and Democratic leaders, I have studied the way voters think and feel, talking to them in plain language. At this point,

I have interacted in person or virtually with more than 50,000 Americans on a range of issues, from taxes and deficits to abortion and immigration.

The average voter is far more worried about jobs than about the deficit, which few were talking about while Bush and the Republican Congress were running it up. The conventional wisdom is that Americans hate government, and if you ask the question in the abstract, people will certainly give you an earful about what government does wrong. But if you give them the choice between cutting the deficit and putting Americans back to work, it isn't even close. But it's not just jobs. Americans don't share the priorities of either party on taxes, budgets or any of the things Congress and the president have just agreed to slash—or failed to slash, like subsidies to oil companies. When it comes to tax cuts for the wealthy, Americans are united across the political spectrum, supporting a message that says, "In times like these, millionaires ought to be giving to charity, not getting it."

When pitted against a tough budget-cutting message straight from the mouth of its strongest advocates, swing voters vastly preferred a message that began, "The best way to reduce the deficit is to put Americans back to work." This statement is far more consistent with what many economists are saying publicly—and what investors apparently believe, as evident in the nosedive the stock market took after the president and Congress "saved" the economy.

So where does that leave us?

Like most Americans, at this point, I have no idea what Barack Obama—and by extension the party he leads—believes on virtually any issue. The president tells us he prefers a "balanced" approach to deficit reduction, one that weds "revenue enhancements" (a weak way of describing popular taxes on the rich and big corporations that are evading them) with "entitlement cuts" (an equally poor choice of words that implies that people who've worked their whole lives are looking for handouts). But the law he just signed includes only the cuts. This pattern of presenting inconsistent positions with no apparent recognition of their incoherence is another hallmark of this president's storytelling. He announces in a speech on energy and climate change that we need to expand offshore oil drilling and coal production—two methods of obtaining fuels that contribute to the extreme weather Americans are now seeing. He supports a health care law that will use Medicaid to insure about 15 million more Americans and then endorses a budget plan that, through cuts to state budgets, will most likely decimate Medicaid and other essential programs for children, senior citizens and people who are vulnerable by virtue of disabilities or an economy that is getting weaker by the day. He gives a major speech on immigration reform after deporting more than 700,000 immigrants in two years, a pace faster than nearly any other period in American history.

The real conundrum is why the president seems so compelled to take both sides of every issue, encouraging voters to project whatever they want on him, and hoping they won't realize which hand is holding the rabbit. That a large section of the country views him as a socialist while many in his own party are concluding that he does not share their values speaks volumes—but not the volumes his advisers are selling: that if you make both the right and left mad, you must be doing something right.

As a practicing psychologist with more than 25 years of experience, I will resist the temptation to diagnose at a distance, but as a scientist and strategic consultant I will venture some hypotheses.

The most charitable explanation is that he and his advisers have succumbed to a view of electoral success to which many Democrats succumb—that "centrist" voters like "centrist" politicians. Unfortunately, reality is more complicated. Centrist voters prefer honest politicians who help them solve their problems. A second possibility is that he is simply not up to the task by virtue of his lack of experience and a character defect that might not have been so debilitating at some other time in history. Those of us who were bewitched by his eloquence on the campaign trail chose to ignore some disquieting aspects of his biography: that he had accomplished very little before he ran for president, having never run a business or a state; that he had a singularly unremarkable career as a law professor, publishing nothing in 12 years at the University of Chicago other than an autobiography; and that, before joining the United States Senate, he had voted "present" (instead of "yea" or "nay") 130 times, sometimes dodging difficult issues.

A somewhat less charitable explanation is that we are a nation that is being held hostage not just by an extremist Republican Party but also by a president who either does not know what he believes or is willing to take whatever position he thinks will lead to his re-election. Perhaps those of us who were so enthralled with the magnificent story he told in "Dreams From My Father" appended a chapter at the end that wasn't there—the chapter in which he resolves his identity and comes to know who he is and what he believes in.

Or perhaps, like so many politicians who come to Washington, he has already been consciously or unconsciously corrupted by a system that tests the souls even of people of tremendous integrity, by forcing them to dial for dollars—in the case of the modern presidency, for hundreds of millions of dollars. When he wants to be, the president is a brilliant and moving speaker, but his stories virtually always lack one element: the villain who caused the problem, who is always left out, described in impersonal terms, or described in passive voice, as if the cause of others' misery has no agency and hence no culpability. Whether that reflects his aversion to conflict, an aversion to conflict with potential campaign donors that today cripples both parties' ability to govern and threatens our democracy, or both, is unclear.

A final explanation is that he ran for president on two contradictory platforms: as a reformer who would clean up the system, and as a unity candidate who would transcend the lines of red and blue. He has pursued the one with which he is most comfortable given the constraints of his character, consistently choosing the message of bipartisanship over the message of confrontation.

But the arc of history does not bend toward justice through capitulation cast as compromise. It does not bend when 400 people control more of the wealth than 150 million of their fellow Americans. It does not bend when the average middle-class family has seen its income stagnate over the last 30 years while the richest 1 percent has seen its income rise astronomically. It does not bend when we cut the fixed incomes of our parents and grandparents so hedge fund managers can keep their 15 percent tax rates. It does not bend when only one side in negotiations between workers and their bosses is allowed representation. And it does not bend when, as political scientists have shown, it is not public opinion but the opinions of the wealthy that predict the votes of the Senate. The arc of history can bend only so far before it breaks.

Critical Thinking

1. Why, according to Drew Westen, is good storytelling a critical part of being a good political leader?

2. At what point in what Westen calls a "cycle of history" did Obama enter the presidency? Which predecessors of his became president at similar points in history?

3. According to Westen, in what way(s) was Obama's "half-stimulus" bill "truly decisive"?

4. Why, according to Westen, do most Americans have little idea of what President Obama stands for?

5. What explanations does Westen offer for why President Obama seems so inclined to compromise and half-measures?

DREW WESTEN is a professor of psychology at Emory University and the author of *The Political Brain: The Role of Emotion in Deciding the Fate of the Nation.*

Bullied Pulpit

Why the White House wasn't able to fight the "Obamacare" Lie.

DAVID CORN

In the Spring of 2009, as the titanic fight over President Barack Obama's health care proposal was beginning, Frank Luntz—an infamous Republican consultant who specializes in the language of politics—drew up a confidential 28-page report (PDF) for congressional gopers on how they could confront, and defeat, Obama on this crucial issue. He suggested that they use a particular phrase: "Government takeover of health care." And they did. Again and again, for the entire months-long debate. During one *Meet the Press* appearance, Rep. John Boehner (R-Ohio), then the House minority leader, referred to Obama's plan as a "government takeover" five times (without once being challenged).

It was a clear falsehood. Obama's system relies on private insurance and the market—especially after he abandoned a public option—albeit with additional government regulation. *PolitiFact.com,* a fact-checking site operated by the *St. Petersburg Times,* declared Luntz's formulation the "Lie of the Year" of 2010. (Luntz didn't have to make an acceptance speech.) Yet the line stuck. A Bloomberg poll conducted as Congress approved the legislation found that 53 percent of American adults believed it amounted "to a government takeover." A *USA Today*/Gallup survey indicated that 65 percent thought the new law would expand government's role in health care "too much." Several months later, a Gallup poll found that 10 percent selected "government involvement in health care" as the No. 1 health care problem facing the nation—over access or cost. In 2008, only 1 percent had cited government interference as the top problem.

Though Republicans lost the legislative war, they had Luntzified the debate and won the battle to define the health care measure through a Big Lie. This was significant: It established a foundation for the right's counterattacks—including the 2010 congressional elections, the ongoing effort to repeal or curtail the law, and the burgeoning 2012 campaign.

So why did two measly words come to bedevil the most powerful man in the world? What could Obama and his crew have done to stop the fabrication from taking root and growing into poison ivy?

"Nobody has the exact answer to that," says Anita Dunn, who was White House communications director in 2009. But surprisingly, she notes that it's "much easier" for a presidential candidate to combat disinformation than for a sitting president to do the same—no matter that the latter has the most commanding bully pulpit in the world.

A campaign can call into action allied bloggers, social-media networks, and millions of supporters who share a common and simple goal: to get this guy elected. A campaign can also run paid ads, while a president depends on the conventional media to convey his message. (The Obama presidency was expected to address this handicap by converting the mammoth grassroots effort of the campaign into an ongoing political force—a conversion not effectively realized.)

What's more, on the campaign trail, the penalty for lying—though not always applied—can be higher. A fib that's widely exposed can define the public's view of the prevaricating candidate. That's much less of a problem for, say, a member of Congress with a safe seat or an advocacy group making a false claim against a White House proposal.

Perhaps most importantly, notes Bill Burton, a former deputy press secretary in the Obama White House, the entire communications operation of a campaign has one aim: Promote the candidate, and defend against untrue assertions. "In government," he says, "that's one of *many* things a communications team is responsible for." And it's not a fair fight—even if one side is the White House. "You had monied interests spending 200 million against health care reform," Burton says. "And we're up against a million fractured groups and voices."

So what's a president to do?

Actually, it's pretty basic. "First, you have to get as many of your own people as you can muster calling a lie a lie," says Dunn. "Second, try to get referees, like fact-checking organizations, to weigh in. Third, keep doing it." She notes that none of this is easy, particularly No. 3: "The press doesn't want to repeat every day, 'Look, the Republicans are still lying about it.'"

Of course, the Obama administration and its defenders did all that. They went on cable shows, did newspaper interviews, tweeted and Facebooked, and generally tried, as Burton puts it, to "find every single avenue into Americans' living rooms." They cited *PolitiFact* and other independent sources confirming that the government-takeover line was false. They kept at it for months—make that *years*. But they couldn't vanquish the lie.

Dunn recalls that on the day that Obama signed the health care measure into law, she was traveling in Florida and watching local TV. Before the signing ceremony, a local station did a long interview with a GOP congressman. He warned of how horrible this government takeover of health care would be; he complained that taxes would go up and people would not be able to choose their doctors. "We didn't have anything to counter that," she says. "The president has a pretty big bully pulpit, but you can't have him come out on an hourly basis saying, 'It's not a government takeover.'"

A small fuss ensued on the house floor; The republicans were essentially claiming that calling a lie a lie was a lie.

Mark Twain is said to have once quipped, "A lie can travel halfway round the world while the truth is putting on its shoes." That's even truer today: "There's this whole phenomenon of an internet fact," notes Dunn. "If something is not immediately and vigorously denied, and is repeated over and over, it becomes a fact because it turns up on Google." Lanny Davis, who did damage control for the Clinton White House (and, recently, himself, when news reports noted that he was working for African tyrants), argues that "search engines take misinformation and put it into an echo chamber. Trying to counter it is the functional equivalent of having your hair full of honey and bees, and you're trying to whack the bees with your hands."

Davis recalls an episode in the fall of 1997—pre-Google, but just as the internet was becoming a factor in political communications—when he was working in the White House. A reporter for *Insight,* a conservative magazine, approached him about a story alleging that President Bill Clinton had arranged for dozens of friends and donors to be buried in Arlington National Cemetery, including a contributor who had served as US ambassador to Switzerland. Davis said he would check it out and get back to the reporter, and he contacted the secretary of the Army. The reporter didn't wait. He posted the article, and it became a right-wing sensation. Conservative talk-show hosts went wild. Congressional Republicans—including House Speaker Newt Gingrich—vowed investigations. The story was locked in: Clinton had sold burial plots in Arlington.

In fact, it turned out, the president had recommended burial waivers for four people, including former Supreme Court Justice Thurgood Marshall. None were donors, and the ambassador in question was not among them. But it took Davis and the White House two days to sort out the facts. By then, the story had gone global. "I was getting calls from around the world," Davis says. "We couldn't do anything at that point, just make sure that the truth was written down somewhere" for posterity. You can't win in such a situation, he says: "If you're lucky—and do everything possible—maybe you get to a draw. And that's if you're very lucky."

Republicans are doing their best to ensure that the White House doesn't reach that level of luck with health care. Earlier this year, after Rep. Dan Lungren (R-Calif.) made a speech on the House floor decrying the health care law, Rep. Earl Blumenauer (D-Ore.) noted that *PolitiFact* had called the government-takeover accusation the top lie of 2010. Lungren interrupted to request that Blumenauer's comment be stricken from the record for impugning another member. A small fuss ensued on the House floor; the Republicans were essentially claiming that calling a lie a lie was a lie. After legislators reviewed the remarks, Blumenauer asked to withdraw his own statement because Lungren had not specifically referred to a government takeover this time (though he had in the past). "I apologize if the person who said 'government takeover of health care' was not you," Blumenauer said. "It is repeated so often by my Republican friends, including the speaker of the House, time and time again, that sometimes I get confused."

Critical Thinking

1. What two words were used—misleadingly, according to David Corn—to describe the health care reform act that President Obama signed into law early in 2010?

2. Why is it easier for a presidential candidate to respond effectively to misinformation than it is for a president?

3. What are three things that a sitting president should do to try to combat misleading information that is critical of him or his policies?

4. What is Mark Twain's famous quip about lies and truth?

From *Mother Jones,* May/June 2011, pp. 30–31. Copyright © 2011 by Mother Jones. Reprinted by permission of the Foundation for National Progress.

Studying the Gipper

What Barack Obama can and can't learn from Reagan's blithe spirit.

Ronald Reagan would have turned 100 next month. That may be one reason why the White House let it be known that when Barack Obama spent his Christmas vacation in Hawaii, his holiday reading list included Lou Cannon's "President Reagan: the Role of a Lifetime", a whopping biography of more than 800 pages. But the Reagan story may be on Mr Obama's mind for other reasons as well.

Like Harry Truman's and Bill Clinton's, the Reagan presidency is remembered as an example of how a president can do big things even when government is divided. On taking office in 1981 Reagan had a slim majority in the Senate but the Democrats controlled the House. This is the mirror image of the predicament that Mr Obama is having to confront only now, after two luxurious years of having a majority in both chambers. Like Mr Obama, Reagan inherited an economy in greater distress than America had experienced since the 1930s. More than 7 percent of workers were unemployed and inflation was north of 12 percent. But by the time he and Nancy retired to Bel Air in January 1989, the man known as the Gipper (after an early role in Hollywood) was basking in an approval rating of 64 percent, the highest of any departing president since Franklin Roosevelt. Little wonder that Mr Obama fancied dipping into Mr Cannon's biography for a tip or two.

Tearing Down That Wall

And yet the Reagan story contains no simple formula that Mr Obama can copy to be sure of an equally happy ending to his own presidential adventure. In big ways and small, the world of the 1980s was altogether different. History will remember for ever that the Soviet Union began to unravel on Reagan's watch, helped on its way both by the affable cold warrior's determination to overawe the "evil empire" with a vast hike in military spending and by the unexpected rapport he established with Mikhail Gorbachev. No remotely comparable foreign-policy triumph is available to Mr Obama. It was Reagan's good luck to become president when the Soviet system was rotting from within. Mr Obama's bad luck is to have the job at a time when America's new Chinese rival is not only rising but has also become Uncle Sam's principal creditor.

The economic parallels may be a bit closer. Unemployment rose in Reagan's first two years, as in Mr Obama's. Like the Democrats last November, the president's party was thumped in the mid-terms of 1982. Reagan's approval ratings two years in were in fact lower, at below 40 percent, than Mr Obama's, which have lately moved back up to around 50 percent. By 1984, however, a rebound brought about by steady policy (combined with a notably weak opponent in Walter Mondale) enabled Reagan to proclaim "morning in America," just in time to be re-elected in a landslide. By 2012 employment may have grown enough for Mr Obama to copy this trick, though it typically takes longer to create jobs in the aftermath of a recession produced by a financial collapse.

Among Republicans, time has burnished Reagan's place in the pantheon of presidents. His mantra that government was the problem rather than the solution was revolutionary for its time. But the revolution he made was decidedly incomplete. Having promised to boost military spending, cut taxes and balance the federal budget, he found the third of these promises beyond his reach. Redeeming it would have been possible only by cutting deep into entitlements, especially Social Security (pensions), an assault on the New Deal that Congress would not countenance and he did not press. Instead he sent eight unbalanced budgets in succession up to the Hill, the government spent more money than it raised, the budget deficit soared from $74 billion *in* 1980 to $220 billion in 1986 and America turned from a creditor into a borrower. The stern new fiscal conservatives taking their seats in the House this week would surely not have approved.

Reagan's two terms saw plenty of other failures. Ethical standards inside his administration were often lax. He oversaw a humiliating military retreat from Lebanon, the scandal of Iran-Contra, a too-timid response to the AIDS epidemic and a lot of inept deregulation, some of which contributed to the savings and loans crisis that led to a taxpayer bail-out under the first President Bush. He achieved almost nothing in education or health, and failed to restrict abortion as he had promised conservatives, probably insincerely.

Why are so few of the failures remembered? Craig Shirley, who worked to re-elect Reagan, argues that everyone always understood what he was about and where he was trying to go. That is unusual in a president. Mr Obama may burn with no less ardent a desire to be a "transformative" president: in 2008 he got into hot water with Democrats for praising this aspect of the Reagan presidency. But Mr Obama's complicated aspirations for America are harder to understand than Reagan's straightforward mission to shrink the state and battle communism, though admirers often glossed over the fact that federal spending as a share of GDP did not in the end shrink that much (from 22.2 percent to 21.2 percent).

Perhaps the hardest thing for Mr Obama to accept about Reagan is that Americans warmed to him not just because of what he did but also because of the sort of person he was. Mr Cannon argues that his political magic did not reside only in his happiness and folksy charm. His greatness was that "he carried a shining vision of America inside him." He had a simple belief that nothing was impossible in America if only government got out of the way. In rejecting the idea of limits, says Mr Cannon, he expressed a core conviction of the nation. Mr Obama does not share this belief, and is perhaps right not to. The idea that nothing is impossible in and for America is an illusion. But Americans have never thanked their presidents for telling them so.

Critical Thinking

1. What was different about the world that President Reagan faced from the international situation in which President Obama is operating?
2. What similarities in economic affairs did both President Reagan and Obama face?
3. Why are so few of Reagan's failures remembered?
4. What are some key differences on a personal level between Reagan and Obama that may help account for Reagan's greater success as president?

When Congress Stops Wars
Partisan Politics and Presidential Power

WILLIAM G. HOWELL AND JON C. PEVEHOUSE

For most of George W. Bush's tenure, political observers have lambasted Congress for failing to fulfill its basic foreign policy obligations. Typical was the recent *Foreign Affairs* article by Norman Ornstein and Thomas Mann, "When Congress Checks Out," which offered a sweeping indictment of Congress' failure to monitor the president's execution of foreign wars and antiterrorist initiatives. Over the past six years, they concluded, Congressional oversight of the White House's foreign and national security policy "has virtually collapsed." Ornstein and Mann's characterization is hardly unique. Numerous constitutional-law scholars, political scientists, bureaucrats, and even members of Congress have, over the years, lamented the lack of legislative constraints on presidential war powers. But the dearth of Congressional oversight between 2000 and 2006 is nothing new. Contrary to what many critics believe, terrorist threats, an overly aggressive White House, and an impotent Democratic Party are not the sole explanations for Congressional inactivity over the past six years. Good old-fashioned partisan politics has been, and continues to be, at play.

It is often assumed that everyday politics *stops* at the water's edge and that legislators abandon their partisan identities during times of war in order to become faithful stewards of their constitutional obligations. But this received wisdom is almost always wrong. The illusion of Congressional wartime unity misconstrues the nature of legislative oversight and fails to capture the particular conditions under which members of Congress are likely to emerge as meaningful critics of any particular military venture.

The partisan composition of Congress has historically been the decisive factor in determining whether lawmakers will oppose or acquiesce in presidential calls for war. From Harry Truman to Bill Clinton, nearly every U.S. president has learned that members of Congress, and members of the opposition party in particular, are fully capable of interjecting their opinions about proposed and ongoing military ventures. When the opposition party holds a large number of seats or controls one or both chambers of Congress, members routinely challenge the president and step up oversight of foreign conflicts; when the legislative branch is dominated by the president's party, it generally goes along with the White House. Partisan unity, not institutional laziness, explains why the Bush administration's Iraq policy received such a favorable hearing in Congress from 2000 to 2006.

The dramatic increase in Congressional oversight following the 2006 midterm elections is a case in point. Immediately after assuming control of Congress, House Democrats passed a resolution condemning a proposed "surge" of U.S. troops in Iraq and Senate Democrats debated a series of resolutions expressing varying degrees of outrage against the war in Iraq. The spring 2007 supplemental appropriations debate resulted in a House bill calling for a phased withdrawal (the president vetoed that bill, and the Senate then passed a bill accepting more war funding without withdrawal provisions). Democratic heads of committees in both chambers continue to launch hearings and investigations into the various mishaps, scandals, and tactical errors that have plagued the Iraq war. By all indications, if the government in Baghdad has not met certain benchmarks by September, the Democrats will push for binding legislation that further restricts the president's ability to sustain military operations in Iraq.

Neither Congress' prior languor nor its recent awakening should come as much of a surprise. When they choose to do so, members of Congress can exert a great deal of influence over the conduct of war. They can enact laws that dictate how long military campaigns may last, control the purse strings that determine how well they are funded, and dictate how appropriations may be spent. Moreover, they can call hearings and issue public pronouncements on foreign policy matters. These powers allow members to cut funding for ill-advised military ventures, set timetables for the withdrawal of troops, foreclose opportunities to expand a conflict into new regions, and establish reporting requirements. Through legislation, appropriations, hearings, and public appeals, members of Congress can substantially increase the political costs of military action—sometimes forcing presidents to withdraw sooner than they would like or even preventing any kind of military action whatsoever.

The Partisan Imperative

Critics have made a habit of equating legislative inactivity with Congress' abdication of its foreign policy obligations. Too often, the infrequency with which Congress enacts restrictive statutes is seen as prima facie evidence of the institution's failings. Sometimes it is. But one cannot gauge the health of the U.S. system of governance strictly on the basis of what Congress does—or does not do—in the immediate aftermath of presidential initiatives.

After all, when presidents anticipate Congressional resistance they will not be able to overcome, they often abandon the sword as their primary tool of diplomacy. More generally, when the White House knows that Congress will strike down key provisions of a policy initiative, it usually backs off. President Bush himself has relented, to varying degrees, during the struggle to create the Department of Homeland Security and during conflicts over the design of military tribunals and the prosecution of U.S. citizens as enemy combatants. Indeed, by most accounts, the administration recently forced the resignation of the chairman of the Joint Chiefs of Staff, General Peter Pace, so as to avoid a clash with Congress over his reappointment.

To assess the extent of Congressional influence on presidential war powers, it is not sufficient to count how many war authorizations are enacted or how often members deem it necessary to start the "war powers clock"—based on the War Powers Act requirement that the president obtain legislative approval within 60 days after any military deployment. Rather, one must examine the underlying partisan alignments across the branches of government and presidential efforts to anticipate and preempt Congressional recriminations.

During the past half century, partisan divisions have fundamentally defined the domestic politics of war. A variety of factors help explain why partisanship has so prominently defined the contours of interbranch struggles over foreign military deployments. To begin with, some members of Congress have electoral incentives to increase their oversight of wars when the opposing party controls the White House. If presidential approval ratings increase due to a "rally around the flag" effect in times of war, and if those high ratings only benefit the president's party in Congress, then the opposition party has an incentive to highlight any failures, missteps, or scandals that might arise in the course of a military venture.

After all, the making of U.S. foreign policy hinges on how U.S. national interests are defined and the means chosen to achieve them. This process is deeply, and unavoidably, political. Therefore, only in very particular circumstances—a direct attack on U.S. soil or on Americans abroad—have political parties temporarily united for the sake of protecting the national interest. Even then, partisan politics has flared as the toll of war has become evident. Issues of trust and access to information further fuel these partisan fires. In environments in which information is sparse, individuals with shared ideological or partisan affiliations find it easier to communicate with one another. The president possesses unparalleled intelligence about threats to national interests, and he is far more likely to share that information with members of his own political party than with political opponents. Whereas the commander in chief has an entire set of executive-branch agencies at his beck and call, Congress has relatively few sources of reliable classified information. Consequently, when a president claims that a foreign crisis warrants military intervention, members of his own party tend to trust

him more often than not, whereas members of the opposition party are predisposed to doubt and challenge such claims. In this regard, Congressional Democrats' constant interrogations of Bush administration officials represent just the latest round in an ongoing interparty struggle to control the machinery of war.

Congressional Influence and Its Limits

Historically, presidents emerging from midterm election defeats have been less likely to respond to foreign policy crises aggressively, and when they have ordered the use of force, they have taken much longer to do so. Our research shows that the White House's propensity to exercise military force steadily declines as members of the opposition party pick up seats in Congress. In fact, it is not even necessary for the control of Congress to switch parties; the loss of even a handful of seats can materially affect the probability that the nation will go to war.

The partisan composition of Congress also influences its willingness to launch formal oversight hearings. While criticizing members for their inactivity during the Bush administration, Ornstein and Mann make much of the well-established long-term decline in the number of hearings held on Capitol Hill. This steady decline, however, has not muted traditional partisan politics. According to Linda Fowler, of Dartmouth College, the presence or absence of unified government largely determines the frequency of Congressional hearings. Contrary to Ornstein and Mann's argument that "vigorous oversight was the norm until the end of the twentieth century," Fowler demonstrates that during the post–World War II era, when the same party controlled both Congress and the presidency, the number of hearings about military policy decreased, but when the opposition party controlled at least one chamber of Congress, hearings occurred with greater frequency. Likewise, Boston University's Douglas Kriner has shown that Congressional authorizations of war as well as legislative initiatives that establish timetables for the withdrawal of troops, cut funds, or otherwise curtail military operations critically depend on the partisan balance of power on Capitol Hill.

Still, it is important not to overstate the extent of Congressional influence. Even when Congress is most aggressive, the executive branch retains a tremendous amount of power when it comes to military matters. Modern presidents enjoy extraordinary advantages in times of war, not least of which the ability to act unilaterally on military matters and thereby place on Congress (and everyone else) the onus of coordinating a response. Once troops enter a region, members of Congress face the difficult choice of either cutting funds and then facing the charge of undermining the troops or keeping the public coffers open and thereby aiding a potentially ill-advised military operation.

On this score, Ornstein and Mann effectively illustrate Bush's efforts to expand his influence over the war in Iraq and the war on terrorism by refusing to disclose classified information, regularly circumventing the legislative process, and resisting even modest efforts at oversight. Similarly, they note that Republican Congressional majorities failed to take full advantage of their institution's formal powers to monitor and influence either the formulation or the implementation of foreign policy during the first six years of Bush's presidency. Ornstein and Mann, however, mistakenly attribute such lapses in Congressional oversight to a loss of an "institutional identity" that was ostensibly forged during a bygone era when "tough oversight of the executive was common, whether or not different parties controlled the White House and Congress" and when members' willingness to challenge presidents had less to do with partisan allegiances and more to do with a shared sense of institutional responsibility. In the modern era, foreign-policy making has rarely worked this way. On the contrary, partisan competition has contributed to nearly every foreign policy clash between Capitol Hill and the White House for the past six decades.

Divided We Stand

Shortly after World War II—the beginning of a period often mischaracterized as one of "Cold War consensus"—partisan wrangling over the direction of U.S. foreign policy returned to Washington, ending a brief period of wartime unity. By defining U.S. military involvement in Korea as a police action rather than a war, President Truman effectively freed himself from the constitutional requirements regarding war and established a precedent for all subsequent presidents to circumvent Congress when sending the military abroad. Although Truman's party narrowly controlled both chambers, Congress hounded him throughout the Korean War, driving his approval ratings down into the 20s and paving the way for a Republican electoral victory in 1952. Railing off a litany of complaints about the president's firing of General Douglas MacArthur and his meager progress toward ending the war, Senator Robert Taft, then a Republican presidential candidate, declared that "the greatest failure of foreign policy is an unnecessary war, and we have been involved in such a war now for more than a year. . . . As a matter of fact, every purpose of the war has now failed. We are exactly where we were three years ago, and where we could have stayed."

On the heels of the Korean War came yet another opportunity to use force in Asia, but facing a divided Congress, President Dwight Eisenhower was hesitant to get involved. French requests for assistance in Indochina initially fell on sympathetic ears in the Eisenhower administration, which listed Indochina as an area of strategic importance in its "new look" defense policy. However, in January 1954, when the French asked for a commitment of U.S. troops, Eisenhower balked. The president stated that he "could conceive of no greater tragedy than for the United States to become involved in an all-out war in Indochina." His reluctance derived in part from the anticipated fight with Congress that he knew would arise over such a war. Even after his decision to provide modest technical assistance to France, in the form of B-26 bombers and air force technicians, Congressional leaders demanded a personal meeting with the president to voice their disapproval. Soon afterward, Eisenhower promised to withdraw the air force personnel, replacing them with civilian contractors.

Eventually, the United States did become involved in a ground war in Asia, and it was that war that brought Congressional opposition to the presidential use of force to a fever pitch. As the Vietnam War dragged on and casualties mounted, Congress and the public grew increasingly wary of the conflict and of the power delegated to the president in the 1964 Gulf of Tonkin resolution. In 1970, with upward of 350,000 U.S. troops in the field and the war spilling over into Cambodia, Congress formally repealed that resolution. And over the next several years, legislators enacted a series of appropriations bills intended to restrict the war's scope and duration. Then, in June 1973, after the Paris peace accords had been signed, Congress enacted a supplemental appropriations act that cut off all funding for additional military involvement in Southeast Asia, including in Cambodia, Laos, North Vietnam, and South Vietnam. Finally, when South Vietnam fell in 1975, Congress took the extraordinary step of formally forbidding U.S. troops from enforcing the Paris peace accords, despite the opposition of President Gerald Ford and Secretary of State Henry Kissinger.

Three years later, a Democratic Congress forbade the use of funds for a military action that was supported by the president—this time, the supply of covert aid to anticommunist forces in Angola. At the insistence of Senator Dick Clark (D-Iowa), the 1976 Defense Department appropriations act stipulated that no monies would be used "for any activities involving Angola other than intelligence gathering." Facing such staunch Congressional opposition, President Ford suspended military assistance to Angola, unhappily noting that the Democratic-controlled Congress had "lost its guts" with regard to foreign policy.

In just one instance, the case of Lebanon in 1983, did Congress formally start the 60-day clock of the 1973 War Powers Act. Most scholars who call Congress to task for failing to fulfill its constitutional responsibilities make much of the fact that in this case it ended up authorizing the use of force for a full 18 months, far longer than the 60 days automatically allowed under the act. However, critics often overlook the fact that Congress simultaneously forbade the president from unilaterally altering the scope, target, or mission of the U.S. troops participating in the multinational peacekeeping force. Furthermore, Congress asserted its right to terminate the venture at any time with a one-chamber majority vote or a joint resolution and established firm reporting requirements as the U.S. presence in Lebanon continued.

During the 1980s, no foreign policy issue dominated Congressional discussions more than aid to the contras in Nicaragua, rebel forces who sought to topple the leftist Sandinista regime. In 1984, a Democratic-controlled House enacted an appropriations bill that forbade President Ronald Reagan from supporting the contras. Reagan appeared undeterred. Rather than abandon the project, the administration instead diverted funds from Iranian arms sales to support the contras, establishing the basis for the most serious presidential scandal since Watergate. Absent Congressional opposition on this issue, Reagan may well have intervened directly, or at least directed greater, more transparent aid to the rebels fighting the Nicaraguan government.

Regardless of which party holds a majority of the seats in Congress, it is almost always the opposition party that creates the most trouble for a president intent on waging war. When, in the early 1990s, a UN humanitarian operation in Somalia devolved into urban warfare, filling nightly newscasts with scenes from Mogadishu, Congress swung into action. Despite previous declarations of public support for the president's actions, Congressional Republicans and some Democrats passed a Department of Defense appropriations act in November 1993 that simultaneously authorized the use of force to protect UN units and required that U.S. forces be withdrawn by March 31, 1994.

A few years later, a Republican-controlled Congress took similar steps to restrict the use of funds for a humanitarian crisis occurring in Kosovo. One month after the March 1999 NATO air strikes against Serbia, the House passed a bill forbidding the use of Defense Department funds to introduce U.S. ground troops into the conflict without Congressional authorization. When President Clinton requested funding for operations in the Balkans, Republicans in Congress (and some hawkish Democrats) seized on the opportunity to attach additional monies for unrelated defense programs, military personnel policies, aid to farmers, and hurricane relief and passed a supplemental appropriations bill that was considerably larger than the amount requested by the president. The mixed messages sent by the Republicans caught the attention of Clinton's Democratic allies. As House member Martin Frost (D-Tex.) noted, "I am at a loss to explain how the Republican Party can, on one hand, be so irresponsible as to abandon our troops in the midst of a military action to demonstrate its visceral hostility toward the commander in chief, and then, on the other, turn around and double his request for money for what they call 'Clinton's war.'" The 1999 debate is remarkably similar to the current wrangling over spending on Iraq.

Legislating Opinion

The voice of Congress (or lack thereof) has had a profound impact on the media coverage of the current war in Iraq, just as it has colored public perceptions of U.S. foreign policy in the past. Indeed, Congress' ability to influence executive-branch decision-making extends far beyond its legislative and budgetary powers. Cutting funds, starting the war powers clock, or forcing troop withdrawals are the most extreme options available to them. More frequently, members of Congress make appeals designed to influence both media coverage and public opinion of a president's war. For example, Congress' vehement criticism of Reagan's decision to reflag Kuwaiti tankers during the Iran-Iraq War led to reporting requirements for the administration. Similarly, the Clinton administration's threats to invade Haiti in 1994 were met with resistance by Republicans and a handful of skeptical Democrats in Congress, who took to the airwaves to force Clinton to continually justify placing U.S. troops in harm's way.

Such appeals resonate widely. Many studies have shown that the media regularly follow official debates about war in Washington, adjusting their coverage to the scope of the discussion among the nation's political elite. And among the elite, members of Congress—through their own independent initiatives and through journalists' propensity to follow them—stand out as the single most potent source of dissent against the president. The sheer number of press releases and direct feeds that members of Congress produce is nothing short of breathtaking. And through carefully staged hearings, debates,

and investigations, members deliberately shape the volume and content of the media's war coverage. The public posturing, turns of praise and condemnation, rapid-fire questioning, long-winded exhortations, pithy Shakespearean references, graphs, timelines, and pie charts that fill these highly scripted affairs are intended to focus media attention and thereby sway the national conversation surrounding questions of war and peace. Whether the media scrutinize every aspect of a proposed military venture or assume a more relaxed posture depends in part on Congress' willingness to take on the president.

Indeed, in the weeks preceding the October 2002 war authorization vote, the media paid a tremendous amount of attention to debates about Iraq inside the Beltway. Following the vote, however, coverage of Iraq dropped precipitously, despite continued domestic controversies, debates at the United Nations, continued efforts by the administration to rally public support, and grass-roots opposition to the war that featured large public protests. Congress helped set the agenda for public discussion, influencing both the volume and the tone of the coverage granted to an impending war, and Congress' silence after the authorization was paralleled by that of the press.

Crucially, Congressional influence over the media extended to public opinion as well. An analysis of local television broadcast data and national public-opinion surveys from the period reveals a strong relationship between the type of media coverage and public opinion regarding the war. Even when accounting for factors such as the ideological tendencies of a media market (since liberal markets tend to have liberal voters and liberal media, while conservative districts have the opposite), we found that the airing of more critical viewpoints led to greater public disapproval of the proposed war, and more positive viewpoints buoyed support for the war. As Congress speaks, it would seem, the media report, and the public listens.

As these cases illustrate, the United States has a Congress with considerably more agenda-setting power than most analysts presume and a less independent press corps than many would like. As the National Journal columnist William Powers observed during the fall of 2006, "Journalists like to think they are reporting just the facts, straight and unaffected by circumstance." On the contrary, he recognized, news is a product of the contemporary political environment, and the way stories are framed and spun has little to do with the facts. In Washington, the party that controls Congress also determines the volume and the tone of the coverage given to a president's war. Anticipating a Democratic Congressional sweep in November 2006, Powers correctly predicted that "if Bush suffers a major political setback, the media will feel freed up to tear into this war as they have never done before."

With the nation standing at the precipice of new wars, it is vital that the American public understand the nature and extent of Congress' war powers and its members' partisan motivations for exercising or forsaking them. President Bush retains extraordinary institutional advantages over Congress, but with the Democrats now in control of both houses, the political costs of pursuing new wars (whether against Iran, North Korea, or any other country) and prosecuting ongoing ones have increased significantly.

Congress will continue to challenge the president's interpretation of the national interest. Justifications for future deployments will encounter more scrutiny and require more evidence. Questions of appropriate strategy and implementation will surface more quickly with threats of Congressional hearings and investigations looming. Oversight hearings will proceed at a furious pace. Concerning Iraq, the Democrats will press the administration on a withdrawal timetable, hoping to use their agenda-setting power with the media to persuade enough Senate Republicans to defect and thereby secure the votes they need to close floor debate on the issue.

This fall, the Democrats will likely attempt to build even more momentum to end the war in Iraq, further limiting the president's menu of choices. This is not the first instance of heavy Congressional involvement in foreign affairs and war, nor will it be the last. This fact has been lost on too many political commentators convinced that some combination of an eroding political identity, 9/11, failures of leadership, and dwindling political will have made Congress irrelevant to deliberations about foreign policy.

On the contrary, the new Democratic-controlled Congress is conforming to a tried-and-true pattern of partisan competition between the executive and legislative branches that has characterized Washington politics for the last half century and shows no signs of abating. Reports of Congress' death have been greatly exaggerated.

Critical Thinking

1. In what ways is Congress able to influence the conduct of military action?

2. What evidence suggests that partisanship lies at the center of the domestic politics of war?

3. What are some of the advantages that a president has in exerting influence during wartime?

4. What congressional reactions to the Vietnam War illustrate congressional opposition to the presidential use of force?

5. How can Congress's opposition or support of military action affect media and public perceptions of war?

WILLIAM G. HOWELL and **JON C. PEVEHOUSE** are Associate Professors at the Harris School of Public Policy at the University of Chicago and the authors of *While Dangers Gather: Congressional Checks on Presidential War Powers.*

The Case for Congress

According to opinion polls, Congress is one of the least esteemed institutions in American life. While that should come as a shock, today it's taken for granted. What can't be taken for granted is the health of representative democracy amid this corrosive— and often unwarranted—distrust of its central institution.

LEE H. HAMILTON

Several years ago, I was watching the evening news on television when the anchorman announced the death of Wilbur Mills, the legendary former chairman of the House Ways and Means Committee. There was a lot the newscaster could have said. He might have recounted the central role Mills had played in creating Medicare. Or he might have talked about Mills's hand in shaping the Social Security system and in drafting the tax code. But he did not. Instead, he recalled how Mills's career collapsed after he was found early one morning with an Argentine stripper named Fanne Foxe. And then the anchorman moved on to the next story.

One of the perks of being chairman of an influential committee in Congress, as I was at the time, is that you can pick up the telephone and get through to a TV news anchor. Which I did. I chided the fellow for summing up Mills's career with a scandal. And much to my surprise, he apologized.

Americans of all stripes like to dwell on misbehavior by members of Congress. They look at the latest scandal and assume that they're seeing the *real* Congress. But they're not. They hear repeatedly in the media about missteps, but very little about the House leader who goes home on weekends to pastor his local church, or the senator who spends one day a month working in a local job to better understand the needs of constituents, or the many members who labor behind the scenes in a bipartisan way to reach the delicate compromises needed to make the system work.

I don't want to claim that all members are saints and that their behavior is always impeccable. Yet I basically agree with the assessment of historian David McCullough: "Congress, for all its faults, has not been the unbroken parade of clowns and thieves and posturing windbags so often portrayed. What should be spoken of more often, and more widely understood, are the great victories that have been won here, the decisions of courage and the visions achieved."

Probity in Congress is the rule rather than the exception, and it has increased over the years. When I arrived in Congress, members could accept lavish gifts from special interests, pocket campaign contributions in their Capitol offices, and convert their campaign contributions to personal use. And they were rarely punished for personal corruption. None of that would be tolerated now. Things still aren't perfect, but the ethical climate at the Capitol is well ahead of where it was a couple of decades ago. And, I might add, well ahead of the public's perception of it.

During my 34 years in the House of Representatives, I heard numerous criticisms of Congress. Many seemed to me perceptive; many others were far off the mark—such as when people thought that as a member of Congress I received a limousine and chauffeur, or didn't pay taxes, or was entitled to free medical care and Social Security coverage. When people are upset about Congress, their distress undermines public confidence in government and fosters cynicism and disengagement. In a representative democracy such as ours, what the American people think of the body that's supposed to reflect their views and interests as it frames the basic laws of the land is a matter of fundamental importance. I certainly do not think Congress is a perfect institution, and I have my own list of ways I think it could be improved. Yet often the public's view is based on misunderstanding or misinformation. Here are some of the other criticisms I've heard over the years:

Congress is run by lobbyists and special interests. Americans have differing views of lobbyists and special-interest groups. Some see them as playing an essential part in the democratic process. Others look at them with skepticism but allow them a legitimate role in developing policy. Most, however, see them as sinister forces exercising too much control over Congress, and the cynicism of this majority grew during the recent wave of corporate scandals, when it was revealed how extensively companies such as Enron and Arthur

Andersen had lobbied Congress. The suspicion that Congress is manipulated by powerful wheeler-dealers who put pressure on legislators and buy votes through extensive campaign contributions and other favors is not an unfounded concern, and it will not go away, no matter how fervently some might try to dismiss it.

That said, the popular view of lobbyists as nefarious fat cats smoking big cigars and handing out hundred-dollar bills behind closed doors is wrong. These days, lobbyists are usually principled people who recognize that their word is their bond. Lobbying is an enormous industry today, with billions of dollars riding on its outcomes. Special-interest groups will often spend millions of dollars on campaigns to influence a particular decision—through political contributions, grassroots lobbying efforts, television advocacy ads, and the like—because they know that they'll get a lot more back than they spend if a bill contains the language they want. They're very good at what they do, and the truth is, members of Congress can sometimes be swayed by them.

But the influence of lobbyists on the process is not as simple as it might at first appear. In the first place, "special interests" are not just the bad guys. If you're retired, or a homeowner, or use public transit or the airlines, or are concerned about religious freedom, many people in Washington are lobbying on your behalf. There are an estimated 25,000 interest groups in the capital, so you can be sure your views are somewhere represented. Advocacy groups help Congress understand how legislation affects their members, and they can help focus the public's attention on important issues. They do their part to amplify the flow of information that Thomas Jefferson called the "dialogue of democracy."

Of course, Congress often takes up controversial issues on which you'll find a broad spectrum of opinions. Public attention is strong, a host of special interests weigh in, and the views of both lobbyists and legislators are all over the map. In such circumstances, prospects are very small that any single interest group or lobbyist can disproportionately influence the results. There are simply too many of them involved for that to happen, and the process is too public. It's when things get quiet—when measures come up out of view of the public eye—that you have to be cautious. A small change in wording here, an innocuous line in a tax bill there, can allow specific groups to reap enormous benefits they might never have been granted under close public scrutiny.

The answer, it seems to me, is not to decry lobbying or lobbyists. Lobbying is a key element of the legislative process—part of the free speech guaranteed under the Constitution. At its heart, lobbying is simply people banding together to advance their interests, whether they're farmers or environmentalists or bankers. Indeed, belonging to an interest group—the Sierra Club, the AARP, the Chamber of Commerce—is one of the main ways Americans participate in public life these days.

When I was in Congress, I came to think of lobbyists as an important part of the *public discussion* of policy. I emphasize "public discussion" for a reason. Rather than trying to clamp down on lobbying, I believe we'd be better off ensuring that it happens in the open and is part of the broader policy debate. Our

challenge is not to end it, but to make sure that it's a balanced dialogue, and that those in power don't consistently listen to the voices of the wealthy and the powerful more intently than the voices of others. Several legislative proposals have been made over the years that would help, including campaign finance reform, tough restrictions on gifts to members of Congress, prohibiting travel for members and their staffs funded by groups with a direct interest in legislation, and effective disclosure of lobbyists' involvement in drafting legislation. But in the end, something else may be even more important than these proposals: steady and candid conversation between elected officials and the people they represent.

Members of Congress, I would argue, have a responsibility to listen to lobbyists. But members also have a responsibility to understand where these lobbyists are coming from, to sort through what they are saying, and then to make a judgment about what is in the best interests of their constituents and the nation as a whole.

Congress almost seems designed to promote total gridlock. People will often complain about a do-nothing Congress, and think that much of the fault lies in the basic design of the institution. When a single senator can hold up action on a popular measure, when 30 committees or subcommittees are all reviewing the same bill, when a proposal needs to move not just through both the House and the Senate but through their multilayered budget, authorization, and appropriations processes, and when floor procedures are so complex that even members who have served for several years can still be confused by them, how can you expect anything to get done? This feeling is magnified by the major changes American society has undergone in recent decades. The incredible increase in the speed of every facet of our lives has made many people feel that the slow, untidy, deliberate pace of Congress is not up to the demands of modern society.

It is not now, nor has it ever been, easy to move legislation through Congress. But there's actually a method to the madness. Basic roadblocks were built into the process for a reason. We live in a big, complicated country, difficult to govern, with enormous regional, ethnic, and economic differences. The process must allow time for responsiveness and deliberation, all the more so when many issues—taxation, health care, access to guns, abortion, and more—stir strong emotions and don't submit easily to compromise. Do we really want a speedy system in which laws are pushed through before a consensus develops? Do we want a system in which the views of the minority get trampled in a rush to action by the majority? Reforms can surely be made to improve the system, but the basic process of careful deliberation, negotiation, and compromise lies at the very heart of representative democracy. Ours is not a parliamentary system; the dawdling pace comes with the territory.

We misunderstand Congress's role if we demand that it be a model of efficiency and quick action. America's founders never intended it to be that. They clearly understood that one of the key roles of Congress is to slow down the process—to allow tempers to cool and to encourage careful deliberation, so that unwise or damaging laws do not pass in the heat of the moment and so that the views of those in the minority get a fair hearing. That basic vision still seems wise today. Proceeding carefully to develop consensus is arduous and exasperating work, but it's the only way to produce policies that reflect the varied perspectives of a remarkably diverse citizenry. People may complain about the process, but they benefit from its legislative speed bumps when they want their views heard, their interests protected, their rights safeguarded. I recognize that Congress sometimes gets bogged down needlessly. But the fundamental notion that the structure of Congress should contain road blocks and barriers to hasty or unfair action makes sense for our country and needs to be protected and preserved. In the words of former Speaker of the House Sam Rayburn, "One of the wisest things ever said was, 'Wait a minute.'"

There's too much money in politics. When people hear stories about all the fundraising that members of Congress must do today, they come to believe that Congress is a "bought" institution. I've often been told that in our system dollars speak louder than words, and access is bought and sold. By a 4 to 1 margin, Americans believe that elected officials are influenced more by pressures from campaign contributors than by what's in the best interests of the country. But in fact, the problem of money in politics has been with us for many years. It's become so much more serious in recent years because of the expense of television advertising. The biggest portion of my campaign budget in the last election I faced—$1 million, for a largely rural seat in southern Indiana—went for TV spots.

Having experienced it firsthand, I know all too well that the "money chase" has gotten out of hand. A lot of money from special interests is floating around the Capitol—far too much money—and we ignore the problem at our own peril. To be fair, many of the claims that special interests can buy influence in Congress are overstated. Though I would be the last to say that contributions have no impact on a voting record, it's important to recognize that most of the money comes from groups that already share a member's views on the issues, rather than from groups that are hoping to change a member's mind. In addition, many influences shape members' voting decisions—the most important of them being the wishes of their constituents. In the end, members know that if their votes aren't in line with what their constituents want, they won't be reelected. And *that,* rather than a campaign contribution, is what's foremost in their minds.

Still, it's an unusual member of Congress who can take thousands of dollars from a particular group and not be affected, which is why I've come to the view that the influence of money on the political process raises a threat to representative democracy. We need significant reform. We have a campaign finance system today that's gradually eroding the public's trust and confidence. It's a slow-motion crisis, but it is a crisis. It's not possible to enact a perfect, sweeping campaign finance bill today, and perhaps not anytime soon. Yet the worst abuses can be dealt with, one by one.

Critical Thinking

1. What are some of the things that members of Congress were permitted to do thirty years ago, which are no longer acceptable in today's ethical climate?

2. What is the role of special interest groups in Congress, according to Lee Hamilton?

3. What are the benefits of a slow-moving legislative process?

4. How can campaign finance reform address the influence of money in politics?

LEE H. HAMILTON is director of the Wilson Center and director of the Center on Congress at Indiana University. He was U.S. representative from Indiana's Ninth District from 1965 to 1999, and served as chairman of the House Committee on International Relations, the Joint Economic Committee, and several other committees. This essay is adapted from his new book *How Congress Works and Why You Should Care,* published by Indiana University Press.

How to Get Our Democracy Back
There Will Be No Change Until We Change Congress

LAWRENCE LESSIG

We should remember what it felt like one year ago, as the ability to recall it emotionally will pass and it is an emotional memory as much as anything else. It was a moment rare in a democracy's history. The feeling was palpable—to supporters and opponents alike—that something important had happened. America had elected, the young candidate promised, a transformational president. And wrapped in a campaign that had produced the biggest influx of new voters and small-dollar contributions in a generation, the claim seemed credible, almost intoxicating, and just in time.

Yet a year into the presidency of Barack Obama, it is already clear that this administration is an opportunity missed. Not because it is too conservative. Not because it is too liberal. But because it is too conventional. Obama has given up the rhetoric of his early campaign—a campaign that promised to "challenge the broken system in Washington" and to "fundamentally change the way Washington works." Indeed, "fundamental change" is no longer even a hint.

Instead, we are now seeing the consequences of a decision made at the most vulnerable point of Obama's campaign—just when it seemed that he might really have beaten the party's presumed nominee. For at that moment, Obama handed the architecture of his new administration over to a team that thought what America needed most was another Bill Clinton. A team chosen by the brother of one of DC's most powerful lobbyists, and a White House headed by the quintessential DC politician. A team that could envision nothing more than the ordinary politics of Washington—the kind of politics Obama had called "small." A team whose imagination—politically—is tiny.

These tiny minds—brilliant though they may be in the conventional game of DC—have given up what distinguished Obama's extraordinary campaign. Not the promise of healthcare reform or global warming legislation—Hillary Clinton had embraced both of those ideas, and every other substantive proposal that Obama advanced. Instead, the passion that Obama inspired grew from the recognition that something fundamental had gone wrong in the way our government functions, and his commitment to reform it.

For Obama once spoke for the anger that has now boiled over in even the blue state Massachusetts—that our government is corrupt; that fundamental change is needed. As he told

us, both parties had allowed "lobbyists and campaign contributions to rig the system." And "unless we're willing to challenge [that] broken system . . . nothing else is going to change." "The reason" Obama said he was "running for President [was] to challenge that system." For "if we're not willing to take up that fight, then real change—change that will make a lasting difference in the lives of ordinary Americans—will keep getting blocked by the defenders of the status quo."

This administration has not "taken up that fight." Instead, it has stepped down from the high ground the President occupied on January 20, 2009, and played a political game no different from the one George W. Bush played, or Bill Clinton before him. Obama has accepted the power of the "defenders of the status quo" and simply negotiated with them. "Audacity" fits nothing on the list of last year's activity, save the suggestion that this is the administration the candidate had promised.

> **'Audacity' fits nothing on the list of last year's activity, save the suggestion that this is the administration the candidate had promised.**

Maybe this was his plan all along. It was not what he said. And by ignoring what he promised, and by doing what he attacked ("too many times, after the election is over, and the confetti is swept away, all those promises fade from memory, and the lobbyists and the special interests move in"), Obama will leave the presidency, whether in 2013 or 2017, with Washington essentially intact and the movement he inspired betrayed.

That movement needs new leadership. On the right (the tea party) and the left (MoveOn and Bold Progressives), there is an unstoppable recognition that our government has failed. But both sides need to understand the source of its failure if either or, better, both together, are to respond.

At the center of our government lies a bankrupt institution: Congress. Not financially bankrupt, at least not yet, but politically bankrupt. *Bush v. Gore* notwithstanding, Americans' faith in the Supreme Court remains extraordinarily high—76 percent have a fair or great deal of "trust and confidence" in the Court. Their faith in the presidency is also high—61 percent.

But consistently and increasingly over the past decade, faith in Congress has collapsed—slowly, and then all at once. Today it is at a record low. Just 45 percent of Americans have "trust and confidence" in Congress; just 25 percent approve of how Congress is handling its job. A higher percentage of Americans likely supported the British Crown at the time of the Revolution than support our Congress today.

The source of America's cynicism is not hard to find. Americans despise the inauthentic. Gregory House, of the eponymous TV medical drama, is a hero not because he is nice (he isn't), but because he is true. Tiger Woods is a disappointment not because he is evil (he isn't), but because he proved false. We may want peace and prosperity, but most would settle for simple integrity. Yet the single attribute least attributed to Congress, at least in the minds of the vast majority of Americans, is just that: integrity. And this is because most believe our Congress is a simple pretense. That rather than being, as our framers promised, an institution "dependent on the People," the institution has developed a pathological dependence on campaign cash. The US Congress has become the Fundraising Congress. And it answers—as Republican and Democratic presidents alike have discovered—not to the People, and not even to the president, but increasingly to the relatively small mix of interests that fund the key races that determine which party will be in power.

This is corruption. Not the corruption of bribes, or of any other crime known to Title 18 of the US Code. Instead, it is a corruption of the faith Americans have in this core institution of our democracy. The vast majority of Americans believe money buys results in Congress (88 percent in a recent California poll). And whether that belief is true or not, the damage is the same. The democracy is feigned. A feigned democracy breeds cynicism. Cynicism leads to disengagement. Disengagement leaves the fox guarding the henhouse.

This corruption is not hidden. On the contrary, it is in plain sight, with its practices simply more and more brazen. Consider, for example, the story Robert Kaiser tells in his fantastic book *So Damn Much Money,* about Senator John Stennis, who served for forty-one years until his retirement in 1989. Stennis, no choirboy himself, was asked by a colleague to host a fundraiser for military contractors while he was chair of the Armed Services Committee. "Would that be proper?" Stennis asked. "I hold life and death over those companies. I don't think it would be proper for me to take money from them."

Is such a norm even imaginable in DC today? Compare Stennis with Max Baucus, who has gladly opened his campaign chest to $3.3 million in contributions from the healthcare and insurance industries since 2005, a time when he has controlled healthcare in the Senate. Or Senators Lieberman, Bayh and Nelson, who took millions from insurance and healthcare interests and then opposed the (in their states) popular public option for healthcare. Or any number of Blue Dog Democrats in the House who did the same, including, most prominently, Alabama's Mike Ross. Or Republican John Campbell, a California landlord who in 2008 received (as ethics reports indicate) between $600,000 and $6 million in rent from used car dealers, who successfully inserted an amendment into the Consumer Financial Protection Agency Act to exempt car dealers from financing rules to protect consumers. Or Democrats Melissa Bean and Walter Minnick, who took top-dollar contributions from the financial services sector and then opposed stronger oversight of financial regulations.

The list is endless; the practice open and notorious. Since the time of Rome, historians have taught that while corruption is a part of every society, the only truly dangerous corruption comes when the society has lost any sense of shame. Washington has lost its sense of shame.

As fundraising becomes the focus of Congress—as the parties force members to raise money for other members, as they reward the best fundraisers with lucrative committee assignments and leadership positions—the focus of Congressional "work" shifts. Like addicts constantly on the lookout for their next fix, members grow impatient with anything that doesn't promise the kick of a campaign contribution. The first job is meeting the fundraising target. Everything else seems cheap. Talk about policy becomes, as one Silicon Valley executive described it to me, "transactional." The perception, at least among industry staffers dealing with the Hill, is that one makes policy progress only if one can promise fundraising progress as well.

As the focus of Congressional work shifts toward fundraising, policy discussions are becoming increasingly 'transactional.'

This dance has in turn changed the character of Washington. As Kaiser explains, Joe Rothstein, an aide to former Senator Mike Gravel, said there was never a "period of pristine American politics untainted by money. . . . Money has been part of American politics forever, on occasion—in the Gilded Age or the Harding administration, for example—much more blatantly than recently." But "in recent decades 'the scale of it has just gotten way out of hand.' The money may have come in brown paper bags in earlier eras, but the politicians needed, and took, much less of it than they take through more formal channels today."

And not surprisingly, as powerful interests from across the nation increasingly invest in purchasing public policy rather than inventing a better mousetrap, wealth, and a certain class of people, shift to Washington. According to the 2000 Census, fourteen of the hundred richest counties were in the Washington area. In 2007, nine of the richest twenty were in the area. Again, Kaiser: "In earlier generations enterprising young men came to Washington looking for power and political adventure, often with ambitions to save or reform the country or the world. In the last fourth of the twentieth century such aspirations were supplanted by another familiar American yearning: to get rich."

Rich, indeed, they are, with the godfather of the lobbyist class, Gerald Cassidy, amassing more than $100 million from his lobbying business.

Members of Congress are insulted by charges like these. They insist that money has no such effect. Perhaps, they concede, it buys access. (As former Representative Romano Mazzoli put it, "People who contribute get the ear of the member and the ear of the staff. They have the access—and access is it.") But, the cash-seekers insist, it doesn't change anyone's mind. The souls of members are not corrupted by private funding. It is simply the way Americans go about raising the money necessary to elect our government.

But there are two independent and adequate responses to this weak rationalization for the corruption of the Fundraising Congress. First, whether or not this money has corrupted anyone's soul—that is, whether it has changed any vote or led any politician to bend one way or the other—there is no doubt that it leads the vast majority of Americans to believe that money buys results in Congress. Even if it doesn't, that's what Americans believe. Even if, that is, the money doesn't corrupt the soul of a single member of Congress, it corrupts the institution—by weakening faith in it, and hence weakening the willingness of citizens to participate in their government. Why waste your time engaging politically when it is ultimately money that buys results, at least if you're not one of those few souls with vast sums of it?

"But maybe," the apologist insists, "the problem is in what Americans believe. Maybe we should work hard to convince Americans that they're wrong. It's understandable that they believe money is corrupting Washington. But it isn't. The money is benign. It supports the positions members have already taken. It is simply how those positions find voice and support. It is just the American way."

Here a second and completely damning response walks onto the field: if money really doesn't affect results in Washington, then what could possibly explain the fundamental policy failures—relative to every comparable democracy across the world, whether liberal or conservative—of our government over the past decades? The choice (made by Democrats and Republicans alike) to leave unchecked a huge and crucially vulnerable segment of our economy, which threw the economy over a cliff when it tanked (as independent analysts again and again predicted it would). Or the choice to leave unchecked the spread of greenhouse gases. Or to leave unregulated the exploding use of antibiotics in our food supply—producing deadly strains of *E. coli*. Or the inability of the twenty years of "small government" Republican presidents in the past twenty-nine to reduce the size of government at all. Or . . . you fill in the blank. From the perspective of what the People want, or even the perspective of what the political parties say they want, the Fundraising Congress is misfiring in every dimension. That is either because Congress is filled with idiots or because Congress has a dependency on something other than principle or public policy sense. In my view, Congress is not filled with idiots.

The point is simple, if extraordinarily difficult for those of us proud of our traditions to accept: this democracy no longer works. Its central player has been captured. Corrupted. Controlled by an economy of influence disconnected from the democracy. Congress has developed a dependency foreign to the framers' design. Corporate campaign spending, now liberated by the Supreme Court, will only make that dependency worse. "A dependence" not, as the Federalist Papers celebrated it, "on the People" but a dependency upon interests that have conspired to produce a world in which policy gets sold.

No one, Republican or Democratic, who doesn't currently depend upon this system should accept it. No president, Republican or Democratic, who doesn't change this system could possibly hope for any substantive reform. For small-government Republicans, the existing system will always block progress. There will be no end to extensive and complicated taxation and regulation until this system changes (for the struggle over endless and complicated taxation and regulation is just a revenue opportunity for the Fundraising Congress). For reform-focused Democrats, the existing system will always block progress. There will be no change in fundamental aspects of the existing economy, however inefficient, from healthcare to energy to food production, until this political economy is changed (for the reward from the status quo to stop reform is always irresistible to the Fundraising Congress). In a single line: there will be no change until we change Congress.

That Congress is the core of the problem with American democracy today is a point increasingly agreed upon by a wide range of the commentators. But almost universally, these commentators obscure the source of the problem. Some see our troubles as tied to the arcane rules of the institution, particularly the Senate. Ezra Klein of the *Washington Post,* for example, has tied the failings of Congress to the filibuster and argues that the first step of fundamental reform has got to be to fix that. Tom Geoghegan made a related argument in these pages in August, and the argument appears again in this issue. (Of course, these pages were less eager to abolish the filibuster when the idea was floated by the Republicans in 2005, but put that aside.)

These arguments, however, miss a basic point. Filibuster rules simply set the price that interests must pay to dislodge reform. If the rules were different, the price would no doubt be higher. But a higher price wouldn't change the economy of influence. Indeed, as political scientists have long puzzled, special interests underinvest in Washington relative to the potential return. These interests could just as well afford to assure that fifty-one senators block reform as forty.

Others see the problem as tied to lobbyists—as if removing lobbyists from the mix of legislating (as if that constitutionally could be done) would be reform enough to assure that legislation was not corrupted.

But the problem in Washington is not lobbying. The problem is the role that lobbyists have come to play. As John Edwards used to say (when we used to quote what Edwards said), there's all the difference in the world between a lawyer making an argument to a jury and a lawyer handing out $100 bills to the jurors. That line is lost on the profession today. The profession would earn enormous credibility if it worked to restore it.

Finally, some believe the problem of Congress is tied to excessive partisanship. Members from an earlier era routinely point to the loss of a certain civility and common purpose. The game as played by both parties seems more about the parties than about the common good.

But it is this part of the current crisis that the dark soul in me admires most. There is a brilliance to how the current fraud is sustained. Everyone inside this game recognizes that if the public saw too clearly that the driving force in Washington is campaign cash, the public might actually do something to change that. So every issue gets reframed as if it were really a question touching some deep (or not so deep) ideological question. Drug companies fund members, for example, to stop reforms that might actually test whether "me too" drugs are worth the money they cost. But the reforms get stopped by being framed as debates about "death panels" or "denying doctor choice" rather than the simple argument of cost-effectiveness that motivates the original reform. A very effective campaign succeeds in obscuring the source of conflict over major issues of reform with the pretense that it is ideology rather than campaign cash that divides us.

Lobbying campaigns obscure the source of policy disputes with the pretense that it is ideology, not campaign cash, that divides us.

Each of these causes is a symptom of a more fundamental disease. That disease is improper dependency. Remove the dependency, and these symptoms become—if not perfectly then at least much more—benign.

As someone who has known Obama vaguely for almost twenty years—he was my colleague at the University of Chicago, and I supported and contributed to every one of his campaigns—I would have bet my career that he understood this. That's what he told us again and again in his campaign, not as colorfully as Edwards, but ultimately more convincingly. That's what distinguished him from Hillary Clinton. That's what Clinton, defender of the lobbyists, didn't get. It was "fundamentally chang[ing] the way Washington works" that was the essential change that would make change believable.

So if you had told me in 2008 that Obama expected to come to power and radically remake the American economy—as his plans to enact healthcare and a response to global warming alone obviously would—without first radically changing this corrupted machinery of government, I would not have believed it. Who could believe such a change possible, given the economy of influence that defines Washington now?

Yet a year into this administration, it is impossible to believe this kind of change is anywhere on the administration's radar, at least anymore. The need to reform Congress has left Obama's rhetoric. The race to dicker with Congress in the same way Congress always deals is now the plan. Symbolic limits on lobbyists within the administration, and calls for new disclosure limits for Congress are the sole tickets of "reform." (Even its

revolving-door policy left a Mack truck–wide gap at its core: members of the administration can't leave the government and lobby for the industries they regulated during the term of the administration. But the day after Obama leaves office? All bets are off.) Except for a vague promise in his State of the Union about overturning the Court's decision in *Citizens United v. Federal Election Commission* (as if that were reform enough), there is nothing in the current framework of the White House's plans that is anything more than the strategy of a kinder and gentler, albeit certainly more articulate, George W. Bush: buying reform at whatever price the Fundraising Congress demands. No doubt Obama will try to buy more reform than Bush did. But the terms will continue to be set by a Congress driven by a dependency that betrays democracy, and at a price that is not clear we can even afford.

Healthcare reform is a perfect example. The bill the Fundraising Congress has produced is miles from the reform that Obama promised ("Any plan I sign must include an insurance exchange . . . including a public option," July 19, 2009). Like the stimulus package, like the bank bailouts, it is larded with gifts to the most powerful fundraising interests—including a promise to drug companies to pay retail prices for wholesale purchases and a promise to the insurance companies to leave their effectively collusive (since exempt from anti-trust limitations) and extraordinarily inefficient system of insurance intact—and provides (relative to the promises) little to the supposed intended beneficiaries of the law: the uninsured. In this, it is the perfect complement to the only significant social legislation enacted by Bush, the prescription drug benefit: a small benefit to those who can't afford drugs, a big gift to those who make drugs and an astonishingly expensive price tag for the nation.

So how did Obama get to this sorry bill? The first step, we are told, was to sit down with representatives from the insurance and pharmaceutical industries to work out a deal. But why, the student of Obama's campaign might ask, were they the entities with whom to strike a deal? How many of the 69,498,516 votes received by Obama did they actually cast? "We have to change our politics," Obama said. Where is the change in this?

"People . . . watch," Obama told us in the campaign, "as every year, candidates offer up detailed healthcare plans with great fanfare and promise, only to see them crushed under the weight of Washington politics and drug and insurance industry lobbying once the campaign is over."

"This cannot," he said, "be one of those years."

It has been one of those years. And it will continue to be so long as presidents continue to give a free pass to the underlying corruption of our democracy: Congress.

There was a way Obama might have had this differently. It would have been risky, some might say audacious. And it would have required an imagination far beyond the conventional politics that now controls his administration.

No doubt, 2009 was going to be an extraordinarily difficult year. Our nation was a cancer patient hit by a bus on her way to begin chemotherapy. The first stages of reform thus had to be trauma care, at least to stabilize the patient until more fundamental treatment could begin.

But even then, there was an obvious way that Obama could have reserved the recognition of the need for this more fundamental reform by setting up the expectations of the nation forcefully and clearly. Building on the rhetoric at the core of his campaign, on January 20, 2009, Obama could have said:

> America has spoken. It has demanded a fundamental change in how Washington works, and in the government America delivers. I commit to America to work with Congress to produce that change. But if we fail, if Congress blocks the change that America has demanded—or more precisely, if Congress allows the special interests that control it to block the change that America has demanded—then it will be time to remake Congress. Not by throwing out the Democrats, or by throwing out the Republicans. But by throwing out both, to the extent that both continue to want to work in the old way. If this Congress fails to deliver change, then we will change Congress.

Had he framed his administration in these terms, then when what has happened has happened, Obama would be holding the means to bring about the obvious and critical transformation that our government requires: an end to the Fundraising Congress. The failure to deliver on the promises of the campaign would not be the failure of Obama to woo Republicans (the unwooable Victorians of our age). The failure would have been what America was already primed to believe: a failure of this corrupted institution to do its job. Once that failure was marked with a frame that Obama set, he would have been in the position to begin the extraordinarily difficult campaign to effect the real change that Congress needs.

Citizen-funded elections and constitutional reforms to ensure legislative integrity would make it difficult for money to buy results.

I am not saying this would have been easy. It wouldn't have. It would have been the most important constitutional struggle since the New Deal or the Civil War. It would have involved a fundamental remaking of the way Congress works. No one should minimize how hard that would have been. But if there was a President who could have done this, it was, in my view, Obama. No politician in almost a century has had the demonstrated capacity to inspire the imagination of a nation. He had us, all of us, and could have kept us had he kept the focus high.

Nor can one exaggerate the need for precisely this reform. We can't just putter along anymore. Our government is, as Paul Krugman put it, "ominously dysfunctional" just at a time when the world desperately needs at least competence. Global warming, pandemic disease, a crashing world economy: these are not problems we can leave to a litter of distracted souls. We are

at one of those rare but critical moments when a nation must remake itself, to restore its government to its high ideals and to the potential of its people. Think of the brilliance of almost any bit of the private sector—from Hollywood, to Silicon Valley, to MIT, to the arts in New York or Nashville—and imagine a government that reflected just a fraction of that excellence. We cannot afford any less anymore.

What would the reform the Congress needs be? At its core, a change that restores institutional integrity. A change that rekindles a reason for America to believe in the central institution of its democracy by removing the dependency that now defines the Fundraising Congress. Two changes would make that removal complete. Achieving just one would have made Obama the most important president in a hundred years.

That one—and first—would be to enact an idea proposed by a Republican (Teddy Roosevelt) a century ago: citizen-funded elections. America won't believe in Congress, and Congress won't deliver on reform, whether from the right or the left, until Congress is no longer dependent upon conservative-with-a-small-c interests—meaning those in the hire of the status quo, keen to protect the status quo against change. So long as the norms support a system in which members sell out for the purpose of raising funds to get re-elected, citizens will continue to believe that money buys results in Congress. So long as citizens believe that, it will.

Citizen-funded elections could come in a number of forms. The most likely is the current bill sponsored in the House by Democrat John Larson and Republican Walter Jones, in the Senate by Democrats Dick Durbin and Arlen Specter. That bill is a hybrid between traditional public funding and small-dollar donations. Under this Fair Elections Now Act (which, by the way, is just about the dumbest moniker for the statute possible, at least if the sponsors hope to avoid Supreme Court invalidation), candidates could opt in to a system that would give them, after clearing certain hurdles, substantial resources to run a campaign Candidates would also be free to raise as much money as they want in contributions maxed at $100 per citizen.

The only certain effect of this first change would be to make it difficult to believe that money buys any results in Congress. A second change would make that belief impossible: banning any member of Congress from working in any lobbying or consulting capacity in Washington for seven years after his or her term. Part of the economy of influence that corrupts our government today is that Capitol Hill has become, as Representative Jim Cooper put it, a "farm league for K Street." But K Street will lose interest after seven years, and fewer in Congress would think of their career the way my law students think about life after law school—six to eight years making around $180,000, and then doubling or tripling that as a partner, where "partnership" for members of Congress means a comfortable position on K Street.

Before the Supreme Court's decision in *Citizens United v. FEC,* I thought these changes alone would be enough at least to get reform started. But the clear signal of the Roberts Court is that any reform designed to muck about with whatever wealth wants is constitutionally suspect. And while it would take an enormous leap to rewrite constitutional law to make the Fair Elections Now Act unconstitutional, *Citizens United* demonstrates that the Court is in a jumping mood. And more ominously, the market for influence that that decision will produce may well overwhelm any positive effect that Fair Elections produces.

This fact has led some, including now me, to believe that reform needs people who can walk and chew gum at the same time. Without doubt, we need to push the Fair Elections Now Act. But we also need to begin the process to change the Constitution to assure that reform can survive the Roberts Court. That constitutional change should focus on the core underlying problem: institutional independence. The economy of influence that grips Washington has destroyed Congress's independence. Congress needs the power to restore it, by both funding elections to secure independence and protecting the context within which elections occur so that the public sees that integrity.

No amendment would come from this Congress, of course. But the framers left open a path to amendment that doesn't require the approval of Congress—a convention, which must be convened if two-thirds of the states apply for it. Interestingly, (politically) those applications need not agree on the purpose of the convention. Some might see the overturning of *Citizens United*. Others might want a balanced budget amendment. The only requirement is that two-thirds apply, and then begins the drama of an unscripted national convention to debate questions of fundamental law.

Many fear a convention, worrying that our democracy can't process constitutional innovation well. I don't share that fear, but in any case, any proposed amendment still needs thirty-eight states to ratify it. There are easily twelve solid blue states in America and twelve solid red states. No one should fear that change would be too easy.

No doubt constitutional amendments are politically impossible—just as wresting a republic from the grip of a monarchy, or abolishing slavery or segregation, or electing Ronald Reagan or Barack Obama was "politically impossible." But conventional minds are always wrong about pivot moments in a nation's history. Obama promised this was such a moment. The past year may prove that he let it slip from his hand.

For this, democracy pivots. It will either spin to restore integrity or it will spin further out of control. Whether it will is no longer a choice. Our only choice is how.

Imagine an alcoholic. He may be losing his family, his job, and his liver. These are all serious problems. Indeed, they are among the worst problems anyone could face. But what we all understand about the dependency of alcoholism is that however awful these problems, the alcoholic cannot begin to solve them until he solves his first problem—alcoholism.

So too is it with our democracy. Whether on the left or the right, there is an endless list of critical problems that each side believes important. The Reagan right wants less government and a simpler tax system. The progressive left wants better healthcare and a stop to global warming. Each side views these issues as critical, either to the nation (the right) or to the globe (the left). But what both sides must come to see is that the reform of neither is possible until we solve our first problem first—the dependency of the Fundraising Congress.

This dependency will perpetually block reform of any kind, since reform is always a change in the status quo, and it is defense of the status quo that the current corruption has perfected. For again, as Obama said:

> If we're not willing to take up that fight, then real change—change that will make a lasting difference in the lives of ordinary Americans—will keep getting blocked by the defenders of the status quo.

"Defenders of the status quo"—now including the souls that hijacked the movement Obama helped inspire.

Critical Thinking

1. In what ways, according to Lessig, is Congress corrupt?

2. What is now the focus of congressional "work"?

3. Identify some of the fundamental policy failures, according to Lessig, of U.S. national government over the past fifty years.

4. What is, according to Lessig, the "fundamental disease" that afflicts Congress.

5. How, according to the author, might Obama have better approached Congress and government corruption when he became president?

6. What forms could citizen-funded elections take, and what effect would they likely have on Congress?

7. How would, according to Lessig, banning anyone from working in lobbying or political consulting for seven years after leaving Congress alter the influence of lobbying or special interest groups on Capitol Hill?

LAWRENCE LESSIG, a professor of law at Harvard Law School, is co-founder of the nonprofit Change Congress.

Pulling Apart

Congress was more polarized last year than in any other year since *National Journal* began compiling its vote ratings. Overlap between the parties is disappearing.

RONALD BROWNSTEIN

In the long march toward a more parliamentary and partisan Washington, *National Journal*'s 2010 congressional vote ratings mark a new peak of polarization.

For only the second time since 1982, when *NJ* began calculating the ratings in their current form, every Senate Democrat compiled a voting record more liberal than every Senate Republican—and every Senate Republican compiled a voting record more conservative than every Senate Democrat. Even Nebraska's Ben Nelson, the most conservative Democrat in the rankings, produced an overall voting record slightly to the left of the most moderate Republicans last year: Ohio's George Voinovich and Maine's Susan Collins and Olympia Snowe. The Senate had been that divided only once before, in 1999.

But the overall level of congressional polarization last year was the highest the index has recorded, because the House was much more divided in 2010 than it was in 1999. Back then, more than half of the chamber's members compiled voting records between the most liberal Republican and the most conservative Democrat. In 2010, however, the overlap between the parties in the House was less than in any previous index.

Just five House Republicans in 2010 generated vote ratings more liberal than the most conservative House Democrat, Gene Taylor of Mississippi. Just four Democrats produced ratings more conservative than the most liberal Republican, Joseph Cao of Louisiana. Every other House Republican produced a more conservative vote rating than every other House Democrat, even though a substantial number of those Democrats pursued a relatively moderate course overall. Of the nine members who were outliers last year, only one—Republican Walter Jones of North Carolina—is still in Congress. That makes him the only lawmaker in the House or Senate this year to have a 2010 vote rating out of sync with his party.

The results document another leap forward in the fusion of ideology and partisanship that has remade Congress over the past three decades, the period tracked by *NJ*'s vote ratings. For most of American history, the two parties operated as ramshackle coalitions that harbored diverse and even antithetical views. Each party's Senate caucus housed ideological antagonists, such as progressive Democratic titan Hubert Humphrey

of Minnesota and segregationist stalwart Richard Russell of Georgia, or New Right Republican firebrand Jesse Helms of North Carolina and silk-stocking New York City liberal Jacob Javits. Such contrasts are not extinct. But since the early 1980s, they have vastly diminished as the differences within each party have narrowed and the distance between them has widened.

Over that period, "it's just a straight, linear increase" in congressional polarization, says Gary Jacobson, a University of California (San Diego) political scientist who specializes in Congress. "There's a little bit of bumping around in the numbers here and there, but the basic movement is toward the parties moving further and further apart. The 1970s are a high point of all the cross-party [coalitions]. The last three decades are ones of pulling apart."

In 2010, the vote ratings show, the ideological consolidation was greater among Republicans than Democrats. Almost without exception House Republicans generated strongly conservative voting records, regardless of the demography or political leanings of their districts. By contrast, House Democrats from districts that voted for John McCain in 2008 or are dominated by working-class whites produced much less liberal records than their colleagues from districts that strongly supported Barack Obama or are more racially diverse and well educated. In the Senate, just eight Republicans notched a composite conservative score of less than 70, while 21 Democrats received a liberal ranking of less than 70.

The results capture the continued remaking of Congress into an institution defined by much greater partisan discipline and philosophical conformity. Occasionally, legislators can still build idiosyncratic coalitions across party lines, as occurred during some of the votes on the free-wheeling House debate over spending earlier this month. Likewise, a bipartisan group of senators is attempting to build a cross-party alliance to advance the recommendations of President Obama's debt-reduction commission.

But increasingly, on the biggest issues, the parties line up in virtual lockstep against each other, as they did on many of the key measures in the 2010 rankings, such as the Senate votes on health care and financial-services reform. (Even on the House's final vote last weekend on funding the government through September, every Democrat voted in opposition and all but three Republicans voted in support.) All of this is fundamentally changing the way Congress gets things done—when it gets things done at all. "If you are the whip in either party you are liking this, [because] it makes your job easier," says Mississippi Republican Trent Lott, the former Senate majority leader (and before that the GOP Senate whip). "In terms of getting things done for the country, that's not the case."

The Lost World

For those who have come of age in today's hyperpartisan Congress—with its near-parliamentary levels of party discipline on floor votes, jagged ideological confrontations, and dominant role for leadership—it's easy to forget how different the institution looked as recently as the early 1980s, when *NJ* began measuring members' votes on a liberal-to-conservative scale.

The first time *NJ* calculated congressional votes using the scale it employs now, in 1982, the results revealed a Congress that operated in a manner that would be unrecognizable today.

John Danforth, a moderate Republican senator from Missouri, was finishing his first term in 1982. He remembers that soon after he arrived, Russell Long of Louisiana, the venerable Democratic powerhouse who chaired the Senate Finance Committee, gave him a singular piece of advice. " 'Don't ever hold grudges, because your strongest opponent today could be your ally tomorrow,' " Danforth, who retired in 1994, recalled in a recent interview.

That advice made sense in the Senate of those years, because both caucuses were much more diverse and unpredictable than they are today. In *NJ*'s 1982 vote ratings, fully 36 Senate Democrats compiled records at least as conservative as the most liberal Republican, Lowell Weicker of Connecticut. From the other direction, 24 Senate Republicans compiled voting records at least as liberal as the most conservative Democrat, Edward Zorinsky of Nebraska. Zorinsky, in fact, received a rating exactly as conservative as Arizona Republican Barry Goldwater, whose 1964 presidential campaign ignited the modern conservative revival.

The senators with voting records that fell between the most liberal Republican and the most conservative Democrat represented a pool of idiosyncratic, unattached pieces that could be assembled and reassembled in constantly shifting coalitions to pass or block legislation. In such a fluid environment, it virtually defied conceptualization to define a typical Democrat or typical Republican senator.

The Democrats who generated less liberal records than Weicker included New South moderates such as David Boren of Oklahoma and Sam Nunn of Georgia and Old South conservatives such as ancient John Stennis of Mississippi and Harry Byrd of Virginia, as well as coastal neoliberals such as Bill Bradley of New Jersey. The Republicans more liberal than Zorinsky included a phalanx of brainy New England moderates, among them Weicker, William Cohen of Maine, Warren

Guide to *NJ*'s 2010 Vote Ratings

Rudman of New Hampshire, John Chafee of Rhode Island, and Robert Stafford of Vermont, a champion of the modern environmental movement. Issues frequently divided the parties along ideological and regional lines. When Helms pushed a constitutional amendment to allow school prayer, Weicker and Danforth helped lead the fight to stop him.

"The overarching point is that the Senate was comprised of 100 individuals who had a loose binding with the respective parties," says Weicker, who left the GOP in 1990 to win the Connecticut governorship as an independent. "There were more conservative Democrats, more liberal Republicans. You had people who stood on their own two feet."

In the three decades since, *NJ*'s vote ratings have tracked the narrowing of that Senate center. By 1994, the second year of Bill Clinton's presidency, 27 Democrats compiled more conservative *NJ* voting records than the most liberal Republican, James Jeffords of Vermont (who also later left the GOP to become an independent). Just nine Republicans compiled voting records more liberal than the most conservative Democrat that year— Richard Shelby of Alabama; Shelby, too, later switched parties, joining the GOP. In 1999, with Clinton's impeachment looming over the chamber and the parties recoiling in the aftermath of the grassroots conservative backlash against the 1997 balanced-budget deal, *NJ* found no Senate crossover between the parties for the only other time.

By 2002, the second year of George W. Bush's presidency, some overlap returned, but just two Democrats compiled a more conservative voting record than the most liberal Republican, Rhode Island's Lincoln Chafee. (Continuing the pattern, Chafee was elected governor as an independent last November.) Just seven Republicans racked up voting records more liberal than the most conservative Democrat, Georgia's Zell Miller (who never switched parties but did endorse Bush at the 2004 GOP convention).

In 2010, the second year of Obama's term, this process of separation reached another apex, with no overlap between the ideological scores of senators from the two parties. Taking the long view, the trajectory from Ronald Reagan's second year to Obama's is stark: In 1982, 58 senators compiled voting records that fell between the most liberal Republican and the most conservative Democrat. By 1994, the number was down to 34. By 2002 (after touching zero in 1999), it stood at just seven. And now it has returned to zero. "Over the years, there is no question that the middle in the Senate has shrunk considerably," says Lott, now a Washington lobbyist and a senior fellow at the Bipartisan Policy Center.

In the House, as noted earlier, some ideological overlap remains. But the basic story is the same—and in some ways is even more dramatic. In 1982, the days of conservative Democratic "Boll Weevils" and liberal Republican "Gypsy Moths," fully 344 House members received *NJ* vote ratings between the most liberal Republican (Rhode Island's Claudine Schneider) and the most conservative Democrat (Georgia's Larry McDonald). Even as recently as 1999, 226 House lawmakers compiled ratings between the most liberal Republican and the most conservative Democrat. By 2005, the number between those two poles fell to 54. By 2010, the number of members between those two boundaries had shriveled to seven.

The separation between the parties might not always be as pronounced as in the 2010 ratings. Some Senate Republicans (Scott Brown of Massachusetts, say, or Mark Kirk of Illinois) might easily compile more-moderate voting records than Democrats Nelson of Nebraska or Joe Manchin of West Virginia, particularly if both tilt to the right in anticipation of tough 2012 reelection campaigns. As Michael Franc, vice president for government relations at the conservative Heritage Foundation, notes, it may have been easier for Republicans to achieve unanimity in opposition to Obama's agenda than it will be for them to do so while trying to pass their own programs.

Yet, the underlying trend toward the parties pulling apart in Congress is unmistakable, and, in the eyes of many analysts, probably irreversible. "The two parties," says Washington lobbyist Vic Fazio, the former chairman of the House Democratic Caucus, "increasingly are at polar opposites."

Lines of Division

Though the dominant trend is increasing convergence within the parties, and widening divergence between them, the 2010 vote ratings reveal enduring fault lines in each chamber, particularly among Democrats.

The ratings measured 427 House members and 94 senators; the missing House and Senate seats were held by a person (or persons) who did not cast enough votes last year to warrant a score.

The results reaffirm the link between senators' voting records and the behavior of their states in presidential elections. Senators whose states reliably support candidates from the lawmakers' party in White House races have consistently compiled more-ideological voting records than senators whose states often prefer the other party or swing between them. That pattern was vivid again in 2010.

Of the 21 Democratic senators with the most-liberal overall voting records, according to the ratings, 18 were elected from "blue wall" states that have voted Democratic in at least the past five presidential elections. The only exceptions to the

pattern are Senate Majority Leader Harry Reid of Nevada and Ohio's Sherrod Brown, who tied with seven others for the most liberal Democratic score; and first-termer Tom Udall of New Mexico, who tied for the 15th-most-liberal score.

Among Republicans, the 22 senators with the most-conservative vote ratings were all elected in states that voted Republican in at least the past three presidential elections. That group includes the eight who tied for the most conservative score—among them Jim DeMint of South Carolina, John Cornyn of Texas, and Mike Crapo of Idaho. In a striking measure of his repositioning since 2008, Arizona's McCain also tied for the most conservative score among Republicans; as recently as 2001, in the aftermath of his defeat by Bush in the 2000 GOP primaries, McCain had generated the 39th-most-conservative record in the Senate.

In both parties, dissent is more common among the senators elected, in effect, behind enemy lines. These are the lawmakers who are often most interested in exploring compromises that round off the sharp edges of partisan conflict. Overall, the 30 GOP senators, for instance, elected from states that voted Republican in each of the past three presidential elections compiled an average composite liberal score of 17, meaning that as a group they were more liberal than 17 percent of their Senate colleagues. But the three GOP senators elected from states that voted Democratic in each of the presidential contests since 2000—Collins and Snowe of Maine and Brown of Massachusetts—generated an average liberal score more than twice that, 37 percent.

The same holds true for Democrats. The 30 Democratic senators elected from states that voted Democratic in the past three presidential elections compiled an average liberal score of nearly 76. By contrast, the eight Democrats elected from states that voted Democratic for president only once since 2000 compiled an average liberal score of 67, and the dozen from states that have not voted Democratic since at least 2000 amassed an average liberal score of only 60. Except for iconoclastic Connecticut independent Joe Lieberman (who is retiring after next year), all 14 of the Senate Democrats with the most-conservative voting records, relatively speaking, represent states that have not voted Democratic more than once since 2000—a list that includes Nelson of Nebraska, Jon Tester and Max Baucus of Montana, Mark Warner and Jim Webb of Virginia, Kay Hagan of North Carolina, and Michael Bennet and Mark Udall of Colorado.

Those pairings underscore another striking trend in the Senate results: the convergence among the ratings of senators from the same party who represent the same state. Although the gap between senators from opposite parties who hail from the same state (say Democrat Tom Harkin and Republican Chuck Grassley of Iowa) remains large, partisan pairs increasingly follow the same course. For instance, Democrats Carl Levin and Debbie Stabenow of Michigan and Barbara Mikulski and Ben Cardin of Maryland all tied for the most liberal ranking (as did Democrat Patrick Leahy and independent Bernie Sanders of Vermont). The other end of the ideological scale finds the overlap between Tester and Baucus, Webb and Warner, Bennet and Udall. Similar patterns are evident among

Republicans. In all, 22 states were represented by senators whose vote ratings were within 5 percentage points of each other. In only 12 states did senators have vote ratings more than 25 percentage points apart.

This convergence may illustrate the diminished ability of senators to sail a distinct course, independent of the dominant political currents in their state. The frequent pairings suggest that senators are aligning more closely with their state's underlying political balance, or at least the consensus in their party within their state.

Those who break from that consensus face an increasing risk of primaries driven by activists of the Left or Right; three senators—two Republicans and one Democrat—were denied renomination in 2010, almost as many as in the previous 26 years combined. "There is more of a demand in each party for a degree of purity or inflexibility that was not there before," says Danforth, now a lawyer in St. Louis. Lott notes that the growing threat of such primary challenges (at least three more Senate Republicans could face serious opponents in 2012) powerfully reinforces the trend toward partisan and ideological conformity evident in the ratings. "You really need to toe the line," he says. "That affects people's thinking—both Democrats and Republicans."

A Tale of Two Parties

In the House, as in the Senate, Republicans pursued a more unified course in 2010 than Democrats did. The contrast between the parties was arguably even greater in the lower chamber. What's more, many House Republicans compiled conservative voting records regardless of the demographic or political bent of their districts, while Democrats differed substantially based on those factors.

Among Democrats, for instance, there was a clear relationship between their 2010 vote rating and the way their district voted for president in 2008. The 124 House Democrats representing districts where Obama won at least 60 percent of the vote compiled an average liberal score of nearly 81, well above the party average of 70. In stair-step fashion, the average liberal score dropped to 69 for the 48 House Democrats in districts where Obama won between 55 and 59 percent, and to 63 for the 35 in districts that he carried with less than 55 percent of the vote. Most strikingly, the average liberal score of the 47 House Democrats from districts that McCain carried in 2008 stood at just 50—fully 30 percentage points below the number for those holding the safest seats. Of the 50 House Democrats with the most-conservative voting records, 35 were from districts that McCain carried.

Among Republicans, the variation was much smaller. The 52 House Republicans from districts where McCain won at least 60 percent of the vote produced an average conservative score of nearly 83. The 33 members from districts where he won between 55 and 59 percent generated a slightly more conservative ranking of 84, and the number fell only slightly, to 78, among the 54 lawmakers in districts that McCain won with less than 55 percent of the vote. Even the 34 House Republicans from districts that Obama carried compiled an average

conservative score of 72—only about 10 percentage points less than those from the safest seats.

The story is similar when looking at the House through a demographic lens. In 2009, *National Journal* divided the chamber into four quadrants based on whether the share of the white population with college degrees exceeded the 30.4 percent national average, and whether the district's minority population exceeded 30 percent, the level that an earlier *NJ* analysis found to be a revealing dividing line in election results.

In 2010, as in earlier years, House Democrats from districts high in both diversity and education posted much more liberal scores than those from districts low on both measures: the predominantly blue-collar small-town and rural seats represented largely by members of the Democratic Blue Dog coalition. Democrats from the "high-high" districts posted an average liberal score of 79, compared with an average liberal score of 62 for those from the "low-low" districts. In stark contrast, the 84 House Republicans from low-low districts posted the exact same 79.6 average conservative rating as the 30 Republicans representing districts high in diversity and education.

Why did House Republicans display so much more ideological unanimity than Democrats? One reason is that the GOP's sweeping losses in 2006 and 2008 reduced the party mostly to strong Republican seats in the past Congress, leaving few members with an ideological inclination or electoral incentive to cooperate with Obama. Rep. Tom Cole, R-Okla., a former chairman of the National Republican Congressional Committee, says that the ambitious Democratic agenda also helped Republicans coalesce in opposition—in the political equivalent of Newton's principle that every action generates an equal and opposite reaction. "I remember when the stimulus package came up for a vote: There are 178 of us, we just got our clock cleaned, and the normal reaction was to make peace with the winner," Cole says. "And, of course, every single Republican voted no. I remember at the time somebody telling me, because I'm a deputy whip, 'You guys did such a great job whipping that.' I said, 'It really was not hard to whip.' You can't be a Republican and be for this. Our members didn't feel agonized."

But the results also reflect a longer-term dynamic: Although both parties are growing more ideologically homogenous, the trend is affecting Republicans more powerfully and more thoroughly. Democrats remain more of a coalition party than the GOP. The roots of that trend extend to the foundation of each party's electoral base. The Republicans' voting coalition is much more ideologically uniform than the Democrats': About three-fourths of GOP voters identify as conservative, while only about two-fifths of Democrats consider themselves liberal, with the rest calling themselves moderate or conservative. That creates a more consistent set of expectations from the base for congressional Republicans than it does for Democrats, no matter what part of the country they represent.

Because about twice as many voters consider themselves conservatives as liberals, Republicans are typically less dependent on support from moderates to win elections, which further amplifies the conservative influence over the party's elected officials. "The Democrats are always going to be fractious and divided if they want to aspire to majority status," says Jacobson, the political scientist. "That's just the nature of their coalition. The Republicans don't have to be that broad; they can be much more unified. Republicans are now a conservative and very conservative coalition, and their share of moderates is minuscule. The pressure right now is not coming from their centrists; it's coming from their extremists."

The difference is already apparent in the early months of 2011. After last November's landslide, House Republicans hold 61 districts that Obama carried in 2008, but those GOP members are not straying from the party agenda nearly as much as McCain-district Democrats did from their party's priorities over the previous two years. Every House Republican has voted to repeal the Obama health care plan; all but two voted on February 18 to block the Environmental Protection Agency from regulating carbon emissions; and all but three (just one of them from a district that Obama won) supported last week's continuing resolution on funding that imposed the largest domestic discretionary spending cuts in modern times. "The polarization around here, the formation of two homogenous parties at the poles, is really asymmetrical," says Rep. David Price, D-N.C., a former political scientist. "The ideological cohesion and voting discipline represents a homogenization of the Republican Party that just hasn't taken place to the same extent on the Democratic side."

A Parliamentary System

At the broadest level, the trends in *NJ*'s vote ratings over the past three decades track the decline of individualism in Congress. Throughout congressional history, the most respected legislators—from Henry Clay and Stephen Douglas to Lyndon Johnson, Bob Dole, and Edward Kennedy—have been those who through force of personality or intellect have been able to assemble coalitions and forge compromises that would not have coalesced without them. Such personalized acts of consensus-building still occur but much less frequently, and those who try face much steeper walls of resistance to compromise. "You don't have so much individualism [anymore]," says Weicker, now president of the Trust for America's Health.

Primarily, legislators in both chambers (especially the House) are asked to simply be foot soldiers—to support policy choices that their leadership forges, almost always in close consultation with the constituency groups central to the party's coalition. Rather than being heralded as iconoclasts, those legislators who deviate too often from that centrally directed consensus now face pressure from their colleagues; a cold shoulder from leadership; blistering criticism from the overtly partisan media aligned with each side; and, with growing frequency, primary challenges bankrolled by powerful party interest groups. "A lot of these institutions have become [ideologically] monolithic in their own right, and that just reinforces the political divide," the Heritage Foundation's Franc says. "If you are a charismatic senator or House member who wants to change an issue, you are going to be swimming not just against your own caucus but all of these outside interests and the blogosphere."

In all of these ways, Congress functions as a more top-down, parliamentary-style institution—the results of which are evident in the relentless separation between the parties and the decline of mavericks in *NJ*'s vote ratings. Meanwhile, the results from the 2006, '08, and '10 elections suggest that congressional campaigns as well are operating in a parliamentary manner, in which assessments of individual candidates matter less than broad judgments about the two parties. Put another way, increasingly in congressional campaigns (especially for the House), it appears that the color on the front of the jersey matters more than the name on the back. That means members have less ability to separate themselves from attitudes about their party by voting against key elements of its agenda.

That trend screams from the latest House vote rankings. House Democrats who broke the most often from the party's liberal consensus—the agenda that contributed to last November's voter backlash—suffered by far the greatest losses in that election. Among the 81 most liberal House Democrats, just one who sought reelection was defeated (the Democrats lost the seat of one other who retired). By contrast, among the 98 Democrats with the most-moderate scores, 45 who sought reelection were defeated and the party lost the seats of 10 others who retired. Those legislators didn't lose because they compiled more-conservative voting records, but neither was their distancing sufficient to save them from the tide that crested against their party in all but the safest Democratic districts.

"What you're seeing now is, it's harder to survive [a wave]," Price says. "The survival techniques that people adopted in these swing districts are less workable now. The elections become nationalized, and it's a harder environment for members to deploy their usual survival tactics, like constituent service, and being nice people, and all the things members have counted on to protect them."

The 2012 election will test how heavily these patterns extend into races for the Senate, where candidates typically have established more independence from general attitudes about their party, largely because they become better known than House members. Many of the Senate Democrats facing tough races next year compiled some of their party's most conservative voting records—among them Ben Nelson, Bill Nelson of Florida, Claire McCaskill of Missouri, and Tester. But the past three elections suggest that that may be thin insulation unless attitudes about the overall Democratic agenda and Obama improve in their right-leaning states. "One lesson . . . is you cannot localize elections like this," says Matthew Bennett, vice president of Third Way, a centrist Democratic group. "You are a Democrat and an Obama Democrat . . . [and] you had better find a way of explaining what you did and putting in context what he did, because that is going to define you."

One final question raised by the long-term trends in *NJ*'s vote ratings is whether a Congress attuned to these quasi-parliamentary legislative and electoral rhythms is more or less reflective of public opinion than the more fluid and unstructured institution of earlier generations. Bennett says that the polarization evident in the ratings has produced a Congress more divided than the country. "There's been a lot of sorting out that has gone on the electorate, and there's no question that districts and states are brighter hues of red and blue than they used to be," he says. "But in aggregate, the plurality of the electorate is still moderate, and they are the most underrepresented category of voters at the moment."

Cole, the Oklahoma Republican, disagrees. He believes that the hardening lines between the parties in Washington reflect a widening disagreement in the country over "fundamental first principles" revolving around the role of government. "Most of the Republicans I talk to, and my constituents, really believe that what's at stake is, we are going to be a fundamentally different America on the other side of these [Obama] policies, and they feel it really strongly," he says. "It's not created by the system, not created by Washington politicians, but is a really profound debate that is beginning to emerge about what kind of country we are going to be."

With all signs indicating that that debate will roar through Washington for the rest of Obama's term, no one should expect the systematic separation of the parties that defines *NJ*'s latest vote ratings to reverse anytime soon. Pulling apart has settled in as a defining characteristic of political life in modern Washington.

Critical Thinking

1. How did the level of party polarization in roll call voting in Congress in 2010 compare with party polarization in the previous three decades?

2. What does "fusion of ideology and partisanship" in Congress mean?

3. How did party polarization in Congress in the 1970s contrast with the current situation?

4. What does it mean to say that today "Congress functions as a more top-down, parliamentary-style institution"?

5. To what extent does strong party polarization in Congress seem to reflect public opinion in the country at large?

Being Boehner

The speaker is running the House his way, not the way of his recent predecessors.

Major Garrett

On the eve of a potential government shutdown in April, a deal was finally on the table to avert the crisis. House Speaker John Boehner stared at President Obama, Senate Majority Leader Harry Reid, and a retinue of White House and Hill aides knowing that his decision would be the most fateful of his young speakership. He understood that his handling of this first clash with Obama would reverberate for months—and quite possibly define his negotiating authority with the White House and with his 87-member freshman class. The tension was palpable. Boehner, reticent both publicly and privately to delve into the divine, did so now.

"Mr. President, I'd like to go home and pray."

The moment bespoke Boehner's complicated role in Washington's new power structure. Obama can't make big deals without Boehner—as the 2011 budget agreement made clear and as the summer swelter over raising the debt ceiling illustrates. But Boehner can't deal without the backing of his 240-member Republican Conference—or, if he does, he can only shed so many votes and retain his credibility and clout. Boehner's speakership is already a study in contrasts and seeming contradictions.

In day-to-day operations, he defers to committee chairmen to a degree not seen since Democratic Speaker Tom Foley (and Boehner is possibly even more accommodating). But on big-ticket items (passing the 2011 budget, raising the debt ceiling, reauthorizing the USA PATRIOT Act, and even negotiating the lame-duck compromise to extend unemployment benefits and the Bush tax cuts), Boehner centralizes power just as tightly as his predecessors have.

Forget the clichés about tightrope walking: Boehner doesn't so much balance as barter—he trades at the highest levels on the biggest deals from a position of legislative strength as the leader of the House. But he must continuously earn and re-earn that position and the leverage that comes with it from his charges, especially the freshmen and those closest to Boehner who purport to speak and lobby on their behalf—Majority Leader Eric Cantor of Virginia and Majority Whip Kevin McCarthy of California.

It is not by accident that Boehner put Cantor in the room with Vice President Joe Biden to negotiate a debt-ceiling increase and the budget cuts and process reforms necessary to win House passage. Boehner gave up some of his power to protect it. The debt deal must have Cantor's fingerprints on it. Boehner's bartering is not only interparty, it's intraparty. And he has protected his power in surprising ways—for instance by letting his freshmen kill a multibillion-dollar defense project important to his Cincinnati district and favored by other top House Republicans. Boehner could have nullified a House vote to kill the F-35 second-engine project, and at times he was tempted. But he deferred to the House's will and, in the process, gained respect and power that may serve as the glue for a debt-ceiling deal and possibly others down the road (tax reform comes instantly to mind). Boehner, in other words, is changing the speaker's office in subtle and consequential ways.

Aranthan Jones, policy director for then-House Majority Whip James Clyburn, D-S.C., and now a lobbyist and principal with the Podesta Group, said that K Street has begun to abandon its habit of burrowing into House leadership circles—Democratic or Republican—and is instead building more-layered operations that seek access to committee chairmen, subcommittee chairmen, and individual lawmakers who take the lead on certain issues.

"That change, I predict, is going to be with us in Washington for a long time," Jones said.

Perhaps, but first Boehner will have to demonstrate that his style of leadership is effective. He'll be judged not only by how far he advances the GOP agenda in this Congress but also by whether voters reward House

Republicans in 2012 with another two-year majority or sack them as unceremoniously as they did the Democrats in 2010.

His approach is not without risks. If, for instance, Boehner's willingness to allow House Budget Committee Chairman Paul Ryan of Wisconsin to craft a controversial 2012 budget resolution that would transform Medicare proves a political liability for Republicans—as now seems to be the case—Boehner (or his successor) could well conclude that more-centralized power is necessary.

For now, though, the speaker seems intent on fulfilling his pledge to change the way the House operates. Three experiences from his short tenure provide a glimpse into Boehner's bartering-for-power ways.

The Ryan Express

Boehner's model for running the House comes not from any of his recent predecessors, but from Democrat Sam Rayburn of Texas, who presided as speaker from 1940 to 1961 except for two two-year stretches when Republicans were in a majority.

Republicans, not surprisingly, considered Speaker Nancy Pelosi's rule autocratic and dictatorial, and the GOP caucus's antipathy to the Pelosi era knows no bounds. But the new House leadership also heaps scorn on Republican Speakers Newt Gingrich and Dennis Hastert for their top-down ways. "Under Hastert, there was an implementing of the idea of winning with a majority of the majority," said Steve Stombres, Cantor's chief of staff. "There was a premium for having to win every vote. Now, committees are told to legislate. They are not being told what the product is. The change is very much real."

Pelosi, Hastert, and Gingrich all consolidated power in leadership circles, and that consolidation shaped the ways that lawmakers—and K Street lobbyists—functioned. Gingrich set the process in motion, tightening his power by ignoring seniority in appointing committee chairmen, term-limiting them to six years, and increasing the use of leadership-picked task forces to circumvent the committee process. Hastert and then-Majority Leader Tom DeLay demanded that legislation pass with GOP votes and almost never sought bipartisan support on big-ticket bills. They also blocked Democratic amendments to shield Republicans from votes that carried high political risk. That generated deep animosity among Democrats during their 12 years in exile. When Pelosi got the chance, she returned the favor.

"We just shut the process down," said Jones, the former Clyburn aide. "There was a very strong desire among leadership to protect policy. And if you're going to protect policy, you'd better make damn sure the diverse parts of the caucus can rally around it. That means all the committee fights take place around the leadership table. And the fights are high stakes."

These tendencies—generated by Republicans and tightened by Democrats—gave the House an "us-versus-them" edge that intensified partisan divisions and marginalized committees. Under Pelosi, committees still moved bills, of course, but they played a diminished role in crafting them; or if they did write the original bill, the leadership often overrode the committee's draft to appease party factions.

"If you are working the process in committee and you see the leadership change it," Jones said, "you feel disenfranchised."

Today's Republicans say they couldn't use that system if they tried. "You can't get away with leadership-knows-best anymore," said Brad Dayspring, Cantor's spokesman. "Protecting our members from a tough vote is not something we can do anymore."

Perhaps the best example of the new paradigm is the budget resolution that seeks an unprecedented overhaul of Medicare, a plan drafted entirely by Ryan, who worked as a budget aide to then-Rep. Sam Brownback of Kansas during the 1995 Gingrich revolution and served as a back-bencher under Hastert.

"We built the budget over hours and weeks, and brick by brick," Ryan told *National Journal*. "We showed our package to leadership and they said, 'OK.' Usually, it's the other way around. Newt did these working groups that he created to go around the committee system. [Boehner has] been a rock. He's never once tried to talk me out of an idea. He motivates through incentives and encouragement, not fear and intimidation. He's a delegator, not a dictator."

Stombres, a veteran of GOP vote-counting operations, said that the Ryan budget, fraught with political risks that everyone can see, retains a tensile strength because members understand it, believe in it, and watched it being built. "The budget used to be the hardest vote we ever passed, the hardest whip we ever had to do," he said. "This was the easiest budget to pass and the easiest whip we've ever had."

Ryan contends that his budget—now under sustained Democratic attack for its vow 10 years hence to abolish Medicare's fee-for-service benefit system and replace it with vouchers—is a more durable political document because he built it and sold it first to his committee and then to the GOP Conference. Rank-and-file Republicans, especially the tenacious freshman budget cutters, would have revolted had his budget not taken on Medicare, Ryan says.

"We would have been dis-unified," he said. "It's a false presumption to think we would be better off if we had not done this."

Michael Steel, Boehner's spokesman, was more blunt. "We promised people we would be serious about the budget. If we hadn't done this, people would have known we were the same old Washington assholes."

The dominant narrative now—fed by polling data and the surprise GOP loss in last month's special election in New York's 26th District (the most Republican of the party's four remaining Empire State congressional districts and in GOP hands since 1970)—is of backlash and buyer's remorse. Top aides to Pelosi and Clyburn are certain that House Republicans have stamped their own ticket to oblivion. Pelosi now talks in ever-confident tones of taking back control of the chamber, almost entirely on the strength of what she regards as the GOP's Medicare overreach.

"If they had made the Medicare vouchers voluntary, we wouldn't be in this situation," a senior House Democratic aide in Pelosi's inner circle said. "By making it mandatory they gave us all we needed." Top House Democratic political advisers spent weeks badgering party lawyers to bless TV ads proclaiming that House Republicans voted to "end Medicare." The operatives won, and Kathy Hochul, the Erie County clerk, used Medicare to defeat GOP state Assembly member Jane Corwin in the special election.

Amid the wreckage of the New York loss, it's worth remembering that when 40 Senate Republicans voted for the Ryan budget—a group that stretched from old-guard appropriator Thad Cochran of Mississippi to tea party favorite Mike Lee of Utah and through freshman Mark Kirk of Illinois and moderate Richard Lugar of Indiana—they did so *after* that election. If those GOP senators saw a cliff, they edged closer to it, not farther away. So did GOP presidential candidate Tim Pawlenty, who offered a qualified endorsement of Ryan's budget after two days of (to party stalwarts) dissatisfying dodginess. To know that Ryan's handiwork has become something of a litmus test for serious GOP presidential candidates, one only needs to revisit Gingrich's version of Pennsylvania Avenue *Apocalypse Now* when he had to backtrack from his criticisms of the plan.

Flying High, Flying Low

For those skeptics who think that "regular order" and "letting the House work its will" are bubblegum phrases filled with air and easy to puncture, consider this: Boehner allowed the House to rise up and defeat a project near his Ohio district that he has defended for years. That project, a General Electric and Rolls-Royce program to build

a second engine for the F-35 jet fighter, lost every dime of funding when an amendment by Rep. Tom Rooney, R-Fla., prevailed during consideration of the continuing resolution. By a 233-198 vote, lawmakers cut $450 million in Pentagon spending, the largest defense cut approved on the floor and one that shocked and disappointed second-engine backers besides Boehner—among them Cantor and the chairman of the House Armed Services Committee, Buck McKeon of California.

The speaker's position on the second engine was clear. A GE Aviation plant just outside Boehner's district in Evendale, Ohio, employs about 1,000 people, and Boehner and others argued that if the F-35 ever needed greater thrust capacity, the GE-Rolls-Royce engine could and should meet the Pentagon's needs. Defense Secretary Robert Gates opposed the second engine (the project began in the mid 1990s with an earmark written by then-Sen. John Warner, R-Va.), arguing that it siphoned funds from more important defense needs. Presidents Bush and Obama opposed the second engine, and each tried to kill it, losing every time to a seemingly unbeatable regional and bipartisan coalition loyal to the engine's makers and the concept of having a backup if the original engine design, manufactured by Pratt & Whitney, fell short.

But when the House turned against it, Boehner was nowhere to be found. Aides said that he deliberately avoided the floor vote so as not to tilt the outcome. His absence miffed McKeon. The chairman's staff pleaded with Boehner's aides to join the fight, which McKeon feared he might lose amid budget-cutting gusto.

"There were some who felt he should have weighed in on that," McKeon told *NJ*, referring to Boehner. "I didn't ask John to weigh in on it. The opponents just did a really good job. And we didn't do a good job."

Rooney remembers the vote as if it was a dream.

"I thought I was going to lose that day; we had lost by 20 votes the year before. When we got to [the needed] 218, I remember thinking, 'Please, God, no one change your vote.' Afterward, someone came up to me and said, 'You just beat the speaker.' I was like, 'Uh-oh.' I'm still sort of shocked to this day that we accomplished that."

But Rooney said he has paid no price with Boehner or any other House GOP leader. "There was no call to the office. Nothing like that. Under any normal political scenario in the past, there is no way we could have been successful. The speaker had a parochial interest. This does signal a change in Washington."

Rooney feared that the change might be short-lived. He knew that Boehner would negotiate the final deal with Obama and Reid on the continuing resolution and could, at any time, tuck funding for the second engine back in the deal. "I did worry about it," Rooney said.

Reid's staff expected Boehner to do just that. In fact, Democratic Sens. Sherrod Brown of Ohio and Patrick Leahy of Vermont lobbied Reid to give Boehner room to revive the engine. At the start of negotiations on the CR, Reid's chief of staff, David Krone, told Boehner's chief of staff, Barry Jackson, that Reid would green-light moving the second engine into the final compromise. Jackson said no. "The speaker does not believe in micromanaging the Defense Department." Boehner wouldn't ask directly for the second engine to be revived, but that doesn't mean he didn't look for indirect ways to keep it alive.

When the CR negotiations began, Boehner suggested beginning with a defense-spending number that included the 2010 authorization levels—which made room for the second F-35 engine. When Obama and Reid objected, Boehner retreated quickly. When the final deal was announced on April 8, a harried Boehner took questions for more than an hour from House Republicans curious about what was in—or not in—the deal before finally retreating in exhaustion to a side room. There, he answered more questions, as if granting audiences to individual members. Rooney approached, and before he could say a word, Boehner waved him off. "Don't worry," the speaker told the two-term upstart who had bested him. "The second engine is not in the deal."

But time still remained. Lawmakers spent the following weekend going over the deal's fine print. It is often at this stage that favored projects sneak back into legislation, typically bearing no fingerprints. Sometime in this process— the principals cannot agree when—Jackson called Krone with a question long expected. "Is the second engine still available?" Jackson wasn't demanding. He wasn't insisting. But one last time, the most tempting perhaps of the entire process, he was exploring what might be possible. Brown and Leahy and other supportive lawmakers had been hovering around the issue. Krone said it was very late in the process and that Reid's office would have to run the request by Obama, Gates, and White House Budget Director Jack Lew. Jackson told Krone to wait for him to call back. When he did, he withdrew the request.

Krone still marvels at Boehner's restraint. "He never sold out his members. The carrot was there. They thought about it. But they never took it."

Rooney said, "We didn't know what he was negotiating in there." The House had approved dozens of policy riders (something Republicans once opposed on spending bills) and any one or all of them could be tossed out at Boehner's direction. "I thought I was going to be taken out with the tide like everything else. A lot of riders— most of the riders—were dropped. The fact that the second engine was one of the ones he kept in the final deal, I just find that very uplifting."

McKeon disagrees with the outcome. His 2012 defense authorization bill seeks to revive the second engine by allowing GE and Rolls-Royce to fund development on their own and retain access to Defense Department facilities and by preventing any destruction of existing tooling and design. "I don't think the issue is over." McKeon knows that it's up to his committee to turn the tide. Boehner clearly won't intervene, and McKeon says that Boehner's instincts served him well.

"The will of the House is the will of the House," McKeon said. "To overcome that vote just because he was the speaker would have damaged his credibility and undermined his leadership."

Boehner and the Budget Abyss

Obama couldn't deny Boehner time to pray any more than he could force Boehner to produce 218 votes—the second and equally important (though often underappreciated) step in translating a budget deal into legislation. Boehner left the Oval Office on April 7 after making his request. The atmosphere remained tense as he and Reid made their way out of the West Wing. The two had come to know and respect each other during weeks of private negotiations and public fencing over the budget and several near-misses on government shutdowns. Reid sensed that Boehner felt boxed in. Obama had demanded that the speaker call him with his answer by 9 the next morning. As Boehner left the White House, Reid returned to the Oval Office. "I think we need to give him more time, Mr. President."

Krone, Reid's chief of staff, then spoke plainly. "You know he's not going to call, don't you?" Krone said.

"What do you mean, he's not going to call?" Obama said, incredulous. Reid told Obama he could sense that Boehner felt squeezed and would milk the clock before agreeing to a deal.

"He's going to keep his options open as long as he can," Krone told the president.

Reid and Krone's intuition served them and Obama well. Boehner didn't call. Importantly, nobody overreacted. Ultimately, the deal got done late on that Friday, April 8, and each side claimed a hard-fought if unsatisfying victory. Boehner didn't get all the spending cuts he wanted and Obama gave up more than he preferred.

Boehner never wanted a government shutdown, and he had conveyed as much to Reid last December when the speaker ventured across the Capitol to meet with the majority leader in his private office. The venue for that meeting may seem trivial, but Reid considered it a sign of respect and graciousness that Boehner, who had dispatched GOP aides to Nevada to fight Reid's reelection just a month earlier, would venture onto his turf for their first encounter as the Capitol's top power brokers.

"We have to find a way to cooperate," Boehner told Reid. "We have to find a way."

During that December meeting, Boehner turned to his chief of staff, Jackson, and pointed to Reid's new chief of staff, Krone, and said he and Reid would "need you two" to deal with budget and other top-tier negotiations and that the aides would have to operate with candor and trust. And although such talk might strike some freshman Republicans as a preemptive act of surrender, at the same meeting Boehner bluntly declared an end to congressional earmarks, line items of federal spending that senators value highly and were in no mood to jettison. Reid stiffened at Boehner's flat refusal to send any earmarks to the Senate, but he sensed the Ohio Republican's seriousness—and, most important, Boehner's institutional commitment to make things work and find a way to forge deals, not blow them up.

This predilection led to last week's four-year extension of sensitive and at times politically divisive government intelligence-gathering powers under the PATRIOT Act. Reid called Boehner during the House recess while the speaker was in California raising money for fellow Republicans; Reid proposed a three-and-a-half year extension of post-9/11 surveillance powers. Boehner pushed for four years and promised that he would quiet restive conservatives who wanted to make the surveillance provisions permanent.

That deal held despite a minor uprising by Rand Paul of Kentucky and several other Senate Republicans. With the backing of House Republicans, the PATRIOT Act extension had legislative throw weight. Rand's demand for votes on amendments to restrict government access to certain firearm and business records held up passage and forced some uncomfortable policy contortions but, in the end, amounted to little more than a procedural hiccup. At no time did Boehner or Reid square off and challenge each other's commitment to national security, as had happened in earlier debates on the issue. The deal got done—again within hours of the law expiring—but done, just the same.

Before becoming speaker, Boehner told *NJ* that he would give committee chairmen more power, allow rank-and-file members of both parties to offer amendments, and encourage bottom-up legislating through the process of "regular order." Six months into his speakership, he has made significant moves in these directions, restructuring not only House operations but also the way lobbyists approach issues, coalition building, and paths to power.

"The diffusion of power is on both sides of the aisle," Jones, the former Clyburn aide now with the Podesta

Group, said. "K Street has noticed and is changing. The vote structure is so much up in the air now."

One measure of House openness is the growing number of floor amendments and subsequent roll-call votes—the most vivid expression of partisan and policy preferences. So far in this Congress, the House has considered and voted on 437 amendments; six bills have come to the floor with modified open rules allowing for wide, though not unlimited, debate. In the entire 111th Congress, the Democratic-controlled House allowed one bill to be debated under a modified open rule and considered 810 amendments.

Appropriations Committee Chairman Harold Rogers, R-Ky., has promised that the House will debate each spending bill under an open rule, meaning no limits on amendments.

House Democrats grudgingly admit that Boehner's approach has led to more amendments, and longer and more-varied floor debate, but they dispute that the process is as open as Republicans say.

"The question isn't just the quantity of the amendments; it's the quality," said Rep. Jim McGovern, D-Mass., a senior member of the Rules Committee. "Most of what Republicans have been doing is messaging. The bills are written to protect their agenda, so amendments that would get at their priorities are ruled out of order or non-germane. Things are not as open as they say they are, and they're not as fair as they say they are."

Rep. Henry Waxman of California, the ranking Democrat on the Energy and Commerce Committee, flatly rejected the continuing-resolution debate and its dozens of amendments and late-night sessions as meaningless. "That was like a Potemkin village," he charged.

"I'm not sure I understand the criticism," Steel said. "It's arguing that we're not bipartisan and open because Democrats didn't get their way. Open process doesn't mean Republicans are going to vote for Democratic ideas."

On that, McGovern does not disagree. "That's their prerogative. They won. And it doesn't do any good to complain, because nobody is going to listen."

By all accounts, Boehner's handling of Ryan's budget, the CR, the F-35 second engine, and the PATRIOT Act has strengthened his speakership. But the debt-ceiling negotiations bring big challenges. Ironically, it was a legislative loss that has Boehner well situated to deal with the tests ahead. Every House Republican knows that Boehner could have played the prerogatives game and forced the second F-35 engine into law. That he didn't, Republicans say, has given the speaker more flexibility and latitude. He will need all of both that he can get, because the issues and the negotiations will only get tougher.

Critical Thinking

1. How does Speaker Boehner's way of running the House of Representatives compare with the way Speaker Nancy Pelosi and other predecessors operated?

2. How does Speaker Boehner's style differ on "day-to-day operations" and "big-ticket items?"

3. Who was Sam Rayburn and how did his leadership style compare with that of Speaker Boehner?

4. How did Speaker Boehner act when a project involving his Ohio district came before the House of Representatives?

5. How does the number of floor amendments and subsequent roll call votes in the House under Speaker Boehner compare with the number when Nancy Pelosi was Speaker?

Master of the Senate

Mitchell McConnell gets the job done.

ROBERT COSTA

Mitch McConnell would not smile. The rest of the crowd, full of big-name Democrats and liberal activists, nodded and cracked grins as Vice President Joe Biden quoted Edmund Burke, the famed Anglo-Irish statesman, on the nature of compromise. But McConnell, the purse-lipped Senate GOP leader, remained still, unmoved by Biden's invocation of a favorite conservative philosopher.

Days before, Biden and McConnell had crafted an agreement to extend Bush-era tax rates for two years. Now, on a frigid December afternoon, the pair was standing on a dais in the first-floor auditorium of the Eisenhower Executive Office Building. As Biden playfully cited Burke, McConnell wondered why the White House seemed so keen to celebrate the deal, along with the rest of their lame-duck maneuvers.

President Obama, the next speaker, heaped on more praise, hailing the deal as a significant bipartisan achievement and, more subtly, as a game-changing moment for his administration. Obama then strolled to a small table nearby to sign the bill, swarmed and cheered by Democratic allies. McConnell simply looked on, stone-faced.

To the five-term Kentucky Republican, the whole scene was a tad bewildering. For McConnell, what matters in a deal is what you give and what you get—the coldblooded count of concessions versus gains—not how it is brokered. The misty-eyed fixation by the White House and the press corps on the *process* of negotiations missed the point—and the score.

"I was amused at the mainstream media trying to declare the president the 'comeback kid' at the end of the lame duck," McConnell tells me in an interview over the holiday break. Sure, he acknowledges, the president was able to help cut a tax deal, ratify the New START treaty, and repeal the military's "don't ask, don't tell" policy on homosexuality. But the fuss being made over this string of accomplishments, he says, is excessive.

The arms pact and "don't ask" repeal, McConnell argues, both "would have passed" at any point last year. He also swats back the creeping conventional wisdom that Republicans caved at the last minute. "More noteworthy," he says, "was the fact that

we got the president—in a move eerily reminiscent of [George H. W. Bush's] decision to go back on his pledge of 'Read my lips, no new taxes'—to sign a bill extending the current tax rates for two more years, something he had demonized and run against for several years."

A day earlier, McConnell had defeated Senate majority leader Harry Reid's 2,000-page, $1.1 trillion omnibus spending bill, after cajoling nine GOP appropriators off the fence and into opposing the bill. "That was a clear indication that power was shifting already as a result of the November election," McConnell observes. "Now we get to determine how the spending will be done for the balance of the fiscal year. And we've settled the tax-rate question for two years."

For McConnell, decoupling taxes from spending was crucial—enabling Republicans to "concentrate exclusively on spending reductions, without having that linked to tax cuts" in coming months. "It's a distinct advantage for us," he says.

Whatever comes next, you can count on the 68-year-old McConnell to play a starring role. He has the potential to become a Great Compromiser, like Henry Clay, the august Kentucky legislator from two centuries ago whose desk he now occupies; a feared, sharp-elbowed partisan; or, perhaps most likely, a combination of the two. As he begins to manage his newly grown, diverse conference, which includes tea-party freshmen along with Yankee moderates, McConnell becomes an even more pivotal figure in Washington.

Addison Mitchell McConnell Jr. has been enraptured by the upper chamber—its byzantine rules, its heroic ghosts—for decades. Born and raised in Alabama, where he overcame a tough bout with polio, he moved to a middle-class section of South Louisville at age 13. As an undergraduate at the University of Louisville in the early 1960s, he became active in campus politics, serving as student-body president. He tells me that he paid close attention to the Senate from afar, reading about and debating its happenings with classmates. For a young man interested in national politics, the Senate was the center of the universe.

"In those days, John Kennedy had just been elected president," McConnell says. "He had defeated Richard Nixon, who was a former senator. The Senate was thought of as a launching ground for national aspirations." It was, he says, an "endlessly fascinating place, with people that you saw in the news—Everett Dirksen, Mike Mansfield. All of those giants were around."

So it was no surprise that, in the summer of 1964, after graduating with honors, McConnell made his way to Washington. He was pleased to have secured an internship in the office of Sen. John Sherman Cooper, the venerable Kentucky Republican, cross-aisle friend of JFK, and supporter of civil rights.

Up close, McConnell studied how senators interacted, debated, and socialized—figuring out who led and who followed. He realized, early on, that "the Senate is a different kind of institution—designed on purpose to not do things quickly, to force consensus."

After the internship concluded, McConnell trekked to the University of Kentucky's college of law, where he took a degree in 1967. For the ambitious young attorney, there were many options post-graduation, but his taste for Senate life remained strong. He promptly moved back east, this time for a full-time legislative-staff position in the office of Sen. Marlow Cook, a Kentucky conservative who would later gain notice—along with Sen. James L. Buckley of New York and others—for urging President Nixon to resign as the Watergate scandal deepened.

Sen. Lamar Alexander of Tennessee, the current chairman of the Senate Republican Conference and a longtime friend of the GOP leader, says that by 1969, McConnell had made a lasting impression on numerous Senate staffers and Nixon White House aides, as well as Sen. Howard Baker, who would later become Senate majority leader.

"Senator Baker said to me that 'you ought to meet Marlow Cook's young legislative assistant; he's a smart young man and I think you'd like him.' That was Mitch McConnell," Alexander says. McConnell, he reminds us, was not only a top-notch staffer, but a master student of the Senate: Within a few short years, two U.S. senators from Kentucky had become his mentors.

A post in the Ford administration as deputy assistant attorney general followed. Next came an extended stint as a judge-executive in Jefferson County, where he served until his election to the Senate in 1984, when he topped two-term Democratic incumbent Dee Huddleston by a razor-thin margin. That first victory, swept along by the Reagan tide, was hard-fought: McConnell, in a memorable series of ads featuring bloodhounds, chided Huddleston for skipping votes while he appeared on the speaking circuit. He pleaded with voters to "switch to Mitch." It worked.

Once McConnell was back in the ornate chamber, this time as senator, his youthful memories came rushing back, as did lessons learned. But he was not immediately a star.

Retiring senator Kit Bond of Missouri fondly remembers those days in the late 1980s, when he, McConnell, and David Karnes of Nebraska sat together in the back corner of the last row. "Mitch labeled us, at the time, the Not Ready for Prime-time Players," he says.

Over time, as he rose from lowly foreign-relations-committee member to ethics-committee chairman, National Republican Senatorial Committee chairman to whip, and then to the leader's spot in late 2006, McConnell came to view Senate leadership as an art, akin to the work of a "choir director trying to get everybody to sing out of the same hymnbook." Listening, he says, for all of its clichéd simplicity, became his greatest tool.

"Listening is the best quality somebody in my job needs to have," McConnell says. "I'm in the midst of a bunch of very smart people—all a bunch of class-president types, all smart, or they wouldn't have made it that far in American politics. They've all got something important to say. If you're going to be a leader of a bunch of leaders, you better be a good listener."

On and off the floor, McConnell is a picture of placidity—the clammed-up moue, propped between hound-dog cheeks, comes easy and often. But his blue-gray eyes, framed by George Will–style spectacles, are darting spotlights. A slight glance can stop a pesky staffer or wayward senator cold.

Sen. Al Franken of Minnesota, a smirking freshman Democrat, experienced the McConnell treatment in August when he was caught mocking the GOP leader's solemn speech on Supreme Court nominee Elena Kagan. Franken, whose rubber-faced routines made him a comic star in the 1980s, groaned and gasped as McConnell spoke. After clicking off his microphone, an irritated McConnell approached Franken. "This isn't *Saturday Night Live,* Al," he said coolly. A chastened Franken promptly apologized, publicly and privately, and hasn't made much noise since.

Capitol Hill reporters, who loiter in the marble halls outside the chamber, often chuckle about McConnell's poker face. In his oratory, his gravelly, evenly paced southern drawl rarely rises above a low simmer. His walk and talk are also slow and hushed—plodding, dignified, and oft-unnoticed. In almost every sense, he has no "tell," as they say at the card table.

Sen. Jim Inhofe of Oklahoma, an easygoing conservative, says he admires McConnell but wouldn't mind a bit more joviality in GOP dealings. Phil Gramm, the former Texas senator, "was, frankly, more of my style," Inhofe says. "He had more of a sense of humor." McConnell "is aggressive and gets things done. He's very similar to Trent Lott—the same effectiveness, but not as entertaining."

Sen. Jon Kyl of Arizona, the No. 2 Republican in the Senate as GOP whip, says that's part of McConnell's appeal inside GOP circles—that he prefers serious persuasion over backslapping ingratiation. "Our friendship has grown, but he and I would not be natural buddies, per se, in the Senate, if we were not working as closely as we do," he says.

Other McConnell confidants say much of his manner comes from his old-school reserve, forged at the feet of the institution's past masters. Others believe that it is strategic—in a 24/7 media age, one must be careful, and on alert, at all times. Harry Reid, a colleague adds, appears to follow a similar approach, according to which one would rather be icy than in hot water.

All of this has a purpose, says retiring senator Judd Gregg of New Hampshire. McConnell, he tells me, "has an intuitive sense of the Senate" and knows the institution's limits. Never-ending sessions of observing, listening, and pitching senators on bills, whether perched near the cloakroom or in his Capitol office, are more than somber posturing to McConnell, says Gregg. They're the only way to get things done in a chaotic chamber; to become, with little fanfare, the center of gravity.

"He is sort of like [hockey player] Bobby Orr, who knew where the puck was going before the person passed it," Gregg says. "That's the way Mitch is: He sees things long before others do, understands what's coming, and positions his membership to deal with issues as they arrive."

The only place where McConnell appears to loosen up, ever so slightly, is on the Senate floor. That is his home away from home—where he consoles and inquires, twists arms, and counts noses. "I've always got a to-do list of things I've got to talk to various members about," McConnell says. "Some of the most useful time I spend is going around from one member to another. It's an opportunity to be accessible, without going through the formality of scheduling a meeting. It's extremely productive and important."

On rare occasions, McConnell's familiarity with the floor can get the best of his emotions. In mid-December, as retiring senators delivered their farewell speeches, McConnell took to the podium to speak about Gregg. As he made his way through his address, he began to choke up. "When Judd walks out of this chamber . . . when he walks out of this chamber for the last time, he'll leave an enormous void behind," McConnell said, coughing away the catch in his voice.

McConnell sees his low-key mien simply as an out-growth of "focus," a prominent word in his vernacular, and what he calls the "single most important attribute any leader—not just in politics, but in any profession—can possess." In politics, he says, "there are all kinds of things coming at you that are unanticipated every day, and that's certainly true in my job. But if you focus on the things you are trying to achieve, and don't get distracted by all of the other things that are happening all around you, including the completely unpredictable, which occurs so frequently, you've got a much better chance of succeeding."

Focus, McConnell notes, also includes the ability to deal with the political reality as it is, instead of as one wishes it to be. In late January 2009, days after the Obama inauguration, McConnell addressed the National Press Club and offered an olive branch to the new president. Now the top Republican inside the Beltway, McConnell wanted to outline his hopes for the upcoming session—and set the stakes.

"Make no mistake: Some of our new president's proposals will be met with strong, principled resistance from me and from others," McConnell said. "But many of his ambitions show real potential for bipartisan cooperation."

This rhetoric had the shelf life of a milk carton. McConnell says that within days, when the administration began to push for a near-trillion-dollar "stimulus" package, he realized that, regrettably, Democrats, with their two-chamber majority and a popular new president, were in no mood to play ball with Republicans.

"I think learning to work in the Senate requires you to take a different measure of what success is," McConnell says, reflecting upon the past two years. "Frequently it is not passing things, but preventing really unfortunate things from happening."

The relationship between Obama and McConnell became chilly. As the ambitious new president, riding high in the polls, worked to pump billions toward state coffers, unions, and various public-works projects, McConnell decided to shift. He says that he recognized that behind the president's cheery, bipartisan rhetoric lay a bare-knuckle progressive fighter—a force that demanded an able opposition.

In policy lunches and closed-door meetings, McConnell urged his "diminished band" to work to defeat the Obama agenda "to the maximum extent possible." On the stimulus vote in February, three Republicans broke with McConnell's stance against the measure—Sens. Olympia Snowe and Susan Collins of Maine, plus Sen. Arlen Specter of Pennsylvania, who soon switched parties. That fight was but an appetizer, and the president soon moved to begin work on passing a massive, national health-care program stuffed with mandates and spending demands.

"We needed to make sure the American people knew that everybody in Washington didn't think that this was the direction we ought to take," McConnell says. "Only if the American people understood that this was not something that was 'bipartisan' would they have an opportunity to understand the differences, and, hopefully, still prove to be a right-of-center country and make a mid-course correction."

Herding together his caucus in 2009 wasn't easy, especially as Obama, with charisma and savvy, huddled with GOP moderates on health care, trying to sway them to his side. "I'm really proud of my members' staying together," McConnell says. "It was particularly difficult on health care. There was endless effort, month after month after month, by the president and others to pick off anybody they could get, so they could give that awful health-care bill a patina of bipartisanship."

McConnell, his colleagues say, did not shy away from whipping the health-care vote hard, making every effort to ensure that his bloc would hold. By Christmas Eve 2009, when the bill finally reached the Senate floor, Democrats were able to pass it only by a 60-to-39 party-line vote. "Not a single [Republican], in the end, found that enticing," McConnell says. "From Olympia Snowe to Jim DeMint, we had 100 percent opposition. The American people knew where we stood."

With Republicans having gained a majority in the House and new life in the Senate, McConnell sees 2011 as an ample opportunity for the GOP, not only to work to repeal aspects of the Obama agenda, but to chart a new course for the party, away from its past spending excesses. But as a longtime securer of earmarks, and a pal of the Senate's old bulls, he knows that change, albeit important, will most likely come slowly. If the House, under new GOP speaker John Boehner, passes a flurry of bills, Senate Republicans may have to throw cold water on any over-the-top aspirations, all while fighting for a version of the same policy.

Still, McConnell says, conservatives should not worry. Senate Republicans, he says, are prepared to make the most of coming months. He looks forward to seeing others help in articulating the message, too, from DeMint, the firebrand conservative from South Carolina, to rising freshmen and ranking committee members. Sen. Tom Coburn (R., Okla.) and Sen. Mike Crapo (R., Idaho), for example, are often mentioned as potential leaders on the entitlement debate, should both sides choose to move forward.

"There are active inside players and more prominent outside players," McConnell says. Playing the role of choir director–cum–leader means one has to share the spotlight—and the music. When senators speak out against leadership positions, "I don't find it a bother," McConnell asserts. "I don't view our conference as a zero-sum game, in other words, if somebody becomes more prominent, somebody becomes less prominent. We have 47 independent contractors doing their own thing, to the best of their ability. I'm not a dictator." His job, he declares, is "all carrot and no stick. "

And this year, those carrots—the rhetorical kind—could be proffered to his colleagues across the aisle: Twenty-one Democrats and two independents who caucus with them are up for reelection in 2012. "That's the wild card," McConnell says. "How do those, especially from redder states, want to position themselves?"

As for President Obama, he will be forced to "pivot" if he wants to accomplish anything on the Hill. "Let's just discuss some things that we can actually do with this guy," McConnell responds, when I press him to expand on the scope of his hopes. "Look, if he's willing to honor the results of the election, and do things that we would do anyway, which is what happened on the tax bill, why would we say no?"

"If he's willing to engage in significant entitlement reform, we'll be there to help him," McConnell says. And as a student of history, he is more than aware that such cross-party collaboration is politically feasible for both sides, if structured with care.

"Reagan and Tip O'Neill did the last Social Security fix in 1983," McConnell recalls. "I was running in 1984 and the subject never even came up. The reason it didn't even come up was because it was a bipartisan deal. In fact, the best thing about divided government is that it is the time you are most likely to be able to achieve entitlement reform." McConnell pauses. "Now, will the president do it? We will see. Should he? Absolutely."

McConnell's political genius over the last two years, his colleagues say, was realizing that the GOP's growth had to be built around united fights against unpopular bills, not a rebranding or a recalibrated message. As William White, the longtime Senate chronicler, once said, "There are not many times when a Senate leader can afford to 'get tough.'" McConnell, his colleagues say, has mastered that balance, after a lifetime of study of the Senate that began one summer years ago in the office of Sen. John Sherman Cooper.

McConnell is already planning to run for reelection in 2014, when he'll be 72. The Senate life is not just a job, but a calling. In 2006, Teddy Kennedy traveled to the University of Louisville, where McConnell had established a center for leadership studies. Kennedy, another avid student of Senate history, wistfully noted in an address to students that McConnell's mentor, Senator Cooper, "was a giant," and an unlikely, but valued, partner on many issues with his brother, Jack.

"I only wish he hadn't inspired his young aide Mitch McConnell to work so hard to build the Republican party here," Kennedy laughed. McConnell smiled.

Critical Thinking

1. What, according to Senate Minority Leader Mitch McConnell, matters in a legislative deal?

2. Address the "diversity" among the Republican senators for whom McConnell serves as Leader?

3. According to McConnell, how is his low-key style of leadership related to what he calls the "single most important attribute of any leader"?

4. What does McConnell mean when he says that his job is "all carrot and no stick"?

From *The National Review*, January 24, 2011, pp. 37–42. Copyright © 2011 by National Review, Inc, 215 Lexington Avenue, New York, NY 10016. Reprinted by permission.

Congress's Man of the Vines, Including His Own

ERIC LIPTON

NAPA, Calif.—The local wine industry's biggest names—and boldest blends—were gathered here one afternoon in February for the annual auction that is the Napa equivalent of the Academy Awards. There, pouring wine along with well-known figures like Tim Mondavi, was another industry celebrity: Representative Mike Thompson, Democrat of California.

Mr. Thompson, who represents this grape-obsessed district in Congress, is not only the industry's foremost champion in Washington, helping it secure tax breaks, get money for pet projects like the Napa Valley Wine Train or beat back restrictions on direct sales of wine. He is also a vineyard owner, growing 20 acres of sauvignon blanc grapes at his farm north of Napa.

While plenty of lawmakers in Washington act as advocates for particular industries, Mr. Thompson is in business with some of the same companies whose agendas he promotes. His vineyard has been paid at least $500,000 since 2006 by two wineries whose executives have appealed to Congress on legislative matters.

Mr. Thompson could also benefit from his own efforts on the industry's behalf, including a push to increase the value of grapes grown near his vineyard by seeking a special designation from the Treasury Department.

Mr. Thompson's dual role as industry backer and grape producer has drawn some criticism, particularly from his alcohol industry rivals. "Clearly, he has a personal interest in what he is advocating for," said Craig Wolf, president of the Wine and Spirits Wholesalers of America, which has been in a dispute with wine producers over the past year. "And the ethics rules in Congress say you are not supposed to do these kinds of things."

Mr. Thompson called such claims nonsense. Any action he takes is to help the industry, he said, not his tiny vineyard, which he said made only an $18,000 profit last year.

"I'm unapologetic about going to the mat for the wine industry," he said. "That is my job."

Mr. Thompson, 60, is the biggest recipient in Congress of campaign contributions from the alcoholic beverage industry, totaling more than $1.2 million during his seven terms. He is also a founder of the Congressional Wine Caucus, which has nearly 200 members who gather regularly to sample wine and talk about industry affairs.

He lives in St. Helena, a picture-postcard Napa Valley town, down the street from the elementary school he attended with future leaders in the wine industry like Mr. Mondavi. Mr. Thompson's father worked as a vineyard foreman and his mother worked as a bookkeeper for local vineyards. Some of his closest friends—and duck hunting companions—are top local sellers.

His vineyard, most of which he bought in 2002 for $228,000 and which today has an assessed value of about $775,000, is about an hour north of Napa in Lake County, on a quiet road with pear and walnut orchards. One recent morning, the fog had just lifted at the vineyard, leaving the fields still covered with dew as Mr. Thompson headed out to walk his property, his khaki pant legs wet and boots muddy.

"It is looking good," Mr. Thompson told his vineyard manager, David Weiss, impressed with a new weed-clearing machine. "I like what I see."

Mr. Thompson has a reputation for long hours, traveling constantly to the far corners of his sprawling district for community meetings and charity events. That and his down-to-earth manner—he introduces himself to strangers as "Hi, I'm Mike"—explain in part why residents here take offense to any suggestion that his intertwined roles might raise ethical issues.

"He is the hardest working guy I have ever met," said Dennis Cakebread, an owner of the Cakebread Vineyard and a major campaign contributor to Mr. Thompson. "So often people get elected, go to Washington, they get sucked in, and they kind of stay there. That is not what Mike is about."

Many pointed out his family's commitment to the community: his wife works as a nurse at the local hospital, one son is a deputy sheriff, the other works for the Fire Department. California's wine country, they said, benefits from having Mr. Thompson in Washington, not the other way around.

But his relationship with the industry, at a minimum, is complicated.

The bulk of Mr. Thompson's grapes, about 100 tons a year, have been sold since 2005 to Bonterra Vineyards, a winery in Mendocino, Calif., that relies on Mr. Thompson to produce about half its sauvignon blanc. Since last year, an additional 25 tons have been sold to Honig Vineyard of Rutherford, Calif., which blends them with grapes from Napa to produce its own sauvignon blanc.

Bonterra has paid Mr. Thompson an average of $978 a ton since 2005, a price that is somewhat higher than the Lake County average, $877 a ton during the same period. But Bonterra executives said it was in line with what they paid other independent growers.

"To paint a picture, you have to have to have a palette of colors," said Robert Blue, Bonterra's founding winemaker. "Mike helps bring that."

But Mr. Thompson's ties to both companies—as well as to other wineries—go well beyond grape growing.

In a January 2010 letter, he urged the chief of the State Water Resources Control Board to reconsider a proposal that would curtail the ability of vineyards to use river water to feed extensive sprinkler systems designed to prevent frost from damaging grape vines, a practice some blame for recent area fish kills.

The letter was written after a Bonterra executive, David Koball, said he turned to Mr. Thompson's office for help. "Millions of dollars and hundreds of jobs are at stake here," Mr. Thompson wrote in his letter to the state.

In an interview, Mr. Thompson said that he sent the letter because of concerns raised by a number of vineyards. He added that Bonterra was already working to rely less on river-fed sprinklers. His own vineyard uses well water, he added, to combat frost.

Until it was sold this spring, Bonterra had been owned by Brown-Forman, a liquor industry giant based in Kentucky that has contributed at least $40,000 to Mr. Thompson's political campaigns.

Bonterra has joined with the lawmaker to oppose proposed increases in federal excise taxes on wine and liquor, which were considered during the health care debate. Mr. Thompson said he had worked to block such increases on behalf of the industry for more than a decade.

Mr. Thompson also led the charge in recent years to expand or extend a tax break given to vineyard owners who promise never to develop their land.

Mr. Thompson has not applied for the exemption himself, but some of his industry supporters, including Andy Beckstoffer, an independent grape grower, have signed up. That move, Mr. Beckstoffer said in an interview, saves him hundreds of thousands of dollars in federal income taxes.

Mr. Thompson has also gotten involved in local wine issues that could benefit his own farm.

Local growers, with the personal financial help of Mr. Thompson, are preparing to apply to the Treasury Department to create a federally designated wine region called Big Valley, which would include Mr. Thompson's vineyard and others nearby. Called an appellation, the designation is a marketing boon that helps increase the value of the grapes grown there.

Mr. Thompson called the Treasury Department to make sure it rapidly reviews the request when it arrives, according to Shannon Gunier, the Lake County Winegrape Growers association president. "We feel really comfortable we can call Mike and he will carry the flag for us," she said.

Mr. Thompson separately wrote to the federal Department of Agriculture last year on behalf of Lake County to try to get a federal grant to market the county's wine grapes, Ms. Gunier said.

The congressman intervened in similar efforts by other Napa-area wine-growing communities in recent years, and he said there was nothing exceptional about his support for the request that included the region where his vineyard is located.

The biggest industry battle Mr. Thompson has taken up in recent years is still playing out in Washington, a pitch by beer and wine wholesalers for legislation granting states more power to regulate alcohol sales. Their goal is to prevent big box retailers like Wal-Mart from buying beer or wine directly from suppliers, cutting out wholesalers.

Winemakers fear that such a law could also ultimately result in a ban on direct-mail sales by vineyards to customers around the country. Honig Vineyard, for example, generates about 10 percent of its sales through direct mail.

Mr. Thompson pressed fellow lawmakers to oppose the measure, and even testified twice on behalf of the wine industry at Judiciary Committee hearings.

"You can have the best soil, the best grapes, the best climate—like you are looking at out the window right now—and the best wine maker," Mr. Thompson said during an interview at his vineyard. "But if you can't get the wine to the people who want it, it is all for naught."

Mickey Edwards, a former House Republican from Oklahoma who now helps run training programs for young political leaders, said that Mr. Thompson was not the only farmer in Congress, pointing to Senator Jon Tester, Democrat of Montana, who grows barley, lentils and wheat on 1,800 acres.

Ethics rules would not prohibit Mr. Thompson or others from voting on legislation that benefits their industry. But House rules prohibit members from using their position for any personal financial benefit, and in particular urge caution when contacting a member of the executive branch on a matter that might personally benefit the lawmaker.

To comply with the rules, Mr. Edwards said, Mr. Thompson should not be calling the Treasury Department about the appellation issue because it affects his own vineyard.

"That is very questionable behavior, not something you would think most members would be comfortable doing," said Mr. Edwards, who taught at Harvard Law School after leaving Congress. "It is a lack of good judgment, if nothing else."

Mr. Thompson dismisses the criticism as unfounded. He will do anything to help the industry flourish, he said, because that is what his constituents expect of him.

"This is the lifeblood of the district I represent," he said. "Every acre planted in grapes is another acre not planted in houses or strip malls."

Critical Thinking

1. What are the possible problems stemming from Mike Thompson being the owner of a vineyard, a leading supporter of wine industry interests on Capitol Hill, and a member of the U.S. House of Representatives?

2. What is the Congressional Wine Caucus and what is Congressman Thompson's connection with it?

3. What are some of the things that Congressman Thompson has done to support the wine industry's interests?

4. How do winemaker's payments for grapes and campaign contributions to Mike Thompson constitute, in some observer's eyes, a conflict of interest or an ethics violation for the congressman?

Roberts versus Roberts

Just How Radical Is the Chief Justice?

Jeffrey Rosen

Last month, the Supreme Court handed down its most polarizing decision since *Bush* v. *Gore*. The 5-4 ruling in *Citizens United* v. *Federal Election Commission* called into question decades of federal campaign finance law and Supreme Court precedents by finding that corporations have a First Amendment right to spend as much money as they want on election campaigns, as long as they don't consult the candidates. It was precisely the kind of divisive and unnecessarily sweeping opinion that Chief Justice John Roberts had once pledged to avoid.

In 2006, at the end of his first term on the Court, Roberts told me and others that he was concerned that his colleagues, in issuing 5-4 opinions divided along predictable lines, were acting more like law professors than members of a collegial court. His goal, he said, was to persuade his fellow justices to converge around narrow, unanimous opinions, as his greatest predecessor, John Marshall, had done. Roberts spoke about the need for justices to show humility when dealing with the First Amendment, adding that, unlike professors writing law review articles, judges should think more about their institutional role. "Yes, you may have another great idea about how to look at the First Amendment," he said, "but, if you don't need to share it to decide this case, then why are you doing it? And what are the consequences of that going to be?"

Since then, Roberts has presided over some narrow, unanimous (or nearly unanimous) rulings and some bitterly divisive ones. And so, it's been hard to tell how seriously he is taking his pledge to lead the Court toward less polarizing decisions. Then came *Citizens United,* by far the clearest test of Roberts's vision. There were any number of ways he could have persuaded his colleagues to rule narrowly; but Roberts rejected these options. He deputized Anthony Kennedy to write one of his characteristically grandiose decisions, challenging the president and Congress at a moment of financial crisis when the influence of money in politics—Louis Brandeis called it "our financial oligarchy"—is the most pressing question of the day. The result was a ruling so inflammatory that the president (appropriately) criticized it during his State of the Union address.

What all this says about the future of the Roberts Court is not encouraging. For the past few years, I've been giving Roberts the benefit of the doubt, hoping that he meant it when he talked about the importance of putting the bipartisan legitimacy of the Court above his own ideological agenda. But, while Roberts talked persuasively about conciliation, it now appears that he is unwilling to cede an inch to liberals in the most polarizing cases. If Roberts continues this approach, the Supreme Court may find itself on a collision course with the Obama administration— precipitating the first full-throttle confrontation between an economically progressive president and a narrow majority of conservative judicial activists since the New Deal.

The first indications that Roberts might not be as conciliatory as he promised came during his second term, which ended in 2007. During his first term, which his colleagues treated as something of a honeymoon, the Court had decided just 13 percent of cases by a 5-4 margin. But, in the next term, that percentage soared to 33 percent. (It would fluctuate up and down a bit over the next two years.) What's more, the 2007 term ended with unusually personal invective, as both liberal and conservative colleagues expressed frustration with Roberts. That year, during the Court's second encounter with the McCain–Feingold campaign finance law (which it would gut in *Citizens United*), Antonin Scalia accused Roberts of "faux judicial restraint," for chipping away at restrictions on corporate speech without overturning them cleanly. Meanwhile, the liberal justices seemed angry that Roberts was refusing to budge from rigid positions in divisive cases. "Of course, I got slightly exercised, and the way I show that is I write seventy-seven-page opinions," Justice Stephen Breyer told me in the summer of 2007, referring to his angry dissent from Roberts's 5-4 decision striking down affirmative action in public school assignments.

That same summer, I asked Justice John Paul Stevens whether Roberts would succeed in his goal of achieving narrow, unanimous opinions. "I don't think so," he replied. "I just think it takes nine people to do that. I think maybe the first few months we all leaned over backward to try to avoid writing separately." In other words, once his first term ended, Roberts faced a choice: In cases he cared intensely about, he could compromise his principles to reach common ground or he could stick to his guns and infuriate his opponents, who would feel they had been played for dupes. On virtually all of the most divisive constitutional topics, from affirmative action to partial-birth abortion, Roberts stuck to his guns.

There were some exceptions. Roberts managed to steer the Court toward narrow, often unanimous opinions in business cases, which now represent 40 percent of the Court's docket. (Though this didn't require him to significantly compromise his views, since most of these cases were decided in a pro-business direction.) And then, there was last term's voting-rights case, in which Roberts wrote an 8-1 decision rejecting a broad constitutional challenge to the Voting Rights Act and instead deciding the case on technical grounds. For those who wanted to believe that Roberts was a genuine conciliator, this was a powerful piece of evidence. Like others, I praised his performance in the case as an act of judicial statesmanship.

But, in retrospect, the ruling may have been less statesmanlike than it appeared. According to a source who was briefed on the deliberations in the case, Anthony Kennedy was initially ready to join Roberts and the other conservatives in issuing a sweeping 5-4 decision, striking down the Voting Rights Act on constitutional grounds. But the four liberal justices threatened to write a strong dissent that would have accused the majority of misconstruing landmark precedents about congressional power. What happened next is unclear, but the most likely possibilities are either that Kennedy got cold feet or that Roberts backed down. The Voting Rights Act survived, but what looked from the outside like an act of judicial statesmanship by Roberts may have in fact been a strategic retreat. Moreover, rather than following the principled alternative suggested by David Souter at the oral argument—holding that the people who were challenging the Voting Rights Act had no standing to bring the lawsuit—Roberts opted to rewrite the statute in a way that Congress never intended. That way, Roberts was still able to express his constitutional doubts about the law—as well as his doubts about landmark Supreme Court precedents from the civil rights era, which he mischaracterized and seemed ready to overrule.

The voting-rights case may help explain why Roberts didn't take a similarly conciliatory posture in *Citizens United*. After all, one was certainly available. Just as Roberts had implausibly but strategically held in the voting-rights case that Congress intended to let election districts bail out of federal supervision, he could have held—far more plausibly—in *Citizens United* that Congress never intended to regulate video-on-demand or groups with minimal corporate funding. As with the voting-rights case, judicial creativity could have been justified in the name of judicial restraint.

There is, of course, a charitable explanation for why Roberts took the conciliatory approach in one case but not the other: namely, that he felt the principles involved in *Citizens United* were somehow more important and therefore less amenable to compromise. As he told me in our 2006 interview, he has strong views that he, like his hero John Marshall, is not willing to bargain away. Marshall, Roberts said, "was not going to compromise his principles, and I don't think there's any example of his doing that in his jurisprudence."

But a less charitable explanation for the difference between the two cases is that Roberts didn't compromise on *Citizens*

United because, this time, he simply didn't have to. Kennedy was willing to write a sweeping opinion that mischaracterized the landmark precedent *Buckley* v. *Valeo* by suggesting that it was concerned only about quid pro quo corruption rather than less explicit forms of undue influence on the electoral system. (Congress had come to the opposite conclusion in extensive fact-finding that Kennedy ignored.) As Stevens pointed out in his powerful dissent, the opinion is aggressively activist in its willingness to twist and overturn precedents, strike down decades of federal law, and mischaracterize the original understanding of the First Amendment on the rights of corporations. "The only relevant thing that has changed" since the Court's first encounter with McCain–Feingold in 2003, Stevens wrote, "is the composition of this Court"—namely, the arrival of Roberts and Samuel Alito.

Some of Roberts's liberal colleagues have suggested that Roberts is a very nice man but that he doesn't listen to opposing arguments and can't be persuaded to change his mind in controversial cases. If so, he may have thought he could produce a unanimous court by convincing liberals to come around to his side, rather than by meeting them halfway. In the most revealing passage in his concurrence in *Citizens United,* he wrote that "we cannot embrace a narrow ground of decision simply because it is narrow; it must also be right." But the great practitioners of judicial restraint had a very different perspective. "A Constitution is not intended to embody a particular economic theory," Oliver Wendell Holmes wrote in his most famous dissent, in *Lochner* v. *New York.* "It is made for people of fundamentally differing views." Holmes always deferred to the president and Congress in the face of uncertainty. He would never have presumed that he knew the "right" answer in a case where people of good faith could plausibly disagree.

With Roberts apparently content to impose bold decisions on a divided nation on the basis of slim majorities, the question becomes: Is the Court now on the verge of repeating the error it made in the 1930s? Then, another 5-4 conservative majority precipitated a presidential backlash by striking down parts of FDR's New Deal. In January 1937, Roosevelt also criticized the Supreme Court's conservative activism in a State of the Union address. The following month, he introduced his court-packing plan. But, at the end of March—thanks to the famous "switch in time" by swing justice Owen Roberts, the Anthony Kennedy of his day—the Court retreated and began to uphold New Deal laws.

One lesson from the 1930s is that it takes only a handful of flamboyant acts of judicial activism for the Court to be tarred in the public imagination as partisan, even if the justices themselves think they are being moderate and judicious. Although vilified today for their conservative activism, both the Progressive and New Deal-era Courts had nuanced records, upholding more progressive laws than they struck down. As Barry Cushman of the University of Virginia notes, of the 20 cases involving maximum working hours that the Court decided during the Progressive era, there were only two in which the Court struck down the regulations. But those two are the ones that everyone remembers. And, during the New Deal era, Cushman adds, we remember the cases striking down the National Industrial Recovery Act and the first Agricultural Adjustment Act, forgetting that the Court upheld the centerpiece of FDR's monetary policy and, by a vote of 8-1, the Tennessee Valley Authority.

It's hard to imagine a full-scale assault by the Roberts Court on Obama's regulatory agenda because, with the exception of Clarence Thomas, the conservatives on today's Court tend to be pro-business conservatives, rather than libertarian conservatives, and are therefore unlikely to strike down government spending programs (like the bank bailouts and the Troubled Asset Relief Program) that help U.S. business. But it's not hard to imagine the four conservative horsemen, joined by the vacillating Kennedy, reversing other government actions that progressives care about. Later this term, for example, the Court may follow *Citizens United* with another activist decision, striking down the Public Company Accounting Oversight Board (nicknamed "Peek-a-Boo"), which was created to regulate accounting firm auditors in the wake of the Enron and Arthur Andersen scandals. If the Court strikes down Peek-a-Boo, even if the decision is narrow enough not to call into question the constitutionality of the Federal Reserve, it may provoke another sharp rejoinder from Obama that turns progressive rumbling against the Court into full-blown outrage.

It's impossible, at the moment, to tell whether the reaction to *Citizens United* will be the beginning of a torrential backlash or will fade into the ether. But John Roberts is now entering politically hazardous territory. Without being confident either way, I still hope that he has enough political savvy and historical perspective to recognize and avoid the shoals ahead. There's little doubt, however, that the success or failure of his tenure will turn on his ability to align his promises of restraint with the reality of his performance. Roberts may feel just as confident that he knows the "right" answer in cases like Peek-a-Boo as he did in *Citizens United*. But political backlashes are hard to predict, contested constitutional visions can't be successfully imposed by 5-4 majorities, and challenging the president and Congress on matters they care intensely about is a dangerous game. We've seen well-intentioned but unrestrained chief justices overplay their hands in the past—and it always ends badly for the Court.

Critical Thinking

1. At the end of his first year on the Supreme Court, what did Chief Justice Roberts say was his goal for the Court in coming years?

2. Has Roberts made visible progress toward that stated goal?

3. According to Jeffrey Rosen, what are some key implications of the Court's decision in *Citizens United v. Federal Election Commission*?

4. In what ways has the Roberts Court been practicing judicial activism? What lessons might be drawn from a similar period of judicial activism in the 1930s?

Court under Roberts Is Most Conservative in Decades

ADAM LIPTAK

Washington—When Chief Justice John G. Roberts Jr. and his colleagues on the Supreme Court left for their summer break at the end of June, they marked a milestone: the Roberts court had just completed its fifth term.

In those five years, the court not only moved to the right but also became the most conservative one in living memory, based on an analysis of four sets of political science data.

And for all the public debate about the confirmation of Elena Kagan or the addition last year of Justice Sonia Sotomayor, there is no reason to think they will make a difference in the court's ideological balance. Indeed, the data show that only one recent replacement altered its direction, that of Justice Samuel A. Alito Jr. for Justice Sandra Day O'Connor in 2006, pulling the court to the right.

There is no similar switch on the horizon. That means that Chief Justice Roberts, 55, is settling in for what is likely to be a very long tenure at the head of a court that seems to be entering a period of stability.

If the Roberts court continues on the course suggested by its first five years, it is likely to allow a greater role for religion in public life, to permit more participation by unions and corporations in elections and to elaborate further on the scope of the Second Amendment's right to bear arms. Abortion rights are likely to be curtailed, as are affirmative action and protections for people accused of crimes.

The recent shift to the right is modest. And the court's decisions have hardly been uniformly conservative. The justices have, for instance, limited the use of the death penalty and rejected broad claims of executive power in the government's efforts to combat terrorism.

But scholars who look at overall trends rather than individual decisions say that widely accepted political science data tell an unmistakable story about a notably conservative court.

Almost all judicial decisions, they say, can be assigned an ideological value. Those favoring, say, prosecutors and employers are said to be conservative, while those favoring criminal defendants and people claiming discrimination are said to be liberal.

Analyses of databases coding Supreme Court decisions and justices' votes along these lines, one going back to 1953 and another to 1937, show that the Roberts court has staked out territory to the right of the two conservative courts that immediately preceded it by four distinct measures:

In its first five years, the Roberts court issued conservative decisions 58 percent of the time. And in the term ending a year ago, the rate rose to 65 percent, the highest number in any year since at least 1953.

The courts led by Chief Justices Warren E. Burger, from 1969 to 1986, and William H. Rehnquist, from 1986 to 2005, issued conservative decisions at an almost indistinguishable rate—55 percent of the time.

That was a sharp break from the court led by Chief Justice Earl Warren, from 1953 to 1969, in what liberals consider the Supreme Court's golden age and conservatives portray as the height of inappropriate judicial meddling. That court issued conservative decisions 34 percent of the time.

Four of the six most conservative justices of the 44 who have sat on the court since 1937 are serving now: Chief Justice Roberts and Justices Alito, Antonin Scalia and, most conservative of all, Clarence Thomas. (The other two were Chief Justices Burger and Rehnquist.) Justice Anthony M. Kennedy, the swing justice on the current court, is in the top 10.

The Roberts court is finding laws unconstitutional and reversing precedent—two measures of activism—no more often than earlier courts. But the ideological direction of the court's activism has undergone a marked change toward conservative results.

Until she retired in 2006, Justice O'Connor was very often the court's swing vote, and in her later years she had drifted to the center-left. These days, Justice Kennedy has assumed that crucial role at the court's center, moving the court to the right.

Justice John Paul Stevens, who retired in June, had his own way of tallying the court's direction. In an interview in his chambers in April, he said that every one of the 11 justices who had joined the court since 1975, including himself, was more conservative than his or her predecessor, with the possible exceptions of Justices Sotomayor and Ruth Bader Ginsburg.

The numbers largely bear this out, though Chief Justice Roberts is slightly more liberal than his predecessor, Chief Justice Rehnquist, at least if all of Chief Justice Rehnquist's

33 years on the court, 14 of them as an associate justice, are considered. (In later years, some of his views softened.)

But Justice Stevens did not consider the question difficult. Asked if the replacement of Chief Justice Rehnquist by Chief Justice Roberts had moved the court to the right, he did not hesitate.

"Oh, yes," Justice Stevens said.

The Most Significant Change

"Gosh," Justice Sandra Day O'Connor said at a law school forum in January a few days after the Supreme Court undid one of her major achievements by reversing a decision on campaign spending limits. "I step away for a couple of years and there's no telling what's going to happen."

When Justice O'Connor announced her retirement in 2005, the membership of the Rehnquist court had been stable for 11 years, the second-longest stretch without a new justice in American history.

Since then, the pace of change has been dizzying, and several justices have said they found it disorienting. But in an analysis of the court's direction, some changes matter much more than others. Chief Justice Rehnquist died soon after Justice O'Connor announced that she was stepping down. He was replaced by Chief Justice Roberts, his former law clerk. Justice David H. Souter retired in 2009 and was succeeded by Justice Sotomayor. Justice Stevens followed Justice Souter this year, and he is likely to be succeeded by Elena Kagan.

But not one of those three replacements seems likely to affect the fundamental ideological alignment of the court. Chief Justice Rehnquist, a conservative, was replaced by a conservative. Justices Souter and Stevens, both liberals, have been or are likely to be succeeded by liberals.

Justices' views can shift over time. Even if they do not, a justice's place in the court's ideological spectrum can move as new justices arrive. And chief justices may be able to affect the overall direction of the court, notably by using the power to determine who writes the opinion for the court when they are in the majority. Chief Justice Roberts is certainly widely viewed as a canny tactician.

But only one change—Justice Alito's replacement of Justice O'Connor—really mattered. That move defines the Roberts court. "That's a real switch in terms of ideology and a switch in terms of outlook," said Lee Epstein, who teaches law and political science at Northwestern University and is a leading curator and analyst of empirical data about the Supreme Court.

The point is not that Justice Alito has turned out to be exceptionally conservative, though he has: he is the third-most conservative justice to serve on the court since 1937, behind only Justice Thomas and Chief Justice Rehnquist. It is that he replaced the more liberal justice who was at the ideological center of the court.

Though Chief Justice Roberts gets all the attention, Justice Alito may thus be the lasting triumph of the administration of President George W. Bush. He thrust Justice Kennedy to the court's center and has reshaped the future of American law.

It is easy to forget that Justice Alito was Mr. Bush's second choice. Had his first nominee, the apparently less conservative Harriet E. Miers, not withdrawn after a rebellion from Mr. Bush's conservative base, the nature of the Roberts court might have been entirely different.

By the end of her almost quarter-century on the court, Justice O'Connor was without question the justice who controlled the result in ideologically divided cases.

"On virtually all conceptual and empirical definitions, O'Connor is the court's center—the median, the key, the critical and the swing justice," Andrew D. Martin and two colleagues wrote in a study published in 2005 in The North Carolina Law Review shortly before Justice O'Connor's retirement.

With Justice Alito joining the court's more conservative wing, Justice Kennedy has now unambiguously taken on the role of the justice at the center of the court, and the ideological daylight between him and Justice O'Connor is a measure of the Roberts court's shift to the right.

Justice O'Connor, for her part, does not name names but has expressed misgivings about the direction of the court.

"If you think you've been helpful, and then it's dismantled, you think, 'Oh, dear,'" she said at William & Mary Law School in October in her usual crisp and no-nonsense fashion. "But life goes on. It's not always positive."

Justice O'Connor was one of the authors of McConnell v. Federal Election Commission, a 2003 decision that, among other things, upheld restrictions on campaign spending by businesses and unions. It was reversed on that point in the Citizens United decision.

Asked at the law school forum in January how she felt about the later decision, she responded obliquely. But there was no mistaking her meaning.

"If you want my legal opinion" about Citizens United, Justice O'Connor said, "you can go read" McConnell.

The Court without O'Connor

The shift resulting from Justice O'Connor's departure was more than ideological. She brought with her qualities that are no longer represented on the court. She was raised and educated in the West, and she served in all three branches of Arizona's government, including as a government lawyer, majority leader of the State Senate, an elected trial judge and, an appeals court judge.

Those experiences informed Justice O'Connor's sensitivity to states' rights and her frequent deference to political judgments. Her rulings were often pragmatic and narrow, and her critics said she engaged in split-the-difference jurisprudence.

Justice Alito's background is more limited than Justice O'Connor's—he worked in the Justice Department and then as a federal appeals court judge—and his rulings are often more muscular.

Since they never sat on the court together, trying to say how Justice O'Connor would have voted in the cases heard by Justice Alito generally involves extrapolation and speculation. In some, though, it seems plain that she would have voted differently from him.

Just weeks before she left the court, for instance, Justice O'Connor heard arguments in Hudson v. Michigan, a case about whether evidence should be suppressed because it was found after Detroit police officers stormed a home without announcing themselves.

"Is there no policy protecting the homeowner a little bit and the sanctity of the home from this immediate entry?" Justice O'Connor asked a government lawyer. David A. Moran, a lawyer for the defendant, Booker T. Hudson, said the questioning left him confident that he had Justice O'Connor's crucial vote.

Three months later, the court called for reargument, signaling a 4-to-4 deadlock after Justice O'Connor's departure. When the 5-to-4 decision was announced in June, the court not only ruled that violations of the knock-and-announce rule do not require the suppression of evidence, but also called into question the exclusionary rule itself.

The shift had taken place. Justice Alito was in the majority.

"My 5-4 loss in Hudson v. Michigan," Mr. Moran wrote in 2006 in Cato Supreme Court Review, "signals the end of the Fourth Amendment"—protecting against unreasonable searches—"as we know it."

The departure of Justice O'Connor very likely affected the outcomes in two other contentious areas: abortion and race.

In 2000, the court struck down a Nebraska law banning an abortion procedure by a vote of 5 to 4, with Justice O'Connor in the majority. Seven years later, the court upheld a similar federal law, the Partial-Birth Abortion Act, by the same vote.

"The key to the case was not in the difference in wording between the federal law and the Nebraska act," Erwin Chemerinsky wrote in 2007 in The Green Bag, a law journal. "It was Justice Alito having replaced Justice O'Connor."

In 2003, Justice O'Connor wrote the majority opinion in a 5-to-4 decision allowing public universities to take account of race in admissions decisions. And a month before her retirement in 2006, the court refused to hear a case challenging the use of race to achieve integration in public schools.

Almost as soon as she left, the court reversed course. A 2007 decision limited the use of race for such a purpose, also on a 5-to-4 vote.

There were, to be sure, issues on which Justice Kennedy was to the left of Justice O'Connor. In a 5-to-4 decision in 2005 overturning the juvenile death penalty, Justice Kennedy was in the majority and Justice O'Connor was not.

But changing swing justices in 2006 had an unmistakable effect across a broad range of cases. "O'Connor at the end was quite a bit more liberal than Kennedy is now," Professor Epstein said.

The numbers bear this out.

The Rehnquist court had trended left in its later years, issuing conservative rulings less than half the time in its last two years in divided cases, a phenomenon not seen since 1981. The first term of the Roberts court was a sharp jolt to the right. It issued conservative rulings in 71 percent of divided cases, the highest rate in any year since the beginning of the Warren court in 1953.

Judging by the Numbers

Chief Justice Roberts has not served nearly as long as his three most recent predecessors. The court he leads has been in flux. But five years of data are now available, and they point almost uniformly in one direction: to the right.

Scholars quarrel about some of the methodological choices made by political scientists who assign a conservative or liberal label to Supreme Court decisions and the votes of individual justices. But most of those arguments are at the margins, and the measures are generally accepted in the political science literature.

The leading database, created by Harold J. Spaeth with the support of the National Science Foundation about 20 years ago, has served as the basis for a great deal of empirical research on the contemporary Supreme Court and its members. In the database, votes favoring criminal defendants, unions, people claiming discrimination or violation of their civil rights are, for instance, said to be liberal. Decisions striking down economic regulations and favoring prosecutors, employers, and the government are said to be conservative.

About 1 percent of cases have no ideological valence, as in a boundary dispute between two states. And some concern multiple issues or contain ideological cross-currents.

But while it is easy to identify the occasional case for which ideological coding makes no sense, the vast majority fit pretty well. They also tend to align with the votes of the justices usually said to be liberal or conservative.

Still, such coding is a blunt instrument. It does not take account of the precedential and other constraints that are in play or how much a decision moves the law in a conservative or liberal direction. The mix of cases has changed over time. And the database treats every decision, monumental or trivial, as a single unit.

"It's crazy to count each case as one," said Frank B. Cross, a law and business professor at the University of Texas. "But the problem of counting each case as one is reduced by the fact that the less-important ones tend to be unanimous."

Some judges find the entire enterprise offensive.

"Supreme Court justices do not acknowledge that any of their decisions are influenced by ideology rather than by neutral legal analysis," William M. Landes, an economist at the University of Chicago, and Richard A. Posner, a federal appeals court judge, wrote last year in The Journal of Legal Analysis. But if that were true, they continued, knowing the political party of the president who appointed a given justice would tell you nothing about how the justice was likely to vote in ideologically charged cases.

In fact, the correlation between the political party of appointing presidents and the ideological direction of the rulings of the judges they appoint is quite strong.

Here, too, there are exceptions. Justices Stevens and Souter were appointed by Republican presidents and ended up voting with the court's liberal wing. But they are gone. If Ms. Kagan wins Senate confirmation, all of the justices on the court may be expected to align themselves across the ideological spectrum in sync with the party of the president who appointed them.

The proposition that the Roberts court is to the right of even the quite conservative courts that preceded it thus seems fairly well established. But it is subject to qualifications.

First, the rightward shift is modest.

Second, the data do not take popular attitudes into account. While the court is quite conservative by historical standards, it is less so by contemporary ones. Public opinion polls suggest that about 30 percent of Americans think the current court is too liberal, and almost half think it is about right.

On given legal issues, too, the court's decisions are often closely aligned with or more liberal than public opinion, according to studies collected in 2008 in "Public Opinion and Constitutional Controversy" (Oxford University Press).

The public is largely in sync with the court, for instance, in its attitude toward abortion—in favor of a right to abortion but sympathetic to many restrictions on that right.

"Solid majorities want the court to uphold Roe v. Wade and are in favor of abortion rights in the abstract," one of the studies concluded. "However, equally substantial majorities favor procedural and other restrictions, including waiting periods, parental consent, spousal notification, and bans on 'partial birth' abortion."

Similarly, the public is roughly aligned with the court in questioning affirmative action plans that use numerical standards or preferences while approving those that allow race to be considered in less definitive ways.

The Roberts court has not yet decided a major religion case, but the public has not always approved of earlier rulings in this area. For instance, another study in the 2008 book found that "public opinion has remained solidly against the court's landmark decisions declaring school prayer unconstitutional."

In some ways, the Roberts court is more cautious than earlier ones. The Rehnquist court struck down about 120 laws, or about six a year, according to an analysis by Professor Epstein. The Roberts court, which on average hears fewer cases than the Rehnquist court did, has struck down fewer laws—15 in its first five years, or three a year.

It is the ideological direction of the decisions that has changed. When the Rehnquist court struck down laws, it reached a liberal result more than 70 percent of the time. The Roberts court has tilted strongly in the opposite direction, reaching a conservative result 60 percent of the time.

The Rehnquist court overruled 45 precedents over 19 years. Sixty percent of those decisions reached a conservative result. The Roberts court overruled eight precedents in its first five years, a slightly lower annual rate. All but one reached a conservative result.

Critical Thinking

1. In what ways did the appointment of Justice Samuel Alito have a significant impact on the composition of the Supreme Court?

2. How do the Roberts court's decisions striking down laws or reversing precedent differ from those of previous courts?

3. Describe the roles of Justice O'Connor and Justice Kennedy as the court's "swing votes." What key differences have O'Connor and Kennedy displayed while on the Court?

4. How well does the political party of a president nominating a Supreme Court justice predict the ideological nature of the justice's decisions while seated on the court?

5. According to the author, the Roberts court continues along its current ideological trajectory, what types of decisions and outcomes are likely in the future?

Justices Venture into Court of Public Opinion

Defenders say a greater media presence promotes education, but critics question the effect on integrity.

Seth Stern

In a term with few blockbuster cases on the docket, Supreme Court justices seem to be making more news for what they're saying off the bench than what they're doing inside the courtroom.

Justice Stephen G. Breyer hopped from the "Larry King Live" show to "Good Morning America" last fall, promoting his latest book. Justice Antonin Scalia, the court's senior associate justice and conservative stalwart, participated in a closed-door talk on Capitol Hill last week organized by the tea party caucus.

Scalia and Breyer are the highest-profile, but hardly the only examples lately of justices emerging with something of a bang from the usually cloistered world of the court by way of speeches, interviews or memoirs. Their motives vary: Some are trying to burnish the court's image and explain its work; others are proselytizing for their vision of constitutional interpretation; and a few may be trying to sell their books.

But as their media profiles rise and some appear before partisan audiences, the question is whether they risk tarnishing the court's carefully cultivated nonpartisan image and turning themselves into just another species of celebrity.

"Do they want that? What does that mean in terms of their ability to project themselves as neutral arbiters?" asks Richard Davis, a Brigham Young University professor and author of a new book, "Justices and Journalists." "This is a new world for them, and they're going to have to decide what's most important to them."

How they resolve that question is likely to have major consequences for the court's legitimacy. "The Supreme Court is the guardian of its own integrity," the Boston Globe scolded in a Jan. 27 editorial. "That means staying above politics and maintaining an air of dispassionate consideration of constitutional issues."

To be sure, the justices have never been entirely detached from politics, and how much they engage the public has fluctuated over time, says Steven Lubet, a Northwestern University law professor.

In the 19th century, several justices campaigned for president, and Charles Evan Hughes resigned from the court in 1916 after becoming the Republican nominee. "Then, starting in the 1950s, we had a long period when justices were much more reticent, and we tend to think of that as normal because it lasted a long time," Lubet says.

Justice William O. Douglas stood out even by the standards of that time by writing several books and complaining in a 1958 television interview about the impact of McCarthyism on freedom of expression. But it was still something of a novelty when Harry Blackmun agreed to appear on a new cable news channel called CNN in 1982, and William J. Brennan Jr. sat for interviews with almost every media outlet that asked around the time of his 80th birthday in 1986.

In the last five years, though, such bookings have become more frequent. Breyer's November appearance on CNN's "Larry King Live" show was a return engagement. Three justices sat for interviews with "60 Minutes" in recent years—including Clarence Thomas, who also appeared on talk radio shows hosted by Rush Limbaugh and Laura Ingraham during a media blitz promoting his 2007 memoir. In a break with the tradition of new justices maintaining a particularly low profile, Sonia Sotomayor signed a contract for a book about her early life last July, less than a year after joining the court.

Penning memoirs and doing interviews can humanize the justices and reinforce respect for the court if the justices come off as erudite and use such opportunities to offer insight into the institution, legal experts say.

But they also risk eroding the aura that surrounds the court as a somewhat mysterious institution apart, says Barbara Perry, author of "The Priestly Tribe: The Supreme Court's Image in the American Mind"

"Do you really want to go on 'Larry King Live' just after Lady Gaga has been there? Do you want to be that popular, or do you want to stay on NPR and Jim Lehrer?" she asks.

Partisan Crowds

Of greater concern, legal experts say, are signs that some justices are branching out from their traditional audiences of judges, lawyers, students and civic groups to more partisan crowds. Liberal groups have criticized Samuel A. Alito Jr., for instance, for speaking at fundraisers for the American Spectator, a conservative political magazine, and the Intercollegiate Studies Institute, a conservative educational organization.

This month, Common Cause called on the Justice Department to examine whether Thomas and Scalia should have recused themselves from a Supreme Court case because they attended a private retreat of conservative businessmen and political activists organized by two billionaire industrialist brothers, Charles and David Koch.

Common Cause argued that the Koch brothers stood to benefit from the court's decision last year rolling back limits on corporate campaign contributions. Thomas and Scalia said in a statement that they had each spoken at dinners at the Koch retreat and that their expenses were paid by the Federalist Society, a conservative legal group.

Thomas has also faced questions about his wife's involvement in a conservative political group, Liberty Central, that she helped found in 2009 and that opposes the health care overhaul law—challenges to which are virtually certain to come before the court.

Common Cause also took issue with Scalia's decision to accept an invitation from Minnesota Republican Rep. Michele Bachmann to speak to lawmakers last week. The talk, which was also attended by a handful of Democrats, proved to be no different than similar appearances he has given to other groups of lawmakers in the past without causing controversy.

In many ways, Scalia has become the archetype for the modern celebrity justice, who is as comfortable speaking in public as he is at oral arguments, where he has emerged as one of the most talkative and combative justices on the bench since joining the court in the fall of 1986.

"Antonin Scalia is in some ways the justice of the future, in that he figured out fairly early on it was not worth his time and effort to write opinions only for his colleagues," says Sanford V. Levinson, a law professor at the University of Texas at Austin. "He realized that the job of a modern justice is, in essence, to try to create or support mass movements that share your constitutional vision, and I think that's what Scalia has been doing for 20 years."

Scalia, who once made it a practice to bar reporters from public appearances, acknowledges that he has made a concerted effort in recent years to engage the public via the media.

"I've sort of come to the conclusion that the old common-law tradition of judges not making public spectacles of themselves and hiding in the grass has just broken down," Scalia said in a C-SPAN interview in 2008. "So if I am going to be a public figure, I guess the public may as well get their notion of me firsthand than filtered."

Breyer has sought to be a liberal counter-weight to Scalia, albeit one who is a far less colorful speaker and commanding public presence. His two books offer an alternative to Scalia's vision of originalism as the proper way to interpret the Constitution. Breyer and Scalia have often done events together, including an appearance last November at Texas Tech University attended by 4,500 people.

The more voluble Scalia has occasionally gotten into trouble by commenting on issues pending before the court. He recused himself from a 2004 case dealing with the Pledge of Allegiance after suggesting in a speech that a lower court's decision was wrongly decided.

Legal experts say justices who appear before partisan crowds and speak about their own views risk undermining the court's legitimacy. "The beauty of the institution has been their ability to say, 'We're above that, we're not susceptible, we don't have lobbyists coming into the Supreme Court building. . . .'" Davis says. "But it becomes more difficult for people . . . to buy the argument that they are really disinterested if you hear them in various settings talking about their personal views."

Where to Draw the Line?

Justices have very little formal guidance in deciding the boundaries of where to speak and what to say publicly. The federal judicial code of conduct, which bars lower federal judges from engaging in political activity, isn't binding on justices. The federal law on conflicts of interest has no enforcement provision.

"As a result, justices are left to judge their own acts of misconduct," says Jonathan Turley, a George Washington University law professor.

Turley says justices should generally "allow their opinions to speak for them," avoid writing books and limit themselves to speaking at judicial conferences and commencements about the legal profession in broad terms.

"I don't see why this is asking so much of justices," Turley says. "I would think these justices would be incredibly honored by their selection to a nine-member court. The price is that you do live a somewhat cloistered life. It doesn't mean that you're cut off from the public. You can still speak, but you do not engage in this type of commentary and debate."

Others, however, question whether such a monastic approach is realistic. "We live in an era of much greater transparency now," says Deborah L. Rhode, a Stanford Law School professor. "There's more of an expectation—part of that is a function of technology and the 24/7 news cycle and the kind of pressure to gain more public insights into the workings of the court."

Ironically, the one place where justices seem to feel little urgency to adapt is their own courtroom. The court continues to bar cameras from televising their proceedings, even after the retirement of David Souter, the justice who most vehemently opposed the idea, and the arrival of four baby boomer justices, all of whom seemed open to the idea at their confirmation hearings.

Critical Thinking

1. What sorts of activities by current Supreme Court justices have made them more visible to the public than their recent predecessors seemed to be?

2. Why is Justice Antonin Scalia said to be the "archetype for the modern celebrity justice" and how does Professor Sanford V. Levinson explain Scalia's public activities in the context of his role as a modern justice?

3. What is the risk, according to some observers, to the Supreme Court's legitimacy that stems from the greater public visibility of current justices?

Marking Time
Why Government Is Too Slow

BRUCE BERKOWITZ

In recent years we have been witness to a portentous competition between two determined but dissimilar rivals on the international scene. In one corner we have al-Qaeda, founded in the early 1990s, the transnational Islamic terrorist organization led by Osama bin Laden. In the other corner, we have the government of the United States of America, established in 1787, at present the most powerful state on the planet. The key question defining this competition is this: Who has the more agile organization? Al-Qaeda, in planning and executing a terrorist attack, or the United States, in planning, developing and executing the measures to stop one?

Let's look at the record. Sometime during the spring of 1999, Khalid Sheikh Mohamed visited bin Laden in Afghanistan and asked if al-Qaeda would fund what came to be called the "planes operation"—the plan for suicide attacks using commercial airliners. (Mohamed had been mulling the plot since at least 1993, when he discussed it with his nephew, Ramzi Yousef, one of the terrorists behind the first World Trade Center bombing and the attempted Philippine-based effort to bring down a dozen U.S. airliners over the Pacific in 1995.) Bin Laden agreed, and by the summer of 1999 he had selected as team leaders four al-Qaeda members—Khalid al-Mihdhar, Nawafal-Hazmi, Tawfiq bin Attash (also known as "Khallad") and Abu Bara al-Yemen.

These four team leaders entered the United States in early 2000 and started taking flying lessons that summer. The so-called "muscle" hijackers, the 15 terrorists tasked with overpowering the crews on the targeted flights, began arriving in April 2001 and spent the summer preparing for the September 11 attack. So from the point in time that a government contracting official would call "authority to proceed" to completion, the operation took approximately 27 months.

Now let's track the U.S. response. U.S. officials began debating options for preventing future terrorist attacks immediately following the September 11 strike. Congress took a year to debate the statute establishing the Department of Homeland Security. George W. Bush, who originally opposed creating a new department, changed his mind and signed the bill into law on November 25, 2002. A joint House-Senate committee finished the first investigation of intelligence leading up to the attack in December 2002. The 9/11 Commission issued its report on July 22, 2004, recommending among other things the establishment of a Director of National Intelligence and a new National Counterterrorism Center. President Bush established the NCTC by Executive Order on August 27, 2004.

Adoption of the Intelligence Reform and Terrorism Prevention Act, which embodied most of the Commission's other proposals, took another three months. The measures it authorized—including the creation of a Director of National Intelligence—lay fallow until a second commission, investigating intelligence prior to the war in Iraq, issued its own report four months later. The new Director was sworn in on April 21, 2005. Total response time, charitably defined: about 44 months, and implementation continues today.

Obviously, planning an attack and adjusting defenses to prevent a subsequent attack are not comparable tasks. Still, it is hard to avoid concluding that organizations like al-Qaeda are inherently nimbler than governments, especially large and highly bureaucratized governments like ours. As things stand now, terrorists can size up a situation, make decisions and act faster than we can. In military terms, they are "inside our decision cycle."

Recall July 7, 2005, for example, when terrorists bombed three London Underground trains and a double-decker city bus, killing 52 commuters. The four bombs exploded within a minute of each other, an operationally and technically challenging feat that is a hallmark of al-Qaeda attacks. A "martyrdom video" proclaiming allegiance to al-Qaeda and taped months earlier by one of the bombers, Muhammad Sidique Khan, soon surfaced on al-Jazeera. Khan apparently made the video during a visit to Pakistan, and investigators concluded that an earlier trip to Pakistan in July 2003 also had something to do with the attack. If so, then the planning of the London attack required two years, possibly less.

Organizations like al-Qaeda are inherently nimbler than governments, especially large ones like ours.

Again, it may seem unfair to compare a government bureaucracy, American or British, with a network of loosely organized, small terrorist cells. But unfairness is the point: Terrorists will *always* make the conflict between us as "unfair" as possible, avoiding our strengths and exploiting our vulnerabilities however they can. So will insurgency leaders and rogue dictators, who also happen to be surreptitious WMD proliferators; narco-traffickers and money launderers, who aid terrorists either wittingly or inadvertently. The U.S. government and similarly arrayed allies will simply lose battle after battle if our adversaries absorb information, make decisions, change tactics and act faster than we can.

Reading the 9/11 Commission Report one cannot help but be struck by how often simple delay and chronic slowness led to disaster on September 11. President Clinton told the Commission that he had asked for military options to get rid of bin Laden in late 1999. But General Hugh Shelton, Chairman of the Joint Chiefs of Staff, was reluctant to provide them. Secretary of Defense William Cohen thought the President was speaking only hypothetically. The one person who could have given a direct order to cut through the resistance and ambiguity, President Clinton himself, did not do so. He thought that raising his temper wouldn't accomplish anything, so he allowed himself to be slow-rolled, and the issue went essentially unaddressed.

The problem wasn't just at the top, however. Down below in the bureaucracy, things were just as bad—case in point, the Predator. The now-famous robotic aircraft was originally built for battlefield reconnaissance and was later modified to carry missiles. The U.S. Air Force had flown Predators in the Balkans since 1996, but Afghanistan was trickier. The aircraft had a limited range and thus needed a remote base and data uplinks to get the information back to Washington. It took until July 2000 to work our these details, and two more months to deploy the Predator over Afghanistan.

Predator operators thought they spotted bin Laden in September 2000, but U.S. officials disagreed over rules of engagement. National Security Advisor Samuel Berger wanted greater confidence in bin Laden's location before approving a strike, and he worried about civilian casualties. At the same time, Air Force leaders were reluctant to carry out what looked to them, not unreasonably, like a covert operation, and the CIA was reluctant to undertake a direct combat operation—or to violate the Executive Order prohibiting assassination.

These disagreements dragged into 2001 as the Bush Administration took office. Then President Bush put everything on hold while National Security Advisor Condoleezza Rice directed a comprehensive plan to eliminate al-Qaeda. George Tenet, the Director of Central Intelligence, deferred the legal over whether the CIA could take part in an attack until the Administration had prepared its new strategy. So it went, until the clock ran out and the terrorists killed nearly 3,000 people.

Or take the inability of the Immigration and Naturalization Service (INS), as it existed on September 11, 2001, to track the whereabouts of known terror suspects and to report relevant information about their attempts to enter the country to other Federal agencies. The INS failed to meet its homeland security responsibilities partly because Congress systematically underfunded it. But even worse, the INS had failed to disentangle its different functions; keeping some people out of the country while letting others in. Meanwhile, everyone—the White House, Congress, the bureaucracy—failed to agree on a solution that both dealt with illegal immigration while also allowing entry to laborers essential to the American economy. The security problem flowing from this failure is obvious: As long as underfunded bureaucrats are unable to regulate the enormous flow of illegal immigrants seeking work, they will never be able to detect and track the few truly dangerous people trying to enter the country.

Of course, the story of the run-up to 9/11 is an oft-told one. Yet almost everyone seems to miss the core problem from which all others followed: There was always time for another meeting, another study, another round of coordination. Virtually no one was worrying about the clock—about whether *time itself mattered.* It's not that every concern raised didn't have some legitimate rationale (at least within the legal-bureaucratic culture that characterizes the U.S. government). It's the fact that, while we were working out legal issues, al-Qaeda was developing and executing its plan.

This same problem surfaced again a year later. Just about everyone agrees now that the United States was unprepared for the insurgency in Iraq, but most overlook that someone else was also unprepared: the insurgents. U.S. analysts who interviewed captured Iraqi officials and military officers for the Defense Department have concluded that Iraqi leaders had not prepared a "stay-behind" or "rope-a-dope" strategy. They had never planned to forfeit the conventional war in order to win a guerrilla war later on. Iraqi military leaders believed they would lose the war and just wanted to get it over with quickly. Saddam Hussein's security services and core Ba'ath Party operatives kept the lid on the various sects, tribes and ethnic groups so that they could not plan a guerrilla war either. The result was that *no one* was prepared for an insurgency. The United States, its coalition partners, Ba'athis who had escaped capture, tribal leaders, religious authorities, foreign fighters—everyone was starting from scratch. So when Saddam's statue came down in Firdos Square on April 9, 2003, the question that mattered most was who could organize and execute faster, the would-be insurgents or the U.S. government?

Alas, we were left in the starting blocks. The insurgents organized much faster than U.S. officials could recognize and respond. We were playing catch-up from the beginning, which is another way of saying we were losing.

Things would perhaps not be so bad if the war on al-Qaeda and the war in Iraq were exceptional. In truth, the problem is pervasive and getting worse. "Organizational agility" sounds abstract, but it really boils down to specific questions: How long does it take to deliver a critical weapon or information system? How fast can an agency bring new people on board? How fast can it change its mix of people if it needs to? In short, *how fast can government agencies act—and is this fast enough to stay ahead of the competition?*

The U.S. government is not always woefully slow. The response to the December 2004 Southeast Asian tsunami, for example, was admirably quick and reasonably effective under the circumstances. So was the relief mission that the United States effectively led following the massive earthquake that rocked northern Pakistan in October 2005. However, these few exceptions aside, the U.S. government has become an increasingly ponderous beast, unable to act quickly or even to understand how its various parts fit together to act at all.

Once, When We Were Fast

It was not always so. After the surprise attack at Pearl Harbor, one of the most heavily damaged ships was the battleship USS *West Virginia.* Most of its port side had been blown away. The ship sank rapidly, but on an even keel on the bottom of the harbor. The Navy needed every 16-inch gun it could muster, so Navy leaders decided to repair the ship. It was not easy, but the USS *West Virginia* steamed into Puget Sound in April 1943 to be refitted and modernized. It rejoined the fleet in June 1944, thirty months after it was sunk, took part in several operations and was present for the surrender ceremonies in Tokyo Bay in September 1945. By comparison, after al-Qaeda agents in Yemen damaged the USS *Cole* far less severely with a single improvised bomb in October 2000, it took 16 months to retrieve the still-floating destroyer and complete repairs in Pascagoula, Mississippi. The ship did not then leave its home port in Norfolk, Virginia, for its first deployment until November 2003—37 months later.

World War II offers many examples like the recovery of the *West Virginia* in which organizations worked with remarkable alacrity. Take the effort to build the first atomic bomb. Albert Einstein wrote to Franklin D. Roosevelt on August 2, 1939, alerting him to the possibilities of nuclear weapons. He met with FDR about a month later, which led Roosevelt to establish the Uranium Committee to research military applications of nuclear fission. Vannevar Bush, Roosevelt's science adviser, persuaded the President to accelerate the project in October 1941, as war with Germany and Japan seemed likely. On September 14, 1942, Brigadier General Leslie Groves was appointed director of the new Manhattan Project, marking the formal start of the project to build the atomic bomb. The Trinity test, the world's first nuclear explosion, took place on July 16, 1945, and Hiroshima was bombed on August 6, less than a month later. The entire effort, costing $21 billion in today's dollars, developed three different means of producing fissile material, two bomb designs and three devices.

Or consider the Office of Strategic Services, the predecessor of today's CIA. President Roosevelt appointed William Donovan as his "Coordinator of Information" in July 1941, and the OSS was itself established in June 1942. Harry Truman disbanded it in September 1945. In other words, the entire history of the OSS—what many consider the Golden Age of American intelligence—spanned just 37 months. In that short time it recruited, trained and deployed a workforce of about 13,000 people. William Casey, directing OSS espionage in Europe, stood up his entire network in about 18 months. By comparison, after 9/11 Tenet said on

several occasions that it would require five years to rebuild the CIA's clandestine service.

Or recall the war in the Pacific. The Battle of the Coral Sea was fought in May 1942, the Battle of Midway a month later. Within six months of Pearl Harbor, the U.S. Navy had destroyed five Japanese carriers, along with most of Japan's naval aircraft and aviators. It has taken us longer just to get organized for the so-called War on Terror (to the extent that we *are* organized for it) than it did to fight and win World War II.

Delivering the Product

Everything else today is moving faster, thanks to jet airliners, interstate highways, the computer and the Internet. But government, including the parts responsible for national security, is moving slower, and it's getting worse.

Everyone knows, for example, that weapons have been getting more expensive per unit, but few realize that it now also takes much longer to get a weapon into the hands of the warfighter. In the early 1940s, it took 25 months to get a new fighter like the P-47 Thunderbolt into action from the time the government signed a contract for a prototype. In the late 1940s, this delay had grown to about 43 months for an early jet fighter like the F-86 Sabre. By the 1960s, the F-4 Phantom required 66 months, and its 1970s replacement, the F-15 Eagle, 82 months. The latest fighter to enter service, the F-22 Raptor, traces its development to a prototype built under a contract signed in October 1986. The prototype first flew in September 1990, and the production model entered service in December 2005—a total of 230 months, or about 19 years. Put another way, that comes to slightly longer than the typical career of an officer in the U.S. Air Force. (The new F-35 Lighting II, which will replace the F-16, is slated to require "just" 15 years from signing the contract for the prototype to when it enters service. We'll see.)

One might think the problem with jet aircraft is a result of the growing technical complexity of modern fighter aircraft, but that argument does not hold up. No rule says that the more complex a technology is, the longer it takes to deliver. Government aircraft of *all* kinds take longer to develop, and longer than their commercial counterparts. Compare a military transport, like the C-17 Globemaster III with the new Boeing 787 Dreamliner. The C-17 required 12 years to enter service, while the 787—more complex than the C-17 in many respects—will take just four. And the 787, for example, will require a little *less* time to develop than its predecessor from the early 1990s, the 777.[1]

The problem holds for most weapons other than airplanes, too—ships, tanks, electronic systems and so on. Threats are changing much faster than we can develop the means to counter them. This is why some officials occasionally say we have to anticipate requirements further into the future. But that's simply unrealistic. When you try to forecast two decades ahead because your weapon takes twenty years to develop, it isn't analysis: it's fortune telling.

The ever-slowing pace of government appears in other ways, as well. Simply getting a presidential administration into place is a stellar example. According a 2005 National Academy of Sciences study, every Administration since Kennedy's has taken longer than its predecessor to fill the top 500 jobs in government. In the 1960s it took just under three months; today it is three times as long. A new administration isn't up and running until almost a year after the election that put it in office. How can a team possibly win the Big Game if half the players don't show up until the end of the first quarter?

That is more or less what happened in 2001 as al-Qaeda was preparing 9/11. The Bush Administration's Cabinet Secretaries were confirmed and ready to go when the new President was sworn in on January 20, 2001, but that was about it. The Administration didn't nominate Paul Wolfowitz to be Deputy Secretary of Defense until February 5, and he had to wait until March 2 to be confirmed and sworn in. Wolfowitz's wait was comparatively short; most positions took longer to fill. Richard Armitage, nominated for Deputy Secretary of State, waited until March 23, 2001. Six months passed before the top Defense Department leadership was in place. Douglas Feith, the Under Secretary of Defense for Policy—as in "policy for combating terrorists"—was *last* to be sworn in, in July 2001.

What is so depressing about the National Academy of Science study is that the problem just keeps getting worse. If top officials have to wait two or three months at the beginning of an administration, candidates for positions at the assistant secretary level in the middle of a term can often wait six months or more. Further down the food chain, bringing on new staff is paced largely by how long it takes to obtain a security clearance. For civil servants, this can take almost a year, for government contractors, the average is about 450 days.

Why?

What explains this bureaucratic torpor? In part, government is slowing down because more people insist on getting involved. Ever more congressional committees, lobbyists and oversight organizations vie to get their prerogatives enacted in a law, regulation or procedure. As the participants multiply, workloads expand and everything slows down.

At another level, it's because there is more obligatory paperwork to handle—financial disclosure in the case of officials, cost justification in the case of contracts, quality assurance documentation in the case of hardware. At yet another level, it's because all organizations have standard procedures that never seem to get shorter or more flexible; quite the reverse. New procedures are almost always cumulative, accreting in ever thicker layers of bureaucratic hoariness. Indeed, we may be seeing a classic case of "organizational aging," a phenomenon perhaps first defined by economist Anthony Downs back in 1967.

In his classic book, *Inside Bureaucracy,* Downs observed that when organizations are first established, they have few rules, written or unwritten, and because new organizations tend to be small, they have a flat, short chain of command with little hierarchy. As time goes by, alas, organizations add personnel. Since managers can oversee only a limited number of people, they develop a reporting hierarchy, which adds to the time and difficulty of making a decision. More members are in a position to say "no," and the joint probability of "yes" diminishes. This translates into the well-known bureaucratic adage, "Where

there's a will, there's a won't." The fact that people expect promotion to positions with greater responsibility (and pay) also encourages the establishment of more management slots with the selective power to say "no," or just to kibbitz. Either way, the process takes more time.

Also, as organizations mature, they develop dogma—sometimes written, sometimes simply part of the organization's culture. This, of course, is exactly what bureaucracies are supposed to do: simplify decisions and improve efficiency by adopting rules. This is fine, until the rules become cumbersome or no longer appropriate to the situation—which is exactly what is happening today.

But the most insidious problem of all is that as organizations mature their character changes. New organizations with few rules offer lots of challenge and risk, so they tend to attract risk-takers who want to make their own rules. Mature organizations with well-defined rules and missions, on the other hand, attract the "Organization Man"—the sort who wants to plug himself in and carry out tasks as set forth in an official, approved job description.

This is why it is somewhere between ironic and pointless to hear critics complain that this or that long-established government organization needs to become less risk-averse and more innovative. Inevitably, they are speaking to people who, by self-selection, are where they are *precisely because they are risk-averse.* They *like* the way things are; they would not otherwise have joined the organization and stayed with it. Organization Men are no less patriotic, dedicated or capable than risk-takers; they're just temperamentally opposite.

If we are serious about gaining agility, we will clearly have to break some china. Improving agility means more than just rearranging boxes on an organization chart, though that is mostly what we have tried to do. There have been countless studies on how to streamline contracting, speed up background investigations, shorten the process of nominating and confirming appointees, and so on. None of these recommendations will ever amount to anything unless we find a way to produce a new mix of people who can develop new ways of doing things, and attract the kinds of recruits who thrive on doing just that.

It's easy to get lost in the day-to-day specifics of why it takes so long to get anything done in the American national security community today. It is far more important to recognize that the underlying theme connecting all the sources of our sloth is that we are trying to balance risk with speed, and there is rarely a champion for speed. The risks that concern people take many forms—that some group will be underrepresented in a decision, that a design or work task will be flawed, that a secret will be compromised, that someone will cheat the government, that an official will have a conflict of interest. Whatever the specifics, we lose agility every time we manage risk by adding a step to reduce the probability of something bad happening. Rarely does anyone with responsibility, opportunity or power say that we should accept more risks so that we can act faster.

It is easy to argue for doing something to avoid some hypothetical bad thing happening. It is much harder to argue that one can take so many precautions against some kinds of risk that other kinds of risk actually increase due to an organization's diminished capacity to act in a timely fashion. The real question is, or ought to be, how much speed do we want to sacrifice in order to reduce certain kinds of risk? There is no single, objective answer to such a question, but without advocates and mechanisms for greater speed, we will be protected against risk so well that arguably our most dangerous adversaries will beat us every time.

Examples of Speed and Success

Lest we be *too* pessimistic, there are cases—including a few fairly recent ones—in which government organizations moved out smartly on national security missions. These cases show us what we need to do if we want organizations to move fast. Consider, for example:

- *The U-2 aircraft:* In the 1950s, the United States needed a higher-flying airplane to take pictures of Soviet military facilities. The CIA gave Lockheed authority to proceed in December 1954; the aircraft flew its first reconnaissance mission over the Soviet Union in July 1956. Total time required: 18 months.
- *The Explorer 1 satellite:* Desperate to match the Soviet Sputnik I launched in October 1957, the Defense Department authorized the Army Ballistic Missile Agency to prepare a satellite for launch on November 8, 1957. Werner von Braun's team launched it three months later, on January 31, 1958.
- *The GBU-28:* At the start of Operation Desert Storm in 1991, the Air Force discovered it did not have a bomb that could penetrate Iraq's deepest underground shelters. To pack enough kinetic energy, the bomb had to be long, streamlined and heavy. The Air Force Research Laboratory took surplus gun barrels from eight-inch howitzers as a casing, filled them with explosive, bolted an existing laser guidance system to the front end, and—after assigning it an official Air Force designation—delivered a bomb in 27 days.
- *JAWBREAKER:* President Bush asked for options to respond to the September 11 attacks. The CIA presented its plan two days later to use Northern Alliance forces as a surrogate army. CIA units, called "JAWBREAKER," arrived in weeks, and Kabul was taken on November 14, 2001.

These programs are all related to national security, but they are as different from one another as one can imagine. One is an aircraft development program, one a space research mission, one a weapon system and one a covert paramilitary operation. The Army, Air Force and CIA are all represented. Two were in wartime, two in peacetime. Yet they share some common features, the most important of which seems to be that someone was willing to bend rules and take responsibility for getting things done. This is a logical—even a *necessary*—condition for speed.

Every organization has a "natural" maximum speed defined by its standard procedures, which are designed to reduce risk. Some are formal, others implicit. Together they establish the organization's operations—who has to confer with whom, who can approve, what materials have to be prepared and so on. Organizations usually operate well below this optimum speed, but in principle one could analyze any organization and then assess whether it can act faster than its competitors. It is hard to measure maximum speed precisely, but it is easy to identify most of the "hard points" that constitute it, like the one official or office lying in the critical path of workflow. Conversely, when government organizations have moved faster than their normal maximum speeds, it's almost always because someone either bent the rules or managed to evade them. Consider the cases cited above.

In developing the U-2, the CIA avoided the constraining pace of the annual Federal budget cycle by using its special authority to spend money without a specific appropriation—the first time the CIA had used that authority to develop a major system like an aircraft. The CIA also wasn't bound to Defense Department regulations, so rather than use the arduous military acquisition and contractor selection process, the CIA simply chose Lockheed.

Lockheed's famous "Skunk Works," in turn, shortened or eliminated many steps a military contractor would usually take. For example, by having all its people working in one location, an engineer could ask metal workers to adjust the design on the spot with a conversation rather than a meeting, and follow up with documentation later. This would violate normal Defense Department acquisition regulations.

The Army also broke rules in building the Explorer 1 satellite—specifically, the rule saying that the Army wasn't supposed to build satellites. The Defense Department and White House had given the Navy that mission. Major General John Medaris, the Army Ballistic Missile Agency director, "went out on a limb," as he put it, and set aside hardware that later gave the Army the ability to get off a quick shot after the Soviets launched Sputnik.

The U-2 and Explorer 1 also had something in common: They "stole" a lot of technology from other programs, using them in ways that no one had originally intended but that sped up the process. The U-2's design was in many ways just like that of the F-104 Starfighter that Lockheed had designed earlier for the Air Force, but with longer wings and a lot of weight cut out. The rocket that launched Explorer 1 was based on an Army Redstone ballistic missile, which, in turn, was an updated V-2 that the Army's German engineers had developed during World War II.

In the case of the GBU-28, the Air Force Development Test Center team compressed a development program that would ordinarily have taken two years into less than two weeks by taking engineering shortcuts and a more liberal approach to safety. For example, it tested the aerodynamics and ballistics of the weapon with a single drop, rather than the usual thirty.

Note that it required an individual with the *authority* and *inclination* to make the decision on how to interpret a contract or a standard. If a person could not legally give approval, the organization would not have followed his direction. If a person had not been willing to use his authority (and, in the process, accept responsibility), nothing would have happened, either—which brings us to JAWBREAKER.

CIA officers like Gary Schroen, who first went into Afghanistan to prepare the operation immediately after 9/11, had largely acted on their own initiative in the 1990s when they kept up personal contacts with Northern Alliance figures like Ahmed Shah Masoud. After the Soviets were defeated in the U.S. supported guerrilla war from 1980 to 1989, the CIA had turned its interest elsewhere. Schroen's contacts and experience in the region greased the re-establishment of the relationship when the United States decided to retaliate against al-Qaeda and the Taliban.

After the fighting started, the CIA was fortunate to have officers on hand with admitted inclinations for focusing more on results than procedures. Gary Berntsen, who took command of JAWBREAKER as the fighting began, once described himself as a "bad kid" from Long Island who graduated second from the bottom in his high school. Once in the CIA, he bragged about his "grab-'em-by-the-collar" approach.

As Admiral Ernest King supposedly said about wartime, "When they get in trouble, they send for the sons of bitches." If you don't have SOBs on staff and a way to get them to the front line, organizations will plod along at their routine pace. True, if everyone broke the rules all the time, there would be no rules. But one of the keys to a fast organization that can beat its opponent to the punch is almost always a willingness to break the rules. This is nothing new. It was said often in the 19th century that Paris sent officials into the French countryside not to enforce rules, but to decide judiciously when and how to ignore them.

How to Get Faster

If we want more speed and agility, some lessons are clear. We must: Make sure U.S. national security organizations have a legal mechanism for bending or breaking existing rules; make sure they have the means for having such rule-benders at hand; make sure these rule-benders exercise influence; and make sure they don't get out of control. (Even unofficially designated rule-benders need *some* clear lines of accountability.)

We need to allow responsible senior officials to put the government in overdrive when it's really important.

Basically, we need to allow responsible senior officials to put the government into overdrive when it's really important. With the possible exception of the operating forces of the military and their counterparts in the intelligence community, even top officials lack this ability today. This encourages other kinds of risks: workarounds. Cabinet secretaries who need to get decisions fast and begin operations expeditiously know that they cannot entrust such matters to the standing bureaucracy. But workarounds and shortcuts spite the institutional memory of an organization and court disaster from ignorance. Iran-Contra is a good example of a workaround gone wrong. The only way to avoid such dangers is to make the responsible bureaucracies faster only when they really need to be fast.

There is always a tension between orthodoxy and innovation, and between direct command and checks and balances. There is no sure-fire way to ensure the best mix. But we don't seem to be close now, or even trying to get closer. Ultimately, our willingness to balance different sorts of risk must be a political decision, in which voters can turn incumbents out and try something else if they are dissatisfied. But if we don't at least have the foundation for rule-bending, they will never get that choice.

What then, should we do? First, to build agility into the key parts of the U.S. government, Congress will clearly have to cooperate. That's the system; that's the Constitution. It is therefore folly for any administration to try to steamroll the legislators—as the then-popular Bush Administration did from about 2002 to 2004, such as when it shunted aside congressional concerns that the Iraq insurgency was gaining steam rather than entering its "last throes," or that U.S. forces did not have the resources to deal with the worsening situation. Accepting these concerns and criticisms quickly would have both improved the situation and solidified support for the effort by getting Congress' "buy in" on the record.

Second, we should consider establishing a small number of powerful "bottleneck breakers" in the Executive Office of the President. Senior experienced officials could be designated by the White House, formally or informally. The important thing is that officials down the line know that these bottleneck breakers are acting at the behest of the president to make sure his policies are carried out. Unlike the too-familiar "czars" that have been given responsibility for drug enforcement, energy conservation and, most recently, the war in Iraq, these officials would know how, and be given the authority, to work quickly and quietly with the Office of Management and Budget. It would take only a few examples of a sequestered budget line, a dismissed appointee or a transferred senior executive to give these bottleneck-breaker envoys the implicit power they require. The very existence of such EOP envoys, and the only occasional demonstration of their authority, would work wonders with hidebound, risk-averse bureaucrats.

Other measures that would counter the natural tendency of bureaucracies to slow down come readily to mind:

- Requiring senior civil service executives to periodically do a tour in a different Executive Branch department. This would make them more familiar with conditions in other departments, so they could anticipate what might slow down an action. It would also build social networks that could help clear these impediments.

- Create an "up or out" system of promotion for senior executives resembling the approach used in the military to create a dynamic that keeps the bureaucracy from getting too settled.

- Adopt a mandatory, congressionally approved, periodic de-layering of bureaucracies.
- Increase the number of Schedule C appointments to give new administrations a better ability to rattle cages. We need not repeal the Pendleton Act completely, but the trend in most sectors of the economy is toward "at will" employment. As an employee rises higher in the organization, it should be easier to move or remove him or her.

One could think of other measures in the same vein, and some have. The point, however, is that if we do not do *something* to increase the speed of government, we will be sure to fall behind future events, get beaten to the punch, and lose ground to our most ruthless competitors. Given the stakes in today's world, that is a loss we cannot afford.

Note

1. Also consider today's automobiles, which are much more complex than earlier models. Like jet fighters, cars today go faster and handle better. They can also locate their current position and tell you how to reach your destination—all while meeting ever-tougher safety and emissions standards. Yet the time required to develop a car and get it into the showroom *is getting shorter all the time.* Toyota is best at about two years,

and it is trying to cut this time to 12 months. Ford and GM are trying to keep up, but still take one to two years longer than Toyota—one reason they have been taking a beating in the market.

Critical Thinking

1. Why are actors like terrorist organizations often more agile than governments?
2. What is organizational agility? What are some of the specific factors that affect organizational agility?
3. What are several World War II-era examples of U.S. government nimbleness? How does government performance in today's war on terror compare with earlier nimbleness?
4. What are some reasons why government bureaucracy has become so slow?
5. Identify some recent examples of U.S. government agility and success. What, according to the author, can be done to improve the speed and agility of the U.S. government?

BRUCE BERKOWITZ is a research fellow at the Heaver Institution at Stanford University. He was Director of Forecasting and Evaluation at the Department of Defense from 2004–05.

Legislation Is Just the Start

The new financial reform law is a good reminder of how much takes place in Washington after a bill gets signed. In the nation's capital, says former Congressman Lee Hamilton, "legislation is just the start."

Lee Hamilton

You might imagine, now that President Obama has signed the massive financial reform package into law, that the issue is behind us. Hardly. In a way, the President's signature was just the starter's pistol.

This is because, despite its length—over 2000 pages—and the many months of negotiations that went into crafting it, the financial overhaul measure leaves countless issues to be resolved later by federal regulators and the lobbyists who will try to influence their decisions. It is a textbook example of the limits inherent in a legislative product, and of the manner in which Congress relies on a mix of concrete action and ambiguous ball-punting to cobble together a majority.

The law undoubtedly changes the nation's financial landscape. It creates a new Bureau of Financial Consumer Protection; strengthens regulation of financial holding companies; regulates derivatives; places new limits—the so-called "Volcker Rule"—on the amount of money a bank can invest in hedge funds and private equity funds; buttresses the Securities and Exchange Commission; and tries to discourage excessive risk-taking.

It is also filled with the sorts of compromises the legislative process demands. The "Volcker Rule" was written off, watered down, and then somewhat re-strengthened on its way to passage. The consumer protection agency was initially to be a standalone regulator, but then was placed within the Federal Reserve in order to calm some concerns. The language on derivatives went through a complex series of balance-seeking negotiations between those who wanted highly restrictive regulation and those who opposed it.

The result is a grand and sweeping law that nonetheless leaves many issues unresolved and much room for interpretation in the future. When you have such ambiguities in new statutes—as is frequently the case—it amounts to an invitation to further struggle on the part of the bureaucrats who must give shape and form to the ideas contained in the measure, and the lobbyists whose clients have much at stake in the results.

According to an analysis by the U.S. Chamber of Commerce, the measure calls for 350 rules to be formulated, 47 studies to be conducted—which is Congress' way of signaling action on an issue without actually making any decisions—and 74 reports. The creation of new entities—the consumer protection agency, a board of regulators to assess risk in the financial system—also will engender much executive-branch maneuvering and back-and-forth with Congress as they're set up and staffed.

Moreover, lobbyists don't stop work when a law is passed; in some ways, that's when their work truly begins, as they strive to build relationships with the regulators who will oversee their industry and try to influence the regulations that will soon enough begin to flow from various executive-branch agencies.

The difference, of course, is that for all its faults, Congress is a relatively transparent and accountable institution. What takes place in regulators' offices is far less visible. As the activity surrounding financial reform now passes beyond public view, political considerations will become less important but the stakes will grow higher. Out of the public's eye, the special interests' influence will grow, and arguments about how to interpret the language contained in the law will blossom—and, inevitably, spill over into the courts. For years to come, there will be enormous demand for lawyers capable either of making sense out of ambiguous legislative language, or of making the strongest possible arguments in favor of interpretations that just happen to favor their clients.

Yet in the end, it's the executive branch that benefits most from what Congress has done. The entire measure is a significant gift of power to federal agencies and financial regulators, who now have to make decisions about how they intend to wield their power. You can already see how significant their role will be in the early maneuvering over who might head the new Bureau of Consumer Financial Protection: each possible appointee, who must be approved by the Senate, would approach the job differently, and in the weeks following the bill's passage the nuances of their approaches were probably the hottest single topic of debate over breakfast, lunch and dinner tables in Washington.

It is important to remember, in the end, that the authority to act is not the same as acting. That is why, while Congress made some important decisions in the process of crafting its bill, the true import of the financial reform package will only reveal itself gradually. There is an old saying in Washington that "nothing is ever decided for good there." For legislation, that's certainly true.

Critical Thinking

1. How does the 2010 financial reform law signed by President Obama promise to change the nation's financial landscape?

2. What were some of the compromises contained in the financial reform legislation?

3. What are some of the government actions necessary in the aftermath of the financial reform act? Who is responsible for doing most of these tasks?

4. How many rules, studies, and reports are said to be mandated by the law?

LEE HAMILTON is Director of the Center on Congress at Indiana University. He was a member of the U.S. House of Representatives for 34 years.

From *Center on Congress at Indiana University*, August 9, 2010. Copyright © 2010 by The Center on Congress. Reprinted by permission. Lee Hamilton is Director of the Center on Congress at Indiana University. He was a member of the U.S. House of Representatives for 34 years.

UNIT 3

Process of American Politics

Unit Selections

Learning Outcomes

After reading this Unit, you will be able to:

- Identify different institutions, processes, and groups that are generally thought to serve as links between American citizens and their government.

- Identify and analyze recent changes in the American party system and assess the likely effects of those changes on the practice of American democracy.

- Outline alleged shortcomings in the way American elections are conducted and assess whether they impair the practice of democracy in the United States to any significant extent.

- Cite important points about American interest groups that appear in this unit and assess whether they work to the advantage or detriment of democracy.

- Identify and analyze recent changes in media that relate to the way that the American political system functions and decide whether each of the changes you have cited is likely to improve or harm the practice of American democracy.

- Summarize the challenges that contemporary newspapers are facing, the rise of the Internet, and the popularity of partisan media outlets such as Fox News and MSNBC and determine which of these phenomena will have the most significant long-term effects on the way the American political system functions.

- Summarize the role that money plays in the practice of American democracy and assess the extent to which it plays a harmful role. If you conclude that money does play a harmful role, recommend what steps should be taken to remedy the situation. If you conclude that money's role in American democracy is not harmful, defend that position.

According to many political scientists, what distinguishes more democratic political systems from less democratic ones is the degree of control that citizens exercise over government. This unit focuses on institutions, groups, and processes that can serve as links between Americans and their government.

The first three sections address parties, elections, voters, interest groups, political movements, and the role of money in campaigns and governing. Recent changes in these areas may affect American politics for decades to come, and these changes are the major focus of selections in these sections. The fourth section addresses media, the role(s) that they play in the American political system, and how they are changing.

One noteworthy development in the past few decades has been growing polarization between the two major parties. Republican and Democratic members of Congress have both become more likely to toe their party's line in opposition to the other party, with partisan voting increasingly becoming the norm on Capitol Hill. Some decry this increase in partisanship, while others think that sharper and more consistent policy differences between Democrat and Republican officeholders will make elections more consequential.

Incumbents' advantages in winning re-election to both the House of Representatives and the Senate have grown in recent years. In turn, despite Americans' dissatisfaction with President Bush and his Republican supporters in Congress, most observers emphasized how difficult it would be for Democrats to regain majority control of the House and Senate in the 2006 congressional elections. But Democrats *did* win control of both houses that year, illustrating what many consider to be a good example of American democracy at work. In the 2008 elections, Democrats, led by presidential candidate Barack Obama, won an even larger majority of seats in each house of Congress. In 2010, however, in the midst widespread dissatisfaction with President Obama and the much-heralded rise of the Tea Party movement, Republicans turned the tables on Democrats, regaining control of the House and making big gains in the Senate. Notwithstanding these recent election results, incumbency advantages—including the way House districts are drawn, name recognition, and easier access to campaign contributions—are likely to remain a concern for those who would like to reform the democratic process in the United States.

Besides built-in advantages for congressional incumbents, the American electoral system suffers from all sorts of other shortcomings. Many of these problems became apparent during the controversy over the outcome of the 2000 presidential election, and reform measures were enacted in both Congress and many states. Despite some improvements in the way elections are conducted in the American political system, many aspects of U.S. election mechanics still seem inferior to election mechanics in many other western democracies.

Campaign financing became a major concern after the 1972 presidential election. Major campaign finance reform laws passed in 1974 and 2002 (the latter is the so-called McCain-Feingold Act) have been aimed at regulating the influence of campaign contributions in the electoral process, but they have met, at best, with only partial success. The history of these and

© The McGraw-Hill Companies, Inc./Christopher Kerrigan, photographer

other major campaign finance laws is intertwined with a handful of Supreme Court decisions that have ruled parts of the laws as unconstitutional. In its controversial 5-4 ruling in *Citizens United v. Federal Election Commission* in January 2010, the Supreme Court voided one key element in the McCain-Feingold Act that was aimed at restricting corporate spending in campaigns.

As recent bribery and corruption scandals make clear, the fundamental challenge of how to reconcile free speech, the freedom of an individual to spend money as he or she wishes, the costs of campaigns, and the fairness of elections remain. In the summer of 2007, Barack Obama publicly pledged to accept public financing—and the accompanying requirement that a candidate who accepts public financing can spend only the sum provided by the government if he became his party's nominee. A year later, Obama changed his mind, and became the first presidential general election candidate to decline public financing since it became available beginning with the 1976 election. Obama made this decision because he was advised that he could raise more than three times as much money from supporters as the sum provided through public financing, and that advice turned out to be correct. Democratic candidate Obama *did* raise and spend more than three times as much money as his general election opponent, Republican John McCain, who accepted public financing and the accompanying spending limit. A noteworthy irony is that most Democrats have been stronger proponents of campaign finance regulation and public financing than most Republicans, notwithstanding McCain's longstanding leadership in reform efforts.

This unit also treats the roles of interest groups in the American political process and their impact on what government can and cannot do. "Gridlock" is a term usually applied to a policymaking situation that is thought to result from "divided government," wherein neither major party controls the presidency and both houses of Congress. But gridlock—and favoritism in policymaking—can also result from the interaction of interest groups and government policymakers. The weakness of parties in the United States, compared to parties in other Western democracies, is almost certainly responsible for the unusually strong place of interest groups in the American political system. In turn, one can wonder whether the current era of stronger, more disciplined parties in government will eventually contribute to the weakening of American interest groups.

Selections in the fourth section address how media—old and new—shape political communication and political behavior in the American political system. Television and radio news broadcasts and newspapers are not merely passive transmitters of information. They inevitably shape—or distort—what they report to their audiences and greatly affect the behavior of people and organizations in politics. Television talk shows, radio talkback shows, and thirty-minute "infomercials" have entered the political landscape with considerable effect. In 2004, televised attack ads financed by so-called 527 committees targeted both parties' presidential candidates and seemed to affect voters' views. In 2008, Barack Obama's campaign perfected some of the Internet fundraising techniques pioneered in 2004 by Howard Dean while unsuccessfully seeking the Democratic party's presidential nomination. Obama's remarkable run for the presidency included his vanquishing and outspending Democratic rival Hillary Clinton, who herself raised and spent more money on her nomination campaign than any candidate in history— *except* Obama. Then, as mentioned above, Obama outspent John McCain by a more than three-to-one margin in the general election campaign.

As already noted, one key to Obama's extraordinary fundraising prowess in 2007–2008 was the Internet, the medium that has revolutionized many aspects of American life. In addition to facilitating fundraising, the Internet played another role in the 2008 campaign by hosting political YouTube segments that played to large segments of the population, including some who mostly avoided traditional news media outlets. Finally, as selections in the fourth section of this unit show, online news reports and commentaries are threatening the very existence of traditional hard-copy newspapers.

Student Website
www.mhhe.com/cls

Internet References

FiveThirtyEight
http://fivethirtyeight.blogs.nytimes.com
The Gallup Organization
www.gallup.com
Poynter Online
www.poynter.org

Real Clear Politics
www.realclearpolitics.com
Tech President
techpresident.com

Polarized Pols versus Moderate Voters?

Stuart Taylor Jr.

What explains the ever-more-bitter ideological polarization that roils our politics today? Is it a reflection of an ever-more-bitterly polarized public? Or are most Americans relatively moderate and thus poorly represented by their immoderate political parties and elected representatives?

These questions have been the subject of lively debate among political scientists in recent years. Now comes Morris Fiorina, a scholar at Stanford University and the Hoover Institution, with a new book announcing its thesis in the title: *Disconnect: The Breakdown of Representation in American Politics.*

Fiorina is the leading exponent of the view that the public is no less moderate and no more polarized than in the past, and thus is ill-served by fervently liberal and conservative elected representatives and political activists.

The Fiorina book will not end the debate about what he has called "the myth"—and other political scientists insist is the reality—of a deeply polarized electorate. But the author does cite new evidence that our elected representatives cleave more dramatically to the left and right ends of the political spectrum than those they purport to represent. He also helps illuminate the causes of the undoubted polarization of political elites over the past generation while adding some insights, such as why many self-described conservative voters are less conservative than you might think.

Some fundamental points are undisputed. So close to unanimity have Republicans been in opposing President Obama's major domestic initiatives that "one would have to look as far back as the 1890s to find party-line voting so sharp on the most salient legislative issues of the day," as Pietro Nivola of the Brookings Institution observed in a recent paper. So internally homogeneous have the political parties become that almost every Republican in Congress is to the right of almost every Democrat. More important, perhaps, the vast majority of Republicans are so far to the right of the vast majority of Democrats in Congress that the moderates who once played a critical role in brokering compromises have virtually disappeared.

And the congressional culture of the 1950s and early 1960s, "where Democrats and Republicans generally treated each other with civility during working hours—and many drank, played poker, and golfed together after hours—is long gone," Fiorina writes.

The disagreements among political scientists focus on whether, as Fiorina argues, the vast majority of voters "appear to be little changed in their moderate orientation from those citizens of a generation ago."

That's the premise of his thesis that in America today, there is a disconnect between an unrepresentative political class and the citizenry it intends to represent, with "a relatively moderate electorate" forced to choose between "relatively extreme candidates."

A new book portrays "a relatively moderate electorate" forced to choose between "relatively extreme candidates."

Fiorina rests his arguments largely on surveys, including the following.

- The percentage of Republican delegates to nominating conventions who identified themselves as "very conservative" has risen from about 12 percent to more than 30 percent since 1972, and the percentage of "very liberal" Democratic delegates has grown from about 8 percent to nearly 20 percent. By contrast, surveys of the general public show little change in "very conservative" and "very liberal" percentages.

- Surveys of voters' views on a range of major issues show "a nonideological public moving rightward on some issues, leftward on others, and not moving much at all on still others" between the 1984 and 2004 elections.

- The incendiary issues—including abortion, gay marriage, and gun control—that command so much political energy and media attention fall far down the list when voters are asked what they think are the most important issues facing the country. Meanwhile, despite all the talk of a culture war, Republicans as well as Democrats have become more accepting of homosexuality in general.

- Members of the public express much more ambivalence on divisive issues than do members of the political class. Indeed, Fiorina writes, most voters "may not want a clear choice between a constitutional prohibition of abortion and abortion on demand . . . between launching wars of choice and ignoring developing threats."

- "Americans are even less ideological than their self-characterizations would suggest," Fiorina adds. He notes that when voters are questioned about specific issues, only one-fifth of those who call themselves conservatives take right-of-center positions on both economic and social issues—while fully one-third "do not actually have conservative policy views" on *either* economic or social issues. (By contrast, 62 percent of self-identified liberals take liberal positions on both economic and social issues.)

The surprising number of not-really-conservative self-described conservatives also casts doubt on the importance of the long-standing preference for "conservative" over "liberal" in voter self-identifications—40 percent to 20 percent in a recent Gallup Poll. Apparently, Fiorina suggests, many Americans whose actual views are not very conservative "hear or see the latest liberal silliness and figure, 'If that's liberal, I must be a conservative.' "

Other political scientists, including Alan Abramowitz of Emory University, have written detailed rebuttals of Fiorina's vision of the electorate.

Nivola said in an interview, "The nation's political parties are polarized from top to bottom." In a recent paper, he cited polls showing that the gaps between the liberal leanings of most Democratic citizens and the conservative leanings of most Republicans in today's world are large indeed: 76 percent of Democrats versus only 31 percent of Republicans thought that the government should guarantee health insurance for all Americans; 62 percent of Republicans versus only 25 percent of Democrats opposed the Obama administration's efforts to help financial institutions from failing; 59 percent of Democrats versus only 36 percent of Republicans thought that we should be willing to pay higher prices to protect the environment; and 66 percent of Republicans versus only 33 percent of Democrats thought that the U.S. must win the war in Afghanistan.

Nivola and others also cite data suggesting that red states have gotten redder and blue states bluer in recent decades, both in the lopsidedness of their votes for Republican and Democratic candidates and in other measures such as church attendance and attitudes toward abortion, gun control, and other social issues.

To some extent the critiques of Fiorina's arguments are over matters of degree. "No knowledgeable observer doubts that the American public is less divided than the political agitators and vocal elective office-seekers who claim to represent it," Nivola and William Galston, also of Brookings, concede in their introduction to a 2006 book of essays titled *Red and Blue Nation.* And more than one-third of Americans call themselves independents and eschew identification with either party.

"The number of deeply committed ideologues in America, though difficult to measure precisely, probably isn't much larger today than at earlier points in our history, which is to say minuscule," my *National Journal* colleague Ronald Brownstein wrote in his 2007 book, *The Second Civil War.* "What's unusual now is that the *political system* is more polarized than the country. Rather than reducing the level of conflict, Washington increases it."

The decline of patronage jobs and other material rewards as a major motivation for political engagement, the increasing importance of party primaries dominated by the most-intense partisans, and the displacement of smoke-filled rooms by "power to the people" activism, Fiorina writes, "had the unanticipated and perverse effect of making American politics less representative." The

reason was that "political power and influence were transferred to political activists who were not like most people," and who were less interested in representing the views of constituents than in imposing their ideological "view of a better world on the rest of society."

Demographic changes also drove the polarization of the political parties. These changes included the migration of blacks to the North; the growth and Republicanization of the Sun Belt; the political mobilization of conservative evangelicals; the rise of suburbs; the fading of broad-based associations such as Rotary and Kiwanis clubs as points of contact between representatives and their constituents; and the replacement of these clubs by advocacy groups for causes such as peace, race, environmentalism, feminism, abortion, and gun control plus their conservative counterparts.

And in a "disturbing feedback loop," Fiorina says, those who are most open-minded often withdraw from politics for fear of introducing "conflicts into their relationships with others in their work and social circles."

One result is that politicians focus more on ideology and the demands of their party base than on solving problems. Another is that "disinformation and even outright lies become common as dissenting voices in each party leave or are silenced." All this "makes voters less likely to trust government."

Fiorina is not optimistic that institutional reforms can improve problems so deeply rooted in demographic change. But he does hope that social changes now at work—especially the fading force of the divisive convulsions of the 1960s—might depolarize our politics somewhat.

The fading force of the divisive convulsions of the 1960s might depolarize our politics somewhat.

Meanwhile, it would be nice if more politicians and activists would heed the wisdom of one of our greatest judges, Learned Hand: "The spirit of liberty is the spirit which is not too sure that it is right."

Critical Thinking

1. What evidence does political scientist Morris Fiorina use to support his thesis that there is a disconnect between elected politicians and the American public?

2. What contrary evidence do other political scientists present?

3. Why, according to Fiorina, are elected politicians more polarized than the voting public today? What roles have demographic changes, decline of patronage jobs, increasing importance of primaries, and the like played?

4. In what sense(s) is government less representative of the American people because of "polarized pols"?

Limited War

How the age of austerity will remake American politics.

Thomas B. Edsall

In this election, you can glimpse the brutish future of American politics. This new age of brutishness may or may not include the Tea Party. But, even if the Tea Party dissipates, the anger undergirding it will not. The Tea Party has expertly articulated a widespread grievance: that the government is redistributing money from hardworking Americans to the idle and undeserving. Of course, this is hardly a new charge. But it takes place in a new context—an age of growing austerity, where this complaint will acquire an ever-sharper edge and battles over the scarce resources of the state will erupt in spectacular skirmishes.

Politics has, in some sense, always been a resource war—and in American politics it has usually taken the form of one political party promoting a social safety net and the other party decrying how hard-earned tax dollars unjustly finance those benefits. But, while that debate was intense, it was in some sense resolvable. For decades, our political system has been able to fund an array of social programs while keeping taxes relatively low. The American economy grew at a sufficient pace that it could rather effortlessly bankroll a state that satisfied divergent interests.

But that broad, unintentional compromise is no longer sustainable. We're entering a period of austerity, far different from anything we've ever seen before. The predictions, especially the ones formulated by sober, nonpartisan analysts, are eye-popping. Earlier this year, a Congressional Budget Office report estimated that the debt as a percentage of GDP would approximately triple by 2035. Put another way, debt will come to exceed 185 percent of GDP. That's far worse than Greece's current perilous condition, a crisis that has been portrayed as the *reductio ad absurdum* of fiscal indiscipline.

Like the David Cameron government in Britain, or any number of other states across Europe, we'll soon be forced to reckon with the fact that our economic viability depends on some combination of shrinking the state and raising revenue. If we were careful planners—and, of course, we're not—we would begin by saving about 5 percent of GDP each year. Next year, for example, we'd have to make tax increases and spending cuts add up to about $700 billion. Over time, the total costs would prove immense: raising everyone's tax bill by at least 25 percent (and probably a lot more than that) or eliminating about 20 percent of the federal budget (the approximate current size of Social Security, for example).

Even if you assume that a crisis is distant—or assume that we'll avert it by letting the Bush tax cuts expire and further containing health care costs—the anxieties about deficits are already acute. Both parties are posturing to assume the mantle of fiscal conservatism, a trend that the success of the Tea Party will only exacerbate. And by December, Obama's deficit commission will release its findings, further propelling this debate to the fore.

With resources shrinking, the competition for them will inflame. Each party will find itself in a death struggle to protect the resources that flow to its base—and, since the game will be zero-sum, each will attempt to expropriate the resources that flow to the other side. This resource war will scramble our politics. Each party will be forced to dramatically change its calculus and remake its agenda. And if you thought our politics had grown nasty, you haven't even begun to consider the ugliness of the politics of scarcity.

At first glance, the Democrats have the most to lose in this new struggle. They have spent decades trying to recover their image from the excesses of the McGovern era, repositioning themselves as something more than an aggregation of aggrieved—and needy—interest groups. Even Barack Obama, the most liberal president in decades, packaged himself as post-partisan candidate, rather than as a warrior on behalf of unions or minority groups. "There's nothing liberal about wanting to reduce money in politics," he said during the campaign. "There's nothing liberal about wanting to make sure [our soldiers] are treated properly when they come home." This pitch worked well. The public basically considered him a man of the center—a perception that rested on many years of Democrats shaking off the caricature (and reality) of paleo-liberalism.

But, for all the gains the party has made, the age of scarcity risks reversing them. It's precisely the Democratic Party's historic base—minorities, labor, the poor—that will take the greatest hit in coming years. You can already begin to see signs of this. Even when Congress approved an economic stimulus bill in August, it coupled spending on health care and teachers' salaries with deep cuts in food stamps. It reduced benefits for a family of three by $47 per month, according to one estimate.

Or take state government, which is really the vanguard of the crisis. The austerity hammer has fallen hard on Democratic constituencies. According the Center on Budget and Policy Priorities, at least 31 states have slashed programs that provide low-income children and families access to either health care or health insurance. Peruse almost any state budget and you'll find further shredding of the safety net. Idaho's Department of Health and Welfare has closed nine of its 45 field offices; Georgia has cut funding for low-income family support programs by 7 percent. And that's all merely a prelude to a looming apocalypse. In their next budgets, 24 states will face a shortfall of at least 10 percent—and it's not hard to imagine where they will trim to cover that gap.

One of the most obvious targets of cuts will be public-sector workers—the very unions that provide the Democrats with their most significant muscle. Indeed, it's hard to overstate the money and manpower that the public-employee unions provide to the Democrats at election time. Just this election cycle, they have donated $12,561,042 to the Democrats. But these public-sector workers—so easily lampooned as bureaucrats—also happen to be unpopular. Even blue states, like New York and New Jersey, which are largely sympathetic to labor unions, have turned against the public employees in this fiscal crunch, according to the recent findings of pollsters.

So as governments consider firing more of these workers, it places Democrats in an uncomfortable defensive position. Do they stand by this swath of their unpopular base? This drama has already transpired in places like California, which recently saved $1.5 billion by furloughing state employees and scaling back their benefits. The union hardly acceded to these proposals. As the state mulled the massive cuts, one union leader notoriously told Democratic legislators, "We helped to get you into office, and we got a good memory; and, come November, if you don't back our program, we'll help to get you out of office." She may have needed to be that blunt. In California, too, the electorate has no love for public workers. A majority, according to a recent Rasmussen poll of likely voters, view them as a "significant" strain on the state budget—an opinion that Republicans like Arnold Schwarzenegger and Meg Whitman have aggressively channeled.

The Democratic base is already applying massive pressure on its politicians to resist cuts. The labor-funded Campaign for America's Future recruited 50 progressive leaders who signed a statement that urged: "We should be strengthening, not slashing, vital programs like Medicaid, Unemployment Compensation, the Supplemental Nutrition Assistance Program (food stamps) . . . and other programs and services crucial to struggling lower-income and middle-income people in every corner of our country." Such anxieties over austerity explain why liberals have savaged Obama for creating a deficit commission in the first place. Arianna Huffington has fumed, "Maybe progressives and the middle class need to sort of face up to the fact that the president is not that much into them, that he would rather hang out with Larry Summers, or flirt with Olympia Snowe. . . . Remember, he set up a deficit commission before he set up a jobs commission."

Unfortunately, defending against these cuts exposes all sorts of political vulnerabilities. This year's elections offer a preview of how Republicans intend to use the vulnerability of these programs to attack Democrats. That is, there's some indication that they will return to the racially tinged backlash politics of the '70s and '80s. Newt Gingrich, who has re-emerged as a particularly active rhetorician for the Tea Party, has supplied a large number of phrases redolent of that era. He has described the Democrats as the "party of food stamps." That's a slightly softer version of the line trumpeted by Glenn Beck that explicitly decries Obama for acting out a "deep-seated hatred for white people or the white culture."

Ugly identity politics—and racially tinged attacks—will accompany austerity.

It's a miserable predicament for a party. These social programs are the very reason for its existence. Yet, the party's political survival has depended on its speaking in a low voice about them. In an age of austerity, that is no longer possible. Republicans will try to force Democrats to defend these programs—with all the attendant baggage. And if they don't take up the cause fervently enough, their base will force their hand, espousing the unattractive identity politics that Democrats thought they had escaped.

Austerity will produce unlikely political strategies on the other side of the aisle, too. Take the Tea Party's stance on entitlements. Ostensibly, the Tea Party has stoked an anti-government moment—following in the footsteps of conservatives who have spent generations trashing the New Deal. That's what made it so strange to hear Republican candidates like Mississippi's Alan Nunnelee, a favorite to rip that state's first congressional district from a Democratic incumbent, release a pledge promising to never privatize Social Security. Countless other Republicans have thrashed their Democratic opponents for supporting a $500 billion cut in Medicare. Karl Rove's campaign group has accused Pennsylvania Congressman Joe Sestak of voting to "gut" the program. Another conservative front group, 60 Plus, has run ads against Democrats around the country alleging that their votes to cut Medicare "will hurt the quality of our care."

These ads do not grow from any conservative epiphany about the philosophical virtues of government benefits. They stem from a clever bet about how scarcity will reshape generational politics. For many years, the anxieties of seniors redounded to the benefit of Democrats. When Democrats issued jeremiads about the perils of Social Security privatization, older voters responded with fear. Democrats have maintained a double-digit advantage on Social Security for well over a decade. An NBC/*Wall Street Journal* poll in October 2006 found that the public invested greater trust in Democrats on Social Security by 28 points. Remarkably, that gap now stands at four points, a statistical tie.

How did the Republicans eliminate this time-tested disadvantage? They have replaced the Democrats as the great students of entitlement anxiety. Republicans understand that one axis of the resource war will be generational. All of their vows to defend Medicare are coupled with attacks on Obama's health care reform. They implicitly portray Democrats as waging an age war—creating a massive new government program that transfers dollars to the young at the expense of the elderly. Republicans have cleverly stoked the fear that Obama is rewarding all his exuberant, youthful, idealistic supporters by redistributing resources that are badly needed by the old.

But the voters over 65 that Republicans are pursuing are largely a subset of their most important voting bloc: whites. Republicans have staked the entirety of their electoral future on them. And just as they have exploited seniors' anxiety about scarcity, they have done the same with the white population as a whole. In fact, whites may be the most anxious group this political season. (Only 59 percent of whites believe "Americans will always continue to be prosperous and make economic progress"—while 81 percent of blacks and 75 percent of Hispanics continue to profess faith in the future.) This anxiety is the reason that Republicans have spent so much time talking about the menace of immigration—even though many of them once viewed Hispanic voters as a potential pillar of their future coalition.

The rise of illegal immigration as an issue this cycle doesn't correspond to material facts. The number of aliens pouring across the border is not increasing. On the contrary, the recession and improved enforcement have drastically reduced it. What is increasing is anxiety about resource competition. And that's exactly why immigrants cause so much agitation: They are perceived by many voters as one giant, undeserving resource suck. In June, Gallup asked, "Which comes closer to your point of view, illegal immigrants in the long run become productive citizens and pay their fair share of taxes, or illegal immigrants cost taxpayers too much by using government services like public education and medical services?" Among all voters, 62 percent perceived immigrants as a resource drain. Among Republicans, the number concurring with that dim assessment rose to 78 percent. You'll often hear Republican immigration proposals—rewriting the Fourteenth Amendment's guarantee of citizenship, for instance—dismissed as political suicide. I would argue that it shows the GOP's astute understanding of the new zeitgeist.

It goes without saying that Republicans will also be waging a war on behalf of the affluent and corporations. They have been stunningly successful at walking away from recent budget fights in those states granting even further tax cuts to business interests. In California, for instance, they managed to secure a $30 million tax break for Humboldt Redwood Company, owned by one of the state's wealthiest, not to mention most influential, families. And, even as the state increased tuition at public universities by 32 percent—and as state parks are actually running out of toilet paper—Republicans have skillfully managed to avoid a corporate tax hike. In fact, they protected a $1.4 billion corporate tax cut by agreeing to merely postpone it for two years.

All of which is to say that the age of scarcity poses it own risks to Republicans. They are relying on a group in long-term demographic decline (whites) and pursuing policies on behalf of a group that hardly seems deserving of limited resources (the affluent)—and are attempting to woo another group (the elderly) with demagoguery that betrays their core principles about limited government.

But, for all the risks that resource competition poses to the political parties, the risks are much greater to our political system. There's no doubt which groups will prevail—and which will fall—in these wars. We can already see that the politics of scarcity will inflict the greatest wounds on the poor. The political vulnerability of programs serving impoverished minority constituencies is self-evident. The suffering caused by these cuts is a tragic consequence of this new dynamic. We will not have conceived cuts in a spirit of the common good, or with any eye to creating sound policy, but out of a sense of gamesmanship and the mean-spiritedness that is integral to intense competition over a shrinking pie.

Social schisms in this country have always been real. Yet, we've embedded an ideal of solidarity into our state, a sense of moral obligation. Not a European ideal of a safety net, but a very American ideal. There's been a sense of optimism in our politics and our social policy because we've never perceived social success in this country as zero-sum. We're now witnessing the erosion of that belief—an array of anxieties and a creeping distrust that will sap the optimism from our system, perhaps the most crucial quality in making us an exceptional nation.

Critical Thinking

1. Outline the period of austerity into which the United States is entering.

2. Why do Democrats have the most to lose in the new era of increasingly scarce resources?

3. What does it mean to say that "one axis of the resource war will be generational"?

4. How do whites, the aged, and the affluent figure into Republican party tactics and why does each of these groups pose a risk for Republicans in the coming age of scarcity?

Thomas B. Edsall holds the Joseph Pulitzer II and Edith Pulitzer Moore Chair at the Columbia Graduate School of Journalism.

Reagan's Lasting Realignment

It shapes politics still.

Michael G. Franc

Gallup polls consistently show that the American public esteems Ronald Reagan as much as or more than any other president. Admittedly, such polls tend to favor recent presidents, along with those whose faces appear on our currency, but even so, Reagan usually manages to outpoll Bill Clinton, JFK, FDR, Lincoln, and the founding fathers. Reagan stands out so strongly not just for his economic and geopolitical achievements, but also because he realigned the American electorate both ideologically and on a partisan basis in ways that are unique in the period following World War II. Equally important, he did this by governing from a clearly articulated set of principles—strong bedrock values to which he returned time and time again to educate and, ultimately, persuade Americans.

Since Gallup first asked Americans about their party preference, the president's political party has almost invariably lost ground during his years in office. This comes as no surprise; everyone wants to be on the same team as a newly elected president, but once in office, presidents face challenging situations that can require them to act in ways that burn their political capital.

Even during the unique political circumstances presented by World War II, and later amid the worshipful media coverage of JFK's Camelot, the president's party lost ground. The largest Democratic losses occurred during LBJ's five years in office, which were marked by the rapid legislative march to his Great Society along with the frustrations of Vietnam. Those identifying as Democrats dropped by a full nine percentage points, while Republican identification inched up two points. Democrats incurred modest setbacks in party identification during the Carter and Clinton administrations, when Republicans posted net gains of three and two points, respectively.

Likewise, Americans moved toward the Democratic party when Republicans controlled the White House. Net Democratic gains were two points during the Ford administration, three points under the Eisenhower and George H. W. Bush administrations, six points under George W. Bush, and seven points under Nixon.

Ronald Reagan stands out as the lone exception to this rule. The percentage of Americans identifying as Republican increased by three percentage points between 1981 and 1988 (from 27 percent to 30 percent), while the Democrats' fortunes plummeted six points, from 41 percent to 35 percent. And as a Pew Foundation study points out, this "probably understates Reagan's overall legacy, as GOP identification had already spiked four points (and Democratic identification fallen four points) between 1980 and 1981."

It is too early to know what effect Barack Obama's presidency will have on his party's fortunes, but it's not too early to draw some preliminary conclusions. In 2008, 36 percent of Americans identified with the Democrats and 28 percent with the Republicans, the largest partisan advantage for the Democrats in over two decades. These numbers prompted a widespread burst of liberal gloating. We were told that America's dalliance with market thinking and its fixation on individual liberty had run their course. America was moving inexorably toward collectivism and would soon resemble "a modern European state" like France. The GOP became the subject of what amounted to political obituaries. "These days," *Time* opined, "Republicans have the desperate aura of an endangered species."

Liberals often remind us that President Obama inherited many problems when inaugurated. But his most debilitating inheritance may have been this triumphalism and the arrogance it inspired, which led him to pursue the most ambitious liberal policy agenda in decades.

Obama's first year saw many Democratic legislative accomplishments, chief among them a budget that contemplated tripling the national debt over the next decade. The American people were ambivalent, because they saw little or no benefit—and considerable harm—accruing from Obama's marquee legislative achievements. The next year Obamacare passed, and its unpopularity hurt the Democrats even more. Not surprisingly, then, after two years in office, one out of every seven Democrats had left the fold. Identification with the Democratic party fell from 36 percent to 31 percent, while the GOP share of the electorate ticked up modestly, from 28 percent to 29 percent Gallup characterizes this six-point shift in only two years as "notable." Other national surveys, such as those conducted by the *Washington Post*/ABC News and the *New York Times*/CBS News, recorded even steeper net Democratic declines.

How does this record compare with that of Reagan's first two years? In 1980, party identification averaged 45 percent for the Democrats and just 23 percent for the GOP. During his first year in office, Reagan fired thousands of striking air-traffic controllers, convinced Congress to enact his historic budget and tax cuts, retooled our military, and reversed virtually every aspect of Pres. Jimmy Carter's failed national-security strategy. The mainstream media and Washington's insiders roundly ridiculed these initiatives and warned that they would lead to further economic stagnation and even a full-scale nuclear war. The American public disagreed. They rewarded the Republicans with a four-point gain in party identification while setting Democrats back by the same amount.

Like our current president, Reagan assumed office during very challenging times. During his transition, a team of advisers wrote:

> 1980 may well have been the most crucial year for the American economy in half a century. . . . No American President since Franklin Roosevelt has inherited a more difficult economic situation.

Sound familiar? As with Obama, Reagan's early years in office were dominated by a nasty recession—falling GDP accompanied by double-digit unemployment, interest rates, and inflation.

And, as with Obama, the recession was slow to dissipate. After nearly two years, voters had realized no dividends from the historic Reagan spending and tax cuts. But even after losing back some of 1981's gains in 1982, the GOP was still up two percentage points since Reagan had taken office. Contrast that to the Democrats' six-point decline in party identification during Obama's first two years.

Of course, we know the rest of the Gipper's story. With his economic plan in place, the economy took off, and his arms buildup cast the die for the ultimate fall of the Soviet empire and international Communism. Not surprisingly, Republican fortunes took off. Identification with the GOP surged from 24 percent in 1983 to 29 percent in 1984 and 32 percent in 1985. It would remain at 30 percent or higher for the rest of the decade. The Democrats' party identification experienced a decline every bit as dramatic as the Republican gains, falling from 43 percent in 1983 to 34 percent in 1985, where it remained virtually unchanged throughout the 1980s.

Reagan's success did more than just revive the fortunes of the Republican party. It also led to a renaissance for American conservatism. Surveys conducted since 1972 by American National Election Studies (ANES) tell the story. In 1980, 28 percent of Americans identified as conservative and 17 percent as liberal. Throughout the 1980s the percentage of liberals remained more or less constant, but the percentage of Americans claiming the conservative label increased steadily, rising to 29 percent in 1984 and reaching 32 percent at the end of Reagan's tenure in 1988. Before Reagan, the conservative total had hovered between 25 and 27 percent. Since his departure from the Oval Office, it has been at 30 percent or higher in all but one of the ANES surveys.

Reagan's success did more than just revive the fortunes of the Republican party. It also led to a renaissance for American conservatism.

The greatest lesson from the Reagan years is that not only must a president's agenda achieve results, but the agenda must be in sync with America's ideological center of gravity, which has long been located on the right. Given the historical norm in which there are roughly three self-described conservatives for every two liberals, that is a daunting challenge for a liberal president. The single greatest factor distinguishing Obama's first 24 months from Reagan's was his decision to advance a relentless big-government agenda at a time when conservative attitudes and values favoring limited government were on the rise. Both the 2010 exit polls and Gallup's extensive surveys indicate that conservatives now account for roughly 40 percent of the electorate while only 20 percent acknowledge being liberal.

Another significant change in the political terrain since the early 1980s: There is now a nearly complete alignment of partisanship and ideology. Three decades ago, a significant minority of Democrats—many of them in elective office—were conservative, and overt liberals were not uncommon among the ranks of elected Republicans. No longer. Today, as ANES surveys have found, the overwhelming majority of Republicans describe themselves as conservative, and most Democrats claim the liberal mantle, though they are a smaller proportion of their party than conservative Republicans are of theirs.

The ongoing debate over the size of government will take place on conservative rhetorical ground. President Obama understands this. He routinely associates Obamacare with conservative values such as "self-reliance," "rugged individualism," "our fierce defense of freedom," and "healthy skepticism of government." His standard stump speech during the 2010 campaign channeled Reagan to the point of being intellectual-property theft:

> I've never believed that government has all the answers to our problems. I've never believed that government's role is to create jobs or prosperity. I believe it's the drive and ingenuity of our entrepreneurs, our small businesses, the skill and dedication of our workers, that has made us the wealthiest nation on earth. I believe it's the private sector that must be the main engine of our recovery.

Obama speaks in this—our—language not because he wants to, but because he has to. Skepticism of government is at a half-century high, and Americans are more willing than ever to embrace limited-government solutions to our existential debt crisis.

The battle can be won.

Critical Thinking

1. What almost always happens to a president's political party—specifically, the percentage of Americans identifying with his party—during his years in office?

2. What president is the sole exception to this phenomenon since World War II?

3. What effect did Reagan's presidency seem to have on American conservatism?

4. What, according to Michael Franc, is the "greatest lesson" from the Reagan years?

Mr. Franc is vice president of government studies at the Heritage Foundation.

America Observed

Why foreign election observers would rate the United States near the bottom.

ROBERT A. PASTOR

Few noticed, but in the year 2000, Mexico and the United States traded places. After nearly two centuries of election fraud, Mexico's presidential election was praised universally by its political parties and international observers as free, fair, and professional. Four months later, after two centuries as a model democracy, the U.S. election was panned as an embarrassing fiasco, reeking with pregnant chads, purged registration lists, butterfly ballots, and a Supreme Court that preempted a recount.

Ashamed, the U.S. Congress in 2002 passed the Help America Vote Act (HAVA), our first federal legislation on election administration. But two years later, on November 2, more than 200,000 voters from all 50 states phoned the advocacy organization Common Cause with a plethora of complaints. The 2004 election was not as close as 2000, but it was no better—and, in some ways, worse. This was partly because the only two elements of HAVA implemented for 2004 were provisional ballots and ID requirements, and both created more problems than they solved. HAVA focused more on eliminating punch-card machines than on the central cause of the electoral problem, dysfunctional decentralization. Instead of a single election for president, 13,000 counties and municipalities conduct elections with different ballots, standards, and machines. This accounts for most of the problems.

On the eve of November's election, only one-third of the electorate, according to a *New York Times* poll, said that they had a lot of confidence that their votes would be counted properly, and 29 percent said they were very or somewhat concerned that they would encounter problems at the polls. This explains why 13 members of Congress asked the United Nations to send election observers. The deep suspicion that each party's operatives had of the other's motives reminded me of Nicaragua's polarized election in 1990, and of other poor nations holding their first free elections.

Ranking America's Elections

The pro-democracy group Freedom House counts 117 electoral democracies in the world as of 2004. Many are new and fragile. The U.S. government has poured more money into helping other countries become democracies than it has into its own election system. At least we've gotten our money's worth. By and large, elections are conducted better abroad than at home. Several teams of international observers—including one that I led—watched this U.S. election. Here is a summary of how the United States did in 10 different categories, and what we should do to raise our ranking.

1. Who's in Charge? Stalin is reported to have said that the secret to a successful election is not the voter but the vote counter. There are three models for administering elections. Canada, Spain, Afghanistan, and most emerging democracies have nonpartisan national election commissions. A second model is to have the political parties "share" responsibility. We use that model to supervise campaign finance (the Federal Election Commission), but that tends to lead either to stalemates or to collusions against the public's interest. The third, most primitive model is when the incumbent government puts itself in charge. Only 18 percent of the democracies do it this way, including the United States, which usually grants responsibility to a highly partisan secretary of state, like Katherine Harris (formerly) in Florida or Kenneth Blackwell in Ohio.

2. Registration and Identification of Voters. The United States registers about 55 percent of its eligible voters, as compared with more than 95 percent in Canada and Mexico. To ensure the accuracy of its list, Mexico conducted 36 audits between 1994 and 2000. In contrast, the United States has thousands of separate lists, many of which are wildly inaccurate. Provisional ballots were needed only because the lists are so bad. Under HAVA, all states by 2006 must create computer-based, interactive statewide lists—a major step forward that will work only if everyone agrees not to move out of state. That is why most democracies, including most of Europe, have nationwide lists and ask voters to identify themselves. Oddly, few U.S. states require proof of *citizenship*—which is, after all, what the election is supposed to be about. If ID cards threaten democracy, why does almost every democracy except us require them, and why are their elections conducted better than ours?

3. Poll Workers and Sites. Dedicated people work at our polling stations often for 14 hours on election day. Polling sites are always overcrowded at the start of the day. McDonald's hires more workers for its lunchtime shifts, but a similar idea has not yet occurred to our election officials. Poll workers are exhausted by the time they begin the delicate task of counting the votes and making sure the total corresponds to the number who signed in, and, as a result, there are discrepancies. When I asked about the qualifications for selecting a poll worker, one county official told me, "We'll take anyone with a pulse."

Mexico views the job as a civic responsibility like jury duty, and citizens are chosen randomly and trained. This encourages all citizens to learn and participate in the process.

4. Voting Technologies. Like any computers, electronic machines break down, and they lose votes. Canada does not have this problem because it uses paper ballots, still the most reliable technology. Brazil's electronic system has many safeguards and has gained the trust of its voters. If we use electronic machines, they need paper-verifiable ballots.

5. Uniform Standards for Ballots, Voting, Disputes. The Supreme Court called for equal protection of voters' rights, but to achieve this, standards need to be uniform. In America, each jurisdiction does it differently. Most countries don't have this problem because they have a single election commission and law to decide the validity of ballots.

6. Uncompetitive Districts. In 2004, only three incumbent members of Congress—outside of House Majority Leader Tom DeLay's gerrymandered state of Texas—were defeated. Even the Communist Party of China has difficulty winning as many elections. This is because state legislatures, using advanced computer technologies, can now draw district boundaries in a way that virtually guarantees safe seats. Canada has a nonpartisan system for drawing districts. This still favors incumbents, as 83 percent won in 2004, but that compares with 99 percent in the United States. Proportional representation systems are even more competitive.

7. Campaign Finance and Access to the Media. The United States spent little to conduct elections last November, but almost $4 billion to promote and defeat candidates. More than $1.6 billion was spent on TV ads in 2004. The Institute for Democracy and Electoral Assistance in Stockholm reported that 63 percent of democracies provided free access to the media, thus eliminating one of the major reasons for raising money. Most limit campaign contributions, as the United States does, but one-fourth also limit campaign expenditures, which the Supreme Court feared would undermine our democracy. In fact, the opposite is closer to the truth: Political equality *requires* building barriers between money and the ballot box.

8. Civic Education. During the 1990s, the federal government spent $232 million on civic education abroad and none at home. As a result, 97 percent of South Africans said they had been affected by voter education. Only 6 percent of Americans, according to a Gallup Poll in 2000, knew the name of the speaker of the House, while 66 percent could identify the host of *Who Wants to Be a Millionaire?* Almost every country in the world does a better job educating citizens on how to vote.

9. The Franchise. The Electoral College was a progressive innovation in the 18th century; today, it's mainly dictatorships like communist China that use an indirect system to choose their highest leader.

10. International Observers. We demand that all new democracies grant unhindered access to polling sites for international observers, but only one of our 50 states (Missouri) does that. The Organization for Security and Cooperation in Europe, a 55-state organization of which the United States is a member, was invited by Secretary of State Colin Powell to observe the U.S. elections, yet its representatives were permitted to visit only a few "designated sites." Any developing country that restricted observers to a few Potemkin polling sites as the United States did would be roundly condemned by the State Department and the world.

On all 10 dimensions of election administration, the United States scores near the bottom of electoral democracies. There are three reasons for this. First, we have been sloppy and have not insisted that our voting machines be as free from error as our washing machines. We lack a simple procedure most democracies have: a log book at each precinct to register every problem encountered during the day and to allow observers to witness and verify complaints.

> McDonald's hires extra workers at lunchtime, but this has not yet occurred to our election officials. Poll workers are exhausted by the time they start counting votes.

Second, we lack uniform standards, and that is because we have devolved authority to the lowest, poorest level of government. It's time for states to retrieve their authority from the counties, and it's time for Congress to insist on national standards.

Third, we have stopped asking what we can learn from our democratic friends, and we have not accepted the rules we impose on others. This has communicated arrogance abroad and left our institutions weak.

The results can be seen most clearly in our bizarre approach to Iraq's election. Washington, you may recall, tried to export the Iowa-caucus model though it violates the first principle of free elections, a secret ballot. An Iraqi ayatollah rejected that and also insisted on the importance of direct elections (meaning no Electoral College). Should we be surprised that the Iraqi Election Commission chose to visit Mexico instead of the United States to learn how to conduct elections?

Critical Thinking

1. What is the central cause of the multiple shortcomings in the way that U.S. elections are conducted?
2. What are the three models used for administering elections in a democracy? What are the drawbacks of the model used by the United States?
3. What are the advantages of a nationally administered election system?
4. What three reasons does Robert Pastor give for the poor U.S. performance in conducting elections?

ROBERT A. PASTOR is director of the Center for Democracy and Election Management and a professor at American University. At the Carter Center from 1986–2000, he organized election-observation missions to about 30 countries, including the United States.

From *The American Prospect*, vol. 16, no. 1, January 4, 2005, pp. A2–A3. Copyright © 2005. Reprinted with permission from Robert A. Pastor and The American Prospect, Washington, DC. All rights reserved. www.prospect.org

Six Myths about Campaign Money

The Supreme Court's ruling in *Citizens United* has spawned arguments that oversimplify money's real role in politics.

ELIZA NEWLIN CARNEY

When the Supreme Court decided in January to toss out the decades-old ban on direct corporate and union campaign spending, U.S. politics changed overnight. In *Citizens United v. Federal Election Commission,* the high court ruled 5–4 that unions and corporations could spend money from their vast treasuries on campaigns. The decision applies to for-profit and nonprofit corporations alike, scrambling the deck for political players of all stripes.

The ruling also intensified the never-ending political money wars: Democrats have fought in vain to push through a broad new disclosure bill, and Republicans have renewed their systematic legal assault on the remaining campaign finance laws. The Court, in a deregulatory mood, appears eager to dismantle the rules still further. At the same time, voters are unusually engaged in the campaign finance debate.

It's a critical turning point in the world of election law, but advocates fighting over free speech versus corruption remain as polarized as ever. Both sides trot out arguments that oversimplify money's real role in politics and make it harder to identify solutions and common ground. Each of the following six myths contains a grain of truth but papers over important nuances. Inevitably, regulating democracy is messy and complicated. The solution rarely can be reduced to a sound bite; there often is no silver bullet.

Corporate Money Will Now Overwhelm Elections

President Obama has been among those sounding the alarm that corporations, in the wake of *Citizens United,* will swamp campaigns with private money.

"This ruling opens the floodgates for an unlimited amount of special-interest money into our democracy," Obama declared in his weekly radio address shortly after the ruling. "It gives the special-interest lobbyists new leverage to spend millions on advertising to persuade elected officials to vote their way, or to punish those who don't."

Reform advocates toss around big numbers and dire warnings. They point to ExxonMobil's $85 billion in profits in 2008 and note that if the company spent just 10 percent of that on politics, the outlay would be $8.5 billion. That's three times more than the combined spending of the Obama and McCain presidential campaigns and every single House and Senate candidate in that election.

So far, however, no such corporate spending tsunami has materialized. If anything, labor unions have jumped in more quickly to exploit the new rules, dumping millions of dollars into Arkansas's Democratic Senate primary and other high-profile races this year. One reason may be that, unlike corporate executives, union leaders don't risk offending shareholders and customers if they openly bankroll candidates.

Actually, neither unions nor corporations will shift vast new resources into campaigns, some political scientists argue. The reason? These players could spend any of their money on politics, through issue advertising, even before the *Citizens United* ruling. Their one constraint was that they had to avoid explicit campaign messages, such as "vote for" or "vote against." The high court's ruling will make such issue advocacy less common because corporate and labor leaders are free to pay for unvarnished campaign endorsements and attacks.

"I don't think you're suddenly going to find 1 percent of corporate gross expenditures moving into politics, largely because there were so many ways to spend that money before," says Michael J. Malbin, executive director of the nonpartisan Campaign Finance Institute. Even before the ruling, about half of the states permitted direct corporate and union campaign expenditures—yet that money didn't appear to overwhelm state races.

To be sure, corporate campaign spending often flies below the radar, in both state and federal elections. Corporations tend to funnel their money through trade associations and front groups, making it hard to trace. New business- and GOP-friendly groups have cropped up, pledging to spend tens of millions of dollars in the coming election. Moreover, it's still early: Most big spending doesn't surface until the last two months before Election Day. And the post-*Citizens United* landscape is so uncertain that its real impact may not be felt until 2012, some experts predict.

Still, ominous talk of exponential campaign spending hikes is starting to look overstated. In the short term, at least, the ruling may do more to change the nature of political spending than its volume.

The *Citizens United* Ruling Won't Change Much

In the absence of an obvious corporate money surge, some analysts have downplayed the *Citizens United* ruling's importance, arguing that it does little to alter the political playing field.

"In a lot of ways, this decision is more marginal than cataclysmic in terms of what it will do to the campaign finance system," election lawyer Joseph Sandler, the former Democratic National Committee counsel and a member of Sandler Reiff & Young, maintained in a conference call the day the Court ruled. The decision's fans have tended to pooh-pooh the public reaction as so much hysteria and hyperbole.

But, in fact, the ruling has sweeping, long-term ramifications, election-law experts and even some conservatives say. Although spikes in corporate and union spending have yet to materialize, the decision signals a turnabout on the Supreme Court and a seismic shift in constitutional and campaign finance law.

That's because the Court's action sets legal precedents that threaten other long-standing pillars of the campaign finance regime, from disclosure rules to party spending curbs, the foreign-money ban, and even contribution limits. *Citizens United* is but one of dozens of campaign finance challenges that conservatives have brought and continue to bring before the high court, emboldened by its deregulatory tilt under Chief Justice John Roberts.

Some of these challenges have fallen short. In *Doe v. Reed,* the Court in June tossed out a suit brought by conservative activist James Bopp Jr. challenging state disclosure rules for voters who sign ballot petitions. Also in June, the Court turned back a Bopp-led challenge to the federal ban on soft (unregulated) money. In *Republican National Committee v. Federal Election Commission,* Bopp had argued that the RNC should be free to collect soft money for independent spending that's not coordinated with candidates.

Still, the high court all but invited further challenges that may succeed down the road. It concluded, for example, that if Bopp could show that petition signers had been harassed, the disclosure rules may, in fact, violate the Constitution. *RNC v. FEC* may also be back. That case was an "as-applied challenge," limited to specific circumstances. But the Court left the door open to a broader, facial attack on the soft-money rules.

"I have little doubt that if a facial challenge is brought to the soft-money provisions, the justices will be ready to hear it," says Richard L. Hasen, a professor at Loyola Law School in Los Angeles.

Most important, the high court's *Citizens United* opinion articulates a new, unusually narrow view of what constitutes corruption. The majority abandoned the position, upheld in previous Supreme Court cases, that campaign finance limits may be justified on the grounds that big money gives its donors "undue influence" or "access."

"The fact that speakers may have influence over or access to elected officials does not mean that these officials are corrupt," the majority opinion states, explaining that only quid pro quo corruption may be regulated. If access and ingratiation are not corruption, Hasen notes that places contribution limits, among other regulations, in serious jeopardy.

"It's a very narrow definition of corruption that is going to have, I predict, a range of very negative consequences across the campaign finance spectrum," he says. The upshot: After several decades of straddling the fence on political money but largely upholding regulations, the high court has shifted sharply in favor of free speech. Over time, disclosure and public financing may be the only regulations that this Court finds constitutional.

Congress Is More Corrupt than Ever

Given the public's disgust with government these days, it should come as no surprise that most voters think that Washington lawmakers are in the pocket of special interests.

In one poll, nearly 80 percent of respondents told a bipartisan team of researchers earlier this year that members of Congress are controlled by the groups that help fund their political campaigns. By contrast, fewer than 20 percent said that lawmakers "listen more to the voters." Such attitudes cut across the political spectrum, according to pollsters at Greenberg Quinlan Rosner Research (D) and McKinnon Media (R), which conducted the survey.

Yet leading political scientists have found the exact opposite; they've hunted in vain for proof of a correlation between money and votes over a period of decades. In study after study, "the evidence is scant to nonexistent" that political action committee contributions affect roll-call votes, says Stephen Ansolabehere, a professor of government at Harvard University.

Ansolabehere says he began his academic career convinced that campaign contributions "are an important leverage point for corporations and interest groups." But after reviewing some 80 political science analyses spanning several decades, from the 1970s through about 2005, he admits that he was forced to reconsider. The vast majority of studies, he says, conclude that "the probability of success of a bill was unaffected by total contributions."

What really sways lawmakers, the studies suggest, are constituents and party affiliation. "Constituent need trumps all," Ansolabehere says. "And party is also very important. So once you factor in parties and constituents, there is just not much room there for contributors and interest groups to have much influence."

True, reform advocates—and many lawmakers—say that such ivory-tower analyses don't square with real life inside the Beltway. Direct PAC contributions, which these academic studies target, represent only a small slice of the political money pie. Independent campaign expenditures and largely unregulated issue ads play a growing role, as do "bundled" contributions that lobbyists round up to curry favor with candidates.

Policy-making, of course, goes way beyond simple roll-call votes. Millions in corporate profits can ride on whether a bill is postponed, amended, or even scuttled—decisions that take place at the margins and behind closed doors, and leave no trace.

One political scientist who thinks that these academics are "out of their minds" is Rep. Mike Quigley, D-Ill., elected on the heels of the scandal that ousted Gov. Rod Blagojevich, D-Ill., now awaiting a verdict in his corruption trial. Quigley has a master's degree in public policy from the University of Chicago, but he takes issue with his fellow academics.

"I don't need that degree to help me understand the connection between money and policy decisions," he says. "It's very hard to prove an actual quid pro quo. Although some [politicians] are stupid and go over the top, most are careful." Quigley adds that he has heard his House colleagues wonder aloud how their votes will affect PAC contributions: "Members think about their constituencies, of course. But they're also thinking about the PACs."

Even so, reflexive public cynicism overlooks new rules and attitudes since the Watergate era, when donors carried around briefcases stuffed with cash. Lawmakers now face contribution limits and reporting rules; the soft-money ban enacted in 2002; and the stricter ethics and lobbying rules imposed in 2007 after the Jack Abramoff lobbying scandal.

The atmosphere has changed, too. Ethics-compliance teams and seminars are de rigueur at lobby shops and on Capitol Hill, and the Internet has made it easier for follow-the-money watchdog groups, reporters, bloggers, tweeters, and even average citizens to connect the dots.

"I think the people up on the Hill are bending over backwards to make sure they don't even approach the lines that have been set by the Honest Leadership and Open Government Act and the Senate ethics rules," said William J. McGinley, a partner at Patton Boggs who specializes in political law. "And I think the culture has changed quite a bit."

There is no shortage of controversies, of course—witness the recent Office of Congressional Ethics investigation into more than half a dozen lawmakers who collected donations from Wall Street donors within 48 hours of the House vote on financial services legislation. Still, popular caricatures of a widely corrupt Congress tar all lawmakers with the same brush even as politicians arguably face more-exacting rules, expectations, and public scrutiny than ever.

Money Equals Speech

If money were really speech, as conservatives like to argue, then virtually all election laws would be unconstitutional.

That is not the case—at least not yet.

Certainly, the First Amendment exhorts that "Congress shall make no law . . . abridging the freedom of speech, or of the press." In their systematic legal challenge to virtually the entire campaign finance regime, free-speech champions invariably quote this mandate. In its *Citizens United* ruling, the Supreme Court acknowledges that political speech "is central to the meaning and purpose of the First Amendment."

But even this deregulatory high court has not gone so far as to conclude that all election rules violate the Constitution. Contribution limits, for one, are a constitutional means "to ensure against the reality or appearance of corruption," the *Citizens United* majority found. The Court also left other key rules, including the soft-money ban and the disclosure laws, firmly in place.

In equating money with speech, conservatives cast political contributions in a rosy light. More campaign spending is invariably better, they insist, because donations underwrite ads and communications that enrich the public dialogue. Given how much corporations spend on commercial products such as potato chips, foes of regulation argue, U.S. elections actually cost remarkably little.

"This case will lead to more spending in political elections," enthused former FEC Chairman Bradley Smith, a professor at Capital University Law School and the chairman of the Center for Competitive Politics, shortly after the *Citizens United* ruling. "We expect to see more speech. We think that's a good thing."

But even if blatant corruption is not rampant on Capitol Hill, as many voters presume, private money potentially distorts policy-making—if for no other reason than that lawmakers must devote so much time to begging for it. American democracy, after all, is not fast-food advertising.

"If large concentrations of wealth can move easily and freely, and increasingly without transparency, through the political system, it's bound to have some influence on the nature of those decisions," says Thomas Mann, a senior fellow in governance studies at the Brookings Institution. "It doesn't have to be a quid pro quo to harm the political system."

Over time, the Supreme Court's logic in *Citizens United* may, in fact, lead it to dismantle all but a few core regulations, as some scholars predict. But we're not there yet. In the meantime, limiting campaign cash remains constitutional, and unfettered private money cannot be genuinely equated with freedom of speech.

Disclosure Is the Silver Bullet

In throwing out the longtime corporate and union spending bans, Associate Justice Anthony Kennedy assured that disclosure laws would safeguard against abuses.

"With the advent of the Internet, prompt disclosure of expenditures can provide shareholders and citizens with the information needed to hold corporations and elected officials accountable for their positions and supporters," Kennedy wrote for the majority in *Citizens United*.

Yet Kennedy's idealized vision of transparency is at odds with the real world of politics, many scholars argue. For one thing, no law requires corporations to tell shareholders whether they're spending treasury money on elections, points out Monica Youn, counsel to the democracy program at New York University School of Law's Brennan Center for Justice.

"Justice Kennedy's decision assumed a background of disclosure laws that simply didn't exist," she says. "When corporate spending does occur, it tends to be covert and to be very hard to track."

Indeed, disclosure rules are particularly spotty when it comes to independent campaign expenditures. Unlike PACs that donate directly to politicians, which must exhaustively report every penny that comes in and goes out of their coffers, groups that spend money independently of candidates need not tell much about their funding sources.

Such independent spenders must report only the money explicitly *earmarked* for an ad. That means that overhead costs paid for by a corporation or a union might never see the light of day. Money transfers between committees also routinely obscure funding sources. For their part, nonprofit advocacy groups, which are increasingly a magnet for political money, face virtually no reporting requirements.

These loopholes prompted Sen. Charles Schumer, D-N.Y., and Rep. Chris Van Hollen, D-Md., to write a broad disclosure bill in response to *Citizens United.* The measure would block big spenders from hiding behind shadowy groups with patriotic names, the lawmakers said, by forcing those running campaign ads to report their top donors and appear in on-air disclaimers.

But the bill died by filibuster in the Senate last month after winning approval in the House. Controversial provisions involving government contractors and foreign-owned corporations hurt the so-called Disclose Act—Democracy Is Strengthened by Casting Light on Spending in Elections. Republicans assailed it as pro-union, and critics blasted a last-minute exemption for the National Rifle Association and other big national groups.

The Disclose Act's real problem, however, was that it imposed elaborate reporting rules not only on unions and corporations but also on all incorporated groups—including advocacy and nonprofit organizations on the Left and Right. It's one thing, it turns out, to require politicians and political parties to publicly report their activities; it's another to ask grassroots groups to do the same.

This helps explain why Republicans, having argued for decades that disclosure is the solution to regulating political money, have reversed course. If anything, conservatives are pushing for less transparency, not more, in a series of legal and regulatory challenges. Disclosure is under fire, says Richard Briffault, a Columbia University law professor, in part because it is taking center stage as one of the few remaining campaign finance restrictions that this Supreme Court appears likely to uphold.

"Disclosure has many values," Briffault says. "But we are becoming more aware of the down sides of disclosure, and we may need to focus more carefully on what we need to know."

It would be nice if disclosure could offer up a clean, popular solution to the campaign finance mess. But like so many facets of election law, disclosure is turning out to be incomplete, complex, and controversial.

Public Financing Will Never Happen

It's true that public financing fixes in their current form will probably not win approval in this Congress, or even the next.

But the mantra that public financing will *never* pass overlooks some important recent developments.

- An innovative model for public financing that would provide multiple matching funds to reward candidates for collecting small, low-dollar donations has the potential to resuscitate the debate and bridge partisan divides.

- Advocates are better funded and organized than ever. A pair of good-government groups has pledged to spend $5 million this year and as much as $15 million over the next 18 months on a high-profile lobbying and advertising campaign to promote the Fair Elections Now Act to publicly fund congressional candidates. The House version of this bill has 159 co-sponsors, and 30 more will soon sign on, its backers say.

- Voters are unusually angry about political money. Anti-Washington sentiment; the *Citizens United* ruling; and high-profile lobbying wars over health care, Wall Street, and climate-change legislation have all thrust special-interest money into the public eye. Voters overwhelmingly object to the *Citizens United* decision, and a majority of them support the Fair Elections Now Act, recent polls show.

Outside the Beltway, "people seem much unhappier with the system than I can recall," observes former FEC Chairman Trevor Potter, president of the nonpartisan Campaign Legal Center. "And I think that inevitably pushes public funding, and new forms of the match, to the forefront."

Public financing faces big hurdles, of course. A Republican takeover of one or both chambers on Capitol Hill this fall will kick the can farther down the road. Recession and unemployment may make it harder to convince voters that lawmakers deserve what critics call taxpayer-financed campaigns.

Half a dozen states offer public financing to statewide and legislative candidates, but even these efforts are under fire. Recent lawsuits, including one heading for the Supreme Court, challenge state rescue funds that give more money to publicly financed candidates who face deep-pocketed opponents. If these suits prevail, fewer candidates may want to participate in the system.

The Achilles' heel of both the presidential and the state public financing models is that they impose spending caps on candidates who opt into the system. That makes the money unappealing and explains why presidential candidates, including Obama, have abandoned public financing.

This problem, however, is easy to fix: Simply drop the spending caps. Leading political scientists argue that it's time to adopt a "floors-not-ceilings" approach that matches small donations without limiting spending. Such a model appeals to some conservatives and may move to the fore if the high court continues to roll back existing rules.

"There's donor fatigue, there's candidate fatigue, and there's lobbyist fatigue," says ex-Rep. Bob Edgar, D-Pa., the president of Common Cause, which has teamed with Public Campaign to push for public financing. The two groups just launched their first wave of TV ads. It may be a quixotic quest, but slowly, over time, public financing may gain traction.

Critical Thinking

1. Why is a large increase in corporate spending on elections not likely to occur in the aftermath of the *Citizens United* ruling?

2. What consequences will the Supreme Court's narrow definition of corruption in the *Citizens United* case have on campaign financing?

3. What do academic analyses conclude about the effect of PAC contributions on Congressional votes? What do those who disagree with these studies argue about?

4. Why is disclosure not an effective response to the anticipated increase in corporate influence on elections following the *Citizens United* decision?

5. What three reasons, according to Eliza Carney, suggest that public financing of elections is still a possibility?

The American Presidential Nomination Process: The Beginnings of a New Era

BRUCE STINEBRICKNER

Let me start with two points that provide essential context for considering significant changes occurring in the American presidential nomination process today. First, in every presidential election since 1860 (that is, in the last 37 presidential elections) either the Democratic or Republican candidate has won and become president of the United States. Thus, the presidential nomination process serves to identify the *only* two individuals who ultimately have a chance to become president of the United States. Second, since the introduction of presidential primaries in the early twentieth century, the American people have played a much bigger role in the American presidential nomination process than their counterparts in any comparable nomination process in the world.

These two points testify to the importance and uniqueness of the American presidential nomination process. But the process by which major party candidates for president are nominated has not remained static since the introduction of presidential primaries early in the twentieth century, much less since the time of President George Washington. The presidential nominating process has sometimes changed suddenly on account of deliberate and focused reform efforts, and sometimes at a more measured and evolutionary pace.

I begin this article with an overview of the history of the presidential nomination process in the United States, identifying four distinct eras and laying the groundwork for the suggestion that we are entering or about to enter a *fifth* era in the way major party presidential nominees are chosen. Second, from the vantage point of November 2007, I identify the major changes that have arrived—or are arriving—on the scene, tracing their origins back to 2004 or 2000 as needed. Third, by assessing the likely consequences of these changes, I make the case that they represent more than minor revisions or routine evolution of the presidential nomination process. Instead, I argue that a sea change—a major transformation—in the process seems to be at hand.

Four Eras in the Presidential Nomination Process
The First Era: The Congressional Caucus Era (ca. 1800–1828)

Revolutionary War hero George Washington became the first president of the United States, serving two terms in office after having been elected unanimously by the Electoral College in 1788 and again in 1792. After Washington retired, party caucuses in Congress (that is, meetings of all the members of Congress who identified with each party) assumed the function of nominating presidential candidates. In six consecutive presidential elections from 1800 through 1828, every successful candidate had first been nominated by his party's congressional caucus. This first era in the presidential nominating process—the Congressional Caucus era—came to an end in 1831–1832, when parties began to hold national nominating conventions to choose their presidential candidates.

The end of the Congressional Caucus era—which some pejoratively called the "King Caucus" era—is significant. Had members of Congress continued to control the presidential nomination process, a key distinction between the American system of government and the parliamentary system of government would probably not have emerged. At the heart of parliamentary systems such as those in Great Britain, Australia, Japan, Italy, and India lies the relationship between candidates for prime minister (and prime ministers) and members of the lower house of parliament. As these systems have come to operate today, a party's members in parliament choose their leader, and that leader becomes the party's candidate for prime minister. Voters play a decisive role in selecting the prime minister by choosing between the parties, their policy positions, and their prime ministerial candidates in general elections. The end of the Congressional Caucus era in the United States severed the direct link between Congress and presidential nominations. In turn, the relationships between Congress and American presidential candidates, on the one hand, and parliaments and prime ministerial candidates in parliamentary democracies, on the other, developed in fundamentally different ways.[1]

The Second Era: National Conventions of Party Regulars or Activists (ca. 1831–1908)

By ending the direct and controlling role of members of Congress in choosing their parties' presidential candidates, the introduction of national nominating conventions in 1831–1832 marked the beginning of the second era in the history of the nominating process. From 1831 to the early twentieth century, delegates to national nominating conventions were individuals active in party organization affairs at the state and local levels. Party officeholders such as state and county party chairs as well as other party regulars became delegates. The national conventions were gatherings of party organization people—that is, party leaders and other party activists—from all the states, with each state party sending a number of delegates roughly proportional to the population of that state in comparison with other states.

In the twentieth century, two significant changes in the methods for selecting delegates to the parties' quadrennial national conventions gave birth to the third and fourth eras in the history of the presidential nomination process.

The Third Era: The "Mixed System" for Choosing Delegates to National Conventions (ca. 1912–1968)

In the early twentieth century, state governments introduced what has been called "the most radical of all the party reforms adopted in the whole course of American history"—the direct primary.[2] Accompanying the introduction of direct primaries for such offices as member of the United States House of Representatives, governor, state legislator, and mayor, was the introduction of presidential primaries by a number of states. A key objective was to reform, revitalize, and enhance American democracy.

Presidential primaries to choose delegates to national nominating conventions were used by twelve states in 1912. From 1916 through 1968, between thirteen and twenty states used presidential primaries, with roughly 35% to 45% of delegates (a minority, but a significant minority nevertheless) to the national conventions typically being chosen in primaries.[3] Because the remaining delegates were party organization activists, this era in the history of the presidential nominating process has been called the "mixed system."

Although reformers had managed, for the first time, to introduce mass popular involvement in choosing a sizable proportion of delegates to national conventions, their efforts did not result in all delegates being selected by voters in primaries. Even this "mixed system," however, introduced mass involvement in the process for nominating presidential candidates to an unprecedented extent and to a degree unrivalled in the nomination process for any other nation's highest elected government office.

In practice, since no candidate of either party's nomination was likely to win every delegate chosen in presidential primaries and, until 1936, Democratic convention rules required a successful candidate to win two-thirds of the delegates' votes, major party nominees during the "mixed system" era typically had to gain substantial support among those delegates coming from states that did not hold presidential primaries. Even so, "inside" and "outside" strategies for winning a party's nomination were possible. A candidate could concentrate on gaining support directly from the party organization regulars who would be attending the relevant national convention, an "inside" strategy illustrated by Hubert Humphrey's successful 1968 candidacy for the Democratic presidential nomination. Alternatively, a candidate could emphasize the primaries and seek to show sufficient electoral appeal in primary states to convince party leaders and the rest of the delegates to support his candidacy. Candidate Dwight Eisenhower used an "outside" strategy in winning the Republican presidential nomination in 1952, and candidate John F. Kennedy did likewise in winning the Democratic nomination in 1960.

The last year of the "mixed system" era, 1968, was a tumultuous and violent year in American politics. Opponents of the Vietnam War supported the anti-war candidacies of Senators Eugene McCarthy and Robert Kennedy for the Democratic presidential nomination. Kennedy was assassinated in June 1968 and, even though McCarthy or Kennedy had won virtually all the presidential primaries while taking strong anti-war positions, the "mixed system" left McCarthy with substantially less than a majority of delegates at the 1968 Democratic convention in Chicago. Adopting an "inside" strategy in seeking the Democratic party's presidential nomination that year, Vice President Hubert Humphrey did not oppose American involvement in the war being waged by his patron, President Lyndon Johnson, and did not compete in a single presidential primary. Yet Humphrey was duly nominated as his party's presidential candidate. The selection of Humphrey marked the end of the "mixed system" that had made his nomination possible.

The Fourth Era: The Plebiscitary Model for Choosing Delegates to the National Convention (1972–present)

Anti-war opponents of Hubert Humphrey waged vigorous protests in the streets of Chicago outside the 1968 Democratic convention and were violently subdued by Chicago police under the direction of Mayor Richard Daley, a Democrat and a leading supporter of Hubert Humphrey's nomination. As a consolation prize of sorts, the convention voted to establish a reform commission, which came to be known as the McGovern-Fraser Commission, reflecting the names of the two Democratic members of Congress—Senator George McGovern and Congressman Donald Fraser—who, in succession, chaired the commission.

The Commission's charge was to look for ways to make the selection of delegates to future Democratic conventions more transparent and democratic.

The McGovern-Fraser Commission uncovered and reported many interesting—some might say scandalous—points about how delegates were selected in various states and made recommendations about how to reform the system. The recommendations went into effect in 1972 and served to democratize the selection of delegates to the national conventions. (Even though the Commission was a Democratic party body, implementation of its recommendations affected the presidential nomination process for both major parties.) Presidential primaries were used to select a clear majority of delegates to national conventions. Those states not using primaries were required to open their party-run delegate selection procedures to all registered voters identifying with either party. These procedures became known as the "caucus/convention" alternative to presidential primaries, an alternative that Iowa, among other states, adopted. In effect, the McGovern-Fraser reforms completed the work of the early twentieth-century reformers, and a new era in the nominating process—the Plebiscitary Model—began in 1972, four years after the "mixed system" had led to the tumultuous and violence-marred nomination of Democrat Hubert Humphrey in Chicago. The name for this new era emphasizes the newly dominant role that the mass electorate could play in the reformed presidential nomination process, since "plebiscitarian" comes from the Latin word "plebs," which refers to the "common people."

A Closer Look at the Operation of the Plebiscitary Model

My central contention in this article is that changes in the functioning of the presidential nomination process in the first decade of the twenty-first century have been so significant that they signal or foreshadow the pending arrival of a new era, the *fifth*, in the history of the presidential nomination process. A brief examination of selected characteristics of the process in operation under the Plebiscitary Model will provide essential background for subsequently considering the major and noteworthy changes that are becoming apparent in 2007–2008.

My earlier discussion of the "mixed system" (ca. 1912–1968) and the "plebiscitary model" (1972–present) addressed changes in how delegates to national conventions were selected in the states. The "mixed system" began when a sizable minority of states introduced presidential primaries to select delegates to the national convention, thus opening the presidential nomination process to the public to an extent that was unique among the world's democracies. The "plebiscitary model" reformed the "mixed system" in ways that led a majority of states to adopt presidential primaries and required the remaining states to make their party-based caucus/convention systems accessible to all registered voters identifying with the relevant party.

Timing and Scheduling

By the 1950s, New Hampshire had established the "first-in-the-nation" status of its quadrennial presidential primary. Two decades later, Iowa successfully laid claim to scheduling its precinct caucuses, the initial stage of its caucus-convention system that operated over several months, shortly before the New Hampshire primary *and* before any other state started its delegate selection process. This Iowa-New Hampshire sequence has begun the delegate selection processes of the fifty states in every presidential election year since 1972. Candidates, news media, campaign contributors, pollsters, political activists, and the attentive public have all paid disproportionate attention to campaign activities and outcomes in these two states.

The sequence of other states' delegate selection processes has been more variable than the Iowa-first/New Hampshire-second part of the schedule, but a noteworthy phenomenon called "Super Tuesday" emerged in the 1980s. "Super Tuesday" came to refer to a Tuesday in March a few weeks after the New Hampshire primary on which a number of states (initially, mostly Southern states) scheduled their presidential primaries or caucuses. One initial objective was to increase the impact of "moderate" Southern states in the selection of the Democratic presidential nominee. With the introduction of Super Tuesday and ensuing variations in which states participated in Super Tuesday in a given presidential election year, the idea of more deliberately self-conscious and self-serving scheduling seemed to catch on. Some states (like California) that had traditionally held their delegate selection processes "late" (that is, in April, May, or June) began to schedule their selection processes earlier. These movements contributed to a phenomenon called "frontloading," which refers to crowding more and more state delegate selection processes into the months of January, February, and March, rather than having them spread out over the traditional February-through-June period.

After the Plebiscitary Model took hold in 1972, the sequence of delegate selection processes in the states seems to have become more visibly contentious among the states, the bunching of a number of states' primaries and caucuses on a single day became more prevalent (not only on "Super Tuesday," but on other single dates as well), and more delegate selection contests were "front-loaded" to the January-March period, while fewer occurred in April through June.

The "Invisible Primary"

Besides the acceptance of an Iowa–New Hampshire–Super Tuesday sequence in states' delegate selection processes, other expectations about broader matters of timing and scheduling in the presidential nomination process also developed. In the 1970s an observer coined the term "invisible primary" to refer to the activities of candidates and relevant others in the year or so *before* delegate selection processes began in Iowa and New Hampshire early in a presidential election year.[4] The "invisible primary" was, of course, not an actual presidential primary; that is, it was *not* an election run by a state government in which registered voters choose delegates to a national nominating convention. *Nor* was it "invisible." But the term, especially the word "invisible," is helpful in understanding how the presidential nomination process has been changing in the early twenty-first century.

The term "invisible primary" conveyed the largely unnoticed—at least by the general public and to some extent news media—activities in which would-be presidential candidates engaged in the years before presidential general elections.

Would-be candidates met with party leaders, high-ranking government officials, potential campaign contributors, and the like to gain support for their possible candidacy. But typically the would-be candidates did not openly declare their candidacies until late in the year preceding a presidential general election, and media attention was sporadic and not particularly intense. To the average American, these activities were all but "invisible." Even so, the "invisible primary" was hardly irrelevant to the outcome of the presidential nomination process that culminated in the selection of the parties' presidential candidates. The resulting campaign experience, fund-raising, and endorsements, not to mention media commentators' impressions and evaluations, presumably influenced candidates' prospects when the actual state-by-state delegate selection processes began.

Campaign Financing

In 1974, in the aftermath of the Watergate scandal associated with President Richard Nixon and his 1972 re-election campaign, Congress passed the Federal Election Campaign Act, initiating a system of campaign finance regulation that continues in its broad outlines to this day. Subsequent court decisions, legislation (most notably, the Bipartisan Campaign Reform Act of 2002, otherwise known as the McCain-Feingold Act), and administrative regulations (issued mostly by the Federal Election Commission, a six-member government body established by the 1974 Act) have left a tangled and complicated set of rules that apply to the financing of campaigns for presidential nominations.

Campaigns for a presidential nomination became subject to a host of reporting and accounting requirements. The amount that individuals could contribute to a single candidate's campaign was limited, and the government provided "matching" funds to candidates if they met certain conditions in their initial fundraising and agreed to accept limits on their state-by-state and overall campaign spending. The system of matching funds was designed to prevent candidates or would-be candidates who lacked reasonably widespread support in a number of states from receiving government subsidies for their campaigns. To become eligible for matching funds, a candidate had to raise $5000 in contributions of $250 or less in each of twenty states. Thereafter, contributions of up to $250 were matched by an equal amount of government funding. These matching provisions were unique to campaigns for presidential nominations and applied to neither presidential general election nor congressional campaigns. And, to repeat for the sake of emphasis, a candidate's acceptance of matching funds brought restrictions, specifically an overall spending limit for the candidate's nomination campaign and a limit on the amount that s/he could spend in each state (based on each state's population).[5]

The era of the Plebiscitary Model began in 1972, but the matching provisions of the Federal Election Campaign Act of 1974 did not take effect until the 1976 presidential nomination contests. Approximately fifty "serious" candidates sought the Democratic and Republican presidential nominations between 1976 and 1992, and only one—Republican John Connally in 1980, who won only one delegate—did not accept matching funds while campaigning for the presidential nomination.[6] In 1996, the issue of matching funds became significant when a very wealthy but relatively unknown candidate seeking the Republican presidential nomination, Steve Forbes, followed in Connally's footsteps and declined matching funds. In contrast, Republican Bob Dole, the well-known frontrunner for his party's nomination, accepted matching funds and their accompanying spending limits. Forbes poured millions of his own dollars into television advertising, which made Dole spend millions of dollars in response. Dole eventually and somewhat easily prevailed over Forbes and other contenders, but, by late March, 1996, he had spent almost all that he was legally allowed to spend until he was formally nominated by his party's national convention during the summer of 1996. This situation, many observers have noted, left him a sitting duck for several months of effective television advertising launched by the incumbent president, Bill Clinton, who had been unopposed for his party's renomination in 1996. In turn, Dole, who could not buy ads to respond to Clinton's barrage until the summer, fell hopelessly behind his formidable Democratic opponent before being officially nominated.[7]

Recent Changes in the Presidential Nomination Process

Three noteworthy recent changes in the presidential nomination process involve timing and scheduling, campaign financing, and interaction between the two: (1) an earlier start to campaigning and other candidate activities, (2) the introduction of "Super Duper Tuesday" in 2008, and (3) what has been termed the "collapse" of the system of matching funds in the financing of campaigns for the presidential nomination.[8] The first and third changes are not attributable solely to the 2007–2008 nominating cycle; both have their origins in earlier years, most particularly in the 2000 and 2004 contests. The second change, the introduction of "Super Duper Tuesday," stems more specifically from the 2007–08 nominating cycle. What I have termed a *sea change* in the process for nominating presidential candidates has been emerging during at least the two most recent presidential election cycles, while the extent and durability of the changes have become significantly more apparent during the on-going 2007–08 cycle.

An Earlier Start

One change in timing is straightforward and has been much reported: Candidates' serious and visible campaigning for presidential nominations was well under way by the beginning of 2007, a full calendar year before delegate selection processes were scheduled to begin early in the presidential election year of 2008. All sorts of activities associated with candidates' attempts to win their parties' nominations have been occurring earlier than in preceding nomination cycles.

Some candidates seeking to be elected president in 2008 declared their candidacies in late 2006. For example, former two-term Iowa governor Tom Vilsack, more than a political nonentity but less than a putative front-runner in the Democratic party's 2008 presidential nomination competition, announced his candidacy in November 2006 and officially withdrew on 23 February 2007. On the other hand, former Senator Fred

Thompson, whose name surfaced as a potentially formidable candidate for the Republican presidential nomination in the first half of 2007, delayed formal announcement of his candidacy until early September. Commentators wondered why he had waited so long to announce and whether it was too late. Major Democratic contenders John Edwards, Barack Obama, and Hillary Clinton, and major Republican contenders Mitt Romney, Rudy Giuliani, and John McCain all announced their candidacies before March 2007.[9]

Nationally televised debates among Republican and Democratic candidates were in full swing during the first half of 2007. By the summer of 2007, a half-dozen debates among Republican candidates and another half-dozen among Democratic candidates had been aired, with a similar number scheduled to occur in the second half of the year. Six to nine candidates participated in each of these events, which varied in sponsorship (from television stations to labor unions to Howard University) and format (from a single moderator to CNN's YouTube-based venture).

Finally, news media provided extensive coverage of nomination campaigns and the like during the period that used to be called the "invisible primary." Candidates' debate performances, poll results, policy positions, campaign fund-raising efforts, and other "horse race" aspects of the campaign were reported, and systematic comparisons of candidates' proposals on issues such as the Iraq war and health care reform were occasionally provided. In the summer of 2007, *The New York Times* conducted interviews with voters across the United States and reported that they were unusually engaged by the early campaigning as well as "flinching at the onslaught of this early politicking."[10]

The Collapse of the System of Matching Funds

In 2000, Republican candidate George W. Bush was the first presidential nominee of either major party who had not accepted matching funds during his campaign for his party's nomination. In 2003, two leading candidates for the Democratic nomination, Howard Dean and John Kerry, followed Bush's lead of four years earlier and opted out of matching funds. The 1996 predicament of Republican Bob Dole that resulted from his acceptance of matching funds and the accompanying spending limits doubtless influenced later decisions by candidates Bush, Dean, and Kerry. By the start of the 2007–2008 presidential nomination cycle, no major contender for either party's nomination was expected to accept matching funds, although eventually Democrat John Edwards decided to do so. By 2007, the path that Republican nominee Bush had taken in 2000 had become the norm for all but one major candidate. In turn, the system of spending limits that depend on candidates' acceptance of matching funds has been undermined and, in effect, probably ended, at least among major candidates.

Several additional observations about the end of the "old" system of presidential nomination financing are in order. In the absence of spending limits that would have accompanied acceptance of matching funds, fund-raising for 2007–08 presidential nomination campaigns grew enormously. Hillary Clinton's 2007 first quarter total of 26 million dollars and fellow Democrat candidate Barack Obama's close second of 25.6 million can be contrasted with 7.4 million, the total for candidate John Edwards, the leading Democratic fund-raiser in the first quarter of 2003, and 8.9 million, Democratic candidate Al Gore's total in the first quarter of 1999.

The maximum that a candidate could receive in matching funds in the 2007–08 nomination cycle was approximately 21 million dollars. When almost all of the front-running candidates of both parties opted out of the matching system, they were concluding that that amount of partial public funding was not a sufficient reason to accept matching funds. More valuable than 21 million dollars of public funding was the freedom not to abide by the spending limits that accompanied the acceptance of matching funds. Through the end of the third quarter of 2007, Clinton had raised 90.6 million dollars and Obama 80.3 million, while the two candidates who were leading the Republican field in fund-raising, Mitt Romney and Rudy Giuliani, had raised 62.8 million and 45.8 million dollars, respectively.[11]

The demise of the "matching" system for financing campaigns for the presidential nomination cannot be attributed solely to the 2007–08 presidential nomination cycle. Foreshadowed by the predicament in which Republican candidate Bob Dole found himself in March 1996, the "collapse" of the matching system is an early twenty-first century phenomenon that culminated in 2007–08.

The Money Primary

Amidst earlier declarations of candidacy (and, sometimes, withdrawals), earlier and numerous televised debates, earlier extensive media coverage, and the collapse of the system of matching funds, a new term was coined to replace "invisible primary" as a name for the early period of the presidential nomination process—the "money primary." Federal Election Commission (FEC) regulations require quarterly reports of candidates' fund-raising activities in the years preceding presidential general elections (and monthly reports in presidential election years). As 31 March 2007 approached, journalists anticipated the required candidate filings and what they would show in fund-raising prowess and contributors' support. News media reported and analyzed candidates' first-quarter filings with the FEC against a background of different fund-raising expectations for different candidates. On the Democratic side, Barack Obama was judged to have performed especially well, raising 25.6 million dollars, just a little less than front-runner Hillary Clinton and substantially more than John Edward's 14 million. On the Republican side, candidate John McCain fell short of fund-raising expectations and prospects for his candidacy were discounted accordingly, while competitor Mitt Romney's stock rose on account of his first quarter fund-raising total of 20.7 million dollars, six million more than the amount raised by the second-place finisher at that stage of the Republican money primary, Rudy Giuliani.[12]

Through all the changes, news media retained their prominent role as assessors of the nominating competition. Years earlier, when the term *invisible primary* applied, news media had been dubbed the "Great Mentioner" because of their role in identifying candidacies that should be taken seriously. For a candidate not to be mentioned by journalists was like being afflicted with a politically terminal illness. In 2007, news media assessments continued to help the attentive public gauge the on-going horse race among candidates. Poll results—both national polls and polls in the early caucus and primary states of Iowa, New Hampshire, and South Carolina—and the results of the quarterly "money primaries" were combined with other information and intuitions to make assessments of who was winning, who was gaining or losing ground, and the like. What seemed new in 2007 was the extent of early candidate activity, including the plethora of televised debates in the first half of the year and especially the salience of the "money primary." Campaigns for the two major parties' presidential nominations seemed to be in full swing early in 2007, nearly two years before the November 2008 general election and a year before the states' delegate selection processes were set to begin in Iowa in January 2008.

Super Duper Tuesday and Related Matters

What should probably, because of the earlier start to full-scale campaigning, be called the *2007–2008* presidential nomination process also brought noteworthy change in the clustering of delegate selection processes in the states. During the 1988 presidential nominating process, sixteen mostly Southern states scheduled their delegate selection processes on a single day in early March that was called "Super Tuesday." Such clustering of many states' primaries and caucuses on a single day continued to occur in subsequent years and "Super Tuesday" became a quadrennial event. In 2004, a second, smaller clustering of states on a single Tuesday in March after Super Tuesday was dubbed "mini-Tuesday."

Prior to 2008, the sequence of delegate selection processes in the states during the era of the Plebiscitary Model typically had the following pattern: Iowa; New Hampshire; and, fairly soon thereafter, "Super Tuesday," which grew beyond its original Southern focus to include more non-Southern states. Super Tuesday was sometimes decisive—and sometimes not—in determining eventual presidential nominees, and outcomes in Iowa and especially New Hampshire continued to play disproportionately influential roles.

The phenomenon of Super Tuesday, coupled with a general tendency in the direction of more and more "frontloading," led in 2008 to what was variously dubbed "Super Duper Tuesday," "Tsunami Tuesday," and even "Unofficial National Primary Day." By mid-2007, at least twenty states that together accounted for more than 50% of the delegates to each national convention had scheduled their delegate selection processes for 5 February 2008, a short time after Iowa, New Hampshire, Nevada, and South Carolina were scheduled to hold their delegate selection processes.

As of this writing in November, 2007, the significance of Super Duper Tuesday remains to be seen, but the outcomes of twenty-odd states' delegate selection processes on that day may well be decisive. In other words, 5 February 2008 may become the functional equivalent of a national presidential primary in which, as a consequence of voters casting ballots in at least twenty states *on a single day,* the presidential nominees of both major parties will be determined.

The idea of holding a succession of regional primaries (for example, four of them, each including a contiguous bloc of states in which approximately one-fourth of the population of the United States lives) or a single national primary is not new. Both ideas have been advocated as possible reforms to the presidential nomination process, often with an eye to reducing or eliminating the disproportionate impact of Iowa and New Hampshire. The creation of "Super Duper Tuesday" on 5 February 2008 resulted from decisions by individual states and small groups of states to hold their delegate selection processes on that date, rather than from any single, coordinated reform effort. As the magnitude and implications of "Super Duper Tuesday" came into focus, California, New York, and Florida, among other states, began to re-think the scheduling of *their* 2008 delegate selection processes.

The outline of the Florida story, as of this writing (November, 2007), bears reporting. In May, 2007, the Florida legislature scheduled its presidential primaries for 29 January 2008. Doing so violated both major parties' rule that only Iowa, New Hampshire, Nevada, and South Carolina could hold delegate selection processes before 5 February 2008. In August 2007, the Democratic national party decided that any Florida delegates elected before 5 February 2008 would not be seated at the 2008 Democratic national convention. In late September, the Florida Democratic Party announced its continuing support for holding the Florida presidential primaries on the forbidden 29 January date.[13] The final outcome of this controversy remains to be seen, but one reporter suggested that it might eventually result in the end of Iowa's and New Hampshire's traditional primacy in the presidential nomination calendar.[14]

A Sea Change and a New Era

I have pointed to three recent and significant changes in the presidential nomination process: (1) earlier sustained and public campaigning by candidates, so that public declarations of candidacies and serious campaigning are well underway two years before a presidential general election, (2) the establishment of what may function as an "unofficial national primary" early in February 2008, which reflects the convergence or perhaps even culmination of two earlier trends: (i) increased "frontloading" of the states' delegate selection processes and (ii) growing inclination of states to schedule their delegate selection processes on a single day a few weeks after Iowa and New Hampshire in an attempt to reduce the disproportionate influence of those two states in the outcome of the presidential nomination process, and (3) the demise of the system of matching funds that had anchored the regulation of presidential nomination campaign financing since the passage of the Federal Election Campaign Act in 1974.

What are the implications of these changes? Why might they matter? A simple answer is that these changes will likely affect the sort of individuals who are likely to be nominated and perhaps those who are likely to run. More specifically, the new era, whose beginnings have, in my view, become clearly visible in the 2007–08 cycle, will give the "dark horse," the underdog, the relatively little-known presidential aspirant, less chance to be nominated.

"Dark horses" emerged frequently enough during the "mixed system" era (1912–1968) to make them a staple of political lore. Sometimes such candidates emerged after an unexpectedly strong showing in important primaries, sometimes after party bosses and delegates at a deadlocked convention turned their backs on the two or three leading contenders and sought a "new face" whom supporters of the leading contenders could accept.

Under the Plebiscitary Model, the dramatic increase in the number of delegates chosen by the mass electorate meant that the outcome of early delegate selection processes, especially in Iowa and New Hampshire, led to successful nominations of Democratic dark horse candidates George McGovern and Jimmy Carter in 1972 and 1976, respectively. Little known Democrat Bill Clinton's nomination in 1992 was also a largely unexpected outcome. Yet each won their party's nomination by successfully navigating the sequence of states' delegate selection processes that operated under the Plebiscitary Model. Carter's first-place finish among candidates in Iowa in 1976 ("undecided" was Iowans' first choice), followed by his win in the New Hampshire primary, put the relatively unknown former governor of Georgia on track to be nominated. McGovern's 1972 and Clinton's 1992 successful quests to be nominated followed roughly similar scripts.

Why does the current sea change in the presidential nomination process threaten such dark horse candidacies? Let me begin with the existence of "Super Duper Tuesday," which may function *almost* as a national primary in 2008. So-called retail politics can work in small states such as Iowa and New Hampshire. The little known candidate can, by dint of arduous campaigning, impress attentive Iowa and New Hampshire voters by shaking hands, attending small meetings in people's homes, knocking on doors, and the like. It has been said (almost surely apocryphally) that an Iowa or New Hampshire voter does not take a presidential nomination candidate seriously until the voter has shaken the candidate's hand at least twice! In such a "retail politics" environment, the advantages of initial name recognition, endorsements from leading national political figures, money, and even campaign organization are less important than in the "wholesale politics" required by big state primaries or multiple-state primaries held on a single day. To the extent that "Super Duper Tuesday" approximates a national primary and the wholesale politics that that would entail, the chances of a dark horse or little-known candidate are lessened. Perhaps, as some observers have suggested, the Iowa-New Hampshire-Nevada-South Carolina-Super Duper Tuesday sequence in 2008 will not result in 5 February 2008 functioning as a national presidential primary. Perhaps it will. Regardless, Super Duper Tuesday seems to constitute movement in the direction of a national primary (or at least a series of regional primaries, which would also require wholesale politics), with such a development working to undermine dark horse candidacies.

The collapse of the system of matching funds also seems to disadvantage dark horse or underdog candidacies. Well-known front-runners typically can raise more money than less well-known underdogs. Even so, the matching system worked to narrow the gap between the campaign resources of front-runners and those of underdogs.

The third change in the presidential nomination process that I have identified—the earlier start of full-scale campaigning and resulting news media attention—might on first glance seem to enhance the chances of potential dark horse candidates. The longer the campaigning, it would seem, the more likely an underdog could out-perform better known opponents and overcome their greater resources both over the long haul and in the face of simultaneous contests in a large number of states on "Super Duper Tuesday." In addition, the argument might continue, if such an underdog performed well in the early going, the resource gap between him/her and his/her better known opponents would likely be lessened.

The counter-argument would run in an opposite direction. The superior resources of the front-running candidates and the earlier start to the campaign make it all the more unlikely that an underdog can win. The front-running candidates have more time during which to effectively spend their resources on TV ads and the like, and more time for their larger and better-financed on-the-ground organizations to produce effects. Moreover, news media identification of the top tier of candidates, based partly on the results of the money primary, has longer to sink in with the mass public and, perhaps, become the received wisdom. Finally, the earlier start to serious campaigning means that an underfinanced, underdog candidate needs to compete that much longer against better known, better financed candidates without the prospect of a headline-grabbing victory or at least an unexpectedly strong showing in Iowa or New Hampshire. Instead, the demoralizing effects of the well-publicized money primary undermine underdogs' credibility, often to the point of no return.

As should be clear, I am less certain about the effects of the lengthened nomination campaign season on dark horse candidacies than I am about the effects of an "unofficial national primary" and the demise of the system of matching funds. But, taken as a whole, recent changes in the nomination process that, in my judgment, constitute—or, at the very least, foreshadow—a sea change seem destined to undermine underdog candidacies.

Before closing, let me do one more brief round of "so what?" analysis. Suppose one wanted to change the operation of the Plebiscitary Model to eliminate virtually any chance of underdog candidates such as George McGovern (1972), Jimmy Carter (1976), and, in the 2007–08 cycle, Democrats Tom Vilsack and Chris Dodd and Republicans Tommy Thompson and Sam Brownback, four seasoned politicians with relevant government experience, but little name recognition among the public. To accomplish such an objective, one might introduce the recent changes in the presidential nomination process identified in this article. The latest sea change in the presidential nomination process may relate especially to the sorts of qualities major party presidential nominees need to have. If widespread name recognition and celebrity status—both of which, to be sure, can result from high profile experience in government, a point that sometimes is overlooked—and/or moneyed connections sufficient to raise vast sums of contributions are to be essential characteristics for a presidential nominee, then the nomination process is moving in an accommodating direction.

Perhaps the fifth era in the history of the presidential nomination process will come to be known as "the post-dark horse era," "the celebrity candidate era," "the national (or regional) primary era," or even "the era after the demise of Iowa's and New Hampshire's primacy." Whatever the new era comes to be called and whatever exact shape it takes, please do not say that no one told you it was coming.

Notes

1. The overview of the history of the American presidential nomination process presented here and continued below draws substantially from Bruce Stinebrickner, "The Presidential Nominating Process: Past and Present," *World Review* 19, No. 4 (October 1980), pp. 78–102.

2. The quotation comes from Austin Ranney, as quoted in Stinebrickner, p. 80. Austin Ranney, *Curing the Mischiefs of Faction: Party Reform in America* (Berkeley, California: University of California Press, 1975), p. 121.

3. For a table displaying exact numbers of states using presidential primaries for every presidential election year between 1912 and 2004, see "Table 3-1 Votes Cast and Delegates Selected in Presidential Primaries, 1912–2004," in *Presidential Elections, 1789–2004* (Washington, D.C.: CQ Press, 2005), p. 104.

4. See Arthur T. Hadley, *The Invisible Primary* (Englewood Cliffs, NJ: Prentice Hall, 1976).

5. For more details, see David B. Magleby and William G. Mayer, "Presidential Nomination Finance in the Post-BCRA Era," in William G. Mayer, ed., *The Making of the Presidential Candidates 2008* (Lanham, Maryland: Rowman and Littlefield, 2008), pp. 141–168. The summary of the matching provisions given here is drawn largely from pp. 142–143.

6. Magleby and Mayer, p. 144.

7. This Forbes-Dole-Clinton account is taken largely from Magleby and Mayer, pp. 149–152.

8. Magleby and Mayer use the subtitle "The *Collapse* of the Matching Fund Program" on p. 149 of their chapter (emphasis added). Martin Frost, former member of the U.S. House of Representatives and former chairman of the Democratic Congressional Campaign Committee, observed early in 2007 that it would not be a surprise if the matching system for presidential nomination process financing "simply disappears" after the 2007–08 cycle. "Federal Financing of Presidential Campaigns May Be History," FoxNews.com, 8 January 2007: 23 September 2007, <www.foxnews.com>.

9. Announcements signaling a candidacy for a party's 2008 presidential nomination often occurred at more than a single point in time. Several candidates made a combination of announcements, presumably to increase the increments of media attention that such announcements were expected to produce. A single candidate's announcements in 2007 might include the following: that s/he was going to make an "important announcement" in a few days, that s/he was going to begin "exploring" whether to become a candidate (or that s/he was forming an "exploratory committee" to "test the waters"), that s/he had "decided" to become a candidate, and that s/he was "formally" declaring his or her candidacy.

10. Adam Nagourney. "Voters Excited Over '08 Race; Tired of It, Too." *The New York Times*, 9 July 2007, A1.

11. Federal Election Commission: 29 November 2007, www.fec.gov/finance/disclosure/srssea.shtml/.

12. "First Quarter 2007 FEC Filings," *Washington Post*: 30 September 2007 <http://projects.washingtonpost.com/2008-presidential-candidates/finance/2007/q1/>.

13. Abby Goodnough, "Florida Democrats Affirm an Early Primary," *The New York Times,* 24 September 2007, A12.

14. "World News", ABC, WRTV, Indianapolis, 24 September 2007, correspondent Jake Tapper: "Democrats are convinced that this is the beginning of the end of the Iowa-New Hampshire monopoly."

Critical Thinking

1. How were major presidential candidates nominated during the early decades of the 19th century?

2. What is a national nominating convention and when did such conventions begin to nominate major party presidential candidates?

3. Why is the third era in the evolution of the American presidential nominating process called the "mixed system"? What elements are in the "mix"?

4. What are the hallmarks of the "Plebiscitary Model" for nominating presidential candidates and what happened in 1968 that led to adoption of this model beginning in 1972? What was the McGovern-Fraser Commission?

5. Why is the Fourth Era's "Plebiscitary Model" given that name?

6. What alternative to direct primaries does the Plebiscitary Model include?

7. What are the most significant recent changes to the presidential nomination process?

8. What are the implications of the collapse of the matching funds system for candidates seeing their party's presidential nomination?

9. What is a "dark horse" candidate? Why does the transformative change in the presidential nomination process that Bruce Stinebrickner expects threaten "dark horse" candidacies?

I want to thank Luke Beasley, Allison Clem, Annie Glausser, Christina Guzik, Kelsey Kauffman, David Parker, Amy Robinson, and Randall Smith for their helpful comments on an earlier draft of this article. I also want to thank Luke Beasley for his work in locating presidential candidates' announcement dates for the four most recent presidential elections.

Three Ways Social Media Will Make or Break 2012 Election Campaigns

Planning a run for office? Here's what you need to know.

Jay Samit

Twitter and Facebook as tools that topple governments? We'd have laughed off that idea a few years ago—but the "Arab Spring" protests prove that social media ignites (and spreads) passion and outrage better than any other communication vehicle. Social media will have a similar game-changing effect on the 2012 elections—in fact, any candidate or issue campaign that expects to succeed needs to make social engagement a critical part of their strategy, or they're doomed to fail.

Television doesn't have the impact it once commanded. The next occupant of the White House isn't going to get elected solely because of a brilliant social-media strategy—but without such a strategy, candidates will not be able to enter a dialog with the majority of swing voters.

Social media made some inroads in the 2008 election, with the Obama campaign using Facebook to build volunteer donor networks and activate the base. In three short years, however, social media has evolved so dramatically, and become so pervasive in daily life for most likely voters, that the fledgling tactics deployed in 2008 look positively ancient. Here's why social media now has the power to make or break campaigns:

Audience: It's not just your kids and it's not just young Obama voters who user Facebook and Twitter. Social-media use by people over 50 is on the rise, and for elections, voters on both sides of the fence rely on social media to connect them to campaigns. According to a January 2011 report from the Pew Internet & American Life Project, Republicans and Democrats used social media to share political information at roughly equal rates during the 2010 midterm election. Facebook has 150 million U.S. users old enough to vote, and the average user has 130 friends. Any way you slice it, the social-media audience is massive, growing, and shares the information that most affects their lives with their family and friends online.

Influence: With the median age of a TV evening news viewer approaching 63 years old, it's possible that voters age 18 to 35 won't even hear a candidate's message—unless it's coming to them through social media. The majority of all internet ad impressions take place on Facebook & Facebook apps. Social-media users rely heavily on their connections for advice on what to eat, wear, watch, and who and what to vote for. Facebook friends' suggestions matter far more than a TV commercial or newspaper editorial. Getting one's message into those billions of news feeds on Facebook is the key to entering the conversation.

Money: Realizing the size and power of social-media audiences, top brand advertisers (both commercial and political) are funneling serious money into online and mobile advertising. Investments in digital advertising for the 2012 cycle have already begun, with the Democratic National Committee/Obama for America allocating significant funds to digital advertising in the first quarter of 2011. And thanks to the recent Supreme Court decision on Citizens United vs. FEC to end a ban on political spending by corporations, the flow of money into campaign advertising—and therefore, into social media—will become a torrent. Thanks to the earned media that is created through viral sharing of political messages, studies of studies have proven social-media engagement advertising as the most cost-effective way to reach a targeted audience at scale.

Social media, and the content that its users share, has become a highly effective way for brands to hammer home messages and build stronger relationships with customers. Global brands such as Microsoft, Procter and Gamble, Coca-Cola and Disney are spending more and more ad dollars on social-media campaigns that engage people—creating a conversation instead of just spraying more banner ads across web pages. And when people interact with these engagements, they're far more likely to share the experience with others in their social networks.

The impact of online engagement and sharing for political campaigns is unprecedented. People who use social networks like to take part in the same activities as their online connections. If they see that their friends are posting photos or checking in at political rallies or sharing candidates' videos, they don't want to be the last to know. It's called "FOMO" or Fear of Missing Out, which social media brilliantly takes advantage of.

Political messages within social media promise to engage users even more deeply than brand messages. Our recent SocialVibe study found that 94 percent of social-media users of voting age engaged by a political message watched the *entire* message, and 39 percent of these people went on to share it with an average of 130 friends online—a rate of sharing that's about double what we typically see for non-political campaigns. This shows you how "share-ripple" goes far beyond the initial audience targeted by the campaign. And 1/3 of friends opened the message—creating millions in free earned media for the candidate or cause.

Local candidates can now use social-media engagement advertising to raise money from like-minded citizens far from their districts. There are many ways to generate excitement for candidates and issues online, ranging from simple emails that include links to Facebook pages and YouTube videos to engagement advertising that trades brand messages for desired content. However, these 2012 campaigns play out online, the key element for success will be sharable content: surveys, videos, "I donated" badges, and check-in rewards, to name a few.

An active and well-informed populace is the key to a strong democracy. Thanks to the power of social media, the 2012 election may be the most participatory election in our nation's history.

Critical Thinking

1. Compare and contrast changes in the likely impact of television and social media on election campaigns in the future.

2. What is the age group of voters who are most tuned into social media?

3. What can be said about audience, influence, and money in the context of social media's likely impact on the coming 2012 election campaigns?

Jay Samit is CEO of SocialVibe, the internet's largest engagement advertising platform. SocialVibe reaches more than 662 million hyper-connected social-media users each month across leading digital, social and mobile properties.

Big Oil's Big Man in Washington

Lobbyist Jack Gerard wants to make the oil industry seem kinder and friendlier. His largest obstacle? Oil companies.

Tory Newmyer

Jack Gerard has pretty much been in crisis mode since taking over as president and CEO of the American Petroleum Institute in November 2008. Shortly after he arrived at the powerful oil-industry lobbying group, President Obama and a wave of Democrats swept into office, promising to fund alternative energy sources and take action on climate change. Last year the BP disaster poured more than 200 million gallons of oil into the Gulf of Mexico, and Gerard spent the summer prepping his members for more than 50 congressional hearings and eight separate investigations related to the spill and its aftermath. Then, in mid-May, executives from five oil companies appeared before a committee of the U.S. Senate and defended their earnings, which could hit record highs in 2011. "Don't punish our industry for doing its job well," Chevron CEO John Watson said. The performance was, by all accounts, a public relations disaster.

Indeed, Big Oil could scarcely be less popular than it is now: Gasoline prices on average are hovering around $4 a gallon, up more than a dollar from a year ago; turmoil in the Middle East and strong global demand contribute to high prices, but try telling that to the guy spending $75 to fill his tank at an Exxon station. President Obama, on the hunt for ways to cut debt, has targeted oil companies' tax breaks, and an NBC/*Wall Street Journal* poll in February found 74 percent of all respondents favor such a move. "Emotionally, no one is on their side," Robert Passikoff, president of the brand-loyalty consultancy Brand Keys, says of the industry. "No one feels bad for the oil companies."

And yet Gerard, a 53-year-old professional lobbyist whose last gig was running a chemical trade association, thinks he can get Americans to support, even root for, Big Oil. As he was putting out fires on Capitol Hill and at the White House, he also reached out to left-leaning groups that haven't been traditional allies, such as the

AFL-CIO and the Congressional Hispanic Caucus, and has even hired the Nature Conservancy's top grass-roots organizer to mobilize a citizen activism campaign for API. Gerard believes he can protect his industry by reminding an increasingly prickly and vocal public—think Tea Party—about how many people his members and affiliates employ. (API says it is responsible for supporting some 9.2 million jobs.)

Key Moments

What happens in the oilfields influences Washington, and vice versa.

- January 1969: A blowout on a Union Oil platform pollutes 30 miles of California beaches.
- July 1979: President Jimmy Carter delivers his "malaise" speech and outlines plans to reduce U.S. dependency on oil imports.
- July 1986: Oil dips under $9 per barrel (in 1986 dollars) after years of increased production.
- August 1990: President George H.W. Bush signs the Oil Pollution act, requiring oil companies to develop disaster-mitigation plans.
- April 2010: Deepwater Harizon explodes in the Gulf of Mexico, killing 11 workers and setting off the worst spill in the nation's history.
- January 1970: Nixon signs the National Environmental Policy Act a response to the Union Oil disaster.
- October 1973: Oil-Producing Middle East countries proclaim an oil embargo against the U.S. in response to its support of Israel.
- March 1989: The Exxon Valdez runs aground in Alaska, spilling at least 11 million gallons of crude.
- July 2010: House Democrats pass a sweeping "spill bill" to address the BP disaster. (It goes nowhere in the Senate.)

Eventually he hopes to have a presence on the ground in every congressional district in the country, so when a policy proposal hits the industry's bottom line, lawmakers from Seattle to Savannah will hear complaints about it from voters back home. The gambit is showing signs of success. A series of API-organized rallies last summer helped derail the "spill bill" Democrats aimed to enact in the wake of the BP (BP) disaster. Now he is hoping the prospect of new jobs will stoke popular zeal for hydraulic fracking—a practice that is raising safety and environmental concerns.

Wooing the American public is just one prong of Gerard's strategy for preserving his members' tax breaks and expanding their access to energy reserves. A lobbyist is only as good as his relationships, and Gerard, a devout churchgoer with eight children, including twin boys adopted from Guatemala, is quite adept at using his personal life to forge bonds with important allies on the Hill. At the same time he's gained unprecedented direct and regular access to the CEOs of his most important member companies, including Exxon's Rex Tillerson and Conoco Phillips' James Mulva.

Gerard often seems clinical, almost professorial, when he talks about the issues he lobbies for. (He asks four times during one interview whether he is boring me, and in a follow-up session in his downtown Washington office he is surprisingly equivocal on the subject of climate change.) But rivals shouldn't mistake his professionalism for lack of passion. Gerard loves a challenge, and nothing could be more of a battle than revamping Big Oil's image. "If I'm playing basketball," the 5-foot-9 Gerard explains, "I want to take on the team who's got the 7-foot-3 guy as opposed to the team that's got the 6-foot-5 guy. Why? Because he's tougher to beat."

"We're putting the true human face on this industry. These are PTA presidents and Little League coaches."

—Jack Gerard, CEO, American Petroleum Institute

Before Gerard agreed to take the job at API two years ago, he made an unusual stipulation for a trade association director. He didn't want to be just a hired gun; he wanted to be a strategic partner with a direct line to the industry's CEOs. He got it—and he isn't shy about using it, keeping in constant contact with his bosses over the phone and by e-mail, much to the chagrin of the oil companies' in-house lobbyists, who don't enjoy the same access. "This can make or break a trade association, having that relationship at the top and having the ability to pick up the phone and talk to someone," he says. Gerard also regularly flies to Houston for meetings with oil executives, and he has found a way to get particularly close to Exxon's Tillerson, who heads API's biggest member company and happens to serve as national president of the Boy Scouts of America. Gerard has been active in the leadership of the D.C.-area organization.

"You sit down for dinner and start talking to somebody, and you find you've got a passion for something similar," Gerard says. "A remarkable thing about humanity is to come together and find those common bonds, and Scouts happens to be one I share with Rex." Tillerson credits Gerard with doing "an exceptional job leading the industry at a very challenging time" by assembling "an effective grass-roots and issue education program that has significantly increased the industry's voice in the national energy discussion."

Indeed, few of Gerard's good deeds go unexploited. He is an active presence in the Mormon church as the equivalent of an archbishop, which gives him ties to Republican Sen. Orrin Hatch—the top GOP member of the Senate's tax-writing committee—and presidential candidate Mitt Romney. Last summer Gerard joined Democratic Sen. Mary Landrieu and a U.S. delegation on a weeklong trip to London and Ethiopia that focused on international adoptions. Landrieu has always been a reliable friend to the oil industry—Louisiana is one of the biggest oil-producing states—but just two weeks after returning from her travels with Gerard she stunned the White House by placing a hold on Obama's nominee to be his next budget director, employing a Senate maneuver to block the appointment. Landrieu explained the move was intended to pressure the administration to lift the moratorium on drilling in the Gulf of Mexico imposed after the spill. The White House blasted Landrieu's ploy as "unwarranted and outrageous," but it relented, lifting the moratorium seven weeks before it was set to expire. Landrieu says the hold was her idea, and she asked Gerard to support her only after placing it. "I'm proud of it," she says, and as for the trip, "when Jack and I travel, we just talk about adoption issues."

The son of a John Deere salesman and a schoolteacher, Gerard grew up in Mud Lake, Idaho (pop. 358). As a child, he memorized the serial numbers on tractors while pitching in at his father's business. The family had a small farm too, and Gerard and his three brothers bracketed their school days by milking Holsteins. Back then there weren't a lot of distractions to complicate his schedule. Now Gerard chalks up his time-management strategy to a three-word formula: "good, better, best." It's a philosophy, he says, that encourages him not to settle for a good use of his time but to strive for the best one. The credo comes from a 2007 speech by a Mormon church leader named Dallin Oaks. Embedded in Oaks' message was an admonition that "to innovate does not necessarily mean to expand; very often it means to simplify."

And so Gerard has simplified API, firing 20 percent of the staff and paring priorities from a sprawling list of two dozen items, including research into alternative energy, to just six, focused on expanding onshore and offshore drilling and blocking proposals such as the Senate Democrats' effort to cut about $21 billion in tax breaks over 10 years. (Most of the money, almost $13 billion, would come from ending the oil giants' eligibility for a manufacturing tax credit, the rest from eliminating a number of smaller, industry-specific deductions.)

As instructive as the fights he picks are those he dodges. On the question of whether climate change is man-made, Gerard not only declines to offer an opinion, he's oblique on whether he has one at all. "I'm not a scientist," he shrugs. Gerard, who actually has been a part of this debate for a decade, going back to his days running the National Mining Association, doggedly steers the conversation to the process for addressing climate change rather than take a position on an issue that's core to his membership. "The view we've taken is that we have a committee that works on it." Asked if that includes a recognition that the phenomenon is man-made, Gerard weaves again: "I'd have to go back and look at the broader principles that have been adopted."

Gerard's rhetorical jujitsu on a hot-button topic dividing the parties—and, to a certain extent, his membership—speaks to a key piece of his mission. He has set about trying to change the perception that Big Oil and Republican politics are inextricably bound, a pursuit that gained urgency when Obama moved into the White House. Gerard acted quickly, hiring Marty Durbin, nephew of the No. 2 Senate Democrat, Dick Durbin of Illinois, to head up API's lobbying team and start opening Democratic doors on the Hill. He organized fly-in lobbying visits by African-American, Hispanic, and female oil workers. And he formed a partnership with the building and construction trades department of the AFL-CIO to tout the job-creating potential of new drilling projects. Informal talks with social-media experts from the Obama campaign prompted Gerard to poach Nature Conservancy's Deryck Spooner to help build a grass-roots army that now claims more than 500,000 members.

Last summer, after the House passed a tough bill to boost safety standards for offshore drilling and remove a liability cap for oil spills, Gerard mounted a round of rallies in regions far from the oilfields. At one, in suburban Chicago, more than 500 union workers assembled for a slick corporate production stage-managed to look like a working-class event. A parade of industry and labor leaders spoke, crediting the oil business for creating American jobs. The rally concluded with a speech by former Chicago Bears coach Mike Ditka, who blended stories of his own hardscrabble upbringing with an appeal for energy independence.

The protest—one of seven that API organized last summer—sufficiently spooked the Senate. "In those smaller media markets, it's a big deal," says retired Sen. George Voinovich, a moderate Ohio Republican. The spill bill barely got a second look when the Senate returned from its August recess. And when Obama in September proposed funding a new $50 billion infrastructure program by repealing Big Oil tax breaks, Voinovich told the President that the industry's on-the-ground vigor would be a major obstacle. Recalls Voinovich: "I told him, 'You've got as much chance as a snowball in hell.'"

Though API is seen as the lobbying arm of some of the world's largest companies (Exxon, Chevron, and ConocoPhillips are Nos. 2, 3, and 4, respectively, on the *Fortune* 500 ranking of companies by revenue), it also includes dozens of small suppliers, and Gerard has started to enlist those companies and other allies in his effort to show how vital the industry is to the economy.

During consideration of the spill bill last summer, API reminded liberal members of Congress of the small vendors that sell everything from boots to helicopter parts to the oil and gas business. Across the country farm bureaus, truckers, grocers, cattle growers, and union locals also got in on the act, piping up in defense of Big Oil. "Jack has done very well at expanding the allies we have in this so people understand how important we are to their industry," says Marathon Oil CEO Clarence Cazalot.

Gerard's tactics will soon be put to the test again as he tries to win local support for horizontal hydraulic fracturing, or fracking. The technique allows drillers to blast a high-pressure cocktail of water, sand, and chemicals into shale rock more than a mile underground. The process cracks the rock and releases the oil or natural gas trapped inside. Some environmentalists and local activists contend that runoff from the practice threatens to contaminate water supplies, a charge the industry denies. Blowback against fracking has been so intense in New York that the state declared a temporary moratorium pending further review. The Environmental Protection Agency is conducting its own study, with results expected next year.

Gaining access to the deposits remains a critical priority for Gerard, and it's easy to understand why. Some of his biggest members—including Exxon Mobil and Chevron—have been getting in on the frenzy by snapping up smaller outfits working in the field. For Gerard, developing the new resources could be a political game changer for the industry, allowing it to ramp up its presence far beyond the traditional confines of oil-rich and gulf states. The largest known oil shale deposit in the world sits underneath Colorado, Wyoming, and Utah—containing an estimated 800 billion barrels of recoverable oil. Another major deposit spans most of North Dakota, into Montana. The Marcellus Shale, containing the largest natural-gas deposit on the continent, underlies New York, Pennsylvania, Ohio, and West Virginia. And a sizable deposit, the Fayetteville Shale, is buried in northern Arkansas.

Gerard touts the employment benefits of starting projects across the map—280,000 new jobs over the next decade by developing the Marcellus Shale alone, and another 340,000 by building the Keystone XL pipeline, a 1,700-mile venture to carry crude from the oil sands of western Canada down to Texas Gulf Coast refineries. All are potential enlistees for Gerard's grass-roots army.

But it turns out that highly paid oil executives aren't the only potential liabilities to Gerard's efforts to put a kinder, gentler face on the industry. As the rally in Joliet wound down, attendee Mike Dalfano, a pipefitting instructor, acknowledged his enthusiasm for the Keystone XL pipeline and the jobs it would create, but he isn't ready to give Big Oil the tax breaks and perks Gerard is seeking to preserve. "The oil companies are profiting quite a bit, and we need to tighten the screws on them."

Presented with Dalfano's ambivalence toward the industry that supports his job, Gerard is nonplussed. He's convinced that Dalfano and millions of others will come around. "We're putting the true human face on this industry, so people understand these are moms and dads, local PTA presidents, and Little League coaches," he says. "That's our challenge. And when the public understands the consequences, they weigh in." Now if only his biggest members could just stay out of the headlines.

Critical Thinking

1. What position does Jack Gerard hold and what was his previous job?

2. What are some of Gerard's key methods for getting the public to support the interests of the organization he heads?

3. On what did Gerard insist before agreeing to accept his current position?

4. What is "fracking" and what is Gerard's objective with respect to it?

Born Fighting

RONALD BROWNSTEIN

A part from his political skills, two forces above all have propelled Barack Obama in his once-improbable quest for the presidency.

One is on vivid display this week: a wave of dissatisfaction with the country's direction that has created a visceral demand for change. That wave has reached towering heights amid the financial crisis roiling Wall Street and consuming Washington. No other candidate has drawn more power than Obama has from that desire to shift course.

With much less fanfare, this week also marked a milestone in the evolution of the second force that has lifted Obama: the rise of the Internet as a political tool of unparalleled power for organizing a vast activist and donor base.

Ten years ago this week, Wes Boyd and Joan Blades, two California-based software developers (their company created the "Flying Toaster" screensaver), posted an online petition opposing the drive by congressional Republicans to impeach President Clinton. The one-sentence petition urged Congress instead to censure Clinton and "move on." Within days the couple had collected hundreds of thousands of names. Thus was formed MoveOn.org, the first true 21st-century political organization.

B orn fighting, MoveOn has become the point of the spear for the Democratic Left through eight years of combat with President Bush over issues from Iraq to Social Security. No group has been more influential, innovative, or controversial in devising the Internet-based organizing strategies that are precipitating the new age of mass political participation symbolized by Obama's immense network of contributors and volunteers. "In the evolution of this, they were there at the very beginning," says veteran Democratic strategist Joe Trippi.

MoveOn's political impact must be measured on two levels: message and mechanics. The group's techniques draw praise in both parties. Boyd and Blades, and later Eli Pariser, a young organizer who has become MoveOn's leading force, recognized that the Internet created unprecedented opportunities for organizing. Traditionally, causes and candidates faced daunting expenses in trying to find like-minded people through advertising, direct mail, or canvassing. But the Internet reversed the equation: Once

MoveOn established itself at the forefront of liberal activism, millions of people who shared its views found it at little (or no) cost to the group.

> **"Our observation was: Whenever we fight, we get stronger."**
>
> —Wes Boyd, MoveOn.org founder

Indeed, MoveOn quickly discovered that the more fights it pursued, the more names it collected—and the more it increased its capacity to undertake new campaigns. "There's this old model of political capital: Every time you fight, you are spending something," Boyd says. "Our observation was: Whenever we fight, we get stronger."

Fueled by this dynamic, MoveOn routinely generates levels of activity almost unimaginable not long ago. Since 1998, it has raised $120 million; it mobilized 70,000 volunteers for its get-out-the-vote effort in 2004, and might triple that number this year. It now stands at 4.2 million members, after adding 1 million, mostly through social-networking sites, this year.

T he purposes to which MoveOn applies these vast resources are more debatable. The group has become a favored target for Republicans and a source of anxiety for some Democratic centrists, who worry that it points the party too far left. On domestic issues, it fits within the Democratic mainstream. But on national security, it defines the party's left flank. MoveOn resisted military action not only in Iraq but also in Afghanistan. And on both foreign and domestic concerns, it often frames issues in terms so polarizing that it risks alienating all but the most committed believers. The group's lowest moment came in 2007 when it bought a newspaper ad disparaging Gen. David Petraeus, the U.S. commander in Iraq, as "General Betray Us" on the grounds that he would attempt to mislead Congress about the war. Petraeus's brilliant subsequent progress in stabilizing Iraq has only magnified the unseemliness of that accusation. "I wouldn't have done the headline the exact same way," Pariser now concedes.

Still, as candidates and groups in both parties adapt its strategies for online organizing, MoveOn can justly claim a central role in igniting the surge in grassroots activism that is transforming American politics. "Regardless of your political convictions, you have to feel like this is a very healthy thing for democracy," Pariser says. MoveOn's causes may divide, but Democrats and even many Republicans are increasingly uniting around the bottom-up vision of political change that these ardent activists have helped to revive.

Critical Thinking

1. What issue led to founding Moveon.org and what year did the organization begin?

2. On what two levels has MoveOn.org had the greatest political impact?

3. Why is MoveOn.org a target for Republicans and a cause for concern among centrist Democrats?

4. How has MoveOn.org changed political activism?

Why They Lobby

WINTER CASEY

Thank You for Smoking, the 2005 film based on a novel by Christopher Buckley, follows the life of Nick Naylor, a chief spokesman for Big Tobacco with questionable morals, who makes his living defending the rights of smokers and cigarette-makers and then must deal with how his young son, Joey, views him. Naylor may have been a fictitious character, but Washington has its share of lobbyists arguing for the interests of industries with a perceived darker side.

The cynical response in Washington is that career decisions and political give-and-take revolve around money: Greenbacks triumph over ethics. There is little argument from lobbyists that their profession's financial rewards have an undeniable allure. But those who represent socially sensitive industries such as tobacco and alcohol have a lot more to say about why, out of all the potential job opportunities, they chose and often "love" what they do.

Representing "sin" industries, such as tobacco, alcohol, or gambling, can provide a challenge like no other.

For some, the job is a result of personal history or connections. For others, lobbying on behalf of a difficult industry provides a challenge like no other. They all make it a point to note that the First Amendment sanctions lobbying: "the right of the people . . . to petition the government for a redress of grievances."

Tobacco

In the film, Naylor works for the Academy of Tobacco Studies, which Buckley based on the Tobacco Institute, the industry's former trade association. Andrew Zausner, a partner at the firm Dickstein Shapiro (which occupies some of the Tobacco Institute's old space), is a registered lobbyist for Lorillard Tobacco, the Cigar Association of America, and Swisher International. He has been working on behalf of tobacco clients for nearly 30 years, ever since he fell into the industry when he was a partner at a New York City law firm that represented Pinkerton Tobacco.

Zausner feeds off the challenge of lobbying for tobacco interests. "The more unpopular the client, the better you have to be as a lobbyist," he declares. "Believing in your client's position makes you a more forceful advocate." Although Zausner doesn't want his children to use tobacco, he notes that the "product has been continuously used in the United States before the United States existed" and says that the industry has a legitimate point of view and a constitutional right to express it.

Beau Schuyler lobbies for UST Public Affairs, a subsidiary of the holding company that owns U.S. Smokeless Tobacco and Ste. Michelle Wine Estates. A former congressional aide to two Democratic House members from his native state of North Carolina—in the heart of tobacco country—Schuyler says that the "opportunity to work internally at one of the oldest continually listed companies on the New York Stock Exchange was just too good to pass up."

Gambling

James Reeder, a lobbyist at Patton Boggs, has spent about half his time over the past decade representing the gambling industry. He insists he didn't seek out this niche, adding, "I tell my grandchildren that gambling is a bad habit . . . and to go fishing."

Shortly after Reeder joined Patton Boggs, a client named Showboat called the firm looking for someone who knew about Louisiana because the company was interested in building a casino there. Reeder happened to be from the Pelican State and was put on the case. He reasoned that Louisiana has always been a home to illegal gambling, and "if the culture of the state supports the industry, [the state] might as well make it legal and reap the benefits and get more tax money." Reeder eventually lobbied in about 17 states to get legislation passed to allow casinos—then mostly on riverboats.

"Whenever you take on one of these vices like booze or gambling and you just pass a law to say it is illegal," Reeder says, "you end up like in Prohibition, when the mob took over the liquor business."

Reeder excelled at lobbying for the gambling industry even though he avoids games of chance. "I don't gamble, because I am not a good card player," he says. "My friends would die laughing because I would go to offices to talk to clients on gambling and I would never go into a casino." If a lawmaker was morally opposed to gambling, Reeder wouldn't argue with him, he says.

John Pappas began working for the industry as a consultant for the Poker Players Alliance while at Dittus Communications. Then the alliance asked him to open its own Washington office.

Pappas calls poker a game of skill that has a rich history in America. He grew up playing cards with family members and friends, and noted during an interview that he would be playing poker with 20 lawmakers that evening at a charity tournament. "Responsibility in all aspects of life is paramount," he says.

Firearms

Richard Feldman's book, *Ricochet: Confessions of a Gun Lobbyist,* has been gaining the former National Rifle Association employee some attention recently. Feldman says that the gun control issue, like most, is not black and white. Working for the NRA, he says, "was the best job I ever had." The "huge power" he was able to wield "in the middle of major political battles" was more attractive to him at the time than the money he earned.

Feldman says he would sometimes play hardball but "didn't hit below the belt" in his pursuit of the gun industry's objectives. "Lobbying an issue that you have some special passion on (guns) is like waking up every day already having consumed a triple espresso," he said in an e-mail to *National Journal.* "On the other hand, if you can empathize with your client's position regardless of the issue, one can be a more convincing advocate, which I've always viewed as the more critical aspect of truly effective lobbying."

John Velleco ran his own painting company before he took a job in 1993 as an intern at the Gun Owners of America. Today, he is director of federal affairs for the 350,000-member group. "Most people, no matter what side of any particular issue they're on, don't always have the time to sort through what's happening in the D.C. sausage factory, so they depend on groups like GOA to keep them informed," he says. "Politicians may not like it, but my job is not to represent the views of the Congress to the people, but the views of American gun owners to the Congress."

Video Games

Because many video games contain a fair share of gunplay and other violence, Entertainment Software Association President Michael Gallagher has had to address complaints that playing violent games causes psychological harm such as increased aggression.

His group lobbies against "efforts to regulate the content of entertainment media in any form, including proposals to criminalize the sale of certain video games to minors; create uniform, government-sanctioned entertainment rating systems; or regulate the marketing practices of industry."

Gallagher, a former assistant Commerce secretary for communications and information in the Bush administration, calls video games a great form of family entertainment. The titles are responsibly rated, he says, and the gaming consoles have easy-to-use parental controls.

"I have been playing video games all my life," Gallagher says, including with his children. He contends that his industry "leads all forms of media when it comes to disclosure on what's in the game" and says that it works with retailers to "make sure minors can't buy games that are inappropriate for them."

Alcohol

Lobbyists who work for the beer, wine, and spirits industries have to deal with a host of negative images, among them drunk-driving accidents, underage drinking, and the effects of alcohol on health.

Lobbyists say their work is protected by the First Amendment—the right to "petition the government for a redress of grievances."

Mike Johnson, a lobbyist for the National Beer Wholesalers Association, acknowledges that alcohol is a "socially sensitive product" and says that is why the industry operates under strict government guidelines.

"I am blessed. I get to represent some great family-owned and -operated businesses that are very active in their communities and provide some really great jobs," Johnson says. "I am completely comfortable one day having a conversation with my son about who I work for, because I can tell him what a great job that beer distributors do in ensuring a safe marketplace and in protecting consumers from a lot of the problems we see with alcohol in other places in the world."

Craig Wolf, president of the Wine & Spirits Wholesalers, calls alcohol a "great social lubricant" that "creates great environments." Wolf got involved in wine-industry issues when he was counsel for the Senate Judiciary Committee. As his job there was ending, Wolf was offered the post of general counsel at the association; he took over as president in 2006.

"The key to advocating for a socially sensitive product is doing business responsibility," Wolf says. "We spend more time and resources [on the issue of] responsible consumption of alcohol then all other issues combined."

Distilled Spirits Council President Peter Cressy says, "I was interviewed for this position precisely because the Distilled Council wanted to continue and increase its very serious approach to fighting underage drinking." As chancellor of the University of Massachusetts (Dartmouth), Cressy says, he was active in "fighting binge drinking on campuses." The opportunity to join the council, which has lobbyists in 40 states, gave him the chance to have a national audience, he says. After nine years with the council, Cressy notes, he "has not been disappointed."

Snack Foods

Nicholas Pyle stands at the policy divide where junk food meets America's bulging waistlines. "I love my job," says Pyle, a lobbyist for McKee Foods, the makers of Little Debbie, America's leading snack-cake brand.

Many of the brand's affordable treats contain a dose of sugar, along with corn syrup, partially hydrogenated oil, bleached flour, and artificial flavor. Little Debbie "has been the target of a number of folks out there who want to paint people as a victim of the foods they eat," says Pyle, who is also president of the Independent Bakers Association. Little Debbie is a "wonderful food, great product, wholesome," with a wonderful image, he says. Pyle explains that he and his children enjoy the snacks.

"The big question of obesity is all about personal responsibility and people balancing [snacking] with a healthy and active lifestyle," Pyle insists. He contends that McKee, a family-owned business, doesn't target children in its marketing. "We market to the decision makers in the household," he says, adding that the company doesn't advertise on Saturday morning cartoon shows.

Snack Food Association President and CEO Jim McCarthy says that lobbying is one of his many duties as head of the organization. "Our belief is that all foods fit into the diet," McCarthy says, and "we don't like the term 'junk food.'" Products made by his segment of the industry—which include potato chips, party mix, corn snacks, snack cakes, and cookies—all contain natural ingredients such as vegetables, nuts, and fruit, he says.

The industry has developed healthier products over the years, McCarthy says, but at "certain times consumers haven't bought these products." He attributes the obesity problem to a lack of exercise and shortcomings in educating people about the need for a balanced diet.

Challenging Stereotypes

No matter what industry they represent, lobbyists interviewed for this article said that a good practitioner of their profession knows all sides of an issue, enabling lawmakers and their staffs to make the best-informed decision. "The system weeds out the bad actors, and the honest folks are the most successful and the longest-lasting," one lobbyist says.

Although many of the lobbyists acknowledge some familiar situations in *Thank You for Smoking*, they insist that the stereotypes are not altogether fair. "I think people don't understand the importance of lobbying to the system. If I don't explain what we do and I am not here to explain it to people, Congress will make uninformed decisions without understanding the consequences to the industry," a former liquor lobbyist says.

"Everyone draws the line in the sand about what they will or will not work on," says Don Goldberg, who leads the crisis communications practice at Qorvis Communications and was a key player on President Clinton's damage-response team. "The line is not set in stone."

"If you don't believe the points you are arguing are the best argument for your client and also that it's truthful, then you shouldn't be in this business," Goldberg continues. "I strongly believe in the First Amendment, [but] I don't believe the First Amendment is the reason to take on clients. The reason to take on clients is, they have a good story to tell and they are honest and reputable organizations."

But James Thurber, director of the Center for Congressional and Presidential Studies at American University, says that at the end of the day, money is a good explanation for why many lobbyists end up in their positions. This is especially true when it comes to tobacco, which was the leading preventable cause of disease and death in the United States in 2007, according to the Centers for Disease Control and Prevention.

For consumers, the message that lobbyists appear to be sending is that the individual is responsible for making the right choices in life. Yet the profusion of advertising, marketing ploys, political rhetoric, and seemingly conflicting studies can be bewildering. And although the financial incentive is ever-present, lobbyists believe they fill a fundamental role in society and deserve some relief from the negative stereotypes.

Critical Thinking

1. What are some of the reasons why lobbyists represent socially sensitive industries?
2. What role does financial compensation play in lobbyists' careers?
3. What fundamental role do lobbyists play in the American political system?

Conservative Juggernaut Melds Politics and Policy

Independent group that funneled millions of dollars to conservative candidates wades into lawmaking process.

JOSEPH J. SCHATZ

Just days after the House passed $62 billion in budget cuts in mid-February, Rep. Jon Runyan received an effusive public "thank you," while Rep. Timothy H. Bishop got a stern public warning.

The missives came in the form of radio ads broadcast in the lawmakers' districts. One praised Runyan, a freshman Republican from south central New Jersey, for supporting "the hard work of reining in government spending" by voting yes on the House GOP plan. The other criticized Bishop, a five-term Democrat from Long Island, for his opposition and for "voting to continue the failed spending policies of Pelosi and Obama."

The ads, which aired as the House prepared to engage in another round of tough spending votes this week, weren't paid for by a trade association, the local Chamber of Commerce, or even an official arm of the Republican Party. They came from the political advocacy group Crossroads GPS. This independent outfit—inspired by top Republican operatives including former Bush White House political director Karl Rove—directed millions of dollars on behalf of the conservative cause in last year's election. It is free not to disclose its donors and is the most visible practitioner of political advocacy these days.

Indeed, while Crossroads made its mark as a campaign-season operation, its founders are now unleashing the group's considerable financial resources in a different direction: the lawmaking process itself. With an eye on the 2012 election cycle, Crossroads is gearing up its advocacy efforts—and keeping the pressure on lawmakers of both parties—amid looming showdowns over government spending in Washington and across the nation.

It has ventured deeper into the policy-making weeds in recent months, filing a Freedom of Information Act request for information on President Obama's plans to develop high-speed rail lines, circulating critiques of the administration's regulatory policies and touting Speaker John A. Boehner's talking points on the economy.

The moves by Crossroads will "help keep members accountable" back in their districts, says Eric Ueland, a longtime Senate Republican aide who now lobbies for the Duberstein Group. "As Crossroads bulks up on policy and politics, they can become a significant independent voice out in states and districts, filling space that the national party can't right now," Ueland says.

Like other independent conservative groups that rose to prominence last year following major changes in campaign finance laws, Crossroads is operating within the law to amplify the GOP message while straddling the amorphous line between politics and policy. With labor unions mobilizing to resist Republican efforts to weaken collective bargaining laws in the states—and fighting spending cuts at the federal level—conservatives welcome the help, particularly in the absence of a financially strong Republican National Committee.

Jonathan Collegio, the communications director for Crossroads GPS and its sister political action committee, American Crossroads, says the organization is preparing to counter expected efforts of unions and other Democratic groups. Crossroads helps to fill a "void" when it comes to the type of nonprofit, anonymous donor organizations that can "engage in issue advocacy and communications in the odd-numbered years," Collegio says. "Early 2011 is a season for policy."

Yet Crossroads GPS is formally organized as a "social welfare" organization under section 501(c)(4) of the tax code—and it does business this way for a reason. It was formed not only to be an issue advocate but also to allow conservative donors to contribute anonymously, as is allowed for this type of group—though Collegio maintains that this is simply a "benefit." To preserve its ability to run political ads as a tax-exempt organization without disclosing its donors, Crossroads GPS must spend the majority of its money on non-political advocacy—though that doesn't prevent it from engaging in battles that have a partisan tinge.

Changed Finance Rules

The Crossroads juggernaut arose last year along with other outside advocacy groups during a confluence of changing campaign finance laws and anger in the business community and among wealthy conservatives over Obama's economic agenda.

The Supreme Court's *Citizens United* decision in January 2010, combined with a later federal court ruling, *SpeechNow.org v. Federal Election Commission,* upended the electoral landscape by eliminating many restrictions on the use of money by corporations and unions for political advertising.

The Supreme Court decision didn't create anonymously financed groups—those have been allowed for years. But, among other things, *Citizens United* altered the rules for 501(c)(4) groups like Crossroads, making it easier for them to run aggressively political ads. Rove and Ed Gillespie, a former RNC chairman and Bush White House adviser, then formed Crossroads GPS as a spinoff of their earlier venture, American Crossroads. They had created the other organization early last year as a 527 "issue advocacy" group to give an expanded voice to conservative donors.

The founders subsequently changed American Crossroads into an "independent expenditure only" political action committee, which must register with the Federal Election Commission and can now receive unlimited contributions.

Together, the two groups spent about $39 million on political advertisements last year, fueled by huge donations from wealthy businessmen such as Texas A Bob Perry to American Crossroads, and millions more dollars in anonymous contributions to Crossroads GPS. These ads ran mostly in states with close congressional contests, such as Colorado, where Democratic Sen. Michael Bennet was locked in a re-election battle.

Post-election, it may be easier for groups like Crossroads to keep within with the letter of the law. The advocacy ads run in congressional districts after the House's spending-bill vote counted as education, not politics, because they were coated in policy-speak.

Anthony J. Corrado Jr., a government professor at Colby College in Maine who focuses on campaign finance issues, says that although policy involvement by groups such as Crossroads has become increasingly common in recent years, these "thank you" ads supporting friendly lawmakers are a new twist.

Some Democrats and campaign finance overhaul advocates argue that distinctions made by the law among these groups are absurd. Some have called for IRS investigations into the groups' activities. Others want the law changed.

Maryland Rep. Chris Van Hollen, who ran the campaign arm of House Democrats in 2008 and 2010 and sponsored legislation last year to force increased campaign finance disclosure, says Crossroads uses its anonymous donations "to protect new vulnerable members who are voting against the interests of their constituents on many of these votes." He calls the practice "a continuation of the campaign and the opening salvo in the next one." To him, "Crossroads GPS is simply a front group for the Republican Party."

Changing the Game

Conservative advocacy groups may seem to be the biggest beneficiaries of the changed campaign finance landscape, but unions, too, are active in the policy arena. In the 2010 cycle, the Service Employees International Union and the American Federation of State, County and Municipal Employees—the biggest public employees union—were the fifth- and sixth-largest outside spenders.

Thea Lee, director of policy at the AFL-CIO, says the union will become engaged "both in D.C. and out in the field" as the budget fight continues. Still, unions simply don't have access to as much money as corporations.

Other conservative groups have also joined the fray in a big way, including Heritage Action for America, a 501(c)(4) spun off by the Heritage Foundation think tank last year to engage in congressional lobbying. The group worked against Senate ratification of the New START nuclear arms agreement with Russia last December and is pushing conservative House freshmen not to fall prey to the pressures of interest groups. "We're in the anti-co-opting business," says the group's chief executive, Michael A. Needham.

Yet Crossroads is by far the heftiest player. Its late February ad buy—which coincided with ads purchased by the National Republican Congressional Committee and the Democratic Congressional Campaign Committee—targeted 12 vulnerable Democrats, defended 10 vulnerable Republicans and cost more than $450,000. That's big money for February of an odd-numbered year. The group's president, Steven Law, said last week that a top priority "is to provide 'field support' for congressional action on issues such as reining in spending, blocking job-killing regulations and dismantling Obamacare."

GOP leaders, who are hoping that voters support their budget-cutting stance, appreciate the assistance. "It's certainly helpful, particularly if the Democrats who run Washington stick to their absurd position that they won't cut a penny of federal spending," said one Republican aide.

And it will be a test of whether the influx of money into the political system since a year ago affects not only who gets elected, but how they go about making decisions.

"It's basically the public lobbying aspect of these groups," says Corrado, who expects more of the same from both ends of the spectrum as budget cuts get more specific and unions get more involved. "It's just the first wave."

Critical Thinking

1. What is Crossroads GPS and what does it do?

2. How did recent court decisions make it easier for groups such as Crossroads GPS to wield influence on various national government officials?

3. How do the independent campaign spending totals of Crossroads GPS and its companion PAC "American Crossroads" compare with totals of other groups during the 2010 election cycle?

From *CQ Weekly*, February 28, 2011, pp. 455–456. Copyright © 2011 by Congressional Quarterly, Inc. Reprinted by permission via Copyright Clearance Center.

The Radical Right Returns

A new generation of conspiracy theorists is following in the footsteps of John Birch Society members and other archconservatives.

PAUL STAROBIN

He was born in Denison, Texas, on October 14, 1890, and raised in Abilene, Kan. He worshipped as a Presbyterian. He was educated at the U.S. Military Academy and embarked on a long military career that took him to the pinnacle of responsibility, as supreme commander of the Allied invasion of Nazi-held Europe in World War II. The war won, his fellow Americans resoundingly elected him to the highest office in the land.

None of these facts about Dwight Eisenhower, known affectionately as Ike, made much of an impression on Robert Welch, a retired candy manufacturer in Belmont, Mass., and the founder in the 1950s of the John Birch Society, an archconservative group sharply focused on the threat of communist subversion. For Welch, a graduate of the University of North Carolina, Eisenhower was "a dedicated, conscious agent of the communist conspiracy." This stark judgment, Welch insisted, was "based on an accumulation of detailed evidence so extensive and so palpable that it seems to me to put this conviction beyond any reasonable doubt."

This history seems depressingly relevant amid a season of scurrilous accusations leveled against the person who now inhabits the Oval Office. The Cold War ended nearly two decades ago, with America the victor, but now a new generation of conspiracy theorists has cropped up. The Radical Right, as the Birchers and their kinfolk were known, is back. The movement has returned, if not to the center of American politics, then to some worrisome place not all that far from the mainstream.

Let's be clear: President Obama's policies, leadership style, and performance record are all fair game for sharp attack in our freewheeling, democratic political culture. But the bill of personal indictment against Barack Hussein Obama the man—that is, the particular spate of accusations that cast him as somehow un-American—is absurd. He was born in the United States, as the Constitution requires the president to be, not in Kenya, as the so-called birthers claim. He is not a Muslim, even though his father was and even though it is not a crime to be a Muslim or, for that matter, an atheist, as other folks suspect him of being. He is not a socialist, although he is a believer in activist Big Government.

Yet such fusillades are, if anything, intensifying, with a raft of insinuations about Obama's character from right-wing assailants in the blogosphere, on talk radio, and from other sources. Amid this battering, the share of Americans who believe that Obama is a Muslim has increased to 18 percent from 11 percent just after his inauguration, according to the Pew Research Center. For his detractors, the label "Muslim" seems to be an indirect way of saying that Obama is un-American, with polls suggesting that about a quarter of Americans believe that most Muslims in the U.S. are not patriotic.

No less weighty a personage than Newt Gingrich, former House speaker, former American history professor, and possible contender for the GOP presidential nomination in 2012, makes the case for Obama as "other." "What if [Obama] is so outside our comprehension, that only if you understand Kenyan, anticolonial behavior, can you begin to piece together [his actions]?" Gingrich told *National Review Online.* "That is the most accurate, predictive model for his behavior."

In offering this comment, Gingrich was echoing a denigrating cover story in *Forbes,* by conservative writer Dinesh D'Souza, who, in reference to Obama's Kenyan-born father, said: "Incredibly, the U.S. is being ruled according to the dreams of a Luo tribesman of the 1950s. This philandering, inebriated African socialist, who raged against the world for denying him the realization of his anticolonial ambitions, is now setting the nation's agenda through the reincarnation of his dreams in his son." D'Souza has defended his piece—which the White House attacked as a "new low"—as "a psychological theory."

Such suspicions about Obama are part of a wider and swelling cluster of anxieties of a traditional nativist type, reflected in an earlier age by citizens worried about the influx of Catholic immigrants in big cities in the North. The core nativist question, a staple of the modern Radical Right, is always the same: Who is a real American?

Today's nativist agenda extends from opposition to the construction of mosques—and not just the one proposed for a site a few blocks from Ground Zero in Manhattan—to calls for repeal of the 14th Amendment provision that automatically grants

The New Nativists

- The return of the Radical Right, circa 2010, also marks the return of what's been called **"the paranoid style in American politics."**
- In the Cold War era, **the seminal shock to the U.S. body politic** was the fall of China to Mao's Communist legions.
- Today's **Radical Right derives its energies** largely from the 9/11 attacks.

citizenship to anyone born on U.S. soil. The rollback cause, agitated by the influx of illegal Hispanic immigrants from south of the border, has been embraced by Republican Sens. Lindsey Graham of South Carolina and Jon Kyl of Arizona.

Although the debate over Muslims and Islam is, in certain respects, quite different from the debate over Latino immigration, a tie binds the two matters: the fear, which a significant chunk of Americans feel but the evidence does not bear out, that the country is being changed for the worse by non-native elements that cannot or simply will not assimilate into traditional American culture.

Thus, there is the phobia that the country is in imminent danger of succumbing to Islamic law, known as sharia, even though 75 percent of the people identify themselves as Christians and less than 1 percent say they are Muslim. That approximates the share of Buddhists and is far less than the 15 percent who say they have no religion.

As for the fear that the U.S. is being overrun by wave after wave of illegal immigrants, the supposed tsunami is actually subsiding because of hard economic times. "The annual flow of unauthorized immigrants into the United States was nearly two-thirds smaller in the March 2007 to March 2009 period than it had been from March 2000 to March 2005," the Pew Hispanic Center found in a recent report.

Prestigious academics have at times given respectable voice to such trumped-up fears. The late Samuel Huntington, who was well known for his view that the post-Cold War world would be defined by a clash of civilizations, came to include America as part of this thesis. "The persistent inflow of Hispanic immigrants threatens to divide the United States into two peoples, two cultures, and two languages," he wrote in an essay for *Foreign Policy* in 2004.

The return of the Radical Right, circa 2010, also marks the return of what the late historian Richard Hofstadter called "the paranoid style in American politics." At the conclusion of his classic essay on the topic, published in the early 1960s and as valid as ever, Hofstadter wrote, "The recurrence of the paranoid style over a long span of time and in different places suggests that a mentality disposed to see the world in the paranoid's way may always be present in some considerable minority of the population." He noted, too, that the political movements exhibiting the paranoid style "are not constant but come in successive episodic waves. . . . Catastrophe or the fear of catastrophe is most likely to elicit the syndrome of paranoid rhetoric."

Tremors

In the Cold War era, the seminal shock to the U.S. body politic was the fall of China to Mao's Communist legions in 1949. China occupied a large place in the imagination of American conservatives, who strived for the conversion of hundreds of millions of souls to the faith of Jesus. China's abrupt shift to the camp of the godless, in league with the Bolsheviks in the neighboring Soviet Union, was precisely the sort of large and disturbing development guaranteed to nourish conspiracy theories. Who lost China? In aggressive pursuit of an answer to that politically loaded question, aspiring right-wing politicians, Richard Nixon among them, built a national fan base.

There were, in truth, some Communist agents in the nation's capital. Historians have generally concluded that Alger Hiss, who served in the State Department, was a Soviet spy, as Whittaker Chambers, whose case was backed by Nixon, alleged. Where the Radical Right went off the rails was in imagining that the entire government had sold out to the Reds—the theme of the 1964 book *None Dare Call It Treason* by John Stormer, a Christian pastor and educator and a John Birch Society member. In selling millions of copies, despite an obscure publisher, the book showed that there was a substantial appetite for such literature. For all the media's attention to the Radical Left that emerged in the 1960s, the Radical Right quite likely played to a far larger audience.

Although few mainstream politicians claimed membership, prominent conservatives sometimes spoke in terms that echoed the movement's vocabulary. When Barry Goldwater, a hard-line Cold Warrior, declared that "extremism in the defense of liberty is no vice," in accepting the Republican Party's presidential nomination in 1964, he invoked the very word, extremism, that defined the Radical Right. It was no accident: Goldwater thought that Robert Welch's characterization of Eisenhower as a communist agent was absurd, but he publicly defended members of the Welch-led John Birch Society, calling them, in 1961, "the kind of people we need in politics."

Today's Radical Right derives its energies largely from the 9/11 attacks, an even bigger jolt than the loss of China to communism a half-century earlier. Nine years after the event, the aftershocks continue to convulse American politics. For a new generation of politicians, "extremism in the defense of liberty" is again no vice. Tom Tancredo, the Republican former House member now running for governor of Colorado as a candidate of the American Constitution Party, has suggested bombing Mecca as a response to any nuclear attack on the U.S. by Islamic terrorists.

The near-total collapse of the banking system and the worst economic downturn since the Great Depression hands today's extremists an agitating ingredient absent from the early decades of the Cold War. With experts pointing to the mounting national debt as a ticking time bomb, a popular "fear of catastrophe"—the incubator for paranoid thinking, in Hofstadter's terms—is a palpable feature of our frazzled culture.

In the 19th century, a rollicking era characterized by boom-and-bust cycles, nativist sentiments had a basis, in part, in economic anxieties. In the mid-1850s, the political fortunes of the militantly anti-Catholic Know Nothing Party—which emerged from the fraternal Order of the Star-Spangled Banner and elected governors, big-city mayors, and scores of members of Congress—were markedly improved by a financial panic in the fall of 1854. Northern white Protestants who made up the party's core saw Catholic immigrants from Ireland and Germany as a threat to jobs and, even more, as a "religious minority thought to be antithetical to American values," with a suspected primary allegiance to Rome, noted Tyler Anbinder, a history professor at George Washington University who specializes in 19th-century American politics.

The Great Depression in the 1930s spawned the noxious spectacle of Father Coughlin, the radio broadcaster whose conspiratorial worldview was infused with the notion that a gullible President Roosevelt was being led down a dark road by conniving Jewish financiers such as Bernard Baruch, "who whispered into his perturbed ears the philosophy of destruction. . . . Did they not, in season and out of season, obstruct our president from driving the money changers from the temple?"

An economic recovery, if and when it arrives in full force, can be expected to take the edge off nativist attitudes. But it is very unlikely that recovery will altogether stanch such sentiments. In the first place, the 9/11 attacks remain as a root source of American fears of the "other," fed by the plausible possibility of new attacks. A core birther concern is Obama's legitimacy as commander-in-chief—an issue that has seeped into areas of the military, with Lt. Col. Terry Lakin, an Army doctor, now facing a court-martial for refusing to serve in Afghanistan on the grounds that his orders came from an ineligible president. Upon signing an affidavit of support for Lakin's demand that Obama produce a birth certificate, retired Lt. Gen. Thomas McInerney, a West Point graduate and frequent Fox News contributor, issued a statement declaring: "Our military MUST have confidence their commander-in-chief lawfully holds his office, and absent which confidence grievous consequences may ensue."

The campaign to sow doubts about Obama's legitimacy has yet to become a McCarthy-era-like drive to indict the entire government as being riddled with enemy agents. "I have here in my hand a list of 205 names . . . known to the secretary of State as being members of the Communist Party and who nevertheless are still working and shaping policy in the State Department," Joseph McCarthy, a first-term Republican senator from Wisconsin, declared in a sensational speech in Wheeling, W.Va., in 1950. But critics on the watch for Islamic subversion are starting to train their sights on the Obama administration's lower-rank officials.

"Shariah: The Threat to America," a new report by the Center for Security Policy, a conservative think tank in Washington, devotes three pages to the proposition that "there is, arguably, no more dramatic example of a senior U.S. government official

failing to perform his duty to know—and, seemingly, to fulfill his oath of office—than that of John Brennan, Homeland Security adviser and counterterrorism adviser to President Obama." The report all but accuses Brennan, an Arabic speaker who formerly served as the CIA's station chief in Saudi Arabia, of being a closeted Muslim, based on comments he has made, such as referring to Jerusalem as "Al Quds," an Arabic name for the city that translates as the "holy place," in a speech earlier this year at New York University's Islamic Center. "Indeed, it is hard to overstate the danger associated with the president of the United States having as his top adviser in these sensitive portfolios someone so severely compromised with respect to Shariah and the threat it poses," the report asserts.

It is not only liberals who view such pronouncements as hyperbolic. "Islam in America is of recent vintage. This country can't be 'Islamic.' Its foundations are deep in the Puritan religious tradition," Fouad Ajami, a Lebanese-born expert on Islam and a supporter of the Iraq war, wrote in a recent *Wall Street Journal* op-ed.

Although Obama has defended the right of Islamic leaders in the U.S. to build a community center, with a mosque, near the site of the twin towers, it's hard to characterize his administration as being soft on Islamic militancy. He retained George W. Bush's Republican Defense secretary, Robert Gates, and approved a major escalation of the U.S. war effort in Afghanistan as his first big national security decision. He made David Petraeus—the architect of the Iraq troop surge and a hero to supporters of that war—his top general in Afghanistan. The Obama administration has ramped up drone attacks on Islamic terrorism suspects in Pakistan and elsewhere—a tactic that human-rights activists have sharply criticized as amounting to an "ill-defined license to kill without accountability."

On top of the national security and economic worries, a third reality is stirring anxieties among some on the Right. The United States is in the midst of a demographic transition in which non-Hispanic, white Caucasians—traditionally the base of the Radical Right—are declining as a share of the total population and are destined to become a numerical minority midway through the 21st century. The evolution is stoking concerns that white people, once the main source of racism, will become the target. In an outburst last year on his Fox News Channel show, conservative commentator Glenn Beck, a white male, called out Obama as a "racist" in reverse—"a guy who has a deep-seated hatred for white people or the white culture."

Beck is teaming up with fellow Fox commentator Sarah Palin at speaking events steeped in nostalgia for a seemingly (and gauzily defined) lost America. At the pair's August rally in front of the Lincoln Memorial, Palin declared, in an apparent swipe at Obama: "We must not fundamentally transform America as some would want; we must restore America and restore her honor." The language of restoration is a staple of nativist rhetoric through the ages. In a 2008 appearance on Fox News, Christine O'Donnell, now the GOP nominee for Senate in Delaware who has modeled herself on Palin, said flatly of Obama, "He's anti-American."

Portrait of Today's Radical Right

It's important to note that nativist sentiments are by no means confined to elements in the Republican Party or parts of the conservative movement. Over the past half-century, the Democratic Party has also been a wellspring of populist nativism, such as that embraced by the race-baiting Alabama Democrat George Wallace in the 1960s. In 1968, Wallace won almost 10 million votes and five Southern states in his bid for the presidency on the American Independent Party ticket. (He later rejoined the Democratic ranks.)

Indeed, the GOP has the greater historical claim as the party of tolerance, with its founding on an anti-slavery platform in the 1850s, a stance that made a vote for the party of the Great Emancipator, Abraham Lincoln, anathema to generations of Southern white Democrats in the post-Civil War era.

In recent decades, however, nativism has been evident largely in various precincts of the Right—and in political party terms, in GOP circles. This raises a host of questions: How big is today's Radical Right? From what parts of society do its members hail? How fast is it growing?

Precise answers are elusive—this is not, after all, a census category. Still, reasonable inferences can be made from the survey data from reputable organizations such as Gallup.

Gallup's standard polling question on political ideology gives respondents five choices to describe their "political views": very conservative, conservative, moderate, liberal, or very liberal. For the most recent poll, published in June, the breakdown was 10 percent, very conservative; 32 percent, conservative; 35 percent, moderate; 15 percent, liberal; and 5 percent, very liberal; with the remaining few percent not answering.

The survey points to the country's broad conservative tilt, even at a time when Democrats control the White House and Congress. At the ideological poles, there are twice as many very conservative Americans as very liberal ones—24 million to 12 million, given an adult population, 18 years and older, of 235 million.

Over the past two decades, moreover, conservative ranks have hardened significantly. Today, very conservative Americans make up 24 percent of all those who view themselves as conservatives; in 1992, the very conservative share of the conservative bloc was only 14 percent. And back then, the very conservative comprised only 5 percent of all Americans, compared with today's 10 percent.

The upshot is that very conservative is a distinct minority strand of opinion in America, but not a tiny one. True, to be very conservative does not make a person, by definition, a member of the Radical Right—at least not in the textbook sense that Hofstadter meant: folks tinged with paranoia about subversive threats to America. The tea party movement tilts very conservative, but its paramount concern with the nation's dire fiscal straits, and particularly the level of government spending, is firmly planted in reality.

Still, even if the Radical Right can be reduced to, say, a mere 5 million of the pod of 24 million very conservative Americans, that equals the number of people who watch Katie Couric, the bane of Sarah Palin, on the *CBS Evening News* on any given night.

Gallup provided additional data to *National Journal* to fill out this portrait. The very conservatives are more likely to be male than are the members of all other ideological groups; are more likely to hail from the South; and are more likely to be 65 and older. The age breakdown between very conservative and very liberal Americans on the dimension of age is particularly telling: The 18-to-29 age group supplies a scant 13 percent of the ranks of the very conservative, but makes up 31 percent of the very liberal pod. The very conservative are also significantly less likely to be college graduates than are the very liberal.

Future of a Political Pathology

For linking conservatives, at least Far Right conservatives, to a "paranoid style," Hofstadter was castigated by critics who called his work a bid to make conservatism not merely disreputable, but psychologically pathological—to consign to the loony bin anyone in America who was not a moderate or a liberal.

Hofstadter, though, took pains to make clear, at the outset of his essay, that "in using the expression 'paranoid style,' I am not speaking in a clinical sense but borrowing a clinical term for other purposes. . . . The clinical paranoid sees the hostile and conspiratorial world in which he feels himself to be living as directed specifically *against him;* whereas the spokesman of the paranoid style finds it directed against a nation, a culture, a way of life whose fate affects not himself alone but millions of others."

The paranoid style, in other words, is foremost a condition of the political culture that waxes and wanes according to circumstances. The style lends itself to opportunists—perhaps Gingrich is one—who take calculated advantage of an environment ripe for the cultivation of paranoid attitudes.

A president, for all the powers of the office, is not apt to find such an environment easy to change. Eisenhower chose to ignore the campaign to vilify him as un-American, which in the end proved a winning strategy. But he had the political leeway, as a military hero with "a huge reservoir of popularity," to take the high road, as a biographer, the historian Fred Greenstein, noted in an interview.

Obama is more exposed to the heat from the Radical Right. For one thing, he lacks the insulation of military service—as did Bill Clinton, whose past as a Vietnam-era draft evader nourished conservative accusations that he was an unreconstructed '60s Leftie. Also, and probably more important, Obama has the misfortune of living in an age in which the media standards of the past have all but crumbled.

Today's mainstream media, including the national television networks, seize on the politically pathological as a spectacle capable of attracting a momentary audience in the frenetic information market in which headlines can easily shift six times a day. NBC's *Today* show, no less, invited Florida pastor Terry Jones, whose Pentecostal church membership numbers only in the dozens, to appear for an interview in New York City, at which he said that he would not, after all, burn the Koran, "not today, not ever." The comment was enough to make the grade for an *MSNBC.com* "breaking news" blip.

In this atmosphere of never-ending carnival theater, the Obama White House finds itself devoting its public opinion-shaping energies to such tasks as correcting misperceptions about the president's religious beliefs. In early September, White House spokesman Robert Gibbs felt obliged to declare that Obama is a "committed, mainstream Christian"—and not the radical "liberation theology" kind of Christian that Fox's Beck was calling him. Score one for Beck.

Will this war of words remain only that—and not morph into the kind of war that claims flesh-and-bone victims? "I fear political violence, political assassinations," Thomas Whalen, a social science and history professor at Boston University, said in an interview. "That's the next step—when you say someone is not an American."

Although Obama, with his seemingly exotic lineage as the Hawaiian-born, Indonesian-raised son of a black father from Kenya and a white mother from Kansas, may be an irresistible target for the paranoids of the Right, history suggests that targets can always be found.

Today Obama; tomorrow, well, how about Mitt Romney, gearing up for another run at the GOP presidential nomination? He is a Mormon—and as such, a member of a church that some Americans, notably some evangelical Protestants, have long viewed as a cult and not authentically Christian. In the run-up to the 2008 Iowa caucuses, anti-Romney robo-calls cited such former Mormon practices as "baptizing the dead." Lee Harris, a political writer who was raised as a Southern Baptist, said in an interview, "Christian fundamentalists have a much more negative attitude toward Mormons than people realize." Noting the importance of the Religious Right constituency in the Republican Party, Harris added, "I find it amazing that people think Romney is going to get anywhere."

If the Cold War era is any guide, at some point the Radical Right will bring forth a Radical Left—a reaction to a reaction. In the 1960s, the so-called New Left gravitated toward its own conspiratorial sense of politics, portraying the U.S. as a serial oppressor of poor nations such as Vietnam under the guise of anti-communism. President Johnson, a Democrat, the architect of the Great Society—the most liberal experiment in politics since the New Deal—and the force behind the passage of landmark civil-rights legislation, became a despised figure for the Far Left. "Hey, hey, LBJ, how many kids did you kill today?" the street protesters chanted.

A new New Left might be finding its own edgy voice. In the pages of *The Nation,* the author Barbara Ehrenreich recently wrote, "The role of the Left should not be to uphold or defend the government, meaning, for now, the corpo-Obama-Geithner-Petraeus state, but to change it, drastically and from the ground up." She added: "As the tea partiers keep reminding us in their nasty and demented ways, these are revolutionary times."

But at this juncture, the fever is mainly on the Right. At some point, the fever will break; it always does. The only question, as ever, is what wreckage it will leave behind.

Critical Thinking

1. What is "the core nativist question"?

2. What is "sharia" and why is it receiving attention in American politics today?

3. What did historian Richard Hofstadter mean by "the paranoid style in American politics"?

4. What does it mean to say that political movements reflecting nativist sentiment or "paranoia" come in successive waves and are not constant factors on the American political scene?

5. What do recent public opinion polls show about the ideological predispositions of Americans today?

Group Think

By embracing radical decentralization, tea party activists intend to rewrite the rule book for political organizing.

JONATHAN RAUCH

Though headless, the tea party movement is not mindless. Its collective brain meets every Monday night. More than 200 leaders of local tea parties—coordinators, as they usually call themselves—join a conference call every week organized by an umbrella group called the Tea Party Patriots, the largest national tea party organization. On one Monday recently, three national coordinators begin the session with a rundown on plans for upcoming rallies. The events are expensive; does anyone have a problem with a search for $1,000 donors? (No one does.) An organizer has put together a manual on what to ask candidates at town hall events. ("That will go to the entire e-mail list.")

The group is polled on whether to hold a second round of house parties throughout the country. (Yes.) A coordinator gives an update on an iPhone app for tea partiers who will be going door to door this fall to talk to voters. (It will use Global Positioning System technology to download walking lists and upload voter data in real time—cutting-edge stuff.)

The floor is then opened. Local leaders propose ideas, announce new tea party groups, float queries, and offer tips. (How can we maximize free publicity? Lawn signs, movie events, and digiprint postcards are cheap and effective.) A newcomer introduces a start-up tea party in Winfield, Ind. A coordinator in nearby South Bend offers a welcome. ("I know all these folks. I want to get you connected with them.")

Rick, from Albuquerque, N.M., asks if the national agenda includes investigating voter-roll irregularities, something his group is concerned about. Mark Meckler, a Tea Party Patriots coordinator and co-founder, weighs in. Newcomers "often don't understand how badly we need *you* to lead the way," he says. "If this is an area of concern to you," he admonishes, "the way the Tea Party Patriots works is that you guys really lead the organization. We're a relatively small group of people who are just trying to help coordinate. We're not in charge; we're not telling anybody what to do. You need to take a leadership role and stand up." Meckler suggests that Rick gather a group of people concerned about the issue and go to work.

Rick gets the message. "We'll get on the *Ning* [social-networking] site and try to take the lead on that."

Will vote fraud emerge as a tea party cause? Maybe, maybe not. Meckler, the closest thing the movement has to an organizational visionary, meant what he said. No one gives orders: In the expansive dominion of the Tea Party Patriots, which extends to thousands of local groups and literally countless activists, people just do stuff, talk to each other, imitate success, and move the movement.

"Essentially what we're doing is crowd-sourcing," says Meckler, whose vocabulary betrays his background as a lawyer specializing in Internet law. "I use the term open-source politics. This is an open-source movement." Every day, anyone and everyone is modifying the code. "The movement as a whole is smart."

Can it work? In American politics, radical decentralization has never been tried on so large a scale. Tea party activists believe that their hivelike, "organized but not organized" (as one calls it) structure is their signal innovation and secret weapon, the key to outlasting and outmaneuvering traditional political organizations and interest groups. They intend to rewrite the rule book for political organizing, turning decades of established practice upside down. If they succeed, or even half succeed, the tea party's most important legacy may be organizational, not political.

Out of Nowhere

The tea party began as a network, not an organization, and that is what it mostly remains. Disillusioned with President Bush's Republicans and disheartened by President Obama's election, in late 2008 several dozen conservatives began chattering on social-networking sites such as *Top Conservatives on Twitter* and *Smart Girl Politics*. Using those resources and frequent conference calls (the movement probably could not have arisen before the advent of free conference calling), they began to talk about doing something. What they didn't realize was that they were *already* doing something. In the very act of networking, they were printing the circuitry for a national jolt of electricity.

The spark came on February 19, 2009, when a CNBC journalist named Rick Santelli aired a diatribe against the bank bailout. "That," Meckler says, "was our source code." The next day, the networkers held a conference call and decided to stage protests in a few cities just a week later. No one was more astonished than the organizers when the network produced rallies in about 50 cities, organized virtually overnight by amateurs. Realizing that they had opened a vein, they launched a second round of rallies that April, this time turning out perhaps 600,000 people at more than 600 events.

Experienced political operatives were blown away. "It was inconceivable in the past" to stage so many rallies so quickly, in so many places, without big budgets for organizers and entertainment, says Grover Norquist, the president of Americans for Tax Reform and a longtime political organizer. Without a hook such as a musical show, he says, "I can't think of anything on the right or the left that mimics those numbers on a local level."

By the summer of 2009, tea parties were springing up all over. Multitudes of activists, operatives, and groups were claiming the tea party mantle, many of them at odds with or suspicious of each other. Believing that coordination was needed, an ad hoc committee emerged from among the core group and, by August of last year, had opened a bank account under the spontaneously chosen name of the Tea Party Patriots.

"Gi-normous"

Today, the Tea Party Patriots is a 501(c)(4) nonprofit group. It has seven national coordinators, five or so of whom draw salaries, which they decline to disclose but say are modest. Three other people get paychecks, according to Jenny Beth Martin, a co-founder and national coordinator.

The organization has no offices, dwelling instead in activists' homes and laptops. Martin says it has raised just over $1 million in the past year, a trivial amount by the standards of national political organizers. About 75 percent of the group's funding comes from small donations, $20 or less, she says.

By conventional measures such as staff and budget, then, the Tea Party Patriots is minuscule. Viewed another way, however, it is, to use Martin's expression, "gi-normous." Lacking dues or bylaws, the network's closest thing to a membership roll is the list of groups that have registered with its website, now approaching 3,000 and spanning the country. The website, teapartypatriots. org, lists almost 200 tea parties in California alone.

Many states and localities have their own coordinators. Dawn Wildman, a national coordinator based in San Diego, doubles as a California state coordinator, hosting two weekly conference calls that typically include about 40 of 180 or so local coordinators. Organizers in Dallas are setting up a tea party in every ZIP code. "If the beauty of the tea party is decentralization," says Ken Emanuelson, a member of the Dallas steering committee, "in large metro areas like Dallas, the decentralization needs to go well below the metro area. It needs to go down into the neighborhoods. We go to our neighborhood groups, and we get our agenda from them." Asked how many neighborhood tea parties exist in the Dallas area, another city-wide coordinator replied, "I don't even know."

Strange though it may seem, this is a coordinated network, not a hierarchy. There is no chain of command. No group or person is subordinate to any other. The tea parties are jealously independent and suspicious of any efforts at central control,

which they see as a sure path to domination by outside interests. "There's such a uniqueness to every one of these groups, just as there's an individuality to every person," Wildman says. "It has this bizarre organic flow, a little bit like lava. It heats up in some places and catches on fire; it moves more slowly in other places."

Lava is a pretty good analogy. Ask the activists to characterize their organizational structure, however, and usually they will say it is a starfish.

Look, Ma, No Head

The Starfish and the Spider, a business book by Ori Brafman and Rod A. Beckstrom, was published in 2006 to no attention at all in the political world. The subtitle, however, explains its relevance to the tea party model: *The Unstoppable Power of Leaderless Organizations.*

Traditional thinking, the book contends, holds that hierarchies are most efficient at getting things done. Hierarchies, such as corporations, have leaders who can make decisions and set priorities; chains of command to hold everyone accountable; mechanisms to shift money and authority within the organization; rules and disciplinary procedures to prevent fracture and drift. This type of system has a central command, like a spider's brain. Like the spider, it dies if you thump it on the head.

The rise of the Internet and other forms of instantaneous, interpersonal interaction, however, has broken the spider monopoly, Brafman and Beckstrom argue. Radically decentralized networks—everything from illicit music-sharing systems to *Wikipedia*—can direct resources and adapt ("mutate") far faster than corporations can. "The absence of structure, leadership, and formal organization, once considered a weakness, has become a major asset," the authors write. "Seemingly chaotic groups have challenged and defeated established institutions. The rules of the game have changed."

Moreover, hierarchies are at a loss to defeat networks. Open systems have no leader or headquarters; their units are self-funding, and their members often work for free (think *Wikipedia*). Even in principle, you can't count or compartmentalize the participants, because they come and go as they please—but counting them is unnecessary, because they can communicate directly with each other. Knowledge and power are distributed throughout the system.

As a result, the network is impervious to decapitation. "If you thump it on the head, it survives." No foolish or self-serving boss can wreck it, because it has no boss. Fragmentation, the bane of traditional organizations, actually makes the network stronger. It is like a starfish: Cut off an arm, and it grows (in some species) into a new starfish. Result: two starfish, where before there was just one.

"We're a starfish organization," says Scott Boston, the Tea Party Patriots' educational coordinator, and a rare paid staffer. He started a tea party group in Bowling Green, Ohio, but then let it slide when he went to school. Filling the gap, another group popped up; now there are two. Groups fuse as well as split. In Dallas, Emanuelson says, if a coordinator burns out, "sometimes another coordinator picks up the reins, but if not, a group can get involved with a nearby group." No one else even needs to know about it.

From Washington's who's-in-charge-here perspective, the tea party model seems, to use Wildman's word, bizarre. Perplexed journalists keep looking for the movement's leaders, which is like asking to meet the boss of the Internet. Baffled politicians and lobbyists can't find anyone to negotiate with. "We can be hard to work with, because we're confusing," Meckler acknowledges. "We're constantly fighting against the traditional societal pressure to become a top-down organization." So why would anyone want to form this kind of group, or network, or hive, or starfish, or lava flow, or whatever it is?

First, radical decentralization embodies and expresses tea partiers' mistrust of overcentralized authority, which is the very problem they set out to solve. They worry that external co-option, internal corruption, and gradual calcification—the viruses they believe ruined Washington—might in time infect them. Decentralization, they say, is inherently resistant to all three diseases.

Second, the system is self-propelling and self-guiding. "People seem to know what the right thing to do is at the right time," Dallas's Emanuelson says. "As times change, then our focus will change, because we're so bottom-up driven. As everyone decides there's a different agenda, that's where things will go."

If a good or popular idea surfaces in Dallas, activists talk it up and other groups copy it. Bad and unpopular ideas, on the other hand, just fizzle. Better yet, the movement lives on even as people come and go. "The message is important," Wildman says, "but people are expendable."

Third, the network is unbelievably cheap. With only a handful of exceptions, everyone is a volunteer. Local groups bring their own resources. Coordinators provide support and communication, but they make a point of pushing most projects back down to the grassroots.

Finally, localism means that there is no waiting for someone up the chain to give a green light. Groups can act fast and capitalize on spontaneity. Equally important, the network is self-scaling. The network never outgrows the infrastructure, because each tea party is self-reliant. And the groups make it their business to seed more groups, producing sometimes dizzying growth.

Ginni Rapini, of the NorCal Tea Party Patriots, holds training sessions in California every six weeks; just since March, she says, more than two dozen tea parties have launched in Northern California alone. Lorie Medina, who acts as recruiter and trainer for the Dallas Tea Party, says she can't count the number of groups she has helped launch or resuscitate; currently, she says, she is rolling out 15 to 20 youth groups in Texas and beyond.

That kind of uncontrolled growth would cause many a hierarchy to collapse. So would a rapid contraction. A network, by contrast, can constantly resize itself as it goes along.

Starfish Can't Catch Flies

Will it work? Is it sustainable? Is it really new?

As to new, yes and no. "There have been many efforts to create decentralized movements before," says Francesca Polletta,

a sociologist at the University of California (Irvine) and a student of political movements. Those efforts, however, have been smaller in scale than the tea party. And, ironically, they have typically been offshoots of the political Left. (Structurally speaking, you could do worse than to think of the Tea Party Patriots as a left-wing organization with a right-wing, or at least libertarian, ideology.)

Polletta and David Meyer, another UC Irvine professor and the author of *The Politics of Protest: Social Movements in America,* cite an assortment of earlier groups that tried to be both ambitious and headless: the Student Nonviolent Coordinating Committee and Students for a Democratic Society in the 1960s; the anti-nuclear-power movement and the Green Committees of Correspondence in the 1970s and '80s.

None proved durable in its decentralized form. The SDS and SNCC succumbed to dissension. The anti-nuke activists lost their issue when nuclear power lost momentum, partly as a result of their efforts. The Greens gradually centralized and now are a national political party. Few decentralized groups, Meyer notes, outlive the issues that brought them together.

One important, if partial, exception is MoveOn.org. It began in 1998 as a small online protest against President Clinton's impeachment, snowballed, and grew still bigger in opposition to the Iraq war. Although those issues are mostly gone, MoveOn is larger than ever. It boasts 5 million members and is a potent political force, able to rapidly mobilize and target political protests and donations.

In more than a few ways, MoveOn.org resembles the tea party movement. It emphasizes people power and civic engagement as a remedy for flawed governance. It owes its existence to new media and relies heavily on that world. It prides itself on following, rather than leading, its membership. "MoveOn.org *is* our members," says Joan Blades, the group's co-founder. "Our job is to listen as well as we possibly can to them. If we decided to do X or Y and that was not supported by our members, it would just fizzle. It wouldn't work."

But here is a difference: In addition to its thousands of volunteers, Blades says, MoveOn has a core staff of about 20, including a national political director, plus another 20 field staffers—all paid professionals.

"I would argue that MoveOn has had far more impact" than the tea party, at least so far, says Ralph Benko, a Washington-based public-affairs consultant and the author of *The Websters' Dictionary: How to Use the Web to Transform the World.* MoveOn strategizes nationally and focuses money and attention on winnable battles. "The reason the tea party isn't yet there is they don't yet make a distinction between friends and foes and persuadables," he says. "They don't yet make a distinction on who they can focus on to change a vote, or how they can change the fortunes of their preferred candidates. As long as they're in 'We hate you all' mode, I don't know if they'll manifest as a powerful national force."

Headless organizations have other problems. They are much better at mobilizing to stop a proposal or person they dislike than at agreeing on an alternative. They are bad at negotiating and compromising, because no one can speak for them, and many of their members regard compromising as selling out. They rely on volunteers, who can wander away or burn out.

"What I see is, every three, four, five months about 10 to 20 percent of your active people trail off," says Medina, the Dallas-based organizer. "Those numbers have to be replaced every few months. It's a continual grind to keep the numbers up."

Leaderless groups also have trouble protecting their brand against impostors, opportunists, and extremists who act in their name and sully their reputation—a vulnerability that the tea party's adversaries are currently doing their utmost to exploit.

"This kind of tenuous balance"—between decentralized structure and national ambitions—"is hard to sustain," Meyer says. "I would suspect the amount of influence they're going to have is peaking right about now, in the current Republican primaries."

It's Education, Stupid

To all of which, tea partiers reply: Just watch us.

"That's what traditional thinking has been," says Tea Party Patriots co-founder Martin, a bustling activist who seems never to pause for breath. "Look where traditional thinking has gotten us—and look at what we've done in just the last three months."

Answering the skeptics, tea partiers point out that bygone efforts at radical decentralization lacked Internet-age networking and communications technologies—without which, of course, the tea party movement could not have arisen in the first place. The Tea Party Patriots' very existence suggests that something new is afoot. One coordinator notes that *Facebook* alone allows the movement to communicate with up to 2 million people simultaneously.

Rogue elements, it is true, cannot be fired or forced into line. But the movement can and does marginalize them by dropping them from the website, excluding them from coordinating meetings, and generally ignoring them. The main body of the movement simply flows around marginal actors, consigning them to irrelevance.

As for the objection that headless groups are bad at negotiating and strategizing and leveraging influence, the Tea Party Patriots' answer underscores the unconventionality of their thinking: *We don't care.*

Well, they do care—some. Sure, they say, replacing bad politicians is worthwhile. Sure, changing policies is a goal. Yes, politics matters. If it didn't, local tea parties wouldn't be pressing their members to run for office and change things from the bottom up, much as religious conservatives did a generation ago. Nor would they be producing and disseminating soup-to-nuts guides on how to hold candidate forums, stage rallies, set up new tea party groups, and conduct get-out-the-vote campaigns, as many are doing.

But, tea partiers say, if you think moving votes and passing bills are what they are really all about, you have not taken the full measure of their ambition. No, the real point is to change the country's political culture, bending it back toward the self-reliant, liberty-guarding instincts of the Founders' era. Winning key congressional seats won't do that, nor will endorsing candidates. "If you just tell people to vote but you don't talk about the underlying principles," Martin says, "you just have to do it again and again and again, in every election."

What will work, they believe, is education: DVDs on American history; "founding principles" training; online reading lists; constitutional discussion groups; cultural and youth programs. In Tennessee, says Anthony Shreeve, an organizer there, groups are giving courses on the Constitution and "socialism and the different types of isms," bringing in speakers from around the state. "Our members have gotten more involved and learned about our local government, how it works, and what kind of influence we can have," Shreeve says. "Education has been the biggest thing."

Not coincidentally, the educational coordinator is among the Tea Party Patriots' handful of paid employees. "Our real mission," says Sally Oljar, a national coordinator, "is education and providing resources to grassroots activists who want to return the country to our founding principles. We recognize that's going to require a cultural change that will take many years to accomplish."

Many years? How many? "We have a 40-year plan," Meckler says. "We don't want to raise another generation of sheeple."

One hears again, there, echoes of leftist movements. Raise consciousness. Change hearts, not just votes. Attack corruption in society, not just on Capitol Hill. In America, right-wing movements have tended to focus on taking over politics, left-wing ones on changing the culture. Like its leftist precursors, the Tea Party Patriots thinks of itself as a social movement, not a political one.

Centerless swarms are bad at transactional politics. But they may be pretty good at cultural reform. In any case, the experiment begins.

Critical Thinking

1. What does it mean to say that the Tea Party movement began as a "network" and not as an organization?

2. What are some pros and cons of being a "leaderless organization"?

3. What are four advantages of the nature of the Tea Party movement, such as it is?

4. What are important similarities and differences between the Tea Party movement and Moveon.org?

5. Do you agree that the Tea Party's greatest legacy may be organizational, and not political?

A See-Through Society

How the Web is opening up our democracy.

MICAH L. SIFRY

It may be a while before the people who run the U.S. House of Representatives' Web service forget the week of September 29, 2008. That's when the enormous public interest in the financial bailout legislation, coupled with unprecedented numbers of e-mails to House members, effectively crashed www.house.gov. On Tuesday of that week, a day after the House voted down the first version of the bailout bill, House administrators had to limit the number of incoming e-mails processed by the site's "Write Your Representative" function. Demand for the text of the legislation was so intense that third-party sites that track Congress were also swamped. GovTrack.us, a private site that produces a user-friendly guide to congressional legislation, had to shut down. Its owner, Josh Tauberer, posted a message reading, "So many people are searching for the economic relief bill that GovTrack can't handle it. Take a break and come back later when the world cools off."

Once people did get their eyes on the bill's text, they tore into it with zeal. Nearly a thousand comments were posted between September 22 and October 5 on PublicMarkup.org, a site that enables the public to examine and debate the text of proposed legislation set up by the Sunlight Foundation, an advocacy group for government transparency (full disclosure: I am a senior technology adviser to Sunlight). Meanwhile, thousands of bloggers zeroed in on the many earmarks in the bill, such as the infamous reduction in taxes for wooden-arrow manufacturers. Others focused on members who voted for the bill, analyzing their campaign contributors and arguing that Wall Street donations influenced their vote.

The explosion of public engagement online around the bailout bill signals something profound: the beginning of a new age of political transparency. As more people go online to find, create, and share vital political information with one another; as the cost of creating, combining, storing, and sharing information drops toward zero; and as the tools for analyzing data and connecting people become more powerful and easier to use, politics and governance alike are inexorably becoming more open.

We are heading toward a world in which one-click universal disclosure, real-time reporting by both professionals and amateurs, dazzling data visualizations that tell compelling new stories, and the people's ability to watch their government from below (what the French call *sousveillance*) are becoming commonplace. Despite the detour of the Bush years, citizens will have more opportunity at all levels of government to take an active part in understanding and participating in the democratic decisions that affect their lives.

Log On, Speak Out

The low-cost, high-speed, always-on Internet is changing the ecology of how people consume and create political information. The Pew Internet & American Life Project estimates that roughly 75 percent of all American adults, or about 168 million people, go online or use e-mail at least occasionally. A digital divide still haunts the United States, but among Americans aged eighteen to forty-nine, that online proportion is closer to 90 percent. Television remains by far the dominant political information source, but in October 2008, a third of Americans said their main provider of political information was the Internet—more than triple the number from four years earlier, according to another Pew study. Nearly half of eighteen-to-twenty-nine-year-olds said the Internet was their main source of political info.

Meanwhile, we're poised for a revolution in participation, not just in consumption, thanks to the Web. People talk, share, and talk back online. According to yet another study by Pew, this one in December 2007, one in five U.S. adults who use the Internet reported sharing something online that they created themselves; one in three say they've posted a comment or rated something online.

People are eager for access to information, and public officials who try to stand in the way will discover that the Internet responds to information suppression by routing around the problem. Consider the story of a site you've never seen, ChicagoWorksForYou.com. In June 2005, a team of Web developers working for the city of Chicago began developing a site that would take the fifty-five different kinds of service requests that flow into the city's 311 database—items like pothole repairs, tree-trimming, garbage-can placement, building permits, and restaurant inspections—and enable users to search by address and "map what's happening in your neighborhood" The idea was to showcase city services at the local level.

ChicagoWorks was finished in January 2006, with the support of Mayor Richard Daley's office. But it also needed to be reviewed by the city's aldermen and, according to a source who worked on the project, "they were very impressed with its functionality, but they were shocked at the possibility that it would go public." Elections were coming up, and even if the site showed 90 percent of potholes being filled within thirty days, the powers-that-be didn't want the public to know about the last 10 percent. ChicagoWorksForYou.com was shelved.

But the idea of a site that brings together information about city services in Chicago is alive and kicking. If you go to Every-Block.com, launched in January 2008, and click on the Chicago link, you can drill down to any ward, neighborhood, or block and discover everything from the latest restaurant-inspection reports and building permits to recent crime reports and street closures. It's all on a Google Map, and if you want to subscribe to updates about a particular location and type of report, the site kicks out custom RSS feeds. Says Daniel O'Neil, one of Every Block's data mavens, "Crime and restaurant inspections are our hottest topics: Will I be killed today and will I vomit today?"

EveryBlock exists thanks to a generous grant from the Knight News Challenge, but its work, which covers eleven cities, including New York, San Francisco, and Washington, D.C., offers a glimpse of the future of ubiquitous and hyperlocal information. EveryBlock's team collects most of its data by scraping public sites and spreadsheets and turning it into understandable information that can be easily displayed and manipulated online.

It may not be long before residents of the cities covered by EveryBlock decide to contribute their own user-generated data to flesh out the picture that city officials might prefer to hide. EveryBlock founder Adrian Holovaty tells me that his team is figuring out ways for users to connect directly to each other through the site. Forums that allowed people to congregate online by neighborhood or interest would enable EveryBlock users to become their cities' watchdogs. If city agencies still won't say how many potholes are left unfilled after thirty days, people could share and track that information themselves.

Such a joint effort is no stretch to young people who have grown up online. Consider just a couple of examples: since 1999, RateMyTeachers.com and RateMyProfessors.com have collected more than sixteen million user-generated ratings on more than two million teachers and professors. The two sites get anywhere from half a million to a million unique visitors a month. Yelp.com, a user-generated review service, says its members have written more than four million local reviews since its founding in 2004. As the younger generation settles down and starts raising families, there's every reason to expect that its members will carry these habits of networking and sharing information into tracking more serious quality-of-life issues, as well as politics.

Cities Lead the Way

Recognizing this trend, some public officials are plunging in. In his "State of the City" speech in January 2008, New York Mayor Mike Bloomberg promised to "roll out the mother of

---

A Sunshine Timeline

1966

FOIA passes. Without the votes to sustain his threatened veto, and with Bill Moyers, his press secretary, urging him on, LBJ signs the bill. But he nixes a press release announcing the new law, and forgoes a signing ceremony, the only time in his tenure he did so. (Ironic footnote: Donald Rumsfeld co-sponsored the bill.)

---

all accountability tools." It is called Citywide Performance Reporting, and Bloomberg promised it would put "a wealth of data at people's fingertips—fire response times, noise complaints, trees planted by the Parks Department, you name it. More than five hundred different measurements from forty-five city agencies." Bloomberg, whose wealth was built on the financial-information company he built, says he likes to think of the service as a"Bloomberg terminal for city government—except that it's free."

Bloomberg's vision is only partly fulfilled so far. A visitor to the city's site (nyc.gov) would have a hard time finding the "Bloomberg terminal for city government" because it's tucked several layers down On the Mayor's Office of Operations page, with no pointers from the home page.

Still, the amount of data it provides is impressive. You can learn that the number of families with children entering the city shelter system is up 31 percent over last year, and that the city considers this a sign of declining performance by the system. Or you can discover that the median time the city department of consumer affairs took to process a complaint was twenty-two business days, and that that is considered positive! Another related tool, called NYC*SCOUT, allows anyone to see where recent service requests have been made, and with a little bit of effort you can make comparisons between different community districts. New York's monitoring tools still leave much to be desired, however, because they withhold the raw data—specific addresses and dates-of-service requests—that are the bones of these reports. This means the city is still resisting fully sharing the public's data with the public.

Compare that to the approach of the District of Columbia. Since 2006, all the raw data it has collected on government operations, education, health care, crime, and dozens of other topics has been available for free to the public via 260 live data feeds. The city's CapStat online service also allows anyone to track the performance of individual agencies, monitor neighborhood services and quality-of-life issues, and make suggestions for improvement. Vivek Kundra, D.C.'s innovative chief technology officer, calls this "building the digital public square." In mid-October, he announced an "Apps for Democracy" contest that offered $20,000 in cash prizes for outside developers and designers of websites and tools that made use of the city's data catalog.

In just a few weeks, Kundra received nearly fifty finished Web applications. The winners included:

- iLive.at, a site that shows with one click all the local information around one address, including the closest places to go shopping, buy gas, or mail a letter; the locations of recently reported crimes; and the demographic makeup of the neighborhood;
- Where's My Money, DC?—a tool that meshes with Facebook and enables users to look up and discuss all city expenditures above $2,500; and
- Stumble Safely, an online guide to the best bars and safe paths on which to stumble home after a night out.

The lesson of the "Apps for Democracy" contest is simple: a critical mass of citizens with the skills and the appetite to engage with public agencies stands ready to co-create a new kind of government transparency. Under traditional government procurement practices, it would have taken Kundra months just to post a "request for proposals" and get responses. Finished sites would have taken months, even years, for big government contractors to complete. The cost for fifty working websites would have been in the millions. Not so when you give the public robust data resources and the freedom to innovate that is inherent to today's Web.

The Whole Picture

So, how will the Web ultimately alter the nature of political transparency? Four major trends are developing.

First, the day is not far off when it will be possible to see, at a glance, the most significant ways an individual, lobbyist, corporation, or interest group is trying to influence the government. Here's how Ellen Miller, executive director of the Sunlight Foundation and a longtime proponent of open government, sees the future of transparency online: "If I search for Exxon, I want one-click disclosure," she says. "I want to see who its PAC is giving money to, who its executives and employees are supporting, at the state and federal levels; who does its lobbying, whom they're meeting with and what they're lobbying on; whether it's employing former government officials, or vice versa, if any of its ex-employees are in government; whether any of those people have flown on the company's jets. And then I also want to know what contracts, grants, or earmarks the company has gotten and whether they were competitively bid."

She continues: "If I look up a senator, I want an up-to-date list of his campaign contributors—not one that is months out of date because the Senate still files those reports on paper. I want to see his public calendar of meetings. I want to know what earmarks he's sponsored and obtained. I want to know whether he is connected to a private charity that people might be funneling money to. I want to see an up-to-date list of his financial assets, along with all the more mundane things, like a list of bills he's sponsored, votes he's taken, and public statements he's made. And I want it all reported and available online in a timely fashion."

This vision isn't all that far away. In the last three years, thanks in large measure to support from Sunlight, OMB Watch (a nonprofit advocacy organization that focuses on budget issues, regulatory policy, and access to government) created

A Sunshine Timeline

1986

In the wake of India's Bhopal disaster, the Emergency Planning and Community Right-to-Know Act mandates development of national and local systems to respond to leaks of dangerous chemicals. Included is the requirement, for the first time, that computerized regulatory information be made public.

FedSpending.org, a searchable online database of all government contracts and spending. The Center for Responsive Politics (OpenSecrets.org), meanwhile, has developed searchable databases of current lobbying reports, personal financial disclosure statements of members of Congress, sponsored travel, and employment records of nearly ten thousand people who have moved through the revolving door between government and lobbying. Taxpayers for Common Sense (Taxpayer.net) is putting the finishing touches on a complete online database of 2008 earmarks.

The National Institute on Money in State Politics, headed by Ed Bender, is filling in the picture at the state level, aiming to give the public "as complete a picture as possible of its elected leaders and their actions, and offer information that helps the public understand those actions," he says. "This would start with the candidates running for offices, their biographies and their donors, and would follow them into the statehouses to their committee assignments and relationships with lobbyists, and finally to the legislation that they sponsor and vote for, and who benefits from those actions."

The incoming Obama administration, meanwhile, has expressed a commitment to expanding government transparency, promising as part of its "ethics agenda" platform (change.gov/ agenda/ethics_agenda) to create a "centralized Internet database of lobbying reports, ethics records, and campaign-finance filings in a searchable, sortable, and downloadable format," as well as a "'contracts and influence' database that will disclose how much federal contractors spend on lobbying, and what contracts they are getting and how well they complete them."

To insure that all citizens can access such a database, we can hope that Obama pushes universal Internet access as part of his investment in infrastructure. As Andrew Rasiej and I argued in *Politico* in December, "Just as we recognized with the Universal Service Act in the 1930s that we had to take steps to ensure everyone access to the phone network, we need to do the same today with affordable access to high-speed Internet. Everything else flows from this. Otherwise, we risk leaving half our population behind and worsening inequality rather than reducing it."

3-D Journalism

A second trend propelling us toward a greater degree of political transparency is data visualization. The tools for converting boring lists and lines of numbers into beautiful, compelling images get more powerful every day, enabling a new kind of 3-D journalism: dynamic and data-driven. And in many cases, news consumers can manipulate the resulting image or chart, drilling into its layers of information to follow their own interests. My favorite examples include:

- The Huffington Post's Fundrace, which mapped campaign contributions to the 2008 presidential candidates by name and address, enabling anyone to see whom their neighbors might be giving to;
- The *New York Times*'s debate analyzer, which converted each candidate debate into an interactive chart showing word counts and speaking time, and enabled readers to search for key words or fast forward; and
- The Sunlight Foundation and Taxpayers for Common Sense's Earmarks Watch Map (earmarkwatch.org/mapped), which layered the thousands of earmarks in the fiscal 2008 defense-appropriations bill over a map of the country allowing a viewer to zero in on specific sites and see how the Pentagon scatters money in practically every corner of the U.S.

The use of such tools is engendering a collective understanding of, as Paul Simon once sang, the way we look to us all. As news consumers grow used to seeing people like CNN'S John King use a highly interactive map of the United States to explain local voting returns, demand for these kinds of visualizations will only grow.

Little Brother Is Watching, Too

The third trend fueling the expansion of political transparency is *sousveillance,* or watching from below. It can be done by random people, armed with little more than a camera-equipped cell phone, who happen to be in the right place at the right time. Or it can be done by widely dispersed individuals acting in concert to ferret out a vital piece of information or trend, what has been called "distributed journalism." In effect, Big Brother is being watched by millions of Little Brothers.

For example, back in August, San Francisco Mayor Gavin Newsom was having coffee at a Starbucks in Malibu when he was spotted by a blogger who took a couple of photos and posted them online. The blogger noted that Newsom was "talking campaign strategy" with someone, but didn't know who. The pictures came to the attention of *San Francisco Chronicle* reporter Carla Marinucci, who identified that person as political consultant Garry South. Soon political bloggers were having a field day, pointing out that the liberal mayor was meeting with one of the more conservative Democratic consultants around. This is *sousveillance* at its simplest.

The citizen-journalism project "Off the Bus," which ultimately attracted thousands of volunteer reporters who posted their work on The Huffington Post during the 2008 election, was *sousveillance* en masse. Much of their work was too opinionated or first-person oriented to really break news, but Mayhill Fowler's reporting of Barack Obama's offhand remarks at a San Francisco fundraiser about "bitter" blue-collar workers

---

A Sunshine Timeline

2003

World Bank begins supporting FOI-related conditions in agreements with some developing countries, but stops short of making right-to-know laws mandatory. According to Privacy International, today roughly eighty-one governments worldwide have some form of FOI law.

---

at least briefly changed the course of the campaign. And there are numerous examples of bloggers and their readers acting in concert to expose some hidden fact. The coalition of bloggers known as the "Porkbusters" were at the center of an effort to expose which senator had put a secret hold on a bill creating a federal database of government spending, co-sponsored by none other than Barack Obama and Tom Coburn. Porkbusters asked their readers to call their senators, and by this reporting process, discovered that Senator Ted Stevens of Alaska was the culprit. Soon thereafter, he released his hold. Likewise, Josh Marshall has frequently asked readers of Talking Points Memo to help him spot local stories that might be part of a larger pattern. It was this technique that helped him piece together the story of the firings of U.S. Attorneys around the country, for which he won the Polk Award.

The World's A-Twitter

The final trend that is changing the nature of transparency is the rise of what some call the World Live Web. Using everything from mobile phones that can stream video live online to simple text message postings to the micro-blogging service Twitter, people are contributing to a real-time patter of information about what is going on around them. Much of what results is little more than noise, but increasingly sophisticated and simple-to-use filtering tools can turn some of it into information of value.

For example, in just a matter of weeks before the November election in the U.S., a group of volunteer bloggers and Web developers loosely affiliated with the blog I edit, techPresident.com, built a monitoring project called Twitter Vote Report. Voters were encouraged to use Twitter, as well as other tools like iPhones, to post reports on the quality of their voting experience. Nearly twelve thousand reports flowed in, and the result was a real-time picture of election-day complications and wait times that a number of journalistic organizations, including NPR, PBS, and several newspapers, relied on for their reporting.

Nothing to Hide

The question for our leaders, as we head into a world where bottom-up, user-generated transparency is becoming more of a reality, is whether they will embrace this change and show that they have nothing to hide. Will they actively share all that is relevant to their government service with the people who, after all, pay their salaries? Will they trust the public to understand the complexities of that information, instead of treating them like children who can't handle the truth?

The question for citizens is, Will we use this new access to information to create a more open and deliberative democracy?

The question for citizens, meanwhile, is, Will we use this new access to information to create a more open and deliberative democracy? Or will citizens just use the Web to play "gotcha" games with politicians, damaging the discourse instead of uplifting it?

"People tend not to trust what is hidden" write the authors of the November 2008 report by a collection of openness advocates entitled "Moving Toward a 21st Century Right-to-Know Agenda." "Transparency is a powerful tool to demonstrate to the public that the government is spending our money wisely, that politicians are not in the pocket of lobbyists and special-interest

groups, that government is operating in an accountable manner, and that decisions are made to ensure the safety and protection of all Americans." In the end, transparency breeds trust. Or rather, transparency enables leaders to earn our trust. In the near future, they may have to, because more and more of us are watching.

Critical Thinking

1. How has the Internet fundamentally changed the way people access and share information?

2. Compare and contrast New York City's and Washington, DC's approaches to sharing information with the public online. What are the benefits and drawbacks of each city's approach?

3. Summarize four major trends in the Internet's influence on political transparency?

4. According to Micah Sifry, why should the national government invest in universal Internet access for all Americans?

MICAH L. SIFRY is co-founder of the Personal Democracy Forum, an annual conference on how technology is changing politics; editor of its group blog techPresident.com; and a senior technology adviser to the Sunlight Foundation.

Governing in the Age of Fox News

The polarization of the American media has deep historical roots—the republic came into being amidst a vigorous partisan press. But the splintering of public attention and the intensification of ideological journalism—in particular, the rise of Fox News—have created unique challenges for President Obama. Is it possible to have partisan media that retain professional standards of reporting?

PAUL STARR

The fight between the Obama White House and Fox News may look like a replay of previous presidential conflicts with the media. After all, antagonism between presidents and elements of the press is a fine American tradition. But the Fox News phenomenon is different, and its development reflects a deeper change in the public itself that presents a new challenge for presidential leadership.

What was once an expansive mass public has lost some of its old breadth and, at its core, become more intense and combative. A growing percentage of people, especially among the young, no longer regularly follow the news in any medium, while those who remain the most attentive and engaged tend to be sharply polarized along ideological lines. On both ends of the political spectrum, people interested in politics increasingly view national leadership through the prism of the partisan media that dominate cable news, talk radio, and the blogosphere.

Before cable and the Internet, the way for a president to reach the national public was through national media that sought to appeal to audiences spanning the partisan divide. The major newspapers, wire services, and broadcast networks controlled the flow of news from Washington and the president's access to the channels of persuasion, yet they operated more or less according to the standards of professional journalism, and the White House could exercise plenty of leverage in its media relations by selectively leaking news and granting exclusive interviews. So despite sometimes antagonistic relations with the press, presidents were able to use it to reach abroad and relatively coherent national public.

But now that the old behemoths of the news are in decline, the unified public they assembled is fading too. Neither the broadcast networks nor the newspapers have the reach they once did, raising concerns about whether the press will be able to serve its classic function as a watchdog over government. That problem also has a flip side. Precisely because the press is often critical of political leaders, it provides them legitimacy when it validates the grounds for their decisions. A press that is widely trusted by the public for its independence and integrity is also a resource for building consensus. Thus when the public

sorts itself according to hostile, ideologically separate media—when the world of Walter Cronkite gives way to the world of Glenn Beck and Keith Olbermann—political leadership loses a consensus-building partner. This is the problem that faces Barack Obama. It is not, however, an unprecedented one.

To most Americans, at least until recently, it had long seemed a settled matter that the media should have no relationship with political parties—but that has not been the norm throughout American history, much less in other countries. In many democracies, newspapers and other media have developed in parallel with political parties (sometimes directly financed and controlled by them), while elsewhere the media have been independent, with no partisan connection. The prevailing model for how American presidents interact with the media has gone through three historical stages. As a young republic (and to a large extent even after the Civil War), the nation had partisan newspapers; the second stage, stretching across the 20th century, was characterized by powerful, independent media outlets that kept their distance from the parties; and in the third stage, we now have a hybrid system that combines elements of the first two.

The founding period in American history created a new and richly supportive environment for the press. Britain and other European states, seeing popular newspapers as a political threat, had limited what they could say and imposed heavy taxes to raise their costs and reduce their circulation. America's Founders, in contrast, believed that the circulation of news and political debate could help preserve their fragile republic. So besides guaranteeing the press its freedom, they excluded it from taxation and subsidized its development by setting cheap postal rates for mailing newspapers to subscribers. The government thereby underwrote the costs of a national news network without regulating its content. Public officials also subsidized specific newspapers they favored, by awarding generous contracts for government printing and paying fees for official notices. Together with subscription and advertising income, the postal and printing subsidies provided the financial basis for a development of the press so rapid that by 1835, the United States, even though it was still almost entirely rural, probably had the highest per capita newspaper circulation in the world.

Under many regimes, government subsidies have made the press politically subservient. But in the United States, the postal subsidies benefited all newspapers without limitation based on viewpoint—and newspapers did clearly express their ideological stances. And because of the separation of powers and the federal system, printing subsidies from different branches and levels of government went to newspapers from different parties. In fact, rather than solidifying incumbent power, the early environment of the press paved the way for two insurgent presidential candidates, Thomas Jefferson in 1800 and Andrew Jackson in 1828.

Jefferson's Democratic-Republicans were the first party to exploit the press environment established by the Founders, and they did so despite adversity. In 1798, during an undeclared war with France, President John Adams's Federalists enacted the infamous Sedition Act, making it a crime to publish "false, scandalous, and malicious writing" about the president (though not about the vice president, who at the time was none other than Jefferson himself, the leader of the opposition). The Adams administration used the act to prosecute leading Jeffersonian editors and close down their papers—but the Jeffersonians more than offset those losses by establishing dozens of new papers in the run-up to the election of 1800. In the process, they demonstrated that the press could serve as a lever for overturning power in the United States.

Political parties at this time were only loose coalitions of leaders; they had no ongoing organization except their newspapers, and in practice, the parties and their newspapers were almost indistinguishable. Local editors were key party organizers, and local party leaders often met in the newspaper office. According to some historians, this partisan press belonged to the "dark ages" of American journalism. But it played a central role in mobilizing political participation and creating a vibrant democracy. And at no time was that more the case than in 1828, when Jackson's supporters built a network of Democratic papers across the country, and voting turnout increased sharply.

Once in office, Jackson established the practice (which lasted until 1860) of having a quasi-official paper that spoke directly for the president and received federal patronage. Still, the press continued to be highly competitive, and the presidential newspaper did not become a stable monopoly. In the 32 years following Jackson's election, 11 different papers in Washington served as presidential organs, and by the 1860s they were so outstripped in circulation by advertising-supported metropolitan dailies that a separate paper representing the president had become obsolete. Beginning with Lincoln, presidents communicated with the public through commercially financed newspapers, though many of these continued to have strong partisan identities.

The rise of the mass press inaugurated a long, second era in presidential communication, spanning most of the 20th century, when national leaders had to adapt to new realities, including the growing role of reporters as independent interpreters of the news and the development of media with national reach. In the late 19th century, presidents literally kept journalists at a distance (reporters had to wait outside the White House gates for news from officials coming and going). Presidents also did not represent themselves, nor were they seen, as the central actors in the nation's politics. Only at the turn of the century, as "congressional government" gave way to a stronger executive, did presidents begin to cultivate the press and make themselves more visible by seizing the opportunities for public persuasion and influence that mass communications provided.

If Jefferson and Jackson were the two breakthrough presidents in the era of the partisan press, the two Roosevelts were their counterparts as presidential innovators in the mass media of the 20th century. Although the shift began under his predecessor, William McKinley, Theodore Roosevelt brought reporters into the White House on a more regular basis, providing them for the first time with a press room. He also projected his influence more widely, giving more speeches than earlier presidents had and making the most of his office as a "bully pulpit." With his charm and energy, Roosevelt infused the presidency with qualities that have served as a model for leadership through the media ever since.

Natural gifts were also critical to Franklin Roosevelt's success. The first Roosevelt, a Republican, had had the advantage of dealing with a press that was predominantly Republican in its sympathies. FDR, however, as a Democrat, was convinced that he needed to circumvent hostile Republican newspaper publishers to reach the public directly. Radio gave him that power. Unlike Herbert Hoover, Roosevelt spoke in a conversational style in his "fireside chats," creating the sense among his listeners that he was talking directly to them in their living rooms.

The advent of television highlighted the personality and performative abilities of the president even more than had radio. What the fireside chat was for FDR, the televised news conference was for John F Kennedy—an opportunity to show off personal qualities to maximum advantage. In the era of the captive mass public, from the 1950s through the '70s—when people had access to only a few TV channels, and the three national networks had a 90 percent share of the audience—the president had command of the airwaves, and the narrative of the evening news typically cast him as the dominant actor in the nation's daily political drama.

For a time, this seemed to be the permanent structure of the news and national politics in the age of electronic media. In retrospect, it was the peaking of the unified national public, the moment just before cable TV and the Internet began breaking it up, bringing the media to another historic turning point.

From the founding era to the late 20th century, the news in America enjoyed an expanding public. In the 1800s, postal policies and advances in printing technology cut the price of the printed word and, together with wider access to education, enabled more Americans to read newspapers and become civically literate. In the 20th century, radio, newsreels at the movies, and television extended the reach of the news even farther.

It was only reasonable to assume, then, that the digital revolution would repeat the same pattern, and in some respects it has; online news is plentiful and (mostly) free. But a basic rule of communication is that abundance brings scarcity: an abundance of media creates a scarcity of attention. So although journalists and politicians have new ways to reach the public, the public has acquired even more ways to ignore them. Politics and other news are at our fingertips, but a lot of us don't want to go there. Between 1998 and 2008, according to surveys by the Pew Research Center, the number of Americans who say they don't get the news in any medium on an average day rose from 14 percent to 19 percent—and from 25 percent to 34 percent among 18-to-24-year-olds. And 2008 was a year when interest in the news should have been relatively high.

Obama's success in using digital media during the election may have led some to expect that as president he would be able to do the same. The job, however, is different. Rallying your activist base may not be the best way to win marginal votes in Congress. What Obama needs to do to win those votes—for example, make concessions to moderate Democrats on health-care legislation—may, in fact, disappoint his most passionate supporters. Mobilizing public support as president, rather than as a candidate, is also a different challenge. Although digital communications have made reaching political supporters cheaper and easier, the fractured nature of the public makes it more difficult to reach both the less politically interested and the partisan opposition.

During what the political scientists Matthew A. Baum and Samuel Kernell refer to as the "golden age of presidential television" in the early postwar decades, close to half the households in the country would watch a primetime presidential TV appearance. As access to cable expanded in the 1980s, the audience started shrinking, and by 1995, only 6.5 percent of households watched one of Bill Clinton's news conferences. Obama started out with comparatively high ratings. According to Nielsen data, 31 percent of TV homes watched his first press conference, on February 9, though that dropped to 16 percent by his fifth, on July 22. His speeches to Congress have drawn a somewhat bigger audience, but the ratings have followed the same trajectory. Nonetheless, the president still has the ability to command wider attention than any other figure in American politics. Obama's health-care speech to Congress on September 9 drew an estimated 32 million viewers, which was down from 52 million for his first address to Congress in February but still far higher than any other political figure could hope to attract.

After a summer when the national debate on health-care reform seemed to be dominated by his opponents—thanks, in no small measure, to Fox News and its one-sided coverage of protests at congressional representatives' town-hall meetings—Obama was able to reverse the momentum. In any conflict, the president's voice can rise above the noise. In any national crisis, eyes will still turn to the president, and citizens will expect him to speak for the nation. On those occasions, if he uses the opportunity well, he remains the country's most important teacher. And that remains Obama's greatest strength in competing with Fox over the direction of the national conversation.

During his presidential campaign, Obama said he would try to repair America's bitter divisions, and he reached out to conservatives on various occasions, such as his visit to Rick Warren's Saddleback Church. American politics has become more polarized, however, for deep-seated historical reasons. With the shift of the South to the GOP, the Republicans have become a more purely conservative party, and the Democrats a more liberal one. If this change in the parties had occurred half a century ago, the dominant news media might have moderated polarizing tendencies because of their interest in appealing to a mass audience that crossed ideological lines. But the incentives have changed: on cable, talk radio, and the Internet, partisanship pays.

Not since the 19th century have presidents had to deal with partisan media of this kind, and even that comparison is imperfect. Today the media saturate everyday life far more fully than they did in early American history. Fox News, in particular, is in a league by itself. In the absence of clear national leadership in the Republican Party, Fox's commentators (together with Rush Limbaugh) have effectively taken over that role themselves. Although they have their liberal counterparts on MSNBC, the situation is not exactly symmetrical, because MSNBC's commentators do not have as strong a following and the network's reporting is not as ideologically driven as Fox's.

Of course, professional journalism, with its norms of detachment, hasn't disappeared, though it's in deep financial trouble. Leading newspapers, notably The New York Times, have a wider readership online and in print than they had before in print alone. Media-criticism blogs and Web sites from varied perspectives serve a policing function in the new world of public controversy. Partisan media are now firmly part of our national conversation, but counter-vailing forces—not just the political opposition and its supporters in the media, but professional journalists and other sources for authenticated facts—can keep partisanship from controlling that conversation. Although most American journalists assume that professionalism and partisanship are inherently incompatible, that is not necessarily so. Partisan media can, and in some countries do, observe professional standards in their presentation of the news. That is where civic groups and the scientific community, as well as media critics and others upholding those standards, should focus their pressure. Some commentators may be beyond embarrassment, but the news divisions of the partisan media are likely to be more sensitive to charges of unsubstantiated claims and loaded language. The yellow press of the 1890s looked equally immune from rebuke—and for a long time it was—but the growth of professional journalism in the 20th century did bring about a significant degree of restraint, even in the tabloids.

No one can put the old public back together again. Walter Cronkite's death last July provoked nostalgia for a time when it seemed all Americans had someone they could trust, and that person was a journalist. But it's not just Cronkite that's gone; the world that made a Cronkite possible is dead. Now we have a fighting public sphere, which has some compensating virtues of its own. As in the early 19th century, a partisan press maybe driving an increase in political involvement. After a long decline, voter turnout in the 2004 and 2008 elections returned to levels America hadn't seen in 40 years. Fox News and MSNBC stir up the emotions not just of their devoted viewers but of those who abhor them; liberals and conservatives alike may be more inclined to vote as a result. Democracy needs passion, and partisanship provides it. Journalism needs passion, too, though the passion should be for the truth. If we can encourage some adherence to professional standards in the world of partisan journalism, not via the government but by criticism and force of example, this republic of ours—thankfully no longer fragile—may yet flourish.

Critical Thinking

1. Why are national news media—including broadcast networks and newspapers—increasingly less able to fulfill their traditional roles as government watchdogs?

2. According to Paul Starr, what are the three stages in the development of news media over the course of American history?

3. Why has Barack Obama's success with digital media during his campaign not been duplicated during his presidency?

4. Can partisan journalism be compatible with professionalism in news media? If not, why not? If so, how?

PAUL STARR is a professor of sociology and public affairs at Princeton University and the author of most recently The Creation of the Media and Freedom's Power.

Serious Fun with Numbers

We're drowning in data, but few reporters know how to use them.

Janet Paskin

The story was already great, even before Daniel Gilbert opened his first spreadsheet. Thousands of citizens in the southern Virginia area Gilbert covered for the *Bristol Herald Courier* (daily circulation: 30,000) had leased their mineral rights to oil and gas companies in exchange for royalties. Twenty years later, they alleged, the companies had not paid, adding up to potentially millions of dollars owed. As Gilbert learned, the complaint was complicated. It involved esoteric oil and gas practices and regulations, a virtually unknown state oversight agency, the rules of escrow accounts—and finally, some very angry people and a handful of very big companies. With these facts alone, he could have written a stellar story giving voice to citizens' complaints, and shining a light on a little-known regulatory agency. That, in many newsrooms, would have been plenty.

But Gilbert, who officially covered the courts for the paper, wasn't satisfied simply to raise the specter of noncompliance. Whenever a well produced natural gas, the energy company was supposed to make a monthly payment into a corresponding escrow account. These payment schedules were public. So were the production records. All Gilbert had to do was match the production records with the payment schedules to see who had—and had not—been paid.

Easier said than done. Gilbert requested the information he needed and received spreadsheets with thousands of rows of information. In Excel, atypical computer monitor displays less than a hundred rows and ten wide columns. Gilbert's data was much too massive to cram into this relatively modest template. So he started with one month's worth of information, using the program's "find" function to match wells and their corresponding accounts. One by one. Control-f, control-f, control-f. It was tedious and time-consuming. There was a story there, he was certain. But control-f would not find it.

What would you do? Could you navigate, process, and make sense of thousands of rows of data? If you have not yet had to ask yourself this question, there is no time like the present.

Most journalists are just like Gilbert, with daily computer skills that include Internet searches, word processing, and maybe some basic calculations in Excel, none of which enables journalists to truly mine large collections of data. Mean-while,

the amount of raw data available to journalists has mushroomed. At the federal level, the Obama administration's "open government" initiative has given rise to new sources like Data.gov, a website devoted to the aggregation and easy dissemination of national data sets. State and local governments have followed suit, making much of the data they collect available online: More elusive tranches of data have been pried loose by non-profit organizations courtesy of the Freedom of Information Act; an inquisitive journalist can download them in minutes. "I'm constantly amazed and surprised about what's out there," said Thomas Hargrove, a national correspondent for Scripps-Howard News Service who often leads data-based research projects for the chain's fourteen newspapers and nine television stations.

Against this backdrop, the ability to find, manipulate, and analyze data has become increasingly important, not only for teams of investigative journalists, but for beat reporters. It is hard to conceive of a beat that doesn't generate data—even arts reporters evaluate budgets and have access to nonprofit organizations' tax returns. What's more, because the universe of data is vast and growing, and the stories that use it are rare, data-based journalism has become a powerful way to stand out in the crowded news cycle. "When you acquire a certain level of data skills and literacy, you can punch way above your weight," says Derek Willis, a web developer at *The New York Times* and author of the computer-assisted reporting blog, The Scoop. "Simply put, you can do things others can't."

Daniel Gilbert convinced his editors he needed training. In return, he won a Pulitzer.

And last but certainly not least, readers *like* data. They like charts and interactive graphics and searchable databases. At The Texas Tribune, which has published more than three dozen interactive databases and usually adds or updates one a week on average, the data sets account for 75 percent of the site's overall traffic.

Of course, news-gathering organizations have to some degree understood the value and power of data for more than twenty years. Bill Dedman's 1989 Pulitzer-winning investigation into the racist lending practices of Atlanta banks relied heavily on database reporting and was widely seen as a validation of computer geeks in the newsroom.

But even after many organizations hired computer-assisted reporting specialists, using data for stories has usually been limited to big investigations and projects. And with good reason: years ago, data-driven stories were almost prohibitively inefficient to write. A reporter had to identify what data he needed and which agency collected them; it often took a FOIA request to secure the data, which tended to arrive in sheaves of dot-matrix-printed paper. It was then up to the reporters to build their databases—by hand.

These days, the main obstacle to more and better uses of data by journalists is not the technology or the ability to access the information, but rather the interests and aptitudes of reporters and their editors.

That's not the case anymore. Agencies maintain and disseminate their data electronically. While there are still plenty of data sets that require diligence, persistence, and FOIA requests, many can be accessed without even speaking with a human being. And in the newsroom, every reporter has a spreadsheet program like Excel or can find one for free online. The logjam, these days, has more to do with reporters' and editors' interests and aptitudes—with their capacity for number-crunching—than it does with technology.

At the Bristol paper, Gilbert clearly needed help. His editor, Todd Foster, had been Gilbert's champion and mentor on the story thus far, but he knew little about managing thousands of rows of data. Neither did anyone else in the newsroom. Gilbert, however, knew who did: Investigative Reporters and Editors. For years, this journalism nonprofit has been running computer-assisted reporting workshops, called Boot Camps, on the University of Missouri campus in Columbia and around the country. At the six-day workshop, Gilbert would learn how to use spreadsheets and a more sophisticated database management program—the two fundamental tools he needed to manipulate the data he had. The only issue was getting Foster to say yes.

That was hardly a slam dunk. Of course, Foster wanted Gilbert to nail down the story. But as one of seven reporters on staff at the *Herald Courier,* Gilbert typically generated three or four stories a week. His colleagues would have to scramble to fill the hole during his absence. Then there was the cost. The *Herald Courier* and its parent company, Media General, were suffering the same economic hardships as the rest of the newspaper industry. In 2009, Media General mandated fifteen furlough days for most of its 4,700-plus employees, equivalent to a 5.8 percent pay cut. Sending Gilbert to Missouri, in this climate, was not an easy sell: tuition for the workshop was $560,

plus travel to and from Columbia, lodging, and meals for a week. The total came to around $1,240, and the reporter would need to use his vacation days to attend.

Still, a potentially important story and six months of work hung in the balance. That weekend, Foster called on the paper's publisher at home, with a few cans of Red Bull and a bottle of vodka in hand. They covered a variety of business issues, and "at the end of the night, I sprung the Boot Camp on him," Foster recalls. "He said, 'Is it worth it?' I said, 'It's worth it. And in April, it might really be worth it.'" Soon Gilbert was on his way to Missouri.

Foster never told Gilbert they expected him to win a Pulitzer for their trouble—at least not in so many words. But the reporter understood that the expectations were high. "They didn't send me there saying, 'Go have fun,'" he notes. "It was more like, 'This better be worth it.' I felt a good deal of pressure to make it count."

This is a fairly standard expectation. Most newsrooms assume that journalists will immediately put their new skills into practice. When Reuters recently sent six beat reporters to one of the IRE Boot Camps, they were all required to pitch a story to work on while they attended the session. "We want to see the stories," said Claudia Parsons, Reuters' deputy enterprise editor for the Americas. "That will be the test."

At the same time, making database skills and training a priority can be tough for overburdened reporters and editors. Nor do journalism schools necessarily give such skills pride of place—in fact, many teach them piecemeal, if at all. At the graduate level, New York University requires students in its Science, Health, and Environmental Reporting (SHERP) concentration to obtain a solid grounding in numeracy. In other concentrations, however, these skills play a smaller role. The Columbia University Graduate School of Journalism offers a handful of relevant classes, including investigative reporting a course called Evidence and Inference, and a new addition, Digital Media: Interactive Workshop, which stresses storytelling through data and interactive presentation. But there is no data course that all students must take in order to graduate. "We don't require every student to know how to use Excel in the same way we require them to know how to use FinalCut Pro or a digital camera," said Bill Grueskin, Dean of Academic Affairs at Columbia. As a result, many students remain stuck at control-f.

What Gilbert learned in Missouri turned out to be indispensable. He took his spreadsheets with him, and learned how to transfer the data from Excel to Microsoft Access, a database management program better suited to large searches. (Funnily enough, Gilbert actually had a copy of Access on his desktop back in Bristol; he just didn't know what it was for.) And he absorbed a basic programming language called Structured Query Language, or SQL, which allowed him to search for specific patterns in his data.

Eventually, Gilbert got his data cleaned and organized enough to be able to write his fundamental query: Show me the accounts that correspond to wells where oil or gas has been produced, but royalties have not been paid. What he found was damning. "Of about 750 individual accounts in escrow, between 22 percent and 55 percent received no royalty payments during months when the corresponding wells produced gas over an 18-month period," Gilbert wrote in the first of an eight-part series. As for royalty payments that *had* been made, $24 million was lying in escrow, in dispute. Over the course of the series, Gilbert explained the history of the dispute, took the state gas and oil board to task, and showed that citizens who were allegedly owed thousands were being told they were entitled to less than a dime. His series spurred the Virginia legislature to investigate ways to distribute the money in escrow to the people who own it. In April, Gilbert won the Pulitzer Prize for Public Service.

After the prize was announced, Foster told Gilbert that the *Herald Courier* had been hearing about the escrow fund and the government mismanagement for years. "Two prior managing editors had spiked the story," Foster said. "Royalties, methane gas, escrow accounts—it's the sexiest story." In these earlier cases, nobody had been able to break through the data roadblock. Gilbert, who moved to Houston in October to cover the oil and gas industry for *The Wall Street Journal,* says that he thought it was a "pretty good story" to begin with. "But the data changed it," he adds. "Instead of just asking the question, I was able to answer it."

Critical Thinking

1. Why has the ability to mine and analyze large collections of data become more important for contemporary journalists?

2. What is the University of Missouri (Columbia)'s Boot Camp?

3. What story led reporter Daniel Gilbert to acquire the ability to manipulate and analyze large collections of data and what prestigious journalism prize did he win for his efforts?

From *Columbia Journalism Review*, November/December 2010, pp. 23–25. Copyright © 2010 by Columbia Journalism Review. Reprinted by permission of Columbia Journalism Review.

UNIT 4

Products of American Politics

Unit Selections

Learning Outcomes

After reading this Unit, you will be able to:

- Rank the six following policy issues facing the United States from *most* to *least* important and explain (and defend) the order in which you put them: energy and environmental problems, comprehensive immigration reform, homeland security against terrorism, the war in Afghanistan, the economy, and the space program.

- Identify the tension or dilemma between, on the one hand, increased government spending aimed at a generally sluggish economy with high unemployment rates, and, on the other hand, huge national government budget deficits and rising national debt. Decide how you would resolve this policy dilemma and explain why.

- Identify the tension or dilemma between, on the one hand, the desirability of making the United States more energy self-sufficient and limiting greenhouse gas emissions and, on the other hand, the U.S. economic woes and the need to continue to use energy to fuel economic growth. Recommend what you would do to resolve this dilemma.

- Summarize the different reasons that the United States engages in military combat and the goals of such military combat. Then summarize the costs of war—broadly conceived (that is, not just economic costs)—for a nation such as the United States. Appraise current United States combat operations in light of your two summaries, doing, in effect, a cost/benefit analysis.

- Explain the growing overlap between what was traditionally thought to be domestic policy (the economy, health care, environment, agriculture, etc.) and what was traditionally thought to be foreign and national security policy (diplomacy, treaties, military combat operations, etc.).

- Bearing in mind the growing financial problems associated with Medicare and Social Security, identify and explain various options for reforming these two programs that are central to the well-being of elderly Americans. Determine and defend what you think ought to be done.

- Compare and contrast the overall policy performance of the American national government during the George W. Bush years (2001–2009) and the Obama years (2009 to date).

Student Website
www.mhhe.com/cls

"**P**roducts" refer to the government policies that the American political system produces. The first three units of this book pave the way for the fourth unit because the products of American politics are very much the consequences of the rest of the political system.

The American economy is almost always a prominent policy issue in the American political system. One of the most remarkable consequences of 12 years (1981–1993) under President Reagan and the first President Bush was enormous growth in budget deficits and the national debt. During the Clinton presidency, the country enjoyed the longest period of continuous economic growth in U.S. history, accompanied by low unemployment and low inflation rates. Continuing economic growth and increased tax revenues led to the long-sought goal of a balanced budget in 1998, amid predictions that the entire national debt would be eliminated within a decade or so. In the last months of the Clinton administration, however, some signs of an economic slowdown appeared. President George W. Bush pushed tax cuts through Congress early in his presidency, the country entered a recession in the second half of President Bush's first year in office, and the 9/11 terrorist attacks accelerated the economic downturn. Large budget deficits returned and the national debt grew accordingly. By 2007, with the costs of the war in Iraq continuing to mount and the retirement of baby boomers drawing ever nearer, the country's fiscal situation was a cause of mounting concern.

In 2008, home mortgage and other financial market problems shook the foundations of the nation's credit and banking systems, bringing Wall Street woes and what came to be called the Great Recession. Meanwhile, the national government's budget deficit soared, and growth in the national debt exceeded that which had occurred during the Reagan administration and the first Bush presidency. By late 2008, it was unclear whether the traditional mainstays of American industry, the Big Three automakers, would avoid bankruptcy, as two of them publicly sought a bailout from Washington in order to survive. Economic problems in the United States reverberated around the globe and many observers suggested that the economic downturn was going to be the worst since the Great Depression.

In its first months in office, the Obama administration concentrated on the country's economic woes. The second half of the $700-billion-dollar Troubled Asset Relief Program (TARP), enacted in the last months of the Bush administration, was used to prop up failing financial institutions as well as General Motors and Chrysler. Moreover, President Obama pushed Congress for a stimulus package to try to get the economy growing again, and the result was passage of a $787-billion-dollar Recovery Act in February 2009.

By late 2009, economic growth had returned amidst continuing high unemployment rates that threatened "a jobless recovery." TARP and stimulus spending, combined with the costs of America's wars in Iraq and Afghanistan and other costs associated with the recession made national government budget deficits reach the highest levels since the end of World War II. While

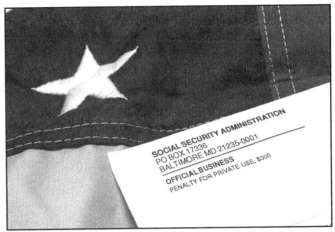

© C. Sherburne/PhotoLink/Getty Images

Obama supporters claimed that his policies had saved the country from another Great Depression, Obama's critics expressed concern about the huge budget deficits, the mounting national debt, and when prosperity and economic stability would return to the United States. By the late summer of 2010, the recovery continued to be weak, with high unemployment figures, an extremely slow housing market, minimal economic growth, and growing fears of a so-called double-dip recession. In this context, it was unsurprising that President Obama's public approval ratings declined to below 50 percent and that Republicans fared well in the November 2010 congressional elections, regaining majority control of the House of Representatives and gaining six seats in the Senate. As many—but not all—political scientists would have predicted, the beginning of a new period of "divided government" in January 2011 seemed to bring heightened policy tensions in Washington. A debt ceiling crisis occurred during the summer of 2011, with an uneasy agreement reached just before the U.S. government was to default. That "uneasy agreement" included the formation of a 12-member congressional "super-committee" charged with producing a set of cost-cutting recommendations for Congress by late November 2011. How this super-committee process will play out is unknown and unknowable as this book goes to press.

Domestic public policy typically involves trade-offs among competing uses of scarce resources. During his 1992 campaign, Bill Clinton called attention to many such trade-offs in the area of health care. As president, Clinton introduced a comprehensive health care reform proposal in 1993. Congress never voted on that proposal, and, while minor changes were made in the nation's health care delivery system during the Clinton years, no comprehensive overhaul was achieved. In his 2007 State of the Union address, President Bush presented several proposals relating to health care, including a change in relevant tax code provisions, but no significant legislation ensued. In 2008, health care reform was a major priority of the two leading candidates for the Democratic presidential nomination, Hillary Clinton and Barack Obama, and Obama's victory over Republican opponent John McCain seemed to make major health care reform of some sort probable, if not inevitable.

After focusing on pressing economic and financial troubles in the first few months of 2009, Congress and the president turned their attention to health care reform more publicly in the summer of 2009. The legislative process seemed to drag on interminably. Not until March 2010 was major health care reform enacted, with Democrats using a parliamentary maneuver called "reconciliation" to sidestep opposition in the Senate from the 41 Republican senators, a number large enough to mount a successful filibuster against comprehensive reform efforts.

The final health care reform enactment included countless tradeoffs and compromises among competing ideas about what ought to be in the bill, the overall price tag, and how to pay for it. Moreover, trade-offs occurred outside the health reform bill as well. By urging Congress to give priority to passing a health care reform bill, President Obama and congressional leaders delayed efforts to pass cap-and-trade legislation to reduce greenhouse gas emissions and to enact immigration reform. In the summer of 2010, Congress enacted the Dodd-Frank Wall Street Reform and Consumer Protection Act. Aimed at curbing financial market practices blamed for the 2008–2009 financial meltdown, this bill was the most comprehensive financial regulatory package since the Great Depression. With congressional elections coming in November, however, Congress and the administration abandoned efforts to enact a major energy and environment bill as well as comprehensive immigration reform. Once again, trade-offs had been at work.

For most of the last half of the twentieth century, the United States and the Soviet Union each had the capacity to end human existence as we know it. Not surprisingly, the threat of nuclear war with the Soviet Union often dominated American foreign policy and diplomacy. During that same period, however, the United States used conventional military forces in a number of places, including Korea, Vietnam, Grenada, and Panama.

The demise of the Soviet Union in 1991 left the United States as the world's sole military superpower, profoundly affecting world politics and U.S. foreign policy ever since. Questions about the appropriateness of U.S. intervention in such disparate places as Bosnia-Herzegovina, Somalia, Haiti, Iraq, Kosovo, and even Russia were at the forefront of foreign policy concerns during the Clinton administration. After the 9/11 terrorist attacks, of course, the George W. Bush administration and the nation as a whole became preoccupied with anti-terrorism efforts and homeland security.

The foreign and defense policy process in the United States raises a host of related issues, including continuing struggle between legislative and executive branches for control. In 1991, after Iraq invaded Kuwait, Congress authorized war against Iraq, which was the first time since World War II that there has been explicit and formal congressional approval before commencement of U.S. military combat operations. In late 1995, President Clinton committed the United States to sending troops to Bosnia-Herzegovina as part of a multinational peacekeeping force. Despite some opposition, Congress passed resolutions supporting the venture. Toward the end of 1997, President Saddam Hussein of Iraq obstructed UN weapons inspection teams in his country, and President Clinton responded by increasing the readiness of U.S. military forces in the Persian Gulf. In late 1998, several days of U.S. air strikes on Iraq followed what was viewed as further provocation by the Iraqi leader.

In the aftermath of the 9/11 terrorist attacks in 2001, Congress supported President George W. Bush in pursuing the perpetrators and launching an assault on Al Qaeda sites in Afghanistan. In the fall of 2002, Congress authorized President Bush to wage war against Iraq if he deemed it necessary to safeguard American security. Early in 2003, U.S. forces invaded Iraq, and critics in Congress and elsewhere suggested that President Bush had made insufficient attempts to gain international support. The initial military success in toppling Saddam Hussein's government has been followed by years of violent insurgency that threatened the legitimacy of Iraqi self-government, killed more than 4,000 U.S. troops and many multiples of that number of Iraqis, and cost hundreds of billions of dollars. Americans' dissatisfaction with the Iraq war seemed a major factor in Democrats' winning majority control of the House and Senate in November 2006, which in turn set the stage for a sharp debate between President Bush and Congress about what to do next and about the proper role of each branch in shaping national security policy.

Barack Obama made his early opposition to the Iraq war a cornerstone of his 2008 presidential candidacy and promised to remove American troops from Iraq in a timely manner if he became president. By late 2008, the Iraqi government declared that American troops should be removed from Iraq within three years. During the transition period between his election and his taking the oath of office on January 20, 2009, Obama announced that he would keep President Bush's Secretary of Defense, Robert Gates, one of whose responsibilities would be to oversee the safe withdrawal of American troops from Iraq. This move suggested that, at long last, American policymakers and the American public were moving toward a bipartisan consensus about ending American military involvement in Iraq. In the second month of his presidency, President Obama announced his plan to withdraw American combat troops from Iraq by August 2010, and the planned withdrawal occurred on schedule 18 months later. But even as his Iraq withdrawal plan was being met with approval by most Americans, in the fall of 2009 President Obama found himself wrestling with various military options in Afghanistan, which ranged, according to some observers, from "bad" to "worse." U.S. military forces in Afghanistan faced a growing Taliban insurgency, and the corrupt Afghanistan government led many Americans to wonder whether mounting American casualties in Afghanistan were justified. In December 2009 the commander-in-chief announced a new plan that would increase the number of U.S. troops in Afghanistan and change tactics used to fight the Taliban. By the end of American combat troop withdrawals from Iraq in August 2010, the additional U.S. troops were in place in Afghanistan, and the nation and the world waited to see whether the new strategy would be successful.

The traditional distinction between domestic and foreign policy is becoming more and more difficult to maintain, since so many contemporary policy decisions have important implications on both fronts. President Clinton's emphasis on the connection between domestic and international economic issues in maintaining what he called national economic security was reinforced at this point. In turn, he worked hard to pass the

NAFTA accord of 1993, which dramatically reduced trade barriers among Canada, Mexico, and the United States. Similarly, President George W. Bush repeatedly noted the connection between, on the one hand, military and diplomatic activities with respect to faraway places like Afghanistan, Iraq, Iran, and North Korea and, on the other, homeland security in the post-9/11 era. In his second inaugural address in 2005, President Bush declared that the liberty and security of Americans at home depend on the "expansion of freedom in all the world."

Two prominent policy challenges facing the Obama administration, economic recovery and global warming, further illustrate the convergence between domestic and foreign policy. With an increasingly globalized economy, the economic health of the United States is inevitably tied to economic conditions around the world. Similarly, no unilateral action by the United States or any other nation to fight global warming can be successful on its own. Strategies to combat climate change can succeed only if pursued on a multilateral or global level. As already mentioned in the opening paragraph of this introduction to Unit 4, the products—that is, policies—of American government are very much the result of interactions among the topics addressed in the first three units of this book: the "foundations," "structures," and "process" of the American political system. Those interactions give rise to the many sorts of policy challenges and tensions that are raised in the Learning Outcomes and the selections in this concluding unit of the book.

Internet References

American Diplomacy
www.unc.edu/depts/diplomat

Cato Institute
www.cato.org

Ezra Klein
http://voices.washingtonpost.com/ezra-klein

Foreign Affairs
www.foreignaffairs.org

Paul Krugman
krugman.blogs.nytimes.com

Tax Foundation
www.taxfoundation.org

The Realities of Immigration

Linda Chavez

What to do about immigration—both legal and illegal—has become one of the most controversial public-policy debates in recent memory. But why it has occurred at this particular moment is something of a mystery. The rate of immigration into the U.S., although high, is still below what it was even a few years ago, the peak having been reached in the late 1990s. President Bush first talked about comprehensive immigration reform almost immediately after assuming office, but he put the plan on hold after 9/11 and only reintroduced the idea in 2004. Why the current flap?

By far the biggest factor shaping the popular mood seems to have been the almost daily drumbeat on the issue from political talk-show hosts, most prominently CNN's Lou Dobbs and the Fox News Channel's Bill O'Reilly and Scan Hannity (both of whom also have popular radio shows), syndicated radio hosts Rush Limbaugh, Laura Ingraham, Michael Savage, and G. Gordon Liddy, and a plethora of local hosts reaching tens of millions of listeners each week. Stories about immigration have become a staple of cable news, with sensational footage of illegal crossings featured virtually every day.

Media saturation has led, in turn, to the emergence of immigration as a wedge issue in the still-nascent 2008 presidential campaign. Several aspiring Republican candidates—former House Speaker Newt Gingrich, Senate Majority Leader Bill Frist, and Senator George Allen—have worked to burnish their "get tough" credentials, while, on the other side of the issue, Senator John McCain has come forward as the lead sponsor of a bill to allow most illegal aliens to earn legal status. For their part, potential Democratic candidates have remained largely mum, unsure how the issue plays with their various constituencies.

And then there are the immigrants themselves, who have shown surprising political muscle, especially in response to legislation passed by the House that would turn the illegal aliens among them into felons. Millions of mostly Hispanic protesters have taken to the streets in our big cities in recent months, waving American flags and (more controversially) their own national flags while demanding recognition and better treatment. Though Hispanic leaders and pro-immigrant advocates point to the protests as evidence of a powerful new civil-rights movement, many other Americans see the demonstrators as proof of an alien invasion—and a looming threat to the country's prosperity and unity.

In short, it is hard to recall a time when there has been so much talk about immigration and immigration reform—or when so much of the talk has been misinformed, misleading, and ahistorical. Before policy-makers can decide what to do about immigration, the problem itself needs to be better defined, not just in terms of costs and benefits but in relation to America's deepest values.

Contrary to popular myth, immigrants have never been particularly welcome in the United States. Americans have always tended to romanticize the immigrants of their grandparents' generation while casting a skeptical eye on contemporary newcomers. In the first decades of the 20th century, descendants of Northern European immigrants resisted the arrival of Southern and Eastern Europeans, and today the descendants of those once unwanted Italians, Greeks, and Poles are deeply distrustful of current immigrants from Latin America. Congressman Tom Tancredo, a Republican from Colorado and an outspoken advocate of tighter restrictions, is fond of invoking the memory of his Italian immigrant grandfather to argue that he is not anti-immigrant, just anti-illegal immigration. He fails to mention that at the time his grandfather arrived, immigrants simply had to show up on American shores (or walk across the border) to gain legal entry.

With the exception of the infamous Alien and Sedition Acts of 1798, there were few laws regulating immigration for the first hundred years of the nation's history. Though nativist sentiment increased throughout the later decades of the 19th century, giving rise to the 1882 Chinese Exclusion Act, it was not until 1917 that Congress began methodically to limit all immigration, denying admission to most Asians and Pacific Islanders and, in 1924, imposing quotas on those deemed undesirable: Jews, Italians, and others from Southern and Eastern Europe. These restrictions remained largely in effect until 1952, when Congress lifted many of them, including the bar on Asians.

The modern immigration era commenced in 1965 with the passage of the Immigration and Nationality Act, which abolished all national-origin quotas, gave preference to close relatives of American citizens, refugees, and individuals with certain skills, and allowed for immigrants from the Western hemisphere on a first-come, first-served basis. The act's passage drew a huge wave, much of it from Latin America and Asia. From 1970 to 2000, the United States admitted more than 20 million persons as permanent residents.

By 2000, some 3 million of these new residents were formerly illegal aliens who had gained amnesty as part of the 1986 Immigration Reform and Control Act (IRCA). This, Congress's first serious attempt to stem the flow of illegal immigration, forced employers to determine the status of their workers and imposed heavy penalties on those hiring illegal entrants. But from the beginning, the law was fraught with problems. It created huge bureaucratic burdens, even for private individuals wanting to hire someone to cut their lawn or care for their children, and spawned a vast new document-fraud industry for immigrants eager to get hold of the necessary paperwork. The law has been a monumental failure. Today, some 11.5 million illegal aliens reside in the U.S.—quadruple the population of two decades ago, when IRCA was enacted—and the number is growing by an estimated 500,000 a year.

The status quo has thus become untenable, and particularly so since the attacks of 9/11, which prompted fears of future terrorists sneaking across our sieve-like borders as easily as would-be busboys, janitors, and construction workers. Though virtually all Americans agree that something must be done, finding a good solution has proven elusive. The Bush administration has significantly increased border enforcement, adding nearly 30-percent more border-patrol agents since 2001 and increasing funding by 66 percent. The border patrol now employs nearly as many agents as the FBI, over 12,000 by the end of this fiscal year (not counting the additional 6,000 proposed by the President in May). But with some 6,000 miles of land border to monitor, that figure represents only one agent per mile (assuming eight-hour, 'round-the-clock shifts). Still, there has been progress: illegal immigration has actually slowed a bit since its peak during the boom economy of the late 1990s—a fact rarely noted in the current debate—though it has begun climbing again.

The latest suggestion is to build a wall along the border with Mexico. Some sections of the border already have 10-foot-high steel fences in place, and bills recently passed by the House and Senate authorize the construction of hundreds of additional miles of fencing along the border in California, Arizona, New Mexico, and Texas. The President, too, has endorsed the idea of a more formidable barrier. The Minuteman Project, a group that fashions itself a citizens' patrol, has volunteered to build the fence on private property along the Arizona/Mexico border. But unless the United States is prepared to build fences on its southern and northern borders, illegal entry will continue, albeit in diminished numbers. (Some 200,000 illegal immigrants—the equivalent of 1.8 million in U.S. terms—now live in Canada; most are Asians, but they are increasingly being joined by Latin Americans who in many cases are hoping to make the United States their ultimate destination.) More problematic for advocates of a fence is that an estimated 45 percent of all illegal aliens enter lawfully and simply overstay the terms of their visas.

So what might alleviate the current situation? Restrictionists claim that better internal enforcement, with crackdowns on employers who hire illegal aliens, would deter more from coming. This might work if we were willing to adopt a national identification card for every person in the country and a sophisticated instant-check system to verify the employment eligibility of each of the nation's 150 million workers. But concern over immigration seems unlikely on its own to spark sufficient support for such a system. Even after 9/11, when some experts recommended national ID's as a necessary security measure, Americans were reluctant to endorse the idea, fearing its implications for privacy.

President Bush has now proposed a tamper-proof card that all foreign workers would be required to carry, though one can envision grave "profiling" difficulties with this, not least when native-born Hispanic and Asian workers are selectively asked to produce such identification. Moreover, an experimental version of a program to require instant checks of work eligibility—now included in both the House and the Senate immigration bills—produced a nearly 30-percent error rate for legal immigrants who were denied employment.

The real question is not whether the U.S. has the means to stop illegal immigration—no doubt, with sufficient resources, we could mostly do so—but whether we would be better off as a nation without these workers. Restrictionists claim that large-scale immigration—legal and illegal—has depressed wages, burdened government resources, and acted as a net drain on the economy. The Federation for American Immigration Reform (FAIR), the most prominent of the pressure groups on the issue, argues that, because of this influx, hourly earnings among American males have not increased appreciably in 30 years. As the restrictionists see it, if the U.S. got serious about defending its borders, there would be plenty of Americans willing to do the jobs now performed by workers from abroad.

Indeed, FAIR and other extremists on the issue wish not only to eliminate illegal immigration but drastically to reduce or halt legal immigration as well. Along with its public-policy arm, the Center for Immigration Studies (CIS), FAIR has long argued that the U.S. should aim for a population of just 150 million persons—that is, about half the current level. If such an agenda sounds suspiciously like views usually found on the Left, that is no accident.

One of the great ironies of the current immigration debate is the strange ideological bedfellows it has created. The founder of the modern anti-immigration movement, a Michigan physician named John Tanton, is the former national president of Zero Population Growth and a long-time activist with Planned Parenthood and several Left-leaning environmentalist groups. Tanton came to the issue of immigration primarily because of his fears about overpopulation and the destruction of natural resources. Through an umbrella organization, U.S. Inc., he has created or funded not only FAIR and CIS but such groups as NumbersUSA, Population-Environment Balance, Pro-English, and U.S. English.[1] The Social Contract Press, another of Tanton's outfits, is the English-language publisher of the apocalyptic—and frankly racist—1975 novel *Camp of the Saints,* written by the French right-wing author Jean Raspail. The book, which apparently had a considerable influence in shaping Tanton's own views, foretells the demise of Europe at the hands of hordes of East Indians who invade the continent, bringing with them disease, crime, and anarchy.

As for the more conventional claims advanced by restrictionists, they, too, are hard to credit. Despite the presence in our workforce of millions of illegal immigrants, the U.S. is currently creating slightly more than two million jobs a year and boasts an unemployment rate of 4.7 percent, which is lower than the average in each of the past four decades. More to the point perhaps, when the National Research Council (NRC) of the National Academy of Sciences evaluated the economic impact of immigration in its landmark 1997 study The New Americans: Economic, Demographic, and Fiscal Effects of Immigration, it found only a small negative impact on the earnings of Americans, and even then, only for workers at lower skill and education levels.

Moreover, the participation of immigrants in the labor force has had obvious positive effects. The NRC estimated that roughly 5 percent of household expenditures in the U.S. went to goods and services produced by immigrant labor—labor whose relative cheapness translated into lower prices for everything from chicken to new homes. These price advantages, the study found, were "spread quite uniformly across most types of domestic consumers," with a slightly greater benefit for higher-income households.

Many restrictionists argue that if Americans would simply cut their own lawns, clean their own houses, and care for their own children, there would be no need for immigrant labor. But even if this were true, the overall economy would hardly benefit from having fewer workers. If American women were unable to rely on immigrants to perform some household duties, more of them would be forced to stay home. A smaller labor force would also have devastating consequences when it comes to dealing with the national debt and government-funded entitlements like Social Security and Medicare, a point repeatedly made by former Federal Reserve Board Chairman Alan Greenspan. As he told a Senate committee in 2003, "short of a major increase in immigration, economic growth cannot be safely counted upon to eliminate deficits and the difficult choices that will be required to restore fiscal discipline." The following year, Greenspan noted that offsetting the fiscal effects of our own declining birthrate would require a level of immigration "much larger than almost all current projections assume."

The contributions that immigrants make to the economy must be weighed, of course, against the burdens they impose. FAIR and other restrictionist groups contend that immigrants are a huge drain on society because of the cost of providing public services to them—some $67 to $87 billion a year, according to one commonly cited study. Drawing on numbers from the NRC's 1997 report, FAIR argues that "the net fiscal drain on American taxpayers [from immigration] is between $166 and $226 a year per native household."

There is something to these assertions, though less than may at first appear. Much of the anxiety and resentment generated by immigrants is, indeed, a result of the very real costs they impose on state and local governments, especially in border states like California and Arizona. Providing education and health care to the children of immigrants is particularly expensive, and the federal government picks up only a fraction of the expense. But, again, there are countervailing factors. Illegal immigrants are hardly free-riders. An estimated three-quarters of them paid federal taxes in 2002, amounting to $7 billion in Social Security contributions and $1.5 billion in Medicare taxes, plus withholding for income taxes. They also pay state and local sales taxes and (as homeowners and renters) property taxes.

Moreover, FAIR and its ilk have a penchant for playing fast and loose with numbers. To support its assessment of immigration's overall fiscal burden, for instance, FAIR ignores the explicit cautions in a later NRC report about cross-sectional analyses that exclude the "concurrent descendants" of immigrants—that is, their adult children. These, overwhelmingly, are productive members of the workforce. As the NRC notes, when this more complete picture is taken into account, immigrants have "a positive federal impact of about $1,260 [per capita], exceeding their net cost [$680 per capita on average] at the state and local levels." Restrictionists also argue that fewer immigrants would mean more opportunities for low-skilled native workers. Of late, groups like the Minuteman Project have even taken to presenting themselves as champions of unemployed American blacks (a curious tactic, to say the least, considering the views on race and ethnicity of many in the anti-immigrant camp[2]).

But here, too, the factual evidence is mixed. Wages for American workers who have less than a high-school education have probably been adversely affected by large-scale immigration; the economist George Borjas estimates a reduction of 8 percent in hourly wages for native-born males in that category. But price competition is not the only reason that many employers favor immigrants over poorly educated natives. Human capital includes motivation, and there could hardly be two more disparately motivated groups than U.S.-born high-school dropouts and their foreign-born rivals in the labor market. Young American men usually leave high school because they become involved with drugs or crime, have difficulty with authority, cannot maintain regular hours, or struggle with learning. Immigrants, on the other hand, have demonstrated enormous initiative, reflecting, in the words of President Reagan, "a special kind of courage that enabled them to leave their own land, leave their friends and their countrymen, and come to this new and strange land."

Just as important, they possess a strong desire to work. Legal immigrants have an 86-percent rate of participation in the labor force; illegal immigrant males have a 94-percent rate. By contrast, among white males with less than a high-school education, the participation rate is 46 percent, while among blacks it is 40 percent. If all immigrants, or even only illegal aliens, disappeared from the American workforce, can anyone truly believe that poorly skilled whites and blacks would fill the gap? To the contrary, productivity would likely decline, and employers in many sectors would simply move their operations to countries like Mexico, China, and the Philippines, where many of our immigrants come from in the first place.

Of equal weight among foes of immigration are the cultural changes wrought by today's newcomers, especially those from Mexico. In his book *Who Are We? The Challenges to National Identity* (2004), the eminent political scientist Samuel P. Huntington warns that "Mexican immigration is leading toward the demographic reconquista of areas Americans took from Mexico by force in the 1830s and 1840s." Others have fretted about the aims of militant Mexican-American activists, pointing to "El Plan de Aztlan," a radical Hispanic manifesto hatched in 1969, which calls for "the control of our barrios, campos, pueblos, lands, our economy, our culture, and our political life," including "self-defense against the occupying forces of the oppressors"—that is, the U.S. government.

To be sure, the fantasy of a recaptured homeland exists mostly in the minds of a handful of already well-assimilated Mexican-American college professors and the students they manage to indoctrinate (self-described "victims" who often enjoy preferential admission to college and subsidized or free tuition). But such rhetoric understandably alarms many Americans, especially in light of the huge influx of Hispanic immigrants into the Southwest. Does it not seem likely that today's immigrants—because of their numbers, the constant flow of even more newcomers, and their proximity to their countries of origin—will be unable or unwilling to assimilate as previous ethnic groups have done?

There is no question that some public policies in the U.S. have actively discouraged assimilation. Bilingual education, the dominant method of instruction of Hispanic immigrant children for some 30 years, is the most obvious culprit, with its emphasis on retaining Spanish. But bilingual education is on the wane, having been challenged by statewide initiatives in California (1998), Arizona (2000), and Massachusetts (2004), and by policy shifts in several major cities and at the federal level. States that have moved to English-immersion instruction have seen test scores for Hispanic youngsters rise, in some cases substantially.

Evidence from the culture at large is also encouraging. On most measures of social and economic integration, Hispanic immigrants and their descendants have made steady strides up the ladder. English is the preferred language of virtually all U.S.-born Hispanics; indeed, according to a 2002 national survey by the Pew Hispanic Center and the Kaiser Family Foundation, 78 percent of third-generation Mexican-Americans cannot speak Spanish at all. In education, 86 percent of U.S.-born Hispanics complete high school, compared with 92 percent of non-Hispanic whites, and the drop-out rate among immigrant children who enroll in high school after they come here is no higher than for the native-born.

It remains true that attendance at four-year colleges is lower among Hispanics than for other groups, and Hispanics lag in attaining bachelor's degrees. But neither that nor their slightly lower rate of high-school attendance has kept Hispanic immigrants from pulling their economic weight. After controlling for education, English proficiency, age, and geographic location, Mexican-born males actually earn 2.4 percent more than comparable U.S.-born white males, according to a recent analysis of 2000 Census data by the National Research Council. Hispanic women, for their part, hold their own against U.S.-born white women with similar qualifications.

As for the effect of Hispanic immigrants on the country's social fabric, the NRC found that they are more likely than other Americans to live with their immediate relatives: 88.6 percent of Mexican immigrant households are made up of families, compared with 69.5 percent of non-Hispanic whites and 68.3 percent of blacks. These differences are partially attributable to the age structure of the Hispanic population, which is younger on average than the white or black population. But even after adjusting for age and immigrant generation, U.S. residents of Hispanic origin—and especially those from Mexico—are much more likely to live in family households. Despite increased out-of-wedlock births among Hispanics, about 67 percent of American children of Mexican origin live in two-parent families, as compared with 77 percent of white children but only 37 percent of black children.

Perhaps the strongest indicator of Hispanic integration into American life is the population's high rate of intermarriage. About a quarter of all Hispanics marry outside their ethnic group, almost exclusively to non-Hispanic white spouses, a rate that has remained virtually unchanged since 1980. And here a significant fact has been noted in a 2005 study by the Population Reference Bureau—namely, that "the majority of inter-Hispanic children are reported as Hispanic." Such intermarriages themselves, the study goes on, "may have been a factor in the phenomenal growth of the U.S. Hispanic population in recent years."

It has been widely predicted that, by mid-century, Hispanics will represent fully a quarter of the U.S. population. Such predictions fail to take into account that increasing numbers of these "Hispanics" will have only one grandparent or great-grandparent of Hispanic heritage. By that point, Hispanic ethnicity may well mean neither more nor less than German, Italian, or Irish ethnicity means today.

How, then, to proceed? Congress is under growing pressure to strengthen border control, but unless it also reaches some agreement on more comprehensive reforms, stauncher enforcement is unlikely to have much of an effect. With a growing economy and more jobs than our own population can readily absorb, the U.S. will continue to need immigrants. Illegal immigration already responds reasonably well to market forces. It has increased during boom times like the late 1990's and decreased again when jobs disappear, as in the latest recession. Trying to determine an ideal number makes no more sense than trying to predict how much steel or how many textiles we ought to import; government quotas can never match the efficiency of simple supply and demand. As President Bush has argued—and as the Senate has now agreed—a guest-worker program is the way to go.

Does this mean the U.S. should just open its borders to anyone who wants to come? Hardly. We still need an orderly process, one that includes background checks to insure that terrorists and criminals are not being admitted. It also makes sense to require that immigrants have at least a basic knowledge of English and to give preference to those who have advanced skills or needed talents.

Moreover, immigrants themselves have to take more responsibility for their status. Illegal aliens from Mexico now pay significant sums of money to "coyotes" who sneak them across the border. If they could come legally as guest workers, that same money might be put up as a surety bond to guarantee their return at the end of their employment contract, or perhaps to pay for health insurance. Nor is it good policy to allow immigrants to become welfare recipients or to benefit from affirmative action: restrictions on both sorts of programs have to be written into law and stringently applied.

A market-driven guest-worker program might be arranged in any number of ways. A proposal devised by the Vernon K. Krieble Foundation, a policy group based in Colorado, suggests that government-licensed, private-sector employment agencies be put in charge of administering the effort, setting up offices in other countries to process applicants and perform background checks. Workers would be issued tamper-proof identity cards only after signing agreements that would allow for deportation if they violated the terms of their contract or committed crimes in the U.S. Although the Krieble plan would offer no path to citizenship, workers who wanted to change their status could still apply for permanent residency and, ultimately, citizenship through the normal, lengthy process.

Do such schemes stand a chance politically? A poll commissioned by the Krieble Foundation found that most Americans (except those with less than a high-school education) consider an "efficient system for handling guest workers" to be more important than expanded law enforcement in strengthening the country's border. Similarly, a CNN tracking poll in May found that 81 percent of respondents favored legislation permitting illegal immigrants who have been in the U.S. more than five years to stay here and apply for citizenship, provided they had jobs and paid back taxes. True, other polls have contradicted these results, suggesting public ambivalence on the issue—and an openness to persuasion.

Regardless of what Congress does or does not do—the odds in favor of an agreement between the Senate and House on final legislation are still no better than 50–50—immigration is likely to continue at high levels for the foreseeable future. Barring a recession or another terrorist attack, the U.S. economy is likely to need some 1.5 to 2 million immigrants a year for some time to come. It would be far better for all concerned if those who wanted to work in the U.S. and had jobs waiting for them here could do so legally, in the light of day and with the full approval of the American people.

In 1918, at the height of the last great wave of immigrants and the hysteria that it prompted in some circles, Madison Grant, a Yale-educated eugenicist and leader of the immigration-restriction movement, made a prediction:

The result of unlimited immigration is showing plainly in the rapid decline in the birth rate of native Americans because the poorer classes of colonial stock, where they still exist, will not bring children into the world to compete in the labor market with the Slovak, the Italian, the Syrian, and the Jew. . . . The man of the old stock is being crowded out of many country districts by these foreigners, just as he is today being literally driven off the streets of New York City by the swarms of Polish Jews. These immigrants adopt the language of the native American, they wear his clothes, they steal his name, and they are beginning to take his women, but they seldom adopt his religion or understand his ideals, and while he is being elbowed out of his own home, the American looks calmly abroad and urges on others the suicidal ethics which are exterminating his own race.

Today, such alarmism reads as little more than a historical curiosity. Southern and Eastern European immigrants and their children did, in fact, assimilate, and in certain cases—most prominently that of the Jews—they exceeded the educational and economic attainments of Grant's "colonial stock."

Present-day restrictionists point to all sorts of special circumstances that supposedly made such acculturation possible in the past but render it impossible today. Then as now, however, the restrictionists are wrong, not least in their failure to understand the basic dynamic of American nationhood. There is no denying the challenge posed by assimilating today's newcomers, especially so many of them in so short a span of time. Nor is there any denying the cultural forces, mainly stemming from the Left, that have attenuated the sense of national identity among native-born American elites themselves and led to such misguided policies as bilingual education. But, provided that we commit ourselves to the goal, past experience and progress to date suggest the task is anything but impossible.

As jarring as many found the recent pictures of a million illegal aliens marching in our cities, the fact remains that many of the immigrants were carrying the American flag, and waving it proudly. They and their leaders understand what most restrictionists do not and what some Americans have forgotten or choose to deny: that the price of admission to America is, and must be, the willingness to become an American.

Notes

1. I was briefly president of U.S. English in the late 1980s but resigned when a previously undisclosed memo written by Tanton was published. In it, he warned of problems related to the "educability" of Hispanics and speculated that an influx of Catholics from south of the border might well lead the U.S. to "pitch out" the concept of church-state separation. Tanton was forced to resign as chairman of U.S. English and no longer has any affiliation with the group.

2. As the author and anti-immigration activist Peter Brimelow wrote in his 1995 book *Alien Nation,* "Americans have a legitimate interest in their country's racial balance . . . [and] a right to insist that their government stop shifting it." Himself an immigrant from England, Brimelow wants "more immigrants who look like me."

Critical Thinking

1. Why has immigration become such a hot topic within the past decade?
2. Why is enhanced border security at best only a partial solution to the immigration problem?
3. What do so-called restrictionists advocate with respect to the problems of immigration, illegal aliens, and the like?
4. What are some of the contributions immigrants make to the U.S. economy? What are some of the burdens they impose?
5. Describe how a market-based guest-worker program might work. Does this type of approach seem feasible?

LINDA CHAVEZ, the author of *Out of the Barrio* (1991), among other books, is the chairman of the Center for Equal Opportunity in Washington, D.C. She is at work on a new book about immigration.

From *Commentary,* July/August 2006, pp. 34–40. Copyright © 2006 by Commentary. Reprinted by permission of Commentary and Linda Chavez.

The Other National Debt

$14 Trillion in the Red? We Should Be So Lucky.

KEVIN D. WILLIAMSON

About that $14 trillion national debt: Get ready to tack some zeroes onto it. Taken alone, the amount of debt issued by the federal government—that $14 trillion figure that shows up on the national ledger—is a terrifying, awesome, hellacious number: Fourteen trillion seconds ago, Greenland was covered by lush and verdant forests, and the Neanderthals had not yet been outwitted and driven into extinction by *Homo sapiens sapiens,* because we did not yet exist. Big number, 14 trillion, and yet it doesn't even begin to cover the real indebtedness of American governments at the federal, state, and local levels, because governments don't count up their liabilities the same way businesses do.

Accountants get a bad rap—boring, green-eyeshades-wearing, nebbishy little men chained to their desks down in the fluorescent-lit basements of Corporate America—but, in truth, accountants wield an awesome power. In the case of the federal government, they wield the power to make vast amounts of debt disappear—from the public discourse, at least. A couple of months ago, you may recall, Rep. Henry Waxman (D., State of Bankruptcy) got his Fruit of the Looms in a full-on buntline hitch when AT&T, Caterpillar, Verizon, and a host of other blue-chip behemoths started taking plus-size writedowns in response to some of the more punitive provisions of the health-care legislation Mr. Waxman had helped to pass. His little mustache no doubt bristling in indignation, Representative Waxman sent dunning letters to the CEOs of these companies and demanded that they come before Congress to explain their accounting practices. One White House staffer told reporters that the writedowns appeared to be designed "to embarrass the president and Democrats."

A few discreet whispers from better-informed Democrats, along with a helpful explanation from *The Atlantic*'s Megan McArdle under the headline "Henry Waxman's War on Accounting," helped to clarify the issue: The companies in question are required by law to adjust their financial statements to reflect the new liabilities: "When a company experiences what accountants call 'a material adverse impact' on its expected future earnings, and those changes affect an item that is already on the balance sheet, the company is required to record the negative impact—'to take the charge against earnings'—as soon as it knows that the change is reasonably likely to occur,"

McArdle wrote. "The Democrats, however, seem to believe that Generally Accepted Accounting Principles are some sort of conspiracy against Obamacare, and all that is good and right in America." But don't be too hard on the gentleman from California: Government does not work that way. If governments did follow normal accounting practices, taking account of future liabilities today instead of pretending they don't exist, then the national-debt numbers we talk about would be worse—far worse, dreadfully worse—than that monster $14 trillion-and–ratcheting–upward figure we throw around.

Beyond the official federal debt, there is another $2.5 trillion or so in state and local debt, according to Federal Reserve figures. Why so much? A lot of that debt comes from spending that is extraordinarily stupid and wasteful, even by government standards. Because state and local authorities can issue tax-free securities—municipal bonds—there's a lot of appetite for their debt on the marketplace, and a whole platoon of local special-interest hustlers looking to get a piece. This results in a lot of misallocated capital: By shacking up with your local economic-development authority, you can build yourself a new major-league sports stadium with tax-free bonds, but you have to use old-fashioned financing, with no tax benefits, if you want to build a factory—which is to say, you can use tax-free municipal bonds to help create jobs, so long as those jobs are selling hot dogs to sports fans.

Also, local political machines tend to be dominated by politically connected law firms that enjoy a steady stream of basically free money from legal fees charged when those municipal bonds are issued, so they have every incentive to push for more and more indebtedness at the state and local levels. For instance, the Philadelphia law firm of Ballard Spahr kept Ed Rendell on the payroll to the tune of $250,000 a year while he was running for governor—he described his duties at the firm as "very little"—and the firm's partners donated nearly $1 million to his campaign. They're big in the bond-counsel business, as they advertise in their marketing materials: "We have one of the premier public finance practices in the country, participating since 1987 in the issuance of more than $250 billion of tax-exempt obligations in 49 states, the District of Columbia, and three territories." Other Pennsylvania bond-counsel firms were big Rendell donors, too, and they get paid from 35 cents to 50 cents per $1,000 in municipal bonds issued, so they love it when the local powers borrow money.

So that's $14 trillion in federal debt and $2.5 trillion in state-and-local debt: $16.5 trillion. But I've got some bad news for you, Sunshine: We haven't even hit all the big-ticket items.

One of the biggest is the pension payments owed to government workers. And here's where the state-and-local story actually gets quite a bit worse than what's happening in Washington—it's the sort of thing that might make you rethink that whole federalism business. While the federal government runs a reasonably well-administered retirement program for its workers, the states, in their capacity as the laboratories of democracy, have been running a mad-scientist experiment in their pension funds, making huge promises but skipping the part where they sock away the money to pay for them. Every year, the pension funds' actuaries calculate how much money must be saved and invested that year to fund future benefits, and every year the fund managers ignore them. In 2009, for instance, the New Jersey public-school teachers' pension system invested just 6 percent of the amount of money its actuaries calculated was needed. And New Jersey is hardly alone in this. With a handful of exceptions, practically every state's pension fund is poised to run out of money in the coming decades. A federal bailout is almost inevitable, which means that those state obligations will probably end up on the national balance sheet in one form or another.

The states have been running a mad-scientist experiment in their pension funds, making huge promises but skipping the part where they sock away the money to pay for them.

"We're facing a full-fledged state-level debt crisis later this decade," says Prof. Joshua D. Rauh of the Kellogg School of Management at Northwestern University, who recently published a paper titled "Are State Public Pensions Sustainable?" Good question. Professor Rauh is a bit more nuanced than John Boehner, but he comes to the same conclusion: Hell, no. "Half the states' pension funds could run out of money by 2025," he says, "and that's assuming decent investment returns. The federal government should be worried about its exposure. Are these states too big to fail? If something isn't done, we're facing another trillion-dollar bailout."

The problem, Professor Rauh explains, is that pension funds are used to hide government borrowing. "A defined-benefit plan is politicians making promises on time horizons that go beyond their political careers, so it's really cheap," he says. "They say, 'Maybe we don't want to give you a pay raise, but we'll give you a really generous pension in 40 years.' It's a way to borrow off the books." The resulting liability runs into the trillions of dollars.

Ground Zero for the state-pension meltdown is Springfield, Ill., and D-Day comes around 2018: That's when the state that nurtured the political career of Barack Obama is expected to be the first state to run out of money to cover its retirees' pension checks. Eight years—and that's assuming an 8 percent average return on its investments. (You making 8 percent a year lately?) Under the same projections, Illinois will be joined in 2019 by Connecticut, New Jersey, and Indiana. If investment returns are 6 percent, then 31 U.S. states will run out of pension-fund money by 2025, according to Rauh's projections.

States aren't going to be able to make up those pension shortfalls out of general tax revenue, at least not at current levels of taxation. In Ohio, for instance, the benefit payments in 2031 would total 55 percent of projected 2031 tax revenues. For most states, pension payments will total more than a quarter of all tax revenues in the years after they run out of money. Most of those pensions cannot be modified: Illinois, for instance, has a constitutional provision that prevents reducing them. Unless there is a radical restructuring of these programs, and soon, states will either have to subsidize their pension systems with onerous new taxes or seek a bailout from Washington.

So how much would the states have to book to fully fund those liabilities? Drop in another $3 trillion. Properly accounting for these obligations, that takes us up to a total of $19.5 trillion in governmental liabilities. Bad, right? You know how the doctor looks at you in that recurring nightmare, when the test results come back and he has to tell you not to bother buying any green bananas? Imagine that look on Tim Geithner's face right now, because we still have to account for the biggest crater in the national ledger: entitlement liabilities.

The debt numbers start to get really hairy when you add in liabilities under Social Security and Medicare—in other words, when you account for the present value of those future payments in the same way that businesses have to account for the obligations they incur. Start with the entitlements and those numbers get run-for-the-hills ugly in a hurry: a combined $106 trillion in liabilities for Social Security and Medicare, or more than five times the total federal, state, and local debt we've totaled up so far. In real terms, what that means is that we'd need $106 trillion in real, investable capital, earning 6 percent a year, on hand, today, to meet the obligations we have under those entitlement programs. For perspective, that's about twice the total private net worth of the United States. (A little more, in fact.)

Suffice it to say, we're a bit short of that $106 trillion. In fact, we're exactly $106 trillion short, since the total value of the Social Security "trust fund" is less than the value of the change you've got rattling around behind your couch cushions, its precise worth being: $0.00. Because the "trust fund" (which is not a trust fund) is by law "invested" (meaning, not invested) in Treasury bonds, there is no national nest egg to fund these entitlements. As Bruce Bartlett explained in *Forbes,* "The trust fund does not have any actual resources with which to pay Social Security benefits. It's as if you wrote an IOU to yourself; no matter how large the IOU is it doesn't increase your net worth . . . Consequently, whether there is $2.4 trillion in the Social Security trust fund or $240 trillion has no bearing on the federal government's ability to pay benefits that have been promised." Seeing no political incentives to reduce benefits, Bartlett calculates that an 81 percent tax increase will be necessary to pay those obligations. "Those who think otherwise are either grossly ignorant of the fiscal facts, in denial, or living in a fantasy world."

There's more, of course. Much more. Besides those monthly pension checks, the states are on the hook for retirees' health care and other benefits, to the tune of another $1 trillion. And, depending on how you account for it, another half a trillion or so (conservatively estimated) in liabilities related to the government's guarantee of Fannie Mae, Freddie Mac, and securities supported under the bailouts. Now, these aren't perfect numbers, but that's the rough picture: Call it $130 trillion or so, or just under ten times the official national debt. Putting Nancy Pelosi in a smaller jet isn't going to make that go away.

Critical Thinking

1. What explains the large amount of state and local debt in the United States?

2. Explain how state pension systems are potentially a large liability.

3. Why is there such a large difference between the stated federal debt figure of $14 trillion and the author's calculation of $140 trillion?

From *The National Review*, June 21, 2010. Copyright © 2010 by National Review, Inc, 215 Lexington Avenue, New York, NY 10016. Reprinted by permission.

In Defense of Deficits

A big deficit-reduction program would destroy the economy two years into the great crisis.

James K. Galbraith

The Simpson–Bowles Commission, just established by the president, will no doubt deliver an attack on Social Security and Medicare dressed up in the sanctimonious rhetoric of deficit reduction. (Back in his salad days, former Senator Alan Simpson was a regular schemer to cut Social Security.) The Obama spending freeze is another symbolic sacrifice to the deficit gods. Most observers believe neither will amount to much, and one can hope that they are right. But what would be the economic consequences if they did? The answer is that a big deficit-reduction program would destroy the economy, or what remains of it, two years into the Great Crisis.

For this reason, the deficit phobia of Wall Street, the press, some economists, and practically all politicians is one of the deepest dangers that we face. It's not just the old and the sick who are threatened, we all are. To cut current deficits without first rebuilding the economic engine of the private credit system is a sure path to stagnation, to a double-dip recession—even to a second Great Depression. To focus obsessively on cutting future deficits is also a path that will obstruct, not assist, what we need to do to re-establish strong growth and high employment.

To put things crudely, there are two ways to get the increase in total spending that we call "economic growth." One way is for government to spend. The other is for banks to lend. Leaving aside short-term adjustments like increased net exports or financial innovation. Governments and banks are the two entities with the power to create something from nothing. If total spending power is to grow, one or the other of these two great financial motors—public deficits or private loans—has to be in action.

For ordinary people, public budget deficits, despite their bad reputation, are much better than private loans. Deficits put money in private pockets. Private households get more cash. They own that cash free and clear, and they can spend it as they like. If they wish, they can also convert it into interest-earning government bonds or they can repay their debts. This is called an increase in "net financial wealth." Ordinary people benefit, but there is nothing in it for banks.

And this, in the simplest terms, explains the deficit phobia of Wall Street, the corporate media, and the right-wing economists.

Bankers don't like budget deficits because they compete with bank loans as a source of growth. When a bank makes a loan, cash balances in private hands also go up. But now the cash is not owned free and clear. There is a contractual obligation to pay interest and to repay principal. If the enterprise defaults, there may be an asset left over—a house or factory or company—that will then become the property of the bank. It's easy to see why bankers love private credit but hate public deficits.

All of these should be painfully obvious, but it is deeply obscure. It is obscure because legions of Wall Streeters—led notably in our time by Peter Peterson and his front man, former comptroller general David Walker, and including the Robert Rubin wing of the Democratic Party and numerous "bipartisan" enterprises like the Concord Coalition and the Committee for a Responsible Federal Budget—have labored mightily to confuse the issues. These spirits never uttered a single word of warning about the financial crisis, which originated on Wall Street under the noses of their bag men. But they constantly warn, quite falsely, that the government is a "super subprime" "Ponzi scheme," which it is not.

We also hear, from the same people, about the impending "bankruptcy" of Social Security, Medicare—even the United States itself. Or of the burden that public debts will "impose on our grandchildren." Or about "unfunded liabilities" supposedly facing us all. All of these form part of one of the great misinformation campaigns of all time.

The misinformation is rooted in what many consider to be plain common sense. It may seem like homely wisdom, especially, to say that "just like the family, the government can't live beyond its means." But it's not. In these matters the public and private sectors differ on a very basic point. Your family needs income in order to pay its debts. Your government does not.

Private borrowers can and do default. They go bankrupt (a protection civilized societies afford them instead of debtors' prisons). Or if they have a mortgage, in most states they can simply walk away from their house if they can no longer continue to make payments on it.

With government, the risk of nonpayment does not exist. Government spends money (and pays interest) simply by typing numbers into a computer. Unlike private debtors, government does not need to have cash on hand. As the inspired amateur economist Warren Mosler likes to say, the person who writes Social Security checks at the Treasury does not have the phone number of the tax collector at the IRS. If you choose to pay taxes in cash, the government will give you a receipt—and shred the bills. Since it is the source of money, government can't run out.

It's true that government can spend imprudently. Too much spending, net of taxes, may lead to inflation, often via currency depreciation—though with the world in recession, that's not an immediate risk. Wasteful spending—on unnecessary military adventures, say—burns real resources. But no government can ever be forced to default on debts in a currency it controls. Public defaults happen only when governments don't control the currency in which they owe debts—as Argentina owed dollars or as Greece now (it hasn't defaulted yet) owes euros. But for true sovereigns, bankruptcy is an irrelevant concept. When Obama says, even offhand, that the United States is "out of money," he's talking nonsense—dangerous nonsense. One wonders if he believes it.

Nor is public debt a burden on future generations. It does not have to be repaid, and in practice it will never be repaid. Personal debts are generally settled during the lifetime of the debtor or at death, because one person cannot easily encumber another. But public debt does not ever have to be repaid. Governments do not die—except in war or revolution, and when that happens, their debts are generally moot anyway.

So the public debt simply increases from one year to the next. In the entire history of the United States it has done so, with budget deficits and increased public debt on all but about six very short occasions—with each surplus followed by a recession. Far from being a burden, these debts are the foundation of economic growth. Bonds owed by the government yield net income to the private sector, unlike all purely private debts, which merely transfer income from one part of the private sector to another.

Nor is that interest a solvency threat. A recent projection from the Center on Budget and Policy Priorities, based on Congressional Budget Office assumptions, has public-debt interest payments rising to 15 percent of GDP by 2050, with total debt to GDP at 300 percent. But that can't happen. If the interest were paid to people who then spent it on goods and services and job creation, it would be just like other public spending. Interest payments so enormous would affect the economy much like the mobilization for World War II. Long before you even got close to those scary ratios, you'd get full employment and rising inflation—pushing up GDP and, in turn, stabilizing the debt-to-GDP ratio. Or the Federal Reserve would stabilize the interest payouts, simply by keeping short-term interest rates (which it controls) very low.

What about indebtedness to foreigners? True, foreigners do us a favor by buying our bonds. To acquire them, China must export goods to us, not offset by equivalent imports. That is a cost to China. It's a cost Beijing is prepared to pay, for its own reasons: export industries promote learning, technology transfer, and product quality improvement, and they provide jobs to migrants from the countryside. But that's China's business.

For China, the bonds themselves are a sterile hoard. There is almost nothing that Beijing can do with them. China already imports all the commodities and machinery and aircraft it can use—if it wanted more, it would buy them now. So unless China changes its export policy, its stock of T bonds will just go on growing. And we will pay interest on it, not with real effort but by typing numbers into computers. There is no burden associated with this, not now and not later. (If the Chinese hoard the interest, they also don't help much with job creation here. So the fact that we're buying a lot of goods from China simply means we have to be more imaginative, and bolder, if we want to create all the jobs we need.) Finally, could China dump its dollars? In principle it could, substituting Greek bonds for American and overpriced euros for cheap dollars. On brief reflection, no Beijing bureaucrat is likely to think this a smart move.

What is true of government as a whole is also true of particular programs. Social Security and Medicare are government programs; they cannot go bankrupt, and they cannot fail to meet their obligations unless Congress decides—say on the recommendation of the Simpson–Bowles Commission—to cut the benefits they provide. The exercise of linking future benefits and projected payroll tax revenues is an accounting farce, done for political reasons. That farce was started by FDR as a way of protecting Social Security from cuts. But it has become a way of creating needless anxiety about these programs and of precluding sensible reforms, like expanding Medicare to those 55 and older, or even to the whole population.

As government programs, Social Security, and Medicare cannot go bankrupt—unless Congress cuts the benefits they provide.

Social Security and Medicare are transfer programs. What they do, mainly, is move resources around within our society at a given time. The principal transfer is not from the young to the old, since even without Social Security the old would still be around and someone would have to support them. Rather, Social Security pools resources, so that the work of the young collectively supports the senior population. The effective transfer is from parents who have children who would otherwise support them (a fairly rare thing) to seniors who don't. And it is from workers who do not have parents to support, to workers who would otherwise have to support their parents. In both cases this burden sharing is fair, progressive, and sustainable. There is a healthcare cost problem, as everyone knows, but that's not a Medicare problem. It should not be solved by cutting back on healthcare for the old. Social Security and Medicare also replace private insurance with cheap and efficient public administration. This is another reason these programs are the hated targets, decade after decade, of the worst predators on Wall Street.

Public deficits and private lending are reciprocal. Increased private lending generates new tax revenue and smaller deficits; that's what happened in the 1990s. A credit collapse kills the tax base and generates more spending; that's what's happening now, and our big deficits are the accounting counterpart of the massive decline, last year, in private bank loans. The only choice is what kind of deficit to run—useful deficits that rebuild the country, as in the New Deal, or useless ones, with millions kept unnecessarily on unemployment insurance when they could instead be given jobs.

If we could revive private lending, should we do it? Well, yes, up to a point there is good reason to have a robust private lending sector. Government is by nature centralized and policy driven. It works by law and regulation. Decentralized and competitive private banks have much more flexibility. A good banking system, run by capable people with good business judgment who know their clients, is good for the economy. The fact that you have to pay interest on a loan is also an important motivator of investment over consumption.

But right now, we don't have functional big banks. We have a cartel run by an incompetent plutocracy, with its long fingers deep in the pockets of the state. For functional credit to return, we'll have to reduce the unpayable private debts now outstanding, to restore private incomes (meaning: create jobs) and collateral (meaning: home values), and we'll have to restructure the big banks. We need to break them up, shrink the financial sector overall, expose and prosecute frauds, and create incentives for profitable lending in energy conservation, infrastructure, and other sectors. Or we could create a new parallel banking system, as was done in the New Deal with the Reconstruction Finance Corporation and its spinoffs, including the Home Owners' Loan Corporation and later Fannie Mae and Freddie Mac.

Either way, until we have effective financial reform, public budget deficits are the only way toward economic growth. You don't have to like budget deficits to realize that we must have them, on whatever scale necessary to restore growth and jobs. And we will need them not just now but for a long while, until we've shaped a strategic program for investment, energy and the environment, financed in part by a reformed, restored, and disciplined financial sector.

It's possible, of course, that all the deficit hysteria is intended to divert attention from the dysfunctions of private banking, and so to help thwart calls for financial reform. Is that giving them too much credit? Maybe. Maybe not.

Critical Thinking

1. According to James K. Galbraith, what are the two ways to achieve "economic growth"?

2. Why, according to Galbraith, do banks favor private bank loans over government budget deficits as a way to fuel economic growth?

3. Outline what is, for Galbraith, one of the "great misinformation campaigns of all time"?

4. How can public debt be a source of economic growth?

5. Why, according to Galbraith, are interest and indebtedness to foreigners not an insolvency threat?

6. What is a "transfer program," and how does the author explain Social Security and Medicare using this concept?

JAMES K. GALBRAITH is the author of *The Predator State: How Conservatives Abandoned the Free Market and Why Liberals Should Too.* He teaches at the LBJ School of Public Affairs at the University of Texas and is a senior scholar at the Levy Economics Institute.

Reprinted by permission from the March 22, 2010 issue of *The Nation*. Copyright © 2010 by The Nation. For subscription information, call 1-800-333-8536. Portions of each week's Nation magazine can be accessed at www.thenation.com

Meet the Real Death Panels

Health care reform is done, but the battle over "entitlement reform" is just beginning—and already, deficit hawks are suggesting that geezers like me need to pull the plug on ourselves for the good of society. Are they looking out for future generations—or just the bonuses of health care execs?

JAMES RIDGEWAY

There's a certain age at which you cease to regard your own death as a distant hypothetical and start to view it as a coming event. For me, it was 67–the age at which my father died. For many Americans, I suspect it's 70–the age that puts you within striking distance of our average national life expectancy of 78.1 years. Even if you still feel pretty spry, you suddenly find that your roster of doctor's appointments has expanded, along with your collection of daily medications. You grow accustomed to hearing that yet another person you once knew has dropped off the twig. And you feel more and more like a walking ghost yourself, invisible to the younger people who push past you on the subway escalator. Like it or not, death becomes something you think about, often on a daily basis.

Actually, you don't think about death, per se, as much as you do about dying–about when and where and especially *how* you're going to die. Will you have to deal with a long illness? With pain, immobility, or dementia? Will you be able to get the care you need, and will you have enough money to pay for it? Most of all, will you lose control over what life you have left, as well as over the circumstances of your death?

These are precisely the preoccupations that the right so cynically exploited in the debate over health care reform, with that ominous talk of Washington bean counters deciding who lives and dies. It was all nonsense, of course—the worst kind of political scare tactic. But at the same time, supporters of health care reform seemed to me too quick to dismiss old people's fears as just so much paranoid foolishness. There are reasons why the death-panel myth found fertile ground–and those reasons go beyond the gullibility of half-senile old farts.

While politicians of all stripes shun the idea of health care rationing as the political third rail that it is, most of them accept a premise that leads, one way or another, to that end. Here's what I mean: Nearly every other industrialized country recognizes health care as a human right, whose costs and benefits are shared among all citizens. But in the United States, the leaders of both political parties along with most of the "experts" persist in treating health care as a commodity that is purchased, in one way or another, by those who can afford it. Conservatives embrace this notion as the perfect expression of the all-powerful market; though they make a great show of recoiling from the term, in practice they are endorsing rationing on the basis of wealth. Liberals, including supporters of President Obama's health care reform, advocate subsidies, regulation, and other modest measures to give the less fortunate a little more buying power. But as long as health care is viewed as a product to be bought and sold, even the most well-intentioned reformers will someday soon have to come to grips with health care rationing, if not by wealth then by some other criteria.

In a country that already spends more than 16 percent of each GDP dollar on health care, it is easy to see why so many people believe there's simply not enough of it to go around. But keep in mind that the rest of the industrialized world manages to spend between 20 and 90 percent less per capita and still rank higher than the US in overall health care performance. In 2004, a team of researchers including Princeton's Uwe Reinhardt, one of the nation's best known experts on health economics, found that while the US spends 134 percent more than the median of the world's most developed nations, we get less for our money—fewer physician visits and hospital days per capita, for example—than our counterparts in countries like Germany, Canada, and Australia. (We do, however, have more MRI machines and more cesarean sections.)

Where does the money go instead? By some estimates, administration and insurance profits alone eat up at least 30 percent of our total health care bill (and most of that is in the private sector—Medicare's overhead is around 2 percent). In other words, we don't have too little to go around—we overpay for what we get, and we don't allocate our spending where it does us the most good. "In most [medical] resources we have a surplus," says Dr. David Himmelstein, co-founder of Physicians for a National Health Program. "People get large amounts of care that don't do them any good and might cause them harm [while] others don't get the necessary amount."

Looking at the numbers, it is pretty safe to say that with an efficient health care system, we could spend a little less than we do now and provide all Americans with the most spectacular care the world has ever known. But in the absence of any serious challenge to the health-care-as-commodity system, we are doomed to a battlefield scenario where Americans must fight to secure their share of a "scarce" resource in a life-and-death struggle that pits the rich against the poor, the insured against the uninsured—and increasingly, the old against the young.

For years, any push to improve the nation's finances—balance the budget, pay for the bailout, or help stimulate the economy—has been accompanied by rumblings about the greedy geezers who resist entitlement "reforms" (read: cuts) with their unconscionable demands for basic health care and a hedge against destitution. So, too, today: Already, President Obama's newly convened deficit commission looks to be blaming the nation's fiscal woes not on tax cuts, wars, or bank bailouts, but on the burden of Social Security and Medicare. (The commission's co-chair, former Republican senator Alan Simpson, has declared, "This country is gonna go to the bow-wows unless we deal with entitlements.")

Old people's anxiety in the face of such hostile attitudes has provided fertile ground for Republican disinformation and fear mongering. But so has the vacuum left by Democratic reformers. Too often, in their zeal to prove themselves tough on "waste," they've allowed connections to be drawn between two things that, to my mind, should never be spoken of in the same breath: *death* and *cost.*

Dying Wishes

The death-panel myth started with a harmless minor provision in the health reform bill that required Medicare to pay in case enrollees wanted to have conversations with their own doctors about "advance directives" like health care proxies and living wills. The controversy that ensued, thanks to a host of right-wing commentators and Sarah Palin's Facebook page, ensured that the advance-planning measure was expunged from the bill. But the underlying debate didn't end with the passage of health care reform, any more than it began there. If rationing is inevitable once you've ruled out reining in private profits, the question is who should be denied care, and at what point. And given that no one will publicly argue for withholding cancer treatment from a seven-year-old, the answer almost inevitably seems to come down to what we spend on people—*old* people—in their final years.

As far back as 1983, in a speech to the Health Insurance Association of America, a then-57-year-old Alan Greenspan suggested that we consider "whether it is worth it" to spend so much of Medicare's outlays on people who would die within the year. (Appropriately, Ayn Rand called her acolyte "the undertaker"—though she chose the nickname because of his dark suits and austere demeanor.)

Not everyone puts the issue in such nakedly pecuniary terms, but in an April 2009 interview with the *New York Times Magazine,* Obama made a similar point in speaking of end-of-life care as a "huge driver of cost." He said, "The chronically ill and those toward the end of their lives are accounting for potentially 80 percent of the total health care bill out here."

The president was being a bit imprecise. Those figures are actually for Medicare expenditures, not the total health care tab, and more important, lumping the dying together with the

"chronically ill"—who often will live for years or decades—makes little sense. But there is no denying that end-of-life care is expensive. Hard numbers are not easy to come by, but studies from the 1990s suggest that between a quarter and a third of annual Medicare expenditures go to patients in their last year of life, and 30 to 40 percent of *those* costs accrue in the final month. What this means is that around one in ten Medicare dollars—some $50 billion a year-are spent on patients with fewer than 30 days to live.

Pronouncements on these data usually come coated with a veneer of compassion and concern: How *terrible* it is that all those poor dying old folks have to endure aggressive treatments that only delay the inevitable; all we want to do is bring peace and dignity to their final days! But I wonder: If that's really what they're worried about, how come they keep talking about money?

At this point, I ought to make something clear: I am a big fan of what's sometimes called the "right to die" or "death with dignity" movement. I support everything from advance directives to assisted suicide. You could say I believe in one form of health care rationing: the kind you choose for yourself. I can't stand the idea of anyone—whether it is the government or some hospital administrator or doctor or Nurse Jackie—telling me that I must have some treatment I don't want, any more than I want them telling me that I can't have a treatment I *do* want. My final wish is to be my own one-member death panel.

A physician friend recently told me about a relative of hers, a frail 90-year-old woman suffering from cancer. Her doctors urged her to have surgery, followed by treatment with a recently approved cancer medicine that cost $5,000 a month. As is often the case, my friend said, the doctors told their patient about the benefits of the treatment, but not about all the risks—that she might die during the surgery or not long afterward. They also prescribed a month's supply of the new medication, even though, my friend says, they must have known the woman was unlikely to live that long. She died within a week. "Now," my friend said, "I'm carrying around a $4,000 bottle of pills."

Perhaps reflecting what economists call "supplier-induced demand," costs generally tend to go up when the dying have too *little* control over their care, rather than too much. When geezers are empowered to make decisions, most of us will choose less aggressive—and less costly—treatments. If we don't do so more often, it's usually because of an overbearing and money-hungry health care system, as well as a culture that disrespects the will of its elders and resists confronting death.

> **You could say I believe in one form of health care rationing: the kind you choose for yourself. When geezers are empowered to make choices about our dying days, most of us will choose less aggressive—and less costly—treatments.**

Once, when I was in the hospital for outpatient surgery, I woke up in the recovery area next to a man named George, who was talking loudly to his wife, telling her he wanted to leave. She soothingly reminded him that they had to wait for the doctors to learn the results of the surgery, apparently some sort of exploratory thing. Just then, two doctors appeared. In a stiff, flat voice, one of them told George that he had six months to live. When his wife's shrieking had subsided, I heard George say, "I'm getting the fuck out of this place." The doctors sternly advised him that they had more tests to run and "treatment options" to discuss. "Fuck that," said George, yanking the IV out of his arm and getting to his feet. "If I've got six months to live, do you think I want to spend another minute of it here? I'm going to the Alps to go skiing."

I don't know whether George was true to his word. But not long ago I had a friend, a scientist, who was true to his. Suffering from cancer, he anticipated a time when more chemotherapy or procedures could only prolong a deepening misery, to the point where he could no longer recognize himself. He prepared for that time, hoarding his pain meds, taking care to protect his doctor and pharmacist from any possibility of legal retribution. He saw some friends he wanted to see, and spoke to others. Then he died at a time and place of his choosing, with his family around him. Some would call this euthanasia, others a sacrilege. To me, it seemed like a noble end to a fine life. If freedom of choice is what makes us human, then my friend managed to make his death a final expression of his humanity.

My friend chose to forgo medical treatments that would have added many thousands of dollars to his health care costs—and, since he was on Medicare, to the public expense. If George really did spend his final months in the Alps, instead of undergoing expensive surgeries or sitting around hooked up to machines, he surely saved the health care system a bundle as well. They did it because it was what they wanted, not because it would save money. But there is a growing body of evidence that the former can lead to the latter—without any rationing or coercion.

One model that gets cited a lot these days is La Crosse, Wisconsin, where Gundersen Lutheran hospital launched an initiative to ensure that the town's older residents had advance directives and to make hospice and palliative care widely available. A 2008 study found that 90 percent of those who died in La Crosse under a physician's care did so with advance directives in place. At Gundersen Lutheran, less is spent on patients in their last two years of life than nearly any other place in the US, with per capita Medicare costs 30 percent below the national average. In a similar vein, Oregon, in 1995, instituted a two-page form called Physician Orders for Life-Sustaining Treatment; it functions as doctor's orders and is less likely to be misinterpreted or disregarded than a living will. According to the *Dartmouth Atlas of Health Care,* a 20-year study of the nation's medical costs and resources, people in Oregon are less likely to die in a hospital than people in most other states, and in their last six months, they spend less time in the hospital. They also run up about 50 percent less in medical expenditures.

It is possible that attitudes have begun to change. Three states now allow what advocates like to call "aid-in-dying" (rather than assisted suicide) for the terminally ill. More Americans than ever have living wills and other advance directives,

and that can only be a good thing: One recent study showed that more than 70 percent of patients who needed to make end-of-life decisions at some point lost the capacity to make these choices; yet, among those who had prepared living wills, nearly all had their instructions carried out.

Here is the ultimate irony of the deathpanel meme: In attacking measures designed to Promote advance directives, conservatives were attacking what they claim is their core value—the individual right to free choice.

The QALY of Mercy

A wonkier version of the reform-equals-rationing argument is based less on panic mongering about Obama's secret euthanasia schemes and more on the implications of something called "comparative effectiveness research." The practice got a jump start in last year's stimulus bill, which included $1.1 billion for the Federal Coordinating Council for Comparative Effectiveness Research. This is money to study what treatments work best for which patients. The most obvious use of such data would be to apply the findings to Medicare, and the effort has already been attacked as the first step toward the government deciding when it's time to kick granny to the curb. Senate minority leader Mitch McConnell (R-Ky.) has said that Obama's support for comparative effectiveness research means he is seeking "a national rationing board."

Evidence-based medicine, in itself, has absolutely nothing to do with age. In theory, it also has nothing to do with money—though it might, as a by-product, reduce costs (for example, by giving doctors the information they need to resist pressure from drug companies). Yet the desire for cost savings often seems to drive comparative effectiveness research, rather than the other way around. In his *Times Magazine* interview last year, Obama said, "It is an attempt to say to patients, you know what, we've looked at some objective studies concluding that the blue pill, which costs half as much as the red pill, is just as effective, and you might want to go ahead and get the blue one."

Personally, I don't mind the idea of the government promoting the blue pill over the red pill, as long as it really is "just as effective." I certainly trust the government to make these distinctions more than I trust the insurance companies or pharma representatives. But I want to know that the only target is genuine waste, and the only possible casualty is profits.

There's nothing to give me pause in the health care law's comparative effectiveness provision, which includes $500 million a year for comparative effectiveness research. The work is to be overseen by the nonprofit Patient-Centered Outcomes Research Institute, whose 21-member board of governors will include doctors, patient advocates, and only three representatives of drug and medical-device companies.

Still, there is a difference between comparative effectiveness and comparative *cost* effectiveness—and from the latter, it's a short skip to outright cost-benefit analysis. In other words, the argument sometimes slides almost imperceptibly from comparing how well the blue pill and the red pill work to examining whether some people should be denied the red pill, even if it demonstrably works better.

The calculations driving such cost-benefit analyses are often based on something called QALYs—quality-adjusted life years. If a certain cancer drug would extend life by two years, say, but with such onerous side effects that those years were judged to be only half as worth living as those of a healthy person, the QALY is 1.

In Britain, the National Health Service has come close to setting a maximum price beyond which extra QALYs are not deemed worthwhile. In assessing drugs and treatments, the NHS's National Institute for Health and Clinical Excellence usually approves those that cost less than 20,000 pounds per QALY (about $28,500), and most frequently rejects those costing more than 30,000 pounds (about $43,000).

It's not hard to find examples of comparative effectiveness research—complete with QALYs—that hit quite close to home for almost anyone. Last year I was diagnosed with atrial fibrillation, a disturbance in the heart rhythm that sometimes leads to blood clots, which can travel to the brain and cause a stroke. My doctor put me on warfarin (brand name Coumadin), a blood-thinning drug that reduces the chances of forming blood clots but can also cause internal bleeding. It is risky enough that when I go to the dentist or cut myself shaving, I have to watch to make sure it doesn't turn into a torrent of blood. The levels of warfarin in my bloodstream have to be frequently checked, so I have to be ever mindful of the whereabouts of a hospital with a blood lab. It is a pain in the neck, and it makes me feel vulnerable. I sometimes wonder if it's worth it.

It turns out that several comparative effectiveness studies have looked at the efficacy of warfarin for patients with my heart condition. One of them simply weighed the drug's potential benefits against its dangerous side effects, without consideration of cost. It concluded that for a patient with my risk factors, warfarin reduced the chance of stroke a lot more than it increased the chance that I'd be seriously harmed by bleeding. Another study concluded that for a patient like me, the cost per QALY of taking warfarin is $8,000—cheap, by most standards.

Prescription drug prices have more than doubled since the study was done in 1995. But warfarin is a relatively cheap generic drug, and even if my cost per QALY was $15,000 or $20,000, I'd still pass muster with the NHS. But if I were younger and had fewer risk factors, I'd be less prone to stroke to begin with, so the reduction in risk would not be as large, and the cost per QALY would be correspondingly higher about $370,000. Would I still want to take the drug if I were, say, under 60 and free of risk factors? Considering the side effects, probably not. But would I want someone else to make that decision for me?

Critics of the British system say, among other things, that the NHS's cost-per-QALY limit is far too low. But raising it wouldn't resolve the deeper ethical question: Should anyone but the patient get to decide when life is not worth living? The *Los Angeles Times*' Michael Hiltzik, one of the few reporters to critically examine this issue, has noted that "healthy people tend to overestimate the effect of some medical conditions on their sufferers' quality of life. The hale and hearty, for example, will generally rate life in a wheelchair lower than will the wheelchair-bound, who often find fulfillment in ways 'healthier' persons couldn't imagine."

Simone de Beauvoir wrote that fear of aging and death drives young people to view their elders as a separate species, rather than as their future selves: "Until the moment it is upon us old age is something that only affects other people." And the more I think about the subject, the more I am sure of one thing: It's not a good idea to have a 30-year-old place a value on my life.

Whose Death Is It Anyway?

Probably the most prominent advocate of age-based rationing is Daniel Callahan, co-founder of a bioethics think tank called the Hastings Center. Callahan's 1987 book, *Setting Limits: Medical Goals in an Aging Society,* depicted old people as "a new social threat," a demographic, economic, and medical "avalanche" waiting to happen. In a 2008 article, Callahan said that in evaluating Medicare's expenditures, we should consider that "there is a duty to help young people to become old people, but not to help the old become still older indefinitely . . . One may well ask what counts as 'old' and what is a decently long lifespan? As I have listened to people speak of a 'full life,' often heard at funerals, I would say that by 75-80 most people have lived a full life, and most of us do not feel it a tragedy that someone in that age group has died (as we do with the death of a child)." He has proposed using "age as a specific criterion for the allocation and limitation of care," and argues that after a certain point, people could justifiably be denied Medicare coverage for life-extending treatments.

You can see why talk like this might make some old folks start boarding up their doors. (It apparently, however, does not concern Callahan, who, last year at age 79, told the *New York Times* that he had just had a life-saving seven-hour heart procedure.) It certainly made me wonder how I would measure up.

> One prominent advocate of rationing has suggested that society doesn't have a duty to help those in their 70s and 80s "become still older indefinitely." You can see why talk like that might lead old folks to start boarding up their doors.

So far, I haven't cost the system all that much. I take several different medicines every day, which are mostly generics. I go to the doctor pretty often, but I haven't been in the hospital overnight for at least 20 years, and my one walk-in operation took place before I was on Medicare. And I am still working, so I'm paying in as well as taking out.

But things could change, perhaps precipitously. Since I have problems with both eyesight and balance, I could easily fall and break a bone, maybe a hip. This could mean a hip replacement, months of therapy, or even long-term immobility. My glaucoma could take a turn for the worse, and I would face a future of near blindness, with all the associated costs. Or I could have that stroke, in spite of my drug regimen.

I decided to take the issue up with the Australian philosopher Peter Singer, who made some waves on this issue with a *New York Times* op-ed published last year, titled "Why We Must Ration Health Care." Singer believes that health care is a scarce resource that will inevitably be limited. Better to do it through a public system like the British NHS, he told me, than covertly and inequitably on the private US model. "What you are trying to do is to get the most value for the money from the resources you have," he told me.

In the world he imagines, I asked Singer over coffee in a Manhattan café, what should happen if I broke a hip? He paused to think, and I hoped he wouldn't worry about hurting my feelings. "If there is a good chance of restoring mobility," he said after a moment, "and you have at least five years of mobility, that's significant benefit." He added, "Hip operations are not expensive." A new hip or knee runs between $30,000 and $40,000, most of it covered by Medicare. So for five years of mobility, that comes out to about $7,000 a year—less than the cost of a home-care aide, and exponentially less than a nursing home.

But then Singer turned to a more sobering thought: If the hip operation did not lead to recovery of mobility, then it might not be such a bargain. In a much-cited piece of personal revelation, Obama, in 2009, talked about his grandmother's decision to have a hip replacement after she had been diagnosed with terminal cancer. She died just a few weeks later. "I don't know how much that hip replacement cost," Obama told the *Times Magazine.* "I would have paid out of pocket for that hip replacement just because she's my grandmother." But the president said that in considering whether "to give my grandmother, or everybody else's aging grandparents or parents, a hip replacement when they're terminally ill . . . you just get into some very difficult moral issues."

Singer and I talked about what choices we ourselves might make at the end of our lives. Singer, who is 63, said that he and his wife know "neither of us wants to go on living under certain conditions. Particularly if we get demented. I would draw the line if I could not recognize my wife or my children. My wife has a higher standard—when she couldn't read a novel. Yes, I wouldn't want to live beyond a certain point. It's not me anymore." I'm 10 years older than Singer, and my own advance directives reflect similar choices. So it seems like neither one of us is likely to strain the public purse with our demands for expensive and futile life-prolonging care.

You can say this is all a Debbie Downer, but people my age know perfectly well that these questions are not at all theoretical. We worry about the time when we will no longer be able to contribute anything useful to society and will be completely dependent on others. And we worry about the day when life will no longer seem worth living, and whether we will have the courage—and the ability—to choose a dignified death. We worry about these things all by ourselves—we don't need anyone else to do it for us. And we certainly don't need anyone tallying up QALYs while our overpriced, underperforming private health care system adds a few more points to its profit margin.

Let It Bleed

What happened during the recent health care wars is what military strategists might call a "bait-and-bleed" operation: Two rival parties are drawn into a protracted conflict that depletes both their forces, while a third stands on the sidelines, its strength undiminished. In this case, Republicans and Democrats alike have shed plenty of blood, while the clever combatant on the sidelines is, of course, the health care industry.

In the process, health care reform set some unsettling precedents that could fuel the phony intergenerational conflict over health care resources. The final reform bill will help provide coverage to some of the estimated 46 million Americans under 65 who live without it. It finances these efforts in part by cutting Medicare costs—some $500 billion over 10 years. Contrary to Republican hysteria, the cuts so far come from all the right places—primarily from ending the tip-offs by insurers who sell government-financed "Medicare Advantage" plans. The reform law even manages to make some meaningful improvements to the flawed Medicare prescription drug program and preventive care. The legislation also explicitly bans age-based health care rationing.

Still, there are plenty of signs that the issue is far from being put to rest. Congress and the White House wrote into the law something called the Independent Payment Advisory Board, a presidentially appointed panel that is tasked with keeping Medicare's growth rate below a certain ceiling. Office of Management and Budget director Peter Orszag, the economics wunderkind who has made Medicare's finances something of a personal project, has called it potentially the most important aspect of the legislation: Medicare and Medicaid, he has said, "are at the heart of our long-term fiscal imbalance, which is the motivation for moving to a different structure in those programs." And then, of course, there's Obama's deficit commission: While the president says he is keeping an open mind when it comes to solving the deficit "crisis," no one is trying very hard to pretend that the commission has any purpose other than cutting Social Security, Medicare, and probably Medicaid as well.

I'd be willing to give up some expensive, life-prolonging medical treatment for my Gen X son, and maybe even for the good of humanity. But I'm certainly not going to do it so some WellPoint executive can take another vacation.

Already, the commission is working closely with the Peter G. Peterson Foundation, headed by the billionaire businessman and former Nixon administration official who has emerged as one of the nation's leading "granny bashers"—deficit hawks who accuse old people of bankrupting the country.

In the end, of course, many conservatives are motivated less by deficits and more by free-market ideology: Many of them want to replace Medicare as it now exists today with a system of vouchers, and place the emphasis on individual savings and tax breaks. Barring that, Republicans have proposed a long string of cuts to Medicaid and Medicare, sometimes defying logic—by, for example, advocating reductions in in-home care, which can keep people out of far more expensive nursing homes.

The common means of justifying these cuts is to attack Medicare "waste." But remember that not only are Medicare's administrative costs less than one-sixth of those of private insurers, Medicare pays doctors and hospitals less (20 and 30 percent, respectively) than private payment rates; overall, Medicare pays out less in annual per capita benefits than the average large employer health plan, even though it serves an older, sicker population.

That basic fact is fully understood by the health care industry. Back in January 2009, as the nation suited up for the health care wars, the Lewin Group—a subsidiary of the health insurance giant United Health—produced an analysis of various reform proposals being floated and found that the only one to immediately reduce overall health care costs (by $58 billion) was one that would have dramatically expanded Medicare.

Facts like these, however, have not slowed down the granny bashers. In a February op-ed called "The Geezers' Crusade," commentator David Brooks urged old people to willingly submit to entitlement cuts in service to future generations. Via Social Security and Medicare, he argued, old folks are stealing from their own grandkids.

I'm as public spirited as the next person, and I have a Gen X son. I'd be willing to give up some expensive, life-prolonging medical treatment for him, and maybe even for the good of humanity. But I'm certainly not going to do it so some Well-Point executive can take another vacation, so Pfizer can book $3 billion in annual profits instead of $2 billion, or so private hospitals can make another campaign contribution to some gutless politician.

Here, then, is my advice to anyone who suggests that we geezers should do the right thing and pull the plug on ourselves: Start treating health care as a human right instead of a profit-making opportunity, and see how much money you save. Then, by all means, get back to me.

Critical Thinking

1. What does it mean to say that health care is treated as a commodity in the United States?

2. What evidence suggests that the U.S. healthcare system is inefficient?

3. What are "advance directives"? How did discussion of advance directives evolve into the rumor of "death panels"?

4. What is a QALY? How are QALYs used as calculations in cost-benefit analyses of health care?

5. How does free-market ideology drive political views on health care? Does the author agree with this approach?

Clean, Green, Safe and Smart

Why the United States needs a new national energy policy.

MICHAEL T. KLARE

If the ecological catastrophe in the Gulf of Mexico tells us anything, it is that we need a new national energy policy—a comprehensive plan for escaping our dangerous reliance on fossil fuels, and creating a new energy system based on climate-safe alternatives. Without such a plan, the response to the disaster will be a hodgepodge of regulatory reforms and toughened environmental safeguards but not a fundamental shift in behavior. Because our current energy path leads toward greater reliance on fuels acquired from environmentally and politically hazardous locations, no amount of enhanced oversight or stiffened regulations can avert future disasters like that unfolding in the gulf. Only a dramatic change in course—governed by an entirely new policy framework—can reduce the risk of catastrophe and set the nation on a wise energy trajectory.

By far the most important part of this strategy must be a change in the overarching philosophy that steers decisions on how much energy the United States should seek to produce, of what sorts and under what conditions. It may not seem as if we operate under such a philosophy today, but we do—one that extols growth over all other considerations, that privileges existing fuels over renewables and that ranks environmental concerns below corporate profit. Until we replace this outlook with one that places innovation and the environment ahead of the status quo, we will face more ecological devastation and slower economic dynamism. Only with a new governing philosophy—one that views the development of climate-friendly energy systems as the engine of economic growth—can we move from our current predicament to a brighter future.

One way to appreciate the importance of this shift is to consider the guiding policies of other countries. In March, I had the privilege of attending an international energy conference at Fuenlabrada, just outside Madrid. I sat transfixed as one top official after another of Spain's socialist government spelled out their vision of the future—one in which wind and solar power would provide an ever-increasing share of the nation's energy supply and make Spain a leader in renewable energy technology. Other speakers described strategies for "greening" old cities—adding parks, farms, canals, and pedestrian plazas in neglected neighborhoods. Around me were a thousand university students—enthralled by the prospect of creative and rewarding jobs in architecture, engineering, technology, and the sciences. This, I thought, is what our own young people need to look forward to.

Instead, we are governed by an obsolete, nihilistic energy philosophy. To fully comprehend the nature of our dilemma, it is important to recognize that the gulf disaster is a direct result of the last governing blueprint adopted by this country: the National Energy Policy of May 17, 2001, better known as the Cheney plan. This framework, of which the former vice president was the lead author, called for increased drilling in wilderness areas, such as the Arctic National Wildlife Refuge, as well as in the deep waters of the Gulf of Mexico. Congress did not permit drilling in ANWR, but it wholeheartedly embraced wider exploitation of the deepwater gulf. To speed these efforts, the Bush administration encouraged the Minerals Management Service to streamline the issuing of permits to giant oil firms like BP to operate in these waters. BP clearly took shortcuts when drilling offshore—thus inviting the blowout on April 20—but it did so in a permissive atmosphere established by the 2001 policy framework.

The 2001 energy plan was devised with substantial input from the energy industry—no representatives of the environmental community were invited to the secret meetings held by Dick Cheney to prepare it—and was widely viewed as a payoff to Bush/Cheney supporters in the oil industry. But it was far more than that: at its core, the plan embodied a distinctive outlook on the role of energy in the economy and how that energy should be supplied. This outlook held that cheap and abundant energy is an essential driver of economic growth and that the government's job is to ensure that plentiful energy is endlessly available. As noted by President Bush at the time, "The goals of this strategy are clear: to ensure a steady supply of affordable energy for America's homes and businesses and industries." But not just any sort of energy. In deference to the executives of Chevron, Enron, ExxonMobil, and the other energy giants that helped elect Bush in 2000, the plan aimed to extend the life of the nation's existing energy profile, with its overwhelming reliance on oil, coal, natural gas, and nuclear power.

However, a strategy aimed at producing more energy while maintaining reliance on traditional fuels was inherently problematic. Although the concept of "peak oil" was not then in widespread circulation, energy experts were becoming increasingly aware of the impending scarcity of conventional oil—i.e., liquid crude acquired from easily accessible reservoirs. Concerns were also growing about the future availability of easily accessible coal and natural gas. The only way to supply more energy while preserving the existing energy profile, Cheney and his allies concluded, was to increase the level of environmental and political risk, whether by drilling in wilderness areas and the deepwater gulf of by procuring more energy from dangerous and unfriendly areas, such as the Middle East, Africa and the former Soviet Union. This became the underlying premise of the 2001 energy plan and underlies much of the global violence and environmental devastation unleashed by Bush during his eight years in office.

Adherence to the Cheney plan has had another significant downside: it has focused energy investment on the extension of the existing energy paradigm rather than on introducing renewable energy systems. Far greater funds have been devoted to, say, deep offshore drilling and the extraction of gas from shale rock than to advancing wind and solar power. As a result, the United States has fallen behind China, Germany, Japan, and Spain in developing next-generation energy systems, jeopardizing our future competitiveness in the global economy.

The philosophy that produced these disasters—"more energy of the existing types at whatever the risk"—must now be repudiated and replaced by a new, forward-looking alternative that stresses innovation and environmental protection. Such an outlook would replace each component of the Bush/Cheney philosophy with its opposite. Instead of growth at any price, it would emphasize energy sufficiency—the minimum amount needed to accomplish vital tasks. Instead of clinging to existing environmentally damaging fuels, it would harness America's ingenuity in the development of new, climate-friendly fuels. And instead of embracing environmental and political risk as a solution to scarcity and excessive greed, it would favor domestically produced, renewable systems that largely eliminate the element of risk. To compress this into a nutshell, the new outlook would favor energy that is "clean, green, safe, and smart."

The philosophy that produced this disaster—'more energy at whatever the risk'—must be replaced with a forward-looking alternative.

What, in practice, would this entail?

First, let's take a closer look at "sufficiency"—the basis for all else. By energy sufficiency, I mean enough energy to meet basic consumer and industrial needs without succumbing to a bias for waste and inefficiency, as is now the case. For example, if X number of American commuters must drive Y number of miles every day to work, sufficient energy would be the amount needed to power the most fuel-efficient personal or public-transit vehicles available, rather than the most inefficient. Likewise, sufficient heating energy would be the amount needed to heat American homes and businesses if all were equipped with the most efficient heating and insulation systems. A wise energy policy would aim to provide whatever is needed when all reasonable measures for efficiency have been factored in—and no more than that. Of course, the transition from inefficient to efficient transportation, heating and industrial systems will be costly at first (the costs will go way down over time), so a wise policy would provide subsidies and incentives to facilitate the transition.

Defining what constitutes sufficient energy will require considerable time and effort. But thanks to visionaries like Amory Lovins of the Rocky Mountain Institute, enough is known about the potential energy savings of various conservation and efficiency initiatives to be confident that our economy can produce more in the years ahead using far less energy. Likewise, Americans can lead equally satisfying lives with less energy use. For example, if every car owner in America drove a gas/electric hybrid or superefficient conventional vehicle instead of one getting about 20 miles per gallon (the current national average), we could reduce our daily oil intake by as much as 4–5 million barrels per day (of a total consumption of approximately 20 million barrels). And if the hybrids were of a plug-in type that could recharge their batteries at night when power plants have surplus capacity, the oil requirement could be reduced by several million more barrels without

requiring additional power plants. Clearly, we don't need more oil to satisfy our transportation needs; we need more efficiency.

By seeking energy sufficiency instead of constant growth, we free ourselves of a tremendous burden. It is impossible to keep expanding the net supply of energy and reduce our dependence on fossil fuels and uranium-powered fission; the only sure way to achieve growth is to supply more of every fuel available. Once you abandon the commitment to growth, however, it is possible to begin the truly critical task: reducing our reliance on traditional fuels while significantly increasing the share of energy provided by alternatives.

To put things in perspective, fossil fuels now provide about 84 percent and nuclear power about 8.5 percent of America's net energy supply; renewables, including hydropower, provide a mere 8 percent. Although the amount of energy provided by renewables is expected to grow in the years ahead, the United States is projected to need so much more energy under its current path—114.5 quadrillion British thermal units per year in 2035, compared with approximately 100 quadrillion today—that it will need much larger amounts of oil, gas, and coal to supply the necessary increase. As a result, says the Energy Department, we will rely more on fossil fuels in 2035 than we do today, and will be emitting greater quantities of carbon dioxide.

Clearly, the existing path leads us ever closer to environmental catastrophe. Only by freezing (and eventually reducing) the total amount of energy consumed and reversing the ratio between traditional and alternative fuels can disaster be averted. A progressive energy policy would aim to achieve a ration of 50:50 between traditional and renewable fuels by 2030, and by 2050 would confine fossil fuels and nuclear power to a small "niche" market.

Accepting the necessity of switching to noncarbon alternatives, what are the "clean, green, and safe" fuels that America should rely on? Any source of energy chosen to meet the nation's future requirements should meet several criteria: it must be renewable, affordable, available domestically, and produce zero or very low amounts of greenhouse gas emissions. Several fuels satisfy two or three of these qualities, but only one—wind power—meets all of them. When located at reliably windy spots and near major transmission lines, wind turbines are competitive with most existing sources of energy and have none of their disadvantages. Solar power comes close to wind in its appeal, possessing great utility for certain applications (such as rooftop water heating); still, electricity derived from existing photovoltaic cells remains uncompetitive with other fuels in most situations. Geothermal, tidal, and wave energy show great promise but will need considerable development to be commercially applicable on a large scale. Biofuels derived from cellulose or algae also look promising, but they, too, require more work. Further out on the development path are hydrogen and nuclear fusion; it will take at least another generation or two before they will achieve widespread commercial utility.

Some within the environmental community argue for short-term reliance on some combination of natural gas, nuclear fission and coal, using the carbon capture and storage process as a "bridge" to renewable fuels, recognizing America's slow start in adopting the latter. While a case can be made for each of these, not one is clean, green, and safe. Natural gas, while emitting less carbon dioxide than other fossil fuels, is increasingly being derived from shale rock through the environmentally risky process known as "hydraulic fracturing" [see Kara Cusolito, "The Next Drilling Disaster?" June 3]. Nuclear fission produces radioactive waste that cannot be stored safely. Likewise, there is no assurance that carbon separated from coal can be stored safely for long periods of time. It follows that a wise policy would seek to leapfrog these technologies and move as rapidly as possible to renewable sources of energy.

With this in mind, the basic goal of a new national energy policy should be to minimize the use of existing fuels while ramping up the development and use of truly green alternatives—which requires not just technological innovation but a concerted effort to bring the new technologies to scale in the market, as Christian Parenti argues. The transition will also require a change in the way energy is distributed. At present a large share of our energy, in the form of oil, natural gas, and coal, is delivered by pipeline, rail, and truck. Most renewables, however, will be delivered in the form of electricity. This will require a massive expansion of the nation's electrical system—and its transformation into a "smart grid" that can rapidly move energy from areas of strong wind or sun (depending on weather conditions) to areas of peak need. A smart grid would also allow people to install their own energy-generating systems—solar panels, wind turbines, hydrogen fuel cells—and sell surplus energy back to the system.

Specifically, this policy would seek to:

- dramatically increase the use of wind power by adding more turbines and by increasing links to an expanded national electrical grid;
- increase the efficiency and cost-effectiveness of solar energy, especially photovoltaics and solar-thermal power;
- accelerate the development of geothermal, tidal, and wave power as well as biofuels derived from cellulose and algae, and expand research on hydrogen fuel cells and nuclear fusion;
- create a national "smart grid" capable of absorbing a vast increase in wind, solar, geothermal, and wave power and delivering it to areas of greatest need;
- spur the development, production, and acquisition of super-energy-efficient vehicles, buildings, appliances and industrial processes;
- accelerate the transition from conventional vehicles to hybrids, from regular hybrids to plug-in hybrids and from hybrids to all-electric automobiles;
- encourage and facilitate greater personal reliance on intercity rail, public transit, bicycles, and walking.

To achieve these goals, the government will have to assemble policy tools and funding devices. All incentives and subsidies for fossil fuel extraction and nuclear fission should be phased out, and like amounts directed toward the development of promising renewables and the further modernization and expansion of the electrical grid. Liberal tax breaks should be awarded to households and small businesses that invest in energy-saving heating, cooling, and lighting systems; similar breaks should be offered for the purchase of hybrid and electric vehicles. Many key initiatives, such as the construction of regional high-speed rail lines, will be costly. To finance such endeavors, taxes on gasoline and other carbon-based fuels should be increased as payroll taxes are decreased, thus encouraging job growth while discouraging carbon pollution; rebates should also be given to cushion the effect on low-income people. In addition, a ten-year, $250 billion energy innovation fund should be established to provide low-interest loans for commercializing promising new technologies being developed at universities and start-up firms around the country; once repaid, these funds could then be used to fund other such endeavors.

The Cheney plan envisioned, among other goals, building 1,000 new nuclear power plants by 2030. By contrast, the new energy policy envisioned here would have the following goals:

- create 5 million jobs through the pursuit of a green energy revolution, with a focus on the construction and manufacturing sectors, as outlined by the nonprofit group Apollo Alliance;
- maximize the nation's energy efficiency—in transportation, heating, electricity, and all other sectors—such that total energy demand declines by at least 50 percent by 2050, as documented in a comprehensive study by Greenpeace International and the European Renewable Energy Council;
- phase out oil consumption, except in niche markets, by 2030;
- formalize the current de factor moratorium on constructing new coal-fired power plants, phase out existing plants as well and halt all coal use by 2020;
- supply at least 75 percent of US electricity from wind, solar, and other renewable sources by 2030 and 99 percent by 2050, as described in the Greenpeace-EREC study;
- shift the US vehicle fleet to all-electric cars by 2035, to be powered with renewable energy;
- reduce US greenhouse gas emissions (from 1990 levels) by at least 90 percent by 2050, as described in the Greenpeace-EREC study.

There is not enough space here to argue the case for each of these specifics, but the essential elements of the new energy policy our nation needs are these: a guiding philosophy, a vision of the intended outcome, an assessment of the possible energy sources, and an outline of tools for implementation. Each of the final three can be modified as necessary to account for global events and scientific advances; but adherence to the first is critical. Adopting an enlightened new philosophy to guide our nation's future energy plans is the single most valuable thing we can do in the wake of the Deepwater Horizon tragedy.

Critical Thinking

1. Why, according to Michael Klare, does the United States need a new national energy strategy?

2. What was the perspective of the 2001 National Energy Policy, known as the "Cheney Plan," on the role of energy in the economy and how energy should be supplied? What have been the drawbacks of following this plan?

3. What is "energy sufficiency," and why is it an important concept in a forward-thinking energy plan?

4. What should be the basic goal of a new national energy strategy, according to the author? What would some of its key points include?

5. What policy and funding devices does the author suggest as a means to implement his vision of a national energy policy?

MICHAEL T. KLARE, The Nation's defense correspondent, is professor of peace and world security studies at Hampshire College. His latest book is Rising Powers, Shrinking Planet: The New Geopolitics of Energy.

A Flimsy Trust
Why Social Security Needs Some Major Repairs

ALLAN SLOAN

I n Washington these days, the only topics of discussion seem to be how many trillions of dollars to throw at health care and the recession, and whom on Wall Street to pillory next. But watch out. Lurking just below the surface is a bailout candidate that may soon emerge like the great white shark in "Jaws"—Social Security.

Perhaps as early as this year, Social Security, which at $680 billion is the nation's biggest social program, will be transformed from an operation that's helped finance the rest of the government for 25 years into a cash drain that will need money from the Treasury. In other words, a bailout.

I've been writing about Social Security's problems for more than a decade, arguing that having the government borrow several trillion dollars to bail out the program so it can pay its promised benefits would impose an intolerable burden on our public finances. But I've changed my mind about what "intolerable" means. With the government spending untold trillions to bail out incompetent banks and the auto industry, it should damn well bail out Social Security recipients, too. But in a smart way.

Why am I talking about Social Security now, when health care is sucking up nearly all the oxygen in our nation's capital? Because Social Security is a big deal, providing a majority of the income for more than half of Americans 65 and up and also supporting millions of people with disabilities and survivors of deceased workers. And because the collapse of stock prices and home values makes Social Security retirement benefits far more important than they were during the highs of a few years ago. And because the problems aren't that hard to solve if we look at Social Security realistically instead of treating it as a sacred, untouchable program (liberals) or a demonic plot to make people dependent on government (conservatives).

Finally, this is a good time to discuss Social Security because the Obama folks say it's next on the agenda, after health care. No one at the White House, the Treasury Department or the Social Security Administration would discuss specifics, however.

It ought to tell you something that Peter Orszag, director of the White House Office of Management and Budget, is a noted Social Security scholar. Alas, he wouldn't tell me what he plans to propose. "Health care first" was all he'd say.

I'd like to show you that Social Security has a real and growing cash problem even as its trust fund is getting bigger than ever, explain how the program really works, and—immodest though it may seem—propose a few solutions.

Social Security has a real—and growing— cash problem.

The Cash Problem

How can Social Security possibly need a bailout when, by Washington rules, it's "solvent" for another 26 years? To understand the problem, look at me. I'll turn 66 next year, which makes me and my wife eligible for full Social Security benefits. They'll be about $42,000 a year for the both of us starting Jan. 1, 2011, and are scheduled to rise as the consumer price index does.

Social Security, which analyzed my situation, values those promised (but not legally binding) benefits at a bit more than $600,000. That is a lot of money, but Social Security is way ahead of us because the value of our benefits is far less than the Social Security taxes we and our employers will have paid by the end of next year, plus the interest Social Security will have earned on that money in the decades since we started working. Those taxes and interest will total more than $800,000 by Dec. 31, 2010. For example, the $5.18 my employer and I paid in 1961—the year I got my card—will have grown to $140 by next year.

I don't have a problem with this disparity. One of the principles of Social Security is that higher-paid folks like me support the lower-paid. That's as it should be, given that the Social Security tax (12.4 percent of covered wages, split equally between employer and employee) is regressive, far more costly as a percentage of income to a $40,000-a-year worker than it is to me. According to the Tax Policy Institute, five of six U.S. workers pay more in Social Security tax (including the employer's portion) than in federal income tax—something that makes it especially important (and only fair) to preserve the program for lower earners, who get old-age benefits of up to 90 percent of their covered wages, while I get only 28 percent.

How can my wife and I pose a problem to Social Security when our benefits are valued at $600,293, while our tax payments plus interest will total $804,686? Answer: Because the obligation is real, but the $800,000-plus asset is illusory, consisting solely of government IOUs to itself.

Now, let's step back a bit—to 1935, actually—to see how we got into this mess. President Franklin D. Roosevelt set up Social Security as an intergenerational social-insurance plan, under which today's workers support their parents (and those with disabilities and workers' survivors) in the hope that their children will in turn support them. It's not a pension fund. It's not an insurance company.

Social Security exists in its own world. In this world, taxes are called "contributions," though they're certainly not voluntary. "Trust funds," which in the outside world connote real wealth bestowed on beneficiaries, are nothing but IOUs from one arm of the government (the Treasury) to another (the Social Security Administration). And "solvency," which in the real world means that assets are greater than liabilities, means only that the Social Security trust fund has a positive balance.

Alas, the trust fund is a mere accounting entry, albeit one with a moral and political claim on taxpayers. It currently holds about $2.5 trillion in Treasury securities and is projected to grow to more than $4 trillion, even as Social Security begins to take in far less cash in taxes than it spends in benefits. For instance, it projects a cash deficit of $234 billion for 2023. But the trust fund will grow—on paper—because it will get $245 billion in Treasury IOUs as interest. The Treasury pays its interest tab with paper, not cash.

"The trust fund has no financial significance," says David Walker, former head of the Government Accountability Office and now president of the Peter G. Peterson Foundation, which advocates fiscal responsibility. "If you did [bookkeeping like] that in the private sector, you'd go to jail."

Let me show you why the Social Security trust fund isn't social or secure, has no funds, and can't be trusted, by returning to my favorite subject: myself.

The cash that Social Security has collected from me and my wife and our employers isn't sitting at Social Security. It's gone. Some went to pay benefits, some to fund the rest of the government. Since 1983, when it suffered a cash crisis, Social Security has been collecting more in taxes each year than it has paid out in benefits. It has used the excess to buy the Treasury securities that go into the trust fund, reducing the Treasury's need to raise money from investors. What happens if Social Security takes in less cash than it needs to pay benefits? Watch.

Let's say that late next year, Social Security realizes that it's short the $3,486 it needs to pay me and my wife for our Jan. 1, 2011, benefit. It gets that money by having the Treasury redeem $3,486 in trust-fund Treasury securities. The Treasury would get the necessary cash by selling $3,486 in new Treasury securities to investors. That means that $3,486 has been moved from the national debt that the government owes itself, which almost no one cares about, to the national debt it owes investors, which almost everyone—and certainly the bond market—takes very seriously.

This example shows you that the trust fund is of no economic value to the government as a whole (which is what really matters), because the government has to borrow from private investors the money it needs to redeem the securities. It would be the same if the trust fund sold its Treasury securities directly to investors—the government would be adding to the publicly held national debt to fund Social Security checks.

Social Security's "solvency" calculations—and the insistence by the status quo's supporters that there's "no problem" until 2036 because the trust fund will have assets until then—assumes that the Treasury can and will borrow the necessary money to redeem the trust fund's Treasury securities. There is also the assumption that our children, who by then will be running the country, will allow all this money to be diverted from other needs. I sure wouldn't assume that.

This whole problem of Social Security posting huge surpluses for years, using proceeds from a regressive tax to fund the rest of the government and then needing a Treasury bailout to pay its bills, is an unanticipated consequence of the 1983 legislation that supposedly fixed the system.

In order to show 75 years of "solvency" as required by law, Congress, using the bipartisan 1983 Greenspan Commission report as political cover, sharply raised Social Security taxes, cut future benefits and boosted the retirement age (then 65, currently 66, rising to 67).

The changes transformed Social Security from an explicitly pay-as-you-go program into one that produced huge cash surpluses for years followed by huge cash deficits. No one in authority seems to have realized that the only way to really save the temporary surpluses was to let the trust fund invest in non-Treasury debt securities, such as high-grade mortgages (yes, such things exist) or corporate bonds. That way, interest and principal repayments from homeowners and corporations would have been covering Social Security's future cash shortfalls, rather than the Treasury's having to borrow money to cover them.

This problem has been metastasizing for 25 years. Now I'll show you why the day of reckoning may finally be here.

Just last year, Social Security was projecting a cash surplus of $87 billion this year and $88 billion next year. These were to be the peak cash-generating years, followed by a cash-flow decline, followed by cash outlays exceeding inflows starting in 2017.

But in this year's Social Security trustees report, the cash flow projections for 2009 and 2010 have shrunk by almost 80 percent, to $19 billion and $18 billion, respectively. How did $138 billion of projected cash go missing in one year? Stephen Goss, Social Security's chief actuary, says the major reason is that the recession has cost millions of jobs, reducing Social Security's tax income below projections.

But $18 billion is still a surplus. So why do I say Social Security could go cash-negative this year? Because unemployment is far worse than Social Security projected. It assumed that unemployment would rise gradually this year and peak at 9 percent in 2010. Now, of course, the rate is 9.5 percent and rising—and we're still in 2009.

Social Security's having negative cash flow this year would be a relatively minor economic event—what's a few more billion dollars when the government's already borrowing more than $1 trillion?—but I think it would be a really important psychological and political event.

Orszag pooh-poohed my thinking when I met with him. He says I'm wrong to harp on Social Security's near-term cash flow—a term, by the way, that he won't use. "I think the real question of Social Security is how we bring long-term revenues in line with long-term expenses," he said, "not whether the primary surplus within Social Security turns negative within the next few years." I guess we'll see.

When you look back at numbers from previous years, you suddenly realize that Social Security's finances have been deteriorating for a long time. Social Security's cash flow (and thus its trust fund balances) has fallen well below earlier projections. Seven years ago, the projected 2009 cash flow was $115 billion. That fell to $87 billion by last year and is now $19 billion. Ten years ago, the trust fund was projected to be $3 trillion at the end of this year, rather than the currently projected $2.56 trillion.

In 1983, the system was projected to be "solvent" until the 2050s. This year it's only until 2036. Social Security's Goss says the major reason is that over the past two decades, the wages on which Social Security collects taxes have grown more slowly than projected. He said Social Security projected them to grow at 1.5 percent above inflation, but they've been growing at only 1.1 percent above it.

The scariest thing, at least to me, is that even as its financials erode, Social Security is as important as ever—maybe more so. Let me elaborate on what I said earlier, about how older people depend heavily on Social Security. It accounts for more than half the income of 52 percent of married couples over 65, and 72 percent of that of 65-and-up singles, according to the Social Security Administration.

What's more, this dependence—which Goss says isn't projected to change—comes despite 30 years of broadly popular self-directed retirement accounts such as 401(k)s, IRAs, 403(b)s and such.

Why haven't those savings accounts reduced dependence on Social Security? Part of the reason is that it takes a lot of money to generate serious retirement income: about $170,000 for a $1,000-a-month lifetime annuity. Inflation protection, if you can find it, is ultra-expensive. Vanguard, which offers a lifetime inflation-adjusted annuity in conjunction with an AIG insurance company called American General, quoted me a staggering price for an annuity mimicking my wife's and my Social Security benefit. Would you believe $774,895?

Another problem is that the stock market has been stinko. Stocks are below their level of April 2000, when the great bull market (August 1982 to March 2000) ended. It's hard to make money in stocks when they've been down for nine years. The Employee Benefit Research Institute estimates that the average retirement account balance of people 65 to 74 was $266,000 in 2007 but had fallen to $217,000 as of mid-June.

Then there's the problem of lost home equity. According to a study conducted for Fortune by the Center for Economic and

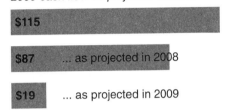

Good Numbers Gone Bad

Social Security will soon take in less cash than it spends, partly because of rising unemployment. Its cash flow will shrink to a projected $19 billion this year, compared with the $115 billion predicted seven years ago.

Shrinking projections of Social Security cash flow for 2009 (in billions)

2009 cash flow as projected in 2002

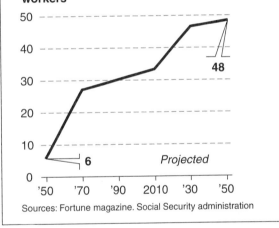

Number of Social Security beneficiaries per 100 workers

Sources: Fortune magazine. Social Security administration

Policy Research, people in the lower-income to upper-middle-income ranges have lost a far greater proportion of their net worth as a result of the housing bust than the most wealthy people have.

The bottom line is that many older people who felt reasonably well fixed for retirement a few years ago now need Social Security more than ever. That makes it even more important to come up with a way to sustain it and to show our children a realistic plan to give them benefits, rather than to rely on the trust fund and the supposed political clout of the geezer class to keep benefits flowing when cash flow goes negative.

So how do we fix these problems? Let me divide it into three categories: what to do, what to change and what not to do.

What to Do

Many of the old standbys: raising the "covered wage" limit, but not to outrageous levels; tweaking the benefit formulas so that high-end people like me get a little less bang for the buck;

modifying cost-of-living increases for us high-end types; and, most important, raising the retirement age to 70, with a special earlier-retirement provision for manual laborers, who can't be expected to work that long.

What to Change

- **The law requiring 75-year solvency.** It's hard to predict what will happen 75 days from now, let alone 75 years from now. But the obsession with 75-year solvency and the status of the trust fund has obscured what's really going on.

This requirement forces Social Security's actuaries—who are among the best and smartest public servants I know—to make all sorts of impossible projections. As we've seen, even one faulty projection—such as overestimating wage growth—can cause substantial problems.

- **The trust fund.** Before the Greenspan Commission-related changes in 1983, the trust fund was a checking account. The workings of Social Security since 1983 have turned it into something it was never intended to be: an investment account. Let's gradually draw down the trust fund by having the Treasury redeem $100 billion or so annually (less than the current interest the fund earns) by giving the fund cash rather than Treasury IOUs, gradually increasing the redemptions. That will let the fund buy assets that will be useful when serious cash-flow deficits hit, assets such as high-grade mortgage securities and high-grade bonds.

That way we'll be bailing out Social Security a bit at a time, which is realistic, rather than in huge chunks, which isn't. Combine that with the lower costs and higher revenues, and today's kids could see that there really is a way they'll get benefits someday.

What Not to Do

- **Depend on taxing "the rich."** One solution you hear in Washington is restoring "covered wage" levels to the good old Greenspan Commission days, when 90 percent of wages were subject to Social Security tax, compared with 83 percent now. Sounds simple and fair, doesn't it? But that would increase the Social Security wage base to about $170,000 from the current $106,800, according to Andrew Biggs of the American Enterprise Institute—at 12.4 percent, a huge new tax to middle-class workers. (And yes, that's middle-class income, not rich-person income, in large parts of the country.)

During his campaign, President Obama proposed (and then dropped) a plan to leave the Social Security wage cap where it is but to apply the 12.4 percent Social Security tax to all wages above $250,000. That—like the 90-percent-level-of-income idea—would be a huge new tax that would weaken support for Social Security among higher-income people. I'm not saying "rich people," because truly rich people generally have huge amounts of investment income, which isn't subject to Social Security tax.

- **Means-test benefits.** It's being done. We'd be making a terrible mistake to means-test Social Security by saying that people above a certain income level can't get it. That would violate the social compact that everyone pays Social Security taxes and everyone gets something.

Besides, Social Security is already means-tested, indirectly. That's because if you have enough non-Social Security income—about $23,000 a year in my case—you pay federal income tax on 85 percent of your benefit.

Given the three pensions I stand to collect from previous employers, I think I hit that level. So, for the final time, let's run my numbers. If my wife and I are in the 28 percent federal tax bracket when we start collecting benefits, we'll be giving almost a quarter of our benefit right back to Social Security.

It would also mean that the $600,000 benefit I talked about earlier would cost Social Security only about $450,000—just 55 percent or so of the $800,000-plus value of our taxes.

I don't mind that big haircut, but I'd be furious if the government decided to just confiscate all the money my wife and I put in over the decades by saying we were "rich" and had no right to any benefits. And I wouldn't be alone.

Given the way health-care reform has bogged down, Social Security may not make it onto the agenda until next year. But it's going to show up sooner or later, probably sooner, because the numbers are so bad that something's going to have to be done. As I hope I've shown, we're going to have to bail out Social Security or risk hurting a lot of low-income older people or putting the whole program at risk by gouging and alienating upper-income Social Security sympathizers like me.

So let's fix this already. By the numbers. And by the right numbers, not fantasy ones.

Critical Thinking

1. Why are Social Security "trust funds" of no economic value to government as a whole?

2. How did the 1983 Social Security cash crisis and resulting legislation implemented to solve it inadvertently lead to the transformation of the system from "pay as you go" into a surplus-deficit cycle, leading to an impending crisis?

3. Explain the reasons why retired people are becoming increasingly dependent on Social Security income.

4. What does the author suggest the government specifically do or change to fix the problems with Social Security?

5. What does the author suggest the government to avoid doing in reforming Social Security?

With reporting by Doris Burke of *Fortune*. **ALLAN SLOAN** is *Fortune* magazine's senior editor at large. His e-mail address is asloan@ fortunemail.com.

What We Don't Know Can Hurt Us

TIM FERNHOLZ

Information is the life-blood of public policy. Identifying a problem is the first step to solving it, and once a solution is in place, we need metrics to understand if the policy is working and how to turn its weaknesses into strengths. Though the data we have today are, unsurprisingly, better than ever, there are still too many dark spots and missing data on a host of important issues. Take, for example, the financial sector. Bank regulators, lacking a clear picture of how predatory mortgage loans are connected to global capital flows, allowed an exuberant bubble to spin into a crash in 2008. It's a reminder that if we can identify gaps in our knowledge, we would be remiss not to close them.

President Barack Obama recognizes the need for better data; he's expressed commitment to scientifically supported policies and filled his administration with wonkishly inclined Democrats. The Dodd-Frank financial-reform bill his administration supported mandates some 67 studies to guide policy-makers' supervision of the financial markets. Obama's signature accomplishment, health-care reform, emphasizes a new commission to gather information about which medical practices are most effective. Conservatives balked, claiming that this data-driven approach was a way to justify taking Grandma off the ventilator. Liberals—and most policy experts—countered that it was a way to make the system more efficient.

This debate isn't just about how to collect new data but also how to interpret the data we already have. A perennial question is how to define poverty; the current measure is pegged to the economy of the 1960s and doesn't reflect today's family finances. A new measure developed by the Commerce Department will paint a more accurate picture of poverty, but it is opposed by conservatives who fear that the results will portray more penury in the United States "propaganda," scoffs the Heritage Foundation. Sometimes, people just don't want to know.

Ignorance, however, is only bliss if you think the government shouldn't play an active role in society; bureaucratic inertia favors conservatives. Though new technology has made sharing and manipulating data easier, the government is playing catch-up in putting information online so the public and academics can put it to good use. In many policy areas, the government isn't just failing at transparency but also usability—data sets don't always lend themselves to apples-to-apples comparisons, making much-needed analysis more difficult to obtain.

We spoke with experts in and out of government to highlight six areas where missing information is preventing us from enacting sound public policy.

Employment
What We Don't Know
How Many Jobs Have Been Offshored

Senate Democrats recently made political hay with the Creating American Jobs and Ending Offshoring Act, a dead-on-arrival proposal that would have penalized companies that send jobs overseas. It's a hot topic, but systematic measures of offshoring are hard to come by. The Bureau of Economic Analysis tracks imports and exports but not the labor impact of trade. The Bureau of Labor Statistics tracks "movement of work," which counts layoffs involving more than 50 workers but not smaller losses. Plus, jobs not created in the U.S. aren't counted. If an auto maker opens a plant in China, rather than in Lansing, or a startup hires a back-office firm in India rather than an in-house accountant, is that offshoring? According to the BLS measure, no. The auto—and office workers might have a different answer. The bureau notes that offshoring of service work, like that bill-processing gig, may be particularly undercounted, due to "a dearth of relevant data." BLS estimates that, as of 2008, some 30 million service jobs were vulnerable to offshoring. If those jobs were lost, we might not know.

What We Don't Know
What Kind of Jobs Are Created by Public Investments

America is spending a lot of money to create jobs, with some $787 billion allocated by the American Recovery and Reinvestment Act, aka the stimulus. We know how many jobs are created or retained with those government dollars—that's a reporting requirement under the law. What we don't know is who's getting them, how long they last, or how much they pay. We also don't know if one job is a single fulltime job or if four people are working 10 hours a week. OMB Watch, a member of the Coalition for an Accountable Recovery, has called for the tracking of the type of work created as well as the wages, health-care coverage, and demographics of stimulus-funded workers. So far, though, those details haven't been recorded.

Recipients of stimulus funds do have to report 99 data points, including information on subcontractors, some executive-compensation data, and other tidbits that please transparency advocates. "This is by far the most transparent federal spending bill in history," says Greg Leroy, executive director of Good Jobs First. "Don't sell it short."—Kat Aaron

Finance
What We Don't Know
How Credit-Card Companies Are Screwing Us

The dismal performance of our country's banks and the resulting bailouts have raised questions about how financiers treat their customers. In the Dodd-Frank bill, a new agency was created to protect consumers from predatory financial products. The problem? We don't have good data on how credit-card companies make their money, especially when it comes to penalty fees. That might not seem like a big deal, but the example of checking-account overdraft fees is useful. After a landmark Federal Deposit Insurance Corporation study revealed that banks make three-quarters of their fee revenue from automatic overdraft penalties, the Federal Reserve created new rules limiting the charges and forcing banks to disclose their policies. Obtaining similar information from credit-card companies would allow for better regulation, and publishing the data would enable customers to understand how much money the companies make off them.

What We Don't Know
How Low-Income People Manage Their Finances

While we fight poverty through education and welfare programs, the only sure-fire way to build a strong middle class is to make certain Americans have the tools they need to build wealth. Encouraging people to save money and use safe credit products requires understanding how they manage their finances. Unfortunately, it's hard to say exactly what low-income Americans do with their money, because we aren't asking enough people the right questions (only in 2007 did we start asking people if they use payday loans) often enough (a three-year gap in a key study means we'll have no data for most of the recession). Most consumer surveys are focused on higher-income Americans, which leaves us unaware of how to help low-income folks climb the ladder. Improved consumer surveys would add more low-income families to the mix, be more frequent, and add questions about fringe financial services. A better picture of family balance sheets would improve government efforts to encourage responsible asset building.—T.F.

Housing
What We Don't Know
The Number of Foreclosures and Evictions

America is almost three years into a massive housing crisis, and astonishingly, the federal government is not tracking foreclosures. The numbers you hear—that one in 75 houses in Las Vegas is in foreclosure, say—likely come from Realty Trac, "the leading online marketplace of foreclosure properties." It's also the country's main source of foreclosure data. Governmental foreclosure-prevention efforts rely on numbers collected by a company whose mission is to help people "locate, evaluate, buy and sell properties." Unsurprisingly, that's not working very well. The much-touted Home Affordable Mortgage Program was projected to save 3 million to 4 million homes, but as of September,

it had permanently modified mortgages for just over 468,000 homeowners. The financial-reform bill included a provision creating a foreclosure database, featuring comprehensive stats on distressed mortgages. The bill, however, didn't specify exactly what the database would track or how it would be paid for.

Anecdotal evidence suggests evictions, too, are on the rise. The National Low Income Housing Coalition estimated in 2009 that 40 percent of foreclosed properties had renters, who were often tossed out by banks when they took ownership. President Obama signed a bill giving such renters certain rights, but without any baseline numbers on pre-crisis evictions and no plan for ongoing measurement, assessing the law's impact is nearly impossible.

What We Don't Know
How a Borrower's Race Affects Home Loans

The Home Mortgage Disclosure Act is a vintage piece of data-generating legislation. The 1975 law requires lenders to report where home loans are made, the race of the borrower, and whether the loan is prime or subprime. Consumer advocates and reporters have used HMDA data to track patterns in mortgage lending, to see whether, for instance, high-cost subprime loans are concentrated in communities of color. When advocates use HMDA to assert racial discrimination in lending, the industry response is often that the disparities in pricing are based on credit scores, not race. Now, under the financial-reform bill, lenders must report a slew of new details, including the credit score and age of the borrower and whether the loan had teaser rates or prepayment penalties, two features common in questionable subprimes. This data may put to rest the heated debate around redlining in the mortgage market.—K.A.

Health
What We Don't Know
Which Drugs and Medical Devices Are Dangerous

The U.S. Food and Drug Administration is charged with protecting public safety by reviewing drugs and devices before they go to the market, but much of the information it collects is not available to the public. Reports of "adverse events"—when a drug or medical device already on the market is causing harm—are incomplete; in many cases, it's necessary to file a Freedom of Information Act request to get the details. Currently, the FDA also does not let us know when a company starts to investigate a new drug or when it decides to put a trial on hold or terminate it. If a company decides to put an end to its investigations because of safety concerns, the FDA doesn't tell us. So if you are, say, a researcher studying a particular drug molecule that's similar to one a company decided to ditch because of a safety issue, you have no way of knowing.

What We Don't Know
The Basics on Food, Drug, and Medical-Device Recalls

When the infant-formula manufacturer Abbott agreed recently to recall certain batches of Similac that may have been contaminated with beetle parts, the FDA made that information available in a new section of its website in a programmer friendly, mashup-ready format known as "XML." The agency, though, had no authority to compel the company to provide basic information on the recall, such as how many cans were affected and where they had been distributed, because all reporting is voluntary. Getting complete information about recalls—whether for food, drugs, or medical devices would be invaluable for public-health experts dealing with an outbreak, journalists reporting on it, and consumers who want to avoid the stuff. Last spring, the agency called for comment on 21 draft proposals to increase agency transparency. We're still waiting to see what the FDA will do.—Nancy Watzman

Education
What We Don't Know
Which Early-Education Programs Work

Experts on early childhood education agree that attending preschool has a positive effect on a child's long-term educational attainment but have no way of tracking which programs produce the best results. A wide variety of preschool programs exist, administered privately or by state or federal agencies. These programs have no uniform way of collecting data, if they collect such information at all, and no system for sharing what they do record with grade schools to track students' progress over time. That means that once students enter grade school, their results can't be linked to their preschool record. Preschools can't monitor how well they are preparing their alumni, and policymakers can't develop an integrated curriculum that accounts for the fact that students move through different education systems. An identification number that tracks students from preschool to the workforce would provide a fuller picture of student experience, but privacy concerns and bureaucratic challenges make such an innovation unlikely.

What We Don't Know
How Much Students Learn in College

Colleges are routinely ranked based on input values like the average SAT score of the entering class, but there is no way to quantify their output—how much they teach students over the course of four years. Intellectual improvement is a subjective value and therefore difficult to quantify. It also varies widely by program. Some degrees may focus on communication skills, while others produce bigger gains in critical thinking. Without any measure of how much students improve, the marketplace for degrees skews away from teaching quality toward reputation. Students can graduate from renowned schools without the skills they need in the workforce, while quality low-profile schools go unrecognized. Tests like the Collegiate and Learning Assessment, which students take during their first year and again when they graduate, offer a potential solution

but are unpopular with colleges wary of having weaknesses exposed.—Sarah Babbage

Campaign Finance
What We Don't Know
Who is Funding Outside Spending

Thanks to the Supreme Court's 2010 ruling in Citizens United and other recent legal decisions, there is an explosion of new election spending by outside groups—$122 million as of early October—much of it by groups with innocuous names like Americans for Job Security, Common Sense in America, and American Crossroads, which counts Karl Rove among its fundraisers and advisers. Reports on who is financing these groups tend to dribble in slowly, and in some cases, when it's a nonprofit group or trade association doing the spending, we may never find out who is spending big money to influence the election. The DISCLOSE Act, which would have given us more information on outside ads, was filibustered by Senate Republicans in September. If the new Congress doesn't take action on this front, come 2012, we'll know even less.

What We Don't Know
Who is Contributing What Until It's Too Late

Most of us can go online to find an up-to-the-minute record of our credit-card transactions, but if we want to know how much cash a Senate candidate collected today, we need to wait weeks or even months. Even though political action committees, House candidates, and party committees must alert the Federal Election Commission electronically within 48 hours of receiving a major donation, Senate candidates still file the old-fashioned way—that is, on actual paper, which then needs to be converted to digital files. That means there is a considerable lag time between filing deadlines and when the information is easily accessible. You can't search and sort last-minute reports of large contributions received on the FEC's website often until three or four days after the reports are submitted. That means that voters may wait until after they fill in their ballots to see who dropped last-minute money into races. There is no technical reason for any of this. We should be able to see political contributions online, in real time.—N.W.

Critical Thinking

1. Why is accurate information "the life-blood of public policy"?

2. Why does the absence of accurate and relevant information in particular spheres tend to favor bureaucratic inertia and thus a conservative approach to national government activities?

3. What are six areas where missing information seems to be preventing sound public policy? What key information is missing in each of the areas?

The Tyranny of Metaphor

Three historical myths have been leading American presidents into folly for nearly a century. Is Obama wise enough to avoid the same fate?

ROBERT DALLEK

In 1952, British historian Denis William Brogan published a brilliantly perceptive article on "The Illusion of American Omnipotence." In the midst of the Korean War, Brogan was not only commenting on Americans' frustration with their inability to prevail decisively against supposedly inferior Chinese and North Korean forces, but also cautioning against other misadventures in which the United States falsely assumed its superpower status assured a military victory in any conflict it chose to fight. Brogan could just as easily have titled his essay "The Omnipotence of American Illusion" in an echo of Friedrich Nietzsche's critique of true believers. "Convictions," the great German philosopher wrote, "are more dangerous enemies of truth than lies."

Brogan and Nietzsche might well have been talking about the last 100 years of American thinking about foreign policy and the convictions—or call them illusions—that have shaped it along the way, across administrations led by men as diverse in outlook and background as Woodrow Wilson, Dwight Eisenhower, and George W. Bush.

There is certainly much about America's world dealings in the 20th century that deserves praise: victory in World War II, the Truman Doctrine, the Marshall Plan, JFK's diplomacy during the Cuban missile crisis, the Camp David peace accords, the Panama Canal treaty, Richard Nixon's opening to China, and détente with the Soviet Union, to mention the most obvious. But a more rounded view would have to include its many stumbles. Three enduring illusions—a misguided faith in universalism, or America's power to transform the world from a community of hostile, lawless nations into enlightened states devoted to peaceful cooperation; a need to shun appeasement of all adversaries or to condemn suggestions of conciliatory talks with them as misguided weakness; and a belief in the surefire effectiveness of military strength in containing opponents, whatever their ability to threaten the United States— have made it nearly impossible for Americans to think afresh about more productive ways to address their foreign problems. Call it the tyranny of metaphor: For all their pretensions to shaping history, U.S. presidents are more often its prisoners.

Universalism: The misguided faith in America's power to transform the world.

Even Barack Obama, who rode his opposition to the Iraq war into the White House and has kept his campaign promise to withdraw U.S. combat troops, is not immune from history's illusions. How could he be? Domestic politics are as much a part of foreign policy as assessments of conditions abroad. But Obama might yet succeed in fending off such pressures. The president is keenly interested in making the wisest possible use of history, as was evident to me from two dinners 10 other historians and I had with him at the White House over the past two years. For despite the many countercurrents confronting him, Obama was eager to learn from us how previous presidents transcended their circumstances to achieve transformational administrations.

Such lessons must weigh heavily as Obama faces his next momentous decision on what to do in Afghanistan while praying that Gen. David Petraeus, the hero of the Iraq surge, can duplicate the feat before the public's patience runs out. So far, the president has avoided either fully embracing the Afghan war or calling for outright withdrawal. His commitment of 30,000 additional troops was meant to reassure America's national security hawks that he is as determined as they are to defend the country's safety from future attacks. At the same time, his promise to begin withdrawing U.S. forces in July 2011 suggests his understanding that Afghanistan could be another Vietnam— a costly, unwinnable conflict that could tie the United States down in Asia for the indefinite future. It might also be, of course, that Obama has serious doubts about the value of sending American soldiers to die in a far-off, impoverished land of little strategic value, but understands that simply to walk away from the conflict carries unacceptable political risks, undermining his ability to enact a bold domestic agenda that is central to his administration and his chances for a second term.

Just as President Harry Truman could not ignore the political pressure from the China Lobby to back Chiang Kaishek's failing regime against Mao Zedong's Communists in the middle of the last century, so Obama is mindful of the political risks of appearing irresolute. Already, his predecessor's U.N. ambassador, John Bolton, has blamed Obama's Afghan withdrawal timeline for sending "a signal of weakness that our adversaries interpret to our detriment." Former Vice President Dick Cheney has referred to the president as someone who "travels around the world apologizing." Bush himself previewed a similar line of attack in a 2008 speech in Israel, in which he criticized Obama and others then calling for engagement with Iran. "We have heard this foolish delusion before," Bush said. "As Nazi tanks crossed into Poland in 1939, an American senator declared: 'Lord, if I could only have talked to Hitler, all of this might have been avoided.' We have an obligation to call this what it is—the false comfort of appeasement, which has been repeatedly discredited by history."

Can Obama escape this trap? To do so, he'll need to study his predecessors' mistakes and learn from those few U.S. presidents who managed to avoid being tyrannized by metaphor. And he'll need to understand how we got here.

America's love affair with universalism, the first of the three illusions, began in January 1918 with President Woodrow Wilson's peace program, his Fourteen Points: the seductive rationalizations for U.S. participation in a "war to end all wars" and make the Western world "safe for democracy." Such high-minded ends appealed to Americans as validations of the superiority of their institutions. They were enough to convince an isolationist America to sacrifice more than 50,000 lives in the last 19 months of Europe's Great War. The 20 postwar years, which saw the rise of communism, fascism, Nazism, and Japanese militarism leading to World War II, gave the lie to Wilson's dreams of universal peace and self-governance, driving Americans back into their isolationist shell until the attack on Pearl Harbor demonstrated that the "free security" provided by vast oceans and weak neighbors no longer guaranteed their country's safety.

Yet Wilson's idealistic hopes for a better world did not disappear on the beaches of Normandy or in the caves of Iwo Jima. If anything, World War II reinforced Americans' unrealistic expectations that they could reduce—if not end—human conflict. Wilsonianism found continuing life in the birth of the United Nations and the triumph of democracy in Germany, Japan, Spain, South Korea, Taiwan, and parts of Latin America. But Wilson's vision was again elevated to a sacred doctrine that repeatedly played America false. Eager to believe that World War II would largely cure countries of their affinity for bloodshed, Americans persisted in seeing the Allies—Britain, China, the Soviet Union, and the United States—as permanent friends acting in concert to keep the postwar peace.

The onset of the Cold War brought an abrupt end to these dreams. But convictions about the irresistible attraction of U.S. institutions encouraged the hope that inside every foreigner was an American waiting to emerge, an outlook that shaped American thinking not only during the years of anti-communist struggle, but all the way up to Bush's rationale for fighting in Iraq. Today, Bush's prediction that the destruction of Saddam Hussein's military dictatorship would transform the Middle East into a flourishing center of traditional American freedoms is proving to be as elusive as Wilson's original grandiose vision. The imperfect U.S.-sponsored regimes in Baghdad—and Kabul too, for that matter—are a far cry from the robust democracies Bush hoped would become the envy of the region. "The survival of liberty in our land increasingly depends on the success of liberty in other lands. The best hope for peace in our world is the expansion of freedom in all the world," Bush said in his very Wilsonian second inaugural address, though U.S. military chiefs in Iraq and Afghanistan have since managed to move the goal posts, promising to establish reasonably pro-American governments that can handle their own security.

Most of the evidence, however, points to an unpredictable future for both countries, where political instability, anti-Americanism, and military coups seem unlikely to disappear. It may be that 10 or 20 or 30 years of U.S. stewardship will bring freedom and prosperity to Iraq and Afghanistan, but Americans have limited patience with nation-building that costs them unacceptable amounts of blood and treasure—and often have a better collective sense of what American power can realistically achieve than the government's best arid brightest. They have not forgotten the Vietnam War, even if, at times, their leaders seem to have.

Indeed, Vietnam is always there as a trap for the American leader, a trap set by the deadly and persistent second illusion—that a failure to combat every act of international aggression is tantamount to appeasement, a return to the failed passivity of the 1930s. This illusion has time and again led the United States into unwise and costly military adventures. While Winston Churchill was marvelously right in saying that Britain had a choice between war and dishonor at Munich in 1938 and that Neville Chamberlain's appeasement of Adolf Hitler would produce both, Munich was never the perfect analogy for dealing with subsequent conflicts, as Churchill himself acknowledged. As he put it in 1950, "The word 'appeasement' is not popular, but appeasement has its place in all policy. Make sure you put it in the right place. Appease the weak. Defy the strong." But for hawks, it is always Munich 1938—no matter whether the aggressor is Saddam Hussein, Slobodan Milosevic, or "Baby Doc" Duvalier—and presidents from Truman to Bush have been led by the appeasement metaphor into misjudgments that have harmed the United States and undermined their presidencies.

Truman, for example, justified his decision to enter the Korean War in 1950 as a way to deter the Soviet Union, which he saw as the architect of the conflict, from future acts of aggression that could touch off a World War III. Truman had reason enough to combat Pyongyang's aggression: South Korea's collapse would have undermined confidence in America's determination to defend Japan and Western European allies. Comparisons between Stalin and Hitler and predictions that Korea was the start of a worldwide communist offensive like the Nazi reach for global control, however, were decidedly overdrawn. But the power of the anti-appeasement proposition was so great in 1950 that one can search in vain for dyssenting voices.

Had Truman aimed simply to restore South Korea's independence, his decision to enter the Korean fighting would look much different today. Instead, he chose to follow Gen. Douglas MacArthur's advice to destroy North Korea's communist regime by crossing the 38th parallel. It was a blunder based on two false assumptions: that the Chinese would not enter the conflict and that if they did, they would be roundly defeated, with the likely collapse of their communist regime. Instead, China's direct entry into the war produced a military and political stalemate, delayed a possible rapprochement with Beijing for years, and destroyed Truman's presidency. With his approval rating falling to 24 percent, he could neither enact his Fair Deal nor maintain public backing for the war.

President Lyndon B. Johnson, of course, was another casualty of the Munich analogy. Recalling the political consequences for his party from the 1949 "loss" of China that right-wing Republicans like Joseph McCarthy used to label Democrats as appeasers of Chamberlain scale, he committed the United States to a war in Southeast Asia even more politically destructive to his administration and the country than any act of passivity might have produced. Johnson came to lament Vietnam's cost to him and his administration, complaining about the "bitch" of a war that distracted him from his true love—building the Great Society.

The failure in Vietnam produced a new metaphor: Fighting a Third World country on hostile terrain was to be avoided at all costs. When George H.W. Bush convinced Congress and the country to oust Iraq from Kuwait in 1991, it was an uphill struggle to persuade Americans that he was not involving them in another Vietnam. Yet he succeeded by invoking that appeasement metaphor yet again: "If history teaches us anything, it is that we must resist aggression or it will destroy our freedoms," Bush explained in making his case for the war. "Appeasement does not work. As was the case in the 1930s, we see in Saddam Hussein an aggressive dictator threatening his neighbors." Such overblown warnings were enough to sell the Persian Gulf offensive, but postwar arguments that America had now kicked the Vietnam syndrome were premature—and may have sown the seeds of his son's disastrous 2003 invasion of Iraq.

The third illusion U.S. presidents often hold is that militarized containment—the belief that containing or preventing enemy aggression depends on a military threat to their survival—is the right way to avoid the traps set by the first two. The core conviction here has been that America won the Cold War because it understood that the Soviet Union was intent on world domination and that the best way to counter its ambitions short of all-out war was to contain its reach for control by a combination of economic, political, and military initiatives that would discourage Moscow from aggression and strain its limited resources to the breaking point, forcing communism's collapse.

From the start, however, containment was a contested doctrine. In his famous "Long Telegram" of February 1946 and "X" article in *Foreign Affairs* the next year, George F. Kennan, who headed the State Department's new policy planning staff, counseled the White House to contain Soviet Russia's "expansionist," "messianic" drive for world control. Kennan later regretted having stated his views in such evangelistic language; it encouraged anti-communists to take his advice as a call for military as well as political and diplomatic action.

In fact, Kennan never believed that Moscow intended a military offensive against Western Europe. In his judgment, Soviet acts of aggression would take the form of political subversion, calculated steps to bring pro-Soviet governments to power wherever possible as Moscow drove to win what it saw as the inevitable competition between communism and capitalism. Kennan's formula for victory was economic aid fostering political stability in countries potentially vulnerable to communism's siren song. He wisely described Soviet communism as a system of state management and controls that would eventually collapse when its inability to meet consumer demands for the sort of material well-being and freedoms enjoyed in the West became evident. Accordingly, he vigorously opposed hawkish Cold War initiatives such as the establishment of the North Atlantic Treaty Organization, armed intervention in Vietnam, and the development of the hydrogen bomb as needless escalations that would only ensure a harsh Soviet response.

Appeasement: The misguided fear that conciliatory talks are a dangerous weakness.

Kennan was a prophet without a following—at least within the U.S. government. Secretary of State Dean Acheson told him to take his Quaker views to a more hospitable setting than he could possibly find in Washington. Kennan found a home in Princeton, N.J., at the Institute for Advanced Study, but vindication would not become fully evident until the close of the Cold War. As his life ended in 2005 at the age of 101, he was convinced more than ever that the tyranny of military containment had done little, if anything, to assure America's victory in that struggle. He saw the invasion of Iraq as another example of misplaced faith in a military solution to a political problem. In a September 2002 interview, a 98-year-old Kennan described Bush's talk of a pre-emptive war against Iraq as "a great mistake."

No postwar U.S. presidents were more mindful of the need to rely on diplomatic and political initiatives in fighting the Cold War than Dwight D. Eisenhower and John F. Kennedy. They understood that Truman's greatest foreign-policy successes were the Truman Doctrine, which committed U.S. financial aid to shoring up Greece and Turkey against communist subversion, and the Marshall Plan, which consisted of multi-billion-dollar grants to support European economies as a bar to communist political gains in Britain, France, the Netherlands, Belgium, Italy, and Scandinavia.

True, Eisenhower and Kennedy were not averse to using subversion to undermine unfriendly regimes in the Middle East and Latin America, as the historical record demonstrates in U.S.

dealings with Iran, Nicaragua, and Cuba during the 1950s and 1960s. Nor were they consistently wise in sanctioning clandestine operations that did not necessarily serve long-term U.S. interests. Both presidents, however, saw the reliance on direct military action to defeat the communists as a step too far. For all the rhetoric in the 1952 campaign about rollback and liberation (Adlai Stevenson has "a Ph.D. from Dean Acheson's cowardly college of communist containment," Richard Nixon taunted), Ike would not unleash America's military power to oust Kim Il Sung's communist regime from Pyongyang, as South Korea's Syngman Rhee and conservative Republicans in the United States urged. Nor would he support Hungary's attempt to throw off Soviet control in 1956 with armed intervention or rely on more than rhetorical threats to deter the Chinese from attacking Quemoy and Matsu, the islands between the Chinese mainland and Taiwan. And he resisted French pressure to intervene with air power to prevent defeat at Dien Bien Phu and the loss of Vietnam, which struck Eisenhower as an effort to involve the United States in a war Paris had already lost and America would not assuredly win.

Kennedy was as cautious as Eisenhower about relying on armed intervention to serve the national interest. Despite intense pressure from U.S. military chiefs in 1961 to rescue the Cuban insurgents at the Bay of Pigs by using American air power against Fidel Castro's forces, Kennedy rejected a direct U.S. part in the fighting. True, the invaders were U.S. surrogates armed and financed by the CIA, but Kennedy wisely concluded that the price of open U.S. intervention would be greater—a barrage of anti-American propaganda in the Third World—than the embarrassment from a defeat. During the 1962 Cuban missile crisis, the demands on Kennedy from his generals to bomb Soviet missile installations and invade the island to topple Castro were intense. But Kennedy insisted on a "quarantine" and diplomatic solution that, as we know now, saved the world from a devastating nuclear war.

Containment: The misguided belief in the surefire effectiveness of military strength.

Kennedy was also a reluctant supporter of expanded U.S. military action in Vietnam. At the same time he increased the number of U.S. military advisors in Saigon from roughly 700 to more than 16,000, he saw a commitment of U.S. ground troops to South Vietnam's defense as a potential trap that could shift the burden of the war to the United States and turn the conflict into another Korea. In the months before he was assassinated in November 1963, he directed Defense Secretary Robert McNamara to lay plans for the withdrawal of the advisors. (He also signed on to a coup by South Vietnamese generals against Ngo Dinh Diem's government, aiming to create a more stable political rule that would reduce the need for U.S. military intervention.) We will never know exactly what Kennedy would have done about Vietnam in a second term, but it seems unlikely that he would have followed Johnson's path.

As Kennedy told *New York Times* columnist Arthur Krock, "United States troops should not be involved on the Asian mainland." He warned Arthur Schlesinger, the historian and presidential advisor, that sending combat troops to Vietnam would place far greater demands on U.S. commitments than the public would tolerate and would not allow him to sustain public backing for other initiatives his administration might hope to take. The history of LBJ's presidency fully vindicates Kennedy's doubts.

Eisenhower and Kennedy have much to teach Obama and anyone else who becomes president; American leaders invariably confront such demands to use military force. The two men could resist that pressure because they were military heroes who could convince the public that they understood the use of armed strength better than domestic hawks urging action. Presidents without military records—like Obama—are at a disadvantage that they need to counter through vigorous rhetoric, a technique deployed with great success by the likes of leaders as Franklin D. Roosevelt and Ronald Reagan.

Counter it they must, for the metaphors that have dominated American thinking about foreign affairs over the last hundred years are not simply objects of historical curiosity. As Obama understands, they remain powerful engines of influence on decision-making about vital questions of war and peace. In trying to forge sensible responses to the challenges posed by Afghanistan, Iran, North Korea, and the persistent Israeli-Palestinian conflict, Obama knows that the shadows of past failures hang over him, whether the misguided belief in turning authoritarian adversaries into Jeffersonian democrats or the false choice of favoring militant containment over anything that even remotely resembles appeasement. His room to maneuver is therefore limited—at least if he hopes to act with the sort of public support required to put across his domestic agenda while also moving boldly to tame international dangers.

Obama seems keenly aware of the main lesson of Vietnam: Don't let the appeasement metaphor, cliché, conviction, call it what you will, lock you into an unwinnable war that destroys your presidency. He appreciates that a grand design or strategy in foreign affairs does not readily translate from one crisis to another. Appeasement was a terrible idea in dealing with Hitler, but avoiding it was never the right argument for crossing the 38th parallel in Korea or embroiling the United States in Vietnam. (After all, a stalemate in the first war and a defeat in the second did not deter the United States from winning the larger Cold War). Nor is Obama persuaded by grand Wilsonian visions of bringing democracy to Iraq and Afghanistan; he has made clear that he does not see military solutions to the problems America faces in those two countries. He has openly described the invasion of Iraq as a "mistake" and seems determined to de-escalate U.S. involvement in Afghanistan as soon as possible.

But no matter how conscious Obama is of the perils of history's traps, he faces no small challenge in convincing political opponents to relinquish the outworn foreign-policy clichés that have been of such questionable service to America's well-being. As Germany's Otto von Bismarck is said to have observed more than 100 years ago, great statesmen have the ability to hear, before anyone else, the distant hoofbeats of the horse of history. More often than not, however, it is the accepted wisdoms—or the wrong lessons of history altogether—that govern the thinking of publics and the behavior of their leaders.

Critical Thinking

1. What are the three historical myths that have, according to Robert Dallek, led American presidents astray in foreign and national security policy for the past century or so?

2. What are examples of each historical myth leading to unfavorable consequences for the U.S. in the world?

3. What experience did Presidents Eisenhower and Kennedy share that advantaged them—in the national security sphere—over presidents such as Barack Obama and George W. Bush?

Presidential historian **ROBERT DALLEK** *is author, most recently, of* The Lost Peace; Leadership in a Time of Horror and Hope, 1945–1953.

Worth Fighting—or Not

In judging which of its dozen major wars America should have fought, *unintended consequences* often outweigh the intended ones.

BURT SOLOMON

War is hell, but it can also be useful as hell. Even if that isn't always obvious at the time. Ponder, for a moment, the War of 1812. When the fledgling United States of America repulsed the British—again—in 1815, the war "felt like a loss or a tie," according to Allan Millett, a military historian at the University of New Orleans. The torch had been put to the Capitol and the White House, and the Battle of Baltimore produced the lyrics of a National Anthem that generations of Americans would struggle to sing. The Americans hadn't won; the British had lost.

Only as the years passed did it become clear that the war had truly served the United States as a Second War of Independence. It forced Britain to respect its former colony's sovereignty; helped to nudge the Spanish out of Florida; persuaded the European colonial powers to accept the Louisiana Purchase and to stop aiding the Indians, thereby opening the way to Western expansion; and prepared the geopolitical groundwork for the Monroe Doctrine. Not for another 186 years, until September 11, 2001, would the continental United States suffer a foreign attack.

"In the long run," Millett judged, "it worked out."

Unintended consequences can also work in the other direction, of course. Consider the following zigzag of events. The humiliating American defeat in the Vietnam War may have encouraged the Soviet Union's adventurism, notably its invasion of Afghanistan in 1979, four years after North Vietnamese troops seized control of South Vietnam. The Afghan mujahedeen eventually drove the Soviets out, with the covert support of the United States, as dramatized in the 2007 movie *Charlie Wilson's War*. The playboy member of Congress, a Texas Democrat, prevailed upon Israel, Egypt, Saudi Arabia, Pakistan, and the U.S. Congress to cough up billions of dollars and untraceable weaponry.

But recall the movie's penultimate scene, when Wilson fails to persuade his fellow House appropriators to spend a pittance to rebuild Afghan schools, in hopes of reconstructing a land left broken by war and occupation. The resulting power vacuum allowed the Taliban to emerge as the mountainous nation's militantly Islamic rulers, offering sanctuary and succor to Al Qaeda as it prepared its terrorist attacks on New York City and Arlington, Va., on 9/11. Surely, the best and brightest who botched the Vietnam War hadn't given the slightest thought to backward Afghanistan or to the World Trade Center's twin towers, which were dedicated just six days after the last U.S. troops withdrew from Vietnam in 1973.

Bunker Hill to Baghdad

Revolutionary War
War of 1812
Mexican War
Civil War
Spanish-American
WWI
WWII
Korean War
Vietnam War
Persian Gulf War
War in Afghanistan
War in Iraq

- All wars, in a sense, are **wars of choice.**
- The smaller wars the U.S. has fought often turned out pretty well: **low cost with high impact.**
- Vietnam is the war from which the **fewest benefits** seem to have flowed, historians say.

Sometimes, the desirability of a particular war will rise and fall over time. When Chou En-lai, the Chinese premier, was asked to assess the French Revolution fought nearly two centuries before, he famously replied: "It is too early to say." Consider the oscillating historical verdicts on the Mexican War. President Polk and Mexican dictator Santa Anna "were as combustible a combo as [Bush] 43 and Saddam," said Philip Zelikow, a historian at the University of Virginia who was a foreign-policy adviser for both Presidents Bush. When the war ended in 1848, it was counted as a clear-cut American success, assuring that Texas would remain part of the United States and adding territories that became the states of Arizona, California, and New Mexico. But after 1850, this territorial expansion reignited the political battles over slavery that the war's opponents (including a one-term member of Congress named Abraham Lincoln) had feared, thereby accelerating the descent into civil war. But that was then. Now, with the Civil War long past, it is hard to imagine the United States without the former chunks of Mexico. At least it was—until Texas Gov. Rick Perry, a Republican, raised the possibility recently that his state might want to secede from the U.S.

With occasional exceptions, the minor wars that the United States has waged from time to time have worked out pretty much as hoped. From the Barbary pirates to Grenada to Bosnia and Kosovo, clear objectives and a sufficiency of military force led to success at a low cost. But in America's 12 major wars during its 233 years of independence, things have rarely played out as expected, in the aftermath of the conflicts if not during them.

Historians, probably wisely, are wary of balancing the costs and benefits of America's past wars and delivering a bottom-line judgment. But if pressed, they'll divide them into a few "good" wars, especially the American Revolution, the Civil War, and World War II; several muddled wars; and a real stinker, Vietnam, the only one that America has lost outright.

Which brings us, of course, to the two wars that the United States is fighting now. There are reasons for hope and reasons for skepticism about the likely outcome of both. The war in Afghanistan, which President Obama has escalated, threatens to become the first war of necessity that the United States loses, especially if the nation next door, nuclear-armed Pakistan, devolves into chaos. In Iraq, the prospect of a reasonably stable, tolerably democratic regime has grown. But even in the unlikelier event that Iraq becomes a beacon of democracy for a mostly despotic Middle East, because of the high costs—including the encouragement of a nuclear-armed Iran and an ebb in American influence—some foreign-policy experts doubt that history will ever judge the Iraq war as worth the fight.

Apples and Oranges

How to judge a war? Let us count the ways.

Thucydides, the historian of ancient Greece who chronicled the Peloponnesian War, categorized wars by the aggressor's motivation for starting them—namely, fear, honor, and interests. In judging the importance of the national interest, "most people put it first, and they're mostly wrong," said Donald Kagan, a professor of classics and history at Yale University. "It's way down the list." Alarm at foreigners' intentions and, especially, feelings of dishonor are more often the main reasons that nations go to war, he says.

Another way of judging the usefulness of a war is by assessing the need for it. In *War of Necessity, War of Choice: A Memoir of Two Iraq Wars,* published in May, Richard Haass distinguishes between a necessary Persian Gulf war, in 1991, when he served on the staff of President George H.W. Bush's National Security Council, and an unnecessary invasion of Iraq begun in 2003, while he directed the State Department's policy planning. A war of necessity, in his thinking, is one that involves a vital national interest and in which military force is the only option that might succeed—judgments that entail "elements of subjectivity," Haass, who is now president of the Council on Foreign Relations, noted in an interview. Rare, after all, is the war that its proponents don't try to sell to the public as essential, even when it isn't. Zelikow, who served as the executive director of the bipartisan commission that examined 9/11, is skeptical of the distinction. "It takes a post facto argument and makes it sound like objective history," he said. "The only war we did not choose is the one that was brought to New York City on 9/11."

Maybe the purest way of judging a war is to contemplate whether it is just or unjust to fight, an exercise most usefully pursued before the shooting starts. Michael Walzer, a political philosopher and

professor emeritus at the Institute for Advanced Study in Princeton, N.J., is the author of *Just and Unjust Wars,* published in 1977 in the wake of Vietnam. The factors in figuring a war's justice are a mix of morality and fact, taking into account whether a nation was attacked or is (credibly) about to be attacked; its efforts to find peaceful solutions; the international or legal legitimacy of its military response; its likelihood of success; and, once a war has begun, the conduct of the fighting.

But these judgments, too, are "different," Walzer acknowledged in an interview, from the practical considerations—measured in lives, treasure, territory, security, and power—that determine whether a nation benefits, on balance, from starting or entering a war. Indeed, neither the justice nor the necessity of a war bears more than an incidental correlation to whether, in hindsight, it was worth fighting. Walzer regards the Mexican War, for instance, as an "unjust war that worked out well," for the United States at least. In Haass's mind, the American Revolution probably ought to be counted as a war of choice, though a "warranted" one that should have been fought. Even a war of choice can be worth fighting—it's just that "the standards are higher," he said—if its benefits sufficiently exceed its costs, measured both in the short and longer term.

"Each had benefits," said Mackubin Owens, a professor of strategy and force planning at the U.S. Naval War College, referring to the major wars that the United States has fought. The problem for decision makers, of course, is that neither costs nor benefits can be known with any certainty—or even good guesswork—in advance. A war's consequences, more often than not, are unfathomable. Even afterward, as any fair-minded historian will attest, it is no easy task to judge. Start with the impossibility of placing a value on the lives lost and disrupted; take into account the improbability of divining the future; and imagine the necessarily speculative character of the counterfactuals—what would have happened had the war not broken out. This is far beyond the reach of any mathematical or actuarial formulation.

Worse, weighing the costs and benefits of a war is an exercise in comparing apples and oranges. Consider the war in Korea, which lasted from 1950 to '53. The U.S.-led combat to repel Communist North Korea's invasion of anti-communist (though autocratic) South Korea proved popular with the American public at first. But that support soured, especially when an armistice settled on virtually the same boundary between the two Koreas that existed when the war began, at the cost of 36,574 American lives. Nonetheless, as the Cold War went on, it became clear that in this first test of resolve after World War II, the U.S. willingness to stand up to Communist aggressiveness cooled Soviet strongman Joseph Stalin's geopolitical ambitions and kept South Korea—and Japan—allied with the West. "I thought it was a just war at the time," Walzer recounted, and "I think it probably helped in the eventual victory over communism."

Andrew Bacevich, a professor of international relations at Boston University, agrees—up to a point. "The initial U.S. response to Korea was a war that we needed to fight," he said. But a crucial mistake was made in conducting it: President Truman's decision to acquiesce in Gen. Douglas MacArthur's desire to invade the North drew Communist China into the war and ultimately produced a stalemate. The consequences, Bacevich said, went beyond the estimated 30,000 additional American Millet to include two decades of enmity between the United States and China—until President Nixon opened the door in 1972—and a failure to exploit the Sino-Soviet schism in a manner that might have weakened the Soviet

U.S. Wars: Worth Fighting?

Historians, if pressed, will divide America's wars into a few "good" wars—especially the American Revolution, the Civil War, and World War II; several muddled wars; and a real stinker, Vietnam.

	Revolutionary War (1775–83)	War of 1812 (1812–15)	Mexican War (1846–48)	Civil War (1861–65)	Spanish-American War (1898–99)	World War I (1917–18*)	World War II (1941–45*)	Korean War (1950–53)	Vietnam War (1964–73)	Persian Gulf War (1990–91)	War in Afghanistan (2001–)	War in Iraq (2003–)
Strategic Benefits	Won independence	Gained recognition of Louisiana Purchase, lessened Indian threat, laid groundwork for Monroe Doctrine	Assured Texas as a state, seized New Mexico, Arizona, California	Preserved the Union, ended slavery	Incorporated Puerto Rico and Hawaii, assured U.S. predominance in Americas	Emerged as world power	Defeated Nazi Germany and Japan	Discouraged Communist aggression, kept Japan and South Korea as U.S. allies	None	Blocked Saddam Hussein from threatening Saudi oil	Ousted Al Qaeda from camps	Created U.S. ally in Arab Middle East
Strategic Cost	Tories punished, Indians harmed	Failed to gain control of Canada	Inflamed debate over slavery	Devastation	Annexation of the Philippines brought conflict with Japan	Diplomatic aftermath led to World War II	Enabled Soviet hegemony in Eastern Europe, Cold War	Led to two decades of antipathy with mainland China	First U.S. defeat, reduced diplomatic influence, caused domestic discord	Left Saddam in power	Destabilized Pakistan	Diminished American influence, emboldened Iran
American Deaths (total serving)	25,324 (290,000)	2,260 (286,730)	13,283 (78,718)	498,332 (3,713,363)	2,446 (306,760)	116,516 (4,734,991)	405,399 (16,112,566)	36,574 (1,789,000**)	58,209 (3,403,000**)	382 (694,550**)	685† (More than 1.9 million troops have served in these wars since 9/11)	4,294†
Financial Cost (in billions of constant 2008 dollars)	$1.8	$1.2	$1.8	$60.4	$6.8	$253	$4,114	$320	$686	$96	$189††	$642††

* Duration of U.S. involvement.

** In war zone only.

† As of May 30, 2009.

†† Does not include $75.5 billion in supplemental war funding requested in April 2009.

Sources: Oxford Companion to American Military History; Defense Department; Congressional Research Service.

Union and bolstered the West. "It sent us down a path," he pointed out, "that cast the decision to go in in a different light." Bacevich cautioned against trying to arrive at "concise judgments" about the desirability of the Korean—or any—War.

The "Good" Wars

The nation's first war, for its independence, was probably its most essential—and successful. King George III had committed "a long Train of Abuses and Usurpations," as Thomas Jefferson detailed in the Declaration of Independence, even as the Founding Draftsman glossed over perhaps the most threatening of the British monarchy's tyrannical acts. Yale's Kagan cited Britain's efforts, from 1763 on, to impose taxes and restrictions that suppressed the commercial ambitions of an entrepreneurial people. Hence the impulse for independence.

Still, only a third of the colonists, historians estimate, supported a rebellion against their British masters; a third remained loyal to the Crown and the rest were ambivalent or indifferent. Many of the Tories paid a price for their loyalty, Bacevich noted, in having to knuckle under or flee. The continent's aboriginal inhabitants likewise did not fare well. Conceivably, the colonists might have acted like their neighbors to the north—Canada waited until 1867 to obtain self-government from Britain without shedding blood—although it is daunting to find anyone who would make that case today.

The Civil War, pitting brother against brother, produced a more vehement diversity of opinion, at the time and ever since. The war was probably unavoidable, most historians say, given the conflicts between the North and the South in their economies—with or without slavery—and their cultures. Had the conflict not broken out in 1861, they suppose, it would have happened later. And by the time the Civil War ended, it accomplished more than its participants had imagined. Early on, President Lincoln declared that he was willing to keep slavery or to end it, in whole or in part, as long as the Union was preserved; the Emancipation Proclamation referred to abolition in the rebellious states as a matter of "military necessity."

Had the South successfully seceded, historians debate whether slavery would have faded out on its own as the soil in the cotton fields was depleted, or, rather, would have spread to states farther west and into Latin America. A popular theme in counterfactual histories posits that the Confederacy and the Union would have reunited eventually. In any event, slavery would presumably have ended sometime (Brazil became the last country in the Western Hemisphere to abolish it, in 1888), although maybe not quickly enough for a slow-changing electorate to choose an African-American president in 2008. But was an earlier end of slavery "worth 600,000 deaths? It's hard to say," concluded Max Boot, a senior fellow at the Council on Foreign Relations. "There wasn't a lot of whooping for joy in 1865. Wars look better when the human costs have faded into history."

"There wasn't a lot of *whooping for joy* in 1865. Wars look better when the human costs have faded into history."

—Max Boot

The classic "good" war, fought by the Greatest Generation, was good ol' Double-U-Double-U-Two. The United States had to be dragged into the Second World War—until the Japanese bombed Pearl Harbor—over the isolationists' objections that the fighting in Europe and Asia was, for a nation protected by oceans, a war of choice. Before it ended, the human costs were staggering, estimated at more than 72 million deaths worldwide, including 405,399 Americans. But the benefits, historians say, were mightier still: the defeat of Hitler's Germany, with its ambitions to control Europe and beyond, and the end of Japan's brutal imperialism across the Far East.

Nonetheless, World War II can be blamed for an unintended consequence—and it was a biggie. The defeat of Nazi Germany left a power vacuum, especially in Eastern Europe, that for nearly a half-century allowed the Soviet Union to have its way. A strong Germany, BU's Bacevich said, would have restrained Soviet aggression, but America's entry ensured Germany's defeat. The United States was drawn into the Cold War, featuring an Iron Curtain, a nuclear arms race, the Berlin airlift, hot wars in Korea and Vietnam, the Cuban missile crisis, and decades of living on the brink of World War III. So which would have better served U.S. interests after World War II: victory by a hegemonic Stalin, or by a genocidal Hitler? Pick your poison.

Wars of Confusion

Something else troubles historians in recounting World War II: It might have been avoided. Winston Churchill, Britain's wartime prime minister and a historian in his own right, described it as a necessary war that shouldn't have been fought.

But it was, and historians blame the sloppy diplomacy that marked the end of World War I. The United States, had it accepted the Treaty of Versailles, would have joined with Britain and France in policing the European peace, presumably to block Hitler from remilitarizing the Rhineland in 1936. That would have prompted the German generals to fire him as chancellor, Kagan said, and "Hitler would never have risen to power." An intransigent President Wilson, unwilling to accept Senate skeptics' reservations about the treaty, is usually accorded the bulk of the blame.

For historians with a taste for slapstick, World War I is the classic case of diplomatic bungling that leads to an unnecessary war. In Lenin's view, both sides were engaged in an imperialist war, trying to carve up spheres of influence. For the European powers, the war proved pointlessly destructive.

But not necessarily for the United States. "The U.S. might have limited the damage of World War I if it had credibly prepared to intervene in 1916 and used that threat to mediate negotiations that leaders on both sides wanted," according to Zelikow. It didn't. But by entering the war in 1917, almost three years after it started in Europe, American troops ended the military stalemate, defeating Kaiser Wilhelm's aggressiveness and bringing the conflict to a triumphal conclusion.

Historians disagree over what might have happened had Germany prevailed. Years later, a German historian found archival evidence that the kaiser's ambitions for a "Greater Germany" extended into Russia and France. The power of a militarily mighty, scientifically advanced, boldly affluent Germany might have blocked—or at least complicated—the emergence of America as a world power. But Walter McDougall, a professor of history and international relations at the University of Pennsylvania, contends that it also would have meant "no Bolshevism, no Holocaust, perhaps no World War II, atomic weapons, or Cold War."

As it happened, WWI fell laughably short of Wilson's idealistic hopes for a war that would end all wars and would make the world safe for democracy. Yet America benefited greatly. Its 19 months at war "gave the U.S. more diplomatic leverage than it probably deserved," military historian Millett said. The war's devastation in Europe held an extra benefit for the United States: It ensured an economic superiority over Germany and Britain, the strongmen of the prewar world, that America has never relinquished.

America's emergence onto the international scene had begun during its previous war. As with World War I, the Spanish-American War of 1898 has given historians fits. Driven by domestic politics in the United States as well as in Spain, it was set off by the typically American blur between idealism and naked self-interest. The Spanish brutalities in Cuba spurred William Randolph Hearst to sell his newspapers by inspiring American intervention in a situation on its doorstep. On a Friday afternoon, after his boss had knocked off for the weekend, the imperialist-minded assistant Navy secretary—Theodore Roosevelt, by name—ordered some battleships moved closer to the Philippines. The result was a quick and relatively bloodless conflict that was "clearly a war of expansion," said Edward (Mac) Coffman, a retired military historian at the University of Wisconsin. It freed Cuba from Spanish rule and, according to Owens at the Naval War College, "basically made it clear that we're the dominant power in the Western Hemisphere. Now we had a seagoing Navy capable of projecting power and an ability to defend the Monroe Doctrine."

The war against Spain probably benefited, on balance, the inhabitants of Puerto Rico and Hawaii by bringing them under U.S. control. But some historians discern a downside in America's trophy of the war. "The annexation of the Philippines created a 'hostage' that the Japanese could attack at will," Millett said. "Long-term, it was a political and strategic disaster," one that put the United States "crosswise" with Japan, fueling an antipathy that exploded on December 7, 1941. The Bataan Death March, in 1942, was another unintended consequence.

Julian Zelizer, a historian at Princeton University, posits a longer-term cost of the Spanish-American War. It was a turning point for the United States, he said, in establishing an "expansionist model" for wielding its influence overseas. He sees in it the roots of another, sadder war seven decades later in Vietnam.

"The annexation of the Philippines created a 'hostage' that the Japanese could attack at will. Long-term, it was a *political and strategic disaster.*"

—Allan Millett, on the Spanish-American War

The Ugliest War

The widely ridiculed "domino effect," so often invoked by Lyndon Johnson in making his case for the Vietnam War, wasn't in itself a stupid idea. "A number of dominoes fell," Graham Allison, a professor of government at Harvard University and former Pentagon adviser, pointed out. Communism's advance in Vietnam ushered in a Communist regime in Laos (which remains in power, as it does in Vietnam) and another, far more virulent version in Cambodia.

Yeah, so? Even if the United States had won in Vietnam, historians say, the benefits wouldn't have been worth the costs. A pro-Western regime in South Vietnam wouldn't have mattered. Thailand and Indonesia would be just about the same. "I lost 58,000 colleagues," said Owens, a Marine veteran of Vietnam who was wounded twice. Tallying up the economic costs and the turmoil in the streets at home, he now concludes that the war probably wasn't worth fighting. ("Though who could say that [the turmoil] wouldn't have happened anyway?") Internationally, the defeat in Vietnam contributed to the image of the United States, which had never lost a war, as a paper tiger.

The miscalculations made in conducting the war are legendary, starting with the "ludicrous" assumption (as Allison put it) among U.S. decision makers that North Vietnam was acting as an agent for China, its enemy of many centuries' standing. A tour of the Hanoi Hilton that showcases John McCain's Navy uniform at the end begins with a guillotine dating from the 19th-century days of French colonial rule. The Americans who decided on the war failed to understand the enemy, a mistake they would make again in Iraq.

"The threat was not real, the death toll was so big, and it affected the U.S. role in the world," Princeton's Zelizer said. "A pretty big catastrophe."

Who was to blame? President Eisenhower comes in for the greatest share from historians. By backing the French as they were being driven out of Vietnam and committing Washington to support a corrupt and unpopular government in Saigon, Yale's Kagan said, Eisenhower made it politically dangerous for Presidents Kennedy and Johnson to back away from Vietnam without seeming soft on communism. In private (though taped) conversations with Sen. Richard Russell, D-Ga., who was a friend, Johnson sounded far more ambivalent about a war that ultimately ruined his presidency and drove him from the White House.

Two Iraq Wars

After the moral morass of Vietnam came the clarity of the Persian Gulf War. When Iraqi troops invaded Kuwait in 1990 and British Prime Minister Margaret Thatcher prevailed on Bush 41 not to go "wobbly," the carefully planned and well-executed war fulfilled Bush's vow: "This will not stand." Kuwait regained its freedom, and Saddam Hussein's forces were forced back across the border into Iraq. With only 382 Americans killed, the United States accomplished a lot at a relatively low cost.

"It would have been a disaster if Saddam Hussein had kept Kuwait," because it would have furthered his progress toward development of a nuclear bomb and destabilized the Middle East, according to Boot of the Council on Foreign Relations. For the United States, something even more vital was at stake. "It was about oil," said Harvard's Allison, citing the fear that the Iraqi dictator would march his troops beyond Kuwait and into Saudi Arabia, in hopes of manipulating the world's—and America's—oil supply. The invasion did not stand. Threat undone.

Yet Bush's famed prudence, reflected in his decision not to chase the Iraqi army back to Baghdad or to oust Saddam from power, took on a different cast during his son's presidency a dozen years later. With a half-million U.S. troops already on the scene, the elder

Bush might have had an easier time changing the Baghdad regime than George W. Bush did. The unfinished business of the first Iraq war led, as events (and perhaps a father-and-son psychodrama) unfolded, to the second, harder war.

The two military ventures showed that the political appeal of a war bears little relationship to its utility. "Iraq I passed the Senate by only five votes and was absolutely right," Zelikow said. "Iraq II passed the Senate by 50 votes and was iffy."

The younger Bush might have tried other, less costly ways to alter Iraqi behavior. An assassination or a coup could have sufficed to change the leadership. Or, Haass wrote, "the United States could well have accomplished a change in regime behavior and a change in regime threat without regime change." The costs of the six-year-long war have exceeded 4,300 American military deaths, a price tag of nearly $1 trillion or beyond—and something less tangible but perhaps more consequential. "Iraq contributed to the emergence of a world in which power is more widely distributed than ever before," Haass maintained, "and U.S. ability to shape this world much diminished."

So, will the potential benefits of the second Iraq war ever be judged worth the price? On that, the jury is out. It could take 10 or 20 or 30 years, foreign-policy experts say, to determine whether the Iraqi government functions as a democracy that is able to bring stability, without a dictator's iron hand, to a nation of sectarian hatreds. Proponents say that the odds of a tolerably good outcome are about even.

But *how* good an outcome is still possible seems harder to gauge. The neoconservative enthusiasts for the Iraq war (along with the likes of *New York Times* columnist Thomas Friedman) envisioned a shining democracy in a reborn nation that would inspire the undoing of Islamic autocracies across the Middle East. Haass believes that such a goal has become "unreachable." Whether anything less would produce enough benefits to make the war ultimately worth fighting will depend, at least in part, on the price. Haass said he sees no plausible scenario by which the direct and indirect costs of the war wouldn't outweigh its benefits. U.S. mistreatment of Iraqi insurgents at Abu Ghraib prison and the indefinite detention of accused enemy combatants at Guantanamo Bay sullied America's good-guy image across the Muslim world (and elsewhere) and surely led to the recruitment of additional terrorists.

Potentially, the most perilous of these costs extend beyond Iraq's borders. The chaos of war and the rise to power of Iraq's Shiite majority have emboldened the imperial ambitions of Shiite-dominated Iran. Moises Naim, the editor of *Foreign Policy*, fears that the Iraq war has encouraged Iran to develop nuclear weaponry, which in turn could inspire Egypt, Saudi Arabia, and possibly Arab Gulf states to do the same. "Is a shining, democratic Iraq," he asked, "worth a neighborhood full of nuclear bombs?"

War(s) of Necessity

Another cost of the Iraq war has been the distractions it has caused, not only in Iran and North Korea, which is pursuing a nuclear program of its own, but also Afghanistan. Barack Obama repeatedly leveled such a charge about the neglect of America's other ongoing war during his 2008 campaign. As president, he has announced the deployment of an additional 17,000 troops to Afghanistan, ousted his top general on the scene, and—in next year's budget, for the first time—has proposed to spend more Defense Department money in Afghanistan than in Iraq. Invading Afghanistan after 9/11 was widely considered necessary, not only to clean out Al Qaeda's camps but also to ensure a stable government that wouldn't give terrorists safe haven again.

"We had to do it, no matter what," Boot said. "Even if it doesn't work, no one will fault Bush [for invading], though maybe for how he fought it." Experts on all sides say that the war is "losable," as Kagan put it, but they're hopeful that it isn't too late to change tactics and win. This was evidently the Obama administration's motivation in recently replacing the cautious American commander in the field with an advocate of counterinsurgency.

Haass, for one, no longer regards the war in Afghanistan as essential to U.S. national security. As long as the American military continues to strike at terrorist-related targets, the United States could accept a "messy outcome" in Afghanistan, he said, one that allows the Taliban to make some political inroads in a civil war. Afghanistan has evolved from a war of necessity, Haass said, into "Mr. Obama's war of choice."

But there is plenty of reason to worry about the deteriorating situation just beyond Afghanistan's borders. In the muddled Afghan war, "what's at stake is Pakistan anyway," military historian Millett said. The nuclear-armed nation, with its shaky democratic government, is facing the Taliban on the doorstep of Islamabad, the Pakistani capital. Should Pakistan's government collapse or if any of its nuclear weapons fall into the wrong hands, the United States could well find itself in yet another war of necessity, one that would prove treacherous to lose.

Critical Thinking

1. What has been the most common result of the small wars the U.S. has fought? What has been the predominant outcome of the large wars it has fought?

2. Why is calculating the potential and actual costs and benefits of a war so difficult? How do "unintended consequences" often overshadow intentions?

3. What wars are widely considered to be "good wars" in U.S. history? What characterizes these wars?

4. What are some of the potential long-term costs and benefits of the current U.S. war in Iraq?

5. What is a "war of necessity" compared with a "war of choice?"

bsolomon@nationaljournal.com.

Back to Normalcy

Is America really in decline?

Paul Kennedy

Where on earth is the United States headed? Has it lost its way? Is the Obama effect, which initially promised to halt the souring of its global image, over? More seriously, is it in some sort of terminal decline? Has it joined the long historical list of number one powers that rose to the top, and then, as Rudyard Kipling outlined it, just slowly fell downhill: "Lo, all our pomp of yesterday/At one with Nineveh and Tyre"? Has it met its match in Afghanistan? And has its obsession with the ill-defined war on terrorism obscured attention to the steady, and really much more serious, rise of China to the center of the world's stage? Will the dollar fall and fall, like the pound sterling from the 1940s to the 1970s?

It is easy to say "yes" to all those questions, and there are many in Latin America, Europe, the Middle East, Asia, and in the United States itself, who do so. But there is another way to think about America's current position in today's mightily complicated world, and it goes like this: All that is happening, really, is that the United States is slowly and naturally losing its abnormal status in the international system and returning to being one of the most prominent players in the small club of great powers. Things are not going badly wrong, and it is not as if America as becoming a flawed and impotent giant. Instead, things are just coming back to normal.

How would this more reassuring argument go? Well, we might start with a historical comparison. In about 1850, as the historian Eric Hobsbawm points out in his great work *Industry and Empire,* the small island-state of Britain produced perhaps two-thirds of the world's coal, half its iron, five-sevenths of its steel, and half of its commercial cotton cloth.

This extraordinary position was indeed abnormal; that is, it could not last forever. And as soon as countries with bigger populations and resources (Germany, the United States, Russia, Japan) organized themselves along British lines, it was natural that they would produce a larger share of world product and take a larger share of world power and thus cut Britain's share back down to a more normal condition. This is a story which economic and political historians take for granted. It is about the tides of history and the shifts of power that occur when productive strength moves from one part of the world to another. It's actually a sensible way of thinking about history over the long term.

So why should we not look at America, and America's present and future condition, in the same calm way? It is of course a much broader and more populous country than Britain was and is, and possesses far more natural resources, but the long-term trajectory is roughly the same. After 1890, the United States had slowly overtaken the British Empire as the world's number one by borrowing critical technologies (the steam engine, the railway, the textile factory), and then adding on its own contributions in chemical and electrical industries, and blazing the way in automobile and aircraft and computer hardware/software production. It was assisted by the good fortune of its geographic distance from any other great power (as Britain was by its insularity), and by the damage done elsewhere by World Wars I and II (as Britain was by the damage done elsewhere by the Revolutionary and Napoleonic wars). By 1945, therefore, America possessed around half of the world's GNP, an amazing share, but no less than Britain's a century earlier when it held most of the world's steam engines. But it was a special historical moment in both cases. When other countries began to play catch-up, these high shares of world power would decline.

In the American case, we might tease out this argument by returning to a point made almost 20 years ago by the Harvard scholar Joseph Nye, that America's strength and influence in world affairs was like a sturdy three-legged stool; that is, the nation's unchallenged place rested upon the mutually reinforcing legs of soft power, economic power, and military power. In all three dimensions, Nye suggested, the United States was comfortably ahead of any other competitor. Global shares of relative strength were being diffused, perhaps, but in no way enough to shake America's dominant role.

How does this assessment look today? Of the three legs to Nye's stool, soft power—the capacity to persuade other nations to do what America would like—looks the shakiest. This is not a measure of strength that can be computed statistically, like steel output or defense spending, so subjective impressions enter into the debate. Nevertheless, would anyone dispute the contention that America's ability to influence other states (such as Brazil, Russia, China, India) has declined during the past two decades? When Nye wrote, he pointed to the significance of popular culture (Hollywood, blue jeans), the dominance of the English language, the increasing standardization of U.S. business (from chain hotels to accounting rules), and the spread of democracy, all as signs of America's influence.

Those were interesting thoughts, but we have since seen that radical students from Ankara to Amsterdam can still wear blue jeans but demonstrate against the United States, and that it is quite possible that a totally free voting system in (say) Egypt, Saudi Arabia, and China would lead to parliamentary majorities highly critical of Washington's policies. The Pew Foundation's regular poll of global opinion suggests diminishing approval of America, despite a short-term upward blip in favor of Obama. Soft power comes and goes very fast.

As to the weakening of the second leg of the stool, America's relative economic and foreign-currency heft, well, a person would have had to have been blind and deaf not to observe its obvious deterioration in recent years. If anything surprises me, it is how fast and how large the relative weakening has been: A truly competitive great power should not have its trade deficits widening so fast, nor its federal, state, and municipal deficits ballooning at such a pace, literally, into the trillions of dollars. It is unsustainable, although that fact has been obscured by the thousands of American economists and investment advisers who emit positive noises to their clients and who themselves simply cannot think strategically. The collective folly of portfolio advisers is compounded by the current congressional baying for China's currency to get stronger and stronger and stronger. Is that what the United States really wants—to get relatively weaker? At a certain stage in the past 500-year history of currencies and power, the Dutch guilder hustled the Spanish escudo off the scene; then the pound sterling hustled the guilder (and franc and mark) off the scene; then the dollar hustled the pound off the scene. What is Washington risking as it presses for a stronger Chinese currency? My apprehension is that it risks a much stronger Chinese political influence in the world.

America's military strengths are, by contrast, still remarkable; at least this one leg of the stool is sturdy. But how sturdy? Well, almost half of the world's current defense expenditures come from the United States, so it is not surprising that it possesses a gigantic aircraft carrier Navy, a substantial Army and Marine Corps that can be deployed all over the globe, an ultra high-tech Air Force, and logistical and intelligence-gathering facilities that have no equal. This is the strongest leg of the three. But it is not going unchallenged, and in several regards.

The first is in the rise of irregular or "asymmetrical" warfare by non-state actors. Anyone who has seen the recent award-winning movie *The Hurt Locker,* about the U.S. Army's uncomfortable and bloody experiences in Iraq, will know what this means. It means that the narrow streets of Fallujah, or, even more, the high passes of the Helmand mountains, equalize the struggle; high-tech doesn't quite work against a suicide bomber or a cunningly placed road mine. General Patton's style of warfare just doesn't succeed when you are no longer running your tanks through Lorraine but creeping, damaged and wincing, through the Khyber Pass. Sophisticated drones are, actually, stupid. They help avoid making the commitment to winning on the ground, and they will eventually lose.

Secondly, there is the emergence, along the historical pattern of the rise and fall of the great powers, of new challenger nations that are pushing into America's post-1945 geopolitical space. Putin's Russia is clawing back its historic zones of control and, frankly, there seems little that Washington can do if Belarus or a kicking-and-screaming Latvia is reabsorbed by the Kremlin. India is intent on making the term "Indian Ocean" not just a geographic expression; in ten or 20 years' time, if its plans are fulfilled, it will be in control. Which is rather comforting, because it will thwart China's purposeful though clumsy efforts to acquire much-needed African mineral supplies. But China, in its turn, and through its very new and sophisticated weapons systems (disruptive electronic warfare, silent submarines, sea-skimming missiles), may soon possess the capacity to push the U.S. Navy away from China's shores. Like it or not, America is going to be squeezed out of Asia.

Overall, and provided the gradual reduction of America's extensive footprint across Asia can occur through mutual agreements and uninterrupted economic links, that may not be a bad thing. Few, if any, Asian governments want the United States to pull out now, or abruptly, but most assume it will cease to be such a prominent player in the decades to come. Why not start that discussion now, or begin a rethink? American hopes of reshaping Asia sometimes look curiously like former British hopes of reshaping the Middle East. Don't go there.

Finally, and most serious of all, there is America's dangerous and growing reliance upon other governments to fund its own national deficits. Military strength cannot rest upon pillars of sand; it cannot be reliant, not forever, upon foreign lenders. The president, in his increasingly lonely White House, and the increasingly ineffective Congress, seem unable to get a harsh but decent fiscal package together. And now, the Tea Party nutcases are demanding a tax-cut-and-spend policy that would make the famous Mad Hatter's tea party itself look rather rational.

This is not a way to run a country, and especially not the American nation that, despite its flaws, is the world's mainstay. This is worrying for its neighbors, its many friends and allies; it is worrying for even those states, like India and Brazil, that are going to assume a larger role in world affairs in the years to come. We should all be careful to wish away a reasonably benign American hegemony; we might regret its going.

But the ebb and tides of history will take away that hegemony, as surely as autumn replaces the high summer months with fruit rather than flower. America's global position is at present strong, serious, and very large. But it is still, frankly, abnormal. It will come down a ratchet or two more.

It will return from being an oversized world power to being a big nation, but one which needs to be listened to, and one which, for the next stretch, is the only country that can supply powerful heft to places in trouble. It will still be really important, but less so than it was. That isn't a bad thing. It will be more normal.

Critical Thinking

1. What are the key parallels between Britain's place in world affairs in the mid-19th century and that of the United States today?

2. What are the three legs of the "three-legged stool" on which a nation-state's status in world affairs is said to rest?

How is the contemporary U.S. faring with respect to each leg?

3. What does it mean to say that the standing and role of the U.S. in world affairs has been "abnormal" for the past half-century or more? What is the title of the piece, "Back to Normalcy," meant to convey?

PAUL KENNEDY is a professor of history and director of international security studies at Yale University. He is the author of *The Rise and Fall of the Great Powers*.

Test-Your-Knowledge Form

We encourage you to photocopy and use this page as a tool to assess how the articles in *Annual Editions* expand on the information in your textbook. By reflecting on the articles you will gain enhanced text information. You can also access this useful form on a product's book support website at www.mhhe.com/cls

NAME: DATE:

TITLE AND NUMBER OF ARTICLE:

BRIEFLY STATE THE MAIN IDEA OF THIS ARTICLE:

LIST THREE IMPORTANT FACTS THAT THE AUTHOR USES TO SUPPORT THE MAIN IDEA:

WHAT INFORMATION OR IDEAS DISCUSSED IN THIS ARTICLE ARE ALSO DISCUSSED IN YOUR TEXTBOOK OR OTHER READINGS THAT YOU HAVE DONE? LIST THE TEXTBOOK CHAPTERS AND PAGE NUMBERS:

LIST ANY EXAMPLES OF BIAS OR FAULTY REASONING THAT YOU FOUND IN THE ARTICLE:

LIST ANY NEW TERMS/CONCEPTS THAT WERE DISCUSSED IN THE ARTICLE, AND WRITE A SHORT DEFINITION:

NOTES

NOTES

NOTES

NOTES